CLEMENT ATTLEE

A Political Biography

by the same author

WHAT HAPPENED IN EDUCATION:
An Introduction to Western Educational History

BRITISH LABOUR AND HITLER'S WAR

CLEMENT ATTLEE

A Political Biography

Trevor Burridge

JONATHAN CAPE
THIRTY-TWO BEDFORD SQUARE LONDON

First published 1985

Jonathan Cape Ltd, 32 Bedford Square, London WC1B 3EL

British Library Cataloguing in Publication Data

Burridge, Trevor
Clement Attlee: a political biography.
1. Attlee, C.R. 2. Prime ministers – Great
Britain – Biography
I. Title
941.082'092'4 DA585.A8

ISBN 0-224-02318-7

The extract from A. P. Herbert's poem, *Man of Mystery*,
appears by courtesy of Lady Herbert.

Phototypeset by Computape (Pickering) Ltd, North Yorkshire
Printed in Great Britain by
Ebenezer Baylis and Son Ltd
The Trinity Press, Worcester and London

Contents

	PREFACE	xi
	INTRODUCTION	1
I	BASICALLY A VICTORIAN	6
II	NOT GOING HOME TO TEA	22
III	THE WORK HAS TO BE DONE	41
IV	NO MORE THE OLD STREET CORNER	56
V	WHAT ABOUT THE RENTIERS?	75
VI	COLLECTIVE SECURITY	96
VII	TOO LATE	116
VIII	NOT WITH A FLOURISH OF TRUMPETS	139
IX	NO MISTAKE THIS TIME	159
X	GETTING ON WITH THE JOB	182
XI	REVOLUTION WITHOUT TEARS	200
XII	NOT AS SIMPLE AS THAT	220
XIII	THE BOMB BECAME ESSENTIAL	234
XIV	THE IRRESPONSIBLE AMERICANS	248
XV	POSSIBLY INDIA	268
XVI	THE MAXIMUM WE CAN DO	289
XVII	TIMES AND SEASONS	313
	NOTES	325
	BIBLIOGRAPHY	381
	INDEX	390

Illustrations

PLATES

between pages 146 and 147

1 Attlee's first visit to 10 Downing Street, 1920
2 Ramsay MacDonald and Arthur Henderson, 1929
3 Oswald Mosley and William Jowitt at the Party Conference, 1929
4 Attlee and George Lansbury, 1931
5 Attlee with Republican forces in Spain, 1937
6 Attlee and Arthur Greenwood, 1939
7 Attlee in the Opposition Leader's room, 1939

between pages 178 and 179

8 Churchill and Attlee, 1941
9 Attlee visiting a munitions factory
10 Sir William Beveridge at Caxton Hall in 1943
11 Molotov talks to Attlee at the UN Conference, 1945
12 Attlee, Truman and Stalin at Potsdam, 1945
13 Attlee leading Ministers to the Service of Thanksgiving for final victory, 1945
14 King George VI with senior members of his new Government, 1945
15 The Labour Government, 1945

between pages 242 and 243

16 Attlee with Ernest Bevin, 1946
17 Attlee with Hugh Dalton, 1947

18 Stafford Cripps and Attlee with the Archbishop of York, 1948
19 Attlee, Pandit Nehru and Dr Malan meet for the Commonwealth Conference, 1949
20 Herbert Morrison in the home of Alice Bacon's mother, 1950
21 Patrick Gordon Walker and Emanuel Shinwell, 1950
22 Aneurin Bevan with fellow rebels, 1951

between pages 274 and 275

23 Attlee on the election trail in 1957
24 Attlee with Hugh Gaitskell
25 Prime Minister Nehru greets Attlee in India, after Independence
26 With President Tito in Yugoslavia, 1953
27 With Chou En Lai in China, 1954
28 A tribute from Durham miners
29 Attlee's statue unveiled in the House of Commons

Abbreviations

COS	Charity Organization Society
CoS	Chiefs of Staff
EDC	European Defence Community
ILP	Independent Labour Party
LCC	London County Council
LPCR	Labour Party Annual Conference Report
LRC	Labour Representation Committee
LSE	London School of Economics
NATO	North Atlantic Treaty Organization
NCL	National Council of Labour
NEC	National Executive Committee (of the Labour Party)
NJC	National Joint Council (of Labour)
PLP	Parliamentary Labour Party
SDF	Social Democratic Federation (became Social Democratic Party in 1907)
SEATO	South East Asia Treaty Organization
SSIP	Society for Socialist Inquiry and Propaganda
TUC	Trades Union Congress
UDC	Union of Democratic Control

Preface

The first time I became aware of Clement Attlee in a significant way was in September 1950. As a young and recent conscript in the RAF, I was in a crowded barrack-room in the North of England laboriously engaged in the evening's domestic preparations for the next day's session on the drilling square. A heavy metallic click from the Tannoy suddenly interrupted the proceedings. There was, intoned the announcer, to be a broadcast from the Prime Minister to which we should all listen. Mr Attlee, in his clipped and precise fashion, then informed us – conscripts and nation alike – that compulsory national service was to be extended forthwith from eighteen months to two years. The news was greeted with incredulity, dismay and loud imprecations. On the following morning, the regular NCOs were all smiles and nasty grins. Nobody, however, either blamed or praised Mr Attlee. He was regarded as the impersonal instrument of some higher authority or fate which had condemned us to six extra months of servitude.

Thereafter, Attlee faded abruptly from view. It was not until over ten years later, when I was a graduate student in Canada examining the 1945 Labour Government's policy towards Germany, that he again became an object of my curiosity. Ernest Bevin may have held the limelight, but Attlee was undoubtedly a prime mover behind the scene. Enlarging my studies to include the Second World War, I found the same rule applied; besides Churchill and Eden, Attlee was a name to be reckoned with. No matter where I turned in British history of the 1940s, there I encountered what to me had been a fairly obscure individual. Still later, when I began to consider the whole of his career, the wonder grew that so little seemed to be known about it.

Attlee lived from 1883 to 1967 and for much of this time was strenuously engaged in politics. Until 1982, when this book was three-quarters written, no full-length study of his life had appeared. It was as if he had managed to perplex his immediate posterity as much as he had his contemporaries, or as if he had become accepted as a worthy but dull figure. Kenneth Harris then published his admirably comprehensive work, authorized by Attlee himself. Somewhat to my relief, I discovered that our approach and aims were very different. I have concentrated in a selective and, what has turned out to be, a partisan way on bringing out Attlee's political significance. I have been encouraged to carry my book to completion, not least by Mr Harris, and I am happy to acknowledge many kind acts of hospitality and friendship by him during the final stages of writing this book.

Because of the length of his career and undemonstrative character, Attlee presents a formidable challenge to any biographer. One is obliged to have recourse to many sources of information about the man and his period, for which I have attempted to provide detailed references. I would like to underline the work of the following authors, from whom I have gleaned much background information: Margaret Gowing, *Independence and Deterrence: Britain and Atomic Energy, 1945–1952*, 2 vols, 1974; B. Donoughue and G. W. Jones, *Herbert Morrison: Portrait of a Politician*, 1973; W. Golant, 'The Political Development of C. R. Attlee to 1935', unpublished B. Litt. thesis, Oxford, 1967, MS. d1263; Paul Thompson, *Socialists, Liberals and Labour: The Struggle for London, 1885–1914*, 1967; Francis Williams, *A Prime Minister Remembers*, 1961; and Philip M. Williams, *Hugh Gaitskell: A Political Biography*, 1979.

Financial support, especially for research trips to the UK, has been generously provided by the Canada Council. The Council has no responsibility for the views expressed here, which only enhances my sense of gratitude. I also wish to record my thanks to the archivists, librarians and their assistants at the Bodleian Library; the British Library; Churchill College, Cambridge; the London School of Economics Library; the Public Records Office; and University College, Oxford. Mrs Irene Wagner and her assistants at the Labour Party Library deserve a special mention.

Lord and Lady Attlee (Clement's son and daughter-in-law), Lady Willis (Clement's sister-in-law, Violet Attlee's twin) and Lady Macdonald (Clement's niece) were gracious enough to discuss Attlee with me, and sustain me with cups of tea. In addition, Lady Attlee has continued our discussions by correspondence. Meeting Clement's relations has been a great pleasure. They provided me with many insights into his happy family life – a fundamental key to his character and politics – but they must be absolved from any responsibility for my interpretations.

I should like to thank my typists, Lise Laberge and Nancy Hough, for the professionalism of their work. Graham C. Greene and his editorial colleagues at Jonathan Cape: Tony Colwell for help with the photographs and, especially, Suzy O'Hare, have given me enthusiastic and valuable support. My thanks to them are coupled with a deep expression of gratitude to the original editors of my text, Marilyn Sims and my wife, Sandra. I have been saved many errors of grammar and style: any faults which remain are mine. To Sandra I would add a particular word of admiration for devoted help in other ways and, perhaps above all, for her general forbearance while I was preoccupied with the present work.

I wish to thank the following for access to and, where necessary, permission to quote from copyright material as indicated: Lord (2nd Earl) Attlee: poems, letters and other writings by C. R. Attlee; British Library Board: J. Chuter Ede Diaries; British Library of Political and Economic Science: Hugh Dalton Diaries and Papers; William Collins Sons & Co. Ltd: Harold Nicolson's *Diaries and Letters: Vol. I; 1930–1939* ed. by N. Nicolson; William Golant: unpublished thesis (see bibliography); The Secretary, The Labour Party: Annual Conference Reports, Labour Party pamphlets, NEC Minutes and Papers; Public Record Office: Cabinet and Prime Minister's Office Papers.

For permission to reproduce copyright illustrations, I am grateful to the following: BBC Hulton Picture Library (nos 2, 3, 6, 10 and 21); Blackpool Gazette and Herald Ltd (no. 16); Life © Time Inc., Larry Burrows (no. 23); Photo Source Ltd (nos 8, 11, 18, 19, 22, 26 and 27); Popperfoto (no. 5); S & G Press Agency Ltd (no. 4); Syndication International Ltd (no. 20); US Army (no. 12). All other photographs come from the Attlee family's archives.

Montreal, 1985 T.B.

One wants in a Prime Minister a good many things, but not very great things. He should be clever but need not be a genius; he should be conscientious but by no means strait-laced; he should be cautious but never timid, bold but never venturesome; he should have a good digestion, genial manners, and, above all, a thick skin.

Anthony Trollope, *The Prime Minister*, 1875–6

Introduction

Like many of his compatriots, Clement Richard Attlee was very fond of detective stories and crossword puzzles. He would travel to Westminster in a third-class carriage, his battered old brief-case containing nothing but two pipes, tobacco and a couple of thrillers. When, as Prime Minister, he undertook a longer journey, his Parliamentary Private Secretary had to collect half a dozen of the most difficult crosswords, which Attlee would solve in a few hours. To his contemporaries, however, Attlee's own character and career presented far more of a puzzle than anything devised by Agatha Christie or Ximenes. Just as Disraeli used to be called the Asian mystery, one newspaper concluded, so Attlee might well be called the English mystery – an incalculable force hidden behind a disarming exterior who achieves an unpredictable success. He would remain, declared another, the great enigma who will fascinate historians and biographers of the future; though the paper gave the impression it meant 'baffle' as much as 'fascinate'.

What was strange about him was that he was so ordinary. Few men could have been more typical and more representative of the average Englishman of his time, class and society. In his character and private life he was so ordinary as to be almost anonymous: had he not existed he could quite easily have been invented. The only gossip available in a public career of over sixty years was in regard to his wife's driving abilities. He made hopeless copy; the journalists were reduced to writing about his 'extraordinary ordinariness'. Their favourite epithet for him was 'colourless'. It seemed highly appropriate that *Time* in 1945 omitted to prepare a coloured cover portrait of him, as had become customary. Instead the magazine reverted to black, white and grey.

Neither *Time* nor Attlee himself had anticipated that he would win the general election. He seemed singularly to lack ambition. His totally unprepossessing physical appearance was on a par with his minimal qualities as an orator. There was 'nothing which his voice and delivery could not make uninspiring;[1] he had an irritating habit of swallowing the tails of his sentences and many of his speeches were, in any case, rather prosaic. King George VI called him Clem the Clam: never, it was alleged, would he use one word where none would do. He made no striking contributions to political theory, nor was he an outstanding party organizer. These shortcomings were bad enough in a Prime Minister; in a leader of a popular mass movement dedicated to drastic social change they defied all expectations.

His personality, according to one informed commentator, was the least impressive among those who had ever held the highest office in the land. On his last election tour a friendly journalist had to be engaged 'to put him over to a new public': Attlee quipped that the twelve labours of Hercules were as child's play compared to such an undertaking. During the Second World War he was referred to as the forgotten minister. For those with a taste for a Latin tag, the term *tertium quid* sprang to mind – 'a third something, especially between mind and matter, or between opposite things.' He was dubbed 'the Prime Minister whom nobody knew . . . often so solitary that no one knew he was there.'[2]

But he *was* there, even if so ubiquitous as to seem invisible. Particularly in the 1940s he was always there, at the centre – some would say the dead centre – of British political life. Those are the dramatic and pivotal years of the 'Attlee consensus': the shadow cast by his slight figure loomed across the decade, if not like a colossus, then at least as 'the sphinx on the totem pole of the British tribes.' By 1951 Attlee had been at the forefront of British politics for sixteen years, five as Leader of the Opposition, another five as a Cabinet Minister second only to Churchill, and six as Prime Minister. He continued to lead the Opposition until December 1955 and died (in 1967) replete with all the honours that his society could bestow on him – First Earl, KG, PC, OM, CH, FRS.

His political opponents were bewildered. If he had got up in the Commons and announced The Revolution, one of them remarked, it would have sounded like a change in a regional railway timetable. He *had* effected a revolution, protested another, but many people hadn't realized it. They had been hypnotized by 'the most successful political dentist in history'.[3] He was 'somewhat of a mysterious figure', pronounced Harold Macmillan. 'Beneath his curiously matter-of-fact and pedestrian replies, the whole great Churchillian fabric began to waver and collapse. Before his sarcastic and down-to-earth approach, imagination, romance, grandeur seemed to wither away.' Churchill confessed himself baffled; he could not follow the workings of Attlee's mind. No one in Churchill's experience of politics had been quite like Attlee.

Attlee's own colleagues were, if anything, in even more of a dilemma. Despite contacts extending over thirty years, Herbert Morrison concluded that he could not claim really to know Clement Attlee. Morrison, moreover, was unable to name anyone, living or dead, in the Labour Party who *had* managed a degree of intimacy with him. He was not, Lord Shinwell stated bluntly, the sort of person with whom one could become intimate. It was very seldom that one could engage in a sustained conversation with him. Michael Foot has observed that for Bevan, Cripps and Dalton, 'the enigma grew ever more incomprehensible with the years. Each in a different way was battered and bruised by the ordeal of politics, whereas Attlee seemed immune, almost disinterested . . . '[4] To Francis Williams, who had collaborated intimately with him, Attlee appeared 'a true solitary who required less than most men the support (or, one might add, the friendship) of others.'[5] By an odd coincidence, when his ashes were interred in Westminster Abbey they were placed but a few feet from those of the Unknown Warrior.

The *Daily Mirror*, a newspaper which supported the Labour Party, declared in its edition of 8 December 1955 that there were *two* Attlees: the public figure 'shy to the point of furtiveness, the man who scuttles on to the platform, looks alarmed by the applause and begins doodling', and 'the backroom Attlee, the tough astute politician, the man with the razor-sharp mind and a waspish tongue.' But was it a wiry toughness, persisted Foot, or just lack of imagination which kept Attlee cool to the point of obliviousness in a crisis? No one had ever unravelled the riddle. A. P. Herbert coined a poem about the phenomenon, called *Man of Mystery*; one verse ran,

> Yet by some shy mysterious art
> He rules the roost, if not the heart.
> It may be 'character' – it may
> Be just his clever, cunning way.

Over the years the mystery remained, but inevitably his stature grew. It was not put down solely to his obvious capacity for survival, an attribute of some standing among democratic politicians. Churchill, in a celebrated story, had no doubt as to the cause – 'if you feed a grub on royal jelly you may turn it into a queen bee.' Macmillan became increasingly aware of Attlee's 'great supremacy over his party and a growing mastery over the House.' Even Aneurin Bevan, a persistent critic, learned a 'new, intermittent respect' for him. Perhaps, like the best wine, Attlee was one of those men who improve with age? Foot, unconvinced but equally unable to settle the matter (to his own satisfaction), fell back on the suggestion that perhaps 'a sphinx was the only emblem which *could* lead the Labour Party.'[6]

In April 1954, a *New Statesman* profile explained that Attlee doodled because his nerves were steadier than those of the men who sought to take his place. He continued to lead the Labour Party chiefly because he was the one man who never doubted that he was the best fitted for the job. His autobiography of that year, a 'lamely written, clumsily constructed book, much of it as boring as the minutes of a municipal gas undertaking' was 'in many ways one of the most egotistical and ungenerous records of a public life ever to be published.' The writer could find examples in every chapter of Attlee's disregard of theories and values which were outside his range. Men and ideas were simply flattened down to the level at which he could comprehend them, with never a qualm that something was being missed. These strictures were entirely wasted on their subject. Having been leader of his turbulent party for nineteen years, he was quite accustomed to the verbal violence of the Left. His skin was as thick as anything Trollope could have desired. Setting aside the sour grapes, the *New Statesman*'s profile also revealed a lack of that historical perspective which is essential to any understanding of the man and his career. Attlee's life spanned what was perhaps the last period in British history when the average Englishman could contemplate his society and the world in straightforward terms. His active years in politics coincided with a succession of uncomplicated 'isms', from liberalism and imperialism to conservatism and socialism. None amounted to a clear-cut ideology, but each was capable of generating a strong sense of moral conviction of the type that Attlee possessed. The success of his career mirrors the growth and eventual triumph of socialist public ethics, as well as the rise to power of the Labour Party. So much is this true that the reader may sometimes wonder: are we dealing with the biography of an individual or with the history of a political party? Attlee himself wrote to Harold Laski in 1944: 'I have neither the personality nor the distinction to tempt me to think that I should have any value apart from the party which I serve.'[7]

Yet there was one thing about the man that eventually impressed itself upon contemporaries; it found expression in the frequent use of the word 'headmaster'. 'I don't suppose there was one of us,' confided a member of Attlee's Cabinet to Williams, 'who didn't feel apprehensive whenever we were summoned to No. 10. It was like being sent for by the headmaster.'[8] Kingsley Martin, the long-time editor of the *New Statesman*, always thought of Attlee in that role – 'a small man in his study watching over the boys, some of them too big for him to handle when they are fresh. They quarrel and fight until they are tired. Attlee calls them in one by one, gives them all a sound caning and restores order.' The journal's caustic profile grudgingly used the term to describe Attlee's custodianship of his Party: despite being favoured early on because of his education and experience, he had 'borne his trust with the stolid conscientiousness of a just headmaster.' And a correspondent of the *Observer* caught the same tone in an account of 7 October of a political meeting in 1951. Attlee 'did not have that air of being more than lifelike which surrounded many British politicians, nor did he display that spurious cheerfulness that suggests everything is fine, just fine.' Instead, he 'looked like a great headmaster, controlled, efficient and, above all, good.' These commentators were indirectly referring to Attlee's greatest quality: moral probity.

He once wrote that a biographer should be in sympathy with his subject, but not a hero-worshipper. In a conventional sense it is exceedingly difficult to make a hero out of Clement Attlee, though some of his qualities are evident enough. That he was efficient, for instance, was well known: an incoming Parliamentary Secretary, Arthur Moyle, was warned that Attlee was ruthless in this regard. Moyle also came to be impressed by Attlee's 'youthful buoyancy, astonishing memory for detail, charming simplicity, quiet courage and toughness'.[9] He was equally renowned for his abilities as a committee chairman, no mean asset for someone involved in twentieth-century administration. The *Manchester Guardian* was convinced that his was the clearest mind in Parliament, perhaps a double-edged compliment. What is certain is that he possessed many of the finer English virtues – genuine modesty, social consciousness, personal responsibility, a profoundly pragmatic and practical mind that owed much of its strength to a suppressed romanticism, and a keen, if dry, sense of humour.

In themselves, these are neither remarkable nor heroic attributes, but in Clement Attlee they were concentrated to an unusual degree. They were cemented by a serene sense of purpose and a loyalty to ideals which, in turn, attracted loyalty. His integrity readily communicated itself to others. It was especially this characteristic, combined with the luck needed by any politician and the rise of the Labour Party, which accounted for an exceptional career. Otherwise he was no more nor less than an archetypal product of his society which, in retrospect, is what gives his career its interest and, indeed, fascination. No one, it will be argued, was more suited to be a democratic socialist leader.

The solution to 'the English mystery' is that there was no mystery. There were no inexplicable deviations, no loose ends in Attlee's life: everything fell neatly into place, almost too neatly for belief. He bemused his compatriots precisely because he so closely resembled a composite of themselves. The name Attlee, he used to explain, was a Saxon word meaning 'at the clearing in the wood': and he can best be considered as a clearing in the tangled wood of twentieth-century politics, a quintessential English clearing. The recent centenary of his birth, accompanied by the crushing defeat of his Party, affords a perspective which might even permit one to discern some heroic elements in the man and his career.

I

Basically a Victorian

When Clement Attlee was born in January 1883,[1] his country was half-way through the period known to historians as 'The Great Depression'. To some extent, the term is misleading: the economic decline was more relative than absolute. But there can be no mistaking the main cause of a certain contemporary despondency: Britain's pre-eminence among the nations had undoubtedly begun to wane, and continued to wane despite the imperial frenzy of the century's last decade or so. The apogee of British power and prestige had been reached in mid-century: during the 1870s the world's economy had taken on a new shape and by the 1880s the years of easy, undisputed British leadership were over.

Agriculture, the oldest and largest industry, had been the first to be affected: its precipitous decline, notably in the grain-producing regions, continued unabated into the 1880s. The landed aristocracy was, politically and economically, pushed on to the defensive: the destitute labourers flocked by the thousand into the towns, thus completing the urbanization of the nation. Then it was the turn of the traditional manufacturing centres to encounter the twin threats of foreign competition and technological innovation; and the mounting anxieties in the former workshops of the world translated readily into social and political conflicts. Class rivalries became embittered; those between employer and employee were soon institutionalized in new forms of organizations. The extension of the adult male suffrage, in 1884, transformed the structures of the old political parties and stimulated the birth of new ones. Two basic tenets of Liberal orthodoxy were challenged, free enterprise from one end of the political spectrum, free trade from the other. Shortly after Attlee's birth the Liberal Party was shattered over the question of Irish Home Rule: as he reached maturity there was a deep rift in the Conservative Party over Tariff Reform. The final years of Queen Victoria's long reign were the most disruptive of national objectives and many traces of her 'homogenous England' would vanish in the process.

Yet none of these disturbances and portents troubled – few even penetrated – the tight cocoon which bound, nurtured and informed the young Clement Attlee's world. The part of society into which he was born was largely aglow in a regenerated vision of Empire, one of hope and glory. For Britannia, indeed, still ruled the waves: between 1884 and 1896 more than nine million square kilometres were added to the Queen's overseas realms. Attlee's first public memory was that of her Jubilee in 1887: the four-year-old helped his elder brother, Tom, to hang out flags on the porch. Ten years later, the imperial cult attained a peak of frenzy and excitement: the two boys witnessed an orgy of pomp and circumstance at the Diamond Jubilee celebrations. Clem came away with an indelible recollection of the 'wonderful display of empire-armed contingents from all over the world ... marching by ...',[2] an entirely appropriate sentiment for someone of his upbringing and education.

Patriotism, he remembered, was deemed the natural emotion of every free Briton. Religion also remained an inspiration and was often linked with patriotism: God was a term which sprang easily to English lips, especially those belonging to the suburban, evangelical middle class. While Attlee grew to manhood, God remained essentially in His heaven, and all was basically right with the world; He would save the Queen for nearly twenty more years after 1883. In her old age, she was almost deified: half a century afterwards Attlee could still write about the 'tremendous shock' caused by her death. Gladstone, the Prime Minister in 1883, also bore a remarkable resemblance, physical and moral, to the Supreme Being. Before he passed on, undoubtedly to higher realms, the aristocracy would manage to provide a tolerable substitute in the august person of Lord Salisbury. A Cecil of the Cecils, last peer to hold the post, Salisbury presided over the nation's affairs during most of Attlee's formative years. That Salisbury did so in a somewhat languid, even cynical, fashion in no way lessened Attlee's enduring admiration for him[3] – which again, was as it should have been.

Foremost among his family's assumptions, he recalled, was that the established order had to be respected and titled people were especially deserving of respect. In comparison, personal political allegiances were of much smaller consequence; after all, as Gilbert jested in 1882, one was either born a little Liberal or else a little Conservative. Attlee's father and an uncle happened to be Liberals, while Clem sided with the majority of his family. Far more important was it to understand that rich and well-to-do people were on the side of the angels. Deserving poor did exist but, normally, poverty was reckoned to be an accompaniment of moral delinquency, thriftlessness or drink. A need for change was admitted, as it accorded with the belief in progress and the theory of evolution: but support for reforms of a philanthropic nature carried the condition that nothing fundamental was to be called into question. And whereas certain successful revolutions elsewhere – along Garibaldi lines for instance – could be praised, violence of the French revolutionary, Cromwellian, Fenian or Chartist varieties was anathema.

The way of life that these attitudes reflected has been aptly described as one 'of Security, of Sedentary occupation and of Respectability'. It bestowed on its followers a tremendous self-confidence which, in many cases, can hardly be distinguished from self-righteousness. But there was also a hard core of optimistic realism to the middle-class Victorian way of life that outlived its social and political assumptions. It produced characters that, to an unusual degree, were harmonious and self-reliant despite the vicissitudes of changing circumstances and opinions. Clement Attlee was an outstanding example; for he was not only a child of the late Victorian era, he was a happy child.

The house where he was born was a typically ugly, roomy and solid construction of the 1870s. As the family prospered, a wing containing a billiard room, a school-house and several spare bedrooms was added. There was a sizeable garden, which the eight children put to good use. The house was situated in Putney, then more of a village or small country town than a suburb of London. There was an old wooden bridge across the river, and Clem's brother Tom (who became an architect) vividly recalled that 'the High Street of old, dark, bricked houses and decorous shops – notably Fairfax House, where the Protector had stayed – [led] up from the river to the steep slopes of Putney Hill with its square, opulent houses in large shady gardens. Beyond them the Heath was still wild, and at its edge watched by great blocks of houses, comfortable, solid, smelling of plum-cake and beeswax; quiet, dignified, set in grounds that were almost small estates, with gardeners' cottages in their far-off corners among cucumber frames and potting sheds.'[4] True, the noise of the London traffic could be heard from the Attlees' garden, but it was the sound of horse hoofs, beating on the paved streets. And though only six miles lay between Putney and Charing Cross, open fields, farms, country pubs and market gardens contributed to the atmosphere of almost rural tranquillity. The automobile had not been invented and direct communication with the city was limited for a time to a single railway line.

Close at hand, on Wandsworth Common, stood another house which figured prominently in Attlee's early upbringing. It belonged to his maternal grandfather and was a more distinctive, Queen Anne building. Several features were guaranteed to stimulate the imagination of young children – an uneven floor, a dining-room window oddly situated over the fireplace, dark and fascinating cupboards, great four-poster beds and a smoking-room devoid of curtains but with swords and daggers on the walls. Some of the rooms were dark, others stuffed with furniture and books. The inevitable garden sported a tennis court, besides the usual complement of sheds and greenhouse. The house, like the way of life it sheltered, was as comfortable as it seemed enduring. Yet the splendid isolation of the burgeoning suburban middle class was to prove as ephemeral as the country's former diplomatic position. The rows of 'mean little white-brick boxes with basements', Tom recorded later, were spreading yearly. The characteristics of the modern development of towns, he concluded bitterly, 'are first its destructiveness and secondly its impermanence'.[5]

That was Tom's retrospective view. When Clem looked back on his early years he was struck by the flood of nostalgic memories, 'mostly happy', that he associated with his congenial environment. They were centred on his family. His grandfather's house, for instance, was also the residence of four unmarried aunts and an uncle who were very kind to the Attlee brood. He was still more fortunate in his parents. His father, contrary in this particular to the stereotype of the domineering Victorian male, did not unduly attempt to constrain or influence the children, not even in their choices of profession. Though tenacious in his Gladstonian radicalism, which included support for Irish Home Rule, Henry Attlee impressed his fourth son as exceptionally broadminded. He had acquired, no doubt, a good deal of tact and discretion in his work as a solicitor, at which he was extremely successful. The culminating point of his career came in 1906 when he became President of the Law Society. Nine years previously he had acquired a second house, a substantial late-seventeenth-century property situated in two hundred acres near the Essex coast. Even so, the Attlees did not quite manage to cross the great dividing line into the upper-middle class: they never possessed a carriage. In all probability they did not aspire to a higher social position. They were content, as well they might be, with their unostentatious but thoroughly agreeable situation.

Henry Attlee came from a line of millers and corn merchants in Surrey and, as a younger son, had been articled at the age of sixteen to a London solicitor. He rose to the top of his firm and added his name to it. That he was a man of ability and character is indicated by his appointment as one of His Majesty's Lieutenants for the City of London. He was perhaps lucky in the timing of his departure from Surrey and his choice of profession. They coincided with the rapid development of South London, a profitable field for city solicitors. Two of his brothers succeeded to the family business, two became brewers in Tooting and one went to Cambridge University and became an Anglican clergyman. Clement Attlee had many cousins on his father's side, including two well-known doctors. Several female cousins became missionaries, as would one of Attlee's sisters.

His mother, Ellen Bravery Watson, came from a more academically minded family. Her father, who had been to Westminster and Caius College, Cambridge, was Secretary of the Art Union of London, a semi-public institution which published art reproductions. T. S. Watson had a white beard and wore a smoking cap, and was Attlee's only living grandparent. He had a son and five other daughters besides Ellen who, in 1870, was to marry Henry Attlee. Watson's wife died early, and Ellen, as eldest daughter, was called upon to play an active domestic role. Her duties do not seem to have adversely affected her education. She acquired a good grounding in English literature, spoke French and some Italian, played the piano, sang, and painted in water-colours.

Attlee's mother epitomized a certain kind of middle-class aesthetic culture that he never ceased to admire. In 1953 he would still describe himself as 'basically a Victorian'.[6] Far from despising Victorian values he positively revered many of them and, given the quality of his mother's attainments, it is easy to see why. One of the goals of his future political philosophy would be the extension of similar attainments to the masses. He did not believe that socialism meant the predominance of working-class culture. 'The conception of a proletarian art and literature which must be sharply distinguished from anything hitherto accomplished in those fields,' he wrote in 1937, 'is quite alien to true Socialism. It results from a sense of inferiority. British Socialists recognize very clearly the danger that exists in the tyranny of the reformer who wishes to make all men in his image.'[7]

Yet in some ways his mother was unduly conservative. She abhorred political discussion – a pattern that Attlee was to follow with his own family, though for the good reason that he had enough of it outside. In any case his wife, like his mother, had little interest in politics: they were each devoted to their respective families. Ellen Attlee, however, carried the cause of family unity to the point of displaying jealousy of members who showed too much independence and who sought friends outside the family circle. Clem and Tom later realized that this attitude tended to make them self-conscious and shy. Tom stated that the great advantage of being one of a large family and of finding constant satisfaction within it was somewhat lessened by 'the effect of too rigid a standard, unintelligently held' and seemed to entail 'an attitude of shy exclusiveness' which lasted beyond childhood.[8] The children, in Clement's tactful words, were not encouraged to have a good conceit of themselves.

The effect was not noticeable for some time. The family was at once united and happy. Religion acted as a strong cement and scepticism was considered sinful. The church, or rather churches, for the Attlees frequented more than one, were naturally of the Anglican persuasion: they varied, as the family prospered, from evangelical to high church in tone. Though there is no evidence that the Attlees were morbidly concerned with the state of their souls, the Sabbath was strictly observed. The regime entailed Sunday-best clothes, morning and evening attendance at church, with an additional Sunday school visit in the afternoon for the children. The Bible was always regarded as inspired, and good works were reckoned an integral part of Christian duty: high-mindedness became a family endowment.

Robert, the eldest child, was to take an early retirement from his profession as a solicitor in order to devote himself to charitable affairs. Even as a girl, the eldest sister,[9] Mary, wanted to go to India as a missionary. She was deterred by Henry Attlee, who liked to have his children about him: after his death she lost no time in repairing to South Africa – her health ruling out her original choice. There she began what could have been considered a life-work except that, at the age of seventy-five, she returned to England and embarked on a campaign for racial unity.[10] All the younger boys became involved in social work, Bernard making a profession of it as a parson. Tom, of whom we have heard already, became a Christian socialist before escaping from what to him were the horrors of London, to end up in Cornwall as a schoolmaster. Laurence, the baby of the family, started a boys' club in Islington then settled down as a family man of his own, becoming a departmental manager in a large india-rubber firm and a devotee of local causes.[11]

Clem's career can also be traced to the Attlee family's concern with doing the right thing, but with him the impulse was focused and strengthened by a reaction against the formal manifestations of religion. His revolt began as a small boy when he was often bored to distraction by the lengthy church services to which the adults attached so much importance. Yet the highly-developed moral sense which these experiences imparted remained intact, though diverted into other channels; he attached an absolute meaning to such words as 'duty' and 'responsibility'. He believed that religion took first place in the influences behind the British socialist movement, if the early work of Robert Owen and the pioneers was excluded, and that this fact distinguished the British movement from those in continental countries. The nineteenth-century habit of Bible reading, in his view, had two particular consequences: it served as an inspiration to the struggle for social justice and equality and, at the same time, because of the variety of interpretations, it was the foundation of the non-dogmatic and tolerant British approach to socialism. The 'natural' British tendency to heresy and dissent, he was to maintain, prevented the formation of a rigid socialist orthodoxy.[12]

The unity of the Attlees did not depend solely on religion: they took great pleasure in each other's company. The family's general conviviality gave its members comradeship and developed Clem's strong sense of community. Enormous pleasure was taken in outings, and charades were as much as part of Christmas as was church-going. The highlight of the year was the annual visit to the seaside, another Victorian invention: for everyone except the hard-working father the summer holidays lasted a whole month. Holidays were spent in Essex after the acquisition of the estate there. Clem's favourite summer pastime was bicycle polo; he also enjoyed tennis, village cricket and rabbit shooting.

Respect and reverence for seniors was a cardinal feature of the establishment and, as seventh child, Clement came very low in the pecking order. The older boys were accorded a certain measure of freedom but the younger children tended to be dominated by the mature females. The latter included a retinue of governesses and domestics and Attlee spent the first nine years of his life at home. Perhaps as a result the future Prime Minister would be known for his courtesy to and about women. His own happy marriage undoubtedly reinforced his early experience and he became an acute observer of the role played by the wives of prominent politicians. He loved family life: it was by choice as well as lack of time that he would have few intimate friends outside his circle of relatives.

For some reason Clement did not attend local day-schools as two of his brothers had done: until he was nine he was taught by his mother and by his sisters' governesses, one of whom was French. He claimed to have been able to recite French with an admirable accent though he admitted that this accomplishment, along with other 'nonsense', was speedily knocked out of him when he went to school. Another governess, a Miss Hutchinson, had a story to tell that was much appreciated by the Attlee family. She had previously been engaged by Lord Randolph Churchill to teach his young son, Winston: one day a maid came into the room and asked her if she had rung the bell, whereupon Winston said, '*I* rang. Take away Miss Hutchinson, she is very cross.'[13] By the time he finally arrived at school, Attlee had acquired the basic three 'r's and a good general knowledge of history, geography and scripture, besides some French and Latin.

This early preparation stood him in good stead. Northaw Place, as his first school was called, was mostly distinguished by what Matthew Arnold would surely have called its philistine atmosphere. Situated near Potter's Bar, in Hertfordshire, it contained forty pupils, all boys, in only two classrooms. Despite their different ages and abilities, the boys worked together. Two sporting clergymen, one a friend of Attlee's parents, ran the place; their true religion was cricket. The order of the day was scripture and cricket – often combined in the evenings, in a game of paper cricket wherein the rival teams were composed of the Kings of Israel and Judah. Intellectually, Attlee got very little out of it, save for coming first in a bishop's examination of the Old Testament. But because of his family education he was one of the best pupils there.

So far as cricket was concerned, Attlee needed no converting: he was devoted to the game. During the last decades of the nineteenth century the rules of golf, lawn tennis, rugby and, above all, cricket were perfected. Organized games became to the middle-class what field sports were to the aristocracy – a psychological as well as a physical outlet. When Kipling came to pour scorn on the entire generation he could think of no phrase more telling than 'the flannelled fools at the wicket'. Attlee would have rejected with contempt any necessary association of his beloved game with fools. In his boyhood the legendary W. G. Grace was still playing and the Test Matches had just begun: for ever afterwards cricketing stories were one of his main items of small talk. As Prime Minister he would sometimes 'laugh his head off' at his own cricket jokes, a colleague recalled, 'and of course those round about him laughed with him even if they didn't understand what he was talking about'.[14] One such person was the celebrated cartoonist, David Low; someone had told Attlee that Low was an Australian, so whenever they met Attlee confined the conversation to cricket, about which Low knew nothing.[15] The difficulty of persuading Attlee to install a new ticker-tape in 10 Downing Street was overcome when someone pointed out to him the prospect of obtaining Test Match scores: he referred to it as 'my cricket machine' and consequently was horrified one day to find it printing out details of Cabinet decisions.[16] Cricket also provided him with a slang vocabulary for awkward occasions; older colleagues would be dismissed, according to Harold Wilson, for the 'reason' that 'Well, you had a good innings. Time to put your bat up in the pavilion.'[17]

Despite his pleasure in cricket, however, Attlee considered later that after four reasonably happy years at prep school he had become 'very much of a prig'. The Victorian child-rearing recipe of family, class, religion and games succeeded completely with him. To this foundation was added, in 1896, the vital ingredient of the English boarding school experience.

Then as now, the function of public school was social as well as academic. Before the sons of the greatly enlarged middle-class were to make their way in the world they had to be turned into gentlemen – assimilated, that is, to the English version of the civilized tradition. But there had been few educational reforms in public schools since 1875.[18] The lofty ideals of Thomas Arnold and his disciples had degenerated into a stereotyped curriculum based on the three 'c's: cricket, Christianity and classics. By the end of the nineteenth century, attendance at public school had become a narrowly social cult, reaching 'a point of religious intensity and crystallized into a fetish-worship'.[19] The system specialized in turning out 'a type admirably fitted for building an Empire . . . men who were sure of themselves and ready to assume responsibility, but devoid of imagination, sensibility and the capacity to criticize what they had been taught to accept.'[20] One authority has it that all the forces in public school in the 80s and 90s worked against the creation of originality of thought or character.[21] The products of these schools have been described as exhibiting 'excessive respect for authority ... obsession with tradition ... [and] prolonged adolescence.'[22] A contemporary account noted that it was 'a great point in Public School Education that boys should be attracted by it ... to the ideas of Law, Order, System, Organization, as distinct from the individual through whom, as the executive power, these things are carried out.'[23]

Haileybury College, during the nearly five years when Attlee was there, was an excellent example of this educational philosophy and practice. Like most of its kind, the school was a fairly recent creation. Founded at the beginning of the nineteenth century by the East India Company, its original purpose had been to provide a suitable education for future managers of the Company. With the dissolution of the Company in 1857, the school closed, but it re-opened five years later as a public school proper. All such schools became thoroughly imbued with the new and stridently imperialistic tone in British life though, perhaps not altogether surprisingly in view of its antecedents, none surpassed Haileybury in this regard. Even before Attlee arrived the school had, in his words, developed 'a great tradition of service in the Army and the Indian Civil Service', but with the advent of the Boer War the imperialist era reached an emotional climax. One of Attlee's teachers was so distressed by the news of the initial British defeats that the boys had to be very careful in his classes. The tension was only broken by the relief of Ladysmith in 1900. The news provoked a collective act of patriotic indiscipline in the school in which Attlee eagerly participated. That he was caned[24] for his part in the celebratory schoolboy march to the local town did nothing to reduce his imperialist ardour. He enrolled enthusiastically in the school's cadet corps and even after three years at Oxford, when the emotional tide of Empire had begun to turn, still believed in 'the legend of the White Man's burden and all the rest of the commonplace of imperialist idealism.'

Attlee did not shine at Haileybury, if only because he was merely average at games. The school was going through a bad patch and suffered from a shortage of pupils. Sanitary provisions were rudimentary and the food poor: the boys were housed four to a room, each boy having a tiny cubicle containing a bed and a desk. The regime, complained a fellow inmate, was 'unnecessarily Spartan. It certainly only suited the virile type of boy who could stand up to more or less tough conditions and who was able to adapt himself to new surroundings.'[25] Attlee, whose slight stature belied an exceptional wiriness, was one of those who could stand up and adapt to the conditions. He was not unduly troubled by the bullying, which was rife, as he enjoyed the protection of his elder brother Tom. The quality of the teaching was indifferent at best, though there were also lectures by special speakers. The headmaster, Edward Lyttelton, whom Attlee rarely met until the Sixth Form, was later selected for the same post at the prestigious Eton. Commenting in 1944 on a book written about Lyttelton, Attlee remarked that he particularly liked the passage in which 'the old man, saying his prayers, broke off to practise a few cricket strokes with his walking stick'. Otherwise Attlee found that the book treated Lyttelton's Haileybury days rather briefly:[26] perhaps there was little to say. Lyttelton was a classicist and though Attlee was in the classics stream his lack of previous preparation in this area proved a handicap which he did not entirely overcome. He did best at history (which was well taught), English and geography, and in these subjects he often came top of his form. He was a voracious reader and acquired a considerable general knowledge, with the notable exceptions of science and technology. He seems to have had no difficulty in passing the entrance examination to Oxford, an achievement limited to a small minority of the more intellectually inclined boys.

In addition to the cadet corps, Attlee was a member of several clubs including the Antiquarian Society, the Literary and Debating Society and a Shakespeare reading group. At the Debating Society in 1901 he opposed a motion that 'the Museums and Picture Galleries should be open on Sundays' which is perhaps more an indication of his conservatism than of his religious views at this period. His first appearance in print was a poem in the school magazine. It was written as an exercise in the Lower Fifth and the subject was the current London cab strike: 'I treated it in a very anti-strike manner,' he remembered. The poem concluded: 'Their wives and bairns must eat; in a little while they'll be more humble and beg for a fare at our feet.'[27] The adolescent arrogance of the tone perhaps also reflects the fact that, towards the end of his schooldays, his mind was tending towards 'a religious scepticism which revolted against the fundamentalist teaching in which I had been brought up' – a reaction which served to distinguish him from his brothers and sisters. So too, he became 'decidedly fed up with public school religion. The whole trend of [his] mind . . . was [now] romantic and imaginative' for which relief, in the shape of university, was close at hand.

Altogether, the main impact of Haileybury on Attlee was social rather than academic. Despite his shyness, which was increased by the predominantly athletic tone of the school, he did not lack friends. One reason was that Haileybury differed from most public schools in that there was not the usual strict separation into Houses: the whole school, with the exception of a single House, took its meals together – hence Attlee could cultivate a wide acquaintance.[28] The fact of having an older brother at the school must also have been an advantage in this regard.

Perhaps what his schooling provided for him best on the social level was not so much a group of friends or an entrée into an old boy network as a personal shorthand of psychology and language. He shared the memories, the sentiments, the jargon and to some extent the nostalgia of the British public-school educated élite. These were political assets later on; even if 'they' were to have difficulty in understanding him, he found it easy to understand and hence to deal with 'them'. His time at Haileybury, he recalled, was 'on the whole enjoyable, though there were considerable periods of black misery'. If he learned one lesson from his first experiences with adversity it was the importance of common and personal loyalties. The effect of his schooldays was to cast him into a psychological mould that would endure to the end of his life. Few things are stranger in the history of the Labour Party than that it should have had as its leader for so long a man who in so many respects was the quintessence of the public school type.[29]

Given the Attlee family's Cambridge connections it is difficult to account for its choice of Oxford as the setting for the boys' university education. Yet partisanship for the latter was made clear to every visitor to the Putney house; with special reference to the annual boat race, one would immediately be asked, 'Are you Oxford or Cambridge?' Clem was to consolidate the prejudice. He became a devoted Oxonian and contributed a footnote to its history. He was the university's first graduate to be elected as a Labour MP. Oxford proved a fitting and splendid climax to Attlee's education. Everyone who was there around the turn of the century was greatly impressed, in retrospect, by the serenity and quiet of the place. It was still the city of dreaming spires and not screaming tyres. The automobile had scarcely been invented and horse-drawn trams still ran down the High; Attlee used William Morris's words to describe it, 'a long winding street and the sound of many bells'. Mainly, recalled Sir Ernest Barker, then a young don, life went by at a walking-pace. The sounds Barker remembered were 'the clop-clop of horses and the rustle of a bird's wings in the skies, with an occasional whistle of a railway engine in the distance.'[30] Bicycles were a recent and costly innovation; the one that Attlee purchased, in 1902, cost him nearly £13, a considerable sum. Gown dominated town, and the district around Oxford was purely rural. The inhabitants showed an appropriate deference, made their own amusements, in their own homes, and 'by and large lived as if Queen Anne were still alive'.[31] The young Attlee succumbed completely to the spell; in later life he often sought to recapture 'the magic of those days and of that city'.

Oxford was also quiet intellectually: a foreign professor used to say that Oxford was not a university at all but a high school for young gentlemen.[32] The fierce doctrinal disputes of the mid-nineteenth century were over: no controversies of comparable excitement had replaced them. The Oxford philosophers such as A. E. Taylor and Harold Joachim were safe, solid and realistic. The prevailing atmosphere, according to the earnest, industrious and intellectual William Beveridge, was one of 'extreme philosophic dilettantism'.[33] Religion, ethics and philosophy, he found in 1898, 'were seen not as guides to moral action, but as subjects for endless metaphysical debate'. The whole place, to his mind, abounded 'with cliques, scandal, envy – pervaded by a refining atmosphere of atheism, cynicism, militant agnosticism and affected indifference to all things in heaven and earth'.[34] Attlee discovered for himself that politics were dull: apart from some active liberalism at Balliol College and some Christian interest in social reform, the university was predominently Conservative. Very little socialist propaganda had penetrated the aged walls. The natural sciences were badly neglected, despite the advent of the Clarendon laboratory; only in chemistry could Oxford be said to be a leading scientific centre.

In contrast to Oxford as a whole, University College, when Attlee joined it in October 1901, was enjoying an exceptionally good period. The run-of-the-mill quality of most of the dons was more than compensated for by the varied abilities of the students. Attlee's companions excelled at every kind of sport – an area in which he continued to be strongly interested: but outstanding athletes were not excused academic effort. The Master of the College ruled his flock 'with a pretty strong hand', not hesitating, for instance, to send down a man who played cricket for England because he had failed his exams. This was a rare occurrence; usually the athletically talented were equally capable at their studies. They included a number of future professors, bishops and top civil servants: several students became Presidents of the Oxford Union at a time when University College contained only 140 members. There was an agreeable absence of cliques: Attlee got to know practically everyone there, and most of them very well. The college's social homogeneity was undoubtedly enhanced by the fact that the students came almost exclusively from public schools.[35]

The undergraduate curriculum was mainly literary and philosophical in character. Greek was retained, in 1904, as a compulsory subject. The most prestigious course was *Literae Humaniores*, known as 'Greats', a combination of philosophy and ancient history: first-class performance here, it was reckoned, would provide a man with an intellectual training on which success in any career could be based. But Attlee, both because of his weak background in classical languages and by inclination, did not follow the 'Greats' pattern: instead, he read Modern History, taking, as his special topic, the Italian renaissance. On the whole, he found his lectures dull. His tutor, Arthur Johnson of All Souls, was an elderly parson of the traditional variety. Johnson's students often found a notice postponing the weekly session; these notices coincided with meets of the Bicester Hunt. It was said of Johnson that he used to teach his pupils in hunting kit, in the interval between tea and changing for dinner.[36] To others, however, he was the 'most beloved of chaplains, whose reading of the service was an education and his rare sermons a delight.'[37] The 'Johner' was sufficiently alive to be obsessed by the Free Trade versus Protection controversy: he was against Protection, while Attlee took the opposite view. And Johnson did send his pupil to a course given by Ernest Barker, whom Attlee was to consider the most stimulating of all his teachers.

Barker taught Attlee on the German Reformation but this was not one of Barker's specialities and he never repeated the course. Writing to Barker some forty years later, Attlee claimed that he still remembered the lectures and quoted a sentence Barker had used to describe the Anabaptists of Munster: 'They indulged themselves in the lusts of lascivious promiscuity.'[38] It seems more likely, however, that what most impressed Attlee about Barker was not the lecture so much as the personality of the lecturer. Barker had been trained in the classics and had a high regard for Johnson who had not; in other respects Barker differed significantly from many of the history dons. He was young, only two or three years older than his students, and came from an unusual social background. He was one of the very rare individuals who had made the transition from a labourer's cottage in Cheshire to the rooms of an Oxford don, and he spoke with a strong regional accent. The Oxford Faculty of Modern History also included historians of the stature of A. L. Smith, H. A. L. Fisher, Charles Oman, E. Armstrong, Sir John Marriott, Professor Pollard, Charles Grant Robertson, Charles Firth, H. W. C. Davies and C. Fletcher. It seems odd that Attlee got so little from them; apart from Barker, he supposed 'old Marriott' to be as good as any. Perhaps the fact that his teachers were mostly Liberals put Attlee off, though Barker too had Liberal leanings.

Attlee was never much of a liberal in either his political attitudes or his psychological make-up. While at Oxford he professed 'ultra-Tory' opinions. He admired 'strong, ruthless rulers' – of whom his special field of study could supply many examples. He also became divorced from religion, and superficially cynical. In part his student worldliness was a reaction to the external constrictions of his early years and a fashionable pose. In addition, Queen Victoria died in the very year in which he went up to Oxford and much of Victorianism rapidly died with her. Liberalism was in decline, and Attlee was disgusted by the way in which the Rosebery and Bannerman factions were fighting each other. There was a huge Tory majority in Parliament: Joseph Chamberlain appeared to him as by far the most attractive politician and the country was still under the jingoistic spell. Among the students of his year, Attlee knew only one who was a Liberal and he, Alec Patterson the future prison reformer, described himself as an 'individualist Liberal'.

Yet despite the fact that the Oxford of the social gospel, as it has been called, flowered just after Attlee left, the university in his time was not completely moribund politically. The glimmerings of a fresh interest and approach were there, if Attlee had cared to investigate. There was, for instance, the Christian group of social reformers associated with the Christian Social Union, but as most of them were either high or low church they had no appeal to Attlee. Religiosity of any kind had become quite distasteful to him, though five of his closest friends became parsons. And at Balliol College could be found William Temple, a future 'socialist' Archbishop of Canterbury and R. H. Tawney, a future socialist historian. It was at Balliol that the secular reform movement originated; an undergraduate there was likely to receive the following advice from the Master: 'Your first duty is to self-culture. You must learn all that Oxford has to teach in this regard. But after that, one thing that needs doing by somebody is to find out why, with so much wealth in Britain, there continues to be so much poverty. And how can poverty be cured?' William Beveridge, the future architect of full social security, never forgot this advice.[39] Only a few years later he was to be found giving a special lecture on the subject at University College:[40] by then the advocacy of positive political action directed at social reform was in full swing. It was of this later Oxford that Attlee seemed to Eustace Percy so typical a son.[41]

He did not get the first-class degree for which Johnson had hoped, though the students who were sent to Barker from other colleges appear to have been those who showed particular promise; among them were Christopher Dawson and Keith Feiling, the future historians, T. E. Lawrence and Harold Laski, In Attlee's case there are several reasons why he had to content himself with a 'good second', if the possibility that he was not of sufficient intellectual calibre is excluded. For one thing, he had no intention of pursuing a life of scholarship: well before his final examinations, he had decided to go in for law and was already eating the required dinners at the Temple. For another, he did not concentrate hard enough or long enough: only at the end did he work flat out.

But Attlee enjoyed himself: he was convinced that no one could have had a happier three years at Oxford than he. After the first year – when he had to overcome his shyness and during which he was forced to live outside the college due to rebuilding – he found he had a wide circle of friends. His background had ensured that he had a number of ready-made friends and acquaintances in colleges other than his own; and his brother Tom, at Corpus Christi, was once again a useful contact. He considered his second year at University to be the happiest and most carefree of his life. Athletic excellence was not necessary to make one an acceptable member of society, enthusiasm sufficed: he played hockey, tennis, bridge and billiards, and also enjoyed sailing and punting on the river. He overcame much, if not all, of his excessive reserve. He read voraciously and widely, extending his earlier love of poetry to include Swinburne and Morris, the Pre-Raphaelites, French and Italian poets. He joined his college's Shakespeare Reading Society and the Literary Society. He also attended some of the Oxford Union debates though, like Lord Rosebery, Sir Anthony Eden, Sir Alec Douglas-Home and Harold Wilson, Attlee was one of those future Prime Ministers who never spoke there. He did summon the courage to speak in his college's Debating Society and at least one occasion has been recorded: he spoke in favour of protection, a Conservative position then but one to which, during the Common Market controversies of the 1960s, he almost returned.

The connection between University College and the wider world of politics was a long-established one. It had begun in the second half of the eighteenth century. Between 1875 and 1885, noted the official historian,[42] it could be said that representatives of almost every shade of English political life had been educated at University College, such as Gladstone, Lord Cross, Forster, Lord Selborne, Lord Salisbury and Sir Stafford Northcote. Attlee's retrospective explanation that, when choosing the Bar as his career, he had at the back of his mind the possibility of entering politics – for which he had a 'sneaking affection' – could well have owed something to the existence of this tradition. In 1902 his college could boast of four Ministers of the Crown, all Conservatives. The public school and university system was largely geared to careers in law and politics, as well as those in the church and executive civil service (at home and in the Empire). To this extent the university had accommodated itself to the vocational demands of the middle-class whose sons now formed the majority of its clientele.

The claim has been made that the success of this educational system is one of the major reasons that England, in contrast to other countries, was able to move from oligarchy to democracy, and then to social democracy without revolutionary violence.[43] Equally, it has often been pointed out that it did little to help the country's industrial efficiency. There can be small doubt that Clem Attlee's future political orientation was extremely influenced by his Oxford experience, in its essence if not in its substance. He turned to socialism precisely because he was so fundamentally – emotionally – conservative. Socialism would appear to him as the best method of preserving and extending the cultural values acquired from his family life and higher education, not as a device for replacing them by revolutionary ones. The seeming paradox is possibly the most distinctive feature of the very English approach to socialism of which Attlee was to be so exemplary a representative.

By exam time, in the summer of 1904, the beauties of Oxford had never seemed so great to him, and he was not thinking of the lusts of lascivious promiscuity. Typically repressed public school romantic that he was, he dwelt on the 'grey old walls, the wonderful green lawns and the shining streams, the spires and domes and quadrangles.' It was time to be gone. The world lay before him, something almost literally true of an Oxford-educated Englishman in 1904, other than in the fields of business and industry.

Attlee's decision to become a barrister was a fairly obvious one. His father's position as a solicitor promised to be a useful stepping-stone to later advancement. But he was not very enthusiastic about any career. He thought rather in terms of some profession in which a living could be made while, in his ample leisure time, he would be free to continue his reading in literature and history, and to learn more of art and antiquities. Oxford had done its work well. Even the Bar was not much of a wrench. The point has been well made that there was 'no easier transition for a young Oxonian from Colleges and quadrangles to life in earnest than by way of the Inns of Court. Once again he sees his name painted at the front of a staircase; he lunches in a Gothic hall, at a long polished table, among colleagues pursuing the same branch of learning: he strolls again upon summer lawns; he belongs to a privileged community'.[44]

Apart from rare exceptions a young barrister could not expect to earn a living at the Bar for several years: parental support was necessary. Attlee was accustomed to such support. At Oxford he kept a record of his expenses; they averaged about £212 per annum. Apparently, he noted, one could do all right in those days on £100 a year over living and college expenses. He certainly did: while there he managed to visit the Continent three times, seeing something of France, Spain, Belgium and Germany, besides taking several holidays in England. It is in the light of this gentle and pleasant conclusion to a favoured youth that the measure of his subsequent conversion to socialism will shortly have to be taken.

II

Not Going Home To Tea

Most of the first twenty years of Attlee's life had been spent in the political shadow of Conservative imperialism: much of the next ten would be dominated by Liberal reform. Both creeds implied some increase in the power of the State: neither conflicted with the public school tradition of service to the community. Attlee was not the only member of his class to come to a different sense of social reality in the decade or so preceding the First World War. But the extent and nature of the shift in his views were unusual: he switched all the way from idealistic imperialism to ethical socialism – without ever being tempted to align himself with that half-way house, the radical wing of the Liberal Party. The transformation in his social and political outlook after he left Oxford was the more profound for not being suddenly or easily achieved. It is perhaps best illustrated by one of his own favourite stories of the period. Joined by a barefoot little girl in a London slum street, he was asked, 'Where are you going?' He replied that he was going home to tea. 'Oh,' was the reply, 'I'm going home to see if there is any tea.' To Attlee, the point of the story was the difference it indicated between 'the comfortable and the insecure classes'; yet by then he himself was no longer going 'home' to tea. Instead, he was taking his tea and re-thinking his view of society in the East End of London.

The importance of the London background to his mental reappraisal cannot be overstated. Infatuated as he had been with Oxford, his sojourn there marked merely a phase in his life, an adolescent and romantic phase. Essentially he was, and remained, a Londoner. It was where he was born and bred, where he was to receive his political baptism, where he was to spend the greater part of his working life and where, finally, he returned to die.[1] His experience of life in that teeming, cosmopolitan capital was to leave its imprint upon him in several ways, none more so than in the reinforcement of the introspective side of his acutely sensitive nature. Moral conversions generally turn people outwards; with Attlee, his family and educational background, allied to the emotional trauma of his London experiences, produced what have been described as 'conflicts of personality that have never been fully resolved, a habit of closing in on himself . . . a compulsion to withdraw into his own private intellectual life and come to solitary conclusions'.[2] One of the most prominent features of his mature personality would be his extraordinary self-control, his ability to isolate his innermost feelings from the necessity of dealing with the world as it is. Pre-war London had much to do with the development of this characteristic.

His fascination with the metropolis had begun in boyhood, with the traffic. The noise, the dirt and the astonishing variety of the thousands of horse-drawn vehicles presented a dramatic spectacle, enlivened by the appalling road conditions of the 1880s and 1890s. Asphalt was both experimental and exceptional: mainly, the surfaces were made of water-bound macadam, except where the density of the circulation entailed the use of concrete slabs. At a time when the horse was king, road-cleaning techniques were primitive, haphazard and largely manual. When it rained, the streets quickly turned into seas of mud, which splashed liberally over the unfortunate pedestrians. Even greater pleasure for small boys was provided by the steam-driven trains of the London Underground Railway, some of whose stations were not unlike Dante's *Inferno*. The advent of the bicycle was an equal source of interest and delight. Attlee could remember the transition from the fashionable penny-farthing to the efficient safety-model which, equipped with cushioned tyres, instantly became the fastest machine on the roads. While he was growing up, the London traffic scene underwent a more drastic revolution. In the last decade of the nineteenth century the tramway system was generally electrified and extended; and by the time that he reported for work in the autumn of 1904, motor-buses had been introduced and the roads improved. There was something overwhelming as well as compelling about his early experience of the big city: one effect was to emphasize the enormity and complexity of the society in which he lived.

These traffic developments represented a more subtle and organic transformation that had come over the capital since Attlee was a boy: they were a corollary to the growth of suburbia which, in turn, had been accompanied by a decline in the population of the inner-city areas. The result was a further separation of the social groups into distinct residential districts. Also, the structure of London government had been reformed and reorganized by the Parliamentary Acts completed in 1889, and the franchise had been extended. Together, these changes had created the potential for new political developments – which were long overdue. Political evolution in London had lagged behind that elsewhere in the country: the city's growth had been too rapid, and the sheer size of the place had made for special difficulties. The problem of class segregation was compounded by a high rate of mobility and a widespread sense of rootlessness. Not to put too fine a point on it, London was a social mess.

No aspect of the city was more distressing than the dire material want of many of its inhabitants. In this respect the capital had mocked the optimistic Victorian ethos of progress. For decades, the general state of the world's most highly-populated and extensive city had been a matter of public concern. The very year of Attlee's birth had seen the publication of a powerful pamphlet, *The Bitter Cry of Outcast London*, which 'had moved the Queen and shook even the party politicians'.[3] It was this and subsequent disclosures which had caused the politicians to act. The conscience of the middle-class had also been aroused: between 1884 and 1900, twenty-six slum settlements had been founded by various bodies of do-gooders. But these had made little overall impact, as the famous inquiry of Charles Booth demonstrated. Begun in 1886 and only completed some seventeen years and seventeen volumes later, his *Life and Labour of the People of London* estimated that a third of the population was poverty-stricken.[4] Booth was able to show that charity was 'largely irrelevant . . . doing little more than relieve the rates.'[5] Despite the move to the suburbs, the inner-city working-class districts remained overcrowded: by the end of the century, far from getting better, the problem of poverty was worse. In East London, eleven out of twelve volunteers for the army in South Africa were rejected as medically unfit.[6]

Such was the underside of the London environment to which Attlee returned; but, for a year, his tight, middle-class world held good. He was able to prolong his carefree, perhaps rather aimless, convivial apprenticeship to life. He began work in the chambers of Sir Philip Gregory, a leading conveyancing counsel of Lincoln's Inn. Here, he found that industriousness and attention to detail counted for more than at Oxford. He learned how to draft documents accurately, a useful training for a future politician. When, at the end of his year with Gregory, he succeeded in passing his Bar examinations without much difficulty, the future boded well. With an eminent solicitor as his father he had every prospect of receiving those initial briefs so essential to later success. Outside the office, life continued to be interesting and enjoyable. He went home for tea to Putney, where most of his family still resided, and where family life was much the same.[7] He played a lot of billiards, his most proficient game; he learned to ride; he joined several of his father's friends on a shoot they had in Sussex. His literary interests were not neglected, and he belonged to the Hazlitt Essay Club. With Tom, his closest friend, he was also a member of a club in Putney where papers were read and discussed on various subjects.

His outlook remained conservative, though away from the rarefied atmosphere of Oxford a hint of the outside world began to make itself heard. His oldest brother, Rob, already professed himself a moderate liberal. Clem and Tom were largely content to peruse papers in which social reform projects were aired though topics such as Co-operation and Co-partnership now figured in their discussions. They realized, too, that Ruskin and Morris were in earnest about certain political and social ideas. But all of this could be safely accommodated under the evangelical Victorian umbrella, the traditional family outlook.

Attlee then made an odd move in terms of a barrister's career, but one which is readily understandable in view of his father's profession. He had passed his legal exams and, before obtaining a proper (paid) post, either he himself – or, more probably, his father – decided that it might be useful if he saw something of the solicitor's side of legal work. Thus for several months he attended his father's office. The move proved to be the turning point of his life. His job was merely to observe the interviewing of clients, but he came quickly to detest it: he experienced what seems to have been the first really powerful emotion of his young, protected existence. The office was dark, dirty and old fashioned; his activity or lack of activity there bored him to distraction. One dreary day in October 1905, he had the idea of paying an evening visit to a part of London he did not know. Accompanied by his younger brother Laurence, an Oxford undergraduate whose term had not yet started, he set out – apparently 'dressed in the finery of the legal profession, silk hat and tail coat'[8] – by train for Stepney, in the East End.

The object of their journey was to inspect a boys' club that their old school had established in Limehouse, a district of the borough. Ostensibly the young men were mildly curious to see what was being done with the money that they and others had subscribed; there seems to have been little other overt motivation. It is difficult, for instance, to detect any deep sense of moral unease, though family tradition must be accounted a strong factor in the direction their curiosity took. On the other hand, it is not too fanciful to suppose that the Edwardian veneer on Victorian civilization had failed to satisfy the psychic needs of these two young gents. We know that Clement, at least, was bored: perhaps he and Laurence unconsciously yearned for new kinds of experience. They might have taken the boat for, say, Africa, in search of the wide open spaces or exotic jungles. Instead they took the easier option of a train to Stepney and eventually discovered the existence of a world as strange and foreign to them as anything that Africa could have offered.

There were no wide open spaces in Stepney, but in its teeming slums, composed of back-to-back houses, there was exoticism aplenty. Among the 300,000 people crowded into fewer than 1,700 acres there were large minorities of 'colourful' Jewish immigrants and Irish Catholics, apart from the indigenous majority of Cockneys.[9] Between 80 and 90 per cent were working class; bourgeois values had little validity. Thrift was impossible, material security unobtainable, sobriety pointless. Some 40 per cent of the employed males were engaged in the tailoring trade, a notorious sweated industry. Large numbers of women were employed in the same business as 'outworkers,' for derisory sums. Many of the other males were dockers or building workers, occupations known as 'casual' because of the daily uncertainty of finding work. Others, railway workers, had more stable employment, but were miserably paid. Ten hours a day for a man was considered a reasonable stint; unemployment was rampant. From a sociological point of view it might have been considered a disaster area, but Attlee was to learn that this was not altogether the case.

He was fortunate in his introduction to the district and its problems. The boys' club that he saw in operation was an unusually good example of what could be accomplished by voluntary social work of a concrete and limited nature. Its object was merely to bring a modicum of healthy recreation and discipline into lives that were obviously lacking in both. The boys were a rough and typical lot, poorly clad and uneducated. They were mostly in blind-alley jobs and would be thrown on the industrial scrap-heap when they were eighteen and had to be paid men's wages. There was nothing exceptional about the evening's activities; the boys were merely drilling, boxing and playing games. The drill was explained by the club's military connection; it formed part of the First Cadet Battalion of the Queen's London Regiment. But there was no formal religious basis to the club, unlike many of the other London middle-class missions to the poor – a fact that appealed to Attlee. Still more attractive to him was the members' evident loyalty to the club, a feeling which Attlee had himself imbibed at school and university, and could instantly appreciate. He learned one other point of lasting value to him that evening. Haileybury House owed much of its vitality and effectiveness to the efforts of one man, Cecil Nussey, a solicitor by profession. What impressed Attlee about Nussey was the latter's sense of justice and the strength of his dedication; he had 'given up his life for the boys'. These qualities, Attlee gradually realized, were of no avail in regard to the key problem – that of the crushing poverty. But in other respects they had a vital contribution to make, one that could not be dispensed with even after massive state-intervention. When he died, the Attlee Memorial Appeal had as its object the raising of money for an investigation into social needs and the encouragement of pilot schemes to support experiments. The Appeal had received his prior approval. It is clear that, although he came to see what the State could and should do in regard to social welfare, he retained his original conviction of the importance of individual initiative and commitment.

His own interest and involvement grew rapidly, though he had a great deal to learn. He had promised Nussey he would pay another visit to the club, and return he did. Within five months he had taken the obligatory commission in the Battalion, but his personal adjustment to the milieu took longer. All the social prejudices of his upbringing and education had to be modified, a process which he was to describe in a book, *The Social Worker*: 'What do they know of England who only the Empire know?' he rhetorically asked, parodying Kipling. He then referred to his own experience:

> Take the case of a boy from public school knowing little or nothing of social and industrial matters who decides, perhaps at the invitation of a friend or from loyalty to his old school that runs a mission, or to the instinct for service that exists in everyone, to assist in running a boys' club. At first he will be shy, then on getting to know the club boys he will find himself with a new outlook and shedding old prejudices. The rather noisy crowd of boys . . . whom he always regarded as bounders, become human beings to him . . .

But, he stressed, it was vital that the interest pass beyond the sentimental, the religious or the financial-support stage: what mattered most was personal involvement.[10]

For him, the process was made more difficult by his shyness, though once he had overcome it, his commitment was immeasurably fortified. He also had to come to grips with the reality of the industrial and social conditions of his protégés: some of them were working eighty or ninety hours a week for five shillings. Many of them nevertheless, he discovered, were fine characters, no different from boys of any other class[11] except that they were up against life at an earlier age. This was a working class, of course, which had not yet been diluted by selective education schemes. Attlee was profoundly moved by the heroism of the daily struggle with poverty, the unselfishness and neighbourly kindness which existed in poor districts. Gradually it dawned on him that his whole scale of values had been wrong and that he could no longer tolerate the 'gross injustices, stupidities and cruelties of the existing system.' Henceforth, he decided, it was up to him to try to find a remedy.

In many respects Attlee was what today would be called a 'late developer'. It had taken him years to find for himself the task that the Master of Balliol had suggested to his students long ago. He was not a natural rebel. He had no personal problems and was not resentful of his background: there were no guilt feelings. Neither was his change of attitude primarily an intellectual one, based on some abstract conception of a new society. He was a man of the greatest self-control: everything in his nature, training, inclination and taste mitigated against any major intellectual or emotional upheaval. His change of heart was rooted in his daily experience of the horrors of life in London's East End, which only subsequently was he to think of as the evils of capitalism. His conversion to 'socialism' was a reluctant one, arrived at by a slow process of elimination of possible alternatives: fundamentally it was an ethical reaction. Even after he had come to look upon socialism as the only general solution, he still felt himself obliged to carry on with his individual and necessarily palliative efforts at social reform. Socialism for Attlee meant fellowship, which implied both individual and State responsibility for society. He did not have the sort of temperament that could dispense with attempts to secure immediate improvements, however small, in favour of a postponed global remedy: action always appealed more to him than theory. He was too conscious of the day-to-day suffering, and of the practical benefits to be gained from any legislation designed to alleviate the condition of the poor, to be overly diverted by a search for philosophical precision. Besides, he found that the Stepney Club was 'absorbingly interesting' and that the boys were 'delightful to know'.

At first he retained his 'strictly middle-class' economic ideas, and his political outlook remained conservative. For a short period he was quite enamoured of the methods of the Charity Organization Society.[12] The COS was an adjunct of the Boards of Guardians established by the infamous Poor Law of 1834, which even Conservatives had come to see as not entirely suitable. The COS restricted its aid to 'loans to tradesmen in difficulties or to artisans who had lost their tools, and gave emigration grants and pensions to the respectable poor. The rest were offered resident relief at the workhouse or nothing.' The COS committees campaigned against free-education, against state-pensions, against the feeding of under-nourished schoolchildren, against the provision by local authorities of winter relief works for the unemployed, against Salvation Army shelters and soup kitchens – all of which they thought eroded self-help.[13] Attlee would tell the story of one COS member, an Anglican parson, who advocated serving starving children *burnt* porridge, in only the most inconvenient places and at the most inconvenient times, in support of the theory.

Such attitudes could not withstand Attlee's growing affection and admiration for his charges. In the summer of 1906 he attended the Battalion's summer camp; already he was devoting three or four evenings to the club. In the autumn of the following year he took a decisive step; he became the residential manager of Haileybury House. For a man of his social position this was the equivalent of crossing the Rubicon and, apart from occasional week-ends, he never returned to tea in Putney. The move to Limehouse allowed him to deepen considerably his knowledge of social conditions; as an evening visitor he had realized that his angle of vision was limited. He was soon appointed to a variety of public bodies, including the Children's Care Committee of a large slum school, which meant visiting the homes.

His change of abode also provided him with an 'opportunity to direct a small society' which, interestingly, he used to decentralize the operation of Haileybury House. He was instrumental in taking the administration away from the exclusive possession of the adults and handing it over to a Club Committee of five, elected by the whole membership. Similarly, a sub-committee of the boys took over the running of the canteen, which resulted in a sizeable profit which was used to assist the poorer boys to pay the Club expenses or the extra fees for camping trips. Attlee started a junior club for boys aged twelve to fourteen, keeping the numbers down to seventy on the principle of trying to influence 'the few rather than the many'.[14] The latter is the first recorded example of his predilection for the immediately practicable over the distantly desirable, which did not affect his rapidly growing awareness of the larger problem. Nevertheless, it was to take him nearly two years before he discovered that he was a socialist. He had to make an enormous intellectual adjustment, 'to effect a revolution in all his conceptions . . . to part with the class prejudices which he [had] taken in as naturally as the air he breathed'.[15]

At first he was simply puzzled, and pursued a number of tacks. He returned to his books, especially Ruskin and Morris, in a new attempt to understand the social philosophy they expressed. At heart he remained a romantic, wanting to have it both ways – hence his brief association with the COS. His ideal social creed would have been one that salved his now uneasy conscience and yet did not entail any major upheaval. Thus, for a while, he turned to Co-partnership and Co-operative ideas, but again his intellectual honesty intervened: these notions begged the fundamental question, that of the role of the State. Here, he ran head on into the cardinal political tenet of his entire upbringing: private property, the sacred basis of society, of law and order, of English civilization itself. To a man like Attlee at this time, the very word 'State' suggested 'the prison, the workhouse and everything that was drab'. On the other hand, the conditions he saw around him every day were as dreary and sordid as anything could be. He was 'burning with anger' about them; nothing in the world, he felt, was as worth doing as trying to alter those conditions. He could no longer afford any illusions about his own work; useful and necessary, it was still 'ambulance work'. *Ergo*, something had to give – his prejudices or the conditions. The more he considered the matter, the more it appeared to him that thorough-going change could only come about through the power of the people, working through their elected representatives. State socialism was the only framework within which a new society could be created. The shock of this discovery, which owed nothing whatsoever to Karl Marx, was enough to send him back to his books. This time he found that many of his literary heroes had also been rebels; if you looked hard enough, rebellion, even socialism, could be made to appear 'respectable'. His word is revealing.

In the autumn of 1907 Attlee, with his brother Tom, joined the Fabian Society. This was not a revolutionary move; the membership, though composed largely of socialists, was eminently 'respectable'. Most Fabians preferred lecturing to middle-class rather than working-class organizations. Interest in the Society, founded in 1884, had been stimulated by the advent of the Labour Party in 1900, but there was no formal consensus as to how socialism might be brought about. The leaders of the London branch, in particular, still believed in 1910 that socialism could be brought about more easily through one of the existing parties.[16] Essentially, the Society was a political debating group, a socialist club for the exchange of ideas. Attlee carried home a vivid memory of his first meeting, attended by Sidney Webb, Bernard Shaw and H. G. Wells, of 'many bearded men talking and roaring with laughter'. Turning to his brother Tom as they left, Attlee wondered, 'Have we got to grow a beard to join this show?'[17]

Tom did grow a beard a little later, but not Clem. The contrast between the rarefied and jovial atmosphere of a Fabian debate and the sociopolitical reality of Stepney was jarring to the commonsensical, earnest Attlee. Having a general interest in ideas did not make him an intellectual, though given his education and middle-class status he might pass as such in the lower echelons of the socialist movement.[18] He afterwards rationalized his hesitations with regard to the Fabian approach to socialism: strong on facts, it 'was always rather weak in dealing with persons. It considered more the organization of things than the life of people. It tended to lose sight of the individual in contemplating the community.'[19] He never totally embraced Fabianism, just as he could never be described as a thorough-going collectivist. Academic socialism had slight appeal for him: his interest was confined to the Fabian diagnosis of capitalism's ills and the particular remedies which emerged from it.

He was even less attracted to the Social Democratic Federation,[20] the second of the three main socialist groups in pre-war London. The SDF was a Marxist-orientated body, and was jealous of its claim to represent the pure gospel of socialism. Not only did Attlee know little or nothing of Marxism in 1907, but the doctrinal exclusiveness of the group which represented it in England would alone have sufficed to repel him. 'I was not a scientific person,' he recalled, 'and was never attracted by Marxism ... I have never had much faith in the belief in the inevitability of socialism. I used to think in my youth: "What is the good of my standing hours and hours at the street corners if the whole thing is inevitable?"'[21]

The third alternative was the Independent Labour Party, a body which responded perfectly to Attlee's needs in 1908. The ILP managed to combine a general socialist objective, 'the collective ownership of the means of production, distribution and exchange,' with a clear tactical aim – that of securing the independent parliamentary representation of working men. In practice, this meant obtaining the co-operation of the trade unions, many of whose members and leaders were far from being socialists. The ILP's lack of any doctrinal exclusiveness was a distinct asset for a time: 'Fervent and emotional,' writes the organization's historian, 'the socialism of the ILP could accommodate, with only a little strain, temperance reform, Scottish nationalism, Methodism, Marxism, Fabian gradualism and even a variety of Burkeian conservatism.'[22] In the end, the lack of doctrinal clarity and a basic structural weakness were to be fatal,[23] but in the early years of the twentieth century they proved to be strengths. Working through its trade union members, the ILP had been able to prevail on a reluctant TUC to summon the special conference in 1899 from which the Labour Representation Committee of 1900 (the future Labour Party) had been formed.[24] Thirty Labour MPs in 1906 gave a much needed boost to the ILP which, by 1909, could claim some 887 branch affiliations and about 22,000 members.[25] Attlee thus joined the group at an opportune moment in its history. The Labour Party itself still had neither a programme nor any provision for individual membership. The ILP was the only vehicle for people like him who wanted to contribute something to the socialist cause at once, not in the nebulous future.

The ILP's *élan* did not last long after 1909. Its original success in establishing the Labour Party had been due at least as much to trade union legal anxieties as to the unions' political ambitions. Subsequently, the Liberal and Labour Parties[26] concluded an electoral pact; and although the pact was secret, radical ILP discontent with the resulting parliamentary collusion soon became widespread.[27] But these political subtleties had little impact on Attlee, who operated largely at grass-roots level. If socialist activity and organization in the country were still in embryo, in London they barely existed. The metropolis was seriously lacking in most of the prerequisites for a labour, not to mention a socialist, movement. Except for the docks, railways and gas works, much of industry was still on a small scale; trade union and co-operative movements were difficult enough to organize, quite apart from the question of political orientation. Between 1904 and 1913 the number of London unions affiliated to the Labour Party actually fell from seventy to fifty.[28] Large numbers of people were employed as domestic workers and were isolated; much the same could be said of the growing number of office workers and commuters. There was also a social gap between skilled and unskilled. The heterogeneous London population was in a state of flux, with results most felt in the poorer districts.

Local factors worked against Labour interests. Abler workers left the slums as soon as possible, depriving localities of a pool of natural leaders.

Community feeling, except at the street or ethnic level, was non-existent. Large areas of the city were untouched by the official gods. Very few Anglican clergymen were socialists and the non-conformist chapels, a source of Labour recruitment in the provinces, were weaker in London than the Anglican church. The London chapels were usually Liberal in political outlook as, for obvious reasons,* were the Irish Roman Catholics. The success of the London Progressive Movement was a further obstacle. (This last was a Liberal-dominated organization that had a long record of co-operation with Labour behind it.)

Even more detrimental to the Labour cause was the fact that the extension of the franchise had had little effect on the London working-class constituencies: by 1911, the inner electorate had only increased from 13.2 per cent to 14.7 per cent of the population.[29] The electoral position of lodgers, for example, was complicated and no doubt many of them failed to take the necessary steps in order to be able to vote. Application for poor relief carried with it an automatic disqualification and all females, of course, were excluded. Also, the system of multiple voting counted against several London boroughs and the working-class vote was heavily penalized by the registration procedures in case of a change of address. Thompson has found that it was common for a quarter or even a third of the electorate to have left a district by the last month of the validity of the register.[30] In terms of parliamentary results, all this meant that in the Tower Hamlets Division of the East End of London (a division which comprised seven constituencies) the Labour Party managed to win only one seat in the pre-war period, George Lansbury's, in December 1910.

The two obvious deficiences of ILP work in London lay in the areas of propaganda and organization: Attlee naturally gravitated to the former. It was here that his ethical impulse could find expression. His associates brought to their task 'an apostolic enthusiasm. It had something of the quality of a religious crusade.' He could taste to the full the quality of his conversion and put his new-found faith to the test. Most ILP London members were working-class and to them Attlee was an outsider. R. C. K. Ensor, a middle-class ILP activist in Poplar, warned a potential recruit like Attlee of what to expect: 'men and women of every grade ... their dialect, their modes of thought, their lack of education ... [would] all bewilder and repel him ... '[31] Yet Attlee revelled in what he called the 'wonderful comradeship'. True, the ILP membership 'tended to be rather puritanical and even pharisaic, while the SDF affected a more worldly attitude. The ILP drank tea where the SDF drank beer.' But the solid core of the ILP, he found, 'consisted of thoughtful and responsible working men and women whose socialism was based primarily on ethics and secondarily on economics.' That was exactly his own position.

*The Liberal Party had adopted its Home Rule policy for Ireland in 1886.

No task was too menial for him. Though he quickly graduated to the level of a street-corner speaker, he also carried the platform, 'called the crowd', buttered bread and collected money in aid of strikers. He saw his own ILP branch increase from an original dozen members to about seventy – resisting, in the process, an attempt by the SDF to break it up. He stood twice for the Board of Guardians and twice for the local council, being 'hopelessly beaten' on each occasion. The burden of his propaganda work was a basic one: he aimed to create an interest in socialism, to persuade people that social reform and an increased standard of living were both possible.[32] In particular, he struck out against the old idea that the poor in a lump were bad: what was wrong with the poor was their poverty.[33] In a newspaper which he helped to produce, *The Stepney Worker*, he suggested the means to eradicate poverty; nationalization of the land, the running of the railways, businesses and factories for the benefit of all, a minimum wage, and fixed rents and taxes to be applied to those able to pay. He found that such a programme was not sufficiently Marxist for the local SDF members, who caused the paper to fold after a few weeks.[34]

Stepney was an exceptionally frustrating experience for a socialist. Of the total population of around 300,000 fewer than 4,000 cast their vote for any national party between 1900 and 1910. Despite its overwhelmingly working-class character, there was little sense of political or social unity in the borough. The population was fragmented into ethnic and cockney elements, skilled and unskilled. Politically, the borough was almost a vacuum: the Liberal Association was defunct; the ILP branch which Attlee joined had been founded only in January 1907; and the only progressive body, an independent Labour League, was almost as weak as the Liberals. Local politics from 1908 to 1914 were dominated by the Union of Stepney Ratepayers, whose policy was to keep the rates as low as possible. Though the borough had a greater number of paupers than the London average, it spent approximately 40 per cent less to maintain them; it has been described as 'a working-class community governed in the interests of the middle-class'.[35] Small wonder that Attlee was so taken with the need for basic propaganda work; the poor he encountered were largely too poor, too tired, too apathetic, too ignorant and too cowed to do anything to improve their collective lot.

He was not, however, so submerged in Stepney as to be completely unaware of the larger Labour context. In the years before the war, this was mostly one of failure. When he became a socialist it had seemed as though it might be otherwise, for the Labour electoral advance of 1906 had been followed, in 1907, by two by-election successes. The first was won by an ILP candidate, in accord with the higher politics of the secret ILP – Liberal Party agreement; the second was a sensational triumph for Victor Grayson who, in defiance of the ILP executive, had stood as an independent Labour candidate. As Secretary of his local branch, Attlee attended the ILP's annual conference at Edinburgh in 1909 which saw the resignations of Keir Hardie, Ramsay MacDonald, Philip Snowden and Bruce Glazier from the National Administrative Council over the Grayson incident. Had Attlee been elected to the NAC, it is probable that he would have sided with the rebels in favour, that is, of a more independent position. But he was not elected, and fell back on his general political tactic that the main task of the ILP was 'to try to wean organized Labour from Liberalism'. He was to see his several personal efforts to persuade his own union, the National Union of Clerks, to join the Labour Party all end in failure. The Clerks had something of a middle-class cachet, but similar attempts by Attlee and his Stepney ILP colleagues in regard to other unions were equally fruitless.

After 1910 there was a decline in membership of the London ILP. Even before then its growth had had little to do with its own efforts: rather, the ILP had grown along with the increased national prestige of the Labour Party in 1906. As the latter apparently became more closely tied to the coat-tails of the Liberals – partly because of Liberal reforms and partly, after the two general elections of 1910, because of the parliamentary situation – so did the fortunes of the ILP in London wane: 'It could get an occasional member elected to the London County Council (one in 1907, three in 1910, one in 1913) but only with Progressive support, and all efforts to win over the Progressive Labour bench . . . failed.'[36] The record for the London Borough Councils was equally disheartening,[37] and the same could be said for Attlee's own work on behalf of George Lansbury's parliamentary campaign in Bow and Bromley, in December 1910. Attlee wrote the election song, sung by the children to the tune of *All the nice girls love a sailor*, and marched down the Bow Road into Mile End carrying a huge placard with the figures of the majority.[38] But the victory soon turned sour; within two years Lansbury resigned the seat in order to fight independently on the suffragette issue, and lost. Attlee could well write in retrospect that he had shared 'the hopes and disappointments incidental to Socialist work in what was then a very backward area'.[39]

As noted, the failure of the Labour movement in pre-war London had a number of causes, of which the weakness of the ILP was only one. The split with the SDF was undoubtedly a contributing factor; according to Thompson such growth as there was in the London socialist movement 'owed much of its character and achievement to the much abused SDF'.[40] Attlee was aware that the SDF contained two distinct elements – a 'fair number of foreigners . . . the nucleus of the future Communist Party . . . ' and some 'very English workers' such as Will Thorne, Ben Tillet and Tom Kennedy, who eventually became loyal and somewhat right-wing members of the Labour Party.[41] There were also the special social and cultural problems that London posed, from a socialist viewpoint. It was only in 1918 that the various obstacles to the formation of a London Labour Party, embracing the whole of the left-wing spectrum, were finally removed. The decisive factor for Labour's electoral opportunities in London, and elsewhere, was the ending of the restricted franchise: McKibbin has persuasively argued that it was 'the 1918 Representation of the People Act, by which 80% of the new voting population was enfranchised for the first time, [which] transformed the conditions under which Labour grew'.[42] In a sense, therefore, the propaganda efforts of Attlee, and others, during the pre-war period were doomed in advance, so far as tangible results were concerned.

Individuals reacted in different ways to this experience. One working-class Cockney, Herbert Morrison, after early disillusionment with the SDF, opted for organizational work. But Attlee's activities were unaffected by the political failure. It mattered little to him that by 1914 much of the early enthusiasm had evaporated[43] and that socialist efforts even in Stepney had waned.[44] His enthusiasm for the cause remained as strong as ever, and he still sought to communicate it to others. The ILP movement provided the best vehicle for him. Perhaps in some ways it acted as a substitute for the organized religion that he had discarded. It certainly contributed to the development of his confidence, and gave him a political education. And the ethical aspects of socialism, on which he put so much emphasis, turned out to be the single point on which all Labour factions could agree.

In any case, during the period before the First World War, Attlee's first preoccupation was his social work. For much of the time, his usual evening routine took him four times a week to the boys' club, only once to the Stepney branch of the ILP. After the autumn of 1907, his permanent residence was Haileybury House, with the sole exception of a year as secretary at Toynbee Hall and a short period of sharing a flat with his brother Tom. He kept his political and social work in separate mental compartments, and this set him apart from other middle-class people who were also engaged in the two fields. For Tom they were intrinsically related. William Beveridge, after his brief experience at Toynbee Hall, quickly came to the conclusion that involvement in social policy was by its nature a highly political activity.[45] And R. H. Tawney, who lasted three years there, became eager for an approach that 'combined education for socialism with organizing workers and marshalling knowledge for the pursuit of state power.'[46] Others argued that though the London poor were too poor for protest or political action of a general nature, they might be galvanized at the grass-roots level in favour of tangible, if limited, objectives. From these humble beginnings a larger, more widespread, popular movement could emerge. The role of the middle-class social worker, on this reckoning, was primarily that of a political midwife; the leadership and initiative of outsiders would, in time, assist the birth of an indigenous socialist movement. Attlee saw the matter in a different light. Not only was he singularly devoid of political ambitions, but the prospect, from a socialist viewpoint, of anything substantial being obtained on the political level seemed to him to be remote. His social work, on the other hand, had its own psychological satisfactions and its own *raison d'être*.

The Social Services Movement of modern times, he explained in his book *The Social Worker*, was not confined to any one class, nor was it the preserve of a particular section of dull and respectable people: it stemmed from a deep discontent with the present society. Sympathy was needed, but so too were understanding and knowledge; the social worker had to get rid of any feelings of superiority. For this reason it was best not to start in relief work; better to begin by working with boys or girls in clubs or Scout groups – this would give scope for exercising whatever talents the social worker might have, be they in singing, playing, dancing, swimming, boxing or gymnastics. 'One does not feel such a fool if there is something to do in this way,' he wrote, 'and one is very apt to feel a fool when starting social work.' People should not be treated as cases or statistics or categories; courtesy and cheerfulness were great assets. Those who couldn't be cheerful, he advised, should try some other kind of work. He warned against the 'survival of the ascetic ideal that the social worker should mortify the flesh, dress in dull – generally black – raiment, and take his or her pleasures sadly ... [They] should not be segregated into a class spending their whole time in mean conditions of life, working long hours, and not mixing in the pleasures of others. They [are] entitled to as much pleasure as anyone else, and if they stick to their work, living, let us say, in the east, and never going up west, they lose power, tend to become narrow and dull, and cease to be as efficient as they might be.'

Attlee was particularly convinced that social workers should strive to see their work in a balanced perspective. There was a danger of middle-class reformers or revolutionaries becoming so impressed with the evil of certain abstractions – such as the capitalist class – that they would readily condemn all methods of social advance that did not directly square with their formulae. All social reformers would be well advised to keep in touch with some form of social work which would bring them into contact with the individual – though he also cautioned that enthusiasm for a particular institution or society could become so great that the evil which had provoked the existence of the institution could be overlooked.[47] Attlee could not identify himself with the poor; the social and educational gulf was too wide. Besides, he had a small private income; he was his own master, if no one else's. But he did endeavour to be accepted by the poor, and such was the strength of the moral imperative which drove and sustained him that he was accepted. It was a notable achievement, and one of which in later years he was justifiably proud: 'Not only did I have countless lessons in practical economics,' he remembered, 'but there was kindled in me a warmth and affection for these people that has remained with me all my life.'[48] That his social work later provided him with secure political roots in a working-class area, an attribute that few middle-class socialists have enjoyed, was an incidental and unforeseen by-product.[49]

He continued to attend Chambers throughout 1908, but by the summer of 1909 he had had enough. William Beveridge, an altogether more intellectually brilliant man, took only three months to come to a similar decision. After an outstanding undergraduate career, Beveridge found the work of a barrister to be solitary, self-centred and intellectually trivial.[50] Attlee's reaction was that there was little to do and he was irritated at wasting time. His father died in November 1908, and Attlee's financial situation somewhat improved: he had just enough independence to be able to take chances. Moreover his social work acquired an additional dimension.

In 1909, the Royal Commission on the Poor Law, appointed by Balfour on his last day in office in 1905, brought down its Report, or rather two Reports. The Commissioners were divided over their recommendations, producing a Majority and a Minority Report. Both agreed that the old system, based on the 1834 Act, had become obsolete, but the Majority merely wanted to transfer the duties of the former Guardians to the local authorities, whereas the Minority, under the direct inspiration of the Webbs, favoured a complete break with the past. They saw the problem of poverty as 'a social condition resulting from the organization of the economy'.[51] The remedy was not cure but prevention; the several categories of poor people – the old, the ill, the unemployed, the widowed, the orphaned – should be assisted by separate and specialized national agencies. But in the political climate of the day neither the proposals of the Majority Report nor those of the Minority were acceptable to the Liberals, in particular Lloyd George, as coming within the realm of practical possibility. Quite unabashed, the Minority Commissioners sponsored a National Committee to persuade all members of society of the need for drastic reform.

Attlee's new job was to organize public meetings all over the country, but his services were frequently called upon as a last-minute replacement for absentee speakers. After three months he accepted the post of Secretary at Toynbee Hall, though he closely followed the rest of the campaign which went on for three years. Not only did it fail, but it has been said of the Royal Commission itself that, 'Never can so important a Royal Commission have produced so little in the way of action, for not even the more moderate suggestions of the Majority Report were enacted.'[52] Some forty years were to elapse before the complete break with the nineteenth-century Poor Law was embodied in the Welfare State, the implementation of which Attlee presided over, with Beveridge producing the blueprints. Meanwhile, the sufferings of the poor continued, and Attlee had no hesitation, a year or so later, in acting as one of the official explainers of the Liberal Government's National Insurance Act of 1911.

Historians have disagreed over whether Lloyd George's Bill can be viewed as the forerunner of the Welfare State. Lloyd George himself considered it to be a start in the universalist direction. On the other hand, the father of the ILP, Keir Hardie, condemned it; to him, the Liberals were only saying, 'We shall not uproot the cause of poverty but we shall give you a porous plaster to cover the disease that poverty causes.' The Bill's cardinal features were the insurance principle and the flat-rate charge, irrespective of amount of income. Yet despite its shortcomings, one writer has argued, the Bill represented a 'tremendously important extension of state aid . . . a major non-socialist injection of social welfare into the British system.'[53] This is how Attlee viewed it; what motivated him was the daily contemplation of the agony caused by material distress. He put his feelings into a poem called *In Limehouse*.[54]

In Limehouse, in Limehouse, before the break of day,
I hear the feet of many men who go upon their way.
Who wander through the city,
The grey and cruel city,
Through streets that have no pity,
The streets where men decay.
In Limehouse, in Limehouse, by night as well as day
I hear the feet of children that go to work or play,
Of children born to sorrow,
The workers of tomorrow,
How shall they work tomorrow
Who get no bread today?
In Limehouse, in Limehouse, today and every day
I see the weary mothers who sweat their souls away:
Poor, tired mothers trying
To hush the feeble crying
Of little babies dying
For want of bread today.

In Limehouse, in Limehouse, I'm dreaming of the day
When evil times shall perish and be driven clean away.
When father, child and mother
Shall live and love each other
And brother help his brother
In happy work and play.

To further this goal of 'happy work and play', Attlee was always ready to put aside his larger convictions and to co-operate in any measures designed to improve the lot of the poor, while still retaining his capacity for detachment. He was once invited to participate in a joint Fabian Society – ILP series of lectures and took Walpole as his topic – a subject somewhat remote from the current concerns of his audience.[55] On another occasion he spoke to an ILP Evening Institute in darkest Bermondsey on the subject of 'Socialism and the Middle Class'.[56] To Ruskin College in Oxford he gave a series of paid lectures on Trade Unionism and other topics. Shortage of money was also probably the reason behind his several applications for other jobs, including two legal posts in the civil service, one with the Church Commission, one with the Charity Commissioners.[57] That he did not obtain a permanent post was partly, he believed, because socialist activities in those days were not looked upon with favour.

Eventually, in 1912, he was appointed to a lectureship in the Department of Social Science and Administration at the London School of Economics. His rival for the post was Hugh Dalton, but Attlee enjoyed the advantages of his practical experience, of being older, and of his contacts with Sidney Webb. The latter, who was Chairman of the Selection Committee, subsequently told Dalton not to be discouraged: 'We thought that, if we appointed him [Attlee], he'd stick to it, but that, if we appointed you, you wouldn't.'[58] Attlee had already acquired a reputation for persistence, though the intervention of the war interrupted his academic career. Both Dalton and Attlee, and Tawney, who all saw military service, found LSE posts afterwards, while Beveridge was named director of the School in 1919.[59] With the publication of his book in 1920, Attlee could no doubt have achieved a respectable academic career in social work, but the desire to do something more practical proved too strong.

On the surface at least, his pre-war activities present an odd picture. He had criss-crossed several worlds, legal offices and courts of law, the London slums, street-corner political platforms and academia. Heeding his own advice to social workers, he had also enjoyed a number of 'cultured' continental holidays, though he had not succeeded in dispelling a nagging sense of personal loneliness. In a poem probably written about this time he confessed:

> My life is passing like a lonely stream
> Winding through meadows flecked with white and gold
> That farseen distant castled hills enfold
> Yearnings and visions, memories of a dream.
> Like tributary brooks my friendships seem
> Into the volume of the river enrolled

So in my heart their added wealth I hold
But still my life is lonely like the stream.
Suddenly a change in this calm life I see
The cataracts and shoals of Love are near
Life is a torrent and within my heart
The calling of another stream I hear
This is the waters meet, never to part
Love let us flow together to the Sea.[60]

On the other hand, he had firmly established his basic values and moral priorities. These were to be given a final definition in the fateful summer of 1914 – when he chanced to be on holiday in Devon with his brother Tom and sister-in-law Dorothy.

III

The Work Has To Be Done

No single act of Clem Attlee's young adult years is more revealing of his character or was more significant for the development of his political views and career than his decision to enlist in the First World War. Most of his ILP friends utterly condemned British participation on grounds of strict principle – socialist, pacifist, or both. Attlee went his own way, and the reconciliation that he would make with his former associates after the catastrophe was inevitably incomplete and temporary.

There was nothing impulsive or casual about the decision he made in the summer of 1914; it followed lengthy discussions with his brother Tom 'on the position of affairs and our own attitudes'. Tom, the Christian socialist, was quite clear on the subject; he was an absolute pacifist, thoroughly prepared to take the consequences. But while appreciating and respecting his brother's views, Clem did not share them. In certain circumstances he was prepared to take up arms: the question to resolve was whether this particular situation constituted sufficient justification. At first, it seemed not; the war would soon be over and would only necessitate the services of the professional soldiers. Kitchener's appeal for 100,000 volunteers, however, made it clear to Attlee that the whole nation would be involved. What should he do? His 'whole instincts as a socialist were against war'; he did not accept the propaganda cry of 'Your King and Country Need You', and he was not convinced of Germany's sole guilt. Moreover, on his return to London – he could not stay on in Devon – he found that several of his political colleagues were certain that the war would lead to unemployment and distress in East London. It was his (socialist) duty to remain there. Despite these arguments, he took the opposite course.

By his own account, he was finally persuaded to enlist by 'the wanton invasion of Belgium and the German actions therein'. Here, he was at one with the predominant national mood, so far as it can be ascertained; in a crisis he discovered that his sense of identification with the nation as a whole counted for more than his 'socialist instincts'. The war also gave him the perfect opportunity for the expression of the service ideal in which he had been raised. 'My point is,' he explained to Tom towards the end of the war, 'that I don't like the work but the community calls on me to be a scavenger – my particular objection to doing the work cannot weigh with me if the work has to be done.'[1] Some people had to serve, and perhaps be killed; he could find no real religious objections to it; he was half-trained already, and single; 'the work had to be done.'

Although those were his conscious reasons, they scarcely do justice to the extraordinary ardour which Attlee devoted to his soldiering. Single he may have been, but at the outbreak of war he was also thirty-one years of age. It was only after the most determined efforts on his part that he was allowed to fight. Initially he was debarred on the grounds that he was too old; then that he already held a commission in the Cadets; still later, when he managed to get himself enrolled in the Inns of Court Officers' Training Corps, there was no certainty that he would be transferred to an active unit. He had to resort to pulling strings by using personal contacts, and was posted to the 6th South Lancashire Regiment. After very active service at Gallipoli and in Mesopotamia, resulting in severe illness and serious wounds, he found himself convalescing in England. There was every chance that he would spend the rest of the war in a training or staff capacity; in fact he was ordered to do the former and was about to be appointed to the latter. Further efforts were required to get himself reposted to his original regiment and so to the Western Front, where he was again wounded.

During the war Attlee rediscovered his erstwhile patriotism – 'the natural emotion of every true Briton'. He found, for instance, that he had no difficulty in relating to his brother officers, despite his socialist views which he made no attempt to disguise.[2] Doubtless, the often daily prospect of sudden death induced a general spirit of tolerance and comradeship, and his colleagues were almost all public-school men. In addition, Attlee possessed the strength that comes from inner conviction. But the core of the relationship was the mutual sense of patriotism, from which Attlee derived a political lesson. 'In time of war,' he noted, 'there is one overwhelming issue which may effect a union of people who differ widely in their conceptions of society but are united in the resolve to defend the particular society to which they belong.'[3] Conservatives and socialists alike had been affected:[4] might not rekindling of this sentiment on the one side be matched by a moderation of social views on the other? His war experiences persuaded him that British patriotic feeling could be mobilized for socialism, provided that the socialists were more tolerant;

and from the moment he obtained a national platform he began to expound this theory.

The opportunity occurred much earlier than he could have anticipated. In November 1922 he would find himself making his maiden speech to the House of Commons and he promptly took as his main theme an appeal to the wartime social unity. The British had then been told, he declared, that every man in the country was valuable. For the first time in 500 years of English history there had been practically no unemployment and, notwithstanding the rationing and food substitutes, living standards had actually been better. Yet now, men who had been fit to be sergeant-majors were reduced to dragging along the street with their hands out for anything they could get. Unemployment struck at the very basis of society. 'Why was it that in the War,' Attlee asked, 'we were able to find employment for everyone? It was simply that the Government controlled the purchasing power of the nation.' As the nation had been organized for war and death, he concluded, so too could it be organized for peace.[5] This was a theme which ran through all his subsequent attempts to define the Labour Party's approach to socialism: for him, it was a patriotic and unifying philosophy. When Attlee used the word 'socialism' it was in a specific, non-cosmopolitan sense: the aim of his book, *The Labour Party in Perspective* (1937), was to show the Labour Party 'as a characteristic example of British methods, and as an outcome of British political instincts.'[6] The socialism that his party preached, he claimed, was 'what the country requires in order in modern conditions to realize to the full the genius of the nation'.[7]

The 'nation' that Attlee himself revered was singularly circumscribed. One of his chapters was entitled 'The England we want to see', but it was southern England that really appealed to him. In 1918 he had chanced to be stationed at Barrow-in-Furness, in Lancashire, 'one of the most dreadful products of nineteenth-century industrialism'. While there he realized that the England he had known and loved in peacetime 'was all south-west of the line between the Wash and the Bristol Channel'. There were some beautiful places north-west of this line; he had seen some of them. But to Attlee, the North spelt the terrible masses of industrialism, Tyneside, the West Riding, the Black Country and that 'abomination of desolation', Lancashire. 'One of the heaviest indictments against the Capitalist system', he would write in 1937, 'is that it is destructive of beauty.' It was not only the crude ugliness that filled him with depression; the people of the North also seemed to lack the manners of the southerner and his 'joy in life'; they appeared 'silent, slow and irresponsive'. He thought nostalgically of the cities of the South; of Salisbury[8] 'with its mellow old red brick houses clustering around that wonderful spire; of the little towns of Somerset and Dorset set in the gaps of the gently sloping hills half-drowned in apple blossom in April'; of Dorchester 'in that rich green valley folded in the heath land with its clear streams and wooded slopes'; of the many little grey towns and villages on either side of the Thames – with 'fairest of all, Oxford'; of Cornwall, South Devon, Surrey, Sussex, Kent, East Anglia and even London with its 'beauty and ugliness and its great warm heart'.[9]

Attlee's experiences during the war both confirmed and modified his socialist views. The main principles of their pre-war socialism would have to remain, he wrote to Tom towards the end of the war, but there had been a danger 'of taking too narrow a view – in that we conceived what appeared to be the ideal life for everybody, with the result that our schemes made them unpalatable to the general public. In fact I think we were too Webby – I am sure I was having a fatal love of statistics and neat structure of society. I think we shall have to allow for greater variety ...'[10] He gave these notions a more considered and sensitive expression in 1935. 'The Socialist conception of society,' he wrote, 'is not that of a mosaic pavement where all the little squares, of no importance in themselves, fit into a pattern designed by an artist, or even of a jig-saw puzzle which allows of greater variety in the pieces.' He thought of it rather as:

> a garden, where are to be found a great variety of flowers, every one of which must have soil, air and space enough to allow it to grow to perfection. In this garden there must be some pruning, lest the coarser growths take all the light and air from the more delicate. The gardener wants variety. The garden, seen from a distance, reveals a general plan and harmony, but viewed closely, every plant is unique. This general harmony is not fixed like a mosaic pattern. It is always changing. Each plant and the garden itself is in a state of becoming. When the pavement is finished the artisan has no more to do. The gardener's work is never done.[11]

The Labour Party also evolved as a result of the First World War. Before it, there had been little consensus either about the Party's function as a political force or in regard to socialism:[12] by the end of the conflict, Labour had become a fully-fledged political party and shortly afterwards equipped itself with a new constitution. Circumstances played the major role in these two developments. The war's demands, which included the mobilization of all resources, moved Labour into a central position on the national stage: several of its leaders were called upon to serve in the coalition governments. This translation owed nothing to socialist theory: like Attlee, the Party merely responded positively to the patriotic call. The key factor was the link with the organized trade union movement; foremost among the Labour patriots were the trade union MPs who took over Party leadership. Ramsay MacDonald was replaced as chairman of the Parliamentary Party by Arthur Henderson the Party's Secretary and an official of the Friendly Society of Iron Founders.[13] His appointment symbolized the growing ascendancy of the trade-union element. In January 1917, a motion was carried at the Party's annual conference that, in future, members of the National Executive Committee should be elected by the vote of the entire conference. The decision struck a deadly blow at the position of the affiliated socialist societies; it destroyed their previous right of separate election to the Executive which, thereafter, would be dominated by the block votes of the unions. In particular, the constitutional change promised to condemn Attlee's political Alma Mater, the ILP, to a backwater. The war fever, in any case, had all but swamped appeals in the name of international utopian socialism. Dissenters had often been ruthlessly persecuted, and there were moments when the ILP hovered on the verge of separating itself from the larger body that it had been instrumental in calling into being.[14] Moreover, the Labour Party and trade union participation in the national war effort tended to favour the 'Webby' approach to socialism, with its doctrine of gradual administrative and institutional penetration. This was the strategy now favoured, for instance, by R. H. Tawney with whom Attlee had had many talks 'behind hedges in France'.[15]

On the other hand, Labour's association with the Government had not been easy, despite the appointment of several Labour ministers. Industrial unrest had continued throughout the war; labour controls and conscription procedures were a constant irritation to the unions. Unofficial shop stewards had begun to rival the official trade union leadership in many workers' eyes. The nature of the war became a source of concern to union leaders who hitherto had shown scant interest in foreign policy; and, as war-weariness grew, so too did the influence of radical groups such as the Union of Democratic Control – which had close connections with the ILP.[16] The turning-point came with the Russian Revolution, an event greeted with great enthusiasm by the Left. Officially, the Labour Party was neutral; Henderson was sent to Russia by Lloyd George with a view to keeping Russia in the war. But on his return, Henderson recommended that the Allies should explore with the Russians the basis for a negotiated peace. He also proposed that delegates from Britain should attend a meeting of the International Socialist Congress at Stockholm, at which it was expected that German socialists would be present. The War Cabinet's rejection of these proposals led to Henderson's resignation, although Lloyd George managed to keep Labour in the Government by appointing another Labour MP, George Barnes, in Henderson's place. Nevertheless, the damage had been done; henceforth Henderson would devote himself to shaping a major reorganization of the Labour Party's structure, to devising an alternative foreign policy,[17] and to preparing a distinctive party orientation.

The immediate fruit was a 'Memorandum on War Aims', drawn up by

Henderson, Sidney Webb and MacDonald and approved by the Labour Party's National Executive Committee and the TUC's Parliamentary Committee. The Memorandum demanded the establishment of a League of Nations and of international machinery to deal with economic problems such as the supply of raw materials.[18] It also 'called for the complete democratization of all countries, the limitation of armaments, the abolition of private arms manufacture, the establishment of an International Court and Legislature, self-determination and the holding of plebiscites to decide territorial disputes'.[19] Hardly 'socialist', the new formulation of foreign policy that was presented as a statement to the Prime Minister in the last days of 1917 did reflect the admittedly uneasy[20] reconciliation between Henderson and MacDonald. Subsequently, Henderson made a special effort to 'weld the Socialist and trade-union elements firmly together'.[21] In 1918 the NEC was expanded to twenty-three seats, four being reserved for women and five for nominees of local Labour parties. Much more important, the Party's New Constitution of that year included the famous Clause IV* on Labour's overall socialist aims – which enabled people like Attlee to continue to associate themselves with the larger body.

In one sense the formula was not as drastic a departure as might appear: the unions had always contained a collectivist element;[22] during and as a result of the war, this element had gained in influence. But it was far from being predominant: the main reason why the unions as a whole accepted Clause IV was because it came in a package which gave them the decisive voice in formulating Labour's future policies. For the unions, the crucial point about the new constitution was not the socialist goal but the abolition of the Party's formerly rigid federal structure:[23] their main concern was to forge an independent political instrument reflecting the upsurge in their power.[24] Clause IV also served the useful tactical purpose of underlining the gulf between the Labour and Liberal Parties.[25] Even the distinguished American political scientist, Samuel Beer, who insists on the ideological significance of the new constitution, concedes that the thrust for power of the organized working class was more important than the adoption of socialism.[26] MacDonald, who took part in the constitutional discussions, angrily noted in his diary that the trade union representatives were determined to control the Party 'with and because of their money. The new constitution is only a new coat of paint – pouring new wine into old bottles'.[27]

Still largely a political innocent, Attlee was perhaps lucky to have been

*'To secure for the producers by hand and brain the full fruits of their industry, and the most equitable distribution thereof that may be possible, upon the basis of the common ownership of the means of production and the best obtainable system of popular administration and control of each industry or service.' Labour Party, *Annual Conference Report*, 1918, p.140.

spared these discussions. Much later, though readily granting that Labour's constitution was 'the result of historical growth rather than of logical planning' and that 'if a fresh start were to be made a simple structure would be built up,' he came to consider that the balance was just about right. He didn't believe, in 1937, that there was need for a great change in the constitution and held that its basis in organized Labour had to remain.[28] These views were, in part, a response to criticism from the Left; but in 1959 he would also be found on the side of those who resisted any tampering with Clause IV: such an exercise was pointless, he considered, 'like attacking the 39 Articles'.[29]

At the end of the First World War Labour withdrew from the Government, despite the opposition of a majority of the Parliamentary Labour Party (PLP) and particularly of some MPs who had become ministers. Armed with its new constitution, its trade union base, provision for individual membership and extra divisional parties, Labour prepared to contest the general election as a distinct national force. The decline of the ILP was not inevitable, though it did not happen at once. So far as Attlee was concerned, a great deal of work remained to be done at his level of operation. He had, however, become more ambitious: he had written to Tom in 1918 that 'this soldiering business is only tolerable when one has a definite unit under one's command'.[30] He looked now for some kind of leadership role in civilian life. His social work would be limited to lecturing at the LSE and to writing his book; he did not return to residence in Haileybury House. After a brief and uncongenial period at Toynbee Hall, he found a dilapidated house in Limehouse which he had repaired and converted into a Labour club, a flat for himself and a second flat for an active Labour family. First an ex-batman, and then another local veteran, looked after his domestic arrangements. The austerity of his bachelor flat was briefly relieved by the resumption of his weekend visits to Putney, where his mother, two sisters and one or two brothers were still living. But in the summer of 1920 his mother and sister, Dorothy, died within a few weeks of each other and the old home was sold and its contents dispersed. With them disappeared his final ties to the scenes of his youth.

He began his political work where he had left off, in Stepney. The local situation had been transformed during his absence. A strong Trades Council had been founded in 1917; the new constitution and expansion of the Labour Party had resulted in the formation of local parties throughout the East End of London. The Liberal stranglehold on the Irish working-class vote had gone with the break-up of the former United Irish League; ex-Irish nationalists stood as Labour candidates in several East End constituencies in the 1918 general election. Yet this favourable development had not benefited the Labour cause in Stepney as much as it might have done, because the old rivalry between the Irish and Jewish factions still existed. There was a need for a neutral individual to contest the local election in Limehouse, long delayed on account of the war. Attlee, with his strong ties and experience, was the ideal candidate.

Though he failed in the London County Council elections held in March 1919, he acquitted himself sufficiently well to be adopted shortly afterwards as the prospective parliamentary candidate for the division. In the 'coupon' election of 1918 the seat had fallen to the same MP who had held it since 1906. But the Labour Party had, at last, put up a candidate who had secured 2,470 votes to the Coalition Liberal's 5,860, with a dissident Conservative obtaining 1,455. Moreover, fewer than a third of the voters had turned out so there seemed a good chance that the seat might be won on the next occasion. When that might be was another question, and Attlee was not a man who marked time. He threw himself into a remarkable number of local political activities which, besides enhancing his future national prospects, had an interest of their own for him.

The LCC elections were hardly out of the way before campaigning for the borough elections began. As the parliamentary candidate, it was thought that Attlee himself should not stand, but he did the next best thing: he wrote the election address and took charge of the campaign. Compared with the previous borough election, there were now three times more people on the electoral roll. Yet Labour had not merely to make a good showing; it was essential to gain the majority so as to move the time of the Council meetings to the evening, when working-class Labour members could attend. The result was a revelation: out of sixty seats, Labour won forty-two, and in Limehouse there was a complete sweep. No Labour man had ever been a councillor there before, and apart from two former Liberal councillors who had defected to Labour, there was a dearth of experience. There was also rivalry between the three local Labour parties who had temporarily combined to fight the election, as well as the previously mentioned ethnic cleavage. It was in these circumstances, to be repeated later in a different framework, that Attlee was co-opted as Mayor. He had found his most appropriate political niche right at the start of his career – as the impartial yet dedicated chairman of a very heterogeneous Labour body.

Thoroughly accustomed by his military service to giving orders and making on-the-spot decisions, he immediately made his mark. The *East London Observer* in December 1919 noted that his comments on any statement not in order were made in 'intensely concentrated – almost curt – precise and unmistakeable sentences, like the slamming of a railway carriage door . . .'[31] The hardest and most valuable work of the borough councillor is done in committee, he wrote in 1920, 'and the man who thinks he can make a show of speeches in full meeting reported by the press without thoroughly mastering the work in committee will find himself disillusioned.' Once the procedural and organizational work had been mastered, however, a councillor could obtain the 'very human satisfaction' of 'getting things done' and 'seeing them work,' which was possible in a small area. He pointedly concluded that the borough council ought not to be despised as a training ground for the social reformer or the aspirant to parliamentary honours.[32]

In his statutory year of office as Mayor, Attlee acquired a formidable experience of local government. He was heavily engaged in the vigorous reforming work of the Stepney Council, which included the fields of health, taxation, poor law administration (he was co-opted on to the Board of Guardians), and housing. In effect, and within the limits of the local authority's jurisdiction, he presided over the introduction of a municipal welfare state. The first requirement was money, which Attlee as Chairman of the Valuation Committee was instrumental in procuring. Tax evaluations of industries and public houses in the borough were raised by 45 per cent. The funds thus obtained were devoted to a variety of new services. Whereas, in 1919, some 139 applicants were supplied with free milk, by 1920 this figure had risen to a total of 6,429 families. Five new maternity and child welfare clinics were created where previously there had been none. A corps of health visitors was established and the number of landlord prosecutions on health grounds increased from 5 in 1919 to 176 the following year. Refuse was collected regularly, again for the first time, and extra provision made for public baths and wash-houses, libraries and highway improvements. The council employees were paid a fair wage and the Mayor given a salary, to put the post in future within the reach of a working individual.[33] The infant mortality rate, Attlee was to record proudly in his autobiography years later, was brought down to 'one of the lowest in London'.[34] Nor did his local government work cease when he relinquished the mayoralty. Before this happened he was elected as an alderman and, for another year, was a member of 'almost every public body in the borough'.[35] Because of his unusual availability for a Labour councillor, and also on account of his enthusiasm, he was in demand as the Stepney Council's representative on a number of external bodies.[36] His most valuable experience was his involvement with the supply of electricity. Beginning as chairman of the Stepney undertaking, he became vice-chairman of the body overseeing the provision of electricity for local authorities throughout London and the Home Counties.

Until 1922, Attlee was mainly concerned with politics at the local level, but the larger framework could not be ignored. A single municipal council was powerless to alleviate the problem of unemployment: Attlee called a National Conference on behalf of London mayors which sent a deputation to the Prime Minister. Nothing came of it except that the accompanying march, containing a large number of ex-servicemen, nearly turned into a riot. The social aspirations aroused by the war propaganda had quickly turned sour in the economic cycle of boom and bust and Attlee shared the widespread bitterness. As Mayor of Stepney he took part in a social welfare conference held in Oxford: an observer recalled that he was 'also a major, a trim Cheltenham-like figure, with an accent as close-clipped as his moustache. He rose. One instinctively expected a prosy report on slumming. One prepared to doze. Instead a jet of flame shot up. The neat little figure shook with passion. He poured out a stream of fervent invective about rich and comfortable philanthropists. He ended up with the words of Tolstoy: "You will do everything for the poor except get off their backs" . . . it was an unexpected excitement. An outraged audience of comfortable philanthropists drowned him in jeers and boos. The handsomely caparisoned Lady Bountiful from Berkshire who sat next to me asked sorrowfully, "Who would have thought it of him? He looked such a little gentleman." '[37] In the gentlemanly columns of *The Times* Attlee gave vent to his feelings in a more acceptable manner. Despite the announcement of a great housing programme by the Government, he caustically commented, every attempt by his council to take any action had been thwarted by the Ministry of Health; 'actions suggested to the council by the Ministry one month [were] turned down the next'. Either there was some influence at work 'endeavouring to prevent local authorities from carrying out their duties in the provision of housing accommodation, or . . . Messrs Dilly and Dally [had] not yet been demobilized.'[38]

Attlee's 'socialist instincts' were rekindled by these experiences, though there was as yet small inspiration to be found in the Labour Party. If the Labour vote had dramatically increased from 371,772 in December 1910, to 2,385,472 in 1918, only 63 MPs had been elected.* The election had come too soon for the Labour organization: most of the leadership had been defeated and the poor quality of the successful candidates was quickly apparent. Even if the Labour Party had won a majority in 1918 it was not clear how it would have dealt with the economic difficulties; the knowledge for specific policies was lacking. This was supposedly the Fabian Society's province and it was under the Society's auspices that Attlee wrote and lectured on the subject of local government. He was rewarded by election to the executive committee of the Fabians, doubtless as a worthy rather than outstanding thinker. He could not have been thrilled by what he found there, as by 1923 he had publicly testified to the fading of his interest in the Fabian approach. Significantly, he published his views in the ILP's paper, *Socialist Review*.[39]

At this stage in his career he still found the ILP more emotionally

*Election statistics used in this book have been taken from David Butler and Jennie Freeman, *British Political Facts*, 3rd edn, 1969. Readers are advised to consult the several works of F. W. S. Craig for a more detailed analysis.

satisfying and more intellectually interesting than any other group. It had regained something of its old crusading vitality, mainly on account of its stand on foreign policy – and Attlee now shared its views. So too did the Labour Party, which had also adopted its broader socialist position. What the ILP urgently needed was to re-define its political identity and role, a need which corresponded almost exactly with Attlee's own situation. There was another reason for his renewed interest in the ILP. Between April 1918 and April 1920, membership had increased from 30,000 to 45,000, and the new members brought with them new talents and fresh perspectives. Among the recruits, for instance, were a number of middle-class, southern English intellectuals and publicists such as Arthur Ponsonby, Norman Angel, E. D. Morel and J. A. Hobson. Originally attracted on account of foreign policy, they soon demonstrated their opposition to the old ILP leadership, with the exception of MacDonald. The leader of the critics was Clifford Allen, and for a while Attlee was one of his most earnest supporters. Their principal aim was to advance the notion of workers' control in industry and, in so doing, to formulate a more explicit commitment to socialism. Their efforts culminated in December 1921 with a statement that stressed two points, 'the guild idea of workers' control and the need to secure the conversion of society as a whole to socialism'.[40] At the ILP's annual conference in April 1922, Attlee moved an amendment proposing that the internal management of each industry should be in the hands of the workers – and 'a programme with a strong Guild Socialist flavour was adopted.'[41]

But his radicalism had definite limits. In the immediate post-war period, the ILP appeared to him as a *moderate* socialist body. He insisted that, in contrast to the SDF, the ILP had never been tied to a rigid gospel. Rather it had been in a continual state of evolution in accord with the progress of socialist thought, though perhaps overly dependent on the 'mental food provided for it by the Fabian Society'. The anti-capitalist movement, he argued, had always comprised two schools, collectivist-socialist and individualist-anarchist, and the particular function of the ILP had been '*to take the middle way between the two extremes*.'[42] It was as a protagonist of the middle way that he had rejected Marxism, and his initial reaction to the news of the revolution in Russia had been entirely consistent with this view. He wrote to Tom that it was 'rather appalling but quite explicable,' adding that he could imagine 'the state of the country run by the Whitechapel branch of the SDF'.[43] That he later supported British recognition of the Soviet Union and an Anglo-Russian agreement was not due to any change of mind in regard to communism; it was simply a case of accepting an accomplished fact. Besides, Russia was a potential market and the cause of world security would be furthered by agreement. His sense of realism also caused him to maintain that Russia need not pay debts incurred under Tsarist rule – how could she? Here he would differ from the First Labour Government, but he thoroughly approved the Labour Party's rejection of the British Communist Party's request to affiliate in 1920.[44]

In his last years with the ILP he felt increasingly obliged to emphasize the differences, as he saw them, between socialism and Marxism. Socialism, he wrote, 'stands for the application of principles of social justice to the economic organization of society. It claims that the present system of Capitalism has failed to provide the material basis for a good life and that as a phase of industrial evolution it must be replaced by a co-operative commonwealth based upon common ownership and control of the means of life.' However, while agreeing that the economic interpretation of history had been 'one of the most illuminating ideas of the modern world,' he warned that – important as that aspect was – 'it must not be overstressed at the expense of other factors in the making of modern civilisation.' The socialist had to beware of reading into the past the conditions of the present; in particular, 'a one-sided examination of history, wherein the whole of it is considered as a class struggle and all events are referred to a single cause, leads to a distorted view and a stunted conception of human nature.'[45] The socialist historian had to deal with every side of human activity, and would be 'interested no less in the struggle of mankind to gain freedom of thought and escape from the bondages of superstition than with his various contrivances for gaining economic freedom.'[46] Attlee was also very conscious of the danger of an over-centralization of power which should not, he wrote, be counterbalanced by weaknesses in local government administrative bodies.[47]

His partiality for a pluralistic society, containing several decision-making bodies of various types, was one of the reasons which led him to favour a measure of workers' control in industry. The post-war revival of the guild socialist movement, he wrote in an article in 1923, represented the 'revolt of the individual' against 'the all-embracing state and the domination of the consumer.' No form of society that left 'the worker a wage-slave, even though a slave to society' was satisfactory to him. Direct workers' participation in the management and organization of industry was not only just but would also enhance their social stature, increase their sense of responsibility, compensate for tedium and be good for morale.[48]

Attlee's interest in guild socialism had been stirred by the shock to his own morale caused by his wartime stay at Barrow-in-Furness; but though subsequently believing that the guild socialists 'had a reasonably good case,' he never subscribed totally to their ideas.[49] At the ILP's 1922 annual conference he pointedly dissociated himself from one of guild socialism's leading advocates at the time, G. D. H. Cole. Attlee preferred to stress 'that industry needed a new morale and incentive which would be supplied when the profit motive was replaced by worker control

– with the state as a referee between the contending demands.'[50] He developed the argument in his 1923 article. 'The capital difficulty of all schemes of social reconstruction,' he believed, 'was that of getting the necessary incentive to involve effort in the worker.' Under capitalism, at least in theory, the only incentive was self-interest; socialism, on the other hand, based on nationalization and municipalization with control by the consumers, depended on 'a general desire for the common good'. Attlee did not deny the potency of this incentive, but delicately suggested that, by itself, it was 'apt to wear somewhat thin'. It was fine for those doing responsible and interesting work: for the man who was only a cog in a great machine something else was needed. The concept of workers' control had arisen precisely from the fact that experience had shown the need for a new industrial incentive. At the same time, the State and local bodies had enough to do: 'it was an error to assume that social problems could best be met by the concentration of all activities into one grouping, ... the geographical'. A socialist system presupposed a number of groups, not hostile and not mutually exclusive, functioning for particular purposes corresponding to human needs.[51] Thus the task of eliminating capitalist control, he explained to trade unionists, belonged to political democracy, whereas the work of organizing the new industrial order belonged to industrial democracy. Each industry should be considered a public service, managed internally by the workers in 'one big all-embracing Union,' though there would be room for subsidiary groupings and the system would vary from industry to industry. Not only was it imperative to put an end to inter-union disputes, but the whole industry of the country had to be regarded as a unity; no one section would be allowed to take advantage of its economic position as against all other sections.[52]

Here of course was the rub: in the final analysis the State would have to be the arbiter and Attlee's acceptance of the fact set him off from the dogmatic guild socialists. He was adamant that the ILP had 'not swallowed all the doctrines of Guild Socialism, nor had been swallowed by Mr Cole': Cole had 'rather run to death his theory of organization by function,' had 'over-elaborated his social structure,' and had not 'fully realised the necessity for some central organization coordinating the activities of the various functional bodies.'[53] Moreover, Attlee warned, the exact delimitation of work between the different groups in a socialist society was not easy to lay down. It would have to be found by experience, and the ILP constitution – for which Attlee was partly responsible – frankly admitted this.[54] Trade unionists, for instance, were both producers and consumers, wanting both better wages and lower prices. As a municipal administrator, Attlee had had personal knowledge of the conflict, and he was aware of similar problems encountered by co-operative societies. Cole had, nevertheless, caused Attlee to revise his previous ideas as to the future industrial structure of society. Hard thinking would be required in devising the appropriate mechanism for 'setting the latent goodwill in all of us' to work. It was easy to ignore fundamental differences, but not helpful. Phrases about the community were all very well for criticism and propaganda; but in the 'Great Society of today' one of the hardest things was to evoke the community spirit. Advantage had to be taken of every grouping that bound man to man.[55] After his election to Parliament in November 1922, Attlee would gradually come to the conclusion that, so far as the Left was concerned, the Labour Party was the most important of the groupings that bound people to each other: for it alone had any chance of using the State as a referee in the national interest.

In January 1922 Attlee was married. His bride, Violet Helen Millar, was the sister of an old Oxford friend, Cedric. Accompanied by Mrs Millar, as respectable custom then dictated, the three had spent a month's holiday together in Italy. Attlee proposed two weeks after returning to London; Violet was twenty-five and he thirty-eight. The marriage took place in Hampstead where the Millars resided, and proved a huge success. Violet was in every respect a suitable companion.[56] She came from a similar social and family background: her deceased father had been a successful businessman, she and her twin sister were the last-born of six boys and five girls, and she had been educated at a private boarding school. She would be devoted to her husband and own family. A first child, a girl, was born a year or so after the marriage, and a son and two more daughters would follow in the next seven years.

Unlike their parents, Violet and Clem had to get by with a minimum of domestic assistance, which bore heavily on Violet.[57] Clem soon fell a victim to the demands of public life: 'I have been married 32 years,' Mrs Attlee said shortly after his retirement, 'and usually had no husband in by 2 a.m. as he normally did not return until the 12.07 a.m. train from Paddington.'[58] Clem was to admit that domestic labour had been difficult to come by and that this had 'meant a pretty drastic change in the way of life for many middle-class families'; yet he had met 'many people who, reared in the comfort of former days, do not resent the change but acknowledge that the old class system was bad and make the best of the new'.[59] His wife's views on the topic have not been recorded though, within the limits of her self-imposed domesticity, she seems to have been a woman of fairly strong character. She was not, for instance, intimidated by Field-Marshal Montgomery who once attempted to give her instruction in one of her favourite pastimes, croquet.[60] When Attlee became Prime Minister, she kept a strict eye on all his engagements and could be very critical of any procedure she thought inappropriate.[61] She was perfectly happy with her role – telling one of Clem's secretaries, 'I know what I'm like; I don't know what would have become of me if I hadn't been married to the best man in the world.'[62] Perhaps her most suitable quality was her lack of interest in politics: 'I'm just not political,' she declared.[63] Attlee could relax completely at home. But it was not to be found in Limehouse, an area he knew from experience as unsuitable for bringing up a family. He and Violet first established themselves in Woodford, some seven miles away, and within a year he was elected to Parliament.

IV

No More The Old Street Corner

Attlee's marriage, his removal to the suburbs and his election to Parliament were soon followed by the responsibilities of office. No doubt he looked back to his life in Stepney with more than the nostalgia he had expressed when working temporarily as a civil servant:

> No more the old street corner
> Where the busy traffic plies
> No more the dear old platform
> And the cause that never dies
> I've got a government job now . . . [1]

Henceforth, he had the chance to influence affairs at the centre. The Labour Party was beginning to come into its own. Nationally, the resumption of party politics after the war had been partially postponed by the continuation of Lloyd George's coalition into the general election of 1918. Afterwards the by-elections had hinted that political allegiances might be shifting: between 1918 and 1922 Labour gained fourteen seats, two not in working-class areas, and accumulated large votes in several other suburban constituencies.[2] But the opportunity that presented itself in 1922 was to be of a different order. The election of that year, for the first time since 1910, constituted a proper test of individual party strengths: the Conservatives decided to break away from the Prime Minister's suffocating embrace and the coalition fell apart. Still better from Labour's point of view, the Liberals promptly split into two factions. Labour had gone some way to completing its internal re-organization: it was prepared to contest over two-thirds of the parliamentary seats. It was finally ready if not for power, then at least to make an independent bid to become one of the two main parties.

This last was the chief result of the election: Labour replaced the Liberal Party as the second party in the State. The Conservatives won 345 seats, Labour 142 and the two Liberal factions combined 116. The voting figures told their own story. The Conservatives gained the most votes, as they were to do throughout the interwar period, but Labour came second in popular esteem – and the difference was only 5.5 million to 4.2 million, with the Liberals a close third. Since 1918, Labour's vote had doubled and a new framework for British politics had been established, though two further general elections within three years would be necessary before the pattern became fixed.

Labour's period of comparative innocence as a party thus came to an end. The focal point shifted from the street corners to the Palace in Westminster. There, His Majesty's Opposition presented an odd spectacle. Previously, Labour MPs had been largely working-class; now the PLP contained a solid phalanx of professional and middle-class people and even some from the upper class. On social grounds, Labour could claim that it was a genuinely representative national party, a movement of opinion rather than of class and, therefore, a potential government.[3] In terms of political cohesiveness – of policy, of agreed priorities, of structural unity – the picture was much less clear. Attlee's own position was, in several respects, a good example. He had conducted his campaign in Limehouse largely on the basis of rhetoric. The real contest, he had written in his election address, was between capital and labour: Liberals and Tories had parted company merely to deceive the British electorate again. He stood for 'LIFE against WEALTH' and claimed the right of every man, woman and child in the country to have the best life that could be provided. Just as men had been conscripted for war, so too must wealth be conscripted for peace. He demanded work, homes and justice for all and, into the bargain, 'NO MORE WAR AND NO MORE SECRET DIPLOMACY'. The peace treaties had to be scrapped.[4]

How these things were to be achieved was another matter. Like thirty-one other Labour MPs, Attlee had been sponsored by the ILP, who could claim something like 100 individual members in the PLP. They were a group of individualists: there were pacifists and non-pacifists, traditional elements such as Philip Snowden and the critics, like Attlee, associated with Clifford Allen. These had been joined by a colourful and more radical group from Scotland, known shortly afterwards as the Clydesiders. No one could tell if they could collaborate with each other, or with the rest of the Labour MPs. Nor was the discipline of power available to weld the PLP together; instead it was the heady delights of opposition which awaited it, though no longer of the street corner variety. The wider Labour Party was in little better shape: barely sufficient for electoral purposes, Henderson's hectic re-organization had yet to prove itself adequate for the next stage in the Party's progress. Inside and outside Parliament, Marquand has written, 'the "movement" was full of fissures . . . between the trade unions and the ILP, between the ILP and the Divisional Labour Parties, between different unions and different sections of the same union, between intellectuals and manual workers, between pacifists who had been in prison during the war and patriots who had spoken from recruiting platforms, between "Right" and "Left", between respectability and revolt.'[5] The miracle was that the Party existed at all as a national force.

In these circumstances a great deal obviously depended on the quality of the leadership. The initiative was seized by the ILP whose radicals, especially, wanted a change. J. R. Clynes, a trade union leader who had served enthusiastically with Lloyd George during the war and who had succeeded a Scottish miner, W. Adamson, as Chairman of the PLP in 1921, was not regarded as inspiring. Ramsay MacDonald in contrast, after his opposition to British participation in the war, had all the heroic qualities and many others: he now came into his own. Attlee supported his candidature, though Emanuel Shinwell noted that Attlee 'never evinced any enthusiasm for MacDonald as some of the Clydesiders and I did . . .'[6] At the PLP meeting, MacDonald only obtained sixty-one votes to Clynes' fifty-six, but the significance of the decision was at once recognized: an official party announcement proclaimed him Chairman or Leader,[7] consonant with his parliamentary position as head of the major opposition party. Hitherto, Labour had had seven chairmen in its twenty-two years of existence, including MacDonald in the three years prior to the war: thereafter, he would retain the post for longer than anyone else until Attlee took over in 1935.

One of MacDonald's first actions as Leader of the PLP was to appoint Attlee as his (unpaid) Private Parliamentary Secretary. There was no personal bond between them, but MacDonald needed Attlee's respectability. W. Golant, a student of Attlee's early political career, has suggested that MacDonald was responsible for Attlee's being referred to as Major, 'because it gave added emphasis when an ex-soldier favoured disarmament . . . Attlee was the kind of person MacDonald wanted the Party to be associated with'.[8] Attlee was also one of the select band of Labour MPs who possessed a university education and administrative experience.

The appointment had several effects on Attlee's career; he had to acquire a knowledge of how the Commons functioned and the scope of his political interests was widened. The extra work load forced him, in the summer of 1923, to abandon his paid position at the LSE. He became a professional politician and his contributions to theoretical discussions and publications diminished rapidly. His appointment also meant that he was obliged to consider politics and policies from the angle of Labour's national leadership. The acquisition of office in 1924, to be followed by his nomination to the Indian Statutory Commission in 1927 and a further official interlude in 1930–1, would all weigh in the same direction. Rhetoric had to be discounted; the broad feelings of outrage which had carried him into Parliament became of less consequence than the ability to organize and to make informed criticism. Abstract ideas had to be translated into practical policies. In order to secure the greatest possible Labour support, compromise was unavoidable: loyalty to the wider Labour Party took precedence over affiliation with minor coteries.

Quite apart from theoretical differences, Attlee was an odd-man-out among ILP radicals and traditionalists. Unlike the majority of the post-war intake, he was not a new convert aglow with sudden conviction; his war service equally distinguished him from the traditional ILPers. In 1918 the question of how the work was to be done in Parliament had been academic; only three ILP members had been elected. The 1922 and the December 1923 general elections – which saw the ILP's parliamentary representation rise so considerably – meant that the question had to be answered. From his central position, Attlee was especially well placed to observe the damaging impact of particularism on the presentation of a coherent Labour position. And although individual membership of the ILP continued to grow, reaching a peak in 1925,[9] he was one of several members who caused their parliamentary candidatures to be transferred to the Labour Party in 1926.[10] For him, the ILP had accomplished its mission.

Attlee could not and did not forget the efforts of the pioneers who had paved the way for the existence of the Labour Party. They had derived their inspiration, energy and courage from a mystical conception of human relationships and society. This socialist vision had to be retained because it was the essential precursor to any serious work. But the changed conditions of political life required that the ultimate goal be pushed into the background – a difficult transition which, unlike many idealists, Attlee was able to make. In the Commons he put the confidence and self-control that he had gained on the street corners and in the trenches to effective use. The bitterness that had marked his maiden speech, when he had accused the Tories of ruining future generations as well as the present one by their policies,[11] was succeeded by a competent debating style. His second speech demonstrated his potential as a solid, dependable parliamentary performer: it also indicated that he was not a man to be easily intimidated, and contrasted favourably with an emotional and confused effort by George Lansbury. The issue, an inflammatory and potentially dangerous one, was tailor-made for Attlee; he had to oppose a Government motion that it was of 'the utmost importance that a strict control be maintained over alien immigration'. His tactic was to lower the tension. He began by making play with the differences in Conservative attitudes to poor and rich immigrants: then he referred to the historical advantages that had accrued to England from the admission of Flemish and French weavers, the Dutchmen who had come over with William III and the Germans with the House of Hanover. Next, he poured scorn on the 'patriotism' of employers who had not hesitated to import aliens as strike-breakers. He followed this by the assertion that, in any case, the whole basis of the motion was false: there was no tremendous increase in the number of aliens as their immigration and emigration just about balanced. Nor did persons of foreign birth often come on to the Poor Law; the Jewish Board of Guardians, an 'admirable institution', for example, looked after its own people. He was interrupted by a Conservative MP, Sir Herbert Nield, who alleged that the borough of Stepney had been positively ruined by alien incursion: 'Wherever you go you will find the music hall and entertainment bills printed in Yiddish . . . the poor wretched creatures ought never to have been allowed to settle down in one district like that . . . ' Attlee calmly deflated his opponent: the motion was nationalistic hypocrisy; the proposed Act was really designed to prevent trade-union organization among persons of alien birth. As for the charge that some of the immigrants were 'revolutionaries', Attlee taunted that there were quite as many 'home-grown, wild and dangerous' ones as there were of the imported variety. But he agreed that control and regulation of immigration were necessary.*[12]

Attlee could also enjoy himself on a subject that would have been tricky for most ILPers. The topic was a proposed cut in the money allocated to education in the army. He recalled, in a Commons committee debate on the Army Estimates, how he had nearly spoiled the career of a young officer: the colonel had asked him what sort of a man the officer was, and Attlee had inadvertently replied that he was a clever fellow. The story led him to assert that the war had demonstrated 'the utter failure of the thinking branches of the Army to realize the modern conditions of warfare.' He was all in favour of economy – in fact he thought the time had come for armies and war to be done away with – but 'the thing that has been very well economized in these Army Estimates has been the brain power.' If there had to be an army, he wanted a young, intelligent and non-class restricted body – hence the necessity of a general education so that those retired could move on into other occupations.[13] His speech was probably spontaneous, and his confidence was

*In June 1950, he would set up a mixed Cabinet committee of ministers and officials to review 'the means which might be adopted to check the immigration into this country of coloured persons from the British colonial territories'. The non-white population was then estimated at 30,000, of whom 5,000 had arrived since the end of the Second World War. The Cabinet accepted the committee's conclusions that restrictions were unnecessary for the time being. (P. Hennessy and K. Jeffery, 'Unnecessary immigration controls rejected in 1951', in *The Times*, 2 January 1982).

equally apparent when he spoke in April 1923, against the second reading of a Special Constable Bill. 'Formerly,' he said, 'we had special constables when there was a period of riot or disturbance. Now we are to have the constables first ... the right honourable Gentleman', he added, indicating the Home Secretary, 'has got the wind up.'[14]

He revealed his interest in international and imperial topics mostly by means of parliamentary questions – on the advent of fascism in Italy (his first inquiry),[15] on the French Air Force, the American debt, the entry of British ships into Smyrna harbour and on political prisoners in India. It was in regard to India that he made his final speech in his first Parliament – which also, apart from the period when he was engaged on the Indian Commission, turned out to be the last one he would make as a backbencher. In July 1923 he took the opportunity of a debate on an East-India Loans Bill to affirm his opposition to the current notion of imperial preference. An amendment proposed that a loan of £50 million for the construction of railways and irrigation works in India should be given on condition that at least 75 per cent would be spent in Britain. Despite Lloyd George's advocacy, the amendment was defeated: for once, Attlee spoke and voted on a winning side. He described the sense of the amendment as being that of 'gombeen man', the village money-lender who compelled all the villagers to repay their loans by spending them in his shop at his prices: it was bad economics and bad imperialism, a remarkable way of keeping the Empire together.[16] Afterwards, Attlee's speeches would be usually couched in the more calculated terms of a minister or shadow-minister, but he had had time to display most of his oratorical skills. These included a moderate tone, brevity, succinctness, simplicity of language, common sense – occasionally enlivened with a cutting or sarcastic remark – and concentration on the subject. Not extraordinary in themselves, they were rare and notable qualities in the PLP of the 1920s – many of whose members were apt to get emotionally carried away.

The general election that Stanley Baldwin called for December 1923 surprised Attlee as much it did every other British politician. Baldwin's motives are still obscure; he had a huge majority and four possible years of office in front of him. The King tried vainly to make him change his mind.[17] It may be that it was Baldwin's fear of increased unemployment which caused him to raise the issue of imperial preference, both inside his own party and among the electorate at large.[18] Attlee, at any rate, had hardly returned from a late summer holiday in the country – necessitated by the illness of his wife following the birth of their first child – when he found himself plunged into electioneering once again. He had no difficulty in overwhelming his single Conservative opponent by 6,000 votes; Limehouse had become a Labour stronghold and the two other Stepney constituencies were also won. These results were part of a pattern;

Labour gains came mainly in areas where the Party had remained unusually weak even in 1922 – in London alone fifteen additional seats were won.[19] In the country as a whole, Labour's vote did not rise appreciably even though eleven extra seats were contested. The old cry of Free Trade had served to unite the Liberals, who polled 4.3 million votes compared with Labour's 4.4 million. The Conservatives seem to have actually increased their poll by some 38,000 votes, but the constituency situation turned against them, resulting in a loss of eighty-seven seats.[20] Labour benefited most: its small gain in votes (some 200,000) was worth more than forty extra seats, mostly in industrial areas. Within the Party, thirty-nine MPs had been sponsored by the ILP, and thirty-nine by local Labour parties – this last a gain of over twenty since the 1922 election: trade-union representation moved up from 85 to 101.[21] Altogether, Labour held 191 seats, the Conservatives 258 and the Liberals 159: it was in these unprepossessing circumstances that Labour came to hold office for the first time.

The Party had no choice. The majority of the voters had clearly rejected the Government's tariff proposals on which the election had been held. The Liberals soon supported a Labour motion of no-confidence and the King was clear that his constitutional duty required that the leader of the second largest party be asked to form a government.[22] Should MacDonald have refused the invitation, the Liberals would have attained office once again and 1922 could have been written off in popular estimation as a fluke: Labour would have lost its painfully acquired status of chief Opposition party and would have been relegated to the position of a parliamentary group. All the Party's executive bodies – the NEC, the General Council of the TUC and the PLP leadership – agreed with MacDonald's argument:[23] they realized that if the ostensible election issue had been that of Free Trade versus Imperial Preference, the long-term issue was the struggle between the Labour and Liberal parties to capture the reform position in a political system that left little opportunity for a third party. Attlee produced two other reasons for Labour taking office. 'The British elector,' he wrote, 'is very sceptical of anything which he has not seen,'[24] while the rank-and-file Labour member not only had the tremendous emotional lift of seeing the 'distant dream become a reality', he also 'had to face responsibility'.[25]

In practice, 'facing responsibility' in domestic affairs meant doing very little. Not only had the Government no mandate for drastic reform, it had no programme: the 1918 statement 'Labour and the New Social Order' was, in Attlee's words, merely 'a declaration of faith and aspirations' with no indication of priorities.[26] MacDonald's choice of ministers also cast doubt on the PLP's executive ability: he did not confine himself to Labour ranks, the venerable George Lansbury was passed over, and only one radical ILPer was deemed fit for full ministerial office, John Wheatley.

Attlee's appointment as Under-Secretary of State for War was a routine promotion following his stint as MacDonald's Private Parliamentary Secretary. Unlike his immediate chief Stephen Walsh, the Secretary, Attlee had service experience, but neither appointment would last very long. Both Walsh and Attlee got on well with the military, some of whom Attlee had known in the war.[27]

He soon learned what the acceptance of office entailed. The Government's sole piece of positive domestic legislation was a Housing Act, promoted by Wheatley, that provided government aid for building municipal houses. But the effects of the Act were necessarily delayed beyond the Labour Government's term of office and the ILP backbenchers soon grew restless. They rebelled on several occasions, notably in March 1924. In that month thirteen Labour MPs voted against the Government over the Service Estimates, and as many as forty-five over a Trade Facilities Bill. Attlee was not among them: as a junior minister he was precluded from such a course. Much of his time was taken up by strenuous attendance at the House where he had plenty of opportunities to observe the internal weaknesses of the PLP caused by its factions.

Otherwise, his War Office appointment was not onerous and aroused little rivalry. Attlee could explain to a contented Commons that the military authorities were satisfied that Germany was disarmed and that the British Army was not intended to be a great continental-type force; its function was mainly to serve as a nucleus for the support of the various garrisons and commitments around the world.[28] He gained some useful knowledge of how a government department operated – and of how positions of responsibility could induce a spirit of compromise. He was obliged, for instance, to resist a demand from some Labour members that the right of appeal on legal grounds from army death sentences be increased. His argument, a standard departmental one, was that the effect of such a demand would be to narrow all appeals down to points of law, whereas most successful appeals had been made on other than strictly legal grounds.[29] Personally, Attlee wanted to reduce or even abolish the death penalty that army courts-martial could impose. In April 1924, he wrote a memorandum proposing a reduction in the number of offences which were punishable by death under the Army Act, and it was on the basis of this document that the Act was amended in the following year: some five categories under which a court-martial could impose the death penalty were removed.[30]

But if not a thrilling appointment, the War Office in 1924 could provide some amusement. On one occasion, Attlee was dining in the officers' mess at Woolwich with a miner's MP, Jack Lawson. Their careers had previously intertwined: Lawson had also been a Parliamentary Private Secretary to Ramsay MacDonald after the 1922 election. Now they were both at the War Office, Lawson as Financial Secretary, and it was in their official capacities that they were in the officers' mess. A propos of nothing, Attlee observed, 'That great chandelier must look fine when lit up.'

'Yes,' was the reply.

'Have you been here before?'

'Yes.'

'When?'

'The last time I was here I was serving these tables as officers' orderly on fatigue, after "stables".'

This was too much for Attlee. 'My fellow-member of the Army Council,' Lawson remembered, 'nearly needed a doctor to take the stitches out of his side.'[31] In 1945 Attlee would appoint Lawson to be Secretary of State at the War Office.

The area where the Labour Government scored its greatest success was in foreign policy. Given the Party's reputation of being preoccupied with domestic affairs the achievement might appear ironic; it certainly proved so in terms of electoral consequences and future international developments during the inter-war period. Yet in foreign policy, as Attlee was to point out, Labour had a 'well-established policy' and a determined leadership.[32] MacDonald, who elected to be his own Foreign Secretary, wanted 'to re-establish relations of confidence and co-operation with France and Italy: to break the deadlock over reparations; to secure a French evacuation of the Ruhr; and to reintroduce Germany into the comity of nations. He wished to further the cause of general disarmament by strengthening the machinery of international arbitration: and to bridge the gulf that, politically and commercially, sundered Great Britain from Soviet Russia.'[33] These were large and to some extent perhaps imprecise aims but, except for the last, they reflected a broad segment of English opinion.[34] They equally, in striking contrast to domestic policy, represented a serious attempt to transform Labour principles into detailed policies and, with the one exception, they were largely achieved. As already indicated, Attlee ascribed the failure to conclude a commercial and general treaty with the Soviet Union mainly to 'the faulty tactics of the rulers of the USSR'.[35] But he would have gone further than MacDonald, as he did not think that Russia either could or need pay Tsarist debts. The Anglo-Soviet negotiations, coupled with the Campbell affair and the Zinoviev letter,[36] opened the way for the Opposition parties (reluctantly in the case of the Liberals) to bring down the Government on the basis of a Red Scare. Labour could reasonably claim that it had been duped out of office and MacDonald, whose uneven handling of the Russian issue was obscured by the use to which his opponents put it, could preserve his reputation.[37]

In the general election of October 1924, Labour increased its vote by over a million but took only 151 seats. The Conservatives polled an extra 2½ million votes and obtained 419 seats, a huge majority. The chief losers were the Liberals: their votes declined to 2.9 million and the number of Liberal seats dropped catastrophically to forty. With its 5.3 million votes Labour moved incontestably into second place, though the result disappointed many of its partisans. Despite a series of encouraging by-election results between 1924 and 1929, there was a turning away of Labour interest from the parliamentary to the industrial scene – highlighted by the General Strike of 1926.

Attlee's own career pursued its tranquil and upward course for a time. In Limehouse, in a three-cornered contest, he had a comfortable majority of 6,000 over the Conservative candidate and an absolute one of 3,000. His status as an ex-minister and Labour's loss of forty seats earned him a virtually permanent position on the Opposition front bench. He had won his place in the PLP hierarchy without having to struggle for it and would have nearly three years in which to establish himself there. During this time he was made one of the Temporary Chairmen of Committees of the Commons which gave him the opportunity to master the details of parliamentary procedure; he also became a practised parliamentary performer.

The two subjects on which he was a recognized expert, local government and electricity, were Conservative weak spots. On the first, Attlee could also appeal across party lines to local pride and interests, comparing British local government favourably 'with the method on the continent'. He did not want, he said about a Board of Guardians Bill, 'to see our local government swept away by nominees of the Government being sent to do local work instead of people of the locality'. The Bill was one of a large number of steps adopted in recent years 'to crib, cabin and confine our local governing authorities', and he sought to defend their rights whatever their political complexion.[38] On his second speciality he could exploit a certain confusion in the Government's policy: it was torn between the need to placate private interests and the necessity of ensuring some order in and control over electricity supply. The Government's attitude was further complicated because the private interests were sometimes in conflict. 'If our British manufacturers were wise,' Attlee could assert, 'they would see to it that the control of prime movers was in the hands of the public authority which is going to give them the best service at the lowest possible cost.'[39] The Government had considerable difficulty in refuting his arguments: on one occasion Attlee successfully moved a motion putting off the Second Reading of a Bill for six months.[40] His approach was the more effective because of his open-minded attitude to the actual nature of public control: 'We do not pin ourselves down to any particular form of nationalization and particular form of organization of industry,' he remarked (notably, in view of later developments in the Labour Party), 'indeed, we know perfectly well that the various forms of industry in this country must have a separate and distinct organization according to their needs.'[41] He nevertheless remained convinced that electricity would have to come under some kind of public ownership and control, not limited to generation and distribution: the manufacture of machinery and appliances would also have to be included.[42]

Attlee's knowledge of local government and electricity provision derived from his continuing involvement in both: he was a Stepney alderman and chairman of that borough's electricity committee. It was in these capacities that the General Strike of 1926 put him to a severe test. The councillors, as owners and operators of the local electricity company, were caught in an invidious situation. They had both legal and moral obligations to the community but the Stepney Labour councillors could hardly use strike-breakers – as did other electrical undertakings. Attlee searched desperately for a solution. He tried vainly to persuade the Electrical Trade Union to desist, on the grounds that a dockland area was a special case: he then negotiated directly with the TUC, obtaining an agreement allowing light but no power, except for the hospitals. But the compromise could only work if individual consumers restricted their use of electricity to lighting purposes; so Attlee's committee announced that those who used power would have their connection severed, otherwise the remaining workers would join the strike. His actions brought the full weight of Conservative vindictiveness down on him and his fellow Labour members of the committee, though not the other members. In January 1927, Attlee and his colleagues were charged with conspiring with the London branch of the Electrical Trade Union 'to further the interest of those taking part in the General Strike' by not providing power. The engineering firm which brought the charge sought material compensation because the company, after using power, had been immediately disconnected. The High Court found the charge proven, even though the firm had its own generating plant and probably suffered little inconvenience.

Attlee was personally liable for over £300 – a sum which would have bankrupted him. He was still dependent on his private income – about £300 per annum – to make ends meet: a second child, Felicity, had been born in 1925 and his son, the present Earl Attlee, would arrive in 1927. Substantial additions had to be made to his house in Woodford and his way of life included a two-seater car in 1925,[43] and family holidays: in 1926 he also accompanied two of his brothers on an extended trip to Gallipoli, Greece and Italy.[44] He made two decisions: first, to appeal, and second to leave politics and seek a job if the appeal failed.[45] Luck was with him: before the appeal was held, Attlee and his colleagues were publicly accused by a Conservative member of the LCC of deliberately depriving the London Hospital of its power supply during the strike and of conspiring to create a scarcity of coal in Stepney by keeping the borough's lights burning during the day. Attlee made the most of the opening: in a letter to *The Times* he replied that his accuser had merely to consult with the non-socialist members of the Stepney committee about his efforts to maintain the power supply to the hospital; as regards the lighting, it was regulated automatically, and even if all the street lights had been left on for a whole day the additional consumption of coal would have only been 38 lbs! Political spite and technical ignorance, he concluded, had led to his accuser making a fool of himself.[46] When the appeal was heard, he was in India. Attlee's case was well handled by a friend who had been in chambers with him. The court found that the jury had been misdirected: there was no evidence of malicious conspiracy to support the General Strike and, in any event, the previous judgment could not stand because action had not been taken within six months of the offences complained about. It had nevertheless been a close thing. Golant points out that though Attlee had said he did not call on the Government to run the electricity supply because he feared 'rioting and damage to property', the only attempt to interfere with the running of a power station had been in Fulham, where no damage was done.[47] Attlee, typically, did not let the uncertainty of the appeal affect his other work in local government. In 1927 he took an active part in the formation of the London and Home Counties Electrical Authority, of which body he became vice-chairman.

Attlee's activities in the Commons between 1924 and 1927 were not restricted to local government and electricity. He also spoke on Service matters, making two points in a debate on the Air Estimates in February 1926 which he was to repeat in the late 1930s. A defence scheme, he insisted, could not be considered *in vacuo*; it had to be related to some apprehended danger and linked with foreign policy. And there had to be more co-ordination among the military services: 'Why should we have eight Ministers of the Crown representing the fighting services?' he asked.[48] On the subject of electoral procedure he took a conservative view. He was opposed to the Government's proposal to do away with the tradition whereby an MP who was appointed minister had to fight a by-election: and he also thought that an MP who changed parties should go before the electors again.[49] One celebrated MP who had changed sides prior to the 1924 election was Winston Churchill, and Attlee came into direct conflict with him in June 1925. Speaking on a Finance Bill, Attlee accused the Conservatives of always confounding capital with private ownership of capital: 'The real poverty of this country at the present time,' he stated, 'is that it lacks the ownership of capital in public hands.' There was a great deal in private hands and not nearly enough in public ownership; 'As in Russia,' the new Chancellor of the Exchequer (Churchill) sarcastically retorted. Attlee replied in kind: he conceded that his knowledge of Russia was not as great as Churchill's, 'My knowledge of Gallipoli comes from taking part in a campaign there, and his knowledge of Russia comes from the campaign which he waged against her.' There was no immediate response, but that the barb had struck home was evident in Churchill's speech: he went out of his way to attack Attlee, and a further exchange followed.[50]

Outside the Commons, Attlee's parliamentary reputation was recognized by his being invited to contribute several articles to *The Encyclopaedia of the Labour Movement*:[51] his topics were Air Force, Army, Conscription, Compensation and Confiscation (he strongly favoured compensation; nationalization and redistribution of wealth had to be kept separate), Electricity, Local Government,[52] London Government and National Defence. Though not of the first importance, it was a respectable list of subjects and testified to the steady growth of his career and standing in Labour circles. Both of the latter were put at risk towards the end of 1927 by his sudden appointment as one of the two Labour members of a Statutory Commission on India.

The question of India was a particularly delicate one in Labour circles. In 1925 some ILPers had persuaded Labour's annual conference to approve a resolution affirming India's right to equal status with the other Dominions, and the need for a conference representative of the various parties in India.[53] The following year the ILP came out in support of total Indian independence, a position identified with several Communist front organizations with whom the Labour Party was on terms of open hostility. Labour's own executive had been unwilling that the Party be represented on the Statutory Commission unless Indians were included, though MacDonald managed to persuade the NEC to drop its resistance if a committee set up by the Indian legislature were to consult with the Commission. The former Prime Minister was in fact in a doubly awkward position: his Government had agreed – in imperial fashion – that Indian forces should be earmarked for use in defence of the Persian oil fields, should need arise, as British forces stationed in Iraq were to be reduced by Anglo-Iraq agreement;[54] and, as the Indian Press realized, the role of the Indian army and the question of Indian Defence were considered crucial to any discussions affecting her future.[55]

MacDonald's original selection of two Labour members for the Commission was thus politically orientated: he chose two senior Party figures, J. H. Thomas and William Graham, but they could not be spared. He then turned to two men who had also been concerned with the defence problem, Stephen Walsh, the former War Secretary, and Attlee, who in 1926 had spoken against an extension of the Anglo-Iraq treaty.[56] When Walsh, too, declined to serve on account of ill-health, Attlee became almost indispensable. He was not chosen, as A. J. P. Taylor has it,[57] because he could be so easily spared from the Commons. MacDonald was determined to ensure that 'the best or most representative people'[58] be chosen, and Attlee qualified on each count. Attlee was keenly aware that it was not a very promising assignment for a professional politician at the beginning of his career and with three children to support: he knew that making a report on the facts of the Indian situation was certain to arouse the ire of many Labour MPs. But 'the work had to be done': he accepted the appointment on the explicit understanding that, if Labour came to power, his domestic opportunities would not be affected.[59]

The nature of the political and personal risk he was taking soon became evident. Indian opposition to the Commission increased, and a boycott was threatened. George Lansbury, speaking for the NEC, pledged the 1927 annual conference to Dominion Home Rule for India and insisted that the Commission should command Indian confidence.[60] After the Commission's membership had been announced in the autumn, MacDonald had to make further efforts to defeat attempts to remove Attlee and Vernon Hartshorn (the ex-Postmaster General who had replaced Walsh) from the Commission.[61] Before the Commission departed for its first visit to India in January 1928, Attlee had to drop his other political activities. On his return, he found that the compiler of the Hansard Index (in April) could no longer spell his name correctly.[62] During his second and longer tour, from October 1928 to April 1929, domestic politics took a not unexpected turn: the Government's term of office came to an end and Baldwin called a general election, the first to be based on universal franchise.

Women now had the vote and in most constituencies outnumbered men:[63] the total electorate had risen by seven million. Labour put up 571 candidates for the 615 seats at stake and, like Attlee, a large proportion of those candidates were sponsored by divisional Labour parties:[64] among the successful ones the trade-union sponsored MPs were in a minority.[65] Attlee himself had no trouble in winning his seat, despite his absence from the country. In a four-cornered contest he had an overall majority of over 7,000 votes and an absolute one of nearly 3,000 again. His party was not so fortunate; though Labour won the election, its victory was seriously flawed. To Labour's 8.3 million votes and 288 seats the Conservatives polled 8.0 million and obtained 260 seats. The Liberals, with a single undisputed chief (Lloyd George) and a radical new programme, piled up 5.3 million votes: however, because of weaknesses in local organization the Liberals secured only fifty-nine seats.[66] For Labour, the election's message was clear: it still depended primarily on the working-class vote in industrial constituencies and the next electoral challenge would be to win outside them.

The Party did have a new programme but, far from being an advance on the 1918 statement, *Labour and the Nation* (1928) was 'in some ways a retreat'.[67] Prepared largely by R. H. Tawney, the document boldly stated the Party's claim to be a national and not a class party,[68] yet otherwise left a great deal to be desired. Drawing the lessons in 1937, Attlee pointed out that even the summary ran to four pages and contained seventy-two proposals, with no indication as to which of them was to be given priority. Large powers of discretion were accorded to the Leader, and 'every malcontent' was given 'unlimited opportunities of charging the Party with breaches of faith for not implementing all these promises.'[69] Labour's electoral success in 1929 was basically due to the swing of the pendulum against the Government during a time of chronic unemployment,[70] coupled with MacDonald's ability to paper over the cracks in Labour's policies.[71]

In the early summer of 1929, preoccupied as he was by the Indian problem, Labour's deficiencies escaped Attlee's notice. Never an economics expert, he was out of touch with the latest thinking emanating from the ILP. That group had vainly attempted, in 1927, to impose a remarkably prescient programme on the Labour Party. *Socialism in Our Time* advocated 'a system of family allowances, to be paid for by taxation; the nationalization of the Bank of England, to secure control of credit and monetary policy; and Government bulk purchase of foodstuffs and raw materials.' But these were only the trimmings. The core of the report was a proposal to 'introduce a national minimum wage and to set up an Industrial Commission to reorganize the industries unable or unwilling to pay it. The resources needed to pay higher wages . . . could not come from taxation. They could come instead from higher production which higher wages could call forth.'[72] A combination of these proposals with Lloyd George's platform of massive public works and a deliberate budgetary deficit anticipated Keynesian economic theory and the mixed and managed welfare economy that Attlee's own government would put into effect in 1945. In 1929 Attlee and the bulk of the Labour Party were not ready for these ideas: they were more concerned with the ILP's disruptive tactics within party ranks. Indeed, the ILP's programme had been put forward primarily as a power-play, not on its merits. As such it was rejected and the ILP then retaliated by demanding that its sponsored candidates at the election pledge themselves to support its policy.[73] This attitude back-fired: Attlee would subsequently blame the ILP for causing those other Labour MPs who also became discontented with the lack of a domestic policy nevertheless 'to rally to the support of the Government'.[74]

Besides believing that the ILP programme would be electorally disastrous, MacDonald considered it to be a totally false conception of the ILP's role. The original and proper function of the ILP had been that of propaganda, in the best sense. The walls of capitalism would not fall from external attacks but from internal changes in intellectual and moral desires. Labour's Leader worried lest too much emphasis on material improvements undermine the Party's spiritual values: capitalism had been condemned by the socialist pioneers both because the distribution of wealth was unjust and even more because the quality of life under it was inhuman.[75] Attlee shared this view. He always insisted that Labour's brand of socialism was not that of a conscious minority trying to force its will on a reluctant nation. Labour was an undogmatic, democratic party. The changes that it sought, he wrote in 1935, could not be imposed from above: 'A Government may transform the outward forms of society, but it requires the active co-operation of the citizens to give life to those forms.'[76]

But whether Attlee agreed with MacDonald's decision to accept minority office a second time is less certain. There were, he argued in retrospect, three possible courses open:

> to refuse office, to accept office and invite defeat by putting forward a Socialist programme and placing the onus of rejecting it on the Liberal Party, or to come to some agreement with the Liberals on a programme which would secure joint action in the House. The first was hardly practical politics at that time, and might well have meant another General Election, which the Party could not then have afforded, while it would have lost ground through what would have been held to be lack of courage and unwillingness to accept responsibility. The second, while open to the same danger of making probable another General Election, would have been a good fighting policy, and, in view of the economic trend of the period, have been the wisest tactics. The third offered considerable possibilities, but had its own disadvantages in the difficulty of securing at the same time support of the Simonite (Right Wing) Liberals and of the Left Wing of the Labour Party. United action on a bold and challenging programme might have given good results.[77]

Attlee was being only slightly disingenuous: co-operation with the Liberals might have produced good results, but the political price would have been too high. The problem was not so much that of securing the support or acquiescence of right-wing Liberals and left-wing Labourites: a Party which could still contain people as disparate in their economic views as Snowden and the Clydesiders could surely have come to terms had it wanted. But Labour did not want to come to any terms which would have the effect of bringing the Liberals back to national politics, especially the party led by Lloyd George. Attlee was always convinced that Labour's way to power would have to be at the expense of the Liberals and, like many members of his Party, probably felt both contempt for, and fear of, Lloyd George. The latter, he had written to his brother in 1918, was someone who mistook 'vulgarity for democracy' and had done so throughout his career.[78] Further, Attlee regarded the

Liberals as just another capitalist party. Had he been consulted, it seems likely that he would have opted for the second choice in 1929 – accept office, put forward a 'Socialist programme', and risk defeat. The paucity of Labour's finances would not have been an insurmountable obstacle.[79]

Of course, he was not consulted and whatever his private hesitations might have been Attlee proved a loyal, if not very enthusiastic, Government supporter. He had no personal reason to favour MacDonald who, despite his promise, passed over Attlee when choosing the ministerial team. The Prime Minister's main interest was foreign affairs, the importance of which Attlee respected: he afterwards defended the Government's accomplishments here as being 'very great', though attributing them to Arthur Henderson, the Foreign Secretary.[80] Attlee's time was mostly taken up by the writing of the India Commission's Report: between the Government's formation, in June 1929, and his appointment in November 1930 as Chancellor of the Duchy of Lancaster, he spoke on only two occasions from the backbenches. As Chancellor of the Duchy, and as Postmaster General from March to August 1931, he confined his parliamentary remarks to debating speeches attacking the Conservative opposition,[81] to the prolonged passage of an Agricultural Land (Utilization) Bill,[82] and to Post Office matters.

Behind the scenes Attlee increasingly shared the widespread Labour unease that dogged the Government's timid footsteps. During the election campaign, all parties had agreed that the foremost problem of the day was unemployment.[83] Shortly after Labour took office, the Wall St Crash of October 1929 precipitated the collapse of the international economy and turned the problem into a nightmare. The number of workless, normally around 1.5 million in the 1920s, soared to 2.5 million by the end of the decade. The perennial Labour debate between those who favoured a cautious ameliorative approach to the cure of the nation's ills and those who believed in a thorough-going 'socialist' solution was fired anew. Attlee's interest in polemic had waned but he gradually came to realize that MacDonald's socialism had, in practical terms, passed the point of no return. The Prime Minister was too old, too tired and too lonely: his appointment of George Lansbury to a cabinet post had been purely a sop to the left wing – other ILPers, even the previously successful Wheatley, were rigorously excluded. Lansbury, however, found an unlikely ally in Oswald Mosley, a former Conservative turned Labour MP, and together they submitted to the Government in May 1930 a plan of action. The plan was largely prepared by Mosley and the ideas it contained were neither original nor revolutionary: they included various provisions to increase purchasing power, to expand credit, to protect the home market, to restrict and cheapen imports and to rationalize industry. Nevertheless they met with a flat refusal at the hands of an economically orthodox cabinet. Mosley resigned his post as Chancellor of the Duchy of Lancaster and Attlee was appointed in his place.

MacDonald probably believed that Attlee was not the sort of man who would make trouble but, to make absolutely certain, the function of the post was changed. Attlee's role was to be that of general adviser to the Government. He became, as he described it to his brother Tom, 'a sort of tip-horse put on to help pull various wagons'.[84] As such, he was but one of a number of people and groups serving the same function,[85] and as the Government took no real heed of anything except traditional advice the net result of Attlee's work was more to concentrate his own thoughts than to influence Government policy. Attlee was not an economist and the economic issues, as Marquand has indicated,[86] were by no means as clear-cut as hindsight might suggest. Attlee's contributions merely reflected, at a prosaic level, the piece-meal and confused edging towards a more comprehensive solution that his abler peers were trying to put together. He had no hope that anything significant could be done which might remove the worldwide depression immediately.[87]

Attlee's specific areas of concern were industrial reconstruction and agriculture, though he also assisted MacDonald on imperial policy. The memorandum on industrial reconstruction that Attlee, together with the economist Colin Clark, submitted to MacDonald was content to sketch out a broad plan that would have required a majority Labour administration to implement. The essence of the plan involved large-scale State control and direction of the economy. Industry would be regulated by massive control of finance, transport and power; it would also be assisted by a National Investment Trust which would be the centre of a system of regional planning authorities. In agriculture, Attlee aimed at stimulating home production by the restriction of imports, guaranteed prices to farmers and cheaper marketing facilities to consumers.[88]

The most valuable lesson he derived from this work was a greater realization of the huge gap that existed between socialist aspirations and a specific series of proposals – arranged in order of priority – that a future Labour Government could reasonably hope to enact. In the autumn of 1930 he became an active member of a small group of socialists who met privately to consider the problem. There was a necessity, it was believed, not only for calling attention to what had been promised, but also for suggesting ways and means of carrying these promises into effect.[89] From these meetings emerged, firstly, the Society for Socialist Inquiry and Propaganda, whose members were dubbed the 'Loyal Grousers', and then the New Fabian Bureau (in March 1931), of which Attlee became chairman. Attlee's work on agriculture caused him to fall foul of the Chancellor of the Exchequer, Snowden, who was a strict free-trader: Attlee insisted that unless the Government set up an import board or a quota for agricultural imports a very serious situation would arise, 'worse than over the Mosley memorandum'. He described Snowden's argument against the quota as being 'fatal to any project whereby a special position is given to any branch of British industry. It applies equally against the Beet Sugar Subsidy, the Coal Bill and most Socialist proposals.'[90] The hitherto impeccably loyal Attlee was showing distinct signs of restlessness and it may be that his activities were a factor in MacDonald's decision, in March 1931, to saddle him with the responsibility of a much criticized department, the Post Office.

Attlee's brief tenure of this post – some six months – was sufficient to demonstrate how much he yearned for something to do, how much he preferred action to theory. He had a 'great time'[91] there, even though most of it was spent in mastering the intricacies of such a large organization – the largest employer in the country. His own input was a curious one: he aimed 'to raise the status of the selling organization, illuminatingly called the Contact Branch, to a level with that of the administrative and technical side of business, and to develop a publicity service'.[92] The result was an advertising campaign to push telephone sales. He also had the opportunity to refine his views about nationalized industries. Previously, many socialists had taken it for granted that they should all be run like the Post Office as a department of State with a minister directly responsible to Parliament. Attlee had already indicated his doubts about the desirability of over-centralization in general and the need for a variety of approaches to nationalization: his Post Office experience convinced him that efficiency and morale in nationalized industries would be improved by removing them from direct political control and interference, especially by the Treasury. He could have pointed to the absurdity of the Postmaster-General being asked, as he was, about whether or not Yspythy Ystwyth should have a sub-post office.[93]

As soon as his second period in government ended he urged that the head of the Post Office, whether an individual or a public board, should be taken away from Parliament. General overseeing functions could be exercised by the Minister of Transport, but day-to-day operations should be allowed the same sort of flexibility as that found in other business concerns.[94] His was no longer the point of view from the street corners: by the beginning of the 1930s, Attlee's socialism had assumed a markedly practical character. Yet his reaction to the momentous political developments of the second half of 1931 was to show that his commitment to 'the cause that never dies' was as firm as ever.

V

What About The Rentiers?

The collapse of the second minority Labour Government in August 1931 threw the Party into a state of shock. The groundswell of optimism which had accompanied the Party's steady rise during the 1920s was checked, and the weaknesses in Labour's programmes were brutally exposed. The increased parliamentary representation, Attlee later rationalized, had been mostly due to the differences in capitalist ranks which had 'caused Labour men and women to think that more progress in the conversion of the electorate had been made than was actually the fact. In 1931 Capitalism closed its ranks and showed the real situation.'[1] But it was not the collapse itself that produced the trauma so much as the way in which the collapse came about. The most enduring effects of what Attlee and most other Labourites considered as MacDonald's betrayal concerned the psychology of the leadership.[2] The very fabric of future policy and decision making, as well as the Party's power structure, were affected. MacDonald's actions had another result of great consequence: Clement Attlee was eventually thrust into prominence. The value to Labour of his hitherto unnoticed qualities would be emphasized because of the contrast with those of MacDonald. Indeed, just as it was said of Bonar Law that he 'became Prime Minister of England for the simple and satisfying reason that he was not Mr Lloyd George',[3] so too could it be said of Attlee that he became Leader of the Labour Party because he was not Ramsay MacDonald. Attlee's personality, solid and reassuring, would act as a healing antidote to bruised psyches, particularly as his actions in 1931 revealed that his commitment to the cause was quite unshakeable.

Prior to the financial crisis, MacDonald had been leader of the parliamentary party for nine years. At the Party's annual conference in 1930, despite the rumblings of discontent with the Government's performance that existed on several levels,[4] he had scored a remarkable oratorical and political triumph. It was not Labour that was on trial, he had declared, it was the system under which they lived: it had broken down everywhere, as it was bound to break down. He concluded his speech with a peroration that stirred the hearts of all who heard it,[5] and one that would return to mock him for the rest of his days. Appealing for a renewal of the socialist faith while cautioning that they could expect to see only the foundations of the new society laid in their lifetime, he proclaimed that 'the temple will rise and rise and rise until at last it is complete, and the genius of humanity will find within it an appropriate resting place'.[6] They were the last words MacDonald would ever address to the Party's chief assembly. In the harsh light of the cherished Leader's comportment and actions during the following year, the flowery phrases would echo ironically down the decade. Conversely, Attlee's controlled and commonsensical speeches would eventually command a hearing and sympathy they might not otherwise have had.

The international financial emergency responsible for Labour's downfall began in early July 1931, when the German banking system virtually ceased to exist. President Hoover's hurried proposal for a year's moratorium on reparations payment came too late to save the drain in German funds, and anyway misfired on account of French delay. Britain's turn soon came as foreign creditors rushed to withdraw their money, a substantial amount of which was tied up in Germany.[7] By August, a quarter of British gold reserves had gone[8] – from an economy which, by the conventional wisdom of the time, was already in trouble.

Snowden, the Labour Chancellor, had inherited an unbalanced budget from his predecessor, Winston Churchill, and had vainly tried to correct it. Early in the summer of 1931, two special committees established to examine the economic and financial situation had drawn attention to the decline in the balance of payments and had recommended slightly increased taxation coupled with heavy cuts in government expenditure. Two Labour members of the second of these committees, which was headed by a City financier, Sir George May, had disagreed, favouring instead increased government spending to stimulate consumer demand. But the majority's guiding principle was the traditional one of restoration of international confidence in the pound, expressed and symbolized in the maintenance of sterling's parity with gold, and it was this principle which had carried the day.

The choice put to the Labour Cabinet was between abandoning the gold standard and obtaining fresh loans in Paris and, especially, New York. However, the American bankers would require definite evidence of Britain's credit-worthiness – a balanced budget: and to achieve the latter, it was said, cuts would have to be made in the rate of unemployment benefit, among other items. The issue boiled down to going off gold or cutting the meagre dole handed out to the unemployed to keep them alive, a course that was adamantly rejected by the TUC. MacDonald's Cabinet, after attempting agonizingly to solve the dilemma by other measures and continuously harassed by the leaders of the opposition Conservative and Liberal parties, reached the point of no return in the evening of 23 August. Eleven members favoured a 10 per cent cut in benefit and nine were opposed, some to the point of resignation. It was clearly the end of the road for the Labour Government even though, according to his biographer, MacDonald did not decide on the formation of a National Government until the following morning.[9]

So far as minor figures like Attlee – journeying in from the Essex coast where he had been on holiday – [10] were concerned, the die had been cast. He was one of the junior ministers summoned by MacDonald on 24 August to hear the Prime Minister's version of the situation. Unusually, Attlee fortified himself for the encounter by lunching in an extravagant restaurant with Hugh Dalton, one of the ablest of the new Labour MPs. They drank a bottle of red Burgundy and Attlee impressed his host by being 'hot against J. R. MacDonald, for his indecision and his inferiority complex, especially in all economic questions, and hotter still against Snowden who, he says, has blocked every positive proposal for two years'.[11] The radical group of ILP MPs, the Clydesiders, would have been impressed: most of them expected Attlee to side with MacDonald when the National Government was formed.[12] They were taken in by his reserve. Yet Attlee's spontaneous reaction at the crowded meeting in the Cabinet Room during the afternoon of 24 August was completely in character. He set aside the economic arguments; he did not even doubt the validity, in the circumstances, of an appeal to national pride. What struck him was simply the inequality of the sacrifices demanded: the question he asked MacDonald was, 'What would be done to the rentiers?' The reply was that no answer was possible before a Budget statement:[13] cutting unemployment benefit apparently came into a different category. Attlee at once concluded that the Prime Minister and his friends had betrayed their mission. Some Labour MPs, including Herbert Morrison,[14] had hesitated to go into Opposition again. A majority of the Labour Cabinet had accepted the cuts in unemployment benefit but had refused for party political reasons (especially because of the TUC's opposition), to join with MacDonald in putting them into effect. Attlee's sense of morality was deeply offended. Within a matter of days he formally resigned his office.

MacDonald himself was fully aware of what he was doing, but attempted to explain it away as a clash of priorities. He had previously admitted to the Cabinet that the proposals as a whole represented the negation of everything that the Labour Party stood for, yet he was satisfied that they were necessary in the national interest.[15] No one could have been more open to persuasion on these grounds than Clement Attlee, for if MacDonald had given proof of his capacity during the war to put what he considered the national interest above that of party loyalty,[16] so too had Attlee. Indeed, given that they had both been more emotionally tied in pre-war days to the ILP than to the Labour Party, it can be argued that Attlee's demonstration had been the stronger one. Even in 1931 Attlee was still ready, in his letter of resignation, to acknowledge that the Prime Minister's action in forming a National Government had been taken solely 'in the endeavour to serve the country'.[17] Nor did Attlee's reaction owe anything to economic reasoning though, as is now known, it happened to be economically correct. There is no evidence that he was among the very few people at the time who were opposed to maintaining the gold standard. In fact Attlee collaborated in the preparation of Labour's 1931 election manifesto, *Labour's Call to Action*, which declared that a balanced budget was the first condition of sound national finance.[18] But however much it could be argued that the Labour Government was the victim of circumstances over which it had no control, the question of how the effects of those circumstances might be mitigated within the United Kingdom was one which pushed Attlee back to the source of his socialist inspiration. He stood for 'LIFE against WEALTH'.

The full impact of the events of August 1931 on the Labour Party took some time to reveal itself; it was not lessened by the huge irony that, after the cuts had been made and a new deflationary (though not entirely inegalitarian)[19] budget had been passed, the country was still obliged to go off the gold standard. The former Labour ministers were caught in a fine state of disarray in the Commons. As a result, power in the Labour movement slipped out of the hands of the PLP and even further into those of the TUC. The recriminations in the Commons were still going on in early October and, while most of the Party's leaders were heading north to Scarborough for the annual conference, Attlee was left in charge of the Parliamentary rearguard.

Opening the debate on a third reading of one of the Finance Bills designed to give effect to the budget, on 2 October, he went after Snowden, now Chancellor in the National Government. The budget, Attlee accused the former ILPer, penalized the poor more than the rentier class; it did nothing to tackle the country's most serious problem – that of debt; it would not even preserve free trade. To Snowden, a staunch free-trader and a master of invective, Attlee's words were as the proverbial red rag to the bull. Realizing what was coming, two of the Government back-benchers went out of their way to compliment him on his boldness. One, George Lambert, was a Gladstonian Liberal and had known Attlee's father. The other, the Marquess of Hartington, recalled that he had first met Attlee as a soldier serving in a regiment which had suffered very high casualties; now, Hartington asserted, Attlee belonged to a force which was about to suffer similar losses. Hartington's remark would apply equally to the general election which was shortly to be called.

Snowden duly demolished Attlee with the same ease with which MacDonald's National Coalition was to vanquish the Labour Party. The Chancellor could make great play with the fact that though Labour was now, in Attlee's words, 'wholly opposed' to the Bill, the measure was exactly the one the Labour Party would have introduced had they been in power. On a personal level, Snowden reminded Attlee that he was among the Labour MPs who, with only twenty exceptions, had voted for the establishment of the May Committee. Attlee had already been led to the clumsy interjection that he did not (now) support the May Committee.[20] Snowden rammed home the point that the economies proposed by the Committee and accepted by the Labour Cabinet required a national government for their implementation. His implication, of course, was that Labour had run away from responsibility – the sorest point of all with Attlee.

The more Attlee dwelt on the moral significance of what MacDonald had done, the more his outrage increased. A few days after the confrontation in the Cabinet Room on 24 August he was talking to Jack Lawson and Lawson's daughter on the porch of the House of Commons, when MacDonald approached: according to Lady Lawson, Attlee then raised his voice, saying, 'And Esau sold his inheritance for a few pieces of silver.'[21] To his brother in December, he wrote: 'I fear J. R. M. has completely gone. He revels in titled friends. He will have a rude awakening soon, I think.'[22] In the Commons in June 1932 Attlee uncharacteristically burst out that he had followed the Prime Minister for five and twenty years only to be told at a moment's notice that MacDonald proposed to go over to the enemy.[23] For Attlee, a significant point to emerge during the controversy over the tariff question which came to a head in October 1932, was what the Ottawa Agreements revealed about MacDonald's actions in August 1931. The Agreements indicated that MacDonald had changed his mind long before August, which had merely been the occasion for betrayal and not the beginning. For if, as MacDonald had said, when he had set up the Ottawa Conference he knew and was persuaded that there had to be taxes on foodstuffs there, 'then he either deceived his colleagues; or he deceived the Dominions' Prime Ministers; or he had made up his mind that if Ottawa was to be a success, he would have to have colleagues who believed in food taxes.' Attlee consoled himself with the thought that the last had been heard about MacDonald's former Labour colleagues running away.[24] But in 1935 Attlee could still be found savagely denouncing his old leader as a 'political nudist, a man who had shed every rag of political conviction he ever had'.[25]

The combined effect of the economic crisis and the electoral defeat in 1931 caused Attlee to doubt for a time whether Labour's moderate and evolutionary tactics of the 1920s had been wise. MacDonald's approach to the evils of capitalism had assumed that the system could be infinitely squeezed:[26] in 1931 it appeared that capitalism was on the brink of breakdown. To Attlee and others, the situation seemed to call for a return to first principles. The next few years were to witness 'a process of theoretical stocktaking and prescription among British socialists unparalleled in the history of the Labour Party.'[27] 'We want', Attlee explained to his brother in November 1931, 'to get the Party away from the immediate and on to basic socialism. I think the shake-up will ultimately prove the salvation of the Party.'[28] For a brief period he toyed with the ideas and spoke the language of revolution: he took an active part in almost all the discussion groups which sprang up. His involvement was partly a compensation for his frustration during the last months of the Labour Government, besides being a reaction to the apparent gravity of the economic crisis. It may also have served to camouflage the guilt feelings created as a result of MacDonald's actions and the revelation of Labour's intellectual shortcomings. The revulsion from MacDonaldism, Attlee would write in 1937, caused the Party (in which he could have included himself) 'to lean rather too far towards a catastrophic view of progress and to emphasize unduly the conditions of crisis which were being experienced and to underestimate the recuperative powers of the capitalist system'.[29]

At the same time, 1931 reinforced Attlee's suspicions that fine-sounding slogans and theories were no substitute for specific policies. His was thus a double quest: he sought both a re-emphasis on socialist goals and a definite plan of action 'so that when we are next returned we shall know exactly what we want to do, how to do it, and through what persons to carry it into effect.' It was, he admitted to Tom in an unconscious reference to Labour's past shortcomings, 'a big job'.[30] Yet the older quarters of the Party had to bestir themselves and show that they meant 'to act and not sit still and just carry on'.[31]

In the immediate light of 'MacDonaldism', a reassertion of socialist goals appeared more urgent than the preparation of plans. A Society for Socialist Inquiry and Propaganda (the SSIP) had already been founded in June 1931. Though definitely left-wing, the Society had not alarmed the Labour movement:[32] Ernest Bevin, the most forceful and powerful trade union leader, became its chairman. When Attlee was elected a member of the Society's executive in May 1932, he took care to insist that it should not become a political party but remain Labour's propaganda arm. More precisely, he thought that the Society should supply propaganda and research in conjunction with, and on behalf of, the Party: members might even control Labour's propaganda and literature posts. But in the excitement of the high summer of that year he was moved to suggest that the SSIP 'should train people to take over the commanding positions in the army and navy in the event of a revolution' and that 'organized bands of members' should be capable of 'taking over certain jobs in an emergency'.[33] By then, the ILP had split apart and had ended its historic link with the Labour Party 'leaving a political vacuum on the Labour Left'.[34] A substantial minority of the former ILPers being unwilling to enter the political wilderness, it was decided that they should amalgamate with the SSIP. The result was the formation of the Socialist League, a body top-heavy with left-wing intellectuals and remote from the Labour mainstream. Attlee's adhesion to the League was undoubtedly the most extravagant of his post-1931 actions. Bevin prudently dropped out during the negotiations but Attlee remained to play a prominent part in the League's greatest triumph, which was won in the first week of its existence.[35]

Attlee openly supported those League members who, at the Labour Party's 1932 annual conference, challenged the National Executive. Sir Charles Trevelyan proposed a resolution that a future Labour government, either with or without a clear majority, should at once promulgate definite 'socialist' legislation. Arthur Henderson resisted it for the Executive, saying that it would be a 'profound mistake' to tie the Party's hands in advance. Attlee countered by insisting that conditions had changed since 1929. A period had come to an end: events of the past year had shown that 'no further progress can be made in trying to get crumbs from the rich man's table.' The people whom Labour represented had to be clearly told that they could not have socialism without tears, that they would be opposed by every vested interest, that there would be another crisis and that they had to have a short-term plan to deal with that crisis. There was no use waiting until their mandate had become exhausted; they had to strike while the iron was hot and before their supporters and the voters had been scared.[36] The resolution was carried.

It was, to be sure, a rhetorical victory, which corresponded to the prevailing Labour mood.[37] Attlee did not join the Socialist League's national council and had little to do formally with the organization after its first virtuous months.[38] He would certainly have objected to the League's belief 'that politics needed to be examined in terms of class conflict and that the Labour Party should adopt a distinctively class approach to political issues.'[39] While not denying that a class struggle existed, he considered that it was not as clear-cut as some theorists assumed. He enjoyed the irony that the League's champions of the working classes were themselves almost exclusively middle-class in origin and had little contact with the working class, organized or unorganized.[40] Yet he could still, in March 1933, be found giving a lecture under the League's auspices on the subject of 'Local Government and the Socialist Plan', which followed an address by Sir Stafford Cripps.

Attlee prefaced his remarks with five assumptions:
(1) that a majority socialist Government had been returned to deal with a critical situation in which the problem of unemployment had not been solved; (2) that the Government had successfully challenged the House of Lords; (3) that the financial system had been nationalized and foreign trade nationally controlled; (4) that emergency measures had been taken to give the Government 'wide powers' to overcome the slowness of the legislative process; and (5) that the detailed national administration had been separated from the function of major strategy which would be carried out by a central planning body working under a 'small Cabinet of superior direction'. The dominant themes of his lecture were those of crisis and practicality. A socialist Government, he argued, would be judged by its ability to deliver the goods during the critical period of transition and not by the theoretical perfection of its plans for the future. In the rather desperate circumstances which Attlee believed would attend the advent of a Labour Government, the important thing would be not to act 'with the most scrupulous regard to theories of democracy or exact constitutional propriety, but to get on with the job'.

In order to get the economy moving again, active co-operation would be required from the local government agencies, but he doubted whether, as these were then constituted, they could function as direct instruments of the central government. Normally he favoured the retention of considerable local autonomy, but in a time of rapid and fundamental change this tradition would have to be temporarily suspended. The national government would have as its priorities such items as an intensive housing and slum clearance campaign; land settlement and utilization involving reclamation, drainage, rural housing and agricultural equipment; extensive electrical provision in the countryside; transport re-organization and railway modernization as part of a unified system; the provision of amenities such as parks, etc., and the extension of education. All these would impinge upon the complicated network of local authorities, hence the need for temporary new machinery to facilitate short-term recovery. Attlee proposed the division of England and Wales into ten administrative regions for the purpose of translating the national government's emergency plan into action. Each region would be under the overall direction of a socialist commissioner, to be assisted by a planning committee and a staff of experts. Any recalcitrant local authority would have to be 'ruthlessly superseded'. In addition to regional co-ordination there would have to be co-ordination between regions, in accordance with the national plan: there would be no use, for instance, in sinking social capital into areas which might subsequently be found economically redundant. Attlee's scheme was based on the principles of national necessity and economic sense, but he also stressed the importance of local participation where possible in the interim period, with a return to a 'full exercise of democracy as soon as the Socialist state [was] in being'.[41]

Attlee's lecture formed part of a series, given by members of the Socialist League in the early months of 1933, which corresponded closely with his previous opinion of what the SSIP's role should be, namely the provision of research and propaganda. His participation may also have owed something to his close relationship with Cripps at this time. Their association had begun in the Commons after the 1931 election where Attlee, Lansbury and Cripps 'worked together with the greatest harmony', for a while. In addition, Attlee found Cripps 'a most warm-hearted and generous friend and a delightful companion'.[42] Cripps was a man of several parts, of which the least developed was his politics. Son of a former Tory MP turned Labour Cabinet Minister in his old age, Cripps had a first-class grounding in science, had been an outstanding factory director in the war and had then achieved an extraordinary reputation as a lawyer. He was also a deeply committed Anglican. Persuaded in 1930 to become a Labour MP, he moved rapidly to the Left, becoming chairman of the Socialist League in June 1933. And though Attlee soon learned to become wary of Cripps's political naivety, he never lost his respect for Cripps which, after the Second World War, was confirmed in a further political relationship.

They had already, in January 1931, collaborated on a document entitled 'The Joint Stock Banks' which they presented confidentially to the Finance and Trade Committee of the Labour Party's Executive. The policy of gradualism was denounced: Attlee and Cripps recommended that Labour openly declare its intention to nationalize the joint stock banks. In their opinion, nationalization of the Bank of England and indirect control over the private banks would not be sufficient to ensure a socialist Government's survival – let alone the achievement of any substantial part of its programme. 'The moment to strike at Capitalism,' they concluded, '[was] the moment of taking power, when the Government [was] freshly elected and assured of . . . support.' The blow to be struck had to be a fatal one, not one which merely wounded and therefore turned a sullen and obstructive opponent into an active and deadly enemy.[43] At the Party's 1933 annual conference, Attlee also supported an amendment proposed by Cripps to an NEC Report on 'Socialism and the Condition of the People': among other things, Cripps's amendment called for (1) the immediate abolition of the House of Lords, (2) passage of an Emergency Measures Act, (3) a revision of Commons' procedure and (4) an economic plan for industry, finance and foreign trade.[44] Attlee argued hotly that 'everything else you are putting through is useless if you cannot get them passed'.[45] Bevin disagreed, saying that it was wrong to create resistance 'as an excuse for not going through with our own measures', and the amendment was referred to the NEC for consideration. In January 1934, a careless reference of Cripps's about the necessity of overcoming probable resistance from Buckingham Palace (should the King refuse to consent to the abolition of the Lords) provoked uproar in the press and considerable annoyance among Labour Party leaders, yet Attlee continued to support him.[46] Later that year, Attlee and Cripps rallied to the defence of Harold Laski, who had been invited to deliver a series of lectures in Moscow and had come under public attack.[47] But Attlee's relationship with Cripps was by then more personal than political.

The League's affiliation to the Labour Party, in September 1933, re-opened the dilemma formerly posed by the ILP. In the minds of many trade unionists and of several NEC members the League was 'a body of dangerous dissidents';[48] that same month the TUC rejected the League's programme *in toto*. For tactical reasons the Labour Party conference postponed judgment but Attlee failed that year in his first bid to secure election to the NEC. The incipient conflict between the Party and the League was precipitated by the League's actions which increasingly demonstrated the body's real aim – converting the Party rather than the electorate at large. The research aspect of the League's work was 'virtually dropped'[49] and there was an intense effort to build up the number of branches.[50] Labour's unprecedented victory at the London County Council elections, in March 1934, underlined the danger presented by the League to the party. The victory was organized and orchestrated by Herbert Morrison, and its political message was the value of moderation. Like Attlee, Morrison had had the intention in 1931 of moving Labour to 'a real socialist Left' and between 1932 and 1933 gained a reputation of being 'almost a socialist intellectual'. But after his brief flirtation with extremist theorizing, Morrison had returned to gradualism and had clashed with Lansbury, Cripps and Attlee.[51] Morrison's suggestions, which had favoured the setting up of public corporations run by experts rather than direct nationalization of industries, had had a mixed reception by trade union leaders; yet he had been re-elected to the NEC in 1932, and he and the equally pragmatic Hugh Dalton headed the poll in 1933.

As soon as the League's covert aim became clear, Attlee's support for the group diminished. From March 1933 he was in any case heavily engaged in the Commons with the long debate over Indian Constitutional Reform, which reinforced his practical bent. Never in the full sense an intellectual, he was temperamentally inclined to seek practical compromises rather than sterile confrontations. The vehemence and personalization of party disputes particularly distressed him: 'I wish people would not always want to be straffing their friends instead of their enemies,' he would write plaintively to Tom in 1934.[52] He also realized that the staggering problem of Labour unity could only be resolved by the construction of a bridge between idealists and pragmatists, a bridge which had to be founded on the strength of organized labour. And why not? The TUC had been rock solid in its opposition to MacDonald's economic proposals on 21 August 1931.[53]

Subsequently, the TUC, together with the extra-parliamentary party, had proceeded to take full control of Labour's parliamentary wing.[54] Having little contact with the trade-union movement, Attlee was not chosen to sit on the new parliamentary executive following MacDonald's desertion; nor, as noted, was he successful in his 1933 attempt to gain a seat on the NEC. However, the short-lived nature of his radical lapse ensured that the setback to his extra-parliamentary career was equally temporary. He became a member of the remodelled National Council of Labour (the NCL), on which the trade unions were in the majority, and it was here he began his acquaintance with union leaders. The Council's task of reconciling TUC and Labour Party policy where there was divergence or overlapping was very much to his taste. He was also co-opted on to the NEC's Finance and Trade, and Constitution, sub-committees. In 1934 he secured formal election to full NEC membership. The votes strongly reflected union opinion. Attlee still came behind Morrison and Dalton but Cripps, still ostentatiously left wing, only just made it.[55]

Left-wing influence in the Labour Party during the 1930s on domestic issues was limited by three factors. In the first place, the anti-Left, cautious trade-union element predominated in the Party's main committees. Secondly, the decade turned out in the end to be modestly prosperous. If the traditional industrial centres were at a standstill, new ones flourished. Expectation of life increased, the purchasing power of the pound rose slightly – as did the average wage – and the bank-rate dropped sharply from 6.2 to 2 per cent. Above all, after January 1932 the unemployment figures began to decline. The gradual economic improvement, coupled with the penetration of Keynesian doctrines, suggested that capitalism could be squeezed further and that a mixed economy was possible. Neither Labour's 1935 general election manifesto nor the 1937 *Immediate Programme* included any 'of the radical critiques of Labour's central assumptions',[56] though the 1937 *Programme* did contrast sharply with Conservative economic thinking. Thirdly, the growing deterioration of the international situation eventually subordinated or subsumed domestic issues altogether – and greatly facilitated the resolution of Labour's differences in this area.

So far as Attlee was concerned, the catastrophic approach at home lost any appeal it might have had for him when he considered what was happening abroad, where a genuine catastrophe was in the making. At the 1934 conference he spoke for the NEC on foreign policy, and he had a confession to make: he had changed his (formerly ILP) mind about unilateral disarmament. He also thought that lining up exclusively with Socialist countries would not remove the menace of world war.[57] The extent of the distance he had put between himself and the Left generally, not just the Socialist League, was apparent from the conference's division over foreign policy (to be dealt with in the next chapter). The Left obtained some 673,000 votes against 1,519,000 in favour of the NEC's position. Much of Attlee's time during the second half of the 1930s would be spent in trying to reduce this split.

Before the 1934 conference, the NEC had also approved a new statement on domestic policy, *For Socialism and Peace*, again drafted by R. H. Tawney, who was much closer to Attlee's way of thinking than the League's ideologists. Tawney's approach to socialism, like Attlee's, was a moral one, grounded not in 'efficiency, or order, or the symmetry of a perfect social machine, or even of abundance, but ... [in] a right order of social relationships, the unending and unmeasurable goal of which is human fellowship.'[58] His document, as amended by the NEC, though more socialist in tone than *Labour and the Nation* of 1928 and its 1931 successor, *Labour's Call to Action*, scarcely revealed a revolution in Labour's economic thinking. On the other hand, it did include more precise and extensive proposals for nationalization, including the Bank of England and the joint stock banks – in deference to the 1932 conference's decision – and public ownership in general was given a high priority. It also envisaged a National Investment Board and a forty-hour week. But the League was not satisfied and tabled some seventy-five amendments, reduced by the Standing Orders Committee to twelve, which sought to get the Party to commit itself to 'a decisive advance within five years towards a Socialist Britain'. They were all massively rejected.[59]

For good measure, the NEC in 1934 appended a further document on *Parliamentary Problems and Procedures*, another indication that the radical ardour of 1931 and 1932 had faded. Though the current methods of operation were condemned as 'antiquated and unsuited to modern conditions', there was nothing particularly extremist in the proposals for accelerating parliamentary business. On this issue at least, a compromise had even been worked out beforehand with representatives of the League, including Cripps. An immediate attack on the Lords, J. R. Clynes explained to the conference, was considered by the NEC to be 'bad tactics'. It would throw the Party into the 'whirlpool of constitutional policy and conduct, and would prevent any proceeding on our part with the great economic and social lines of policy with which we want to deal.' A House of Lords veto on legislation would be overcome and, in any case, a Labour Government during its term of office would take steps to abolish the Lords as a legislative chamber. As regards emergency powers, the NEC document stipulated that these would be used only if an emergency situation accompanied or followed a Labour victory, and only for a limited time: such powers 'would have a definite and clear relationship to the character of the emergency created, and they would be operated with a view to the most rapid return possible to the process of normal government'.[60]

These policy developments would probably have come about in any case. After the radical flourish of the early 1930s, they represented a return – with only slight modifications – to the pragmatic trend discernible in the 1920s. The most prescient contribution of the radical period to Labour thinking in the end came from Attlee. It was one which addressed itself directly to what had happened in the Party in August 1931. As a result of the MacDonald episode, many radicals had called for stronger Party controls on the freedom of action of a future Labour Prime Minister: Attlee showed how it might best be done. 'The essential quality in a P.M.,' he wrote in 1932, 'is that he should be a good Chairman, able to get others to work ... ' The Cabinet should be composed not of department heads, but of representatives of various functions, such as Finance, Economic Planning, Social Services, External Relations, Defence, Law and Order, plus the Secretary of State for Scotland (as had become customary) and perhaps the Minister of Agriculture. The Prime Minister's job would be to reconcile differences of opinion and be the ultimate arbiter of the decisions in the light of the interim socialist plan that had been accepted by the electorate.[61] What, in other words, a Labour Government required at the top was a catalyst rather than a stimulant, someone who could co-ordinate rather than provoke, a team-leader rather than a one-man-band. It was the recipe which he had used successfully at Stepney, and which he would follow in 1945.

His views in 1932 on the premiership reflected his preference for a clearly-defined, democratically acceptable form of socialism and they also forecast the attitude he would adopt to his Party when he became its leader. 'I am not prepared,' he wrote in 1937, 'to arrogate to myself a superiority to the rest of the movement. I am prepared to submit to their will, even if I disagree. I shall do all I can to get my views accepted, but, unless acquiescence in the views of the majority conflicts with my conscience, I shall fall into line, for I have great faith in the wisdom of the rank-and-file.' By rank and file, Attlee did not mean 'that small proportion of people who are continually interested and active in politics': he was referring rather to the broad mass of people who were content with nominal membership and support of the Labour Party.[62] Their views were expressed, notably, by the trade unions. Another lesson he had learned from the fiasco of 1931 was that any major departure from the advice of the TUC spelt political disaster for the Labour Party. He might also have considered in 1937 that Bevin, the outstanding representative of collective wisdom, had been right in 1925 in his unsuccessful effort to prevent the Party from taking office again as a minority government, right in 1931 on the economy, and right again in 1935 on rearmament.

While the Labour movement was thus digesting the wider impact of the events of August 1931, parliamentary life tended to be pushed into the background. Attlee himself was taken aback both by the date and result of the 1931 general election. MacDonald had written to all the junior ministers on the 24 August that the new Government was not a Coalition but 'a co-operation between individuals who are banded together to avoid the disaster. No parties are involved in it, and as soon as the country gets on an even keel again, the Government will cease to exist'.[63] As there was no sign of recovery in September, Attlee must have presumed that the Government would carry on: he arranged to move house in October, from Woodford to a larger place with a good-sized garden in Stanmore.[64] His move testified to a certain confidence in his personal prospects. MPs' salaries had not been increased since 1911,[65] but he had become accustomed to receiving the emoluments of a junior minister and there seemed every prospect of further advancement in the not too distant future.[66] Neither did his campaign in Limehouse give him any particular anxiety; 'the election pursued its usual quiet course and it did not appear that anything unusual was in the wind.' It was only after returning to his new home on polling day, 27 October 1931, that he realized a political landslide was in the making. Even then he could not have guessed the extent of the Labour rout; he 'decided to sleep on it'.[67] The following morning he was to discover that 'one of the greatest reversals in British electoral history'[68] had taken place.

MacDonald's decision to form a National Coalition and to appeal to the country for 'a doctor's mandate' revealed in the most dramatic fashion that the time for a socialist consensus on a national scale was not yet ripe. His Coalition, largely dominated by the Conservatives, obtained 67 per cent of the votes cast – some 14½ million – and the colossal, almost embarrassing, number of 554 seats out of a total of 615. Labour, in spite of its 6½ million votes, was massacred: the Party obtained a derisory forty-six seats and the ILP, who had fought a separate campaign, a mere five. Although the total Labour vote had declined only 6.3 per cent compared with 1929,[69] the constituency pattern had swung abnormally against the Party. But unlike most of his colleagues Attlee was not affected: he managed to retain his seat – by a meagre 551 votes. These votes were more influential in the shaping of his future political career than his forays into the realms of theory: his victory was almost certainly due to the personal loyalty he had built up with his constituents over the years. Labour's strength depended on the number of votes it could secure; policy-making, in the final analysis, had to be governed by the same criterion. Socialism without a sufficient number of socialists, or people willing to support socialist programmes, was a nonsense. Even in Stepney in 1931, Labour narrowly lost its two other seats. Elsewhere, the damage was greater. With the single exception of George Lansbury, all the older generation of Labour's parliamentary leaders who had not defected were eliminated and, except for Stafford Cripps, so too were all the younger ones. At the first meeting of the survivors, Lansbury was unanimously elected chairman and Attlee deputy chairman of the PLP.

Luck certainly played a part in Attlee's advancement: in what outstanding political career has it not? There can be little doubt, as the unlucky Dalton has pointed out,[70] that almost any of the former ex-Ministers on the NEC, or Herbert Morrison, would have been chosen as chairman or deputy chairman in preference to Lansbury or Attlee. Both were London MPs, and had anyone from a provincial constituency been available, one at least would have been excluded, probably Attlee. He had been on neither the National nor the late Parliamentary Executive Committee. But no one else was available. The new parliamentary party was composed mostly of inarticulate trade-union stalwarts, especially ex-miners.[71] Even Cripps, not yet left wing, who had only a year's parliamentary experience and who had hesitated for twelve days before deciding not to join MacDonald,[72] was soon invited to share Lansbury's room at the Commons.

Together, Lansbury, Cripps and Attlee made up a parliamentary Labour triumvirate, but the differences in their roles would be as great as their personalities. Lansbury may have 'proved a more successful Mark Antony than anyone could have expected,'[73] but he was seventy-two, not in the best of health and inclined towards a 'woolly-minded sentimentality'.[74] His absolute pacifism would also prove an increasing irritant to the trade union leaders who controlled the Party. Similarly, while Cripps may have been 'the perfect Octavius, cold, remorseless in the pursuit of his enemies and never deflected from his argument,'[75] he was also a very busy and successful lawyer given, in his political utterances, to the exaggerated language of the recent convert. He had something akin to genius for provoking needless controversy. Alone of the three, Attlee proved to be a most assiduous, conscientious and dependable parliamentary performer: even the denigrating Foot admits that 'Lepidus ... performed his errands with such peremptory agility and despatch that he seemed to make himself indispensable.'[76] In the course of four and a half years Attlee attracted a loyalty from his fellow MPs equal to that which he had won from his constituents. He did so because he understood, more than his two colleagues, that leaders have to work with people as they are. He was also more aware of the responsibilities of his position: in the Commons, he reminded the Party's 1935 annual conference, 'you cannot take up a negative attitude; you have to deal with realities'.[77]

From 1931 to 1935, the parliamentary rank and file Labour members came to have great confidence in Attlee, whose Commons career was thus transformed as a result of the 1931 election. In fact, while many of his radical associates devoted themselves to internal Party wrangles, Attlee was carrying an enormous parliamentary burden. He was required to speak several times a week on a variety of subjects. In 1932 he filled more columns of Hansard than any other MP, a notable feat for so laconic a speaker. He had ample opportunity to perfect his mastery of Commons procedure, a skill which earned him the respect of colleagues and Government supporters alike. In December 1933 he became the temporary Labour Leader in the Commons, though in a somewhat back-handed fashion. Lansbury broke his hip and offered the job to Cripps, who refused.[78]

Attlee's overall thesis on domestic affairs was a simple one – the need for a comprehensive policy of economic recovery. There could be no return, he argued, to the pre-war position in relation to the rest of the world and only Government intervention could bring about the reorganization of industry. The omissions in the King's Speech in this regard, he declared in the debate on the Address in November 1931,[79] were more important than what it contained. As no one knew better than himself the gaps in Labour's own economic policy, it was just as well that two subsidiary themes were available to him: these were the nature of the 1931 election campaign, described by the *Manchester Guardian* as '... the shortest, the strangest and the most fraudulent of our time',[80] and the obvious division in Government ranks over the free trade-versus-protection issue. One of the election stunts had been a scare about the security of Post Office Savings Bank deposits under a Labour Government and, as a former Postmaster-General, Attlee was well equipped to make a detailed refutation of the charge. He found unexpected support from Winston Churchill who had no quarrel with the 'temper' of Attlee's speech.[81] Attlee's temper at this time, as previously noted, was reserved for the unfortunate Ramsay MacDonald.

Officially, Labour steered a neutral course between the protagonists of tariffs and free trade: neither position, Attlee explained to the Commons, should be regarded as an end in itself.[82] Privately he considered at the end of 1931 that 'a genuinely Tory protectionist government would be better than this cross-breed animal';[83] he had himself indicated to MacDonald in 1930 the desirability of protecting British farming interests by limiting imports.[84] These views did not prevent Attlee from berating the Government's tariff proposals: they were totally divorced from any sound plan for building up the economy[85] and their imposition without a general policy for the stimulation of domestic consumption was a mistake.[86] In any case, all attempts to seek a favourable balance of trade in the absence of an agreement over inter-Allied debts and reparations were futile: Britain was suffering not so much from an attack on its trade by particular foreign nations as from the fact that the whole world was suffering from a slump and decrease in purchasing power, due largely to currency and exchange problems.[87] Nor did he attach much importance to the notion of imperial preference: it was no longer precisely true that the British Empire was composed of mutually complementary units.[88]

In principle, Attlee was correct: the debate between protectionists and free traders had become more or less obsolete when Britain went off gold. There was, however, the immediate economic problem to be faced; here, while his Party was attempting to get a policy together, Attlee could only stone-wall with taunts that they were, anyway, living in 'the twilight of the capitalist system'.[89] In reality, he was exercised by the complexity of the financial tangle: he joined a private dining-club where City men could 'meet and instruct the Labour leaders in the mysteries of finance so that they would not make a hash of it when they came to power'.[90] By the end of 1932, his expertise, along with his acceptance of certain Keynesian ideas, had noticeably improved. Yet he still claimed that ' ... we Socialists are the true preservers of Western ideas ... [Unless] your capitalism can be brought into accord with the ideal of social justice to the ordinary man, then a great deal of what many of us hold, what I myself hold, to be most precious in our Western civilization will go down before the irresistible rush of the discontented.'[91] And he was still groping towards some idea of patriotic consensus: action to relieve unemployment, he insisted, could be taken on an entirely non-party basis. The memory of what had been done during the war was never very far below the surface of his mind; when the will had been there, the money had been found.[92] How to achieve a similar accord in peacetime? During the 1930s Labour did not find a convincing answer – as the loss of the 1935 general election, despite four years of massive unemployment, would seem to indicate. The Party's political task was two-fold, Attlee concluded in 1937: it had firstly, 'to convert to its faith many millions of workers who still [clung] to Capitalism'; and secondly, 'to persuade many members of the classes which [depended] in the main on their own work for their livelihood that a true community of interest [was] based on fellowship in service, not on participation in profits.'[93]

These objectives were another reason why he put the accent on general principle in his post-1931 Commons speeches on domestic policy. Nothing much had come from going off gold, he reiterated in April 1932; the budget had not been balanced.[94] What Labour and other people demanded was that plans should replace chaos; only state action would suffice to rectify the situation and he was not concerned to discuss the limitations of such action, which were merely a matter of degree.[95] Where, in his estimation, effective action had been taken – as in the case of the Post Office – he was unstinting in his praise.[96] Unemployment – the domestic subject in which, along with agriculture,[97] he took a special interest – was another matter.[98] Here he found humbug and hypocrisy,[99] class legislation and a clear indication that the values of the Government differed from those of the Opposition.[100] The latter included a number of Liberals who before and after 1935 were voting with Labour on the unemployment issue. But after that year's election Attlee could leave the domestic front largely in the hands of his additional colleagues.

Labour's electoral failure in the 1930s was mitigated on domestic matters by the fact that the national Government's abandonment of free trade in 1932 involved a further shift in the orientation of British capitalism. The deflationary and conservative character of the Government's overall position partially concealed the implications of a series of supplementary policies that necessarily had to accompany the introduction of a comprehensive system of tariffs. They included 'the provision of capital investment loans and direct subsidies; organized marketing and guaranteed agricultural prices; the promotion of cartel organization in a widening range of industries; some extension in the scope of public ownership; and efforts to promote economic recovery in particularly hard-hit regions.'[101] Labour could well argue that these, and other measures, were inadequate; nevertheless, they implied that the State did accept some responsibility for the direction of the national economy. MacDonald's consensus was far from the one envisaged by Attlee, but it was a step in that direction and one which a narrow concentration on Labour Party fortunes could easily overlook. Attlee was to admit as much in 1937.

After 1935 Attlee's main domestic concern was to establish Labour's democratic character with the electorate, especially the middle class. He contributed to several symposia[102] on the nature and necessity of democracy, though he stipulated that personal and political liberty could only, in twentieth-century conditions, be maintained by a large measure of economic equality.[103] He emphasized that 'There was no privilege in the ranks of Labour. Every member . . . [had] the full right of taking part in making decisions and of choosing the men and women who [would] be candidates for election to any office.'[104] In 1937, the Party's constitution was changed so as to permit the constituency parties to elect their own members to the NEC and the number of seats was increased from five to seven.[105] At the same time, the 1937 annual conference confirmed the NEC's decision to disaffiliate the Socialist League, which dissolved itself shortly afterwards. Individual Labour Party members were free to advocate policy changes within the party framework; they could not contravene Conference decisions by joining external bodies which organized public campaigns against those decisions.[106]

The same conference also unanimously approved a short-term policy statement, *Labour's Immediate Programme*, which was moved by Attlee. The proposals, he said, were the result of a great deal of research, and marked a new stage in the Party's development. Long programmes were characteristic of a minority movement which included 'every kind of demand in an attempt to get various crumbs from a table at which it cannot hope to sit,' whereas a short programme indicated that 'we are now demanding the right to sit at the table.' Such a programme combined ameliorative measures and fundamental changes, both of which a mandated government could put into effect within the normal life of a Parliament.[107] The various items in the *Immediate Programme* were familiar ones: they included a commitment to the nationalization of the Bank of England, but there was no mention of the joint stock banks; a National Investment Board would be set up and there would be no return to the gold standard. Land should belong to the people and the use of it be controlled in the public interest, but full-scale nationalization was not envisaged and the small householder and owner-occupier would be left in undisputed possession of his home. Transport would be co-ordinated on a national scale, but only the railways and such other transport services as were suitable for public ownership would be nationalized. The coal, electricity and gas industries, however, would be taken over completely by the State. The various social services would be extended and large schemes of public development undertaken, with the distressed areas receiving particular attention.[108] In this balanced fashion were the controversies of the early part of the decade formally settled.

Whatever may be thought today of Labour's 1937 *Immediate Programme*, it marked a clear break with traditional economic thought, then still averse to Keynesianism. Attlee himself remained as convinced about the ultimate socialist goal as did any Colonel Blimp about imperialism. Either one had the vision, a compelling impulse towards the creation of a redistributive and egalitarian society, or one did not. This is one reason why he would have nothing to do with those Liberals who also spoke the language of social reform. It also partly explains why he welcomed an invitation to summarize his political philosophy from the Left Book Club.

Founded in 1936, the Club was very much a left-wing body. It has been described as 'closely associated with the Communist Party, providing a prolific propaganda backing for Communist campaigns to Spain and for all united and popular fronts ... '[109] Yet the significance of the Soviet purges had not been digested by the British left-wing intelligentsia, who concentrated on the spectacle of fascism. Attlee probably took the same view about the Club's members as he had done about the pre- First World War SDF, namely that there was a sizeable English element among them who could be persuaded to come over to Labour. Not one of the Club's book selection committee was a card-carrying member of the Communist Party. Gollancz, the driving force, was an old-fashioned socialist idealist and pacifist, rather like George Lansbury. Harold Laski was on Labour's NEC and it was he who proposed Attlee's name to Gollancz. Attlee had sent a message to the Club's Albert Hall rally in February

1937, stating that 'Socialism could not be built on ignorance and the transformation of Great Britain into a Socialist state [would] need the active cooperation of a large body of well-informed men and women' – for which reason he considered the Club's success to be 'a most encouraging sign'.[110]

The influence game was a tricky one. The third member of the Club's committee was John Strachey, then a fellow-traveller, and he thought a book by Attlee might be very useful as a tactical move.[111] Attlee's luck held. *The Labour Party in Perspective* came out in August 1937 just before the Club ran into headlong conflict with the Labour Party.[112] The book achieved a sale of over 50,000 copies[113] and was translated into several languages.[114] In 1949 it was republished, unchanged: in a Preface, Francis Williams could happily point out the connections between what Attlee had advocated twelve years previously and what the post-war Government had actually carried out.[115] Meantime, Strachey had joined the Labour Party, becoming both an MP and a minister in Attlee's administration.

The central theme of Attlee's book was the historic continuity between the Labour Party's evolution and that of the British tradition. His party, he claimed, was 'the inheritor of the achievements of those who fought for liberty in the past':[116] British socialism's aim was 'to give greater freedom to the individual,'[117] though State action was now required to turn this goal into a practical reality. But perhaps sufficient indication has already been given of Attlee's insistence on democratic and constitutional methods, the lack of rigidity in his conception of socialism – its essentially evolutionary, practical, non-violent and spiritual character, its antagonism to ideological orthodoxy, its mistrust of over-centralization, of uniformity and of any attempt to suppress criticism. In 1937 he was obliged to make a further qualification: the circumstances in which Labour would come to power could include 'a time of acute tension in international relations which would necessarily absorb a great amount of its attention and energy'. And indeed, in the decade's final years he had to concern himself less with British rentiers than with foreign fascists.

Yet, if the Labour Party's electoral experience in the period was largely one of failure, Attlee could find cause for some satisfaction in 1937. 'Looking back over the past thirty years', he wrote, 'the most striking feature in the mentality of the people of this country has been the change in their attitude to social questions. The assumptions have altered. Propositions indignantly rejected in the nineties have now passed into common acceptance ... in judging the work of the Labour Party it is essential to bear in mind not only direct, but indirect, results of the work. Those who count progress only in terms of seats won and of the growth of the numbers of the professed adherents of the Party miss the real significance of what has happened. The outstanding thing is not so much the growth in the strength of the forces which attack the citadel of Capitalism as in the loss of the outworks, the crumbling of the foundations, and the loss of morale of the garrison.'[118] The modern socialist's task had become harder but at least the rentiers were on the defensive.

VI

Collective Security

If Attlee could find some consolation for Labour in the development of domestic affairs during the 1930s, the same was not true in the international sphere. His Party's parliamentary status of hopeless opposition acted as a double handicap – both in regard to influencing Government policy and in terms of Labour being able to present a coherent alternative to it. Only once, in 1935, did Labour succeed in making a slight momentary impact, and that was due mainly to Attlee himself. His thesis was consistent and simple. Too simple, many people thought, in view of the complexity of the international problem and of his party's somewhat convoluted posture. He stood for 'collective security'. Afterwards, when the 'devil's decade' had ushered in a brave new world of war, his opinions would require little justification. The sole satisfaction he could derive from his pre-war efforts was being able to observe, in 1944, that 'those who had advocated collective security had been right.'[1] It must be accounted a tragedy that his views were not heeded earlier and did not have more effect. They can hardly be said to have been less realistic than the policies pursued by the various 'National' administrations headed successively by MacDonald, Baldwin and Neville Chamberlain. Had it not been for German military mistakes, those policies would have led to Britain's defeat.

Few topics in recent British history have attracted more intensive scrutiny than that of foreign policy in the 1930s. The underlying question is 'Could the Second World War have been avoided?' Understandably, the bulk of the research has been devoted to the policies of the parties in power. The Labour Party's position as a whole has received rather less attention while Clement Attlee's interpretation of that position has been almost ignored. Yet his views were much more representative of Labour's attitude to international affairs than the other dissident strands in Party opinion which have often been cited.

Before the First World War, international policy had been of secondary concern to the fledgling Labour Party. Such statements on the subject as were made were largely the work of socialist theorists,[2] at a time when Labour was not officially socialist. In 1907, the Party's application to join the Second International had been blocked for a year because the European socialists were not very happy about Labour's 'aloofness from Marxism, particularly from its insistence on class warfare'.[3] In a general way, Labour can be said to have been opposed to any sort of warfare, class or nationalist, imperialist or capitalist; it was also anti-militarist. But these attitudes had never amounted to a clear policy; the most definite gesture Labour made was its eventual subscription to the International's watered-down resolution on recourse to some form of direct action if war threatened.[4] When war came, the resolution, the International and all the slogans fell by the wayside; the bulk of the Party – including, as we have seen, Attlee – fell massively in step with the war effort: Labour also began to consider foreign policy seriously.

From 1914 to 1922, 'issues of war and diplomacy were dominant in the Party's councils';[5] a determined attempt was made, at the urging of the UDC and the ILP, to translate what had previously been vague attitudes into more specific policies. In the forefront came a demand for the revision of the Peace Treaties and, not without certain hesitations, support for the League of Nations.[6] The concomitant idea of collective security – in its most positive form of a pooled defence system – tended to be blurred in the widespread revulsion against anything smacking of war, such as conscription and military establishments. No security problem, of course, existed in the 1920s: but even so, Arthur Henderson, who was mainly responsible for Labour's acceptance of the League, insisted in 1924 that force might be one day needed to maintain international order. The point was fully recognized by the Party in 1929,[7] and Labour never became pacifist. In 1936, a climactic year in Labour's attitude as a Party to foreign policy,[8] Dalton could point out that the minority Labour Government in 1931 had defeated a pacifist proposal which would have almost eliminated the Air Force – by 12 to 248 votes, of which 163 plus two tellers were Labour.[9]

The Party did not base its post-war practice of foreign policy on any systematic or dogmatic theory. During its two brief spells of office in the 1920s Labour had to take into account the realities of power. Ramsay MacDonald's efforts, in 1924, to obtain French acceptance of the Dawes Plan (a reparations scheme which was based on Germany's capacity to make current payments, but which did not include any reduction of the total) clearly compromised the Party's blanket condemnation of the Peace Treaties, a condemnation which had included the very principle of reparations. Labour recognized the fact of the Russian Revolution (by its extension of diplomatic status to the Soviet Government), and it also proposed Germany's admission to the League (in September 1924). When Attlee reviewed Labour's first experiences in trying to implement foreign policy, he particularly stressed the Government's attempt to strengthen collective security by its initiative in what became known as the Geneva Protocol.[10] That several of these initial experiences proved rather frustrating did not lessen Labour's renewed efforts, from 1929 to 1931, to promote the cause of international reconciliation. MacDonald concentrated on Anglo-American relations, while Arthur Henderson (the Foreign Secretary) devoted himself to European questions. A paper agreement was concluded in the early months of 1931 by Britain, the US and Japan for the reduction of proposed increases in naval forces. Relations with the USSR, which had been broken off by the Conservative Government, were resumed and a commercial treaty signed; the French withdrew their forces of occupation from the Rhineland, and preparations were begun for a general disarmament conference. Britain under the second Labour Government agreed to compulsory arbitration of disputes by the Permanent Court of International Justice at the Hague.

Attlee had no doubt that the general orientation of Labour foreign policy in the 1920s was sound. Although his personal activity in external affairs towards the end of the decade was monopolized by India, he had enormous respect for Arthur Henderson, 'the chief builder of the Labour Party'.[11] In Attlee's opinion, Henderson 'entered the Foreign Office with a perfectly clear idea of what he wanted to do and how to do it'. The Foreign Secretary had realized the 'old objective of the Labour Party, the substitution of compulsory arbitration in place of war, and the world had taken a big step forward on the road from anarchy to international government'.[12] The somewhat strident tones in Labour's attitude to foreign policy before and immediately after the war had given way to a quieter note of optimism. The question of frontier revision, for example, had lost its primacy of place in the criticism of Versailles:[13] the Party had moved steadily towards full support for the League.[14] In short, a pragmatic and realistic approach had become the order of the day.

The turmoil of the 1930s put this approach to the severest of tests, but did not substantially change it. True, the Party's structure permitted heated debate at all levels and its emotional inheritance was re-triggered by the stresses and strains of the period. Quite apart from events abroad – the Japanese invasion of Manchuria in 1931 and the coming to power of Hitler in 1933 – Labour was still reeling from the shock of 'MacDonaldism' during the first half of the decade. And internal confusion was compounded in the case of foreign policy by the fact that two of the three parliamentary leaders held extreme views. Lansbury was an avowed pacifist 'with Marxian undertones, opposed to the very existence of the

League which he regarded as a society of rich powers banded together against the have-nots':[15] Cripps considered the League to be primarily an instrument of capitalism. Nevertheless, effective power in the Party remained in the hands of the trade unions, who stuck determinedly by the League. So too did Attlee, the odd man out in the political triumvirate. His problem was how to emphasize the underlying Labour consensus without splitting the Party. That he was not cast in the heroic mould was an advantage, and he came very close to making the majority Labour position the national one. Had Labour succeeded in obtaining power in 1935 there can be little doubt that the resulting Government would have pursued a foreign policy along the lines he indicated if only because such a Government could only have been formed on the basis of 'moderate' support in the country.

The distinctiveness of Attlee's approach to the problem of foreign policy, as contrasted with that of Labour's two other parliamentary spokesmen, became apparent as early as March 1932. Leading for the Opposition in a debate on the Army Estimates, he referred to the difficulty of considering provisions for a single service without knowing what the Government's overall defence policy was. He could understand, he stated in pointed contrast with Labour's official Leader, a defence programme based on certain realities of alliance or hostility between the nations of the world. He could also understand a programme based on the fact that the British had certain obligations under the League of Nations that they should be prepared to fulfil. What he could not understand was the several indefinite policies put forward by the ministers responsible for the various defence agencies. The trouble with haphazard and unconcerted defence organization, he added in reference to the National Government's zest for economy, was that it produced a minimum of security for a maximum of expenditure.[16] Later in the same month, when the Air Estimates were being considered, Attlee admitted to a deep interest in flying; he believed that every kind of aviation would undergo enormous development, and he wanted to see the creation of an international civil authority to control it.[17] Despite his other political preoccupations, the time and energy he devoted to international developments underwent a sharp increase. In May, he was one of the Party's delegates to a Joint Disarmament Conference held in Zurich by the Labour and Socialist International and the International Federation of Trade Unions – the first of several such visits to the continent. The contacts he made in Zurich may have impelled him, in June, to utter a solemn warning: the situation in Germany, he told the Commons, was one of the 'utmost possible danger' – and he was not 'trying to raise a scare'.[18] The following month found him anxiously inquiring about the relative strengths fixed by the Treaty of Washington in number and tonnage of naval arms, battleships and aircraft carriers of the five naval powers[19] – not a typical interest of a Labour Party politician in the summer of 1932.

In the country at large, in 1932, as well as in the Labour Party, 'pacifist sentiments, a vague belief in the League as a guardian of peace, and a disbelief in the possibility of a European war were still dominant, and remained so until 1935'.[20] The League's Lytton Commission, set up to investigate the Sino-Japanese dispute, reported in October 1932, condemning the Japanese invasion of Manchuria, refusing to accept the Manchukuo puppet regime and proposing the granting of Manchurian autonomy under Chinese sovereignty. The Disarmament Conference that had been established in February, presided over by Arthur Henderson, had broken down for the time being[21] and the League was still considering the Lytton Report: reparations had been abandoned in June and Hitler had not yet come to power. When Attlee made his first important intervention in the Commons in November, therefore, the international situation was in a state of considerable flux. The motion that he introduced was content to demand, as an essential preliminary to success at the forthcoming World Economic Conference, that the British Government support an immediate, universal and substantial reduction of armaments on the basis of equality of status for all nations, and that it maintain the Covenant of the League by supporting the findings of the Lytton Commission. On this last issue the Labour motion was not far removed from the Government's own aims, however dilatory its pursuit of them.[22] But the tone and nuances of Attlee's speech in November 1932 were striking: he insisted that 'the Manchurian question [was] the acid test of the League of Nations against attack'. Unless it was settled satisfactorily, he warned, the League would lose its moral authority, the world would slip back to the old system of individual armaments and sectional alliances, and France and Germany would not accept disarmament. He defined Labour's foreign policy as that of *full* support of the League, acceptance of the principle of equality of status – *provided there was not rearmament*, the abolition of private manufacture of arms, the international inspection of arms factories and, as a first step, the internationalization of civil aviation.[23]

He was in deadly earnest about the League and its collective security role, despite the hesitations and ambiguities that could be found in the Government's attitude, in public opinion generally and in his own Party. Writing to his brother Tom on New Year's Day 1933, Attlee indicated that the air posed the greatest threat to British future security, but that the sea would be the easiest element on which to base an international force. Apart from Japan, which had to be considered as an outlaw for the moment, there were only three powers concerned with the sea: Britain, France, and the US. Once these powers had combined their navies, Britain and France could form the nucleus of an international air force and air service. The adhesion of the US and Russia, together with the smaller neutrals who would have no option but to follow, would compel Japan and Germany to join – thus creating the embryo of a future World State. The basis of such an organization would have to be the surrender of a large degree of national sovereignty and the revision of the Peace Treaties – which might sound visionary. But nothing else, in his opinion, could prevent war. Transport was the key and it was there that a beginning could and should be made.[24]

In 1933, the British preferred to muddle along. In February, the Oxford Union passed its famous resolution that 'this House will in no circumstances fight for its King and Country'. During the year, the Government was to present two comprehensive plans to the resumed Disarmament Conference. Also in February, a joint meeting of the NEC and the General Council of the TUC demanded the application of an arms embargo in the Far East and an economic boycott of Japan if that country persisted in its defiance of the League of Nations, but there was no mention of military sanctions.[25] That same month, referring to the Sino-Japanese dispute, Sir John Simon (the Foreign Secretary) stated that '... in no circumstances [would the] Government authorize the country to be a party to the struggle'.[26] Simon was undoubtedly expressing a majority opinion. Lansbury rhetorically replied in the Commons that '... all the sanctions, all the obligations of the Covenant ought... to be carried through,'[27] but the effect of his remark was largely nullified by the ambiguities (consonant with his pacifism) in the rest of his speech.[28] Lansbury was already at odds with the NCL over the League.[29]

In these unpropitious circumstances, Attlee's intervention in the Army Estimates debate in March was oblique but still noteworthy. Though protesting against the size of the Estimates, one of his major criticisms of them was that they appeared to him to take no account of 'the changed conditions that [were] likely in the event of war occurring again'. He wanted to know to what extent 'the whole question of infantry, artillery, tanks and so forth, [was] being considered in the light of modern warfare.'[30] In so far as several antediluvian Tories were still arguing the merits of cavalry[31] – an idea which was beyond Attlee's comprehension if there was to be another European war[32] – he certainly had a point. More significant in retrospect was his capacity to speculate, in a deceptively detached fashion, about what to most people in Britain – a few cavalry men and specialists apart – was still unthinkable: another war.

March 1933 was also the month during which Hitler assumed full dictatorial powers in Germany; and Attlee reacted immediately. The rise to power of the Nazi Party, he told the Commons in April, had added a wholly new dimension to the international situation. Some might regard the Hitler movement as simply the resurgence of crude nationalism, a revitalization of Germany's national life; to Attlee it foretold 'the reintroduction of death in the near future'. He was concerned to draw out the implications for international relations of what was going on inside Germany. The Labour Party had never denied the need for a revision of the Peace Treaties, but Germany had to be told straight out that, if she wanted any revision, she had to come 'with clean hands'. No one in Britain would now entrust any minority to Germany: he thought that the House and country 'ought to say that we will not countenance for a moment yielding to Hitler and force what was denied to Stresemann and reason'. What was the Government going to do for democracy, he asked, particularly in Austria? It was no use avoiding the issue by saying that it was a matter for the League – because Britain had the biggest influence there. The re-arming of Germany was a dangerous suggestion. Labour believed in the reduction of armaments, but *an essential preliminary of disarmament was security*. The world had to be prepared to take a strong line on the Sino-Japanese dispute or this would cut at the very root of disarmament: it would be said that there was no security for a member state of the League.[33]

Three disparate observers went out of their way to comment favourably on Attlee's speech: Sir Austen Chamberlain, a former Foreign Secretary, forcibly agreed that no concessions should be given to the new Germany; Colonel Wedgwood, an independent-minded and iconoclastic Labour MP, declared that Attlee and Chamberlain's speeches – or the events that had caused them – had killed the revision of the treaties; while Winston Churchill hoped that Attlee's words would have an influence 'far beyond the limits of this country'.[34] Their opinions and hopes unfortunately turned out to be mistaken, though not because of any retraction by Attlee. He did not shrink from drawing the obvious corollary to his speech in March: the frustration of the Disarmament Conference, he argued (in June), had been very largely due to the failure to make security effective, and the frustration would continue until there was actual proof that the League could provide security. It was of course possible to give grave reasons for not taking action in the Far East, but he did not believe in buying off militarism by concessions. The German Government should be warned that the kind of thing happening in Austria and on the Austrian frontier would not be tolerated.[35] During the year, Hitler replaced disarmament as the main issue in foreign policy for Attlee.

Inside his own Party, however, he was in a subordinate position. The effect of 1931 had been to emphasize political 'purity' which, for some time, appeared to be personified by Lansbury and Cripps in foreign as well as domestic affairs. Attlee was very conscious of the question of Party morale – 'how best to convince its members that the movement had a future'.[36] The answer could hardly be to push internal differences too far, hence the Party's – if not Attlee's – ambivalence over sanctions. The articulate pacifist minority were unwilling even to contemplate the thought of the League becoming involved in military action, while the propaganda efforts of the Socialist League – with part of which Attlee had some sympathy – reached their climax in 1933. Dark suspicions of the possibility of the capitalist and imperialist British government equipping itself with arms readily allied themselves with pacifist sentiments. At the Labour Party's 1933 annual conference, held in the first days of October, a Socialist League-inspired resolution pledging the Party to take no part in war was – as the result of a procedural tangle – accepted.[37] Shortly afterwards, a Labour candidate won a sensational by-election on what appeared to be a pacifist platform.[38] Labour was also firmly attached to Henderson's continued efforts to promote schemes of disarmament at Geneva, though these received a decisive setback later in October when Germany simultaneously withdrew from both the Disarmament Conference and the League of Nations.

The Labour movement, Attlee commented wryly to his brother in November, had not really made up its mind whether it wanted to take up an isolationist attitude or whether it would take the risks of standing for the enforcement of the decisions of a world organization against individual aggressor states.[39] Neither, for that matter, had the Government, though Baldwin intimated later in November that if agreement on disarmament was not forthcoming, Britain's defences could not remain indefinitely as they were.[40] Even the trade union leaders, long accustomed to the conduct of negotiations based upon shrewd calculations of strength, were more concerned in 1933 to call attention to the internal threat posed by the advent of the fascist movement rather than to the external one.[41] Attlee, nevertheless, began before the year was out to stress the second of the alternatives that he had described to his brother. When two Government MPs succeeded, in December, in forcing a debate on the desirability of Britain joining an International Police Force under the League, he took the political risk of giving the suggestion his full support. The League was no use without force behind it to settle disputes, he roundly declared, though such force ought also to be envisaged as part of a deliberate attempt to build up a World State. He rather daringly gave the British Empire as an example of the sort of international security which could be extended.[42] And at the year's end he was revealingly stating his belief that, together, Britain, the US and Russia could form the biggest bulwark for peace in the world.[43]

With Lansbury temporarily out of the way due to illness, the tone of Attlee's speeches on foreign affairs became increasingly forceful, largely, it can be assumed, in the attempt to sway his own Party as much as to influence the Government. The latter's disarmament proposals, he insisted in February 1934, were really a proposal for the rearmament of Germany. German equality was being conceded too late, and to force rather than reason. Belief in a collective security system meant that obligations had to be met – 'you have to be prepared to act'.[44] There could be no disarmament without security, he reiterated in March; the Labour Party was not out for war but the position brought about by successive Governments meant that the possibility of war had to be faced if commitments to the League were to be carried out. A system of pooled security could not be built up unless one was prepared to take certain risks.[45]

It has to be admitted – he later admitted it himself[46] – that the weight of his argument was diminished by the fact that Labour continued to vote against the Service Estimates until 1937. There was a simple explanation: voting against the Estimates no more implied opposition to all armaments than voting against education supplies meant that Labour was opposed to education. A vote against the Service Estimates, in parliamentary terms, was nothing more than a convenient and customary way of registering a lack of confidence in the Government's defence policy as a whole, and the foreign policy on which it was based. That such a vote may have served to disguise, to some extent, the Labour ambiguities on the subject – which lasted until 1935 – was again perfectly normal. An Opposition is not required to disclose the hypothetical details of its alternative actions were it in office. Within the limits imposed by his Party's ambivalence, Attlee attempted to meet the criticism of his Party's voting behaviour: Labour's objection was to *national* armaments; the Party could only agree to armaments if they were part of a system of pooled security to be used by the League for keeping the peace of the world; and in so far as that system did not presently exist they were not prepared to vote for the Estimates.[47] In the course of 1934, the slightly disingenuous element in this argument was to be clarified.

Meanwhile, as the cumbersome process of Party reorientation was proceeding, Attlee contrived to give a clear indication of his own views on defence policy. Whatever view might be taken of the possibilities of war, peace or disarmament, he told the Commons in March, the effectiveness of whatever defence position was adopted still had to be considered; the question of the co-ordination of staff training, for example, he regarded as of the utmost importance.[48] He took the initiative in raising the subject of Imperial Defence in the course of a debate on the Consolidated Fund Bill. The reason he did so, he explained, was to give the Prime Minister or some other Cabinet minister the opportunity to reply for the Cabinet on defence as a whole, instead of splitting the subject into a series of disjointed debates on particular Services. Setting aside views on general international policy, Attlee was concerned to know whether the arrangements for the co-ordination of national defence were the best available. He launched into his familiar plea for a unified Ministry of Defence and wondered – without 'arguing it at the moment' – whether too much was being spent on the Navy and too little on the Air Force. He drew attention to the fact that British defence arrangements had not only to take account of Britain's position as part of a world organization but also as 'the centre of a far-flung Commonwealth of Nations, with the necessary policing of the Empire.' He denied the argument that, in these circumstances, the Minister of Defence would have to be a superman; the problem could be solved administratively by a division between general policy-making and departmental administration. He would like to see 'the nucleus of a defence staff built up from all three services': without some co-ordination large sums could be spent for years on defence purposes which were utterly useless.[49] Winston Churchill began his remarks by saying that he very largely agreed with Attlee's 'gracious speech',[50] though it was Churchill's own oratory which gained the House's attention at the time, and subsequently. In sharp contrast with both, the Government spokesman, MacDonald, was content to waffle – undoubtedly reflecting the general public mood of ambivalence.

Attlee persisted, and later in the year was able to note some success in terms of a changed Labour attitude. It had become increasingly recognized, he was able to write, that 'whatever may be the force of public opinion – and it would be a mistake to underestimate it – and whatever may be the possibilities of financial and trade embargoes, there must be an eventual possibility of armed intervention against an aggressor'. He made the observation in a pamphlet outlining his conception of an international police force. He urged the members of his Party to give careful thought to the idea which, in his view, should begin with the creation of an international air force. It was 'futile sentimentality to believe that paper restrictions against bombing [would] be effective in a struggle for national existence'; his answer to pacifist objections was that the success of an international air force would lie not in its use but in its non-use.[51] By the summer of 1934 the Party's attitude had hardened. Attlee welcomed the attempt to make an Eastern Locarno, as one way of building up some kind of collective security. The Labour Party, he announced, was 'convinced that, in the absence of a world scheme of pooled security, *the policy of reducing national forces in return for international guarantees of security backed by international forces may be promoted by States within the League concluding regional arrangements* under Article 21 of the Covenant and in conformity with the Covenant.' It was essential that Europe get a breathing space if anything was to be done with regard to disarmament. Events in Germany had profoundly disturbed conditions on the Continent. Although he did not agree with the dictatorial nature of the government in Russia, it at least was stable and non-aggressive; he wanted the British Government to take the strongest possible line to get Russia into the League.[52]

The NEC was at last ready, in October, to present a lengthy statement on 'War and Peace' to the 1934 annual conference. The Policy Committee had been working on it for nearly three years;[53] in the last twelve months Attlee had been co-opted on to the Committee. The document inevitably tried to secure the maximum possible acceptance by the Party and, in the main, was a re-statement of traditional Labour attitudes and aims. There was, however, no mention of the previous pledge that Labour would not take any part in any war; instead the document specifically recognized 'that there might be circumstances under which the Government of Gt. Britain might have to use its military and naval forces in support of the League in restraining an aggressor nation which declined to submit to the authority of the League and which flagrantly used military measures in defiance of its pledged word.'[54] Labour would also be prepared to find the terms on which the US might co-operate with the League in regional security arrangements. The document warned that the lack of a trade union movement in Germany, Austria and Italy and its weakness in Japan meant that reliance on the hope of general strike action was quite unrealistic. Naylor has concluded that 'War and Peace' marked 'a significant change in Labour's approach to the methods by which a socialist foreign policy might be implemented'.[55] The Labour hierarchy indicated that, until the emergence of a new international socialist society, the system of collective security, in its broadest interpretation, was essential if peace was to be preserved.

The document did not go unchallenged. The Socialist League purists rejected the use of force under the existing League of Nations because that body represented (despite the addition of Russia) the economic conflicts of the capitalist system.[56] Lansbury refused to speak on the 'Peace' section[57] of the statement, and offered to resign during the Conference.[58] Attlee had a difficult time defending the NEC policy and his speech to the Conference was not one of his best. As noted in the previous chapter, he admitted that in the light of fresh experience he had changed his mind in regard to unilateral disarmament, which was much easier to advocate in England than on the Continent. The Party could not wash its hands of responsibility for its socialist comrades and workers in other countries, but he could not accept the suggestion that the socialist countries should be lined up separately: 'The danger of that is that all the other countries may strike at you, and you may divide the world in a great war.' He agreed that there could be no ultimate peace without world socialism, but things had to be dealt with as they were. The menace of world war was not far away. He was opposed to national forces of any kind – which could be superseded by the internationalization of aviation (as he hoped). Nor did he envisage a League of Nations with limited liability and a minimum of control; the creation of a World State remained the goal.[59] But his attempt to placate all sections of the Party – the NEC 'was not spoiling for a fight in 1934'[60] – did not succeed. No fewer than 673,000 votes were cast against the 1,519,000 favouring 'War and Peace'. Attlee and his like-minded NEC colleagues still had to take account of their own Party's situation.

European developments in 1935 proved crucial for the League and also served to expose the British Government's half-hearted attitude to that body, though Labour was to reap no substantial electoral benefits. During the first half of the year Hitler's rearmament drive and Mussolini's preparations for an attack on Abyssinia became evident. The British Government prevaricated on the diplomatic front, still seeking to come to some accord with Hitler, while announcing, in March, its intention to increase spending on armaments. Together, these attitudes implied that the Government had abandoned any faith it might have had in the League and collective security. Attlee was incensed: defence depended upon policy and the Government's announcement, he charged, demonstrated that 'We are back in a pre-war atmosphere. We are back in a system of alliances and rivalries and an armaments race'.[61] Hitler's actions later that month, including the restoration of conscription and a public declaration that a German Air Force was already in existence, supplied confirmation which gave a jolt to British public opinion. One cause of an unusual slump in the Labour vote at a by-election, a report to the NEC noted, was that the growing war atmosphere was shaking people's faith in the ability of the League to guarantee security; the passion for peace which had given Labour such a powerful plea in earlier elections was not so effective under the shadow of Hitler's threats even though the successful Conservative candidate was himself a League supporter.[62] Attlee redoubled his parliamentary efforts. Britain, he told the Commons in May, was now paying for the failure to deal fairly with the post-war position when Germany was disarmed. The real significance of the rise of Hitler and Mussolini was a move back to power politics, and the menace of Germany in particular was more than that of 'a certain state rearming, it [was] . . . a denial of the fundamental principles of western civilization.' He would not agree to the handing over of colonial or any other people to Nazi rule. Labour stood by the collective system and wanted the Covenant strengthened.[63]

The great question was 'How?' The Government's decision to embark on an expansion of the British Air Force threatened to put Labour at a serious political disadvantage; a joint meeting of the PLP, the NEC and the General Council of the TUC to discuss this project, presided over by Lansbury, took place on 21 May 1935. Several of the participants questioned whether an expansion of the Air Force should be opposed.[64] Attlee stressed the need for pressing forward with a system of collective peace and pooled security – with reductions in armaments – as compared with the exclusive development of National Defence. For the TUC, who wanted an enlarged Air Force, Citrine slyly recorded his complete agreement with Attlee's views 'as to the necessity for pressing the Government to pursue more actively the establishment of a collective peace system'.[65] The TUC members were not merely cognizant of the German question; their urging of action in regard to Italy was made precisely because of the potential effect on Germany.[66] Attlee was in an awkward position, clearly estranged from both Lansbury and Cripps. But the pacifist Lansbury was still Leader, and his views appeared to command significant support; Cripps had adopted and was leading the Socialist League's ideological resistance to the League and collective security. The much revered Henderson was still at Geneva and Hitler further confounded Labour and other opinion by making an apparently conciliatory speech on the same day as the joint meeting.[67]

The answer to Hitler, Attlee told the Commons the following day, should not be just rearmament, though Labour believed the country should be prepared to make its contribution to collective security. If Germany or Italy, or any other country, was preparing to use her armed strength to gain her own ends, then she had to be restrained by all the Powers of the League and not by Britain alone or by any group of allies.[68] He was the first senior Labour politician openly to broach the tricky question of Abyssinia – tricky both in terms of Labour's internal conflict and in terms of foreign policy considerations which indicated caution in respect of adding to potential enemies. In early June 1935, Attlee used the Adjournment Debate to declare that the tension between Italy and Abyssinia was 'a test of the reality of the League and of the Covenant'. It was also an opportunity for re-establishing the League's authority and the rule of law in Europe. Mussolini ought to be told that the matter affected British honour and vital interests. Refusal to accept the League's authority constituted a refusal by an aggressor, and in that event Mussolini should be told that Britain would be bound under the Covenant not only to give no assistance whatever to an aggressor but to act against one. Attlee's suggestion was that, if Italy acted, the Suez Canal should be closed.[69]

Opinion within his Party and outside it was now coming round to his point of view. The Advisory Committee on International Questions (of which Attlee was a member) reported in July that there was no conceivable excuse for the League not to act in regard to Italy, and this was especially true of Great Britain, for geography had placed the decisive power in her hands. Italy could not send troops or supplies to Eritrea or Somaliland without going through the Suez Canal or the Straits of Gibraltar and both could be closed by the Royal Navy. And unless the members of the League upheld the Covenant in the present case there would be nothing left of the Covenant or the Kellogg Pact (of 1927, wherein all the nations had renounced war as an instrument of national policy). True, 'the diehards in all countries are certain to denounce with great vigour the bloody-minded pacifists who desire to make war to stop war.' But, the report continued, 'in this particular case the risk of war involved in upholding the Covenant is still extremely small.' Mussolini had never yet dared to stand against Great Britain. In any case it was impossible to conceive any application of the Covenant in which the risk of loss of British life would be so small. The Navy would be able to exert its power almost bloodlessly.[70] The NEC adopted a resolution on 24 July 1935, later endorsed by the General Council of the TUC, calling upon the Government to make immediate proposals in an open meeting of the League at Geneva, and to declare that it would discharge its duties and obligations under the League 'without fear or favour'. Attlee had already made a pointed attack in the Commons on Hoare, the new Foreign Secretary. The Government had reduced the League to a farce. What had most disturbed Attlee in recent years had been British concern not with what was right but with the effect of any action on another aspect of foreign affairs. No attempt had been made in Europe to stand up for the rule of law; he had lived to see 'a most terrible example of drift, and drift that [was] leading on again to war'.[71]

Attlee had come very close to the expression of a general British view, too close for the comfort of the new Prime Minister Stanley Baldwin, who had replaced MacDonald on 7 June. On the whole, by-elections had provided some indication of a persistent and heavy decline in Conservative support and the beginning of a swing to Labour despite the internal quarrels.[72] Towards the end of June 1935, the results of a national ballot organized by the League of Nations Union, of which Attlee was a member, revealed a very strong current of opinion in favour of the League and the collective security concept. The prevailing mood was pacific rather than pacifist; a clear majority supported the application of military sanctions, if necessary.[73] One of the Baldwin Government's first actions had been the conclusion of a naval pact with Germany, outside the auspices of the League, which in effect had 'allowed' Germany to build as many warships as she could. A subsequent attempt to conclude a private deal with Mussolini fell through. The Government then suddenly rediscovered its faith in the League. In September, Hoare announced that Britain was after all fully committed to the League and collective security – provided that the burden really was a collective one. The following month the general election was called for November. In the meantime Labour went a long way towards clarifying its policy, though too late to have any considerable effect on the result of the election. Lansbury managed to confuse matters almost to the end: just before the summer adjournment he stated that Labour stood by the League in the Abyssinian dispute though he personally would not use the British Fleet.[74] Cripps resigned from the NEC in September. Earlier that month, the TUC had overwhelmingly approved a declaration that 'all the necessary measures provided by the Covenant should be used to prevent Italy's unjust and rapacious attack upon the territory of a fellow member of the League'.[75] The Party's pacifists became increasingly alarmed at the trend and the stage was set for the famous confrontation at the annual conference which assembled in Brighton on 30 September 1935.

The conference is best remembered for Bevin's personal attack on Lansbury, who publicly opposed the NEC's resolution reiterating Labour's full support of the League to restrain the Italian Government: 'It is placing the Executive and the Movement', Bevin charged, 'in an absolutely wrong position to be taking your conscience round from body to body asking to be told what you ought to do with it.'[76] Attlee's more measured defence – and assertion – of Labour policy has been overlooked, although it was that which had provoked Lansbury to an extreme and pathetic affirmation of his utopianism: – 'Attlee says we have the compulsion of the police and of the law. Some day even that will pass away, when justice between man and man comes into being'.[77] Attlee had heard the like in private from his brother Tom for more than twenty years; he referred the conference to his parliamentary experience of the past four years where 'you cannot take up a negative attitude; you have to deal with realities'. Just as he had had to stand against those who thought the League should be a mere debating society, so too could he say that he had confronted those who wanted to make it the instrument of capitalist and imperialist policies. He was at a loss to understand why people seemed to think the issue of sanctions had only just arisen. The whole structure of the League had been built up on the enforcement of law, though the force necessary in the last resort was only determined by the force of the lawbreaker. The point was the proper use of force for ensuring the rule of law. Non-resistance was not a political but a personal attitude which was not a feasible policy for people in positions of responsibility.[78] He also set himself to refute two other fallacies: Cripps had argued that 'the central factor in our decision must turn, not so much on what we as a country should do, or should not do, but upon who is in control of our actions'.[79] Attlee replied: 'Does not the same thing apply if a Socialist Government is in power? Are we to have the anti-socialists saying 'we would enforce sanctions but we cannot entrust it to a Socialist Government"?' That, in Attlee's opinion, meant the acceptance of the totalitarian state – that nothing could be done unless all the people of a state thought and acted the same way. The same argument was being applied by Cripps to the League.

The third fallacy that Attlee denied was the argument that support of collective security meant departing from the real work of the Labour Movement, the building up of socialism. He found the idea parochial; socialism could not be built in an anarchic society. Besides, socialists had to realize the element of truth in what their opponents said: the 'National'

Government was moved by various motives, some imperialistic and some pro-League; those on that side were not all black. Labour was not in any case following the Government's lead – rather the Government was 'tardily and very doubtfully beginning to do what we have been demanding for the past four years'. The dispute was not between Great Britain and Italy, but between the League and an aggressor state. It could be said that the League was just an alliance, but it was a very big alliance. The present issue was whether the nations – some capitalist, others not – who were really interested in peace could get together and form a group inside the League. At the same time, Labour policy went far beyond Government policy: it sought to abolish international armies altogether, to abolish the idea of the sovereign state, to develop political and economic unity. Labour had to keep this full programme, of which sanctions were but a small part.[80]

Attlee's was far and away the most balanced speech in the debate; but though the NEC's resolution was approved by 2,168,000 votes to 102,000, he still came only third in the balloting for membership of the NEC.[81] The six elected members, however, were all in favour of sanctions and the ballot proved to be the last that Attlee would face. Italy attacked Abyssinia within twenty-four hours of the conference's adoption of the NEC's resolution, and the National Council of Labour informed the delegates on 4 October that they had asked for an immediate summoning of Parliament to hear the Government's proposals in the face of aggression.[82] Four days later, Lansbury resigned and Attlee was again called upon to replace him as Labour's acting parliamentary leader.

He was aware that the defeat of the pacifist and extreme left at Brighton did not mark the end of the internal Party controversy. A hundred constituency organizations had been included in the minority vote and the Left were determined to renew the conflict.[83] His own standing in the Party outside Parliament, and in the country at large, was not great.[84] The League declared Italy to be an aggressor and established a committee to recommend economic sanctions, which turned out to be derisory. When Parliament reassembled on 22 October, Hoare confirmed that, from the beginning of the current discussions at Geneva, there had been no consideration of military sanctions: no such measures formed any part of British policy.[85] Attlee's reaction was to stress that his Party was prepared to support 'such an amount of armaments in this country as is necessary to fulfil our obligations and responsibilities under the League' – but Parliament had never been asked to provide armaments for these purposes.[86] He quoted from a blunt speech by Citrine to the TUC Conference which had argued in favour of putting at the League's disposal sufficient military, naval, and aerial forces to make sanctions work. For his pains Attlee was contradicted by Lansbury, who was now taking his conscience to other bodies.

Baldwin's reply to Attlee, in effect, was to announce that a general election would be held in November 1935. The Conservatives had neatly stolen Labour's clothes;[87] the Prime Minister could even use as one of his election slogans, 'The Socialist Policy Means War!'[88], and pledge his word that there would be no great armaments.[89] Labour had gone 'Right', and the Conservative Party 'Left'; the electorate was understandably confused. Turn-out on election day was lower than at any time since December 1923,[90] though this can also be attributed to the inclement weather and the belief that the result was, in any case, a foregone conclusion.[91]

Attlee has been blamed for being an indifferent, ineffective campaigner,[92] but it is difficult to see how another Labour leader could have produced a more favourable result. Apart from the foreign policy issue, his lack of charisma was but one of a number of factors in the Party's defeat. The domestic situation had improved; unemployment was down, wages had generally increased (except in the coal industry where the employees' politics could be taken for granted), housing construction was up and the Government had announced a new spending programme. The spectacle of Labour splits over policy and leadership – the resolution in regard to foreign policy had hardly been made early enough, or in a fashion calculated to inspire confidence – was compounded by bad organization, serious financial difficulties and overwhelming opposition in the press and on the radio. Despite the fact that domestic politics in Britain between the wars were based mostly on class allegiances, the election results demonstrated not only that Labour had failed to make any real inroad into the vital middle ground but also that it had not managed to capture the working-class vote. It was almost as if Labour 'lacked the will to win the election':[93] the Party barely managed to recoup the votes it had lost in 1931. Baldwin's National Party retained 11.8 million votes, worth 432 seats, against Labour's 8.3 million, which translated into 154. The Opposition Liberals, more divided than Labour, were routed, taking only 1.4 million votes and 21 seats. The ILP and the Communist Party were all but annihilated, though by concentrating their efforts in a few areas they obtained respectively 4 and 1 seats.

Perhaps Attlee's preoccupation with foreign policy did not help the Labour cause. In late May he had gone to Smethwick where an important speech was expected and had chosen to speak on 'the Sino-Jap Dispute' – a topic 'infinitely remote from his audience both in time and space'.[94] Throughout the election campaign, Attlee was 'clearly most distressed by what he considered Baldwin's appropriation of Labour's foreign policy'.[95] Before it began he stated that 'Where you have politicians, who at a moment's notice throw over all their principles and join with the other side thus shaking faith in democracy, and where you have responsible statesmen, instead of giving the country the opportunity of forming a calm judgment on policies, going to the country on stunts of one kind or another there too you have the destruction of democracy.'[96] He was acutely aware that the Tories had well chosen the moment of apparent bipartisanship on foreign policy to divert attention away from other issues. According to Cowling,[97] when the Unemployment Act was passed in 1934 it had seemed even to Conservatives that the Government was *intending* to be harsh: the pre-electoral about-turn on foreign policy brilliantly succeeded in neutralizing the potentially vote-winning domestic topic, and in 'thwarting the Opposition'.

Attlee's formal accession to the leadership of the Labour Party after the election now seems inevitable: it did not appear so in 1935. The time was clearly ripe for the Party to select a 'permanent' head, though no one could have foreseen how long the appointment would actually last. Including Attlee himself on a temporary basis, there had been four leaders in the previous five years: of these, MacDonald had been expelled, Lansbury had resigned and Arthur Henderson[98] had died during the course of the 1935 annual conference. J. R. Clynes, another revered character from the past who had regained his parliamentary seat in 1935, declined to stand for the leadership – which left Attlee the sole remaining senior parliamentary figure. But there were two other candidates, both of whom were solidly working-class in origin. Arthur Greenwood possessed a strong Party background and wide administrative experience; he was highly self-educated and was head of the new TUC and Labour Party Research Department. Defeated at the 1929 election, he had been found a seat in 1931 and he obviously had serious claims. He also had two weaknesses: one was drink, the other that he had been closely associated with those trade unionists who had sought Lansbury's head.[99] The third candidate was Herbert Morrison who, though supported by many of the Party's middle-class intellectuals,[100] had equally alienated an influential number of trade unionists, especially Bevin:[101] and Morrison had yet to prove his worth in the Commons. Attlee, on the other hand, had been virtually forced, from 1933, to be a Party conciliator, a sort of social worker to the Labour Party. He could count on the support of most of the Labour MPs who had been in Parliament from 1931 to 1935. On the first ballot he received 58 votes, to Morrison's 44 and Greenwood's 33: on the second he was preferred by 88 Labour MPs to 48 who favoured Morrison.

Typically, Attlee did nothing to promote his candidacy. The worst that Dalton, a Morrison activist, could say was that on the day of the election Attlee '[ran] around with slightly nervous grin, eagerly greeting everyone.'[102] Tom Williams, who seconded David Grenfell's motion proposing Attlee, was amazed to learn afterwards 'that there had been massive campaigning, accompanied by a welter of intrigue, discreet dinner and cocktail parties, conspiracies and a touch of masonic influence thrown in' on behalf of the other candidates.[103] The fact that Attlee had led the Party into a lost election was not held against him: the NEC had been worried months before about the electoral situation,[104] over 100 extra seats had been won, and Labour's percentage of the vote (38.1) was more than ever before. Above all, Attlee threatened no one. Dalton wrote in his diary that 'a little mouse shall lead them',[105] but this was sour grapes. Labour's recent history had effectively demonstrated that the Party required an adroit chairman rather than an overbearing leader. The antipathy to a leonine character may have begun as a reaction to MacDonald, but in 1935 there were also the examples of Lansbury and Cripps to conjure with; Morrison, too, was suspect on this account.[106] Asked at the PLP meeting whether he would give his full time to the job – a question aimed at Morrison as chief executive of the LCC – Attlee could kill two birds with one stone: he replied, 'If I'm elected, I shall carry on as before.' When the decision had been made, he was still reassuring: it was only for one session, he stressed, and he wouldn't complain if a change was made later.[107] His victory marked another turning point: the first Labour leader with a public-school background owed his position initially to working-class MPs. On the second ballot his majority came from a more socially mixed group; nearly half of Labour's 154 seats had been won by candidates other than those sponsored by trade unions.[108] Attlee's election proved that, at least within the Labour Party, class origins did not matter.

Until the Baldwin Government's sudden announcement of its support for a League of Nations-based foreign policy, Attlee had believed that a firm Labour position here would provide the political opportunity the Party needed for achieving office: indeed, Labour's stand on foreign policy has been said to have given the Party 'a respectability that it might not otherwise have regained so quickly after 1931'.[109] Just how accurate Attlee's intuition had been became evident a few weeks after the election. With the Cabinet's approval, Hoare promptly reverted to the former unilateral approach; the offer to Italy was revised, in Mussolini's favour. The French premier, Laval, was prepared to go still further in recognizing Italian designs on Abyssinia. British public opinion was appalled: the Hoare-Laval deal provoked 'the greatest explosion over foreign affairs for many years, perhaps the greatest since the campaign against the "Bulgarian horrors" in 1876'.[110] Hoare was obliged to resign – and Attlee's national consensus was in the making: he jumped at the chance offered by the Government's cynicism. What had most nettled him since 1931 had been the accusation that Labour had run away from responsibility, had put Party before Country. It was this belief, more than any other, that he had realized would have to be overcome before Labour could have a real prospect of power. Now the shoe was on the other foot: his subject in December 1935 was that of national honour.

Exceptionally, he spoke for nearly an hour in the Commons, deliberately seeking to identify Labour's pro-League attitude with that of British integrity: 'If you turn and run away from the aggressor, you kill the League . . .' he charged, 'and you kill all faith in the word of honour of this country.' He specifically drew attention to the risks involved in collective security – the better to dismiss them on the grounds that there was nothing in any special pleading about the difficulties of the time that could justify the British dishonouring their word.[111] Though counter-productive in immediate parliamentary terms,[112] Attlee's remarks denoted that a new stage in the parliamentary struggle had been reached: his Party had recovered its confidence and had gone over to the attack. He had already, in his first speech as Leader of the Opposition, taken a similar approach to domestic affairs: his argument had been that Labour's policies were based just as much on expediency, that is British interests, as they were on justice.[113] Labour may have lost the 1935 election but, in retrospect, Attlee had squarely put his party on the road to 1945.

VII
Too Late

As Leader of the Opposition from 1935 to 1940, Attlee had an unenviable task. Foreign affairs predominated. The Government's majority was unassailable and its responsibility for decision-making complete. For a time, Labour continued to wrangle. All Attlee could do was to expose the weaknesses in the Government's policy while trying to repair or contain those of his own Party. He could see no alternative to a foreign policy based on collective security, though he naturally hoped that the League could secure peace without having to resort to force. The Government's duty was to give the lead, commit itself and accept the risks. Far more was at stake than Abyssinia, important as that aspect was: 'The whole question, not merely with regard to aggression in Africa, but with regard to aggression in Asia or Europe, or anywhere in the world,' he declared in February 1936, 'is whether the aggressor is going to get away with it.' One of the mistakes made before the First World War had been precisely that the British position had not been made absolutely clear. He realized that the Government could not have imposed oil sanctions right away,[1] but they should have made a perfectly plain statement of where they stood. The question of sanctions constituted a clear test and he sensed 'the old Adam in Eden' who had replaced Hoare as Foreign Secretary.[2] After the German occupation of the Rhineland (in March 1936), Attlee was to have the qualified satisfaction of seeing Winston Churchill come fully round to his point of view: 'We should endeavour now with great resolution', Churchill pronounced 'to establish effective collective security'. How Labour would have rejoiced, Attlee responded, to have had Churchill's eloquence on their side five years previously. When he looked back on those years the thought uppermost in Attlee's mind was 'too late'.[3]

His Party was also tardy in facing up to what was involved in effective collective security. The deepening international crisis prolonged Labour's recovery from MacDonaldism. Pacifism may have been in decline after 1935 but the Hoare-Laval deal gave momentary force to the Left's argument that the 'the League of Nations was an imperialist sham.'[4] The British Government, it could be maintained, was not to be trusted at all, especially with armaments. Attlee was to find himself harassed from both wings of the Party, the one strongly in favour of re-armament, the other adamantly opposed. While carrying the major burden of representing Labour defence policy to the Commons and country, he had to attempt to prevent his Party splitting apart. As a result, his and Labour's efforts to come to grips with the defence issue provoked much criticism at that time and subsequently. But such criticism overlooks Labour's opposition status: not a shell, ship, plane or tank was lost to the nation or League because of the Party's tactical and philosophical difficulties. In 1937 Churchill would remind the House of his father's dictum: the business of an Opposition was to oppose everything, propose nothing and turn out the Government. If, by an unfortunate combination of circumstances, the Opposition was occasionally forced to support the Government, that support should invariably be given with a kick and not with a caress.[5] This was far from being Attlee's attitude but Churchill's point is not entirely irrelevant in the parliamentary context, particularly when the emotional gulf between the parties was so wide.

Shortly after Attlee's assumption of the leadership, Labour began to take a serious interest in defence for the first time. There was a need, as Attlee later put it, to get 'an informed opinion'[6] which was a difficult undertaking in the absence of much official or confidential contact between the Opposition and Government, or even, in Government circles, between insiders and outsiders. The important discussions about defence took place 'in the back rooms'[7] of both sides. Early in 1936, the NEC formed its own Defence Committee, composed largely of Labour MPs and others who had either served in the Service Ministries or who had some military experience. Attlee was the obvious chairman; the Committee's task, he proposed, should be fourfold: (1) to formulate a definite policy on defence; (2) to reach definite opinions on the form that modern war on an important scale would be likely to take (including types of equipment and the relative importance of the three Services); (3) to prepare a policy of financial allocation to the three Services within an aggregate expenditure; and (4) to build up a general body of informed opinion on Defence matters.[8] An indication of how urgent the subject was considered may be gathered from the fact that the Committee met some five times in February 1936 alone. It had its own research facilities which, after a while, were supplemented by leaks from senior serving officers.[9]

The Committee's immediate duty was to report to the NEC, for whom, by 4 March 1936, a long and detailed paper on defence problems had been drawn up, probably by the same Party officials who were assisting the Defence Committee. The paper contained several annexes on the defence expenditure of various countries as well as that of the UK. It concluded that it was 'imperative upon Great Britain to undertake the diplomatic preparations necessary with the end of concluding a Treaty of non-aggression and mutual assistance associated with the sanctions system of the Covenant and including a definition of the aggressor in an international conflict to cover the whole of Europe.' Echoing what Attlee had said in the Commons, the paper argued that 'uncertainty about what Great Britain would do certainly operated in German Public Opinion to make the Great War possible' and that there should be 'no uncertainty now'. The worst of all policies was one of compromise in Europe between isolation and collective action. Britain could not take the risk of standing alone even against Germany and, whatever the calculation of political probabilities, 'it would be criminal for any Government to neglect the dangers in the present situation'. An object of British foreign policy had to be to prevent Poland from being drawn into the German orbit. A powerful British Air Force might turn the balance against Germany. It would be impossible to deny that, relative to its national income, Great Britain was spending less on armaments than any Great Power or any second-class power in Europe. The Nazi ideal of a Greater Germany could not be attained without war. Finally, the document insisted 'it would be illusory to think that there is any economic solution for present ills (even if it were capable of immediate realization) which would satisfy the appetites of Japanese, German or Italian imperialism'. The militarist was not a rational animal – if he were he would not be a militarist.[10] Attlee was in substantial agreement with the Report. Following his speeches in the Commons and these private committee meetings, he was invited to address the Imperial Defence College, the Naval Staff College and other Service bodies.[11] But the issue of what political tactics his Party should adopt was another matter.

The sobering arguments and detailed statistics being prepared behind the scenes raised the question of whether the PLP should abandon its practice of formally voting against the Service Estimates. Great pressure was applied both inside and outside the NEC, from the trade union representatives, Hugh Dalton and certain of the Party's officials, for the NEC to alter course. Attlee resisted this pressure, not only because of the effect on Party unity: it was not merely a Labour matter, he insisted in a written memorandum to the NEC,[12] but one which went to the heart of parliamentary procedure. Votes had always been directed to the *policy*, not the actual provision of supply: these votes had never been taken as voicing a desire for the abolition of the Services until the present year, when Baldwin had so exploited them in the country. Moreover, if it was decided not to vote against the Service Estimates in future it would be necessary to cease voting against any Supply Estimates – for henceforth, a vote against the Home Office would mean that Labour wanted to abolish factory inspection. Nor could the question be solved by moving token reductions in the Estimates as that would indicate that Labour wanted less spent on the Services, '*although we really desire more*' (my emphasis). Motions of reduction or against Estimates were the historic method of insisting that redress of grievances preceded supply. If such votes were to be interpreted literally in future there would be many occasions, Attlee warned, when Labour would be unable to register an opinion in the division lobby. He later considered the views expressed in his memorandum to have been 'perhaps unwise and pedantic';[13] but the only alternatives were either to abstain or to vote with the Government, courses guaranteed to harden the divisions inside his Party. In 1936 neither Labour as a whole nor the country was ready to contemplate the possibility of war.

The NEC meeting on 4 March 1936, to which Attlee submitted his memorandum, had been called to consider the Government's publication on the previous day of a White Paper announcing a general but still relatively modest increase in the provisions for all three Services.[14] The meeting was followed in the afternoon by a gathering of the three Labour executive[15] bodies over which Attlee presided. He rather vaguely declared that there was general agreement on fundamentals. Citrine, for the TUC, was adamant that nothing should be said in the Commons which could be interpreted as a desire to make concessions to Hitler, though there was no possibility of Attlee doing so. In his next speech to the Commons on 9 March, Attlee again hammered the point that there was no plan for defence co-ordination, which the Government tacitly admitted a few days later by the appointment of a Minister for that purpose.[16] He also drew attention to the fact that defence was still being discussed in complete isolation from the rest of the Empire, and that there was no distinction between collective and national security.[17] The PLP ignored his advice about voting: only token reductions in the individual Service Estimates were moved and, on the main Estimate, the Party abstained.[18]

Meanwhile on 7 March the Germans had occupied the Rhineland. On the 20th, Attlee took part in a conference with the International Federation of Trade Unions, the Labour and Socialist International and the International Trade Secretariat which passed a vigorous motion aimed directly at Fascism and Hitler: collective security had to be organized as the peace of the world was threatened.[19] Perhaps it still wasn't too late? Unknown to Labour, the French (with the ratification of the Franco-Russian Treaty on 27 February 1936) had vainly tried for two weeks prior to the occupation of the Rhineland to conclude a military alliance with

Britain.[20] No one can say what the effects of such an alliance might have been,[21] but it is now known that the extent of German rearmament was grossly exaggerated at the time. Hitler said that, had the French ordered a general mobilization, the Germans would have withdrawn with 'our tail between our legs, for the military resources at our disposal would have been totally inadequate for even a moderate resistance.'[22]

On 26 March Attlee stated that the occupation of the Rhineland was a serious breach of a Treaty obligation. He rejected the plea that Germany could be excused because of evils suffered in the past from the Treaty of Versailles. The German people had suffered, but 'you cannot run an orderly system' on the basis of unilateral action. Peace in Europe was indivisible: the danger of the immediate situation was that it would only produce a patched-up peace, with another crisis next year.[23] Unfortunately he discovered that oral support (reiterated in April)[24] from Churchill and his minute group of rebel Tories was one thing, support in the voting lobby another. After the announcement in June that sanctions had been abandoned against Italy, Attlee's motion of censure was accepted by the Liberals, but not Churchill. The Government had indeed killed the League, Attlee concluded, though Italian policy had only been the final betrayal: 'If you can't beat Signor Mussolini when you are standing in company with 52 other nations,' he said with scorn, 'you will not have much chance if you are prepared to defend the British Empire single-handed.' There was no security in isolation. Baldwin could only reply that he had told one of his colleagues a year previously that one of the greatest difficulties he would have to face would be to keep himself from being thrust into war by the Opposition.[25]

Perhaps the only satisfaction available to Attlee in 1936, and it was a slight one, was the rapid evaporation of Baldwin's reputation.[26] It has been suggested that Labour's convolutions on the Service Estimates during the year were a 'godsend to the Government, since [they] gave a specious excuse for its evasions and half-measures, despite its large majority and its responsibility for leadership.'[27] However, the Government did not need any excuse; it was determined for a variety of reasons to avoid becoming entangled in any action that might lead to war. Both Baldwin and Neville Chamberlain were convinced that British public opinion would not support any kind of sanction in pursuit of foreign policy objectives.[28] The quality of Baldwin's insight into international affairs may be gathered from his reply to a delegation of eighteen senior Tory backbenchers and peers who saw him on 28 July in order to urge improvements in the country's military preparations. The Prime Minister declared: 'I am not going to get this country into a war with anybody for the League of Nations or for anybody else ... [if] the Russians and Germans got fighting and the French went in as allies of Russia owing to that appalling pact they made, you would not feel you were obliged to go and help France would you? If there is any fighting in Europe to be done, I should like to see the Bolshies and the Nazis doing it.'[29]

By January 1937, Churchill had become sufficiently alarmed about the international situation to organize – in co-operation with trade union leaders and others – a campaign on behalf of 'Arms and the Covenant'.[30] On New Year's Day he, together with Lloyd George, the Archbishop of Canterbury and other notables, had no difficulty in obtaining the signatures of Attlee, Dalton and Philip Noel-Baker to a joint declaration entitled 'The Covenant and Military Action.' War could still be avoided, the document stated, 'if the Members of the League would make plain their determination to fulfil their obligations under the Covenant and to take any measures required for the prevention or repression of aggression including, if necessary, military action.' These words could have been taken almost verbatim from any of Attlee's speeches in the previous five years. In the Commons in January 1937 he could do little but repeat himself: ' . . . if democracy was to survive, it had to be prepared to stand up to the dictators . . . Labour recognized that there was a danger of war that had to be faced.'[31] The difference in 1937 was that the tide of opinion within his Party would finally come to accept this unpalatable possibility.

Labour's difficulties in 1936 were compounded by the outbreak of the Spanish Civil War in July, which sparked a further resurgence of the Left and general mistrust of the Government. Forgetting its actions in March, the PLP voted against the total Supplementary Estimates for the fighting forces on 20 July; a week later, it voted against the final stages of the total Supply Estimates.[32] Attlee's previous counsel, at least in terms of political tactics, must now have appeared sound. The PLP came to their decision by only 57 to 39, with another 60 Labour MPs either absent or not voting;[33] but Attlee knew that the bulk of Labour opinion against entrusting the Government with arms – and in favour of Cripps's position – lay in the constituency parties.[34] The Socialist League still retained its affiliation with the Party. Perhaps encouraged by the formation of the Popular Front Government in France in June, a movement began in the summer of 1936 for a United Front of all the Left – to 'fight' against Fascism, Reaction and War; one of the agitators' specific demands was for unconditional opposition to rearmament.[35] On the other hand, at yet another joint meeting of Labour's executive bodies, held in September at Plymouth, Ernest Bevin proposed that the time had come for the whole policy of the Labour Movement on the menace of war to be looked at anew: he declared that an announcement to this effect would be made to the TUC. There could be no doubt about what was in his mind: rearmament. The NEC appointed a special sub-committee to draft a resolution on the international situation which, after review by the NEC, could be presented to the Party's annual conference. Attlee was a member of the sub-committee[36] but the statement it prepared was rejected by the NEC and another committee appointed. Finally, after further discussion and amendment a resolution was approved,[37] a patent compromise that failed to satisfy either the Right or Left. While the armed strength of the countries loyal to the League had to be 'conditioned by the armed strength of the potential aggressors,' the resolution also stated that the Party declined to accept responsibility for a 'purely competitive armaments policy' and therefore reserved complete liberty to criticize the Government's rearmament programme.

At the 1936 annual conference held in Edinburgh from 5 to 9 October, Cripps had no difficulty in pointing out that the NEC's resolution permitted several interpretations. There was also confusion, perhaps deliberate, on the part of NEC speakers[38] between Labour's policy as an Opposition and what a Labour Government would do. If a Labour Government came to power, declared Hugh Dalton, it 'would be compelled to provide an increase in British armaments'. The high hopes of 1931 had all been dashed. Five years ago Britain had been secure in the military, naval and air sense; that security had now gone. Since Labour had left office, the international situation had changed; 'the central, brutal fact in Europe was that of German rearmament,' and the time had passed for vague, humbugging phrases. The Fascist States had to be told, 'there is a limit; thus far and no further.'[39] Morrison, however, who also spoke on behalf of the NEC, put the emphasis on Labour's role as an Opposition. The Party couldn't vote for the Government's armaments policy, he repeated, because it was a nationalistic and competitive one, not guided by any enlightened foreign policy. In any case, the conference did not have the authority to decide how the PLP should vote on the Estimates, which was a matter of parliamentary tactics.[40] Bevin vigorously objected, describing Morrison's speech as one of 'the worst pieces of tight-rope walking' he had ever seen at the conference. It was unfair to 'pass the buck' to the PLP, and he ominously warned that the one thing he did not want to see was the trade unions taking one line and the rest of the Party another. For Bevin, the resolution had marked 'a clear departure' from the votes on the Estimates that had been given in the House during the past few months. The trade unions feared Fascism; Bevin knew the type of man Hitler was.[41]

The chore of responding on behalf of the NEC to the debate fell to Attlee. His speech was inevitably a rather strained effort; there was something in it for everyone, though it was not as ambiguous as Morrison's. He made an attempt to answer certain specific questions that had been raised. Security did mean building up sufficient forces, including those of the loyal members of the League, to deal with potential aggressors. Yet there was nothing in the resolution that bound the PLP, whose voting tactics were its own prerogative. Labour did not support the Government's rearmament policy, yet it was wrong to suppose that

Labour should oppose every kind of armament and every kind of military activity so long as there was a capitalist Government. Labour declined to give the Government a blank cheque, but that did not mean that no arms were necessary or that present armaments or last year's armaments were the exact amount required. Armaments and foreign policy issues were inseparable, which is why Labour would continue to oppose the Government on both.[42] The NEC resolution was carried by 1,738,000 votes to 657,000: the size of the opposition vote accounts for Attlee's attempt to take heed of its views.

On the emotional level the Edinburgh debate on defence was overtaken and overshadowed by the Spanish situation. Originally, Labour had accepted the Government's policy of non-intervention in Spain,[43] a policy actively supported by the socialist French Prime Minister.[44] Just before the 1936 conference, Labour's National Joint Council had voted eleven to eight in favour of non-intervention.[45] Arthur Greenwood of the NEC justified this position to the 1936 conference by saying that any alternative would involve (1) a free trade in arms, benefiting the rebels; (2) the fall of the *Front Populaire* in France; and (3) the possible enlargement of the conflict into a European War. Dalton, Bevin and other trade union leaders were also concerned with the 'terrible insufficiency of British armaments in the face of the German danger'[46] and hence thought that Britain could not afford to send arms to Spain. But a number of conference delegates argued that, because of German and Italian intervention there, the non-intervention policy, adopted on the assumption that it would be adhered to by all parties, was dead. Attlee pleaded that the reports of foreign intervention had first to be verified and, if proven, any subsequent action had to be international action if it was to be effective.[47] Opposition to non-intervention, however, was widespread in the Party and the Left found an exceptionally impressive spokesman in Aneurin Bevan.

After a formal vote on the question, which the NEC won by 1,836,000 votes to 519,000, the conference's mood was further stimulated by speeches from Spanish fraternal delegates. The NEC hastily decided to send Attlee and Greenwood to London, to consult the new Prime Minister, Neville Chamberlain. As a result, and after further heated NEC meetings, a statement on which Attlee had actively collaborated was made by him to the conference: it declared that if non-intervention was proved to be broken, the British and French Governments should forthwith restore to the Spanish Government the right to buy arms. Attlee emphasized that the NEC were prepared, in the event of foreign intervention, to go beyond the mere abrogation of the Non-Intervention Agreement. The NEC would urge that Britain and France, without necessarily waiting for the agreement of other Powers, should act to ensure that the Spanish Government received arms.[48] Cripps was content to have the NEC add a clause declaring its own conviction that the Fascist Powers had broken their pledges of non-intervention, and Attlee's statement, was then carried unanimously. In a sense, therefore, the Left's new preoccupation with Spain paved the way for Labour's reversal of its votes on rearmament and its eventual united entry into the war against Germany in 1939. It was precisely this possibility that Attlee stressed in his explanation of the NEC's statement: Labour had to be absolutely clear, he said, that they were prepared to face any risks that could come from Government action.

Thus Attlee's efforts in 1936 to keep his party together were not completely unsuccessful, though he could do little to bridge the gap between the radicals with their strong support in the local parties, and the trade union faction backed by the bloc vote and majority NEC support. The latter were bound to get their way in the end. Attlee's tactic of delaying and dissembling the conflict was the only option to him in his bid to ensure the maximum possible Labour unity when the moment of decision could no longer be avoided. Events played into his hands. As the international crisis deepened, the armaments issue faded and left-wing opposition to the NEC split. The left-wing's United Front Campaign never really got off the ground; divergences among the Socialist League, the ILP and the Communist Party were too great. Factional rivalries in Spain and the impact of the Soviet purges and show trials gradually caused what remained of the Left to disintegrate. The sole remaining threat to the Labour Party came from the Socialist League whose leaders, after Labour's annual conference in 1936, began openly to defy Labour Party directives. But the enthusiasm of the League's leaders for the United Front Campaign greatly exceeded that of their followers. Early in January 1937 the NEC warned that the League might be disaffiliated; this was done on 27 January.[49] Inside the NEC there was a move to expel the rebels individually from the Labour Party, which put Attlee to great trouble. 'Stafford [Cripps] and Co.,' he explained to Harold Laski in February 1937, 'have played into the hands of every Right-wing influence in the party besides offending a vast mass of members who are not Right-wing but who will not stand for the flouting of Conference decisions.'[50]

Attlee was such a member and he thoroughly agreed with the several Party edicts pronounced against any association with the Communist Party. There was another aspect of the question which he put to Laski: 'The real difficulty will be in meeting the argument that the offenders against party discipline are prominent and for the most part middle-class people and that they should not be treated differently from rank-and-file members who offend and are dealt with by their local parties for infractions of discipline. I fight all the time against heresy-hunting, but the heretics seem to seek martyrdom.' Indeed, the NEC waited only until the London County Council elections were out of the way before declaring, on 24 March 1937, that members of the Socialist League would be ineligible for Labour Party membership from 1 June. Morrison and Attlee tried to postpone the decision, but were outvoted.[51] The League dissolved itself in May, leaving as its 'most enduring legacy' the weekly paper, *Tribune*.[52] It is probable that Attlee, by the middle of the year, had become weary of the debate and his own efforts to find a *modus vivendi*. Self-criticism was a healthy thing, he wrote in *The Labour Party in Perspective*, so long as it did not lead to a paralysis of the will. There was a danger that a party might be so concerned about its own health that it could become a political valetudinarian, incapable of taking an active part in affairs. It might even discuss its own internal condition to such an extent that it disgusted all those with whom it came in contact.[53]

Between the Party conferences of 1936 and 1937, Labour's executive bodies held numerous sessions to arrive at a generally acceptable policy on international policy and defence. Faith in the League of Nations evaporated, and the last-minute attempt by Churchill and others to revive it in the first months of 1937 rapidly failed.[54] Attlee himself had declared, in June 1936, that none of the smaller States in Europe were going to trust any more in collective security under the League – which might survive as 'a debating society' but had been killed by the Government.[55] Internal party surveys revealed an equally harsh, brutally realistic attitude. One of them, a memorandum prepared by the International Department for the Advisory Committee on International Questions in December 1936, took for granted that the League, as an instrument for the prevention of war, had been destroyed. The Party had to revise its whole peace policy; it had to recognize that a major European war within the next few years was 'a very real probability'. Such a war could not be localized in east or west. Mussolini might be thoroughly opportunistic but Hitler's intentions had been clearly set out in *Mein Kampf*, a volume which, until it was repudiated, had to be given preference over diplomatic documents.[56] Labour, the Party's International Secretary insisted, in April 1937, had seriously to consider what military guarantees it would give, to whom and under what conditions, etc: these matters were fundamental to the Party's foreign policy.[57]

While the debate went on, Attlee could be almost grateful that parliamentary attention was focussed in December 1936 on the abdication crisis. His major Commons intervention in 1937 was to denounce, in June, the non-intervention policy in Spain as a 'farce'. It had not removed international tensions because it had not been honestly tried: in such difficult matters it was always the first step that counted; firmness at the start would have prevented the extension of intervention. He asked the Foreign Secretary what he proposed to do to restore the world situation. Stung by the laughter which greeted the question, Attlee tartly added that he had been brought up to think that the British Foreign Secretary had a certain responsibility.[58] Meanwhile, Labour was changing its parliamentary tactics. The Party divided the House on the individual Service Estimates in March (by moving token reductions), but by July, prior to the total Estimates being presented, decided it would henceforth abstain from any further divisions on military provisions, though voting as usual against all other Estimates involving policy.[59] The final PLP vote to abstain on the Service Estimates was carried against the wishes of the PLP executive, almost certainly including Attlee, by 45 to 29. Though only half the Labour MPs participated, Attlee 'scrupulously refused to entertain a manoeuvre to reconsider the decision.'[60]

Independently of the PLP, Labour's Joint National Council had been reviewing the whole question of the Party's position on foreign policy and defence. The logistical and logical background was provided by William Gillies, Secretary of Labour's International Department and a convinced rearmer. The Council's report, *International Policy and Defence*, was published in July 1937 and attracted wide comment in the press.[61] Its premise was that the League had proved ineffective and, pending reform, would remain so: its conclusion was that if a new British Government were to accept its recommendations, the next war could be prevented, the arms race stopped and the League made strong again. Such a government would have to be powerful in order to make any appeal to the Fascist States. Until international change had been brought about, there could be no reversal of the rearmament programme. Grievances should be listened to and a new system of political security and economic opportunity offered to all nations, but aggressors had to be confronted, through a reinvigorated League, 'with an emphatic superiority of armed force'. The aggressors seriously threatening peace were Germany, Italy and Japan. Tactfully, the report, though describing itself as a policy for the Labour Movement, limited its recommendations to what a Labour Government should do: it did not attempt to prescribe the political tactics for an opposition party. At its general meeting in September, the TUC adopted the report by a huge majority of 3,544,000 to 224,000.[62] This vote settled the issue.

During the debate on 'International Policy and Defence' at the Labour Party's annual conference, held in Bournemouth from 4 to 8 October 1937, the main protagonist was Ernest Bevin and the main opposition speaker Aneurin Bevan. This time, Bevan's argument that the restatement of the Party's foreign policy was simply a guise under which the Movement was being committed to support of the Government's rearmament programme[63] fell on deaf ears: a motion to refer the report back was defeated by 2,169,000 votes to 262,000. As consolation, the Left were gratified to see the Party's acceptance of a revised representation of the constituency parties on the NEC; they were now allowed to elect their representatives directly to the Executive, and their number was increased from five to seven.[64] The Left were also mollified by the conference's unanimous declaration of support for the Spanish people and for a national campaign against non-intervention. At the same time, the NEC's disaffiliation of the Socialist League and its rejection of a 'United Front' policy were confirmed. Attlee's main contribution at the conference was to introduce Labour's 'Immediate Programme' on domestic policy. He also moved an emergency resolution condemning Japanese action in China. Both propositions won unanimous approval and the net result of the conference was that the Party was more united than it had been for years.

Tired as he was of the internal wrangling, he did his best during the year to pour oil on troubled waters. Two trips abroad helped to consolidate his unique position in the Party. In August he visited the Soviet Union for two weeks, and though he acknowledged the superficiality of his impressions they were not completely unfavourable.[65] In December he went briefly to Spain,[66] where he was photographed giving the clenched fist (anti-fascist) salute. The British Battalion of the International Brigade that had been formed on a volunteer basis to assist the Spanish Loyalists included a 'Clement Attlee' Company. On his return he found that a Tory MP had accused him in the Commons of breaking an undertaking he had given not to take part in any activities liable to be interpreted as being inconsistent with the Government's non-intervention policy. He hotly denied the charge in a personal explanation to the House and the affair was dropped.[67] These activities did him no harm with the Left and after October 1937 he was free, in any case, to devote himself to the parliamentary and national arenas.[68]

These continued to be exceedingly unpromising. Chamberlain's majority remained intact and his character was abrasive. Attlee thought 'the man was no good ... absolutely useless for foreign affairs – ignorant and at the same time opinionated.'[69] Chamberlain's appeasement policy, however, as far as can be ascertained, was highly popular in the country.[70] British opinion in the main hoped against hope for the best, which was to say non-involvement in war: 'One half of England,' it has been aptly remarked, 'did not know whether it supported appeasement from fear of war or fear of revolution, while the other half shouted collective security without being very clear whether they were demanding a war against fascism or holding on to the last hope of peace'.[71] Yet Attlee had been clear, and so too now was Churchill. 'What is so ridiculous about collective security?' Churchill rhetorically asked in March 1938, and replied: 'The only thing ridiculous about it is that we have not got it.'[72] But he was only one of a small minority of Conservative MPs, and one with a long reputation for waywardness. More significant Tory dissent began in February 1938, with the Foreign Secretary's resignation. Viscount Cranbourne, the Under-Secretary, joined Eden in an action described by Attlee as courageous, though he would have had 'even keener sympathy for them . . . if they had resigned at the time of the Hoare-Laval Agreement.'[73] The effect of Eden's action was considerably lessened politically by the weakness of his speeches explaining it.[74]

To some extent, Attlee himself contributed to the deepening of the impasse between the parties by his insistence on the continuity of Labour's policy. He was no doubt irritated by Chamberlain's claim that the situation had changed completely since the last election.[75] After the Nazis had taken over Austria, Attlee rubbed the lesson in: such action showed the futility of thinking that dictator States could be dealt with on the assumptions that usually prevailed in international relations. The event knocked down the house of cards that the Prime Minister had been building. The whirlwind that the Government was reaping, he continued, sprang from the wind sown by the Chancellor of the Exchequer. Manchuria, the Rhineland, Abyssinia, Spain, China, Austria – what next? There had to come a time when it was necessary to stand firm, unless all Europe was to be thrown into the melting pot. The need was not for separate bargaining with separate dictators, it was for a return to League principles and policy.[76] Churchill agreed: 'It seems to me quite clear that we cannot possibly confine ourselves only to a renewed effort at rearmament . . . I affirm that the Government should express in the strongest terms our adherence to the Covenant of the League of Nations and our resolve to procure by internal action the reign of law in Europe . . .' There had to be a moral basis for British rearmament and British foreign policy.[77] Again, the words could have been Attlee's own – from five years previously. He could only add that nothing was quite so dangerous as a policy of weakness, drift and uncertainty: Chamberlain's policy merely meant a postponement of war.[78] In the nine weeks before 4 April 1938, there were no fewer than thirteen debates in the Commons on foreign affairs which culminated in a Labour vote of censure, and the inevitable crushing Government majority. True, the Liberals sided with Labour, and Churchill and Eden did not vote; but there was no sign of any significant anti-Chamberlain move on the part of dissident Conservatives.

Attlee was rightly sceptical that there would be any important division in Tory ranks.[79] Only Hitler, first after Munich and then decisively in May 1940, could break the political barriers. Still, in the course of 1937, Churchill came to agree fully with Labour on foreign policy and, in turn, before the year was out, Attlee could indicate privately his accord with Churchill on rearmament.[80] From the end of 1937 Labour behaved more and more like a potential government[81] and it was the Party's stand on foreign policy, coupled with Chamberlain's failure in this area, that was mainly responsible.

On the subject of rearmament, Attlee tried to come to some confidential arrangement even with Chamberlain despite their differences. Attlee informed the Prime Minister on 11 January 1938 that there were a number of points he wanted to raise about Air Force preparations but that, owing to their nature, he did not want to do this in open debate. Chamberlain suggested that Attlee send him a note, which he did; the note posed a series of detailed questions about training, organization, aircraft and so on, to which Chamberlain replied that the Minister of Air, Lord Swindon, would discuss all of them confidentially with Attlee as a fellow Privy Councillor.[82] This course was not satisfactory to Attlee; he did not have the technical qualifications to pronounce on the adequacy of the replies, he wrote to Chamberlain on 23 January. Moreover, even if he was so qualified, should he be unsatisfied he would have no option but to press for a public inquiry. He thus proposed that a confidential inquiry be made by qualified and independent persons.[83] Chamberlain rejected this suggestion, whereupon Attlee had no option but to make his request in public. Everything seemed to have been thought of, he complained in the Commons in March, but nothing seemed to have been done.[84] The only result of Labour and the Churchill rebels' criticism of the country's weaknesses in air defence was the dismissal of the Secretary of State for Air. A proposal by Cripps for the creation of a Ministry of Munitions along the lines established during the First World War – which indicated a remarkable change of mind on Cripps's part – was turned down.[85]

Churchill still voted with the Government but in May he joined with Attlee, Dalton and the Liberals to give the new Minister for Air a thorough roasting. Attlee was smarting from a renewed charge by Chamberlain about Labour voting against the Estimates in the past: 'Let him [the PM] go to his Chancellor of the Exchequer [Simon] and ask him why he voted against the entire Army, Navy and Air Force Estimates in 1928. Let him ask his Minister of Labour [Ernest Brown] why he voted against the Estimates and let him ask his Minister of War [Hoare-Belisha] why he voted against the Estimates. What he [the PM] said was one of those half-truths which are worse than lies ... It is untrue that a vote against an Estimate in this House means ... that there should be no provision. It is well known that it is a vote against policy.'[86] Attlee then collected himself and proceeded to more pertinent matters: he alleged that the Government's defence programmes were insufficient and in any case not realized. There was a general failure to concentrate on essentials and the organization of defence was inappropriate. He disputed various details in the provisions for the Air Force.

Under Attlee, Labour's Defence Committee was preparing a long memorandum on the subject. The Committee was aided considerably by leaks from insiders and the memorandum was given to the Prime Minister in June. Churchill also pressed for an inquiry. For their part the TUC leaders had begun a series of meetings with Government officials between March and May in the course of which Citrine had suggested the setting up of 'some sort of Council of State to include some representative of the trade union movement, for the purpose of enabling representatives of interests other than the Government to appreciate the international situation and its implications'. Chamberlain rejected the idea as 'a dangerous innovation', but he did agree to meet the TUC's General Council in March. He then emphasized that it was no good spending time arguing whether or not Britain should give guarantees or take part in collective security action unless the country was in a position to take action. He referred to French military weakness, especially in the air, and the weakness of other possible friends in contrast to Germany's 'great military strength'. At best, Italy might be neutralized; Japan could not be forgotten, and there was no use relying on the USA. He shared the natural dislike of all Englishmen for dictators and their methods, and would be only too pleased if British forces were sufficient to enable them to threaten effectively. But the central weakness was the air; London was particularly exposed and he couldn't take any risks. The union leaders were impressed but they remained dubious about the overall aim of Government policy, were extremely dissatisfied with the official attitude to Spain and were not pleased with the Anglo-Italian Agreement, concluded in April, which recognized the Italian conquest of Abyssinia in return for Mussolini's promise to withdraw from Spain.[87] The sole area of agreement was the necessity of accelerating the rearmament programme, and even here Chamberlain failed to make much of it.

During the summer, the international situation sharply deteriorated. Ostensibly the crisis concerned Czechoslovakia, a country that Chamberlain famously described as being one about which 'little was known.'[88] Yet as long ago as March 1936, Dalton had asked Chamberlain (then the Chancellor of the Exchequer) about the Government's attitude 'in the event of unprovoked aggression by Herr Hitler in either Czechoslovakia or Poland'. The reply had been that such action 'would, of course, immediately come under the notice of the League of Nations' by whose obligations Britain would be bound: peace in Europe, Chamberlain had added, could not be divided,[89] but his subsequent actions demonstrated otherwise. Attlee happened to be personally acquainted with several Czech socialists and also knew Dr Benes, the President, and Jan Masaryk, the Czech Minister in London, very well.[90] In February 1938 the NCL declared its uncompromising opposition to any agreement with either Fascist Italy or Nazi Germany on the basis of the partition indicated by Chamberlain and, in particular, demanded an immediate assurance to Czechoslovakia that Great Britain and the other League Powers would fulfil their obligations to maintain her integrity and independence.[91]

By April, however, Labour's Advisory Committee on International Questions felt obliged to sound a note of caution. There was now 'the fearful doubt about Russia's real strength and real loyalty to the League' since Stalin had swept away so large a proportion of the higher command in the army, navy and civil government. Without Russian power, 'the League's sum would not come out'. Moreover, if Germany struck in Czechoslovakia, Italy and Japan might strike elsewhere; Czechoslovakia would be weak in any case if Germany could organize an economic boycott. French power to aid Czechoslovakia was greatly reduced by the fortification of the German frontier, and British sea power could not be made effective 'on the coast of Bohemia'. Nor did Labour know exactly how 'criminally negligent' the Government had been in regard to passive defence – i.e. air raid defence and storage of food. The Government might reckon the risks of calling a halt to the aggressors in 1938 would be even graver than in 1940 (when the defence position would be stronger). Labour lacked some of the materials for making a judgment, but the risks were evidently so great that Party spokesmen ought to be extremely careful in pressing for more explicit guarantees to Czechoslovakia than the Government had felt able to give. The Advisory Committee was equally hesitant in regard to Spain: it was now almost too late to make any resolute stand and the Government was fervently opposed to doing so, since, amongst other concerns, it might accelerate whatever Hitler had in store for Czechoslovakia.[92] This gloomy prognostication had little effect on Attlee. At the beginning of September, he subscribed to the reaffirmation by Labour's three executive bodies of a policy of resistance to German demands; the British Government, moreover, should inform Germany that Britain would unite with France and the USSR if Czechoslovakia were attacked, and Parliament should be recalled.[93]

By then it really was too late. Chamberlain went his own well-known way, though after the first of his three visits to Hitler he did consent to see a Labour delegation consisting of Walter Citrine, the TUC's General Secretary, Dalton and Morrison. Citrine began by saying that Labour was unanimous in its hostility to severing Czech territory and handing it over to Germany; the Party also believed that a joint indication of opposition to German policy on Czechoslovakia on the part of Britain, France and Russia would deter Hitler. Chamberlain explained that it was precisely the extent and completeness of German military preparations that had decided him to go to Germany. There was every reason to believe that if he had not done so, and if his action was not followed by a solution acceptable to both the Sudeten-Germans and Germany, there would be a move into Czechoslovakia. He then turned to the alternative – some form of war. Even if the British people were prepared to fight for Czech self-determination and the war was won, Czechoslovakia could not be restored to its present state. But neither he nor Hitler thought that France would participate. The French Air Force only had 21 planes equal to German planes, of which there were 500. Russia was also unlikely to do anything effective, and Britain could not face an immediate conflict with Germany, Italy and Japan, combined, as it would be, with complications in Palestine and India. Dalton replied that to give way to Hitler then might mean that he would think it worth while to try something else when the British situation would be still weaker. Chamberlain insisted that one of the choices was between 'a war today as a certainty against a possible war in years to come.' He evidently made an impression. Dalton said that by their declaration the Labour leadership had thought they were backing France and Russia; it seemed that they had been misled. Citrine added that the delegation was now in an embarrassing position; other Labour leaders 'would still be wanting to stand up to Hitler' and he, Dalton and Morrison were not really in a position to tell them that Britain was unable to do so. Chamberlain advised that their best course was to tell a selected circle of their Labour colleagues what they had heard about the position of France and Russia.[94]

One member of that circle who was not convinced was Attlee. Citrine (according to Dalton) had for some time thought that Chamberlain 'had a pretty good answer to [Labour's] questions and criticisms', and had had some rows about this with Attlee who had sworn at him.[95] Attlee had also resisted any idea that the Spanish Government should be pressed to seek mediation for peace terms, in view of the fact that neither Britain nor France could send any substantial amount of arms.[96] He had 'rather vigorously' snubbed another Labour figure – the pacifist Noel-Buxton – who in July wanted the Labour Party to issue a declaration urging the Czech Government to make large and speedy concessions.[97] However, Attlee thought it right that the Czechs should be kept fully informed. The day after the delegation's encounter with Chamberlain, he summoned Dalton to his house in Stanmore to meet the Czech Socialist Minister of Social Welfare. Dalton explained Labour's call to the British Government to join with France and Russia in warning Hitler – adding that British action would depend on France moving.[98] But two days later, on 20 September, it became clear that Attlee and his circle were as determined to resist Hitler as ever. An NCL declaration recorded that Labour viewed with dismay the reported proposals of the British and French Governments for the dismemberment of Czechoslovakia as a response to the threat of German military action; they constituted a 'shameful betrayal of a peaceful and democratic people' and a dangerous precedent for the future.[99] Churchill phoned Attlee that same day saying that the declaration did honour to the British nation, whereupon Attlee curtly replied, 'I'm glad you think so.'[100]

Attlee's curtness was probably due to his belief that time had run out for any parliamentary upset, at least for the moment. In April there had been talk among rebel Conservatives of a new Coalition Government, with Churchill as PM and Eden as Foreign Secretary and including a strong Labour and Liberal representation in the Cabinet. The go-between had been Kingsley Wood who had found Attlee not unfavourable to the idea. Such a government was to have made a definite commitment to Czechoslovakia and an active approach to Russia. But the notion depended on there being a large Conservative breakaway from Chamberlain and Attlee had soon changed his mind,[101] presumably calculating (correctly) that the breakaway would not come.

Before Chamberlain left to see Hitler a second time, Attlee and the Deputy Leader, Greenwood, called on the Prime Minister. It was a disagreeable interview, Attlee reported to the NCL: the PM was becoming steelier and steelier, smiling less and snarling more. They had cross-questioned Chamberlain on the details of the plan for the partition of Czechoslovakia, but it seemed that no details had been arranged. Nothing had been worked out about the minorities; there were no guarantees for the Czechs. Attlee told Chamberlain: 'You have abandoned these people completely. You have made a complete and abject surrender. All Eastern Europe will now fall under Hitler's sway. We are all full of the most profound disgust, and this is one of the biggest disasters in British history.'[102] The three Labour Executives passed a resolution on 21 September expressing their humiliation at the Czech Government's statement of acceptance (as a result of the Anglo-French pressure). The settlement was a shameful surrender to Hitler, amounted to the virtual destruction of the Czech State, sacrificed vital British interests and the sanctity of international law, and would not bring peace. Hitler's ambitions did not stop at Czechoslovakia. There was no longer a frontier in Europe which was safe. Hitler's present triumph would be a starting-point for further warlike adventures which in the end would lead to a general conflict.[103] Later that day the NCL sent a deputation to Halifax, the Foreign Secretary, to reiterate these views. Attlee did not go. The deputation said that the NCL did not accept the suggestion that France and the Soviets were unwilling as well as unready to go to the assistance of Czechoslovakia. What was now proposed was no longer self-determination for a minority but the complete dismemberment of the State. The NCL were not nervous about the future if a determined stand was now made against Germany. Hitler's internal position was not strong, and the alleged strength of German rearmaments was exaggerated.[104]

On arrival in Germany, on 22 September, Chamberlain found that Hitler indeed wanted more: the Anglo-French proposals did not suffice; the areas to be ceded to the Reich had to be handed over at once, which was too much for the Czechs. That same day Attlee phoned Churchill at his London flat, where a meeting of a few Tory rebels was taking place, saying Labour would come in with them.[105] In London, trenches were dug in the parks and a plan prepared for the evacuation of schoolchildren. Labour attempted to stiffen British public opinion with a published letter to the PM; the PLP approved the leadership's actions in the crisis, with only half a dozen pacifist dissidents.[106] On 27 September the fleet was mobilized. Parliament was recalled the following day, and it was while Chamberlain was nearing the end of his speech that Hitler's third invitation for him (along with Daladier, the French MP, and Mussolini) to visit Munich was announced. There could be no mistaking the general relief, which Attlee did not share. He said only that everyone welcomed the PM's statement that a fresh opportunity had arisen which might lead to the prevention of war. No chance of preserving peace that did not sacrifice principles should be neglected.[107] Chamberlain, however, returned to London waving his celebrated piece of paper, signed by Hitler and himself, which stated that the agreement over Czechoslovakia and the Anglo-German Naval Treaty were symbolic of their peoples' desire never to go to war with one another again. Attlee believed that war had now become inevitable:[108] he responded, in the Commons, with the finest speech he had yet made,[109] one of the finest he would ever make.

Attlee denied that 'peace in our time' had been established; instead there was 'nothing but an armistice in a state of war', and humiliation. It had not been a victory for reason and humanity, but for brute force. A gallant, civilized and democratic people had been betrayed and handed over to a ruthless despotism. He felt as he had on the night that Gallipoli had been evacuated, he added, in a reference that could not fail to catch Churchill's ears: 'There was sorrow for sacrifice; there was sorrow over the great chance of ending the war earlier that had passed away. There was, perhaps, some feeling of satisfaction that for a short time one was getting away from the firing [line] but there was the certain and sure knowledge that before very long we should be in it again.' The events of the last few days had constituted one of the greatest diplomatic defeats that Britain and France had ever sustained. Hitler had overturned the balance of power in Europe without firing a shot. Chamberlain had been described as the man who saved the peace, but he was also the man who had brought them into the danger of war. The price of peace had been paid by the Czechs, and their armaments were to be handed over to the Germans. The cause of the crisis was not a minorities problem or (sarcastically) 'the wonderful principle of self-determination': it was because Herr Hitler – whom Attlee called a gangster – had decided to dominate Europe. The degeneration in the world was due to two things: (1) the failure to deal with the political and economic injustices arising out of the follies of the Peace Treaties; and (2) the failure to deal with force. The background to the present crisis was to be found in the history of the past seven years and in these matters it was the early steps which counted: the Government had never tried to get together the Powers that might have stopped the crisis. The USSR had been cold-shouldered, though French weakness here had been even greater than that of the British Government. But was the policy Chamberlain's or the Government's? Chamberlain, at any rate, had been the dupe of the dictators: Britain had been left isolated. Attlee warned that the USSR might well hold aloof in future when it considered what little trust could be placed in the Western democracies. Britain's potential allies had all gone except France, which was in the position now of a second-class State. All that remained from British policy were two promises, one from Hitler, the other from Mussolini. Seven years of National Government had brought the British to a more dangerous and humiliating position than at any time since the days of Charles II. There were only two sources of consolation – the calm of the people during the crisis and the universal detestation of war. Attlee concluded by calling for 'a real peace conference' which would include the USA and the USSR.[110] On the Opposition's censure motion no Conservatives actually voted against the Government, though some 30 abstained.

'There was the root of the trouble,' Attlee commented in retrospect, '... you could never get the revolting Tories up to scratch ... You couldn't get them to vote against the Government.'[111] Cripps thought otherwise, and abandoning or, rather, broadening his conception of a Unity Campaign after Munich, 'looked to Dalton, Attlee and Morrison to concert a national agreement with Churchill' and other Tories. Dalton was game as always for intrigues but also concluded that a major Conservative revolt was not in sight.[112] Inside the Labour Party, the post-mortem on Munich and its implications for Labour policy included very careful consideration of possible political alliances. A paper prepared for the Party's Policy Committee on 8 October suggested that 'a continuance of the [Government's] present pro-German policy may lead to serious dissensions in the Tory Party'.[113] A further document, submitted to the Policy Sub-Committee in November, defined the dissident Tory Group as 'strong in leadership, numerically weak in adherents, but with many secret sympathizers, and which is therefore potentially quite strong'. This group's foreign policy in some ways approached that of the Labour and Liberal Parties and did provide material for those interested in promoting a unification of opposition forces. It could be that, at the next general election, a majority of the electorate would like to overthrow Chamberlain but would not be prepared to accept even Labour's *Immediate Programme* as the price. Labour had to consider whether the national and international situations were so serious as to change its aim of a majority Labour Government to one of co-operation in appropriate and agreed areas with other anti-Chamberlain groups. Prior to Munich Labour had rejected the idea of a Popular Front on the grounds that (a) it would not succeed electorally and (b) it would not succeed either as a government: the document suggested that these assumptions might no longer hold good, and outlined the form a particular anti-Chamberlain grouping might take. An immediate decision had to await further political developments, but should Labour meanwhile think about relaxing its hitherto 'exclusive' attitude? The Sub-Committee's reaction was fairly evenly mixed, pro and con, and nothing came of the discussion.

Attlee thought that the form of coalition suggested was not then a likely one, but he was not doubtful as some other speakers had been about the possibility of a Tory split. His own experience led him to believe that this was by no means impossible, particularly if the situation got worse. He was worried that a movement of opinion was developing in the Labour Party and the country which might, in circumstances of utmost seriousness, crystallize itself into something like a Centre Party or association, which would be very damaging for the Labour Party. He also thought that there should be consideration of the position which might arise if, after a general election, the present Government was returned to power with a majority of 30–50 and continued its present policy. In that case Labour might be approached by a group of dissident Tories sufficiently large to reverse the Government's small majority. Labour would have to think 'very seriously and very responsibly about the answer it would make to such an offer'. At the same time, he wished to emphasize that in any possible coalition, Labour would necessarily be by far the strongest partner and he thought therefore that it should not be Labour who would make sacrifices, but the dissident Tories and those Liberals supporting them.[114]

In contrast to Attlee's statesmanlike approach, Cripps's maladroit tactics served only to complete the Party hierarchy's annoyance with him. In January 1939 he wrote a memorandum to the NEC, calling for an all-party and group alliance against the National Government: it was rejected by 17 votes to 3, with Attlee voting with the majority.[115] Later that month the NEC expelled Cripps from the Party altogether along, in March, with a few other Popular Front advocates.[116] Attlee told the annual conference in May: 'It has been suggested that somehow or other the Labour Party ought to have accessions of strength, from very odd quarters sometimes, before they can govern this country. I believe that is entirely untrue.'[117] There is little evidence that a Popular Front at that time would have been especially popular in the country and Attlee preferred keeping Labour's powder dry. He was also determined that, when the time came, Labour views on the running of the country would matter most.

After Munich, the Labour executive undertook lengthy reviews of the strategic and defence situations. A small group of the Defence Committee, under Attlee's chairmanship, prepared a detailed report, completed in January 1939, on the organization of a future Ministry of

Defence.[118] In the Commons he continued his condemnation of the Munich Agreement, calling attention to the plight of the various refugees from Nazi persecution.[119] He was completely unimpressed with the results of Chamberlain and Halifax's visit to Rome in January; he could not understand the PM's conviction of Mussolini's good faith towards Spain.[120] After Chamberlain's announcement, in February, that Britain now recognized General Franco's Government, Attlee launched a bitter and even vicious attack on the Prime Minister.[121] Such an entirely uncharacteristic act reflected the depth of his own and the entire Left's emotions in regard to the issue which, more than any other, had divided Labour from all Conservatives, including the dissidents, in the period 1936–39.

Attlee's health and stamina throughout the 1930s had been remarkable; he seems hardly to have missed a single parliamentary division and virtually lived at the House of Commons when it was in session. But from March 1939 he was increasingly unwell. His illness was due to a bungled prostate gland operation. He had to be operated on again, necessitating a lengthy convalescent period as the final months of peace elapsed.[122] His voice was thus rarely heard as Hitler marched into Prague and when, with the British guarantees to Poland and Rumania, appeasement apparently died. His last major speeches in the Commons before the war were devoted to two issues which seemed peripheral to the German question but which, in fact, went to the heart of his attitude to international affairs and the related defence question during the 1930s. In April he denounced the Italian invasion of Albania, an action which neatly underlined his oft-expressed view that peace was indivisible and that the word of the Fascist dictators could not be trusted. Even Chamberlain now confessed doubts about Italian intentions. Attlee added: 'If you want to build up a system of collective security, you must get unity between Great Britain, France and the USSR.'[123] These had always been the League's big Powers. The second issue was the hardy one of conscription. After some hesitation caused by his knowledge of the Labour movement's certain reaction[124] and his four-month-old promise that there would be no conscription in peacetime, Chamberlain announced a limited measure on 26 April. In March, the NCL had reaffirmed its traditional position against conscription on the solid grounds that it was unnecessary. Attlee went further: conscription was positively detrimental. Voluntary service had not been fully tried and would give better results; forced service would produce dissension at home.[125] Often misrepresented, Attlee's attitude was later proved sound: allies, not men, were required. The actual measure was in any case little more than a gesture. During the war, when conscription was considerably enlarged, with Labour approval, it would be found that all sorts of highly skilled men essential to the war effort had been swept into the net and attempts had to be made to demobilize them.

The Party's 1939 annual conference, held in Southport at the end of May largely in Attlee's absence – he had a relapse of his illness at the conference – contained no surprises. The NEC's decisions regarding Cripps, an anti-government coalition, and its foreign and defence policies were all confirmed by overwhelming majorities. Despite the lack of confidence in Chamberlain's Government, the Party resolved to continue its co-operation with the Voluntary Service scheme. Before, during and after the conference, Labour continually advocated the making of – as the chairman of the annual conference expressed it – 'a union against aggression of the three most powerful members of the League of Nations,'[126] though whether any British Government could have managed it at that stage must remain a matter of conjecture. What is certain is that the Conservative Government did not really try. Attlee recovered sufficiently to make a brief intervention: the team on the Treasury Bench was the weakest he had ever seen; it had dillied and dallied at a time of crisis. Driven from a policy that had totally failed, it had crept back to try to adopt in a feeble way Labour's own policy.[127] It was 'too late'. Attlee spent the last few months of peace in acute physical pain. They were months both of convalescence and of preparation for the most arduous and important years of his political career.

VIII

Not With A Flourish Of Trumpets

During the Second World War the change in the climate of British public opinion, of which Attlee had briefly dreamed in the last war, finally took place. Labour patriotism converged with a more moderate Conservative social outlook. The shared dangers and efforts of total war, especially at home, brought about a broad sense of national purpose, of mutual values and of community feeling. Whether the war experience actually produced the change or merely revealed an underlying tendency which the years of inter-party strife had obscured is perhaps debatable. Whether it would outlast the war could not be foreseen. Nevertheless, for Attlee the shift represented an historic opportunity, the absolutely vital preliminary to any substantial social advance. Without it, socialists would always be begging for crumbs from a rich man's table: with it, they would be sitting at that table. More precisely, the formation of the Coalition Government meant to Attlee that a way was at last open for reformist ideas to permeate political life. In comparison, the devising and engineering of specific measures incorporating the new mood was of secondary importance. He saw his role as that of a facilitator, one whose major task was to smooth the way for permanent change. And such was his success that the overall result has been dubbed 'Attlee's consensus'.[1]

It was not, nor in the circumstances could it be, a fully-fledged socialist consensus. Attlee certainly believed, as he told the Commons in November 1939, that the war could not be won without 'a good deal of practical socialism,'[2] but he also feared that its continuation would ruin many of the social gains for which Labour had striven. Indeed, within a few months of the Churchill Coalition taking office, the country verged on bankruptcy; by 1945 the economy on which Labour's *Immediate Programme* had been based was shattered. Yet there had been no alternative to resisting Hitler.[3] After the Coalition had been formed, there were also political reasons which prompted Attlee to tell the NEC in March 1942 that Labour 'should not try to get Socialist measures implemented under the guise of war'.[4]

Nevertheless, according first priority to the maintenance of the Coalition and the prosecution of the war did not preclude taking advantage of prevailing opinion to effect a substantial improvement in the lot of the poorer classes. Attlee's preferred tactic was the discreet, adroit and persistent advocacy of Labour policies, and the promotion of Labour colleagues in every branch of government. His approach did not please the radicals who thought in terms of an open, direct confrontation with the status-quo forces. Harold Laski's strictures provoked Attlee, in January 1941, into a vivid explanation of his technique: 'I am sufficiently experienced in warfare,' he riposted caustically, 'to know that the frontal attack with a flourish of trumpets, heartening as it is, is not the best way to capture a position.'[5] To him, the quiet conceptual revolution that he was doing his best to promote was infinitely more important than legislative achievements. He was able, in 1944, to tell Laski that, whatever the political complexion of the post-war government, it would 'inevitably have to work a mixed economy'. He had witnessed the acceptance by the leading politicians and economists of 'the conception of the utilization of abundance', which had coloured all discussions on home economic policy. What he, and others, had been vainly advocating since 1931 was now accepted, and was the basis of conversations with the Dominions and Allies. The doctrine of full employment followed automatically, but the crucial point to Attlee's mind was 'the extent to which what we cried in the wilderness five and twenty years ago has now become part of the assumptions of the ordinary man and woman'.[6]

The political watershed can be dated precisely: 10 May 1940. It was on that day that Labour's NEC formally resolved that the party would take a 'full and equal share in a new Government', but not one headed by Neville Chamberlain.[7] The emissary who brought or, rather, telephoned the bad news to the Prime Minister was Attlee; he had already indicated as much to Chamberlain the previous day, before leaving for Bournemouth, where the NEC was preparing for the Party's annual conference. During the night the Germans had begun their attack on the Low Countries, but the military emergency brought no reprieve for the *ancien régime* – for whom 10 May turned out to be Black Friday.[8] It brought Labour and Clement Attlee on to the centre of the political stage. Once again, a great turning-point in British twentieth-century domestic politics was due to a crisis over foreign policy.[9] But this time the outbreak of war had been anticipated by the Opposition, and Chamberlain was defeated because of doubt as to whether he really wanted to win. Labour's self-confidence had been growing since 1935; and though an electoral truce was arranged in September 1939, the Party subsequently would have little to do with the Government. The continuance of the truce had been deliberately made subject to Labour's discretion.[10] Attlee had warned the Party in January against making any blanket assumption that there would be no appeal to the electorate during the war.[11] In May common sense ruled out any election, but Labour, as Paul Addison has observed, 'were not in reality *given* office; they broke in and took it, on terms of moral equality'.[12] Attlee was crystal clear: 'We are going in' [to Churchill's government] he explained to the 1940 annual conference, 'as partners and not as hostages'.[13]

It had been by no means certain that Labour would agree to serve under Churchill. Attlee had his doubts; Churchill's earlier record was against him.[14] Several Labour figures expressed a preference for Halifax[15] – which was the only reason why Attlee can be said to have favoured the Foreign Secretary.[16] Attlee had let it be known that he would not refuse personally to serve with Churchill,[17] as his telephone call in 1938 had already indicated. In Attlee's opinion, Churchill stood head and shoulders above any other possible Prime Minister. Attlee's own war experience and his readings in history had convinced him that the Prime Minister should be a man who knew what war meant – in terms of high strategy, of the personal suffering of the man in the line and in terms of 'that crucial issue' – how the generals got on with their civilian bosses.[18] In any case, the matter had been virtually decided on 9 May by Halifax's refusal to serve: within an hour of the NEC's resolution of the following day Chamberlain resigned, leaving Churchill as sole contender. Invited by the King that evening to see if he could form a government, Churchill at once summoned Attlee – who intimated that he would join a government under Churchill, but only as Leader of the Labour Party, not as an individual.[19] Churchill accepted Attlee's stipulation, perhaps the more readily because of his high regard for Attlee's war and parliamentary experience.[20] He and Attlee at once agreed on a preliminary list of names for the new War Cabinet – themselves, Greenwood, Halifax and Chamberlain. There was also ready agreement that night about the Service Ministers, one from each party:[21] Churchill could assure the Sovereign that a new government could be formed. It merely remained for Attlee, on 12 May, to telephone the NEC in Bournemouth to say that he and Greenwood proposed acceptance of Churchill's offer. The proposition passed by 17 votes to 1 – a resounding affirmation of Labour's patriotism, and also of the hierarchy's confidence in their Leader. Further appointments were arranged in London before Attlee and Greenwood left to rejoin their NEC colleagues. The next day Attlee described the decisions to the full conference and they were approved by some 2,413,000 votes to 170,000.

One of the reasons for Attlee's unobtrusiveness during the war was that he was ubiquitous. Wherever one looks among the highest echelons of the Coalition government, there one finds his name. As a founding member of the War Cabinet, he was immovable: only he and Churchill sat in it from beginning to end. Attlee's position was doubly impregnable: unlike the other members, including the Prime Minister, the Labour leaders (Attlee, and Bevin who joined the Cabinet in October) were there because they represented interests indispensable to the conduct of the Government. Attlee deputized for Churchill, being formally designated as Deputy Prime Minister in February 1942. His position was unique in another way: apart from a brief period as Dominions Secretary when the role of that department was critical,[22] he alone among Cabinet ministers had no departmental responsibilities. He operated freely over the full range of affairs, domestic, foreign, military and imperial: he sat on every committee of importance, creating several of them himself. The powerful committee was his natural element. His first job, with Greenwood, was to review the entire machinery of government: they found a great mass of committees, and proceeded to scrap most of them. In their place were substituted a smaller number of ministerial bodies, of which two became paramount – the Defence Committee and the Lord President's Committee. Attlee sat on both from their inception to the termination of the Coalition: he was deputy chairman of the former, often taking the place of an absent or ill Churchill; he took over the chairmanship of the latter (which co-ordinated all aspects of home affairs) from Sir John Anderson in September 1943. With the single exception of Chamberlain, who died in November 1940, Attlee was the only Cabinet minister to sit on both these bodies. Altogether, a better apprenticeship for a future Prime Minister could not have been devised.

Attlee's first action as a member of the War Cabinet was to veto Churchill's proposed appointment of Chamberlain as Leader of the House. The motivation was political rather than personal, for the two men soon found that they could work together after all.[23] This particular example of wartime co-operation was more a response to the immediate military crisis than to anything else, and the same applied to the Emergency War Measures Bill which, introduced to the Commons by Attlee on 22 May 1940, went through all its stages in a single day.[24] More indicative of the growing consensus was a decision of the War Cabinet's Food Committee the following month: it approved a scheme for free or subsidized milk to mothers and their children under five years of age, which had been ruled out in August 1939 as 'financially impracticable'.[25] The rapid eclipse of the Treasury increased enormously the power and efficiency of the changed committee system. Attlee was well aware of what was happening, Churchill rather less so: Churchill wanted to win the war so badly that he did not care what fiscal means were used. In fact, Churchill's casual attitude towards economic planning eventually irritated Attlee: some heed had to be taken for the morrow: 'I doubt,' he wrote to Churchill, 'whether in your inevitable and proper preoccupation with military problems you are fully cognisant of the extent to which decisions have to be taken and implemented in the field of post-war reconstruction before the end of the war. It is not that persons of particular political views are seeking to make vast changes. *These changes have already taken place*.'[26]

Churchill's nominees in the Coalition were often personal cronies such as Beaverbrook and Cherwell, non-party figures such as Anderson and Woolton, or Conservative 'rebels' such as Eden and Macmillan. Labour's representation, thanks to Attlee, was out of all proportion to its parliamentary strength: besides assiduously securing particular posts for leading Labour figures[27] – and thwarting the careers of certain Conservatives[28] – he worked hard to bring forward younger Labour politicians. The number of junior ministerial posts held by Labour increased from eight in 1940 to seventeen by 1945: his success here, he later reflected, was one of his most noteworthy achievements as Leader of the Labour Party. Equally important, he considered, had been his ability to keep the Labour members of the Government together as a team during the war period[29] – no small feat. Personal relations among the chief Labour figures, Addison has observed, were so troubled that it is a wonder they exerted the collective influence they did.[30] The ever calm and collected Attlee turned out to be the ideal catalyst. Few people were more surprised and impressed than Hugh Dalton, who had begun the war with a very low opinion of Attlee's leadership qualities.[31] Within a year of being in office Dalton began to change his opinion: 'Whenever the pressure in the pipe gets too great, I see this little man, who is always most loyal, unruffled and understanding on my affairs,' he recorded.[32] Others, and not only Labour politicians, came to similar conclusions.[33] Attlee was a man with whom everybody could work, and who could get others to work together. But only insiders could appreciate his qualities: in comparison with Churchill, who achieved a monopoly of the heroic role, Attlee came across publicly as a shadowy figure.

His habit of always arguing 'from what has been done to what may be done'[34] infuriated Labour's left-wingers. For them the war had to be seen in conventional revolutionary terms. It was, Harold Laski fulminated, merely a stage in an immense revolution in which the war of 1914, the Russian Revolution and the counter-revolution on the Continent were earlier phases.[35] The thesis had several implications, one of them being the absolute necessity of securing radical domestic changes during the war itself. Attlee was soon warned that a minority of the Party would try to re-create the position of 1929 and 1931, 'when those members of the Party who were in the Government were treated as if they had no real connection with the Party'.[36] The Coalition had scarcely been formed before Aneurin Bevan accused Attlee and Greenwood of timidity: 'They are much too conscious of the strength of the Tory majority in the House of Commons and too little conscious of its weakness in the country.'[37] In October 1940, Laski published an 'Open Letter to the Labour Movement' in the Labour *Daily Herald*,[38] urging the Movement to demand a statement of war aims from the Government – which amounted to an implicit attack on the leadership. For his pains Laski was made to apologize to a special meeting of the NEC: 'in all the circumstances' he now felt that 'probably the publication [of the letter] was unwise and liable to misunderstanding considering the relation he held to Mr Attlee as Leader of the Party.'[39] It was this incident that provoked Attlee to explain his 'not with a flourish of trumpets' approach. There was an odd sequel to Attlee's letter. Thoroughly chastened – for the moment – Laski attempted to pull off an extraordinary deal with Churchill. Labour's ideological spokesman proposed a continuation of the National Government after the war, under Churchill's leadership, with a domestic programme very similar to that which Attlee's own government was later to enact. Rebuffed by Churchill,[40] Laski became further embittered against his Party's Leader.

For Attlee the war was first and foremost a fight for spiritual values: '... no sophistry, no talk about imperialism and the rest of it [could] alter that fact', he told the delegates to the Party's annual conference in June 1941. 'There was nothing more foolish than to represent that our people do not understand what they are fighting for ...' he added, 'they know what Hitlerism means ...' Indeed they did; for by then the nightly arrival of German bombing planes had become a feature of British life. 'The cause for which they were fighting,' he concluded, 'was the cause of civilization against barbarism.'[41] The War Cabinet had already, in August 1940, agreed to set up a Committee on War Aims with Attlee as chairman and Bevin as a member.[42] This committee had at once recognized that there was a demand for a statement of the general principles and objectives for which the British were fighting, and that it should be issued as soon as possible,[43] but agreements on its terms had proved a different matter. There was no shortage of suggestions: one draft prepared by Harold Nicolson and Halifax, and approved by Duff Cooper, the Minister of Information, advocated a federal structure for post-war Europe and increasingly socialist measures at home. Churchill vetoed the proposal on the grounds that 'precise aims would be compromising, whereas vague principles would disappoint.'[44] Thereupon the committee had decided to postpone its meetings and faded away.[45]

Contrary to what the Left believed, Attlee's acquiescence had not been due to timidity. His overriding concern was, and had to be, national unity. Neither Labour's position in the Government nor Churchill's were as yet secure, because of the close presence of the Chamberlainites. The only certainties in late 1940 were the menace of Germany[46] and the Prime Minister's resolve (which Attlee absolutely shared) not to give way before that menace. His experience in late 1940 and early 1941 as chairman of the War Aims Committee must have persuaded him that any immediate statement would have done more harm than good to the preservation of the Coalition. Moreover, in view of the way the wind of change was evidently blowing, he could afford to bide his time. There was also another factor: the destroyers-for-bases arrangement with the US portended future changes that were realized in the course of 1941. Attlee was determined that Labour's voice be heard in any international dealings. Still, he let it be known in government circles, in July 1941, that a more positive and revolutionary statement of war aims ought to be officially formulated and put before the country. The statement should admit that the old order had collapsed, and ask people to fight for a new one. Otherwise, it looked as if the British were fighting a conservative war with purely negative objectives.[47]

Next month Churchill initiated the Atlantic Charter, 'vague principles' notwithstanding. Attlee and the rest of the Cabinet asked that a paragraph about social security be included, an addition which was acceptable to both Churchill and Roosevelt.[48] The Charter was not meant to be taken seriously, being regarded by the Labour ministers and by Churchill as largely an instrument of propaganda, a diplomatic tool.[49] A visit to Canada and the US, where he saw the President twice, and every member of the US Cabinet, convinced Attlee of the soundness of Churchill's approach: 'The Atlantic Charter has set out the principles upon which the Free Peoples intend to proceed,' he reported to the Cabinet in November 1941, 'it would not be wise to attempt to elaborate those principles in any public statement or document ... Too much concentration on post-war problems affords an opportunity for those who will not face up to war to salve their consciences by planning a new world.'[50]

In one sense, Attlee could afford to be sanguine. Open as his turbulent Party was to debate, even during the war, the leadership was always in an unassailable position of authority. The beginning of hostilities had coincided with a marked improvement in Labour's structural cohesion:[51] when Attlee and Bevin joined the new Government in 1940 they took with them control of the Party's political, parliamentary and industrial wings. Any potential danger from those Labour MPs not in the Government and who continued to sit on the Opposition benches was handled by the neat device of appointing an acting and unpaid leader. Other Opposition front-benchers were elected by the PLP rump to form an administration committee whose main function, according to one of its members, was to sustain the Labour leaders in the Government and to preserve the identity and unity of the Party.[52]

Even so, the war's military frustrations, especially during the first half of 1942 when Russia bled and burned while the British appeared to mark time, gave an extra fillip to the critics' voices. On his return in January from Moscow where he had served as Ambassador, Cripps refused an immediate offer of the Ministry of Supply and referred publicly, in February, to the lack of urgency in the country.[53] Beaverbrook also terminated his Government appointment that month and appeared to be out to prove that his campaign for the opening of a Second Front in Europe to help Russia was an issue which could unite the political extremes.[54] Laski made up his mind in March to make Labour break with the Prime Minister,[55] which resulted in a second clash with Attlee and the NEC. After the Party conference in May, when he had the penance of speaking for the Executive, Laski again broke loose. Articles by him appeared in the *New Statesman*,[56] calling for an end to the political truce, and in the popular *Reynolds News*,[57] attacking the Labour leadership. He told Attlee to his face in the NEC that he had lost confidence in Attlee's leadership.[58] Bevan's mouthpiece, *Tribune*, declared that Attlee was 'loyal to the point of self-effacement'; he was no longer 'the spokesman of the movement which had carried him from obscurity into the second position in the land'.[59] More serious was the fact that the revival of party feeling caused other Labour Party activists to turn again to domestic issues. Those Labour MPs not in the Government manifested their grievances on several occasions: in December 1941, some thirty-five of them insisted on carrying to a division an amendment to the Manpower Bill demanding that the transport, coal-mining and munitions industries be nationalized, despite being previously told by Attlee that if a substantial number voted against the Government he would find his position impossible.[60] In the event, only eight did so[61] – just as only eight were to vote against the Government in the famous censure vote in July 1942. But the discontent was still there: Harold Nicolson believed that a dissenting vote of some sixty-three Labour members later that month, on an Old Age Pension Bill, reflected the agitation on the Second Front question.[62]

These difficulties put a heavy strain on the Labour Opposition in the Commons, already in a somewhat anomalous position. Greenwood, now out of office, attempted a closer definition of the Opposition's support of the war effort. He identified three main areas of activity: (1) representing to the Government, and particularly to Labour members of it, opinions, grievances and defects in the Government's organization and administration; (2) bringing to bear on the Government constructive criticism and suggestions with a view to the more effective prosecution of the war; and (3) keeping to the forefront, in order to satisfy the national morale, their primary peace aims. Clearly, these objectives imposed strict limits on the Opposition, but anything closer to the role of a formal Opposition, Greenwood believed, would soon force the Party to leave the Govern-

1 Attlee's first visit to 10 Downing Street. He is leading a delegation of East End mayors to protest to Lloyd George about the failure of the Government's unemployment policy, in 1920

2 Ramsay MacDonald (left) and Arthur Henderson, 1929

3 Oswald Mosley (left) and William Jowitt in Brighton for the Labour Party Conference, 1929

4 (*left*) Attlee, Deputy Leader of the Labour Party, and George Lansbury, 1931

5 Attlee with Republican forces in Spain, 1937

6 Attlee, Parliamentary Leader of the Labour Party, with Arthur Greenwood, Deputy Leader in the House of Commons, 1939

7 Attlee at work in the Opposition Leader's room at the House of Commons, 1939

ment.[63] At the same time, they handed a certain critical initiative to the left-wingers. Laski was quick to prepare a critique of Greenwood's memorandum – to which Attlee replied that the Party should not attempt to get socialist measures passed under the guise of winning the war. He rightly surmised that Laski wanted to insist on a minimum programme of measures being demanded from the Prime Minister, even at the risk of breaking up the Government. 'What would be the effect on the Party,' Attlee retorted to Laski, 'if, in fact, it left the Government?' In his opinion, 'it would be held that the Party had slipped out of responsibility when things looked black'. Labour, in other words, would leave itself open to the devastating charge of being unpatriotic. His intervention settled the matter at the NEC, no vote being taken.[64] But Attlee still had to convince the rank and file. In the Commons he insisted that the Cabinet was not a body of people sitting around listening to one man.[65] He reminded the annual conference, in May 1942, that '... we knew the situation would be full of difficulty. We have had two years of working with this Government and there may be some who think we have turned the corner in this war and can afford to return to Party strife and direct our minds from the objective of winning the war. They make a great mistake.'[66]

The first six months of 1942 were the most hazardous of all for the British. Ultimately, the German attack on Russia and Hitler's declaration of war on the US would prove decisive for Britain, but for a long time in 1942 the predominant question was not whether Britain would win but whether she would survive. Churchill warned in July that 'It might almost be true to say that the issue of the war depends upon whether Hitler's U-boat attacks on Allied tonnage, or the increase and application of Allied air-power, reach their full application first.'[67] Earlier notions, or hopes, that Germany might collapse economically or politically were not fulfilled. Even after American entry into the war, the British Government had no clear ideas about how the war might be won, only about how it might be lost. It was for this reason that the Labour leaders in the Government, including Attlee, were among those most adamantly opposed to the opening of a Second Front in 1942, despite support for the idea from the Russians, Americans, Beaverbrook and officials such as Cadogan, the head of the Foreign Office[68] – not to mention Labour's left wing. It was for this reason, too, that the Labour Executive had to contain the demand for domestic changes that might have put the existence of the Coalition in jeopardy.

At the 1942 annual conference, the NEC had no trouble crushing an amendment that Labour end its association with the Coalition,[69] but met strong resistance to its proposal that the electoral truce be continued. Bevan was especially vehement against this, and his amendment referring it back to the NEC was defeated only by the slenderest of margins, some

1,275,000 votes to 1,209,000. Just over a month later, in July, the Commonwealth Party was founded by Sir Richard Acland and other progressive intellectuals with the precise aim of contesting by-elections on the grounds that 'Britain must change rapidly in the direction of Socialism if she is to win the war.'[70] Cripps, however, proved more flexible. After his rejection of the Ministry of Supply, Attlee at first blocked Cripps's prospects of further advancement,[71] but then relented. Cripps had changed his views about Russian aims,[72] and Attlee probably considered him less of a political liability in the Government than out of it. Indeed, in November Cripps declared: ' . . . broadly speaking, those who join in the united effort from what is generally referred to as the political Left cannot expect in the present circumstances that the Government should introduce legislation for the purpose of bringing about a complete change in our political and economic structure.'[73] His speech coincided with the news of the victory of El Alamein and might have given some pause to Labour rumblings of discontent. But the publication of the Beveridge Report on 1 December provoked an explosion. Attlee vainly insisted in the Commons two days later that 'The Labour Movement, increasingly, through its members has taken responsibility in Parliament and in local councils of every kind.' He conceded that 'Their speeches have tended to change . . . because it was enough in the old days to get up and denounce the existing state of affairs for 50 minutes, and in two minutes to say "The remedy is Socialism", and sit down.' An interruption was heard, to which Attlee rejoined: 'Not everyone, but many did.'[74] A few days later, he admitted that he was 'very conscious of difficulties in the Party.'[75]

In fact, the affair of the Beveridge Report was to put Attlee in the most exposed and dangerous position of his career. In one sense this was ironic, because the public's acclaim for the Report was the war's most outstanding evidence of 'the Attlee consensus.' El Alamein was followed early in 1943 by the news of the great Russian successes at Stalingrad and elsewhere. It became possible to think about planning new worlds, beginning with Britain. The Beveridge Report promised a new world. There was 'a long series of proposals . . . for a national health service, family allowances, full employment and a comprehensive system of social insurance.'[76] It was, in short, a detailed plan for universal social security similar in almost every respect to that proposed by the Webbs in their 1909 Minority Report and so ardently advocated by Attlee. Nevertheless, it might be recalled that when the campaign had failed, Attlee had not hesitated to support Lloyd George's much more limited Unemployment and Health Insurance Bill.

The trouble in 1943 was that, though the Coalition Government expressed sympathy for Beveridge's recommendations in the Commons, it was unwilling to implement them. The recommendations touched off an avalanche of public discussion, and protests at the Government's lukewarm response were not confined to Labour's left-wingers who, on account of the failure of the Second Front campaign, were actually in a state of disarray for the first half of the year.[77] The rest of the Labour Party took up the challenge: when the Report was debated in the Commons, in February, all but two of those Labour MPs not in the Government voted in the Opposition lobby, against the Government's refusal to implement the Report. This was the only occasion during the war when they divided the House on a domestic issue, and they had allies. Of the 121 anti-Government votes, Addison has noted that 97 were Labour, 3 ILP, 1 Communist, 11 Independent and 9 Liberal – 'including David Lloyd George, casting his last vote in support of the welfare state which he had helped to found'.[78] Even a small group of Conservative MPs pronounced themselves in favour of the Report[79] though they did not go so far as to vote in the debate. In the long term the general Labour reaction – the NCL declared its support for the Report[80] – paid solid political dividends;[81] in the short term the Government's attitude caused a serious rift between the Labour Party's ministers and their backbench supporters. The immediate gainers were the Commonwealth Party and those independent Labour candidates who then came forward at by-elections.[82]

For Attlee, the crucial consideration was the survival of the Coalition: the war had still to be won. There was also the question of Churchill's attitude to the Report. Attlee knew that Churchill was under pressure from the Conservative majority[83] (who opposed the Report), and that the Prime Minister might well feel the issue would detract from the task of winning the war.[84] When the Report came before the Cabinet and Commons in 1943, Churchill was ill – which to some extent may account for the fact that he missed the opportunity to associate himself and his party more clearly with the Report, a mistake which was to prove deadly in 1945. But Attlee also knew that Churchill's personal views were by no means completely negative; indeed Attlee had a shrewd suspicion that the real reason why the Beveridge Report was not immediately put into effect was because Churchill intended to enact it himself as the first post-war Prime Minister.[85] In 1943 Churchill did the next best thing to implementing the Report: he indicated that the Government would prepare the necessary legislation, though insisting that only a House of Commons that had received a popular mandate could commit itself to the expenditure involved.[86] In March he went even further; he and his colleagues, he broadcast, must be ranked 'as strong partisans of national compulsory insurance for all classes for all purposes from the cradle to the grave'. In the same speech the PM pronounced himself in favour of full employment, an expansion of the health services, housing and educational development, and the mixed economy. This was, in effect, 'the first popular proclamation of the new consensus'.[87] On the main score, therefore, Attlee could afford to be patient. The things for which he had been crying in the wilderness were evidently coming to pass: there was no need to rock the Coalition boat.

Yet rocking the boat at the wrong time was precisely what Beveridge, like Laski,[88] was doing. The Report's arrogant and egotistical author had a habit of irritating people, especially Labour leaders. Attlee's dislike for him probably dated from the time they had spent together at Toynbee Hall and the LSE; Churchill did not like him either, and had pointedly rebuffed his initial request for employment in the Coalition Government's bureaucracy. Beveridge had then proceeded to annoy Attlee and Dalton 'by treating them as though they were still junior lecturers and he the director at the LSE'; he made the further mistake of underestimating Bevin, regarding him as merely 'a powerful personality without any intellect or comprehension of the facts'. Therefore Attlee and Bevin frustrated Beveridge's first hopes of a government career.

The Report came about because Beveridge was irrepressible. In December 1940 he managed to join Bevin's mammoth Ministry of Labour (after refusing to take charge of a new welfare department), and Bevin was soon anxious to get rid of him. Through an intermediary, Attlee suggested that Beveridge take a Labour peerage, a proposal that appealed to Beveridge's élitism, but offended his political sentiments. While he was dithering, Bevin appointed someone else to the post he most coveted, Director-General of Manpower, and Beveridge became chairman of a departmental committee set up by Arthur Greenwood to make a survey of all existing social security schemes. It was from this innocuous committee, which Beveridge dominated, that the Report issued. Before its official publication, Beveridge had made another bad reputation for himself in Cabinet circles for criticizing the Government too much, and for courting massive personal publicity for his Report.[89] In addition, Bevin had some specific objections to it[90] and, of all the Labour ministers, only Herbert Morrison in the Cabinet and William Jowitt outside it (as Minister of Reconstruction) could be found to argue for its immediate implementation.[91] Attlee was particularly resentful: 'Beveridge seemed to think the war ought to stop while his plan was put into effect . . . He seemed to imagine he was going to be a leader of the nation or of the House of Commons. Always a mistake to think yourself bigger than you are.'[92] Consequently, a talk Beveridge had with Attlee on 17 March 1943 about the prospect of further government work led nowhere.[93] Furthermore, Beveridge would not be consulted in the domestic policy decisions of the post-war Labour government.[94]

Attlee's opposition to the wartime implementation of the Beveridge Report was not solely due to political considerations or dislike of the Report's author. In 1943 Attlee was thinking in much broader terms.

Particular measures of social reform, however desirable in themselves, had to be fitted into the *general* problem of post-war reconstruction, and it was the Coalition Government's reluctance to move here that concerned him. In June he, Bevin and Morrison addressed a memorandum to the Cabinet on 'The Need for Decisions'. If the Cabinet had been right to refuse to make decisions on piecemeal reforms, such as the Beveridge Plan, the moral could not possibly be to make no decisions at all. In the post-war period, the most urgent need would be to find a home and employment for all those who had served their country. No real progress in shaping Government policy could be made so long as the Cabinet adhered to the principle that decisions involving financial commitments could not be made until the post-war financial position was definitely known. Even when hostilities had ended, it was doubtful if financial forecasting would be much easier. Yet the country would expect physical reconstruction to begin immediately the war was over. Decisions of some kind had to be taken, on the basis of the best available financial estimates, about such items as the use of land, development rights, compensation, water supply, the financing of the building programme, reorganization of transport, heat and power . . . etc. These decisions could not be left until the end of the war.[95] In a personal note to Churchill, Attlee added: 'The changes from peacetime to wartime industry, the alterations in trade relations with foreign countries and with the Empire, to mention only a few factors, necessitate great readjustments and new departures in the economic and industrial life of the nation.'[96]

Attlee's initiative was not without effect. The Treasury, which had previously insisted that no post-war commitments should be made until it was possible to forecast the post-war situation as a whole,[97] began to bend a little. Kingsley Wood, the Chancellor, indicated on 1 July 1943 that, 'greatly daring', he was prepared to let general financial discussions proceed on the basis that in the third year after the war (assumed as 1948) the net national income was likely to reach £7,000 million.[98] Attlee and his colleagues then concentrated on driving a wedge between the Prime Minister and the Treasury. The misunderstandings which had arisen, they insisted, were not between Churchill and the Labour ministers, but between Churchill and the Treasury. They could find no inconsistency between their paper and Churchill's broadcast in March.[99] The argument went on throughout the summer, reaching a new stage when Wood died in September. Churchill's replacement for Wood was not a Conservative Party figure but Sir John Anderson, a non-party civil servant. Similarly, though wanting to make Beaverbrook Minister of Reconstruction, Churchill yielded to Attlee's resistance and appointed Lord Woolton, then a non-party businessman. The most important post on the domestic front, Lord President of the Council, went in September to Attlee himself.[100] He, Bevin, Morrison and Jowitt also became members of the

Cabinet's new Reconstruction Committee. Attlee's tactics were sound: future reform stood a better chance, politically, by being prepared from within the Government. Outside agitation for reform risked, at best, sterility and, at worst, the break-up of the Coalition.

When the reconstruction discussion reached the full War Cabinet, in October 1943, Attlee insisted that unless decisions were taken the Government would lose the power to influence events at the end of the war. He believed there would be a large measure of agreement across Party lines on many issues. Churchill attempted to side-track: he alleged that the Labour Party's 1943 annual conference had stipulated that if the Party called on the Labour ministers to withdraw from the Government after the war, these ministers would resign. Yet the Prime Minister indicated he would consider any matters on which it could be shown that necessary preparations were being held up for lack of Cabinet decisions. Bevin bluntly proposed a political deal: he would accept, for example, the scheme for Agriculture as proposed by the Agricultural Department, if some arrangement could be made about the coal industry. He also thought that electricity and water supply were services that should be brought under some form of national control in the national interest; he added that he was trying to get the TUC to agree to certain post-war labour controls. Clearly, the political log-jam of the inter-war period was breaking down; the top secret Cabinet discussion was broaching the question of the continuation of a National Government after the war and, to judge from the minutes, Churchill had no major objections to the idea. Attlee's consensus was forthcoming, though the time had not yet arrived for detailed policy-making.

Attlee brought the discussion back to reality by emphasizing again that many urgent matters affecting trade and industry raised no Party matters. He resisted an attempt by Lord Cherwell to draw a distinction between those reconstruction plans which had to be carried out and those that were desirable if the means could be found. Attlee argued that the two classes were inseparably connected, giving as an example the building industry, which Churchill himself had just cited as essential. Housing, Attlee pointed out, was largely dependent not only on the location of industry but also on the distribution of purchasing power, which in turn depended on the scheme of social service. He then referred specifically to the items on which decisions were needed – the use of land, development rights and compensation, water supply, the financing of the building programme, reorganization of transport, heat and power, and the budgetary implications of these and similar matters. Churchill, who was now beginning to feel out of his depth, agreed that it would be helpful if a list of four or five major projects could be prepared on which, in the view of the Ministers concerned, decisions were called for but were at present being delayed.[101]

By the next meeting, it became apparent that Attlee and the Labour ministers had won the argument. Churchill was ready with a list of problems for which preparations had to be made to cover the period of transition between the end of the war and the beginning of settled peace; these included demobilization, food, employment, the resumption of the export trade, the restoration of the mercantile marine and the general turnover of industry from war to peace. Food and employment were the crucial issues on which any decisions had to be taken immediately, whether or not they involved legislation and whether or not controversial. He added that there were a number of other matters, such as education, social insurance and rebuilding, about which it should be possible to find a wide measure of agreement; thus plans here too could be made during the war. The War Cabinet expressed its general agreement with the Prime Minister.[102] Other indications of the degree of accord that came to prevail soon followed. Attending the third meeting of the War Cabinet's Reconstruction Committee, Attlee could note that, during a discussion on the cost of maintenance in hospitals for example, there was a general feeling that 'every effort should be made to get rid of the element of individual payment . . . when what was claimed to be a comprehensive health service was being introduced.'[103] In the course of 1944 the Committee held some eighty meetings during which subjects ranging from Acquisition of Land to Workmen's Compensation were discussed.[104]

By the end of the year Churchill had become alarmed at the trend: 'A solid mass of four Socialist politicians of the highest quality and authority, three of whom are in the War Cabinet, all working together as a team, very much dominates this Committee,' he complained in a draft letter to Attlee. 'I feel very much the domination of these Committees by the force and power of your representation, when those members who come out of the Conservative quota are largely non-Party or have little political experience or Party views'.[105] Attlee brushed Churchill's protest aside. Churchill had shown scant respect for his colleagues' views on civil affairs; frequently a long delay supervened before reports of Cabinet Committees could be considered and even then it was exceptional for Churchill to have read them. Half an hour or so would be wasted in explaining what could have been grasped in two or three minutes' reading: 'Not infrequently a phrase catches your eye which gives rise to a disquisition on an interesting point only slightly connected with the subject matter.' Only Attlee could have written to the Prime Minister in such terms.[106]

Churchill was worried lest, in Attlee's words, the socialists were putting something over on him. 'Whenever', Attlee recalled, 'he got wind that a report or memorandum on something outside his ken was coming up, he would get somebody to spy out the land so that he could prepare an onslaught on our "machinations". Winston used to describe this artlessly, as getting a second, highly qualified and objective opinion on the issue. In fact, what he wanted was a hatchet job.' Churchill, however, was unlucky in his choice of hatchet-men. He first chose Lord Cherwell: Attlee countered by suggesting that Churchill put Cherwell on the appropriate committee, after which 'Cherwell saw things very much as we did'.[107] Churchill then tried Beaverbrook and Bracken (the Minister of Information), and only succeeded in drawing a tart response from Attlee: 'When they state their views,' Attlee protested, 'it is obvious that they do not know anything about it. Nevertheless an hour is consumed in listening to their opinions. Time and time again important matters are delayed or passed in accordance with the decision of the Lord Privy Seal [Beaverbrook]. The excuse is given that in him you have the mind of the Conservative Party. With some knowledge of opinion in the Conservative Party in the House as expressed to me on the retirement from and re-entry into the Government of Lord Beaverbrook, I suggest that this view would be indignantly repudiated by the vast majority.'[108] Churchill might have heeded Attlee here; Beaverbrook was not popular among Conservative MPs.[109]

Attlee's irritation with Churchill did not last long: the larger victory over domestic affairs had been won. Attlee also knew that major foreign policy matters remained to be decided and he had a personal interest in seeing these through.[110] There was something else to consider: Churchill would probably win the next election. Another possibility was a continuation of the Coalition after the war, an alternative that Churchill had aired in March 1943. Bevin, Dalton and Morrison were all favourably disposed to the idea at the time,[111] and Attlee almost certainly agreed. In July 1943 Morrison thought that 'the Tories have got the whole political position nicely in their hands.'[112]

But Labour unrest was spreading: many trade union leaders were concerned about the Government's failure to amend the Trade Disputes Act of 1927. Although the NEC rejected in May 1943 a motion by the radicals that the by-election electoral truce be modified in particular circumstances in individual constituencies,[113] the Executive felt obliged, in June, to issue a statement expressing 'great regret' over the Trade Disputes Act matter.[114] Had the Left decided to put its emphasis here it could have caused great embarrassment to the leadership. As it was, while Churchill's popularity as Prime Minister in the Gallup Polls rarely fell below 80 per cent after 1942,[115] the pro-Left vote in by-elections held in 1943 and 1944 increased significantly.[116] The political outlook became perplexing. Morrison, Labour's leading electoral strategist, met the NEC in February 1944 to review the situation. The majority opinion was that the Coalition should continue to the end of the war in Europe but there should be no question of any 'coupon' election so far as Labour was concerned. The awkward question of any future Coalition, its nature and terms, was left over for later consideration.[117]

On 1 March 1944, Attlee circulated his views. He believed that the anti-Government vote in the recent by-elections was due to a number of factors: (1) the accumulation of individual irritations against particular Government actions; (2) the fact that an adverse vote would not effect a change in the Government (thus adding 'a sense of security to the gratification of an impulse'); (3) the attraction for people subjected to many Government regulations of being able to act contrary to the Government's wishes; (4) the fact that a vote for a splinter candidate did not carry with it support for an alternative government; (5) the reluctance of regular supporters of particular parties to vote for natural enemies; and finally, the poor quality of official candidates in many instances. He thought that as the war proceeded all these reasons would grow stronger and the position of the politically minded section of the population would become more difficult. This argument applied particularly to Labour supporters because 'They know the swing of the pendulum is in their direction and *there is undoubtedly a leftward swing, especially in regard to post war problems* [my emphasis]; and as the majority of Government members were non-Labour it was particularly hard for [Labour supporters] to accept it as their Government.' Thoughtful Labourites also saw in the continuation of the electoral truce a danger to established political parties, and a drift away from parties would not express effectively the political thought of the day. Attlee found a parallel here with the failure of organized religious bodies to attract the religious impulse of the younger generation. He noted that Churchill's attempt to meet the by-election difficulties by personal intervention and by urging all parties in the Coalition to greater activity on behalf of the Government had had the opposite effect. Thus the Labour demand for loosening, not tightening the truce, he concluded, stemmed not merely from a partisan point of view but from regard to the general political life of the country, even though Labour was still strongly convinced of the need for a continuation of the Coalition at least until the defeat of Germany. This demand was likely to take the form of asking that all Ministers refrain from taking part in by-elections and of asking for a free fight between various sections supporting the Government and any outsiders who liked to join in.

Having thus summarized the case for loosening the political truce Attlee then tackled the question: What would be the effect of such a demand? On the positive side it would restore the main parties to full activity and remove the sense of frustration. It would bring the electors face to face with rival political theories and programmes for the future, backed by responsible parties, with the restraints thus imposed, as against the irresponsibility of independents: and it would make both parties more careful in their choice of candidates. On the other hand a demand for freely-contested elections would tend to break the unity of the Government and undermine national unity. Ministers would tend to consider war and post-war problems from the angle of immediate political advantage. Auctioneering between the parties on such matters as soldiers' pay and old age pensions would be stimulated. With Ministers out of the fight, parties would tend to invite critics rather than Government supporters to speak and the critics would take the limelight away from the gagged Ministers. There would be a risk of independents of Left or Right extremes slipping in through the disarray in the Government's ranks.

Attlee left no doubt that he valued the preservation of the national consensus, as represented by the Coalition, more than the possibility of short-term political gain. Indeed, the more he considered the extent of the problems that any post-war government would have to face, the more convinced he became that the Coalition should be continued. Ministers should participate in by-elections.[118] He told Dalton privately on 20 April 1944 that the best line about the election at the annual conference would be one of no change in the electoral truce. Labour should fight the first election after the defeat of Germany, but 'it would be a great mistake for this election to come too quickly'.[119] In July 1944, Attlee thought that the annual conference ought to be postponed and that the Flying Bomb offered a good pretext. He and Dalton agreed that it would be much the best if there were no election for six months after the German surrender and only then if they could separate from the Tories without too fierce a quarrel.[120] Attlee was particularly worried that not only Churchill, but also Labour's left wing might cause Labour to lose the election. A large number of people were now property owners of one sort or another, he wrote in a draft of a speech probably intended for an extremely restricted executive Labour group in early 1945: 'In face of this it is time that the Labour Party ceased to mouth Marxian shibboleths about the proletariat having nothing to lose but their chains.' The Party should state in its election manifesto with the utmost emphasis that it would stand absolutely against inflation: 'A silly speech by someone like Aneurin Bevan might easily be used to stampede the electors from Labour.'[121] Attlee's calculation was that the longer the wartime consensus was maintained, the more Labour stood to gain.

Following an NEC discussion in April, the Party's General Secretary, J. S. Middleton, composed a draft paragraph on 'Government and Party Policy'. Something had to be said on the topic in the Labour Party's Annual Report and he invited individual comments from NEC members by return post. His draft was an implicit criticism of Attlee's analysis in March. It referred to the 1942 Labour statement on *The Old World and the New Society* which had declared that it was urgent to lay the foundations of a new social order before the end of the war, especially in view of the 1914–18 experience. Otherwise, there was a grave danger that the peace would be lost a second time. Middleton's draft noted that even though certain measures had been taken, there was still a big gap between Labour's principles and the Coalition Government's policy. Attlee replied that the draft paragraph looked very unrealistic to him. 'No one who acclaimed *The Old World and the New Society*', he added, 'expected that in two years a completely Socialist world or even a completely Socialist Britain would be established . . .' To him, the effect of the draft paragraph was that if Labour continued in an all-Party Government until victory was won they were deliberately inviting a disaster of the first magnitude. 'So what?' Attlee asked. 'The logical answer would be that we must immediately leave the Government and try to get a Socialist majority at the next election,' but this was contrary to the unanimous view of the Executive. The kind of paragraph required was an affirmation of socialist faith coupled with a realization that, while the all-Party Government continued, planning for the interim period had to be based on compromise. '*We might even welcome what has been and is being done*,' he added, '*as showing the influence of the Labour Movement and of the practicality of our ideas*, but perhaps that would be asking for too much.'[122]

The Party's annual conference in 1944 was postponed to December, but the gulf between the leadership and the rank-and-file activists increased as a result, despite the NEC's announcement, on 7 October 1944, that Labour would fight the next election (whenever it came) as an independent party. The straw that broke the camel's back was not a domestic issue. The Prime Minister's handling of the situation in Greece aroused the ire not only of the Left but also of a large segment of liberal opinion.[123] It resulted in a recrudescence of anti-Churchill feeling in the Labour Party and it was in vain that Bevin attempted to explain to the annual conference that the decision about Greece had been a Cabinet decision. Aneurin Bevan made hay with the issue and saw himself elected to the NEC only months after that body had almost expelled him from the Party.[124] Laski again headed the poll in the constituency section. An NEC resolution referring to 'the transfer to the State of power to direct the policy of our main industries, services and financial institutions' that made no mention of nationalization was defeated.[125]

Shortly afterwards, there were increasing clashes along party lines in the Cabinet over reconstruction: 'the only disagreements', Attlee recalled, 'came towards the end when we were considering post-war problems . . .'[126] Stafford Cripps was readmitted to the Party in February 1945. Some Labour ministers, though not Attlee, thought it prudent to safeguard their political positions. Bevin made a public speech in April attacking the Tories. This upset Churchill[127] who, after Roosevelt's death on 12 April, was worried by the prospect of a new crisis in Europe. 'If there is going to be trouble of this kind' (between Russia and the West), he wrote to Eden, 'the support of men like Attlee, Bevin, Morrison and George Hall is indispensable to the National presentation of the case.' Churchill now indicated that he had changed his mind since October 1944, when he had made a formal statement to the effect that it would be wrong to continue Parliament beyond the period of the German war.[128] In the event of an international crisis, he told Eden, 'I should on no account agree to an Election in October, but simply say that we must prolong our joint tenure.'[129]

Attlee shared Churchill's concern about developments in Europe: 'The Russians', he told Dalton on 16 May 1945, 'are behaving in a perfectly bloody way, telling us nothing, but setting up Puppet Governments all over Europe as far west as they can.'[130] Two days later, Churchill formally wrote to the leaders of the Labour and Liberal Parties, proposing a continuation of the Coalition until after the defeat of Japan, or else there would have to be an immediate election. Attlee saw him privately and persuaded him to include a paragraph in his letter, which was destined for publication, about social security and full employment:[131] whatever happened, he wanted to ensure his consensus. The same day, 18 May 1945, Attlee told Bevin and Dalton (again) that he 'was inclined to favour going on'. They replied that they saw the force of the argument but did not think the Conference would agree.[132] They joined Attlee in arguing for acceptance of Churchill's offer to the NEC but were outvoted. Morrison, who had also changed his mind, took the lead in rejecting the offer.[133] When he replied to Churchill on 21 May, Attlee underlined that it was 'precisely on the problems of reconstruction of the economic life of the country that Party differences are most acute.' The Labour ministers resigned before the end of May, and the elections were called for July. Churchill certainly could have been more accommodating but Attlee and most of his colleagues were prepared until the last moment to stay on until the autumn, to deal with the immediate international questions.[134] In effect, the Coalition ended as it had begun – with an accord on international policy.

IX

No Mistake This Time

Contrary to what is often thought, British foreign policy during the Second World War was made by a Coalition and not by an individual.[1] Final determination of British initiatives had, in any case, to wait upon Allied agreement – which in itself limited Churchill's impact. His practice of 'personal diplomacy', however, and perhaps even more his account of it, has tended to obscure the War Cabinet's function in the formulation of policy. Churchill's influence was greatest between 1940 and 1943, when military exigencies mattered more than politics. In the last years of the war, Attlee took at least an equal part in policy-making. The key issue was Germany, and it was here that Attlee's role was pivotal. Just as the term 'Attlee's consensus' has been given to the accord over domestic affairs, so too did the British plan for Germany come to be known as the 'Attlee plan'.[2] The plan, moreover, was accepted by the US and USSR, and formed the basis of the post-war European settlement.

Attlee's interest in and, indeed, preoccupation with Germany owed much to the fact that during the war he drastically altered his views on the subject. At first, he shared the mainstream Labour opinion that the advent of a second war with Germany in less than a generation was primarily Hitler's fault. It was a war into which the Germans, no less than the British, had been forced against their wills. A *Message to the German People* from the NCL on 25 August 1939 reiterated that Labour believed it was not the German people who wanted war, only a handful of their rulers.[3] Even the Polish *débâcle* did not immediately affect this attitude. Socialist 'principle' insisted on the absolute necessity of distinguishing at any given moment between a particular people or nation and the character of its government. Applied, or rather, re-applied after the First

World War, the principle had led directly to a denunciation of the Versailles Treaties. Subsequently, though Nazi methods of overturning those treaties were condemned, the validity of certain German grievances appropriated by the Nazis was not challenged. Labour was never particularly pro-German,[4] but certainly held the view that a non-Nazi Germany was fully entitled to play a part in the shaping of Europe. During the war this view was virtually abandoned. The extent of the change in Attlee's attitude may be gathered from a remark he made to Dalton in January 1943: 'We must make no mistake this time,' he said, 'in rendering Germany unable to repeat her aggressions.' The British had been too lenient with her last time, though he had not thought so then.[5]

Given the manifest failure of Chamberlain's foreign policy, the Labour Party as a whole was obliged to agree by September 1939 that the international enemy was more important than the domestic one. Individually and collectively the Labour reaction to the British declaration of war was one of relief.[6] But this rather curious reaction was compounded of many elements, including the hope that the declaration itself would resolve the Nazi problem. A revolution inside Germany would suffice for the bloodletting.[7] Attlee, however, seems to have had a very early premonition that the war would have to be fought. He certainly had no illusions as to the nature or menace of the Nazi regime. While his deputy, Arthur Greenwood, did not hesitate to write in the *Daily Herald* that the invasion of Poland by the USSR could not be justified,[8] Attlee remained silent for a period not absolutely warranted by his sickness and convalescence. And when, in October, he addressed the Commons, he was noticeably more circumspect about the international situation than other Party leaders had been. 'The fact that Poland has been overrun,' he said, 'is not different from the fact that all of Belgium was overrun in the last war . . . Poland will rise again.' Instead of dwelling on the Russian angle, Attlee preferred to lambast the Nazi regime which was the fundamental cause of the war – a war that had begun long before there was any formal declaration. Deeds, and not words, would be required before there could be any substantial basis for peace, he concluded.[9]

Later in October he underlined that there were three essential difficulties in dealing with what had been called Herr Hitler's peace proposals: firstly, they had been made 'by a man whose word is utterly worthless'; secondly, they had been made after brutal and unprovoked aggression; and thirdly, there was no indication of any change of heart or mind on which hopes for the future could be founded. It was therefore impossible for anyone to discuss usefully the detailed terms of a European settlement. All that could be done was to reaffirm certain basic principles that Labour had laid down long ago. A world that was subject at all times to violence was unendurable: there had to be a new world based on the rule of law and, in particular, a Europe in which the rights of all nations were recognized. Labour sought no Carthaginian peace, but 'a more closely co-ordinated Europe'; Labour wanted disarmament, but disarmament was not possible except in exchange for really effective measures for collective defence. The choice before the German people was '... not of being defeated in war and disappearing as effective members of the European comity of nations. They have the choice of stopping this war, they have the choice of contributing to a great Europe ... But until we get people on whose word we can rely we must with resolution pursue this struggle.'[10]

He had to take into account the fact that there were several opinions within his Party on the international situation. Inside Parliament, the pacifists continued to be over-represented; they may have been down, they were not quite out. Outside Parliament, the left-wingers voiced certain doubts as to the form the war might take, the aims for which it would be fought and its possible outcome. Arguments that the 'war' would end with a German revolution readily allied themselves to the old suspicions regarding British imperialism. Some left-wingers feared that an attempt might be made to turn the war against the Soviet Union. All, both despite and because of the Nazi-Soviet Pact, insisted that the conflict had to be seen in terms that transcended nationalism and imperialism. There was another angle: as Kingsley Martin, the editor of the *New Statesman*, put it to Harold Nicolson, 'We cannot possibly beat both Russia and Germany.'[11]

The anti-Soviet diatribes of the Labour hierarchy (Attlee excluded) undoubtedly exacerbated the Party's international discussions. While the NEC struggled to formulate a generally acceptable position, it fell to Attlee to say *something*. Guided but not bound by a report emanating from Labour's sub-committee on International Affairs, his statement on 8 November 1939 was designed mainly to rally left-wing opinion around the leadership. Although his statement contained nothing new, it was evident that Attlee ruled out any dealing with the Nazis, and there was no mention of Germany's frontiers. The main points were:

1 No dictated peace, revenge or punishment, though restitution to victims of aggression would have to be made.
2 National self-determination.
3 Abandonment of aggression and armed forces.
4 Recognition of religious, racial and national minorities.
5 Creation of an international authority: 'Europe must federate,' said Attlee, 'or perish.'
6 Abandonment of imperialism, and equal access by all nations to markets and raw materials.[12]

Russia's invasion of Finland then provoked what one historian has called 'hysteria in political circles'.[13] Stalin and the USSR were denounced in the most vitriolic terms.[14] There was a danger that the Party would be so far carried away by its righteous indignation on behalf of Finland as to be sidetracked from the attention which, in Attlee's view, had to be paid to Nazi Germany. He took no part in the public Labour rebukes of Russia, which carried the more or less direct implication that Britain should participate actively on the Finnish side. When the NCL decided that a Labour team should be sent to examine the situation in Finland, Attlee's first choice was Dalton, whose anti-German views took precedence over all others. And even though Dalton, understandably, refused such a political hot potato,[15] the only result of the visit was the launching of a joint TUC and Labour appeal to bolster the Party's Aid to Finland Fund. Nor did a 'depressing' Paris meeting with French Socialists in February 1940 cause either Attlee or Dalton to lose sight of the essential priority. A joint resolution did refer to Stalin as 'Hitler's accomplice', but at a follow-up meeting of the Labour and Socialist International in Brussels, Dalton went out of his way to restrain Léon Blum, the French leader. Blum 'was for helping the Finns at all costs, even though this led to war with Russia'; Dalton insisted that he had no mandate for that.[16] Attlee's article on 21 February 1940 in the *Daily Herald* was directed against *British* communists. In early April an editorial in the same paper pointedly commented: 'In wartime a wise nation does not look for extra enemies. We are fighting Hitler.'[17]

In the meantime the Labour hierarchy was still trying to compose an official pronouncement on the war. Attlee would not vote for the document that the NEC considered at a special meeting on 6 February 1940. According to Dalton, Attlee considered that there was too much about Germany and France in the proposals; in particular Attlee had strong reservations about a phrase stating that, in resistance to any potential German aggression, the British and French in the future 'must be not merely allies, but brothers for all time'.[18] He was no doubt troubled about the potential effect of such phrases on left-wing opinion. Presumably in view of his abstention, the document was revised (by Morrison, Dalton and Laski) and published on 9 February 1940 as *Labour, The War and The Peace*. The result was something of a mish-mash. The overthrow of the 'Hitler system in Germany' was deemed essential to the achievement of Labour's domestic and foreign policies, though any attempt to keep Germany an outcast after the war would fail. The French claim to security had to be reconciled with the German claim to equality. The British Government's earlier clumsiness in its relations with the Soviet Union was condemned, but this could not excuse the Russian Government's Pact with the Nazis or its unprovoked attack on Finland. The extinction of the free Finnish democracy would be regarded as an 'intolerable disaster for civilization', though nothing was said about Russo-Finnish frontiers. As regards Germany, Labour believed the most far-sighted and least dangerous policy would be to win the co-operation, as an equal partner, of a Germany 'governed by a political system whose needs and aims run parallel with ours'. Labour was opposed to any attempt from outside to break up Germany, yet the Party recognized that though Hitler and his system had prepared and started the war, he could not continue if the Germans ceased to support him. Nor should the Allies enter into peace negotiations unless it be with a German government which had actually performed, not merely promised, certain acts of restitution, including withdrawal from Poland and Czechoslovakia.

Reluctant as he had been to associate himself with some of the details, Attlee had no fault to find with the most significant part of the statement. The Labour hierarchy now emphasized its acceptance of the fact that the war would have to be fought. 'Victory is our immediate task,' the statement concluded, '. . . either by arms or economic pressure or, better still, by a victory of the German people over the Hitler regime.' The sting was in the tail: 'Victory must come to the *arms* [my italics] of Britain, France and their allies.'[19] Attlee made it clear from February 1940 on that he had no serious hope or belief that a German revolution would contribute substantially to that victory. Both in and out of the Commons Attlee's message was 'that Hitler and his gangsters have – by the most brutal measures – established a very strong hold on the German people'.[20] Hitler's military and economic machine could only be defeated by a more vigorous and efficient organization of the British war effort, including a small War Cabinet composed of ministers without departmental responsibilities.[21] In April, Labour agreed to participate with members of the other two parties in support of the war effort, though Attlee had no thought of going back on the Party's rejection of Chamberlain's offer at the beginning of the war to join the Government.[22]

Teaming up with Winston Churchill in May 1940 was a different matter; Churchill wanted to get on with the war and, in Attlee's judgment, was better qualified than any other man to do it. Proof of Churchill's attitude was soon forthcoming. On 26 May the Coalition's War Cabinet was given an assessment by the Chiefs of Staff of Britain's chances of survival if France collapsed. The crux of the situation was air superiority. To achieve it the Germans would have to knock out the RAF and the aviation factories. German success would thus depend partly on the morale of the workpeople and their determination to stand up to wholesale bombing. It was on the morale factor that Attlee and Churchill were particularly at one, as the following Cabinet meetings revealed. The immediate subject before the War Cabinet on 27 and 28 May was a plea from the French Premier, Reynaud, for a fresh appeal to Mussolini, both through Roosevelt and directly by Britain and France. This time the bait was to be specific territorial concessions in the Mediterranean, which for Britain would have meant the offer of Malta and Gibraltar. Chamberlain, though doubtful of success, wanted to send Reynaud a soft answer, not a blank refusal, so as to keep the French in a good mood. Attlee said that the suggested approach would be very damaging to British morale; he believed that if Britain complied with the French request it would be impossible to rally the British people. Churchill came through loud and clear; even if the worst came to the worst, 'it would not be a bad thing for this country to go down fighting for the other countries that had been overcome by the Nazi tyranny'. Halifax was alarmed by Churchill's fight to the finish attitude,[23] but it was exactly what Attlee had anticipated.

As a member of the War Cabinet and, particularly, as deputy chairman of the Defence Committee, Attlee was exceedingly well placed to observe the way in which Churchill got on with the war. He very much appreciated how Churchill, 'an ex-soldier who had fought with weapons in his hand',[24] compelled the respect of the generals. Not that there were any major disagreements between the politicians and the military chiefs in the Second World War. The generals, in Attlee's opinion, were much more intelligent than their predecessors: 'We always accepted their professional advice. Even Winston did after a struggle. We never moved on a professional matter against them.' Many of those in the Government, Attlee recalled, 'had served in war so we understood something about it, understood the military mind.'[25] Nevertheless, as an old front-line soldier, Attlee could take a certain pleasure in the wrangles between Churchill and the military heads that did occur: 'you needed someone to prod the Chiefs of Staff ... it was a great advantage for someone to be there driving them all the time. Your advisers always tend to say "It can't be done", and it's as well to have someone who'll tell them it can.'[26] He would pay tribute afterwards to Churchill's success in solving 'the deadly problem of civilian-versus-generals in wartime'.

At the same time, he did not overrate the Prime Minister's military abilities; he considered Churchill 'the greatest leader in war this country had ever known,' but 'not the greatest warrior'.[27] What Winston required was 'some strong people around him saying "Don't be a fool over this"'.[28] In the Chief of Staff, Alanbrooke, Attlee believed that the British had such a man, 'the best strategic brain on our side'[29] and 'one of the three great soldier-statesmen of the Second World War'.[30] Indeed, to judge by his sharp post-war appreciations of the leading military figures, English and American,[31] Attlee followed the military mind in its higher manifestations with the same degree of detachment and eye for detail that he had brought to his personal experiences in 1914–18.[32] He thought, for example, that Eisenhower was a poor strategist, though he did not blame him entirely: 'his refusal to push on to Berlin ... was really attributable to American delusions about Russia which Eisenhower, though he shared them, did not create. The Americans were innocents abroad.'[33]

Attlee carried his aggressive attitude towards Nazi Germany into the

War Cabinet; what he wanted to see, he announced at once, was the bombing of Germany.[34] Of course, when France had fallen the question of how victory might eventually be won required rather more than martial enthusiasm. Attlee quickly turned his attention to the efficiency of the intelligence services; he pressed Churchill, in November 1940, to have someone conduct a thorough review of the organization, which was done.[35] He ensured that Dalton got a Special Operations Executive with the object of making the enemy uncomfortable by every means: 'strikes, propaganda, terrorism, riots, boycott and bribery'.[36] For a brief period, as we have seen, he toyed with the notion that a statement on war aims would contribute to the war effort. Attlee did not think, however, that Churchill's extraordinary appointment of Sir Stafford Cripps as Ambassador to Moscow would produce much result: though a useful idea, Attlee recalled later, he did not 'kid himself that our left-winger would have any more influence on Uncle Joe than a right-winger'.[37] But the British had to try anything; a story was soon circulating about the Chief Rabbi of Jerusalem's supposed reply to the question of who would win the war: 'I think, on the whole, the British,' he answered, 'either naturally or miraculously.' Pressed to be more explicit, the learned man added: 'They might win by the help of God, which would be natural, or by their own efforts, which would be miraculous.'[38]

British strategic options were extremely limited. The course followed by Churchill would probably have been adopted by any other Prime Minister. One reason why Attlee in 1942, the war's most difficult year, told the Commons that it was 'quite impossible to take away from the Prime Minister the major responsibility of advising the Cabinet of decisions on strategy'[39] was that he entirely agreed with those decisions. When Hitler turned east, Attlee at first shared the prevailing doubts as to whether Russia could withstand a German attack 'of the blitzkreig variety which had overcome the great French army within a month'.[40] He was convinced that launching a second front in 1942 was impossible. True, the British had got the Americans to agree to a policy of 'Germany First', originally at the level of staff talks between January and March 1941;[41] this was confirmed at the top-level Arcadia Conference held in Washington between December 1941 and January 1942.[42] Attlee had had no objections to the decision, in April 1942, that preparations for military operations in Europe should go ahead without delay.[43] But this decision was in the nature of a temporary obeisance to American views. Earlier that month, Attlee was present as a member of the Defence Committee which had heard the Americans present their plan for a second front. Churchill accepted it, subject to one reservation – the defence of India and the Middle East, and Attlee went out of his way to indicate his accord. The plan, he said, had ushered in a new phase of the war. Hitherto they had been hanging on to the best of their ability; now the time had arrived to wrest the initiative from the enemy. But, he insisted, they had great responsibilities in other parts of the world; it was entirely right that they should safeguard these while concentrating the main striking force in the European theatre.[44]

In fact, a vital British strategic consensus was arrived at in the spring of 1942 and received formal confirmation by the Cabinet in June during Molotov's visit to London. It was decided that there would be no substantial landing in France that year unless (a) it was to be permanent, and (b) the Germans had been previously demoralized by failure against Russia.[45] Any landing in Europe to 'help' the Russians would thus depend upon a prior Russian victory. The decision led directly, though not perhaps inevitably, to the postponement of the second front and to the eventual Anglo-American adoption of a 'Mediterranean strategy'. This so-called 'indirect approach' had the strongest appeal to the veteran of the First World War. Attlee supported Churchill's more controversial idea 'of exploiting our success in Africa and of striking at what he called the soft underbelly of the Axis powers . . . It was entirely in line with the strategic lessons of our past.'[46] He also approved the Alanbrooke-Montgomery plan, once the second front was opened, of a concentrated drive for Berlin, instead of Eisenhower's wider, more gradual advance into Germany.

Whether the Americans – in this or other strategic preferences – were as politically innocent abroad as Attlee in typical English fashion believed, is a matter of conjecture. But they certainly had difficulties in the creation of an efficient foreign-policy-making apparatus: too much, it can be argued, devolved upon the President. This was not the case with Churchill: in Britain all important decisions were taken or approved by a minuscule War Cabinet, in which Attlee's contributions on German policy were to be considerable.

His efforts here set him even more at variance with his Party's radicals than his tactics on social reform. Between 1941 and 1943, Labour was exercised by what Aneurin Bevan identified as a great debate centring on the question, '. . . are we fighting the German people or the Nazis?'[47] From one angle the debate can be seen as a reaction to the frustrated demand for war aims, a demand that the pronouncement of the Atlantic Charter did little to satisfy.[48] But essentially it reflected the theoretical controversy that had dogged the Party for so long over the true nature of a socialist foreign policy. Should or could a Nazi-free Germany be involved in the peace settlement? The longer the war lasted the less likely *and* the less desirable such a consummation appeared to those who, like Attlee, were responsible for getting on with the war.

The continuation of the war, and Labour's active part in its prosecution, had an immediate impact on one element in the purest socialist tradition. In January 1940, the Party's Secretary and National Agent wrote to the constituency organizations that no attacks were to be made on official Party candidates or policy by pacifist members. Pacifists would be treated with the utmost consideration, provided (essentially) they kept their views to themselves.[49] Between the wars – due to the general condemnation of First World War politics, abhorrence of the bloodbath and a widely-held conviction that any repetition would be worse – the pacifist influence had been a strong one. The crushing of the hope that the 'war' in Europe might take the form of an internal German revolution brought this era in Labour politics to an end – symbolized by George Lansbury's death on 7 May 1940.

For the Left the unkindest cut of all was the transformation of Labour's internationalism into open anti-German sentiments. Before the end of 1941, Bevin was writing in the *Daily Herald* that even if the British got rid of Hitler, Goering and others, that did not end the German problem: 'It was Prussian militarism . . . that had to be got rid of from Europe for all time.'[50] In private, Hugh Dalton was quite frank. From the very beginning of the war he desired to see it terminate with a drastic and permanent reduction in the actual and potential power of Germany. 'Others believe,' he confided to his diary in October 1939, 'that there is always a "good old Germany" just around the corner. They hope for just a small change, a Government of Generals, or even a Monarchist restoration, and then all danger will be past. This, too, is an illusion. There is no "good old Germany" just around the corner.' The other side of the European picture concerned Russia, but Dalton – in a very different way from the Left – took a sanguine view. The Russians, he believed, 'had long since passed from Communism . . . had become first Nationalists and now Imperialists', but this did not trouble him. 'Even supposing that the Red Army overran, or got control of, all Poland, part of Germany and the Czech and Slovak lands,' he continued in a remarkable forecast of what was to come, 'so that there emerged a Polish, a German, a Slovak and a Czech Soviet Socialist Republic, I do not feel that this would be a stable constellation, or that it could be run from Moscow. But I would greatly prefer a development of that kind to the continuance of Hitler Germany with its Protectorates.' However, it was 'much too soon to say this, or anything like this in public . . .'[51]

By the following year Dalton felt able to publish a book in which he argued that 'for the last seventy years Germany has been the most regular and the most formidable trouble-maker in Europe.' Nazism, he insisted, was no isolated development: 'More rubbish about "racialism" had been talked, and taught, in Germany than anywhere else, long before this specially poisonous brand of current Nazi nonsense.'[52] Officially, Labour continued to make a distinction between Nazis and German workers until 1942. But in November of that year, Dalton noted with satisfaction that Attlee 'would take away all machine tools from Germany and distribute them among her victims, Poles, Czechs, Russians, etc.'[53] When the almost unbelievable details of the Nazi persecution of the Jews began to be known, the NEC warned (in January 1943) that 'such an unparalleled and stupendous act of barbarism would always be associated with the name of modern Germany.'[54]

The initial British successes in the Western Desert towards the end of 1942, closely followed by the vastly more important Russian victories at Stalingrad and Kursk-Orel, indicated that the time had arrived to move from sentiment to policy-making. The war had already proved that Britain and France together were no match for Germany; thus the logical aim of an all-out war policy was to make a decisive reduction in German power – potential as well as actual. What then would become of Europe? In May 1943 Churchill seized on the idea that Stalin's abolition of the Comintern that month might offer some hope for a mutual agreement with the USSR. He was especially anxious to sound out his Labour ministers for, though thinking the news 'very fine', he wondered if there might be a snag. In any case he wanted to send Stalin a telegram. Attlee's mistrust of Russia had not changed in the slightest. He instantly replied to Churchill, who was in Washington, that the Cabinet unanimously considered that it would be a mistake to send a telegram or make any public comment.[55] Attlee did not share the opinion, prevalent especially in Foreign Office circles and on Labour's left wing, that there was a realistic possibility of post-war co-operation with Stalinist Russia. His first impulse had been to resist the Foreign Office advice that, in order to obtain Russian goodwill, Britain should recognize Soviet claims in Eastern Europe during the war.[56] Only the consequences of Britain's strictly limited strategic role eventually persuaded him otherwise – a victorious Russia would hardly be content with anything less than the frontiers she possessed when Germany attacked her. From November 1941, therefore, Attlee argued that the key to the post-war European situation was to get the Americans actively involved in any peace settlement: his US visit that month convinced him that this possibility did exist and that the British should do everything to encourage it.[57]

However, he and the other members of the War Cabinet had also to take into consideration the possibility that the Americans would refuse, which would mean no European balance of power for some time after the war. Should the Americans not provide any forces for post-war Europe, then the burden would fall on the British. This would leave the Americans free to concentrate their forces in the East which would, in Attlee's view, disrupt the Commonwealth, weaken the Dominions and increase the risk of Big Power rivalry. Thus by July 1943 he concluded that '. . . in the interests of the solidarity of the British Commonwealth we should hesitate again to enter, *without the U.S.* [Attlee's emphasis], into any military guarantees of the Locarno type, i.e. a Continental obligation, not shared by the Dominions.'[58] The impact of air power, especially the use of the Flying Bomb, caused him to moderate this view a year later. In 1943, as he began to contemplate the imponderables of the post-war situation, he stressed the importance of the British Commonwealth as a potential stabilizing factor. 'I take it to be a fundamental assumption,' he wrote to his Cabinet colleagues on 15 June, 'that whatever post-war international organization is established, it will be our aim to maintain the British Commonwealth as an international entity, recognized as such by foreign countries, in particular by the U.S. and the Soviet Union.'[59]

Another obvious factor in the post-war European riddle would be the role of France. During his visit to the US in May 1943, Churchill also asked the Cabinet to consider the elimination of de Gaulle as a political force, probably in deference to the President's strong personal views. Now in July 1940 Attlee had described de Gaulle and his entourage as practically fascist;[60] and in October of the same year he had suggested to Halifax, the Foreign Secretary, that reactionary elements in the governments-in-exile and amongst the Free French should make way for left-wing elements more solidly welded to democratic ideals.[61] But as David Stafford has pointed out, 'the formal and legal commitments accepted by the British government to recognize the exiled groups in London as the legitimate governments of Europe [were] commitments which in the aftermath of Dunkirk it would have been unthinkable not to give ...'[62] It also became clear that even if European resistance movements were largely left wing, anything the British could do to help them depended on some minimal co-operation from the governments-in-exile.[63] This applied to de Gaulle, as well as to the legally recognized governments. When it became evident that the Free French movement led by de Gaulle was the most effective centre of French resistance and that his entourage had been widened, Attlee decided to support him – and this despite Churchill's personal antagonism to the French leader and Roosevelt's vehement and sustained pressure on the Prime Minister to get rid of him. Towards the end of 1941, for instance, de Gaulle succeeded in rallying the support of the inhabitants of St Pierre and Miquelon; Churchill was in Washington and received the weight of American anti- de Gaulle opinion. Attlee telegraphed Churchill in January that the Cabinet felt British public opinion would not understand why de Gaulle was not allowed to occupy French territory which welcomed him. There should be no appeasement of Vichy, whatever the American view.[64]

Subsequently, the Labour ministers' support of a strong France in the future, represented in the interim by de Gaulle, became a basic feature of their European policy. The Cabinet's response to Churchill's request in 1943 to consider the elimination of de Gaulle was an unequivocal no, with Attlee, Bevin and Morrison in the vanguard.[65] A year later, a squabble arose with the Americans about whom Eisenhower was to deal with in France. Attlee wrote frankly to Eden: 'I agree with you in feeling considerable anxiety over the French situation. We have a much bigger stake in France than the USA ... The French are always difficult and never more so when they owe gratitude to others for their deliverance as we saw after the last war. I do not think the President has any real understanding of the French temperament ... nor do I think that his attitude is dictated by a zeal for democracy ... This did not prevent him from running Darlan and afterwards Giraud. I am very sensible how much we owe to the President but this should not lead us to agree to a mistaken policy ... We are the only people in the set up who can speak as Europeans concerned with the future of Europe.'[66] Attlee was very much in favour of de Gaulle's first visit to the liberated French territory in mid-June 1944,[67] which settled the question of de Gaulle's standing in France in a decisive manner.

The new direction that the war took in 1943, coupled with the American announcement at the beginning of the year of the unconditional surrender doctrine, lent a fresh impetus and urgency to the making of policy for Germany. Eden had preceded Churchill to Washington in order to assess American opinion on the matter and when he returned the Cabinet had been given much food for thought. American opinion seemed to favour a joint occupation in order to avoid a division resulting in spheres of influence. But the President favoured dismemberment as the only safe solution of the German problem and Sumner Welles, his influential Under-Secretary of State, was arguing that, for the purposes of military occupation, plans should be devised to make separate divisions among the separate commands corresponding broadly to the areas into which Greater Germany might be broken up. Eden was impressed by Welles's argument,[68] as Attlee would be.

In July 1943, Attlee was also troubled by the failure to specify what kind of German authority the British should or should not treat with. Everyone agreed that there should be no dealing with the Nazis, but Attlee wanted to avoid a repetition of what, in his opinion, had happened after the last war: first the Kaiser had been made the scapegoat for Germany, and then the democratic parties had been made the scapegoat for Versailles – leaving 'the real aggressive elements' untouched. He thought primarily of the Prussian Junker class, with its strong roots in the Reichswehr, and the Civil Service, allied to the masters of heavy industry. There were also aggressive factions in southern Germany, especially in Bavaria. How far these had used the Nazis, or had been used by them, might be open to debate, but it was not out of the question that they might liquidate Hitler and his circle (an unconscious forecast of the July 1944 plot), and come forward as the only body which could save central Europe from anarchy. Last time these forces had maintained themselves because of the Allies' fear of Bolshevism. Attlee insisted that this must not happen again. The Prussian virus had to be eradicated and there was no reason why the big industrial combines should be allowed to continue. It could be, Attlee speculated, that the Russians, Czechs and Poles would liquidate the Junkers, or even that the Germans themselves would deal with some of the aggressive elements. But he was most emphatic that 'very positive action will have to be taken by the victorious Powers if there is to be a new orientation of the German nation'. Neither the encouragement of particularist tendencies, nor a cordon sanitaire, nor the prohibition of aircraft or aircraft factories would suffice. The German industries should be controlled in the interests of Europe and operated in the interests of Central and South-Eastern Europe, though German workers could be permitted good conditions. German officials, however, could not be left in control.[69] Like the Labour left-wingers, Attlee also wanted to see a German 'revolution'; but in his case it was to be one imposed from the top and from outside. He had completely lost any confidence in 'the other Germans': there was no doubt in his mind now that Germany was a 'guilty nation', and would have to be treated accordingly.

The sum of what Attlee was saying in the summer of 1943 may be expressed as follows: Germany had to undergo a thorough social, political and economic change, but this would result in a power vacuum in Europe. Russia would predominate unless the British committed themselves to redressing the balance. If the British did this, the Commonwealth would be endangered by American ambitions. If the choice were between a balanced Europe and a Commonwealth, Attlee preferred to opt for the Commonwealth, particularly in an age of air power which left the homeland vulnerable. The only satisfactory solution would be to persuade the Americans to provide forces for Europe. In that case, a balance of power could be obtained there and, at the same time, the Imperial or Commonwealth connection could be maintained. Having expressed such views, Attlee found himself in very short order chairman of the three sub-committees of the War Cabinet which dealt with the formation of British post-war policy. These committees varied in duration, but each made important decisions.

An *ad hoc* body on Armistice Terms met only once, on 21 July 1943, to consider a single problem: how to exclude the Soviet Union from any significant participation in the conclusion of the Italian surrender while avoiding giving the Russians a pretext to act unilaterally in regard to Finland, Rumania, Hungary and possibly even Germany in the event of a sudden collapse. Attlee had no fault to find with this aim; his sole recorded remark was to draw attention to a paragraph in the draft proclamation to the Italian people, suggesting that it gave the impression that the Fascists might be left in power. When he had been reassured about this – another wording would be recommended instead – the committee proceeded to define the extent to which Russian participation would be acceptable: the Russians would have to be consulted in a general way, but not about the particular Italian authority with whom a surrender agreement should be signed, nor about the details of such an agreement.[70] Brushing aside Stalin's formal protests, the War Cabinet subsequently agreed to pressurize the Americans into not withdrawing war material from Italy, even if it meant a delay of two or three months in the start of the proposed invasion of France.[71]

The *ad hoc* committee was followed, in August 1943, by a ministerial committee on Armistice Terms and Civil Administration and by a War Cabinet committee on the Post-War Settlement. The latter formally approved a total occupation of Germany, in order to encourage decentralization, and the cession to Poland of East Prussia, Danzig and the Oppeln district of Silesia, among other things. There was some criticism, presumably from Labour members and quite probably from Attlee, of the Foreign Secretary's proposals for what was to happen inside Germany,[72] but little could be done in the absence of any further inter-Allied agreement. And, despite the fairly cordial talks at the Moscow Foreign Ministers' Meeting in October 1943, little was actually accomplished except the acceptance of Eden's proposal to set up a European Advisory Commission to consider and make recommendations on European problems connected with the termination of hostilities.[73] Neither the Russians nor the Americans were in such a hurry as the British, whose military weakness relative to that of the superpowers daily became more evident.

It was in these circumstances that Attlee's Armistice Terms and Civil Administration committee, which had spent much of its time discussing Italian policy, decided to give itself a revised composition and wider terms of reference. These were presented to the War Cabinet in a memorandum written by Attlee and approved by the Cabinet at a meeting presided over by him.[74] This was the committee that accepted a recommendation by the Chiefs of Staff that Germany should be divided into three main zones of occupation, split among the three Powers, plus a combined Berlin zone: Britain should occupy the north-west of Germany, Russia the east, and the Americans the south.[75] Ostensibly, it was a short-term plan; but every member of the committee was aware that it could turn out to be the basis for a long-term settlement. The 'Attlee Plan'[76] for Germany represented a triple British insurance policy – against a German resurgence, American withdrawal and Russian intransigence. The plan neatly reflected Attlee's antipathy towards Germany, and his pessimistic analysis of the possible post-war European situation.

The war's later developments, both military and political, did not cause him to modify his sceptical and pragmatic standpoint. There were no fundamental Cabinet disagreements, though Attlee did his best to tone down some of Churchill's more maladroit enthusiasms. He was not enamoured, for instance, of the Prime Minister's desire to continue dealing with Marshal Badoglio's Italian government, which had replaced Mussolini and had brought the Italian Fleet over to the Allies. He protested, in June, about Churchill's attempts to persuade Roosevelt to keep the Marshal in power. Churchill climbed down and a broader Italian government under Ivanoe Bonomi was formed, which included Count Sforza, whom Churchill particularly disliked, but whom the Americans supported. It is highly likely that Attlee enjoyed seeing Churchill stand up to Roosevelt. Attlee was among those Cabinet ministers who feared that Churchill's dream of a special relationship with the US would turn out to mean American domination of Britain. It was no doubt on account of this fear that in April 1944 Attlee had again stressed to the War Cabinet how important it was to make sure that the British Commonwealth spoke as a single unit. If that could be done then the Empire would be in as strong a post-war position as the USA and the Soviet Union: if not, and the Dominions insisted on being dealt with as separate nations, then the position would be much less satisfactory.[77]

For Spain, Attlee had little but contempt: he warned the Cabinet, towards the end of 1944, that Britain was in danger of appearing to be Franco's only external support. On the other hand, in view of what he termed 'Spanish xenophobia', he conceded that it was useless to take overt action to change the regime; instead he contented himself by saying that the British should use whatever other methods might be feasible, especially economic ones, to help bring about Franco's downfall. He was supported by Eden but Churchill thought that Franco should be left to stew in his own juice,[78] a position that was acceptable to Attlee.

Greece, in contrast, was an issue that, mainly on account of Churchill's idiosyncrasy and obtuseness, tested Attlee's phlegm and powers of self-control to the full. He did not object to the Cabinet's initial decision in August 1944 that in the event of a German withdrawal British troops should be sent to Greece. Attlee merely suggested that it might be politically wise to make it appear that the troops were sent for purposes of relief.[79] Nor had he any real doubts about Churchill's intentions which the Prime Minister outlined to the Cabinet on 7 December 1944,[80] and defended in the Commons on the following day as the establishment of a British-type democracy.[81] But Churchill's obdurate support for the Greek king, which no doubt owed something to his famous deal with Stalin,[82] drew a sharp rebuke from Attlee. Conservatives such as Eden and officials like Cadogan were also alarmed at the Prime Minister's handling of the situation.[83] The alternative, proposed by Harold Macmillan (who was in Athens) and widely supported in Cabinet and Government circles, was the appointment of Archbishop Damaskinos as

Regent pending a plebiscite and elections. Churchill insisted that the Archbishop would turn out to be a left-wing dictator, whereupon Attlee retorted that 'We've often heard you say that, but you haven't produced a scintilla of evidence in support of your thesis'.[84] The Prime Minister realized how isolated he was becoming from colleagues and officials, and after a Christmas visit to Athens, accepted the Archbishop.[85]

However, from the moment that British forces became involved in the Greek civil war (in early December 1944), Attlee and the Labour ministers were caught in an extremely delicate political situation. Labour opinion was outraged that Britain appeared to be supporting the dubious Greek monarchy and conservative elements (whose attitude to Fascism was equally suspect), against the groups which had led the resistance to Nazi occupation. The entire weight of the official Labour Opposition was brought to bear against the Coalition, the only time throughout the war this happened on a foreign policy question. Churchill's last-minute acceptance of the Archbishop as Regent (in exchange for which the Greek Communists tacitly agreed to end the civil war) came too late to diminish the fury in the country and in the Labour Party that had been triggered by press reports of the fighting in Greece. Attlee himself had at first been alarmed by these reports,[86] but decided to ride out the storm. Despite Bevin's staunch support, Attlee's position was seriously compromised for a time.

A first debate in the Commons on 8 December 1944 had produced thirty Opposition votes in favour of an amendment criticizing British policy on Greece; only 279 MPs supported the Government and of these only twenty-three were Labour votes.[87] The official Labour Opposition, under Greenwood, abstained. Shortly afterwards, the Party's annual conference took place and, to ward off dissension, Greenwood produced an innocuous NEC motion calling for a ceasefire. The bloc vote of the trade unions ensured its passage but even Bevin's insistence that the Government's policy in Greece was a Cabinet policy and that the British Empire could not just abandon its position in the Mediterranean[88] did not suffice to quell Labour unease. The NCL on 19 December was obliged to pass a unanimous motion regretting the tragic situation in Greece, and calling for all possible steps to be taken to resume negotiations. The following day, Greenwood apologetically raised a second debate (on the adjournment, which did not require a vote) in the House: the Prime Minister, he somewhat ambiguously charged, had not handled the situation as it should have been handled: Greece was a political not a military problem and it was not an isolated one.[89] Prior to yet a third Commons debate, Greenwood led an NEC delegation consisting of Laski, James Griffiths, Aneurin Bevan and Morgan Phillips (Labour's new General Secretary) to explain privately to Churchill Labour's concern. The meeting proved to be a remarkable personal success for Churchill,[90] but had little immediate effect on the furore. The Labour Opposition pressed on regardless with its public attack, despite its private understanding and accord.

Churchill vainly protested that there was no case in his experience, certainly not in his wartime experience, 'where a British Government has been so maligned and its motives so traduced in our own country by important organs of the Press or among our own people'. The Government's policy – in Italy and Yugoslavia as well as Greece – was one of 'Government of the people, by the people, for the people, set up on a basis of free and universal suffrage election, with the secrecy of the ballot and no intimidation.'[91] Attlee, suggesting that it was very difficult 'to get knowledge of all the facts', demanded that 'on the record of this Government, on the known opinions of this Government, we have the right to be trusted to carry out the principles in which we believe.' Aneurin Bevan interjected 'No', whereupon Attlee countered, 'I have stuck a good deal more closely to carrying out the principles in which I believe and in working with my party than has the Hon. Member opposite.'[92] Even the moderate James Griffiths warned Churchill that the trade unions and the Labour movement would have no repetition of 1920: 'This time,' Griffiths stated, 'we are determined that, at the end of this war, there shall be no intervention which we can prevent against working-class and popular movements in Europe, or anywhere else in the world.'[93] The Greek issue caused Churchill's past to be resurrected against him, and undoubtedly destroyed what chance remained of his leading a post-war Coalition: only 340 MPs could be found to support the Government in the lobbies and a large number of Labour MPs abstained. Fortunately for Attlee, the heat over the Greek issue quickly subsided. A TUC delegation that was sent out in January reported in terms favourable to the Government and confirmed Attlee's emphasis on the complexity of the situation.[94]

In itself, the issue of Greek policy was peripheral to the larger problems in international affairs confronting the Government. To someone as engaged in the central question of Germany as was Hugh Dalton, the 1944 annual conference had been 'surprisingly quiet'[95] – and Attlee was still more directly and continuously involved. In April 1944, His Armistice Terms and Civil Administration committee had been given wider terms of reference and a new name, the Armistice and Post-War Committee. It was intended to be a key decision-making body, not only about German policy in the short and long terms, but also for the entire post-war European settlement. The British representative on the European Advisory Commission reported to it and it served as the clearing-house for the various specialized and inter-departmental committees of officials, the Foreign Office and the Chiefs of Staff. By the end of the year it had received and considered no fewer than 127 memoranda, reports and papers, and had met some twenty-three times. Whether Churchill quite expected or realized the influence that the APW Committee and, in particular, Attlee would have, is a moot point. The Prime Minister appears to have been astonishingly innocent of the effort and planning that went into the British proposals on Germany: 'His own account of how the agreements were drawn up,' Sharp comments, 'betrays a great ignorance of the events which took place, and is very unreliable.'[96] Probably, Churchill hoped or expected to shape the broad outlines of the peace settlement by means of 'personal diplomacy': if so, he was disappointed both during the war and after it. He himself downgraded the influence of the Foreign Office, and as a result the influence of the Cabinet committees was enhanced.

The 'Attlee Plan' for Germany, it should be stressed, was not particularly favourable to Russia. Indeed, if one considers that in 1943 when it was devised the only Ally effectively fighting Germany on the Continent was the Soviet Union, it is almost surprising that the plan came to be accepted by the Russians in the end. Roughly speaking, some 40 per cent of what would be left of German territory after the 'extremities' had been lopped off, 36 per cent of the population and 33 per cent of Germany's resources were allocated to the control of the Red Army. The Americans fared even worse; as a wag said later, the British were to get the industry, the Russians the agriculture and the Americans the scenery. The 'Attlee Plan' was derived in the first place from military considerations: these became stronger as the war unfolded, and took into account the fact that after Germany's defeat the most powerful country on the Continent would be Soviet Russia. By July 1944 the Chiefs of Staff had become convinced that not only would the assistance of France and the West European states be necessary for future British security but so too might that of Germany.[97] Given that the USSR would hardly permit the rearmament of a united Germany, the CoS and the Post-Hostilities Staff eventually came to believe that a three-way dismemberment of the German rump – as envisaged in the short term by the 'Attlee Plan' – would also be to Britain's long-term strategic advantage, as against both Germany and the USSR. There was also the hope that one day the British might be able to bring southern as well as north-western Germany within a West European grouping.[98] While very much aware of these views – which horrified the Foreign Office[99] – Attlee's committee insisted that the political arguments for Britain occupying the north-west of Germany were just as strong as any military ones. British vital interests were at stake; it was essential that the north-west European powers be held tightly to Britain.[100]

Although he shared some of the military chiefs' scepticism about the possibility of creating a World Security Organization responsible for keeping the post-war peace,[101] and was highly suspicious of Russian imperialism, Attlee was not as forward-looking in his strategic thinking. He did, however, come to change his mind about the desirability of post-war British involvement in Europe. Two days after the APW Committee had completed a report recommending the establishment of a world council to be backed with force,[102] he presented to the Cabinet a memorandum of his own on 'Foreign Policy and the Flying Bomb'. This was the first paper by any British politician to have addressed itself specifically to the impact of the new weapons on Britain's future strategic situation and, hence, foreign policy. Though no answer to these weapons had yet been found, Attlee considered it obvious that Britain could no longer be indifferent to the political position of the countries from which they could be launched. 'We must deny access to the nearer sites and gain space for dealing with those launched at a longer range,' he insisted. There was no choice in the matter: Britain was now a 'continental Power with a vulnerable land frontier'. The British could not afford to have as a buffer between them and a potential enemy a ring of weak neutral states liable to be overrun quickly. A system of defence had to be created which would deny to a potential enemy bases for launching attacks, and which could furnish positions for British counter-attack. In particular, Attlee stated: 'From our point of view, Norway, Denmark, Holland and France are necessary outposts of Britain and, in as much as Britain is now as she has been for a hundred years a shield for the US, outposts of America as well. Their defence is necessary to our defence and without us they cannot defend themselves . . . Unless we are prepared to shift the centre of the Commonwealth we must ensure that it is in a strategic position comparable to that of Washington and Moscow. We can only do this by bringing into the closest association with ourselves the countries which hold the keys of our fortress.' He concluded that, within a general system of collective security, 'there should be a close military alliance between ourselves and the States above mentioned.'[103]

There was no mention of Germany within Attlee's proposed West European group. Nor did he think that such an organization would be viewed with suspicion by Russia. The most likely enemy in his mind was still Germany – albeit a disarmed and reduced Germany. Neither he nor the Foreign Office appears to have realized that, if a western alliance against Germany was logical, so too was an eastern European alliance. However, no decision about a western bloc was taken by the Cabinet before the Yalta or Potsdam Conferences, and a further factor offering some prospect of an accord with Russia was the British attitude to the Polish question. The Cabinet was resolved that Britain would support Polish claims to territorial compensation in the west – at the expense of Germany and in return for Polish acceptance of the Curzon Line in the east favouring Russia – no matter what the Americans might think.[104] The only qualifications concerned the composition of the future Polish

Government and the exact delineation of Poland's western frontier; but the former was viewed as a bargaining counter, the latter in terms of its potential economic effect on what would be left of Germany (if millions of Germans had to be transferred). The British would go to Yalta hoping that an agreement with Russia over Europe might be secured and they were not to be disappointed. The vital question was Germany, the one for which the war had been fought and the one on which Attlee had been a leading policy-maker.

Apart from his complete accord with the plan to divide Germany, he had gone to great lengths to indicate his conviction that the highly centralized machinery of German government should be smashed, not hesitating in this regard to clash with Eden. There was a choice to be made in British policy for occupied Germany, he had declared in July 1944: they could either aim at restoring normal, orderly and organized life as quickly as possible, providing food and facilities for economic, commercial and industrial revival – subject to disarmament and demilitarization; or they could aim at 'utterly rooting out', at all costs, Nazi influence and the German warlike cult, even if the result at first would be that Germany would feel 'the full impact of military defeat, including loss of territory, influx of transferred populations, political and economic turmoil and so on'. Attlee made it plain that he favoured the second course, though taking it for granted that chaos and economic disorganization would have to be avoided, insofar as it was detrimental to British interests elsewhere, and subject to ordinary considerations of humanity. Even if an extreme view of the German people's responsibility 'for our trials' was not taken, it could still be argued, he felt, that anything that brought home to the Germans the completeness and irrevocability of their defeat would be worthwhile in the end. The provisions of the Atlantic Charter were no obstacle to such a policy, and the only alternative would be a prolonged occupation that neither the British nor the Americans would have the toughness in peacetime to carry through. If they were not careful, the Germans would get away with it again. In any case, there was no normal Germany to re-establish. Apart from the Nazis, the two enduring factors in German national life for the past fifty years had been the Prussian military land-owning caste and the controllers of heavy industry who looked to war or the apprehension of war to provide them with orders. It was vital that the British be quite uncompromising in the early stages of the occupation when the realization of German enormities would be still vivid to the Allies.[105]

On the other hand, it should be stressed that Attlee's 'No Mistake This Time' approach never amounted to a policy of Carthaginian peace. Commenting, in January 1944, on a statement by Churchill to the Cabinet that it had been decided at Teheran that Germany was to be broken up into a number of separate states, Attlee wrote that he did not recall that

8 Wartime partners: Churchill and Attlee, 1941

9 On the home front: Attlee (with gas mask) visiting a munitions factory

10 Sir William Beveridge addressing a public meeting at Caxton Hall in 1943

11 Soviet Foreign Minister Molotov (far left) talks to Attlee at the United Nations Conference, San Francisco, April 1945. Anthony Eden is beside Attlee

12 Attlee, Truman (centre) and Stalin at Potsdam, August 1945

13 Attlee with Churchill and Eden on his left, Morrison on his right, leads the House of Commons to the Service of Thanksgiving for final victory, at St Margaret's Church, Westminster, 15 August 1945

14 King George VI with senior members of his new Government in 1945: from left to right, Morrison, Attlee, H.M. the King, Arthur Greenwood, Ernest Bevin and A.V. Alexander

15 The Labour Government, 1945. It included just one woman, Ellen Wilkinson, Secretary of State for Education

the British had ever been so definite. Though he himself wanted to see the decentralization of Germany and the severance of certain areas, he was sceptical as to the efficacy of a partition enforced by the victors.[106] He was one of the British ministers who vetoed the Morganthau Plan.[107] He had no thought of smashing Germany for its own sake, and was disturbed, in January 1945, to learn that the US occupying forces had refused to give the slightest help to German civilians in making some kind of shelter for themselves in devastated areas. The non-fraternization policy ought to be interpreted intelligently.[108] Moreover, he and other ministers became increasingly preoccupied towards the end of the war with the general European economic picture and its effect on Allied policy for Germany. While Churchill was at Yalta, Attlee sent him a summary of the Cabinet's views, which included the following points:

1 Reparations had to be considered together with, and as part of, any policy of dismemberment.
2 The two objects that the Russians had in mind, the depletion of Germany's manufacturing capacity and the preservation of her capacity to make large annual reparation payments, were essentially incompatible.
3 Britain's own economic situation would only permit the acceptance of certain raw materials, not manufactured goods.
4 Britain was more concerned than either the US or the USSR with the future of Europe, and the creation of a decent Europe was one of the war aims.[109]

Attlee had good cause to pronounce to the Cabinet that the results of the Yalta Conference were highly satisfactory.[110] There had been no dispute as to the necessity of measures for the deNazification, demilitarization and disarmament of Germany. France and the US were to be involved in the German settlement. There was agreement in principle, at least, over dismemberment and reparations, and over Poland. In short, there seemed to be a reasonable possibility of Allied advance along the lines that Attlee, notably, had been advocating. Certain large questions, of course, remained and it was for this reason that Attlee advised Churchill against the idea of making the entire Yalta declaration the subject of a vote of confidence in the Commons. He and the Coalition Government's Chief Whip did not expect trouble from Bevan and company who, anyway, did not count for much, but there was a considerable body of opinion, mainly Conservative, which was worried about Poland.[111] Churchill, nevertheless, exuberantly insisted on his vote of confidence: he argued that the Conference had faced realities and difficulties in so exceptional a manner that the result constituted an Act of State.[112] He eventually obtained his vote, by 413 to 0, but not before an amendment was laid regretting 'the decision to transfer to another power the territory of an ally contrary to the Atlantic Charter ...' and also the failure to ensure that the liberated nations had the right to choose their own governments.[113] Attlee's political estimate proved correct: Bevan and company actually supported the Government against the amendment, which obtained only twenty-five votes. The left-wing journals also took a favourable view of the Yalta settlement: *Tribune* considered that, in certain important respects, it marked an improvement on previous Allied statements, while the *New Statesman* described the decision on Poland as 'statesmanlike'.[114] On the main motion Greenwood, for the official Opposition, announced his general support, though critical of what was going to happen to Poland; Bevan and the Left abstained.

But the Left remained extremely anxious about the German question; this was the ideological rock on which their overall approach to the post-war international situation was fixed and on which it foundered. It was a matter of principle on which the left-wingers would not budge, regardless of fellow Party members or of Russia, or of anyone who appeared to subscribe, directly or indirectly, to the 'guilty nation' theory. On this point Attlee was adamant: 'If you ask,' he said during the Yalta debate in the Commons, 'who is responsible for the movements [of populations], this terrible thing that has smitten Europe, there is no doubt at all that it is the Nazi rulers of Germany and the people of Germany who actively supported them.' He did not suggest that an indictment could be drawn up against a whole people, but neither could a whole people be relieved of responsibility. The central problem of Europe was the German people. They had broken down the old barriers and they could not appeal to the old Europe on the basis of moral laws that they had disregarded or to the pity and mercy that they had never extended to others. He did not believe in treating them as they had treated others, but they would have no right to complain if pieces of their territory were given to the Dutch or Poles.[115]

The Left, on the other hand, continued until the end of the war to view the problem of Germany in a quite different fashion. The reason for the Germans' last-ditch desperation, explained the *New Statesman*, was the absence of any detailed plans for Germany coupled with Eisenhower's 'no-fraternization' order: the Germans were afraid that the Allies' deep-rooted suspicion of each other would allow Germany to lapse through inaction 'into a ruined no-man's-land in which no wheel turns, there are no wages or bread, and pestilence marches with the underground gunmen.'[116] Bevan argued that the best way to keep Germany disarmed was not by impoverishment or dismemberment, which would merely convert Germany 'from a problem into an obsession': the important question was whether the need for security against German military resurgence would be regarded by the victorious Powers as an excuse for national ambitions or as a 'secular task'. If the latter, then the task was simple: the factory inspector, the agent of civilization at home, could solve the problem of security abroad. To base post-war international unity on an alliance to prevent the rise of Germany was 'to substitute a mania for a policy'.[117]

There was, however, a distinct divergence between the groups associated with the *New Statesman* and Bevan's *Tribune* over the attitude to take towards Russia. Though suspicious of the Soviet Union's Polish policy,[118] the *New Statesman* insisted that the Russians would respond to a 'realistic' approach to Germany.[119] Bevan had serious doubts, though in 1944 he thought there was a chance that a socialist integration of Europe might eventually be recognized by Russia as being in her best interest. As a first stage he urged the formation of 'an organic confederation of the Western European nations, like France, Holland, Belgium, Italy, Spain, the Scandinavian nations along with a sane Germany and Austria and a progressive Britain . . .'[120] But when Russia's acceptance of the occupation of Germany became clear after Yalta, *Tribune* became as doubtful of Russian 'realism' as of the West: 'They have, as it were, replaced the old watchword "Workers of the World, Unite!" by a new one: "Workers of the World, divide into three zones!"'[121]

The fact that Attlee's scepticism about the possibility of a post-war agreement with Russia was reinforced by the war's last developments did not cause him to modify substantially his views about Germany. He certainly agreed with Bevin's statement to the Party's annual conference that, while Germany had to be prevented from developing a war potential, sixty to eighty million people could not be left derelict. The Germans had to grow food because neither the United States nor Britain could feed them, even if they wished. At the same time the 60 per cent increase in German industrial war potential under Hitler would have to be controlled and eliminated.[122] Even Cripps, the Left's old hero, was privately advocating a drastic reduction in the German engineering industry, at least during the occupation. All the Labour ministers were agreed that the first priority of German policy should be security, and detailed plans, involving serious restrictions on German industry, had been made to achieve it.[123] Attlee, in particular, could only have been reassured as to the correctness of his views on German and European policy in general, when he heard of Stalin's announcement on 9 May 1945 that he did not intend to dismember Germany after all. At the Potsdam Conference it would be remarked that Attlee and Bevin were 'businesslike and imperturbable', and gave 'confidence to all around them'.[124] They had good reason to consider that the central aim of British wartime policy – the elimination of Germany as the dominating power in Europe – had been achieved in a most satisfactory manner: military victory had been accompanied by the reduction and division of the Third German Reich. This time there had been no mistake.

X

Getting On With The Job

As Labour's leader in the 1945 election campaign, Attlee's task was less winning the election than not losing it. Opinion polls since 1942 had shown a shift to the Left.[1] Polls, however, were not taken very seriously then; Churchill was. What Labour had to do was to remove the Prime Minister from his national pedestal and bring him down to the party arena. Another Labour leader might have been tempted to compete with Churchill for popular appeal; this was obviously impossible for Attlee. Churchill made four election broadcasts, Attlee only one. But Attlee's 'calm dignity' and 'self-effacing style' reinforced the team aspect of the Labour leadership:[2] and the single broadcast he did make was masterly.

In one of those lurches into misjudgment that had characterized his career, the Prime Minister began the campaign by launching his famous accusation that a socialist government 'would have to fall back on some kind of Gestapo, no doubt very humanely directed in the first instance'. Applied to Bevin, Cripps or Morrison in a mudslinging contest, the charge might perhaps have passed muster; applied to Clement Attlee (whom Churchill had just invited to Potsdam), it was ludicrous, a gift from the gods. The Prime Minister, Attlee explained to radio listeners on the following evening, wanted the electors to understand how great was the difference between Winston Churchill the leader of a united nation, and Mr Churchill the leader of the Conservatives: the voice had been that of Mr Churchill, the mind that of Lord Beaverbrook. Attlee thereby established the tone of the campaign. Churchill admitted privately in the course of it that he had lost touch with the national mood: 'I've tried 'em with pep, and I've tried 'em with pap, but I don't know what it is they want,' he told Attlee.[3]

What they did *not* want, the results revealed, was the Conservative

Party. Labour took nearly 12 million votes (47.8 per cent of the poll) and 393 seats;[4] this was a higher number of votes than had been obtained by any party prior to 1945. The Party gained over 200 seats from the Conservatives; almost 80 of these constituencies had never returned a Labour MP and 18 had consistently voted Tory for a century. The most sensational returns came from the English counties, where Labour virtually drew level with the Conservatives.[5] Although the Conservatives polled nearly 10 million votes, and the Liberals 2 million, they respectively obtained only 213 and 12 seats: the electoral landslide has been fittingly compared with those in 1906 and 1832. Doubtless the swing owed much to long-term factors,[6] but there was also the preoccupation with housing and jobs – where Labour's detailed programme *Let Us Face The Future* presumably made more impact than *Mr Churchill's Declaration of Policy to the Electors*.

The Prime Minister's polemics also had the effect of drawing belated attention to Attlee's 'hitherto almost unknown personality'.[7] During the war, Attlee had been eclipsed in the public eye by Bevin, Cripps and Morrison as well as Churchill; and where little is known, little is expected. Consequently, it has been asserted that Attlee's qualities were only made manifest and developed as a result of his exercise of the premiership.[8] He is one of the very few British twentieth-century peacetime Prime Ministers whose reputations have increased while in office. Yet the sixty-three-year-old Attlee did not change after his elevation: there was no need. He possessed three formidable qualifications for the post: unrivalled experience of the whole range of affairs, proven executive ability and complete self-confidence. 'I was acquainted', he noted, 'not only with all the outstanding problems but with the course of events out of which they had developed. I . . . understood the machinery of government, and knew personally the leading figures in the Civil Service and in the Fighting Services . . .'[9] If the first qualification escaped everyone's notice, appreciation of his talent for 'always getting on with the job'[10] was confined to a very narrow circle. In the war it had been mostly a few overworked and exhausted civil servants and generals who had remarked on his efficiency, his ability to get agreement, his decisiveness.[11] One political colleague had observed that when Attlee took the chair at Cabinet meetings 'we keep to the agenda, make decisions and get away in reasonable time' – merely to contrast him with his illustrious predecessor: 'When Churchill presides, nothing is decided: we listen enthralled and go home, many hours late, feeling we have been present at an historic occasion.'[12]

Attlee was totally impervious to such comparisons. He was perfectly aware that he owed his premiership to the fact that he was Leader of the Labour Party – a party that in the Commons 'represented more fully than ever before all classes, all occupations and all the adult age-groups'.[13]

There was 'something strange and romantic'[14] that there should be a Labour Government and a Labour Prime Minister at all: their collective deeds would provide any colour and excitement that was needed. In any case, he considered, whereas war called for 'a national leader', in peacetime 'less forceful characters could take their place'.[15] Men could be led equally well 'by such things as the example of moral or physical courage, sympathy, self-discipline, altruism, and superior capacity for hard work.'[16] These were qualities that he could readily supply; Ernest Bevin neatly summarized them when he introduced Attlee to the PLP's first post-election meeting as 'Nature's gentleman'.[17] Attlee had no doubt that he should accept the King's invitation to form a government. Urged on by Bevin, he brushed aside a last-minute attempt by Morrison and a few others[18] to re-open a leadership contest: 'The idea was fantastic and certainly out of harmony with the feeling of the Party.'[19] He refused to be troubled by any intrigue: the only kind of authority worth having was that which was given without being sought for. 'Men who lobby their way forward into leadership', he believed, 'are most likely to be lobbied back out of it. The man who has most control of his followers, is the man who shows no fear. And a man cannot be a leader if he is afraid of losing his job.'[20]

Not only did he suit the job but the job suited him, in so far as its constant pressures can be said to suit anyone. 'As God has called us to the Papacy,' he said to his wife, recalling Pope Leo X, 'let us enjoy it.'[21] And enjoy it, in his fashion, he did. There was, for example, 'the great advantage of living on the premises', which meant that he saw more of his family between 1945 and 1951 than 'before or since'.[22] While in office, he celebrated two 'outstanding family events',[23] his Silver Wedding Anniversary and his eldest daughter's marriage (in 1947), and became a grandfather. His daily philosophy was, 'One should never worry and one should get the greatest pleasure one can out of things.'[24] He spent as many weekends as possible at his official country residence, where he claimed to have read the whole of Gibbon.[25] At Chequers, too, he played tennis and croquet during the summer, delighted to give children's Christmas parties and habitually wore a dinner jacket and stiff collar for the evening meal: it was there, one presumes, where he was seen to shudder if the port was passed the wrong way round.[26] After 1947, the Attlees took brief holidays in Eire, Wales, Norway and France: 'I found time for relaxation,' he remembered.[27] He found the work-load 'heavy but not insupportable'.[28]

He began his normal routine with a walk in the park, and then worked through the day from 9.30 to 11 or 12 at night: according to his Parliamentary Private Secretary, Arthur Moyle, he never left the Cabinet Room until every paper had been dealt with, whatever the time. Punctuality was one of his prime virtues, and interviews were kept brief. He had a 'deadly mannerism' for visitors who overstayed their allotted time: 'he would place his pipe on the table blotting pad, lift himself out of his chair, look at the clock, take a few deep breaths, and grunt.'[29] His wife kept a close eye on his outside engagements; her vigilance was thoroughly justified because her husband compensated for his lack of public appeal by attending a large number of them. The legislative programme was the heaviest in British parliamentary history,[30] but Attlee also knew how to relax in the Commons. During all-night sittings, he didn't sleep; instead, he would surround himself in his room with 'old *Hansards*, *Who's Who*, *Wisden's Cricket Annual* and *The Times House of Commons Book*' and would muse and indulge his nostalgia.[31] In the debating chamber he was given to doodling freehand geometrical designs with a multi-coloured pencil. Moyle claimed that he could tell whether the occasions were harmonious, stormy or boring from the doodles. Sometimes his doodling was a device for putting opponents off their guard by creating the impression that he was not following the proceedings.[32] At interminable Cabinet meetings, Aneurin Bevan remembered, it was 'a constant source of wonder how he was able to bear the strain . . . with crisis piled on crisis, and no sign of letting up either at home or abroad . . . He was able to call on reserves of strength which were not obvious on the surface, and in the end emerged fresher, or so it appeared, than the rest of us.'[33] Attlee did spend several weeks in hospital during his six years as Prime Minister, once in August and September 1948 with an ulcer and eczema, the second time in March 1951, again with a duodenal ulcer. But around him several of his colleagues were breaking down physically, never to recover.

In the parliamentary system a huge majority is not necessarily an asset: Attlee warned the new PLP from the outset that the selection of ministers – from an abundance of experienced people – would be a difficult task.[34] Yet he had become convinced that the responsibility was one that devolved solely upon the Prime Minister; indeed, if he could not be trusted to exercise this power without 'fear, favour or affection' he was not fit for the post.[35] Such had not been his Party's view in the aftermath of the MacDonald 'betrayal': the 1933 conference had laid down a specific procedure for the Leader to follow in making up his team. In 1945 circumstances ruled out formalities. Attlee had to depart almost immediately for the adjourned Potsdam Conference. Taking only the precaution of obtaining the consent of the old PLP's administrative committee,[36] he went ahead with his initial selection. Some individuals virtually chose themselves, but they did not choose their positions: Bevin and Dalton's preferences were exactly opposite to what they got.[37] Attlee was guided by a number of considerations, of which his knowledge of those concerned and of their party status were the most obvious. On occasions he consulted his senior colleagues though, in retrospect, he thought that when he accepted advice, 'it wasn't very good'.[38] For the most part he dealt with the matter himself – finding it the most difficult of all his duties. One of his concerns was to appoint 'a certain number of solid people whom no one would think particularly brilliant, but who between conflicting opinions [could] act as middlemen, give you the ordinary man's point of view'; another was to balance intellectuals by trade unionists.[39] On the whole, he was chary of experts[40] with the exception of the Exchequer, where he held that 'considerable technical economic knowledge' was necessary in order that Chancellors should not be at the mercy of their permanent officials.[41] Mainly, he relied on his own judgment of character and his political intuition. He had a knack of appointing to office people who had conspired against him. Ellen Wilkinson was made Minister of Education despite the fact that she had actively campaigned against his leadership.[42] George Brown organized a 'plot' to replace Attlee, and was named Under-Secretary of State for Agriculture.[43] Stafford Cripps went into the Cabinet Room in 1947 with a detailed proposal for a change of leadership – and came out with the top economic post. Attlee, complained a disgruntled Morrison,[44] was a master at moving the chessmen on the board. 'It was always clear to me,' Attlee somewhat disingenuously said, 'that certain jobs had to be done, that I had to make up my mind, with the assistance of my colleagues, about who was the best man to do it.'[45] In this regard, ruthlessness was a function of the post;[46] personally he found the dismissal of ministers distasteful and unpleasant.[47] His brusqueness on these occasions served to mask his discomfort: Attlee was much too conscious of his own shortcomings to enjoy the exercise of any authority unwarranted by his public responsibility. He carried his modesty to extremes, sometimes fetching his own cup of tea on the grounds that the messenger was 'probably busy'.[48]

Once appointed, a Minister could be certain of minimum interference, so long as he got on with the job. Attlee's zeal for delegation was comparable with some men's yearning for power, but there was no other way in which the immense legislative programme and administrative burden could have been carried. The Cabinet was pre-eminently a decision-making team, not a forum for argument; in it the Prime Minister was 'undoubtedly the most important member, but not a monarch'.[49] However, his was the major responsibility for ensuring that decisions were made.[50] Rhetoric, Attlee pointed out, was wasted on hard-boiled politicians.[51] Democracy of course meant government by discussion, but it was only effective if you could stop people talking unnecessarily.[52] His precept was supported by his example, which probably established a record for prime ministerial brevity, and also by his method of chairmanship. Sitting with Morrison on one side and Bevin on the other, he would take Morrison's view first and then go around the table, concluding with his own laconic summing-up.[53] There was nothing casual about the procedure. He came prepared, and expected others to do likewise: 'You've said that already! No need to repeat what's in the circulated Cabinet papers! Nothing more to add, I hope? Good!'[54] He was particularly severe on a minister who was unable to give sensible answers to questions about his own department: 'It is no good your coming here so ill-prepared and wasting everyone's time.'[55]

The purpose of his summing-up was to reflect the general view, though he also had regard to Party and public opinion.[56] Had he led in any other fashion the Cabinet might well have fallen apart – to this extent he was a conciliator. But that is not a sufficient description of his role; he controlled the agenda, and in the process of the round-table discussion could make sure of extracting the opinions he wanted when he wanted them.[57] Harold Wilson has stressed the Prime Minister's power when summarizing, provided the chair remains detached.[58] When Attlee summed up, noted James Griffiths, 'he would get to the heart of the matter in a few sentences and there would be no ambiguity about his decision'. The relatively inexperienced George Brown sometimes wondered whether Attlee was summing up for the committee or despite it; like others before him, Brown was impressed by Attlee's incisiveness, which enabled him to sum up the most confused meeting.[59] A change in Attlee's attitude, as Michael Foot has observed, could tip the balance in a wavering Cabinet[60] where votes were rarely taken and only on minor matters. Attlee took pride in his mastery of the art of chairmanship and attempted to instruct his associates in its finer points.[61] He was not only efficient himself, but sought to be the cause of efficiency in others.

The Cabinet was the apex of a committee system whose structure Attlee had sketched out before the war. Complete duplication of the minute War Cabinets being impossible in peacetime, Attlee's aim remained that of keeping his own Cabinets as small as circumstances allowed. He began with twenty members (half of whom had previously been manual workers)[62], and managed to reduce the number to seventeen or sixteen. There was an even smaller, informal group of senior colleagues who were charged with the function of overseeing the entire range of policy. Membership of this group varied from time to time – Bevin and Morrison always being part of it, Cripps, Dalton, Greenwood and one or two others for lesser periods. In addition, within the full Cabinet, two or three ministers were purposely not given departments so as better to perform a co-ordinating role. This was also the main purpose of the Cabinet Committees. Attlee took care to keep the appointment of their chairmen and members firmly in his own hands[63] and, by the end of 1947, himself chaired the three most important: Economic Policy, Defence, and the India and Burma Committee. In general, the system developed from that prevailing during the war, which Attlee had helped to create. Later, as a result of the economic crisis in 1947, Attlee reviewed the structure in some detail.[64] A recent observer has concluded that in the conditions of the time, 'Attlee's pattern of cabinet government functioned well.'[65]

That it did so owed a great deal to Attlee's personal influence, as well as his managerial skills. His governments bristled with able and articulate individuals who thrived on conflict: he rightly regarded his ability to 'adjust relations' between them as one of his major achievements.[66] True, the elements of discord were also held in check by Labour's sense of historic opportunity, its possession of a detailed programme, the continuous economic crisis and by one 'constant attender', the ghost of the 1931 split.[67] Attlee was nevertheless able to draw and hold together a collective effort from people of disparate opinions, temperaments, social backgrounds, ambitions and abilities – the very definition of successful management. The strength of his personality lay in his introspection;[68] perfectly aware of his own limitations, he had a keen eye for those of others. Having no illusions about himself, he had few about his colleagues. His ability to repress his imagination coupled with his modesty gave him a superb self-control which, if it made him seem an almost prosaically practical figure, also produced his air of sympathetic disinterest. He appeared to be more of 'a reasonably impartial umpire' than captain of the team.[69] His relationship with his colleagues, if not one of splendid isolation, was similar to the British balance of power concept of the previous century: the balance that he strove for inside his Cabinets largely excluded himself. Thus his attitude could be decisive.

The great exception to Attlee's detachment was his relationship with Ernest Bevin, which Attlee described as the deepest of his political life.[70] The attraction was mutual and to some extent one of opposites. 'Against the emotional, lurching, instinctive manner by which Bevin reached decisions, Attlee offered an impersonal and dignified authority whose approval was not only necessary but valued.' To Attlee, Bevin epitomized those working-class attributes that he had observed in the young in East London and which had led him to socialism.[71] Attlee positively relished Bevin's celebrated accent. He was very fond of telling the story of how he, Bevin, Hugh Dalton and David (Dai) Grenfell had conferred once during the war. 'Which of us should handle it?' – Attlee asked Bevin. 'You and I' was the answer: or was it, Attlee would joke, 'Hugh and I' or 'You and Dai' or 'Hugh and Dai'?[72] Bevin had most of the qualities that Attlee lacked – egotism, appetite for power and exuberance. They also had two common characteristics – their staunch patriotism and their mutual recognition of loyalty as the highest political virtue: here, public school and trade union values coincided. On a wide range of questions their views had begun to converge in the 1930s and their wartime association had cemented their appreciation of each other's abilities and toughness. Above all, they seem to have realized instinctively that their relationship was one of mutual dependence. During the war they had jointly faced up to political pressure from the Left, and they would do so again. At times, Bevin may have adopted a 'protective' attitude to Attlee, yet he did not like to move far without talking things over with the PM.[73] Attlee could disagree with Bevin on occasion,[74] and Bevin would sometimes lose patience with Attlee,[75] but basically they knew they hung together, and that a large part of the Government and Party's cohesion hung with them.

To his political alliance with Bevin Attlee added a personal one with Christopher Addison, Secretary of State for Dominion Affairs from 1945 to 1947, Leader of the Labour Party in the House of Lords, and also a close neighbour. For six years, Addison's biographers have noted, 'Clem' and 'Chris' reflected on the state of the nation over lunch and tea at weekends at Chequers.[76] Addison, aged seventy-six in 1945, was a wise and extraordinarily experienced old political bird who had no personal ambitions. He had much in common with Attlee, who was to pay him a significant tribute: 'A wonderful man in the House of Commons and House of Lords. No orator. No art.' Attlee added that Addison had been 'one of the most influential men in my time'.[77] Indeed, Attlee appointed Addison to the highly secret body charged with the development of Britain's atomic bomb and nuclear energy programme.[78]

Attlee did not need any other ties in what was the most heterogeneous group of people, individually and socially, who had ever attempted to govern the country. He may have been a pygmy among giants, but all the giants had flaws. He could afford to take his position for granted, taking care only to ensure that any potential rivals had plenty of work to do. Morrison in effect became Deputy Prime Minister and found himself 'faced with a remarkable range of tasks and offices'. He was made responsible for the general co-ordination of the entire domestic front including, until 1947, economic planning. Morrison also supervised the nationalization and future legislation programmes and from time to time was given various *ad hoc* assignments. In addition, he had important parliamentary and Party roles. Afterwards, Attlee could blithely say that Morrison had been a good member of Cabinet,[79] though his final appointment of Morrison as Foreign Secretary was 'a bad mistake'.[80] Morrison was the only leading Labour figure whose personal ambitions equalled or outdistanced his political aims; all his actions had an element of personal calculation. Even the party he gave to mark the Attlees' silver wedding anniversary in January 1947 could be interpreted as calling attention to the Party Leader's advancing years.[81] But Morrison had no luck; soon after the celebration he was the one to be taken seriously ill. In any case, his path to the top was blocked by Bevin's implacable animosity.

Apart from Morrison, all senior Cabinet ministers demonstrated that they were willing to set aside any thought of advancement in favour of the common good. Attlee was more secure than he sometimes seemed. He could also count on the support of most Cabinet members outside the inner group.[82] Cripps might have been glad to see Attlee upset, but Attlee probably understood Cripps better than any of his senior colleagues.[83] Their long acquaintance was social as well as political. Attlee knew how to use Cripps's highmindedness, economic expertise and forensic ability while ensuring that his idealistic impulses were calmed. Cripps's opinions had changed during the war, yet Attlee was still wary of his aptitude for picking 'on sudden ideas';[84] and Attlee could hardly forget that Cripps had only recently rejoined the Party.[85] His solution was to have Cripps serve a political apprenticeship as President of the Board of Trade and then to put him in charge of economic policy. This last choice turned out to be as inspired as was the selection of Mountbatten for India.

Another brilliant appointment was that of Bevan to the Ministry of Health. Attlee made it clear that, despite his wartime rebelliousness, Bevan was starting with a clean slate. He was the youngest member of the Cabinet and the more he could learn the better. One thing that Bevan did learn, his biographer has remarked,[86] was a new, though intermittent, respect for Attlee. The sharp, cryptic manner, Bevan discovered, assisted the dispatch of business; ministers were generally allowed to get on with their work unmolested. Attlee's mind, 'however unadventurous', was usually open and unprejudiced. A case presented with close argument and detailed facts had a good chance of winning on its own merits and Attlee could be won as an ally.[87] There were moments, Foot asserts, when 'the association between the two men trembled on the verge of a warmer friendship'.[88] Attlee's rebuke over Bevan's notorious 'vermin' speech was a masterpiece of discretion and did not affect the relationship: the speech had been singularly ill-timed, had drawn attention away from Bevan's excellent work, and would he please be a bit more careful in future in his own interests?[89] Attlee may have suppressed his own bitter experiences – with the Tory clergyman and the burnt porridge, for instance – but he had not forgotten them. When Bevan resigned in 1951 – the only important Cabinet Minister to do so – Attlee was in hospital. If he had not been, be believed he could have prevented the resignation and Harold Wilson, who also resigned, thought so too.[90]

Despite the size of the Labour majority and the weakness of the Opposition, two factors which almost invited internal disputation, Attlee had little trouble with the PLP over domestic policy. As there was barely room for the Labour MPs to fit into the largest committee room in the Commons, communications between the Government and its backbenchers had to be streamlined. Liaison was mainly in the hands of Morrison, in conjunction with the Chief Whip and Attlee himself. MPs could join a number of specialist groups according to their interests and a committee was established to arrange for ministers to explain Government policy to these groups.[91] Attlee was not exempted from the duty. Dalton was forcibly impressed by Attlee's reception on one occasion: 'There is no doubt', Dalton noted, 'that this sort of speech . . . will have a good effect on the morale of our supporters.'[92] So good was the morale that the PLP's standing orders on discipline were suspended from January 1946 to March 1952, and Attlee could boast to the Party's 1946 annual conference of 'the wonderful spirit and wonderfully loyal support of all our Members in the House'.[93] The Government's relationship with the extra-parliamentary party was equally harmonious, as well it might have been. To an extent unprecedented in British political history the legislation of a government was dictated by a party programme.[94] The nation's difficulties were widely understood and the wartime discipline prevailed for a time.

On two points Attlee was firm. He would not tolerate interventions by theorists in practical politics,[95] and neither would he accept any interference from the Labour Movement at large with the Government's and PLP's tactical independence. Prime Ministers had to deal in terms of priorities.[96] Between 1946 and 1948 the Government's position at the annual conference suffered eight defeats (on minor matters).[97] They made no difference to the Government's policy. Attlee was scrupulous in his respect for the conference's authority,[98] so long as it respected the supremacy of the PLP in its own sphere.[99] From their respective viewpoints, Bevan and Morrison each paid tribute to Attlee's standing with the rank and file;[100] he seemed to Bevan to have an intuitive understanding of the individual member's reactions.[101] Ironically, it was Bevan who found himself most at odds with the conference. In 1947 he had to get the Cabinet to agree that, though the Government accepted the principle of equal pay for men and women, it would be inexpedient to introduce it then; nor could the Government accept another resolution favouring the immediate abolition of the tied cottage system.[102] Bevan had to explain to the Conference the following year that it was quite impossible for 1,000 people, even if it were constitutionally proper, to determine the order in which the PLP and Government introduced legislation into the House of Commons.[103] Attlee was certain that it was not constitutionally proper: 'If you begin to consider yourself solely responsible to a political party you're half-way to a dictatorship.'[104]

He took the same attitude in regard to organized labour. Soon after taking office, he convened a secret meeting with Bevin, Morrison and Greenwood to concert policy for the maintenance of essential services in the event of large-scale industrial disturbance. By January 1946, a plan which involved the use of the Services was ready, and it came before the full Cabinet in March. Though agreeing with the principle of government responsibility, Bevan raised certain objections: preparations, he believed, should not be made in advance, as they would be costly and hypothetical, would become known and would be highly embarrassing politically. Attlee rejected the argument: if left to the advent of an emergency, plans might not only be ineffective but they would probably contain the very defects that the Government wanted to avoid, such as in the choice of persons to assume local responsibility. In addition, failure to make preparations in advance would increase the risk that, at the last moment, undue reliance would be placed on military assistance. Attlee had no difficulty in persuading the rest of the Cabinet.[105] It was first put into operation in January 1947, just before the year's great blizzard; a road haulage strike made it obvious that military transport alone would not suffice for moving essential supplies.[106] As a result of the freeze-up, and with Attlee's approval, the plan was extended to cover emergencies arising from other than industrial causes. There was little discussion, in April, over the Cabinet's decision to send additional troops to unload food ships in Glasgow. Stocks of rationed foods were too low for the Government to permit any interruption in supplies.[107] That same year the Government resisted demands for increases in miners' pay unrelated to productivity.[108]

Attlee was even more unbending in his dealings with unofficial labour. One of his administration's first decisions was to prolong the Emergency Powers Act for five years. The Cabinet approved the use of troops to break an illegal dockers' strike within three months of taking office.[109] States of emergency to deal with other dockers' strikes were proclaimed in 1948 and 1949; Attlee managed to bring the first to an abrupt end with 'a memorable headmasterly broadcast',[110] but troops were used in the second emergency. Attlee declared that it would be 'absolutely intolerable to let the unions gain the power of deciding which ships would be unloaded and which not.'[111] Troops were again sent – under extended Emergency Powers – to take over the London power stations in 1950.

It may be thought that Attlee was simply lucky in the timing of his labour relations. Certainly his Government's actions were greatly facilitated by its overall pro-labour policies. Full employment had been endorsed by the Coalition as a primary responsibility of any post-war administration, but the Attlee Government's skilful and determined implementation of the policy – considering the size of the demobilization problem – was highly impressive. The unions were especially gratified, too, by the speedy repeal of the detested 1927 Trade Disputes Act.[112] In 1949 the TUC's General Council announced that TUC policy had been followed by the Government in all essentials.[113] And Henry Pelling has argued that two most important areas of the trade union way of life remained unchanged during Attlee's term of office: 'One was the voluntary system of collective bargaining which, in spite of the spread of wages councils, still accounted for much the larger part of wages negotiation – the other – was the pattern of union growth and structure.'[114]

But Attlee was quite unwilling to surrender the prerogatives which he had ascribed to Labour's political arm in 1937. The trade unions, he had written, were the backbone of the movement, but the Party represented something more than the needs of organized labour. It was a national party with a Socialist objective. It might conclude that certain immediate demands from a trade union were in conflict with Socialist policy.[115] On the general point Attlee would even risk a clash with Bevin, who was adamantly opposed to any system by which the State attempted to regulate industrial wages or conditions of work. The latter, Bevin considered, should be left to the recognized organizations of employers and employees,[116] despite the fact that the TUC itself had recommended, in 1944, the establishment of a National Industrial Council to advise the Government on all aspects of industrial policy.[117] Attlee took the view that, though it was evidently impossible for the State to assume complete responsibility for wage-fixing, with the new conditions created by the full employment policy and the socialization of important industries, the Government could not leave the matter entirely to employers' and workers' organizations, especially in view of the danger of pressure for wage increases from workers in the sheltered trades.[118] The Cabinet majority supported the setting up of a National Industrial Conference to promote 'communication' between the Government and both sides of industry and, when Bevin was absent in Paris, carried the proposal.[119] The National Joint Advisory Council, as the body was eventually named, came into operation in October 1946.

Consultation and advice, however, were not sufficient. The industrial recovery was too successful and the foreign loans were used up more quickly than anticipated: multiple demands for scarce materials and labour meant inflation. Government action to impose import restrictions, wage controls and wage increases in certain industries could not be avoided. In one sense the extraordinary winter of 1947 bolstered Attlee's thesis because it revealed the extreme delicacy of the entire industrial situation. The shortage of coal forced the suspension of the electricity supply to commercial users in large areas: unemployment immediately jumped and revived all the old fears. Eleven days after the Government had announced the suspension, a new economic policy was published. The *Economic Survey for 1947* 'stressed physical economic planning and for the first time established explicit priorities and production targets for the year, industry by industry'.[120] There had been no specific consultation with the unions beforehand, apart from general talks between the Government and the TUC concerning 'wage-restraint'.[121] In July Attlee warned the Cabinet that the Government had a duty to adopt a positive wages policy, though it should also be borne in mind that in those countries where the Government had intervened in questions of hours and work the results had not been satisfactory.[122]

By August 1947 the decline in Britain's balance of payments took a serious turn. Sterling, according to the terms of the American loan, had been made freely convertible. Morrison was deputed to tell the TUC's leaders that the Government proposed to take certain steps 'which would directly affect work-people and their Trade Unions'. The steps included the reintroduction of the Control of Engagement Order, a request to the General Council to ask member unions to accept an increase in working hours and the establishment by the Ministry of Labour of a branch to collect and collate information on wages and hours. Speaking to the Commons on 6 August, Attlee repeated these proposals and appealed to workers to avoid pressing for wage increases not tied to increases in productivity, especially to avoid asking for wage increases based on differentials.[123] Although the sacrosanct principle of voluntary wages negotiation had not been breached, the implication that it might have to be was evident. The decisive moment came in February 1948; a White Paper was issued which declared unilaterally that there could be no justification for any further wage increases without commensurate increases in productivity.[124] Several altercations followed, requiring Attlee's personal intervention,[125] but in the end the Government got what it wanted, a period of wage restraint which lasted from 1948 to 1950. Attlee had no hesitation about exploiting the Government's position of strength – it could have ended food subsidies and the unions had no alternative but to support it. The unions may have theoretically preserved the principle of free collective bargaining: in practice, they yielded.

That they did also owed something to Attlee's efforts to ensure good industrial relations. Failure to maintain contact with the unions, he believed, had been one of MacDonald's major mistakes,[126] and he did not intend to repeat it. Of the six trade union figures in Attlee's original Cabinet,[127] one was Bevin and another was George Isaacs, a former TUC President whom Attlee made Minister of Labour. Attlee was the first Prime Minister to address the TUC's annual assembly and his theme was the necessity of co-operation, as essential during the period of reconstruction as it had been during the war. Co-operation had to be reciprocal. When the unions complained about his ministers' inadequacies in this regard, Attlee treated his overworked colleagues to a dose of his sarcasm. They were reminded that Neville Chamberlain had urged his ministers to co-operate with the unions in October 1939, and Churchill in 1940: Labour ministers had to be especially vigilant.[128] In 1950 Attlee paid a visit, unprecedented for a Prime Minister, to a trade union leader in hospital.[129]

The amount of co-operation he did receive was nothing short of remarkable. Union support of his appeal in 1948 for wage restraint had no precedent, not even during the war. It was an extraordinary gesture on the part of the TUC leadership, at a time when communist agitation in the rank and file was on the increase. The TUC's General Council also agreed to the continuation of the wartime Order making strikes illegal,[130] and did not insist on the restoration of other pre-war practices. During the winter of 1947 the Council accepted the re-introduction of the 1940 Control of Engagement Order, placing legal restrictions on workers changing their jobs.[131] The number of working days lost by strikes did not exceed 2½ million in any of the years from 1946 to 1951.[132] Attlee's premiership coincided with what might be described as organized labour's finest (peacetime) hour.

The picture was not completely rosy. An appeal by Attlee to the leaders of the miners' union to work an extra half-hour a day as a temporary measure had no effect.[133] The inadequacy of using troops where specialized technology was involved – as at the London power stations in 1950[134] – was an ominous sign of potential difficulties. That year the TUC's General Council itself was unable to withstand a resolution at its annual conference declaring that there was no longer any basis for a restraint on wage applications – despite a speech to the contrary from Attlee.[135] But although problems remained, Labour had got the job done; by 1950 an industrial recovery was under way and the country's trading position had greatly improved, though the cost of living had increased. Attlee had good grounds for regarding 'keeping the confidence of the trade unions' as one of his successes.[136]

In itself, the Parliamentary Conservative Party posed no threat to Attlee's administration from 1945 to 1950. Some 60 per cent of the pre-war Conservative MPs either retired or lost their seats in 1945;[137] those who survived appeared bewildered at the sheer speed with which the Government implemented its domestic programme.[138] The Opposition's clumsy attitude to the National Health Service Bill meant that for the next four years the Conservatives were forced to deny that they were against the Act in principle.[139] The Tory progressives needed time to reorientate the Party's policies:[140] the Industrial Charter, which accepted the general idea of government control and, within limits, measures of nationalization, was not formally endorsed until October 1947.[141] Conservative Party approval of the Welfare State, with some stipulations about tighter administration and reduced costs, had to wait until July 1949.[142] From about 1947 onwards, the Conservatives did manage to find a certain unity of expression – by playing on scarcities and shortages. A Gallup poll in August 1947 indicated that the Labour Party had lost its lead for the first time. But this was a tactical rather than a strategic gain, despite the deterioration of economic conditions. Gains at the Conservative municipal level in 1947 and 1949 were not reflected at the national stage: the Government did not lose a single seat at a by-election from

1945 to 1951, the first such case since 1832. Moreover, after an initial heavy swing from Labour in 1945 and early 1946, the Conservative lead over Labour in the opinion polls rarely exceeded 5 per cent and by 1950 Labour was marginally ahead.[143]

Confused as it was, the Conservative Party nevertheless held a potential ace of trumps. For a few months after the 1945 election Winston Churchill was disillusioned and tired; he preferred writing his war memoirs and making speeches abroad to leading an effective Opposition. But after having his elbow jogged by the 1922 Committee of Conservative back-benchers in November 1945, Churchill was stirred into action. No one would have given anything for Attlee's chances in a parliamentary duel and the Government might have suffered considerable loss of morale and psychological damage on the floor of the Commons. The result, therefore, of Churchill's first major speech in December, on a motion of censure, was a complete surprise. For Churchill 'merely succeeded in setting himself up for Attlee's magnificent *coup de grâce*. Rising brilliantly to the occasion, the Prime Minister delighted his supporters and demoralized the Opposition with a sober and yet extremely forceful counter-attack.'[144] Churchill's speech, Attlee quipped, amounted to a complaint that, having been elected to carry out a socialist programme, the Government was not carrying out a Conservative one. The motion of censure was nothing more than the party move of a politician in difficulties. Churchill had spoken melodramatically of the 'gloomy vultures of nationalization hovering over our basic industries'. Was it his view, Attlee asked, that 'our basic industries are so rotten that they attract the vultures?' Churchill's assertion that the Government's nationalization proposals had diverted attention from the immediate task was 'an example of a static mind'. The Right Honourable Gentleman had gone down the primrose path which, as everyone would remember, led to the eternal bonfire.[145] Attlee's speech, reported *The Times*, was incisive in argument, lively in retort and touched with a playful humour. 'The debate', an editorial writer considered, 'had served the Opposition if at all, only by enabling them to measure the strength of the position they have to assail in the coming months and years.'[146] The *Manchester Guardian*, more than a year later, rated Attlee's performance as the best of his parliamentary career.[147] and Attlee included it in his list of major successes as Labour leader, because it established his debating position against Churchill.[148]

Attlee's debating superiority vis-à-vis the Leader of the Opposition continued to be one of the main and totally unexpected bonuses that accrued to the Government throughout the 1945–51 period. Attlee proved an almost impossible target to hit and, perhaps as a result, his personal standing in the country outran that of his party by 1950.[149] Between January and May of that year, a Gallup Poll revealed, approval of him as Prime Minister increased from 44 to 50 per cent, while disapproval declined from 42 to 39 per cent; the Government's standing, on the other hand, remained unchanged.[150] A speech by him, one journalist commented, 'was like a corkscrew thrust. The more it revolved in the mind, the deeper it went'.[151] This particular reference was to a speech by Attlee on foreign policy, but he has been similarly lauded on domestic matters. In February 1946, for instance, Attlee spoke during the second reading of the debate on the National Insurance Act. 'In his very powerful speech,' a historian has noted, 'Attlee went to the heart of this whole new conception of social insurance and of the completely changed role of Government in employment policy. It was a speech which, for lucidity and unemotional persuasiveness, ranks high among the great contributions to Parliamentary debate.'[152] In November 1946, Attlee could remark almost complacently that, 'We have our debates and opposition but at the end there is not left a little barren controversy, but a good fat volume of Acts of Parliament.'[153] His forte was winding up a debate,[154] and he also excelled at question time 'when both ministers and backbenchers appreciated the merits of brevity'.[155] Against Eden he was less effective: Eden's 'gentlemanly methods ... provoke[d] in him an answering amiability which too often turn[ed] to dullness';[156] but Eden was a lightweight. The important parliamentary duel was with Churchill which took on the character 'of a contest in the bullring with Attlee as a small and nimble toreador teasing and infuriating his magnificent opponent with his sudden barbs.'[157]

After the terrible winter of 1947, Churchill judged the moment ripe for another censure motion, and this time his attack was more vicious. The socialist Government, he thundered, had deemed it their mission to impose their particular ideological formulas and theories upon the rest of their fellow citizens, which amounted to a 'crime against the British State and people'. He accused Attlee and his colleagues of 'mouthing slogans of envy, hatred and malice'; they had 'spread class warfare throughout the land and all sections of society ... [had] divided the nation ... as it never [had] been divided...'[158] Attlee responded by saying that Churchill liked this form of oratorical exercise. Labour enjoyed him 'doing his stuff ... He amuses me a little because he always gets up with such an air of injured innocence.' But Attlee doubted whether Churchill had contributed much to the serious side of the debate. Turning to the Government's Economic White Paper,[159] which had been the occasion for the censure motion, Attlee stressed the necessity for flexibility in the Government's approach to economic policy. Indeed, that there could be any complete blueprint would have been rejected by any member of the Coalition Government. Since Labour had taken over there had been the delays over the peace treaties and the difficulties over the maintenance of the occupation forces, coupled with the uncertainties about the American loan and the problem of post-war shortages. It was the latter that had made controls necessary, and he poured scorn on the sheer simplicity of Churchill's suggestions. The British, Attlee said in effect, just could not go to the US to buy food that did not exist with money they did not have; and the same applied to other commodities. It could even be said, he continued, that the Government's very successes – with demobilization, the reabsorption of industry, housing and repair work – had increased the difficulties of economic planning. Churchill seemed to think that nationalization was desired for nationalization's sake, whereas it was simply a means to an end, 'a fine standard of life for all people, and putting the interest of the community before that of certain private-property interests'.[160] *The Times* parliamentary correspondent noted that Attlee had 'brought a darting liveliness, salted with wit, to his reply . . .'[161] while the historian of the Conservative Opposition considered that Attlee disposed of Churchill's strictures 'magnificently'.[162]

Attlee's success in the Commons mattered far more to him than what the newspapers said. This was just as well for, as one experienced journalist has observed, he had 'a calamitous Press', and was the most derided and underrated of all Prime Ministers that the journalist ever met. The newspapers were 'consistently and irresponsibly political, slanted and prejudiced', but Attlee never once replied in kind.[163] In fact, the extent to which he ignored the media and public relations generally has been accounted one of the Government's mistakes.[164] Attlee allowed the information services to be run down considerably – for reasons of principle as well as economy. When the Cabinet discussed the wartime Ministry of Information in December 1945, he declared that it was 'politically dangerous that there should be a Minister with no other responsibility but the conduct of publicity'. The Ministry was wound up and a more limited Central Office of Information established in its place.[165]

Attlee of course knew that a British socialist Government would arouse great public interest in Britain and abroad.[166] He therefore appointed Francis Williams, a former editor of the *Daily Herald*, to the newly created post of Adviser on Public Relations to the Prime Minister. Williams had a difficult assignment, which lasted only two years. Attlee's first words to him were not encouraging: 'As you know, Francis,' he said, 'I am allergic to the press.' Williams found that Attlee took no interest in what the newspapers had to say about him, 'had no desire to seek out their company and no wish to bribe them with confidences. He took the old-fashioned view that politicians and journalists were likely to do their best work if they were not in each other's pockets.'[167] His reaction to Hugh Dalton's unfortunate Budget leak in 1947 exemplified his attitude: 'Behaved like a fool,' he told Williams. 'Can't see why anyone should want to talk to the press.'[168] He had complete confidence in his adviser, and after making the appointment confined his guidance to seeing Williams each morning in the Cabinet Room for a talk. Williams was also permitted to see all Cabinet minutes and papers, and all important Foreign Office telegrams, though he could not attend Cabinet Meetings; otherwise, he was left to his own devices as to how he should interpret the Government to the world. He could count on Attlee's support, even against a complaint from Bevin.[169]

Attlee was largely ignorant of the working methods of the press; the only way Williams could persuade him to have a ticker-tape service installed in 10 Downing Street was to suggest that Attlee could thereby obtain the lunch-time cricket scores.[170] His reading of the newspapers seems to have been limited to the *Daily Herald*, for Party affairs and to see what his colleagues were saying in public; and *The Times*, for the births, marriages, deaths, appointments and promotions columns and, especially, the crossword – in short, to keep in contact with his private world. He was still a Victorian when it came to the press, James Margach concluded, and 'he judged that as long as he had the support of the country and of Parliament, moving peacefully from its Imperial glory to its home-based role, he did not have to spare a thought for Fleet Street.'[171] Getting on with the job sufficed.

XI

Revolution Without Tears

How to regard what the Labour Governments of 1945 to 1951 actually accomplished? The question has provoked much controversy, but Attlee had no difficulty with it. The description of 'the job' that particularly appealed to him was 'revolution without tears'.[1] He and Dalton were agreed, in 1951, that the first chapter of the socialist story, in law and administration, had been written.[2] There had been 'a great levelling-up' of conditions, 'the mass of poverty had disappeared' and 'a far wider range of opportunity' existed.[3]

The main components of Attlee's 'peaceful revolution'[4] consisted of the Welfare State and the nationalization of approximately 20 per cent of British industry. Neither was intrinsically revolutionary, still less unique. Since the Second World War each has become a characteristic feature of many industrialized countries. In Britain, government provision of welfare and ownership of industry can be traced back to the sixteenth century.[5] Attlee's Victorian social inheritance included a state-run post office and elementary school system, besides municipal utilities of several kinds. Lloyd George and the Liberals had soon added social insurance; and the State's role in the economy and its sponsorship of welfare had grown steadily, mostly at the hands of Conservative administrations. Especially after 1931, social conditions had improved considerably, and just as important in Attlee's mind had been the change in public opinion about those conditions.[6] The war had provided a further demonstration, notably in the case of food rationing, that the British could respond positively to a policy of fair and equal shares. By 1945, it can be argued, the major task for 'socialism' had become more one of finding the right balance between state control or ownership of the economy and private enterprise than that of outright revolution. Many observers have discerned a pattern in these developments, one of continuous social progress coupled with increasing individual liberty. Indeed, this is how Attlee himself generally thought of English history, which may account for the air of normality that he lent to his Government's contributions to the process.

These contributions have been viewed as merely 'completing and consolidating' the work initiated by the Coalition.[7] For someone of Attlee's period and background, it has been suggested, 'any substantial increase in the welfare of the working class was itself a revolution.'[8] We have ourselves noted how he had always been willing to lay aside the visionary element in his socialism in favour of immediate, tangible benefits to the poor. And certainly the changes made by his Government stopped a long way short of what is usually considered social or economic revolution. The class structure was left virtually intact: with one minor exception, no wealth or capital gains taxes were introduced; the mainsprings of financial power and corporation profit were untouched. Whenever, it has been asserted, '"social justice" and "individual freedom", which it was Mr Attlee's declared purpose to reconcile, appeared to conflict, the Labour Party's native liberalism generally ensured that the new "equality" took second place to the older "liberty".'[9] As for nationalization, that of the Bank of England was little more than a technicality; the case for the public takeover of the coal, gas and electricity industries was largely won in advance; the railways were worn out; and the only controversial bill – for the nationalization of steel – was postponed. The economy was not modernized: neither power nor transport were fully integrated into two centralized organizations; inefficient units were not eliminated; unpromising and uncompetitive industries were not reformed; no serious effort was made to take advantage of restricted domestic demand and of the absence of foreign rivals other than the US[10] Instead, the 'once-for-all opportunity of 1945 was largely consumed in cleaning-up capitalism's messes and repairing its worst defaults.'[11]

These, however, are retrospective criticisms; there were few such at the time. Attlee would have readily agreed that his 'revolution' was not perfect: it was not intended to be so. He never imagined that socialism, any more than Christianity, could be imposed by law. He and his colleagues, he wrote, had not been afraid of partial solutions.[12] His philosophy was: show the people the Welfare State and the Mixed Economy and they will like it or, at least, accept it. The nationalization programme probably represented the maximum amount of legislation that could have been passed in the time available and fulfilled the election manifesto. In any case, Attlee did not consider that nationalization in itself was an integral part of socialism. It was one of several possible means to an end: control of the people's economy by the people and for the people. He reminded Churchill that nationalization had never been desired for its own sake, though Attlee had no doubt that the measures put into effect by Labour were necessary. As for workers' participation, he had long discarded the idea. The TUC had rejected it in 1932; Attlee's change of mind dated from his experience at the Post Office. In 1937 he had squarely opted for expert management, subject to general government policy. The workers were not, of course, to be treated as wage slaves, but the exact way of working out their status as 'citizens in industry' depended upon the circumstances of particular industries.[13] Later, he had come round fully to Morrison's managerial approach, with its emphasis on efficiency. Control of the industries nationalized between 1945 and 1951 was vested in the hands of public boards, with parliamentary supervision. If union representatives accepted appointment to the boards they had to sever their formal union ties.[14] Relatively few were so appointed.[15] Attlee somewhat apologetically explained that his Government had tried to get more worker involvement, without much success: 'A hangover from the past, I'm afraid. Some of them still had the old feeling of opposition to any administration. Others frankly said, "Well look, management isn't our job."'[16]

On the other hand, Attlee was clear that Labour's policy between 1945 and 1951 had not been to patch up an old system but 'to make something new . . . progress towards a democratic socialism.'[17] He believed that this had been achieved. And had it not been for 'the grave events which [had] darkened the international scene,' he broadcast in 1951, the British people 'could certainly have looked forward to an even wider extension of the great schemes of social betterment which had been enacted since 1945.'[18] These schemes represented an enormous advance on the piecemeal reforms of the past and they established the principle of universality. They also, in several fundamental respects, went beyond the wartime plans. The revisionist Labour politician, Anthony Crosland, has stressed that 'Social services extended to family allowances, a comprehensive National Health Service and a complete new structure, instead of minor improvements, of National Insurance: . . . in the fields of redistributive taxation, the level of employment, the Distressed Areas problem, the working class standard of living, and government control over the economy, much more was achieved than most pre-war writers ever anticipated.'[19] Crosland's list was not exhaustive. Other measures included the Children's and Legal Aid Acts (passed after the Government had supposedly run out of reformist steam[20]), the Town and Country Planning Act of 1947 and the National Parks Act of 1949, all of which have acquired extra significance with the passage of time. The nationalization programme, comprising the Bank of England, Cable and Wireless, the transport, civil aviation, coal, gas, electricity, railway, iron and steel industries, far exceeded anything proposed by the Coalition

Government. An American historian has even concluded that the Labour Government 'changed the nature of England's problem'. Afterwards, it was no longer a question of poverty or equality but rather the challenge to achieve for all her people a satisfactory standard of living.[21]

That such claims can be made at all is extraordinary. What really justifies Attlee's description of his Government's accomplishments as 'revolutionary' is the economic circumstances in which they were made. The country had been bankrupt for five years. 'Well boys, Britain's broke,' the Ambassador to the US had told American reporters towards the end of 1940, 'It's your money we want.'[22] Before the money was forthcoming (in the form of Lend-lease voted by Congress in March 1941), all fresh purchasing abroad had had to be stopped.[23] During the war it had become apparent that Washington intended to increase the US share of Middle East oil, gain access to British colonial markets, and break the sterling area – and that there was nothing the British could do about it. Pre-war self-sufficiency had depended on two factors: 'invisible income' from overseas investments, shipping, banking and other foreign and imperial financial services; and exports of manufactured goods. In order to recoup wartime losses of invisible income it was estimated that Britain would have to increase the volume of its pre-war exports by about 175 per cent.[24] But the National Debt had more than tripled; industrial plant had either been destroyed or run down because of insufficient maintenance, or had become obsolete; four million houses had been lost or damaged, and housing dominated public demand for labour and scarce materials; five million people were in the armed forces and 42 per cent of the work force (some four million people) was engaged in keeping them supplied. Only two million were producing goods for export and if any more workers had been available the raw materials for them to work on did not exist, neither did the ships to carry extra exports.[25] Shortage of manpower in peacetime was a quite unprecedented problem – as was the fact that Britain in 1945 (with major foreign and imperial commitments) was the world's largest debtor nation.[26] No difficulties of comparable magnitude had ever existed before. Far from being one of the greatest reform periods in British history, the Attlee era seemed destined for economic collapse and chaos. The achievement of those reforms, however they are viewed, demanded revolutionary imagination and determination.

Attlee, in his quiet way, was so determined. He warned his Limehouse electors that the post-war years would not be easy, that they would require from the nation the same resolute spirit as had been shown in the war; he nevertheless assured them that 'a higher standard of life than ever before and a more just social system' could be obtained.[27] And he did not allow the hair-raising financial situation to deflect him from his purpose. Debating the National Insurance Bill in the Commons in February 1946, he tackled the big question directly: 'Can we afford it?' 'Supposing the answer is "No",' he continued, 'what does that mean? It really means that the sum total of the goods produced and the services rendered by the people of this country is not sufficient to provide for all our people at all times, in sickness, in health, in youth and in age, the very modest standard of life that is represented by the sums of money set out in the Second Schedule to this Bill. I cannot believe that our national productivity is so slow, that our willingness to work is so feeble or that we can submit to the world that the masses of our people must be condemned to penury. After all, this is really the payment into a pool of contributions from employers and workers and the products of taxation, and the payment thereout of benefits to various categories of persons. It is a method of distributing purchasing power, and the only validity of the claim that we cannot afford it must rest either on there not being enough in the pool, or on the claim that some sections of society have a priority to take out so much that others must suffer want.'[28]

Prime Ministers have to be optimistic in public; Attlee's optimism was justified. By 1950, exports would rise to 175 per cent of their pre-war volume.[29] Despite 'the shortage of capital for the necessary investment and modernization, and the critical fuel situation . . . Britain made rapid headway in industrial production, notably in such modern technologies as machine tools, chemicals, electronics, aircraft and synthetic fibres.'[30] Capital investment would be 'at a rate higher than many had believed possible – much of it in the basic industries and in previously neglected and vital fields. Production and productivity rose while the average working week was reduced. The annual increase in manufacturing output of 8% and per capita increase in all industry of 3% compared well with any previous period of British industry and with other countries at the time.'[31] The economy, under the system of controls, expanded 'rather faster . . . than it had done for any equally long peacetime period since 1873 at least.'[32] Marshall Aid, the credit that made all this possible, was terminated in January 1951, some fifteen months ahead of schedule. Attlee's administration, another historian has considered, 'effected an economic recovery which was almost on a par with its diplomatic success'.[33] To Attlee, Labour's demonstration that it could govern alone and successfully in such extraordinary circumstances was of revolutionary significance.

His administration's distinctive feature was executive efficiency.[34] As Prime Minister, Attlee's contributions to this efficiency were obviously of consequence. They may not have been heroic; they were as vital as they were continuous and varied. To rehearse them in detail, however, would be tedious and difficult.[35] What may be attempted is an illustration of how he handled some of the inevitable internal crises during the early years of his premiership.

Like Churchill, Attlee's introduction to his position took the form of a Battle for Britain: the nation, Maynard Keynes pronounced in August 1945, was facing a financial Dunkirk. Escape was only possible on three conditions, an intense concentration on exports, immediate and drastic cuts in overseas expenditure and a substantial loan from the US If these were not met, there would have to be an indefinite postponement of the Government's best hopes.[36] The Coalition had been thinking in terms of a gradual transition from a wartime to peacetime economy as soon as the war with Germany was finished; instead, with the sudden collapse of Japan, Attlee was confronted with the abrupt cessation of Lend-lease and dire warnings of epidemic dangers in Europe during the coming winter.[37] His reaction was to put his government on the equivalent of a wartime footing. Financial discussions about the approach to the US became a matter of the utmost secrecy and the Cabinet was bluntly invited to prolong the Supplies and Services Bill for another five years, during which the Executive could exercise emergency powers just as in the war.[38] His ministers were given, in impartial fashion, to understand that the Cabinet's time was not to be wasted by unconsidered policies or parochial controversies.[39] They received regular digests of key statistics and Attlee had his Map Room converted into an operational economic headquarters where a series of charts was put on display.[40] A stream of sundry orders and curt observations began to flow from 10 Downing Street: the rate of release of doctors from the forces was inadequate; speedy reductions in Civil Service departments connected with the war had to be made;[41] the target of 1.5 million people to be demobilized by the end of 1945 was to be accepted; and the provision of shipping 'would be treated like a wartime operation'.[42] He telegraphed President Truman personally in October 1945 requesting the return of Britain's three largest vessels (the *Queen Mary*, *Queen Elizabeth* and *Aquitania*) or an equivalent lift.[43]

No British Prime Minister could possibly have been enthusiastic about the terms of the American loan; equally, no Prime Minister could have rejected them. During the vexed Cabinet discussions of the subject in November and December of 1945, Attlee was largely silent. The running was naturally made by the Chancellor, Dalton, while the main opposition came from Shinwell and Bevan. Attlee's point of view was similar to that of Bevin who, while feeling 'the most profound reluctance to any settlement which would leave us subject to economic direction from the US,' would have preferred 'a straightforward loan without conditions' as Keynes had originally thought possible.[44] But Bevin (and Attlee) were obliged to conclude that the only alternative to acceptance of the American terms was struggling on without American assistance, which would have meant lower living standards than during the war.[45] Shinwell and Bevan denied this conclusion, arguing that the American need for export markets was equal to the British need for a loan.[46] Attlee could only point out that the risk of a breakdown in discussions was not one that a majority of the Cabinet could contemplate.[47] Yet he was uneasy about the Government appearing to commit itself too strongly to the American proposal of an International Trade Agreement; he was concerned about the effect upon Australia and New Zealand.[48] Similarly, though approving the Cabinet's general acceptance of the American demand that sterling be made convertible in fifteen months, he suggested that there was no harm in letting British anxieties be known.[49] 'We were not in a position to bargain,' he ruefully commented later. 'We knew that the convertibility clause was quite impossible and would create difficulties later on and we told the Americans so. But they would not see it and we were forced to accept the fact that without the convertibility clause there would be no loan.'[50] The loan was not finally authorized until July 1946. It was for $3.75 billion plus $650 million for goods in transit at 2 per cent repayable in fifty years beginning in 1951, and it included the Bretton Woods agreement of 1944 which fixed the value of gold to the dollar, and a convertibility of sterling clause. 'Free trade for all the world but not for themselves,' was how Attlee described it.[51] He and Cripps considered that any agreement was better than no agreement; it would have to be renegotiated later.[52]

Until the loan was secured, a bankrupt Britain had to pay for all supplies received from the US and the economic predicament quickly made itself felt. Morrison reported in January 1946 that there would be a manpower shortage of 1.3 million by the end of the year: the defence machine could not be maintained on the current scale and, at the same time, industry be converted to peace production with the requisite speed.[53] The Chancellor and Keynes warned the Cabinet in February that overseas military expenditure had to be reduced immediately; if not, Dalton added, rations and employment would have to be cut. Ministers should realize, said Keynes, that they were 'going down the drain at a great rate' because of political and military expenditures overseas.[54]

Quite apart from the manpower and financial aspects of the economic problem there was also an acute world shortage of food. It was the latter which produced the first important dispute within the Cabinet. The food position in the British zone of Germany became critical and Attlee recommended on 8 March 1946 that the UK should take the risk of advancing a further supply of 75,000 tons of grain to the zone, in the expectation that a replacement could be obtained from the US.[55] The Cabinet reluctantly agreed, only to be informed by the Minister of Food (Sir Ben Smith) on 25 March that the wheat requirements of importing countries for six months ending 30 June exceeded available supplies by about a third; rice supply was even more deficient.[56]

By April 1946 the question of bread rationing at home had to be faced.

No immediate decision was taken, though the size of loaves and biscuit production were reduced in early May. Morrison was then dispatched to Washington to discuss the problem with Truman. He reported that there was certain to be a critical world shortage of wheat from May to September, though he was satisfied that the US authorities were now really determined to increase exports. The Americans would also take over the supply of wheat to the British zone of Germany and agreed to treat India as a special famine case. But they insisted that Britain had to cut its imports up to the end of September by 200,000 tons. Again, the Cabinet had no choice but to accept. Bread rationing now appeared certain.[57] Attlee, who had been intending to sack the Minister of Food at the earliest opportunity, accepted his resignation just before the parliamentary debate.[58] The new Minister, John Strachey, introduced an order on 27 June, approved by the Cabinet, going ahead with bread rationing from 21 July.[59] The decision was reaffirmed on 18 July.

Strachey, however, had been having doubts as to whether this drastic and politically dangerous course was necessary; he received a telegram from Canada, giving a new programme of wheat exports, too late for the Cabinet meeting. On 19 July, therefore, he wrote to Attlee saying that 'in view of these new figures I can advise you that the introduction of bread rationing could be safely suspended.' He was aware that Attlee had very forcibly made the point that Britain's international situation would be weakened if bread rationing were not introduced – 'in the sense that we should weaken our hand in demanding that the Americans should in future take care of needs of the British Zone in Germany'; but Strachey now thought that the feeding of the zone was 'likely to be a much easier problem than it appeared even a week or so ago'. Attlee and other Cabinet ministers were en route to the annual miners' rally in Durham. Morrison was in charge. He wrote to Attlee saying he agreed with Strachey and proposed to call a Cabinet meeting on the following day.

As soon as Attlee could get to a 'scrambler' phone, he called Morrison, taking the precaution of assembling Dalton, Lawson, Bevan and the Chief Whip: they were all convinced it would be a grave mistake to alter the decision. Attlee added that he also thought it a mistake to have called a Cabinet in the absence of at least six Cabinet ministers. He gave a succinct summary of the reasons for going ahead with bread rationing: there was no certainty that shipments would arrive in the UK from Canada or the US, on account of strikes; there was no real assurance about the British zone; the US Administration might think that bread rationing had been introduced to influence the loan debate; he had suspicions concerning the message from Canada, which might have been prompted by certain Opposition statements; the Commons had already decided, and a late change would be taken badly by Labour supporters; the Government would be justly accused of weak handling of the situation; decisions anyway depended not on ascertained facts but on estimates based on various unpredictable circumstances, and prudence was fully justified. Attlee would get the other Cabinet ministers in Durham together in the morning, but he was not prepared to reverse policy without a full Cabinet meeting. Morrison nevertheless went forward with his meeting in London and Attlee learned that Bevin,[60] Morrison, George Hall (the Colonial Secretary) and George Isaacs (the Minister of Labour) all favoured Strachey's recommendation. Those who stuck to the Cabinet's original decision were A. V. Alexander (the First Lord of the Admiralty), Tom Williams (the Minister of Agriculture), Chuter Ede (the Home Secretary), Lord Addison (the Dominions Secretary), and Lord Pethick-Lawrence (the Indian Secretary).

When he returned to London on 21 July, Attlee called a full meeting of the Cabinet. After allowing Strachey to state his case, Attlee proceeded methodically to demolish it. The deciding factor, on 18 July, he pointed out, had not been what would be available from Canada after September but what was likely to be the UK stock position at the end of August. The uncertainties about US ability to deliver grain and about the UK harvest still remained, nor had the situation sufficiently changed to justify suspension of the rationing scheme, which had already made a great impression in the US. Moreover, breakdown of the food supply in Germany or India or any of the British Far Eastern territories might lead the US to divert wheat destined for the UK. Suspension of the rationing scheme would leave the Government open to charges of vacillation, besides making its introduction in the future difficult. The Minister could safely bring the scheme to an end after six weeks or two months if it proved possible. Nor did Attlee see any reason why the Minister should not make public the new figures and take the view that, while encouraging, they did not warrant abandonment of rationing. The Cabinet was convinced.[61] Attlee had had against him three of the most senior Labour ministers – Bevin, Cripps and Morrison – as well as the Minister of Food (Strachey), the Lord Chancellor (Jowitt), the Minister of Agriculture (Tom Williams, who appears to have changed his mind overnight) and the Minister of Labour (Isaacs). Attlee's supporters – Bevan, Dalton, Hall, Shinwell, Chuter Ede, Addison and Whiteley – were all of much lesser political weight.

Strachey again recommended to Attlee in September that bread rationing be abolished, but the Cabinet agreed to continue it for a further period and, by October 1946, Strachey himself favoured its continuation.[62] By then the American Government had announced that it was no longer responsible for procuring food supplies on behalf of foreign countries who, henceforth, would have to use the ordinary channels of trade: this meant higher prices and greater difficulties. In December there was a possibility that the ration might have to be cut; in April 1947

Strachey practically begged Attlee to write personally to the Canadian Prime Minister, Mackenzie King, about the delays in wheat shipments, and even proposed that the extraction rate be increased from 85 per cent to 90 per cent! The Minister of Food received short shrift from Attlee, who curtly refused to write to Mackenzie King or anyone else; the Cabinet vetoed the increase in the extraction rate.[63] Bread rationing was not abolished until July 1948. As it turned out, there was no great shortage of bread; nevertheless the measure was highly unpopular and required political courage of a high order. Attlee had no doubt that the decision to ration bread had to be made. Churchill, had he been Prime Minister, would have done the same thing.[64] But in any case, equitable distribution of basic foodstuffs was what socialism was all about to Attlee.

Britain's economic troubles came to a head in 1947. They were symbolized by the temporary freeze-up of Big Ben during the winter, the severest since 1880–81.[65] They were compounded by political crises abroad, in India, in Palestine and in the British zone of Germany, and by the breakdown of the wartime alliance. Despite the decisions to get out of India, Greece and Turkey (which became known early in the year), the effect of imperial and foreign commitments on the manpower shortage, and on the related question of defence expenditure, remained a constant nightmare.[66] It is certain that no peacetime British government had ever encountered a more daunting set of circumstances. Any Prime Minister was bound to appear wanting. In many ways it is remarkable that Clement Attlee survived; and yet he did so with equally remarkable ease.[67]

Especially during the first half of the year, he was under tremendous pressure. The country's industrial fragility was underlined and exacerbated by the winter. In February, some 4½ million people were temporarily thrown out of work because of the fuel shortage, which was so critical that a report to the Cabinet was made daily. Attlee appointed a special committee under his chairmanship to monitor the situation and also to supervise plans for avoiding a similar crisis the following year. It was immediately apparent that there was no prospect of the UK producing enough coal to meet its needs for two or three years, owing to the manpower shortage.[68] He then ordered Sir Edward Bridges, the Cabinet Secretary, to investigate the division of responsibility and organization in coal production; duplication between the National Coal Board and various Government departments had to be avoided. In March, despite Bevin's known opposition, Attlee asked the Minister of Fuel and Power (Shinwell) to approach the US about the possibility of securing coal imports.[69] The expertise he acquired about the fuel problem helped him to dispose 'magnificently' of Churchill's strictures in the Commons in March, but it could not produce coal. The Conservatives drew level in that month's opinion polls, and subsequently increased their lead.[70] Nor did Attlee's sustained efforts[71] assuage more general misgivings among certain Labour MPs about public relations, industrial efficiency, planning and the Civil Service. It was argued, for instance, that there was excessive employment in less essential industries, and concealed unemployment in others; higher civil servants had too much influence over Government policy, while Civil Service organization and methods were poor. Fortunately, on these matters Attlee could count on the continued loyalty of the trade union MPs, who expressed their complete confidence in the Government.[72]

One reason for that confidence was Attlee's frankness. In January 1947, the Cabinet agreed to defer publication of a White Paper on the state of the economy, fearing that the difficulties and the inadequacy of the proposed remedies would expose the Government to serious criticism.[73] However, within ten days or so, Attlee decided that they must go ahead with the White Paper. The country had to be made fully aware of the situation whatever the political consequences. He supervised the drafting of the White Paper himself. In the murky light of the fuel crisis, still more potentially damaging changes had to be made in the forecasts of coal and electricity production which had been overestimated.[74] When it was published, in February, the *Economic Survey* put its major emphasis on the crucial need to increase production; the problems it revealed tended to belittle party politics, particularly partisan Labour views. It admitted that there were limits to planning and explained frankly that 'the task of directing by democratic methods an economic system as large and complex as ours is far beyond the power of any Government machine'.[75] *The Times* called the *Survey* 'the most disturbing statement ever made by a British Government.'[76]

Stafford Cripps then began a vigorous attempt to shape the direction of the economy – to increase production and divert imports as much as possible away from dollar areas – by a series of government regulations coupled with incentives.[77] There was no hope, however, that these or any other measures could succeed in solving Britain's financial plight.[78] Despite the Marshall offer, made on 5 June, the financial underpinning of the economy collapsed in the early summer. The senior group of Cabinet ministers, Attlee, Morrison, Dalton, Bevin and Cripps, were informed on 17 June that, at the existing rate of withdrawal, the American credits would be exhausted by November – well before the Marshall Plan could come into operation.[79] World recovery continued to be slow and there was an acute shortage of dollars – due to world-wide demand and the fact that American wholesale prices had increased 40 per cent since the conclusion of the Loan Agreement. In Britain, the production of coal and steel had not made up the shortages caused by the weather crisis.[80] As the day of convertibility, 15 July, drew near there was a dramatic run on the pound. On 1 August the Government was forced to adopt a whole new range of cuts in dollar expenditures in a vain effort to shore up the balance of payments deficit.[81] The austerity plan that Attlee presented to the Commons on 6 August included new targets for coal, steel, agriculture and exports, reductions in the armed forces and in dollar imports, reallocation of raw materials, and a control of engagement order. But he was adamant that these measures should not interfere with full employment, social security, the National Health Service or the housing programme.[82] Convertibility had anyway to be suspended on 20 August, and the rationing of foodstuffs increased.

Such was the wider economic background to Labour's debate over iron and steel nationalization, which also reached a climax in 1947. No other domestic proposal proved more divisive, within and without Labour ranks, and none was more of a challenge to Attlee's control of the Government. At issue was 'undoubtedly Labour's most hated legislation.' A highly organized anti-Government campaign in the country was exploited by the Conservative Party in Parliament.[83] Conservative feelings, Attlee thought, were perhaps aroused because hopes of profit in iron and steel were greater than in the other nationalized industries.[84] Conservative tactics probably contributed to a partisan Labour reaction; sensitive 'socialist' nerve endings were touched – at a time when the country's economic fate hung by the finest of threads. Personality conflicts among Labour ministers served to weaken flagging energies. Attlee's handling of the affair incurred the ire of Left and Right at the time, and subsequently. But there was no split.

In one way the Labour dispute was ironic. Attlee's comments in 1937 on the Party's *Short Programme* had made no specific reference to iron and steel nationalization, and the *Programme*, it has been noted, had been posited on the assumption that economic conditions would be 'normal'. The TUC, in 1944, had not given the iron and steel project a very high priority[85] and the NEC, at the 1944 annual conference, had wanted the Party not to commit itself on the subject.[86] Herbert Morrison, in particular, opposed the inclusion of iron and steel in the 1945 electoral programme on the grounds that it was 'too complicated and troublesome' an industry for public ownership.[87] Unlike the other industries on the list, iron and steel had not already come under a measure of public authority and it alone was a manufacturing industry.[88] Nevertheless iron and steel was included in the programme. Contrary to what is sometimes supposed,[89] a blueprint for iron and steel nationalization had been prepared, in 1934; it was this plan which had served as the basis for a scheme Hugh Dalton proposed to the Coalition Government in 1944.[90] During the 1930s the industry had been drastically restructured and by 1939 had become 'the most completely self-cartelized and controlled of any major British industry'.[91] Thus the industry's monopolistic character could be used to support both the demand for complete nationalization and also the argument that close government supervision short of ownership would suffice equally well for socialist goals, particularly in the extremely difficult short-term circumstances. To complicate the discussion, the industry's productivity record during the war had been generally good – which could certainly not be said of the coal industry, whose more urgent need of reconstruction was obvious.[92]

Quite properly, Attlee's preoccupation was with the timing of bringing iron and steel under some kind of state control, rather than with the principle or method. The question of method first arose in March 1946 when the Minister of Supply, John Wilmot, rejected the industry's own modernization proposal and decided in favour of full nationalization. Wilmot's decision was overruled by Morrison's Economic Policy Committee, which feared that the changes would have an adverse effect on productivity. In Cabinet, the combined strength of Bevin, Dalton, Bevan and Cripps prevailed in favour of nationalization over Morrison's opposition. At this stage Attlee was open-minded. A Cabinet Committee was appointed to prepare detailed nationalization plans.[93] Great pressure was then brought to bear by the industry's leaders on the Government, including representations to Attlee himself, against the project. It is probable that the winter of 1946–47, which revealed the fragility of the entire economy, was more influential in shaping his eventual attitude. There was a further practical consideration, unrelated to the issue's merits or demerits. Attlee warned the Cabinet in March 1947 that the provisional programme of legislation for the 1947–8 session would impose too great a strain on ministers and departments, and that it was essential to omit some of the Bills when the final programme was drawn up.[94] After a long Cabinet discussion in April as to whether the nationalization of iron and steel, or that of gas, should be included in the 1947–8 session, Attlee acknowledged that, in the main, opinion favoured the Steel Bill.[95] The chosen method was the simple one of the acquisition of shares in selected companies, all of which would be retained in their current form.[96] Attlee and other ministers, however, not persuaded that the timing and priority were correct, wanted first to proceed with gas. Attlee, in particular, had reached the conclusion that the steel nationalization project at that time would be a mistake.[97] What followed testifies to the weight of his Cabinet influence.

He asked Morrison privately to explore the possibility of finding a compromise with the steel employers, a task which Morrison was not reluctant to undertake.[98] Morrison's report was ready on 21 July 1947,[99] and presented to the Cabinet on the 24th. The Iron and Steel Federation was prepared to accept far-reaching statutory Government control, including the creation of an Iron and Steel Board with powers of future requisitions. These requisitions would take place (if necessary) only after the lifetime of the existing Parliament – which constituted a departure from Labour policy, though the Minister of Supply (Wilmot) and the steel union's leaders were amenable to the proposed compromise. Attlee now stated flatly that, in view of the economic circumstances, it would be inexpedient to proceed with nationalization in the 1947–8 session. The Government would be judged by its handling of the economic situation in the next one or two years; it could not afford to expose itself to the charge of having aggravated the problems by adopting a measure which might make it impossible to obtain the maximum output of steel. His intervention had the desired effect of denting the previous pro-steel nationalization majority. Some Ministers supported Morrison; others, including Bevan, insisted that steel had to be nationalized fully as soon as possible; Dalton indicated that he had changed his mind but did not favour Morrison's plan, while Bevin said that he was now clear that the original [April 1946] plan of nationalizing iron and steel by the acquisition of the industry's physical assets was unworkable.[100] A week later, Attlee declared that the postponement of the original scheme would not amount to a betrayal of the Government's political principles. He considered that both the original scheme and Morrison's compromise would leave the industry in a state of uncertainty which would have an adverse effect on production. He thought, as did Bevin, that there should be further consultation with the unions and that, in the meantime, the immediate need for increased production could be met by the use of the Government's new emergency powers.

Although Attlee now carried the Cabinet majority with him,[101] 143 Labour MPs signed a letter on 4 August urging him to scotch the rumours that the Cabinet was hesitating over the question. Attlee reiterated to the Cabinet three days later (the union leaders had been unable, or had not had enough time, to indicate their views), that to proceed with the original scheme at that time might lead to considerable disturbance in the steel industry. He wanted an announcement made that the Government would not introduce the project in the 1947–8 session. He took this view despite the fact that, as he wrote to Lord Nathan (Labour's Deputy Leader in the Lords), he had 'intimations of resignation whichever course we take', and did not like them. Only if Ministers stuck together would they get through their present difficulties.[102] Once again, he carried the day. Labour supporters were told that while the Government adhered to the nationalization policy, it needed more time for a final decision.[103] By a narrow majority, 81 to 77, with a large number of abstentions or absentees, the PLP agreed and the Labour crisis was over. In October, Attlee formally proposed to the Cabinet that the Gas Bill should be included in the forthcoming parliamentary session's legislative programme, and that of Iron and Steel excluded. Even Bevan now agreed.[104]

During 1947, discussion of Attlee's leadership was inevitable, but the so-called plotting[105] against him did not amount to much more than desultory talk. In effect he had become irreplaceable; any conceivable successor would probably have split the Party, as the years in opposition after 1951 were to suggest. Attlee was in a strong position in 1947: individual ministers had continually to fight each other over steadily diminishing national resources for their own departments. And though apparently willing to grumble,[106] Bevin refused to take any part in the 'plotting'. He would in all likelihood have refused to serve under Morrison, and Morrison under him. At any rate, Attlee's imperturbability was never ruffled. After the August bank holiday he departed for a much-needed holiday in Wales, returning only for the Cabinet meeting that decided to abandon convertibility. When he arrived back in London, Cripps boldly suggested (on 8 September) that Bevin should take over. Attlee responded by making Cripps the Government's chief economic co-ordinator in place of Morrison, and the leadership talk came to an abrupt end. Shortly thereafter Attlee proceeded to make important ministerial changes, which he first put to Morrison in a letter accurately described as 'strikingly authoritative in tone and informative in detail'.[107] So far as the ramifications of the steel issue were concerned, Wilmot was dismissed and Attlee suggested that Bevan become Minister of Supply instead – a suggestion Bevan found no difficulty in resisting! By the end of 1947, the crisis atmosphere in the Cabinet had begun to subside; meetings became less frequent and less heated.

However tense the Cabinet atmosphere at times may have been, the Attleean 'revolution' was constitutionally peaceful. There had been a period when Attlee had thought otherwise. In 1933 he had warned that a Labour Government might not be able to act 'with the most scrupulous regard to theories of democracy or exact constitutional propriety'.[108] From 1945 to 1951 such action was not necessary. Indeed, afterwards he could happily vaunt the constitution's flexibility. Control had passed successively from King to Lords to Commons. Nothing had been sacrosanct and the constitution's responsiveness to changed conditions and the shiftings of political power was precisely what had kept the country from violent revolution.[109] Attlee considered that in order to understand this flexibility, 'to catch the spirit of the constitution', one needed to have been in active politics.[110]

In his case that understanding began with an appreciation of the role of the monarchy, of which he was an unashamed and sentimental supporter. The institution, he wrote, had many practical advantages, notably its representativeness, its stability and its continuity. These assets applied particularly to the domestic scene, where the monarchy precluded to some extent the possibility of the people being carried away by a dictator. Attlee gave this 'establishment' argument a neat twist by maintaining that the greatest progress towards democratic socialism had been made in countries such as Britain, Norway, Sweden and Denmark, and not in republics. He would have thoroughly agreed with Samuel Beer that 'A king or queen is a symbol of the fact that the state is not just a nightwatchman.'[111] The advantages of a monarchical constitution extended also to the Commonwealth, where it served as a symbol of unity to diverse peoples.[112] To this end he welcomed the invitation to the King to visit South Africa, and positively urged him to continue with the tour in March 1947, despite the King's misgivings at being away from the country at such a critical time.[113] Attlee took the chair at the Commonwealth Prime Ministers' Conference in April 1949 which, in an attempt to define the undefinable, agreed in a Declaration to speak of a 'common allegiance to the Crown . . . [the] symbol of their association . . . [the] Head of the Commonwealth'.[114] A measure of Attlee's reverence for the monarchy's symbolic importance was his agreement with the King to restore the Order of the Garter to its original chivalric, Christian and personal status.[115]

According to Attlee, the individual monarch did not have to be a 'genius': it was enough that he be 'a good, ordinary man who understands how to fill an extraordinary position'[116] – a description that also applied exactly to himself! George V, whom Attlee met only briefly, struck him as a 'very fair-minded man – with a very high sense of duty': he made 'an excellent king' despite not having 'unusual intelligence'.[117] Edward VIII was not acceptable: Attlee had several meetings with Baldwin at the time of the abdication crisis and made it clear that the Labour Party would have little sympathy with Mrs Simpson. The objection was not to an American being Queen, it was to Mrs Simpson: a morganatic marriage would not be approved.[118] A leading Conservative MP was convinced that 'the really decisive influence was not the views of the Cabinet or even of the Dominion Premiers, but was that of the Labour movement': he recorded that 'There was not the slightest doubt on the part of Attlee or Bevin that the only alternatives facing the King were renunciation of Mrs Simpson or abdication. No compromise was possible . . . '[119] By contrast, Attlee got his family out of the house by 4.30 a.m.[120] to attend the coronation of George VI, and his expectations of the new King were not to be disappointed. The only time Michael Foot ever saw Attlee emotionally affected in public (and he had frequent opportunities to do so) was when Attlee spoke of George VI's death, with 'tears in his eyes and voice'.[121]

Originally George VI had been upset by Churchill's defeat. Conservative in politics, the King felt uneasy at the prospect of having to deal with 'aggressive Labour ministers'.[122] In fact, he and Attlee must have proved a fine match in mutual shyness,[123] informal as their conversations were. Attlee appreciated that, if he had had the choice, the King would probably 'have preferred the life of a country gentleman interested in farming and field sports'. But Attlee also found that the monarch had a 'real knowledge of industry and understood the mind of working people very well'. He was impressed by 'the picture of family life' that the Royal Family presented though, as Prime Minister, he was a 'little anxious as to where a suitable consort [for Princess Elizabeth] might be found'. In the event, he thoroughly approved of Prince Philip, and he was one of a minority of Labour members on a Select Committee that recommended, in December 1947, an increase of £5,000 p.a. in Princess Elizabeth's allowance, subject to a free vote in Parliament, to which he managed to secure the Cabinet's agreement.[124]

There were only two interventions by the King of any note during Attlee's premiership. The first concerned the King's suggestion of Bevin as Foreign Secretary, which Attlee went out of his way to deny as having any influence on him.[125] The second took place in 1947 when the King expressed his anxieties over the Supplies and Services [Emergency Powers] Bill, fearing that it might be used 'to curtail seriously those liberties which the ordinary British citizen has long regarded as a right . . . ' He was aware that Attlee's attitude in the matter was the same as his own and so long as Attlee headed the Government he knew that 'due regard will be given to the rights of Parliament itself, and that Parliament will be afforded the opportunity of exercising its proper functions of supervising legislation in respect of any orders made under this Bill.' But the King wanted a personal account from Attlee of the purpose and scope of the Bill.[126] Attlee replied that his main intention in introducing the Bill to Parliament had been 'to put it beyond doubt that the powers given by the 1945 Act could not be used for the immediate purposes of the present economic crisis . . . ' This intention had been privately explained to the Opposition before the Bill had been introduced, and the Government had had reason to think that any grave apprehensions on the part of the Opposition had been removed. He was surprised and sorry that Churchill had attacked the Government on the grounds that the Bill was designed for other ends. Both the 1945 and the 1947 Supplies and Services Acts extended the rights of Parliament, by providing that Orders and other Statutory Instruments made under the Defence Regulations should be subject to parliamentary challenge, whereas this had not previously been the case. There was no reference to direction of labour in the Act; these powers already existed and had been used, though with restraint and caution.[127] After his explanation, Attlee found that the King 'became quite happy again'; he realized that Churchill's fulminations were 'only an Opposition stunt and that there was in fact no basis for anxiety'. Attlee could write that he never knew George VI to do anything that was not constitutionally correct and that, under him, the British monarchy increased its popularity and prestige.[128]

In one respect the King did have an important, if indirect, influence on Attlee's decisions. When he called an election in 1951 one of the factors he took into consideration was the King's position: George VI was in poor health and about to depart for a lengthy tour of Australia and New Zealand. Though there were other reasons for Attlee's election decision,[129] he did not think it fair to let the King leave with the possibility of a political crisis hanging over him. After the election, one of the King's first actions was to confer the Order of Merit on his former Prime Minister.

Despite his fondness for the monarchy, Attlee had taken a very different attitude to the House of Lords. We have seen that in 1933 he had favoured its immediate abolition if Labour came to power. In 1937, while acknowledging that the Labour Movement had 'no desire to obscure the economic issues which it presents to the country by staging a constitutional struggle . . . ', his hostility had not weakened, because he thought that the Lords would probably oppose a Labour programme. He stressed that 'Labour would not allow its measures to be whittled away by . . . [Lords] amendments or to be subjected to delay.' He continued to view the Lords as an 'anachronistic survival', considering that it had no federal function and existed to preserve a social system based on capitalism and class privilege. Whatever the case for having a piece of constitutional machinery for the purpose of reviewing and technically amending legislation, he could see none for any constitutional obstacle to the decisions of the people.[130]

In the light of wartime experience, the issue became less significant. The Lords made no difficulties about 'war-socialism', and political goals which had seemed radical in 1937 appeared much less so in 1945. Churchill himself had gone out of his way to create several new Labour peerages, not intended as political honours or as rewards, but deliberately designed 'as a special measure of State Policy . . . to strengthen the Labour Party in the Upper House, where its representation is disproportionate at a time when a Coalition Government of three parties is charged with the direction of affairs'.[131] By the end of the war it had been tacitly agreed between the parties that there was at least a basis for further discussion of Lords reform, and Labour's 1945 Election Manifesto preferred to remain silent on the subject.[132] For almost three years the Lords posed no practical obstacle to the enactment of Labour measures – a situation to which Attlee's adroit appointment of the highly experienced Christopher Addison as Labour Leader in the Lords no doubt made a special contribution.[133]

There was no point in the Lords using the delaying power provided in the 1911 Parliament Act during the Labour Government's first two or three years. Non-financial Bills automatically became law if passed by the Commons in the course of three parliamentary sessions and over a minimum period of two years. It was in the last two years or so of a Parliament's life that the power of the Lords to frustrate legislation approved by the Commons remained significant. Hence, in June 1946, the Cabinet asked the Lord Chancellor to prepare a report on the amending of the 1911 Act,[134] an action which took on much greater importance in the light of the debate on and eventual postponement of the iron and steel nationalization Bill. Attlee was convinced that this Bill would not get through the Lords in time to become law if the 1911 Act stood.[135] Discussion of Lords' reform however, in October and November of 1947, stirred up some of the old Labour feelings. Addison wanted the hereditary right of peers to vote abolished altogether. The Cabinet decided against this suggestion as it would make the proposed reform too wide-ranging.[136] The Bill thus introduced into the 1947–48 session, and eventually passed despite the Lords' objections in December 1949, reduced the delaying powers to two successive sessions and a minimum period of one year. Though agreeing with Addison on the principle of a more drastic change, Attlee sided with the Cabinet majority who favoured passing the Parliament Bill before wider discussions, arousing controversy, could encourage the Opposition to delay its passage.

Addison had made several other proposals, all of which were attractive to Attlee: these included the payment of a reasonable salary to members of the House of Lords (Attlee's Government had already, in 1946, agreed to pay travelling expenses to regular members), the creation of life peers, and provisions to ensure that a House of Lords deprived of its hereditary members should not contain a permanent majority for any one political party. Attlee was not concerned about the logicality of reform. In constitutional matters, there were great dangers in trying to be too logical, he told the Cabinet in January 1948. It was in accord with British traditions to hold on to the past by adapting existing institutions, however illogical that course might be. The House of Lords had been founded on the hereditary principle, but it would be quite in accordance with British constitutional development to retain the House of Lords while abolishing the hereditary principle.[137] For tactical reasons he thought it best that the Government should not initiate discussions about House of Lords reform, though standing ready to consider proposals from other parties. In January 1948, the Cabinet agreed to enter into talks with the Opposition in return for an assurance that the Parliament Bill would either be passed or definitely rejected before the end of the current session.[138] Attlee's view was that it was better to reach agreement with the Opposition about the period of delay to be given to the Lords, both in order to get the Parliament Bill passed, and to reduce the risk of a future Conservative Government upsetting it.[139] Talks among party leaders took place in February, March and April 1948 and a certain measure of common ground was found. The talks broke down over the question of what powers a reformed House of Lords should have, in particular how long it could delay legislation and whether, as the Conservatives wanted, it could force the Government to hold a general election.[140]

It remains to be stressed that the Second Chamber, of which Attlee actually became a member in December 1955, was far different in character from the one whose abolition he had advocated in the 1930s. The new Earl Attlee found that among those few peers who attended, some did so because they liked to keep in touch with politics and old friends, others because they liked to speak; but for most the 'overwhelming incentive' was 'public service'.[141] It might also be added that the Criminal Justice Act of 1948 had abolished the privileges of peers in criminal proceedings. The Labour Government, Morrison has admitted, was not anxious for the rational reform or democratization of the Second Chamber, 'for this would have added to its authority and would have strengthened its position as against that of the House of Commons'.[142] This was also Attlee's view. He much preferred 'revolution without tears'; it was more effective than the other kind.

XII

Not As Simple As That

'Mr Attlee will deal with the international situation on Wednesday morning,' the delegates to Labour's 1945 annual conference (held in May) were briskly and confidently informed. But in this field Attlee's main contribution was to introduce a note of caution into the proceedings. Few people had more intimate knowledge than he of the complexities confronting statesmen at the end of the war. 'I have sometimes heard speeches,' he said, 'suggesting that all international problems could be solved if we could only get a few people sitting around a table and discussing them. Believe me, the thing is not as simple as that.'[1] At the same time, Attlee was not entirely devoid of hope. There was a chance that the organization whose birth he had just witnessed in San Francisco might prove to be the instrument of a more ordered world. If the UN Charter was not perfect, at least it was acceptable to the US and the USSR. To that extent the Charter's basic provisions corresponded to the realities of world power. In any case, it was not the exact provisions that were important so much as the spirit in which they were carried out.[2] The liberation of atomic energy, he told an all-party rally in October 1945, had added a new dimension to international relations; war had become merely a form of suicide. Either mankind set up an organization like the UN and made it work, or it would face appalling consequences.[3] His Government firmly intended to make the success of the UN the primary object of its foreign policy.[4]

In this context, Attlee's appointment of Ernest Bevin as Foreign Secretary appears at first contradictory. Nationalistic to a fault, Bevin sometimes seemed to confuse international with union politics. Rhetorically addressing himself to his 'Russian friends' at the annual conference, he had aggressively declared: 'Round the table we must get but do not present us with *faits accomplis* when we get there . . . The cards should be on the table, face "uppards".'[5] Attlee, equally aware that the most obvious threat to British interests came from the Soviet Union, expressed similar views more diplomatically. Everything depended, he told the conference, on the UK, the US and the USSR working together in harmony; the vital condition for any success was that the comradeship which had won the war should continue into the peace. Power as well as will would be needed to prevent aggression, and Britain had to make her contribution.[6] Power, of course, was what Britain manifestly lacked. Attlee's renewed 'internationalism' in 1945 coincided even more closely than it had done in the 1930s with British interests, and her glaring inability to protect those interests by herself. His cautious 'idealism' and Bevin's robust 'realism' were twin aspects of the same approach.

The Foreign Office argument that a devastated Russia would have solid, material reasons for post-war co-operation remained to be tested; and, in the absence of any clear indication of long-term American policy, Britain had to test the argument. In one way, Russian policy turned out to be less of a difficulty than American: the Soviets behaved much as Attlee and Bevin had expected, whereas for some time it was almost impossible to fathom what the Americans would do. Attlee and Bevin were to discover that the only cards on the table in the next two years were to be British cards, of rapidly declining value. Until the Americans committed themselves Britain could not have a foreign policy so much as aspirations for one. The resulting holding operation required great tact and patience, and these were not among Bevin's outstanding virtues. Often in ill health, he was capable of crude diplomatic lapses. His expertise lay in the areas of negotiation and organization, but at first negotiations failed and he had nothing to organize. Later, his many talents would be put to good use. In the meantime, Attlee's self-control, his restraint in language and temper and, above all, his concentration on the global situation acted as a calming influence, a brake and a point of reference for Bevin. Together they complemented each other admirably.

The immediate British concern was for a permanent European peace settlement. On the resolution of this problem depended the fate of the wartime alliance and the future of international relations. The central issue, politically as well as geographically, continued to be Germany. As regards the larger question of Germany's future as a whole, Attlee was quite unrepentant. Entire generations had been absolutely warped and twisted into barbarism, he told the Labour Conference; great changes over a long time would be needed before the German people would be regenerated and fit to be admitted fully into the comity of nations.[7] But there was also the specific question of the British zone of occupation, and the connection between this and Germany's future as a whole had at first been thought to be reparations. Attlee, in the name of the War Cabinet, had impressed on Churchill at Yalta that reparations had to be considered together with dismemberment. Then, in March 1945, the Chancellor of the Exchequer had warned that reparations and dismemberment ought to be seen as alternative policies. Unless Germany was treated as an economic unit, the burden of underwriting the German economy would fall primarily on the British on account of their occupation of the region most industrialized and least self-sufficient in food. If the Russians were allowed to make up deficiencies in reparations from their zone by taking them from the others, the British would scarcely be able to support their zone in the absence of compensating agreements as to food supplies.[8] Bevin's warning to the Labour Conference in May that the Germans had to be permitted to grow food[9] was quite deliberate; without food from other zones the British zone could not be made to function. Thus the British went to Potsdam determined that their two German bargaining assets, control of most of the German fleet and merchant navy, and the industry in the British zone, would only be traded for food supplies.

When Attlee and Bevin replaced Churchill and Eden at Potsdam, negotiations had reached a virtual stalemate. The *de facto* extension of Poland's frontiers to the Western Neisse river had simultaneously reduced Germany's food-growing area and multiplied the number of mouths to be fed (because of the refugee influx into the German rump).[10] Churchill had refused to recognize the extended frontier, but the general impasse was broken by the Americans.[11] As a result, the Russians and Americans were informed that Britain accepted the new frontiers pending, in the Conference euphemism, 'the final peace settlement'. Attlee and Bevin could do nothing about the western enlargement of Poland at Germany's expense and probably did not desire to do anything, other than to see what the Russians would concede for British recognition.[12] Much more important to Attlee was that the American 'package deal' seemed to denote active US involvement in the European peace settlement. The Americans proposed that the bulk of the Russian and Polish reparations claims should be met from the Russian zone. In addition, the Russians could have 25 per cent of the industrial capital equipment to be removed from the Ruhr as unnecessary to a peace economy on condition they made available an equivalent value in food, coal, potash, zinc, timber, clay and oil products. A further 15 per cent of capital equipment would be transferred without any equivalent. Bevin managed to reduce these percentages and to include all the western zones from where the equipment was to come,[13] though there was a distinct air of unreality to the negotiations as there was no agreement as to the monetary or weight figures on which the percentages would be based.[14] It was also written into the protocol that reparations were 'to leave enough resources to enable the German people to subsist without external assistance' and imports into Germany were to have first claim on German exports.[15]

Certain economic and political principles to govern the treatment of Germany in the initial control period were also agreed to at Potsdam. From the British viewpoint, the most significant economic principle was Article 14, which clearly stipulated: 'During the period of occupation Germany shall be treated as a single economic unit.' The agreed political principles were the negative ones of demilitarization, deNazification and disarmament. The European Advisory Commission – whence the principles had stemmed – was wound up and what remained of its duties was transferred to the Allied Control Council, on which the French were given a seat just as Yalta had given them a zone. The seat included a veto which the French were to use freely. Not a party to the negotiations, the French bitterly resented the provisions made for central administrative German agencies, local self-government and democratic political parties. They were also left out of the naval spoils: the German fleet and merchant navy were divided among the Big Three, except for the submarines, most of which were sunk, with a few being shared out for 'experimental and technical purposes'. It was agreed that the transfer of populations (a far cry from the Atlantic Charter!) was to be carried out in 'an orderly and humane manner'. Most important of all, a Council of Foreign Ministers was created to draw up peace-settlement treaties with Italy, Rumania, Bulgaria, Hungary and Finland, and also to prepare for a peace treaty with Germany, whenever a German government was formed.

Attlee reported these arrangements to his first full Cabinet meeting. Noting that very little had been decided before he and Bevin assumed responsibility for British policy, Attlee's opinion was that, on the whole, the Cabinet 'could be very well satisfied' with the results of the Potsdam Conference. The other Labour ministers agreed.[16] They had, of course, hardly had time to assess the nature of the commitment in the British zone; nor was there any indication that the Americans, within a matter of days, would turn off the Lend-lease tap to Britain itself. Even when the enormity of the British economic predicament had become slightly clearer, Attlee did not hesitate to overrule certain ministerial doubts in regard to occupation policy. On 10 September 1945 Bevin, as chairman of the Cabinet's Overseas Reconstruction Committee, drew up a memorandum on 'The Industrial Disarmament of Germany'. It was based on three assumptions: (1) that Germany would be prohibited for an indefinite period from maintaining armed forces, possessing arms and munitions, or maintaining plant for their manufacture; (2) that Germany would not be further dismembered, 'though important territories would be ceded to neighbouring States', and the Reno-Westphalian industrial district would not be withdrawn from the German economic complex; and (3) that Germany would not be occupied indefinitely but for a sufficiently long period (at least ten years) to allow the changes in the industrial structures proposed in the memorandum 'to have a chance of becoming permanently established'. Britain's immediate purpose was 'to achieve security against the possibility of a future German aggression', the paper explained, and went on to specify 'a drastic policy over a selected field of German industry to eliminate the basis of Germany's war potential'. There was to be no civil aircraft potential and no merchant marine (except coastal and short sea traffic); steel capacity was to be reduced to 50 per cent of the pre-war capacity of 23 million tons per annum; the production of machine tools was to be limited to the requirements of a peaceful engineering industry; the production of ball and roller bearings, ammonia and methanol produced by high pressure hydrogenation, and synthetic oil were all to be eliminated. Furthermore, the list was not regarded as exhaustive; in a few years war potential might be based on quite different industries, the paper stated.[17] When the memorandum came before the Cabinet three days later, there was a fair amount of criticism. Some ministers thought it was too severe, others not severe enough, and some complained that it was too difficult to consider security without looking at the economic aspects. Summing up with his usual skill, Attlee agreed that the Cabinet was confronted with a difficult balance of considerations, but he pointed out that Bevin's proposals dealt purely with the short term and it was urgent that British representatives should have guidance. He recommended that the memorandum be endorsed; the Cabinet concurred.[18]

Attlee had no quarrel with the idea of reparations. He did not intend to go 'soft' with the Germans. Serious warnings about the shortage of food in Europe, and especially in the British zone of Germany, soon reached London. Attlee told the TUC on 12 September that there was bound to be intense distress on the Continent that winter, but he reminded the Congress that the position at home would not be easy.[19] A motion expressing concern about the situation was due to be presented in the Commons on 26 October and the Cabinet met to discuss what line to take. Bevin stated that the debate might develop into a discussion of Russian policy in Europe and thought the time had come to refer publicly to the effect of Soviet food policies. (No food was being sent to the British zone.) But Attlee considered that the principal Government speaker (Bevin) should make a number of other points. The Commons should be told that, as Britain had been engaged for six years in inflicting the greatest possible damage on the German economy, it could not be expected to recover within a few months. Conditions in Germany were bound to be distressing and were likely to get worse during the winter. The Germans had been specifically warned about the consequences of prolonging the war; the resulting conditions were their own fault. The situation had been aggravated by the actions of certain European governments in expelling Germans from their territory. Britain could not materially improve conditions in Germany by herself; any widespread relief had to be organized on an international basis with the co-operation of the food-exporting countries. The Minister of Food who was to reply to the debate could add that the small additional contribution of foodstuffs from Britain was to go to the schoolchildren in the British zones of Germany and Austria.[20] The Russians, in short, who were presumably kept informed of British policy by their spies, had little to fear from Attlee's general attitude to Germany. That they scorned his approach undoubtedly had its effect on his attitude to them later.

During the autumn of 1945 the international spotlight switched temporarily away from Germany – to Washington where feverish loan negotiations were proceeding, and to the Council of Foreign Ministers' meetings, the first of which was held in London.[21] Attlee followed the Council's discussions very closely and did not hesitate to intervene in them. When the London meeting failed, ostensibly for procedural reasons, he wrote a sharp letter to Stalin.[22] But it is doubtful that Attlee was unduly perturbed at this stage by the delay in dealing with Germany. So far as he was concerned, the Germans deserved to feel 'the full impact of military defeat'. Even if he had wanted, there was not much he could have done. During the latter part of the war he had shared Churchill's disappointment at American strategic policy; now he found that the Americans 'had an insufficient appreciation . . . of the entire European situation. They suspected us of being old-time Imperialists and were inclined to think of Russia and America as two big boys who could settle things amicably between them.'[23] Each of the other Allies had its own preoccupations and frustrations in Germany. Molotov's attempt in London to raise the question of reparations had been outvoted[24] and, for France, Bidault had announced that he would oppose any creation of a central German authority until the western frontiers were settled.[25] The British zone was plagued with a multitude of organizational problems,[26] despite Attlee's appointment of a special Minister (John Hynd) to handle them.[27] Moreover, important as the German issue was, British foreign policy interests were not limited to an acceptable solution of that issue alone. These interests involved economic and strategic considerations over a wide area, notably in the Middle East, and appeared almost everywhere to collide with Russian interests or ambitions. On the other hand, American policy away from Europe in 1945 seemed incalculable. In these circumstances the British had to see if the Potsdam agreements on Germany could be made to work.

Some Labour left-wingers had come to another conclusion. In September 1945, the *New Statesman* published two articles by Richard Crossman arguing that Russian non-compliance with the economic principle agreed at Potsdam destroyed any possibility for German reconstruction and Four-Power collaboration; a dismembered Germany, of which at least one half would be alive, was preferable to a Germany united by famine, disease and death. It would be far better to reconstruct the country into an Eastern and a Western State.[28] Failing Russian co-operation, the journal pronounced editorially in October, the only course left for Britain would be to consider how to build up a Western Europe independent of the two superpowers.[29] How this was to be done was not explained, but Bevin conceded in the Commons that same month that perhaps it would have been better not to create zones: all he wanted was a reasonable insurance policy against a renewal of German aggression.[30]

The dilemma that Britain faced in Germany became much more apparent during the winter. In January 1946 Attlee, still without the American loan, was warned by Field-Marshal Montgomery that starvation and disease in the British zone were inevitable if further wheat supplies were not forthcoming. Attlee was compelled to divert additional US wheat destined for Britain to Germany,[31] and soon had to contemplate the possibility of bread rationing at home. Substantial food cuts had to be made in the British zone in March, which were followed by a 10 per cent drop in the output of the zone's most precious resource, coal.[32] Even Dalton, preparing his April Budget on the assumption that the American loan would be ratified, included an estimate of British expenditure on the zone in the next financial year of £80 million, mostly in dollars, and this figure excluded military costs. To compound the diplomatic problem, before the second meeting of the Council of Foreign Ministers in Paris in April, Bevin formally reported that the French, too, did not accept the Potsdam decision to treat Germany in the occupying period as an economic unit.[33] While the meeting was in progress Bevin outlined two alternatives for British policy: either to continue to work towards a unified (though federal) Germany, or to seek to promote the formation of a Western German State or States which would be a bulwark against the spread of Communist influence from the east.[34]

Attlee, however, still took the view, both on general grounds and because Britain lacked the resources to organize the British zone as a stable separate unit, that the dangers of splitting what was left of Germany were greater than those of continuing to negotiate.[35] During an adjournment of the Paris meeting, Bevin, in his way, loyally supported Attlee's opinion: there were most weighty arguments against taking the measures necessary to make the British zone self-supporting; it would mean a complete break with Russia and if Potsdam had to be cast aside he would prefer the Russians to initiate the break.[36] The British and Americans had already suspended reparations deliveries to the Russians, but moves for their resumption went on and social relations on the Allied Control Council remained good.[37] In 1946 it was possible to hope that an East-West rupture might be avoided. Czechoslovakia had a coalition government and in Hungary the Communists were in the minority. When, at the Paris meeting, US Secretary of State Byrnes privately suggested to Bevin that arrangements be made at once for British and American zonal co-operation (the Americans had made the unpleasant discovery that their zone was costing them $200 million a year) to the exclusion of the Russian zone, Bevin replied that it would be a mistake to take an action at that stage which implied a clear division between the two Germanies. Only if the possibility of Russian co-operation had to be abandoned should it be done.[38] The rest of the Cabinet agreed.[39] In March, Churchill had called for an Anglo-American alliance (which had disturbed some leading Conservatives);[40] Attlee, in June, declared to the contrary, 'We do not want in any way to get an exclusive friendship.' It would be fatal to accentuate the line of division between east and west Europe. An attempt had to be made to understand the Russian mind and Russian history. He did not want to accept 'the counsel of despair' that would divide Europe into two absolutely separate camps. The difficulty with Potsdam was that, whereas the British regarded it as laying down some general principles to be applied, the Russians had insisted on importing into the agreement a rigid, literal interpretation. He admitted that, as a result, the British had been placed in a terribly difficult position. The trouble was that the Russians did not understand how democracies worked: the iron curtain, he added in reference to Churchill's Fulton speech, was really 'a curtain between minds'. Attlee did not choose to draw the conclusion that only open minds could deal with each other; instead, he stressed that patience was needed.[41]

Soon after his address to the Commons, Attlee briefly replaced an ailing Bevin during the second half of the Paris meeting which ended on 15 July 1946. The experience was probably conclusive for him and it is now clear that the meeting effectively terminated negotiations with the USSR over Germany. Ostensibly the talks were to be resumed in New York later in the year, but the third Foreign Ministers' meeting did not deal with Germany in detail and the issue was put off until March 1947. Meanwhile, events took their course. A speech by Byrnes in Stuttgart in September 1946 seemed to herald a major shift in American policy, and the trouncing of the Communists in the Berlin municipal elections in October probably served to stiffen the Russian attitude towards the West. Above all, the drastic deterioration in the British zone's economic condition forced the Cabinet's hand.[42] The huge capital investments required to put German industry back on its feet could only come from the US. By the end of 1946, the Anglo-American agreement to fuse their zones, largely on American terms, had been concluded, though only after protracted negotiations. The Americans would not agree to Bevin's demand for a specific assurance that economic fusion would not prejudice the British plan to socialize the heavy industries, nor would they limit the fusion arrangement to one year. But they did agree to look after the currency problem and they would be responsible for the food. These,

Attlee told his Cabinet, were the best terms the British could get.[43] For their part, the Russians ensured that elections in Rumania in November 1946, and in Poland in January 1947, resulted in Communist victories.

Attlee's call for patience in June had been partly prompted by the restlessness inside his own party. Many Labour backbenchers had little better to do than to speculate about foreign policy and their unhappiness was exacerbated by news of conditions in the British zone of Germany. The discontent came to a head in November. On the 8th of that month readers of Labour's main newspaper, the *Daily Herald*, learned that the Germans were 'down to potatoes'; the basic food ration of 1500 calories a day was not being met. Attlee indicated his concern to Bevin (in New York), in a top secret and personal telegram:[44] some of the 'widespread criticism' was due 'to a misapprehension of the inevitable conditions', but he was worried about the quality of some of the British personnel in the zone. A strong body of criticism appeared to be based on personal observation of conditions there, and although he had previously opposed the idea of a Resident Minister, he now thought there was something to be said for it. Bevin, who well knew Attlee's gift for understatement, hastily reassured him that he, too, was worried about the German situation, but asked that no action be taken until he returned. By then, the fusion arrangement had been announced. In the meantime Attlee had to bear the brunt of the Labour criticism himself.

On 18 November, Crossman and fifty-six other Labour MPs signed an amendment to the King's Speech asking the Government to review its foreign policy and provide a 'democratic and Socialist alternative to an otherwise inevitable conflict between American Capitalism and Soviet Communism'. Attlee's patience did not extend to this sort of argument nor to the amendment's proposer, Crossman.[45] He considered the amendment to be 'misconceived, mis-timed and based on a mis-conception of the facts'. Foreign policy could only be carried out in co-operation with other nations. His government did not believe in the forming of groups and opposed them, whether of East, West or Centre: its policy was based on support for the UN. It was entirely untrue that Britain had been subservient to the US or insufficiently ready to co-operate with the Soviet Union. He resented the attacks on Bevin, 'often by people whose services to the causes of Labour and socialism were as dust in the balance compared with Mr Bevin's'.[46] Shortly after the debate a Labour stronghold in Bermondsey was held over Liberal and Conservative challengers, suggesting that the average Labour elector was not unduly alarmed by the Government's foreign policy.[47] In the Commons, however, Attlee's homily was less effective: though no Labour MP voted for Crossman's amendment, the number of abstentions was estimated by *The Times* to be 122.[48]

Relatively little attention was paid to Attlee's curt remarks on

Germany. Britain, he said, had encouraged the Social Democrats there, but not exclusively: people should be able to choose for themselves. In any case, a political party supported by an Occupying Power would lose the support of the German people. Germany would have been in a better position if economic unity had been achieved; perhaps the Government had kept hoping and pressing too long for this.[49] What he did not say was that another of the reasons why the Government had persisted and would continue to strive for much of the following year to see if Potsdam could be made to work was the anti-German sentiment generated by the war, coupled with fear of a future German resurgence. In January 1947 Bevin told Duff Cooper – the ex-Conservative minister who had resigned over Munich and who was now Ambassador to France – that he thought the danger still came from Germany rather than Russia, an opinion which the Ambassador found 'very satisfactory'.[50] The French were almost intractable on the subject until 1949. The Labour Cabinet in February 1947 was resolved to apply a policy of socialization to the coal, iron, steel, heavy engineering and chemical industries in the Ruhr:[51] reduction of German 'war potential' was still very much on the British agenda, despite the difficulties with Russia. Explaining the Government's attitude to the Commons that month, Bevin declared that the problem of Germany had to be approached from two viewpoints: the economic welfare of 66 million people in the centre of Europe and the security of Europe. He was sure that Germany now recognized the effects of defeat and the stupidity of war, but there was a lot of talk about Eastern and Western Powers; he was 'obsessed, above all else, by the possibility of those major Powers having differences which might result in the resurgence of Germany'.[52] In March, prior to the Moscow meeting of the Foreign Ministers, Bevin (no doubt with Attlee's approval) described to the Cabinet the specific aims of his German policy: (1) he wanted to prevent the creation of a strong, centralized Germany and, (2) he sought an upward revision of the agreed levels of German industry. The former would be furthered by a federal system of government and the latter was necessary to prevent additional charges on the British Exchequer.[53]

Neither Churchill nor Labour's left-wingers grasped that a major reason for Attlee and Bevin's prolonged effort to see if Potsdam could somehow be made to work was their desire to preserve the maximum of British influence over the wider international scene. Although seeking and welcoming American involvement in Europe, they could not be certain whether it would be forthcoming or, if so, what form it would take or how long it would last. Attlee's reservations about US understanding of European conditions and political complexities were concurrently being reinforced by his experience of dealing with the Americans over the loan, the atomic bomb and Palestine. In the Far East, his doubts about American policy would extend to the questions of recognition of Communist China and limiting the war in Korea. He never ceased to assert the independence of British policy, within a framework of its ultimate reference to the UN idea. That his aim was frustrated – critically so over Germany – was due to Britain's financial insolvency and Russian intransigence. The nature of these obstacles became somewhat clearer to his left-wingers during the course of 1947.

Their complaints can be said to have culminated in the April publication of *Keep Left*, a pamphlet calling for a more drastic socialist orientation of Government policy, which was as unfortunate in its timing as it was question-begging in its recommendations. Signed by a group of Labour MPs, including Crossman and Michael Foot, the pamphlet argued specifically for the development of the Anglo-French alliance into a European regional security scheme under the UN, and argued that Britain should not have to pay half the cost of the fused German zone. Instead, the authors insisted that Germany should be economically integrated into Europe, a suggestion which must have been read with a mixture of astonishment and derision by Attlee and Bevin in view of what they had been trying to do. An official Labour Party pamphlet answered by pointing out that the cards really were now on the table in the world situation as a result of the Labour Government's efforts.[54] But there was a wide emotional cleavage between Attlee and Bevin and the left-wingers over foreign policy: it concerned their respective attitudes not so much to the US or the USSR as to Germany. While *Tribune* and the *New Statesman* were vying with each other in urging the US to make generous and substantial aid to that country,[55] Bevin in the Commons was saying that Germany should not escape reparations, if Potsdam was carried out. Making public his views regarding the creation of a federal Germany, he added that British policy favoured land reform and public ownership of industry and supported the French claim to the Saar.[56] He had only contempt for his critics, as his 'stab-in-the-back' reference to Crossman and company at the Labour annual conference (in May) made clear. Attlee was content to 'deny utterly . . . the charge made by some people whose subservience to one great power makes them charge us with subservience to another'. He repeated that the British wished to collaborate with all.[57]

Confirmation that American policy was changing had appeared in March, with the announcement of what became known as the Truman doctrine. It had been precipitated by the British intimation that their troops would have to be withdrawn from Turkey and Greece. Earlier that month Britain had concluded a defensive alliance with France, the Treaty of Dunkirk. At the same time, and as important as any other development, was Bevin's report from the Moscow Foreign Ministers' meeting that the Americans had – without consulting him – insisted that the Potsdam agreement on German reparations supplant the talk at Yalta.

Bevin wanted to support the American view, and Attlee most certainly had no objection.[58] On his return, Bevin informed the Cabinet that despite the failure to reach any agreement over the main obstacle, Germany's economic problems, the time had not been wasted. The positions of the various governments had been clarified. It had been made clear to the Russians that the Anglo-American fusion agreement had been forced on the UK and US by Russian refusal to treat Germany as an economic whole. Bevin had not rejected in principle the Russian claim for reparations from current production, only stipulating that the claim could not be considered until the Germans had achieved a balanced economy. With respect to Germany's political future, Bevin reported that the Russians had moved some way towards accepting the British decentralization proposals. It also looked, he could tell the Cabinet at last, as though the Americans were not proposing to withdraw from Europe. Everything would turn on the next Foreign Ministers' meeting, to be held near the end of the year.[59]

The Marshall offer at the beginning of June took much of the wind out of the Labour critics' sails; it was welcomed by almost all shades of left-wing opinion.[60] Yet the grumblings about Germany continued. In July, Attlee received a letter signed by nineteen Labour MPs saying that, though Germany was a vital British interest, the current price could not be afforded. When the loan ran out, the US had to be told that Britain could not afford to pay for imports into the two zones.[61] By then, the British and Americans had virtually reached agreement on new levels of industry for their fused zone, which was seen as part of the plan for European economic co-operation. Bevin was now convinced that West Germany should be treated on the same basis as other countries for the purely practical reason that it would be the best way of ensuring that Germany played a full part in contributing to Europe's economic recovery. However, in view of French reaction, the Government decided that no steps should be taken until September to implement the new plan.[62]

In August it was the turn of the Opposition (with the support of some Labour MPs) to criticize British zonal policy in Germany and Austria. Bevin countered by saying that he had still not accepted the division of Germany or Europe into two zones. The Government intended to make a 'supreme effort' for economic unity at the November conference of Foreign Ministers. He was not going to take the step which was so fraught with danger for Europe and the world without having finally come to the conclusion that there was no other way.[63] By October Attlee was warning that the Government was greatly disturbed at the increasing tension in foreign affairs and at the attitude of the USSR's representatives, which was gravely imperilling the work that was being done trying to build up the UN organization. At the same time, because of the economic crisis, he announced that a substantial reduction in the size of the armed forces had been decided upon for the next eighteen months.[64] Next to Molotov's contemptuous rejection of the Marshall Plan, perhaps the most telling intellectual blow to the left wing was the Fabian Society's publication, in November 1947, of a pamphlet entitled *Foreign Policy: the Labour Party's Dilemma*. A 'Foreword' by Harold Laski confessed that, though the Society's International Committee had set out a year ago to define the outlines of a socialist foreign policy, no agreement could be reached on its major principles.[65]

The failure of the Foreign Ministers' meeting about Germany at the end of the year marked the formal turning point in East-West relations during Attlee's term of office. By then neither Attlee nor Bevin could have had any serious hope that negotiations would succeed. During the conference, Bevin warned the Cabinet that Four Power agreement on the main issues affecting Germany was unlikely and, unless there was a radical change on the part of the Soviet Union, he saw no purpose in continuing discussions through the Council of Foreign Ministers.[66] After it, he told the Commons that the British could not go on as before towards Germany and Austria.[67] In January 1948 he was ready with a detailed set of new proposals for the reconstruction of Western Germany, as the Government could be no party to creating a situation likely to bring about a Communist-controlled Germany on the East European pattern. He told the Cabinet that he had not abandoned hope until the very end of the meeting, but Molotov had overplayed his hand and aggravated the situation. The conflict was 'between the Soviet desire to dominate Europe politically and economically and the desire of the Three Western Powers to put Europe back on its feet again with American backing'. The failure to reach agreement, he warned, 'meant that the division between East and West in Germany, which itself is part and parcel of the same division throughout the world, will continue and is likely to get sharper.'

Even then, however, Bevin intimated that he would continue to insist on the capital reparations plan and would resist any proposal to suspend deliveries to the Soviet Union and her satellites. He added: 'Should we none the less have to agree to suspend all deliveries to Russia, we should only agree that actual delivery of the plant should be deferred but that it should continue to be allocated to the Soviet Union and stored in Germany. I shall offer the most stubborn opposition even to this.'[68] Later that month Bevin was still telling the Cabinet that it was premature to reach any firm conclusions about Western Germany, unwise to place too much reliance on Germany's ultimate willingness to promote a pacific and co-operative policy, and that some dismantling of German industry would continue.[69] It is difficult to avoid the conclusion that, if the mainspring of Russian policy had been a desire of reparations from (and fear of) Germany, then they missed a golden opportunity to come to some agreement with the Britain led by Bevin and Attlee.

Once begun, the process known as the Cold War developed its own momentum. Subsequent diplomatic developments, including the Brussels Treaty, the formation of NATO and the creation of Western Germany, need not be rehearsed here. Apart from the special position of Western Germany, Attlee had envisaged them during the war. Bevin's talent – amounting perhaps to genius – for organization came into its own, and Attlee could well let Bevin get on with *his* job. Attlee's New Year broadcast on 3 January correctly forecast that 1948 would 'be dominated politically by foreign rather than domestic policy'. Although he drew a pointed distinction between the British system and that of either US capitalism or Soviet imperialism, his main indictment was directed against 'the absolutists who suppressed opposition in the name of liberty', in ironic contrast to the European struggles of a century previously.[70] Thereafter, the anti-Soviet tone of his speeches markedly increased: 'Russia was in my young days the supreme example of the police State . . . It is the same today only with a different set of rulers . . . It employs new methods, but in effect the countries of eastern Europe have been brought within its imperialistic sway.' (1 May 1948): ' . . . the responsibility for dividing the world . . . rests squarely on the shoulders of the rulers of the Kremlin. We have to recognize that the Russian use of the veto has blocked all progress at the UN . . . ' (10 April 1949): 'The continued obstruction by Russia has frustrated the efforts of the UN and, further than that, all over the world the agents and supporters of Communism have worked ceaselessly to foment trouble and disorder.' (13 September 1950): 'Nazism has been wiped out in western Germany, but in eastern Germany its followers are enrolled in Soviet-dominated forces.' (27 January 1951).[71]

Attlee did not become completely convinced about American military involvement in Europe until the Berlin crisis of 1948–9, for only then were men, as well as dollars, committed.[72] His approach to foreign policy had been essentially open-minded. He and Bevin had pursued several, not mutually exclusive, courses, from seeing (in close association with the Commonwealth countries) if the UN could be made to work and from trying to come to some accommodation with Russia, to strengthening Western Europe and to getting the US actively engaged in international affairs. All had had drawbacks, Attlee found, especially the attempt to come to terms with the USSR. He had good cause to reflect, at the end of his premiership as at the beginning, that trying to solve international problems by getting a few people sitting around a table was 'not as simple as that'.

XII

The Bomb Became Essential

In retrospect, Attlee's most controversial decision as Prime Minister was on the atomic bomb. He did not act alone. Professor Margaret Gowing, the leading authority, has established that A. V. Alexander, Bevin, Dalton, Greenwood and Morrison were all involved in the decision-making process at one time and another, though not always for the same purposes. Lord Addison and the two successive Ministers of Supply, Wilmot and Strauss (whose department was entrusted with the project), also played significant parts. Nevertheless, it was Attlee who had the ultimate responsibility, and 'no major decisions . . . were taken without his prior approval'.[1] He was fully aware of the bomb's implications for international relations; these implications troubled him more than those of any other decision he made. And yet he had no difficulty in deciding that Britain had to have the weapon. How may his action be explained?

A short answer is that Attlee had little choice. Gowing is quite blunt: 'The most obvious reason why Britain was determined to have an atomic bomb of her own after the Second World War was that her scientists and the refugee scientists living in Britain had invented it.'[2] Alfred Goldberg, the Senior Historian, US Air Force, agrees: 'The atomic energy programme, both in its civil and military aspects, was a logical and inevitable historical evolution. Had there been no other motivation, the sheer momentum of the great scientific effort alone would have been enough to keep the programme going.'[3] This answer, however, reveals nothing about the actual decision, or the way in which it was made, or Attlee's role in it. Despite the fact that several important government documents remain unavailable to the historian, it is possible to be more specific.

The key discussions took place outside the full Cabinet. They were conducted in a series of *ad hoc* ministerial committees presided over by

Attlee. A proper Ministerial Atomic Energy Committee with specific terms of reference was only set up after January 1947, when the Cabinet's own Defence Committee also became more important. But by then the main lines of Government policy had been established. The early machinery for ministerial consultation on the atomic energy project was equally odd; to describe it Gowing has chosen a favourite Attlee word, 'curious'. In large part the machinery began as a carry-over from the war, and subsequently just grew.[4] The key word had been, and remained, secrecy. Churchill had excluded most of his ministers, including all Labour ministers, from any specific knowledge of the atomic bomb. Of those who were privy to the wartime work, only two – Lord Cherwell and Sir John Anderson (neither of whom belonged to any political party) – 'knew continuously and in detail about the whole business'.[5] These were the facts that account for the strangest part of the post-war procedure – Attlee's retention of Anderson's services. Although Anderson sat (as an Independent MP) on the Opposition front bench and often engaged in violent criticism of the Government, as an administrator of the project he was indispensable at first. He was made chairman of an Advisory Committee of scientists, officials and service representatives which reported directly to the Prime Minister when ministerial decisions were called for. However, Anderson's appointment only lasted a year or so as in August 1946 the Advisory Committee was superseded by an Atomic Energy Officials Committee.

It is clear that Attlee supported and even contributed to the general secrecy and oddity of procedure. He did intimate to the Commons in October 1945 that a research and development organization was to cover all aspects of atomic energy,[6] but that was about as far as he went in taking the public into his confidence. He asked for, and received, Churchill's support in ensuring that parliamentary questions about raw materials for atomic research did not reach the order paper; the answer might involve reference to secret agreements with Belgium, Holland and Brazil.[7] The costs of the project were cunningly concealed from Parliament in Ministry of Supply estimates. The news that Britain was making the bomb was not given to the Commons until May 1948, and then in a deliberately oblique fashion.[8] Attlee consulted the full Cabinet less than ten times in six years and then mainly for purposes of information. The only occasions on which the Cabinet actually discussed atomic energy questions were twice in connection with Attlee's visit to Washington in 1945 and once about security. True, Attlee's worries about the confidentiality of his Cabinet's deliberations (and decisions) were not limited to atomic matters; he had to warn his ministers about the effects of unguarded statements on the country's delicate economic situation several times.[9] And the extreme caution on atomic policy, Gowing has explained, had a three-fold purpose: (1) to avoid prejudicing proceedings of the UN

Atomic Commission; (2) to conceal as much as possible from the Russians; and (3) to avoid American charges that the British could not keep atomic secrets.[10] Yet the extent of Attlee's quite uncharacteristic deviousness was remarkable. Gowing asserts that the British policy of secrecy, especially when contrasted with that of the Americans, went beyond rational explanation.[11] There is one plausible reason for Attlee's 'dislike of seeing almost anything about atomic energy in print':[12] his profound sense of unease on the subject.

The explicit decision on the bomb was not taken until January 1947 – by an *ad hoc* committee consisting of Attlee, Bevin, Morrison, Alexander, Addison and Wilmot.[13] According to Gowing, the basic motivation was 'something fundamentalist and almost instinctive',[14] feelings of patriotic pride and fear. Attlee was certainly not immune to the first of these emotions, but his apprehension was of a special kind. The decision was not a response to any immediate military threat, actual or imagined. No bomb could be ready for five years, and no action was taken in 1947 as to the means of delivering the weapon. There was no belief in 1947 that war was imminent; rather, everybody agreed that Britain was peculiarly vulnerable to attack with modern weapons and that the supreme object of British foreign policy had to be to avoid war.[15] Neither Attlee nor Bevin wanted to offend the Russians. In June 1947 they vetoed a CoS proposal that defence policy should be based on the possibility of war with Russia on the grounds that it would be dangerous – 'would tend to bias Britain's outlook in international affairs and would probably lead her to take steps which Russia would see to be directed against her, steps which might precipitate war'. Attlee's concern at the beginning of 1947, which caused him to bestow 'his own priority on the [atomic bomb] project'[16] soon after the decision was made, was with the US.

'We had to hold up our position vis-à-vis the Americans,' he said later. 'We couldn't allow ourselves to be wholly in their hands . . . we had to bear in mind that there was always the possibility of their withdrawing and becoming isolationist once again.' It was for this reason that the bomb 'had become essential'. He added: 'You must remember that this was all prior to NATO . . . We had worked from the start for international control of the bomb. We wanted it completely under the control of the United Nations. That was the best way. But it was obviously going to take a long time. Meanwhile we had to face the world as it was. We had to look to defence – and to our industrial future. We could not agree that only America should have atomic energy.'[17] Pressed explicitly on another occasion to state whether fear of American isolationism had influenced the decision, he reiterated: 'There was always the possibility . . . you never knew what they would do . . .'[18] The question of priority for the atomic weapons programme, he admitted in 1950, was not entirely a *military* problem.[19] Indeed not: for Attlee, the British bomb was a diplomatic tool against the US.[20]

Gowing has acknowledged that there was 'one dominant theme in the history of the British atomic bomb project . . . the relationship between Britain and the US.'[21] The relationship had begun in the special circumstances of the war: in 1941, before Pearl Harbour, the British had persuaded the Americans that the project was feasible and urgently required.[22] Most of the preliminary work had already been done in Britain; in 1946 Attlee would argue to Truman that if Roosevelt had not decided in 1941 to engage the vast resources of the US on the project, the British would have had to make the attempt 'at whatever cost'.[23] Originally, the Americans had welcomed British assistance, but thereafter the relationship had run an irregular course. It was only after 'a great struggle'[24] on Churchill's part at Quebec in 1943 that Roosevelt had agreed to full collaboration. The agreement stipulated that the US and UK never use the bomb against each other, or against third parties without the mutual consent of both signatories. No information was to be given to others, though Canada, already closely associated with British research efforts, became a member of the Combined Policy Committee established under the Agreement. Another clause was that any post-war advantages of an industrial or commercial character should be dealt with between the US and UK on terms to be specified by the President to the Prime Minister. The ambiguities in this clause seemed to have been resolved by an Aide Mémoire signed by Churchill and Roosevelt at Hyde Park (New York) in September 1944: both leaders pledged full collaboration in the development of atomic energy for military and commercial purposes after the defeat of Japan, unless and until terminated by joint accord.[25]

Whether Attlee knew of the second of these agreements during the war is not clear; he must have known about the Quebec Agreement and was aware, though in very general terms, of the atomic energy project. He did not know of the progress made on the bomb. It was not until Potsdam that he and Stalin were informed that the Americans had an atomic weapon, and that it was ready for use on Japan. He had no objections, and that was the extent of the mutual consultation.[26] Attlee was not fully aware of the weapon's destructiveness, but in the war context his attitude would not have been different if he had known.[27] Churchill had taken the precaution of preparing a statement in advance and it was this that Attlee issued on the same day as Hiroshima. The document dealt mainly with Britain's role in the bomb's development; there was no mention of the secret agreements.[28]

Two days later, before the second bomb was dropped over Nagasaki, Attlee made his own views known in a telegram to Truman. Stressing the immediate implications of the new weapon for international relations, he added that he and Truman, 'as heads of the Governments which have control of this great force', should without delay make a joint declaration of their intention 'to utilize the existence of this great power, not for our own ends, but as trustees for humanity in the interests of all peoples in order to promote peace and justice in the world.'[29] Truman's reply made no acknowledgment of mutual control but said he was going to broadcast to the American people on the points Attlee had raised and was sending recommendations to Congress for making atomic energy a powerful and forceful influence towards the maintenance of peace. Attlee was highly pleased and suggested that any joint declaration could wait 'until the means of control and the implications in the field of international relations have been more fully considered by those concerned'.[30] Uppermost in Attlee's mind in August 1945 was the question of control. 'It has to be recognized,' he added to Truman, 'that the emergence of this weapon has rendered much of our post-war planning out of date ... I noticed at Potsdam that people still talked of the line of the Oder-Neisse although rivers as strategic frontiers have been obsolete since the advent of air power. It is infinitely harder for people to realize that even the modern conception of war to which in my lifetime we have become accustomed is now completely out of date.' He did not think that all nations would agree to let the UK and the US keep the bomb a secret. 'The most we may have is a few years' start. The question is what use are we to make of that ... start.' He did not think that an Anglo-American attempt to enforce a world-wide inspection of all laboratories and plants was desirable or practicable. The only course which seemed to him 'to be feasible and to offer a reasonable hope of staving off imminent disaster for the world, [was] joint action by the USA, UK and Russia based upon stark reality. We should declare that this invention has made it essential to end wars.'[31]

Attlee was not being rhetorical. In the absence of any American initiative, he sent a letter to Truman on 25 September, setting out his views at length. He began with the premise that the emergence of the new weapon had brought about a qualitative change in the nature of warfare. He was not aware of any possible means of defence: the only deterrent was the possibility of the victim of an atomic attack being able to retort in kind. He believed that, if mankind continued to make the atomic bomb without changing the political relationships of states, sooner or later the bombs would be used for mutual annihilation. No comfort could be derived from the fact that experience of the manufacturing processes and technical knowledge was then confined to the UK and US, and that only the US possessed the manufacturing capacity. It was not certain that the two Governments' control of the main known sources of uranium and thorium would either last long, or could be defended in principle. A further problem was that the harnessing of atomic energy as a source of power could not be separated from the simultaneous production of material capable of being used in a bomb. The Great Powers were therefore confronted with a situation that had not been envisaged at San Francisco. While it was important to devise means of preventing, as far as possible, the power of producing the new weapon getting into other hands, Attlee was more preoccupied by the implications for international relations; far-reaching changes were necessary, as well as a fresh review of world policy and a new valuation of national interests. He concluded his letter by intimating that it might be essential for Truman and him to discuss 'this momentous problem together . . .'[32] Churchill, to whom a draft of the letter had been shown, reacted in a strikingly different fashion: what, he asked, did Attlee want the Americans to do? In contrast to the sombre Attlee, the former Prime Minister 'rejoiced in American possession of the bomb',[33] and also in Britain's special atomic relationship with the US as the result of the wartime agreements.[34] On the American side, too, no particular urgency to rush into talks was felt: over three weeks elapsed before a reply to Attlee's letter arrived, and it was non-committal. Attlee had to resort to telegraphing his desire for a meeting, which was eventually arranged for November.[35]

The 5 November 1945 happened to be the 340th anniversary of the Gunpowder Plot. It was also the day on which Attlee circulated to his Cabinet colleagues his summary of the issues raised by a British study of the international control of atomic energy.[36] Further, Attlee's memorandum indicated the policy he intended to propose to Truman and Mackenzie King, the Canadian Prime Minister. Because of its significance at the time and later, the document will be paraphrased almost in its entirety.

The British study – by officials – had produced only one firm scheme for control. It proposed to invite all Governments to become parties to a convention pledging themselves (a) not to use atomic bombs except in accordance with (b); (b) to join in immediate and complete sanctions against any country making use of the atomic bomb in violation of (a); (c) to enter into a full exchange of the basic scientific information relating to the use of atomic energy; and (d) to institute effective control of the use of atomic energy on their own territory. The scheme assumed that there was no practicable way of enforcing the prohibition of the manufacture of atomic bombs, or of ensuring their control by an international body. The study argued that the sole solution was one of mutual trust, reinforced by the certainty of swift retribution if the trust was broken.

Attlee found several faults with this scheme which, in his opinion, had to be considered in the light of the UN plan for sanctions against an aggressor. A general renunciation of the use of the bomb seemed to imply war with other weapons, presumably against an aggressor. But if the aggressor proved too strong for the Power or Powers enforcing sanctions and one of them *in extremis* resorted to the use of the atomic weapon, the aggressor, however heinous his aggression, became entitled to the help of all other nations possessing the bomb. They would thereupon turn on the victim of the aggression. Furthermore, renunciation of the weapon would put any computation of strengths of rival nations back into the pre-atomic bomb age; the US would be unlikely to accept this situation at a time when power politics seemed to be in full vigour. Britain was peculiarly vulnerable to attack by atomic bombs; to accept a pledge to join in immediate and complete sanctions against a country using the atomic bomb would be to expose London to annihilation. Could any Government, Attlee wondered, take such a risk? There was as yet no means of knowing whence had come an atomic bomb or who was the culprit. The deterrent effect (of certainty of immediate counter-attack) was lessened; in atomic warfare, the maxim 'thrice is he armed who gets his blow in first' seemed to apply. He concluded his criticism of the officials' study by saying that, though international arrangements had to be based on mutual trust and there had to be a deterrent against aggression of all kinds, this could only be achieved by unqualified support for a point made recently in Truman's statement of American foreign policy, viz: 'We are convinced that the preservation of peace requires a UNO composed of all the peace-loving nations of the world, who are willing jointly to use force if necessary to ensure peace.' Attlee rejected any ideas of specific provisions about who could authorize use of the bomb, with particular reference to the Security Council where the veto could be used to protect a small aggressor or by one of the permanent members to prevent any action against itself.

Attlee, in short, was pessimistic about the possibility of piecemeal solutions. No attempt should be made to restrict the development of atomic energy by any country, because effective control was impossible. The problem posed to international relations by the advent of atomic weapons was fundamentally different from those of the past. The only hope was the setting aside of nationalistic ideas and the creation of international relationships based on the renunciation of war. Atomic weapons would have to be available to restrain aggression, but the best way of achieving such restraint was the determination by all countries who developed atomic energy to live up to the principles of the UN Charter. In other words, where there was the will a way would be found; but without the will, nothing could be accomplished.

The line he intended to take with Truman, the Cabinet was informed, would be based on these views. Attlee agreed with Truman's proposal that there should be a free exchange of fundamental scientific information on atomic energy, but he did not think that there was anything to be gained by sharing the practical 'know-how' with Russia. The US would probably be opposed and, in any case, it would be regarded as a confession of weakness. The establishment of better relations should precede the exchange of technical information. Russia would be able to produce the bomb within a few years, and it was during those years that a real attempt had to be made to build a world organization upon the abandonment of power politics. He also intended to suggest to Truman that all nations should be pressed to institute effective control of the use of atomic energy in their own territories, and that the peace treaties concluded with Germany and Japan should include a provision prohibiting them from making use of atomic energy in any form. The cases of Italy and other enemy satellites should be considered separately. He would express the hope that the US continue the general system of co-operation then existing – with particular regard to the Quebec Agreement, except for the section stipulating that the President was to specify the terms of post-war commercial advantages: here Attlee, in apparent ignorance of the 1944 Aide Mémoire, wished to 'regain [British] freedom'. He also thought that, in view of the relative scarcity of uranium and thorium, no arrangements for the pooling of those materials with Russia should be made, except in return for some substantial advantage.

When he opened the Cabinet discussion of his paper, three days later, Attlee explained that, though power politics might for a time produce an uneasy equilibrium, it was bound to lead in the end to war. He hoped that a general realization of the destructive power of the atomic bomb would bring about a new attitude to international relationships. Britain, at any rate, should grasp the opportunity of establishing on a firm foundation an effective world organization with both the will and the power to preserve peace; otherwise, there was no prospect of controlling the use of the new weapon. The Cabinet did not quarrel with his general thesis. Discussion turned mainly on the question of sharing with Russia the practical knowledge relating to the bomb's manufacture. Some ministers – not identified in the Cabinet minutes – thought that it would be wiser to make an immediate offer to disclose the information to the Soviet Government. The true basis for lasting peace was mutual confidence; Britain should be ready to take risks in creating it. Soviet Russia might well be unwilling to co-operate wholeheartedly in the establishment of a world organization so long as the British and American Governments insisted on keeping to themselves the manufacturing secrets. The present Soviet attitude was due in large measure to their suspicion of the Western democracies, founded to some extent on their pre-war experiences. The urgent need was to remove the causes for that suspicion. There was much to be said for offering full disclosure, linking the offer with discussion of the means of co-operating in the establishment of an effective world organization. Less than a month previously, Bevin had shared this view, which was also the opinion of the British Ambassadors to both the USSR and the US.[37] Attlee, too, had first thought that he and Truman should at once consult Stalin together.[38] But in November, Bevin said he now thought it a mistake to attempt to deal with the atomic bomb in isolation from other weapons. He suggested that Attlee should explore with Truman the possibility of remitting to the UN, as soon as it was established, the task of devising suitable machinery for full disclosure and exchange between all members of the UN of the results of all scientific research. Such machinery might be developed by an extension of the wartime agreements between the principal Allied Powers, for which a UN staff of highly qualified scientists would be required. Attlee welcomed Bevin's suggestion, pointing out that it was necessary to have regard to countries other than Russia. He added, in response to the First Lord of the Admiralty (Alexander), that he did not altogether exclude the possibility of an international convention renouncing the use of the atomic bomb, though it was not the existence of such a convention which had prevented the use of poison gas in the war. A convention would not suffice by itself: the real safeguard was the creation of an effective world organization. Eventually, the Cabinet endorsed the general line of Attlee's memorandum and his view that it was preferable not to put forward any specific agenda or submit any document for the Washington discussions.[39]

The importance of these early Labour reactions to the advent of the new weapons can hardly be overestimated, particularly as the full Cabinet was involved. Gowing has pointed out that they 'contained the seeds of ideas and strategic theories that were to pervade discussions on control for the next twenty-odd years ... They were founded on the truths learned from League of Nations days ... control of any weapons was impossible unless mutual trust existed between nations, while no world organization could be strong unless the leading powers were united in wishing it so to be.' But, Gowing adds, they also underlined 'the paradoxes and dilemmas of a world power in the nuclear age: while waiting for mutual trust to be established and Utopia to arrive, each such power must look to its own interests and make itself as strong as possible in nuclear weapons, even if thereby mutual mistrust was engendered and the chances of ultimate international control diminished. Attlee's own position illustrated the paradox.'[40] He was not yet prepared to give the directive for the production of bombs for which the committee of officials had asked:[41] he had eliminated references to the Russian threat by officials in the draft versions of their paper. Yet before he went to Washington he had accepted the American view that practical know-how, as opposed to fundamental scientific knowledge, should not be shared with the Russians.[42]

There was a practical weakness in the 'full disclosure' argument made by a minority of Attlee's Cabinet colleagues: Britain had almost no manufacturing secrets to share. And the Americans, as it turned out,

16 Attlee with Ernest Bevin, his closest political ally, 1946

17 Attlee with Hugh Dalton, who as Chancellor of the Exchequer was forced to resign for leaking to the Press his budget proposals in 1947

18 Stafford Cripps and Attlee with the Archbishop of York (Dr Cyril Garbett) at the Labour Party Conference, Scarborough, 1948

19 Commonwealth Conference 1949: before South Africa left the Commonwealth over apartheid, Attlee shared a joke with Indian Prime Minister Nehru on his right, and South Africa's Dr Malan in the garden of No. 10

20 Herbert Morrison, after a hard day's electioneering, relaxes before the fire in the house of Alice Bacon's mother, February 1950

21 Two ministers in Attlee's new Government arriving at Downing Street in March 1950: Patrick Gordon Walker, Commonwealth Relations (left), and Emanuel Shinwell, Defence

22 Aneurin Bevan with fellow rebels Harold Wilson (left), Ian Mikardo, Tom Driberg and Barbara Castle, 1951

were unwilling to share their secrets even with the UK. But in November 1945 Attlee still believed that the two countries would fully co-operate, and he could have acted from his own rationale that the UK and the US had only a few years' advance anyway (the Russians exploded a device in 1949, three years ahead of the British). There was also the argument from 'moral principle' that the same minority of his ministers had made, and/or the idea that the British 'should seek to act as mediators and should let [their] views be known to the world. By such means,' the unidentified ministers had continued, 'Britain might succeed in rallying those nations who feared the consequences of growing estrangement between the US and the Soviet Union.'[43] Attlee could not accept these arguments. In 1945 he was grappling with the immediate fate of Western Europe; a peacetime accord with the US had to be his priority.

At first the signs boded well. The eventual Washington Declaration – signed by Attlee, Mackenzie King and Truman – strongly reflected the views Attlee had expressed in his paper. The only protection from the destructive use of scientific knowledge of every kind, the Declaration stated, was the prevention of war. The three leaders said they were willing, 'as a first contribution', to exchange basic scientific information with any nation that would fully reciprocate. They were not prepared to share any specialized information regarding the practical application of atomic energy before effective, reciprocal and enforceable safeguards against its use for destructive purposes, acceptable to all nations, could be devised. To that end, they proposed that the UN should set up a Commission.[44] More important for future Anglo-American relations and the development of British atomic policy was a document hastily signed on the last day of the conference in which Attlee and Truman expressed their joint desire 'that there should be full and effective co-operation in the field of atomic energy between the US, the UK and Canada', and agreed that the Combined Policy Committee and the Combined Development Trust should be continued in a suitable form, to be worked out by the Combined Policy Committee.[45] Sir John Anderson, who had accompanied Attlee, also signed a memorandum with his American counterpart, General Groves, setting out the particular points that the Policy Committee was to consider. Attlee and Mackenzie King thus had good reason to believe when they left Washington that peacetime co-operation between the three countries on atomic energy was all but assured.[46]

The story of how this belief was confounded has been magisterially told by Gowing and does not need to be recounted in detail. In April 1946, Attlee suggested to the US Ambassador, W. Averell Harriman, that until control of atomic energy by the UN became effective, the US should make atomic bombs available to Britain or, at the least, provide the data for production of nuclear energy.[47] Neither was forthcoming and that same year Britain decided to produce fissile material. Despite

Goldberg's belief that the complete rupture of Anglo-American atomic co-operation was foreshadowed long before the end of the war,[48] the passage of the McMahon Act by the US Congress in August 1946, prohibiting the communication of any classified atomic information to any country, came as 'a terrible blow to the British'.[49] Attlee's vain remonstrances culminated in an exceptionally long and irrefutable (there could not be, nor was there, any reply) telegram to Truman on 6 June 1946 in which the entire history of the previous accords was reviewed.[50] But he did not blame Truman personally for the McMahon Act,[51] and the British desperately continued to seek American atomic co-operation, especially because by the end of 1946 it had become almost certain that the UN effort to produce a control scheme for the monster was going to fail.[52]

Britain was prepared to pay a great price for US co-operation – 'to forswear any co-operation, however small, with the Dominions (other than Canada) or any European country'.[53] However, the Americans, for a variety of reasons, did not want the British to make atomic bombs[54] – despite the revival of the 'special relationship' in most other areas between 1947 and 1951 (including, in January 1947, the appointment of the pro-British General Marshall as US Secretary of State, the Marshall Plan of June 1947 and the establishment of NATO in August 1949). The price for even minimal atomic collaboration turned out to be the virtual surrender of independence. In return for American recognition of the British atomic energy programme and an extremely limited technical co-operation arrangement, the British were obliged to give up their right of consent or consultation over the use of atomic bombs in January 1948. And in June of that year, when the Berlin airlift began, the US was allowed to station strategic bombers in the UK. True, it was 'a long accepted axiom that Britain could never again fight a major war alone',[55] an axiom reinforced in August 1949 when Russia exploded her first atomic device; thereafter, both independence and deterrence concepts were at a considerable discount. British deterrence had always been envisaged as minor compared with that of America, yet Britain was not even given enough information about the American strategic plan 'to calculate rationally her own nuclear role'.[56] This last lends support to the contention that in Attlee's mind that role was primarily intended to be a diplomatic one.

Before he left office, Attlee was to have further, chastening experience of the limitations of British influence with the Americans. When North Korean forces crossed the 38th parallel in June 1950, he did not doubt that such 'naked aggression', as he described it to the Commons, had to be resisted by the UN. Since 1948 the Labour Government had been engaged in a military struggle to prevent communist – principally Chinese communist – subversion in Malaya. Yet the Government recognized, in January 1950, the accomplished fact of the communist regime in China itself. Such niceties of distinction appeared to have escaped the notice of many Americans. Soon after the outbreak of the Korean War, Attlee reminded Truman that the global aspects of the political as well as military situation vis-à-vis the communists had always to be kept in mind. He suggested that discussions be held between the UK and the US 'Other Governments, in particular the French, may be concerned,' he added in his message, 'but it will suffice if they are informed as and when the situation demands.'[57] His request bore fruit and the Anglo-American intimacy which had revived in all areas other than that of atomic energy since 1947 seemed to be holding firm. In November 1950, however, when large numbers of Chinese 'volunteers' intervened in Korea against the UN forces led by General MacArthur, the situation took an ominous turn. It was not helped by a maladroit reply at a press conference by Truman to the effect that the Americans would take whatever measures were necessary to meet the crisis, including consideration of the use of atomic weapons. There was widespread alarm in Britain: over a hundred Labour backbenchers signed a letter to Attlee protesting against the possibility of the use of the atomic bomb. Truman, well informed of British fears that the Korean War might escalate into a major conflict,[58] readily acceded to Attlee's extraordinary request for a personal conference. Attlee explained to George VI that 'the unfortunate statements of the President required immediate action'. He thought the Americans realized that 'to get heavily involved in the Far East would be to play the Russian game', but he was also concerned about the broader strategic picture and believed that, unless the US Government co-ordinated its economic policy in terms of world strategy, the British would be unable to fulfil their defence needs.[59]

Attlee put these points in Washington to a President who was having the usual difficulties with the administration, the Constitution and, this time, General MacArthur. Truman, significantly, has provided an almost verbatim account of the discussion in his *Memoirs*.[60] The narrative reveals a waspishly penetrating and effective Attlee whose manner of discussion, Secretary of State Dean Acheson recalled, 'was of the suave rather than the bellicose cross-examiner'.[61] Truman saw the Chinese communists as Russian satellites; Attlee did not agree. To him the Chinese were potentially ripe for 'Titoism'. They were not completely in the hands of the Russians and the aim ought to be to divide the two. Truman, referring to the American differences of opinion on China, stressed that the US could do nothing abroad without solid backing at home; Attlee riposted that it was also essential to keep the United Nations together. He agreed that the UN had to hold on in Korea for as long as it could, but pointed out that sooner or later there would have to be a Far Eastern settlement. China had to be seated in the UN; somewhere, somehow, the Americans would find that they would have to treat with the Chinese communists. It did not pay to pretend that the 'nasty fellow' on the other side did not exist. There was a danger that a limited war in Korea would provoke a demand for a total victory. If China were in the UN it would be possible to use the principles of the UN in dealing with her. Truman said that in the long run the Chinese would realize that their true friends were in London and Washington: 'You won't bring them to that realization,' Attlee countered without smiling (Truman's description), 'if you keep fighting them.' Truman proved no verbal match for Attlee; the President had to rely on the more adroit Acheson to rescue him from several awkward impasses.

On the immediate issues there were no major differences. Both parties agreed that there could be no thought of appeasement in Korea, or of rewarding aggression. The final communiqué also stated that they were always open to seeking an end to the hostilities by negotiation. The British successfully pressed for NATO to be made effective and for Anglo-American consultation over the supply of raw materials for defence purposes. But Attlee learned that having the best of the discussion was of no avail to the British on the most important matters. Sitting alone with Truman while the final communiqué was being assembled, Attlee got the President to agree that, in a sense, the atomic bomb was a joint possession of the US, the UK and Canada, and that Truman would not authorize its use without prior consultation with the other two Governments save in an extreme emergency (such as an attack on the US calling for immediate retaliation).[62] When the gist of the President's promise was revealed to the full conference, Acheson undermined it. The President had had no power to give such a promise.[63] All that remained was the statement: 'The President told the Prime Minister that it was also his desire to keep the Prime Minister at all times informed of developments which might bring about a change in the situation' (requiring the use of the bomb).[64] Once again, as Gowing has underlined, the atomic promise of a President of the US to a British Prime Minister had been broken.[65] And the Americans refused to recognize China.

Thus Attlee could find considerable justification for his view that, while he was Prime Minister, making a British bomb became diplomatically necessary. Nor could he neglect the opportunity for nuclear power that the production of fissile material represented. And the bombs he envisaged were the ones to whose use he had already given his tacit consent during the war. As Gowing has remarked: '. . . it seemed enough simply to have a supply of the primitive type of bomb dropped on Japan.'[66]

However, at least so far as Attlee is concerned, Gowing is less convincing when she adds: 'The remorseless logic of future advances in atomic bomb technology – including the technology of delivering these horrific weapons – was not foreseen at the time or, if it was, was not discussed in high quarters.'[67] By her own account it was foreseen, and discussed. Attlee, we have noted, was already conscious of the impact of the Flying Bomb on British defence and foreign policy. In November 1945 he received a paper from Professor P. M. S. Blackett which argued that a decision to produce or acquire atomic bombs would tend to *decrease* British security. Blackett, an important Government scientific adviser since 1941, had originally accepted the deterrence concept,[68] but afterwards questioned whether Britain could expect to keep up in the technological race. He came to the firm conclusion that the future in atomic weaponry lay with a new category of superpowers to which Britain could not aspire.[69] Attlee disparagingly described Blackett's 1945 paper as a layman's view on political and military matters, though he still sent it to the Chiefs of Staff.[70] In February 1947 Blackett produced a second paper calling for 'a complete reappraisal of Britain's foreign and defence policy in the shadow of the almost certain breakdown of the negotiations for international control of atomic energy.' As a basis for discussion he proposed a policy 'which would renounce atomic bombs and weapons of mass destruction, design forces on defensive lines and in effect adopt a policy of neutrality between America and Russia.' Though there was no ministerial discussion of these proposals, Attlee was sufficiently interested to have two conversations with Blackett about them.[71] Finally in 1949 the Government's Chief Scientific Adviser, Sir Henry Tizzard, also became convinced that Britain should not be making atomic bombs: 'We are a great nation,' he wrote, 'but if we continue to behave like a Great Power we shall soon cease to be a great nation.'[72]

It can be argued, therefore, that what Attlee, in concert with the vast majority of his colleagues, advisers and the general public,[73] did not sufficiently grasp, was that atomic development had its own momentum. But he was informed about that momentum. Already, when he left office, 'the enterprise was entering a far more chilling phase where all kinds of horrible possibilities could be bandied about in terms of military hardware.'[74] All the historian can say is that Attlee stuck to the view he had expressed in 1945: his first words to Truman in December 1950 were how important it was to maintain the prestige and authority of the UN.[75] Attlee had no doubt that the bombs and other weapons of mass destruction would ultimately be used. There was no hope for peace and security without an effective world organization. Everything else, including his own actions, was temporizing.

XIV

The Irresponsible Americans

The ambiguous character of Anglo-American relationships during the first years of Attlee's premiership was perhaps most evident in the case of Palestine. A bankrupt and militarily enfeebled Britain lacked the power to impose a solution: what Attlee wanted, at least until the UN was ready to intervene, was a fully considered and fully-fledged American involvement. Instead the British were treated to a series of arbitrary and piecemeal pronouncements, coupled with implied moral condemnation, by a President whose actions seemed to be derived largely from domestic political calculation, sentimentality and impulse. 'The Americans,' Attlee considered, 'were quite irresponsible.'[1] As Prime Minister, Attlee's responsibility was for British external policy as a whole; he took it for granted that the Palestine issue had to be viewed in the context of the Middle East, India and Europe. In the absence of anything that could be called a comprehensive American policy, he had small choice but to let Bevin attempt to find a negotiated settlement for a problem that was not negotiable. Much, indeed, has been made of the unfortunate Bevin's handling of the affair, though he always acted with the Cabinet's approval. Attlee himself took a more active part than is often supposed; had the Americans been prepared either to share the burden, or even to take it over completely, all the evidence suggests that he would have intervened vigorously and decisively.

He was never, as he later put it, 'a great enthusiast for the idea that Palestine was the one place for the Jews'. He did not believe in 2,000-year claims.[2] On the other hand, his sympathy for the plight of Jewish refugees from continental persecution dated from his early days in Stepney; the reputation he had then acquired as a respected conciliator between different cultural, religious and ethnic groups had led, as noted in a previous chapter, to the launching of his political career. But neither his sympathy nor his subsequent experience moved him to total support for the Zionist cause. He had denounced the British Government's efforts in 1922 to impose strict control over alien immigration into the UK as both hypocritical and an example of 'that extreme nationalism' which was 'ruining Europe and the world'. Zionism, as it developed, could also be interpreted as a variety of extreme nationalism. Attlee always treated the subject with great caution.

In 1935 he did sign an official Labour election statement declaring that the Party had associated itself from the dark days of the First World War with the ideal 'of a National Home in Palestine for the Jewish people'; but the meaning of the famous phrase had been disputed since its original formulation in the Balfour Declaration in 1917. In 1930 Sidney Webb, as Lord Passfield and Labour Colonial Secretary, had issued a White Paper intimating that a National Home in Palestine was not the same thing as Palestine as a National Home.[3] He was contradicted shortly afterwards by Ramsay MacDonald, who affirmed that Jewish immigration into the British Mandated Territory would be limited 'only' by the area's economic capacity.[4] Increased persecution in Europe produced further immigration, and turmoil, in Palestine. In 1937 the British Government accepted, in principle, the recommendation of a Royal Commission headed by Lord Peel to divide Palestine basically between Arabs and Jews, with the British retaining a permanent mandate over the holy places and a corridor to the sea at Jaffa. Labour took the view that the Peel proposals should be first examined by a Joint Select Committee of the House before Parliament was committed; the Party's speakers also stressed the importance of trying to get a Round Table Conference,[5] i.e. a negotiated settlement. Attlee explained that Labour did not want to make the matter a party issue: 'We are solely concerned with having the best way possible of meeting this position in the interests of the Arab people, the Jewish people and the whole world.' He agreed with the Government's suggestion to put the Peel Report first to the League of Nation's Mandates Commission. He did not agree with an amendment by Churchill which would have committed the House in advance to partition.[6] Attlee, it would appear, had already concluded that, in Palestine as in Europe, unilateral British action would be ineffective and undesirable. When the annual conference reviewed the situation in October 1937, a spokesman reiterated that Labour had never been pro-Jew or pro-Arab; it was fair to both sides. Attlee pointedly said that he had nothing to add.[7]

No doubt, also, Attlee generally agreed with Labour's strong opposition to the Chamberlain Government's 1939 White Paper on Palestine. The document's two most controversial provisions were those curbing Jewish immigration into Palestine to 75,000 in the five years after April

1939 and limiting the sale of land to Jewish settlers. What preoccupied Attlee, however, was the manner of the Government's action. Though present during the Commons debate of May 1939, he did not speak; his attitude may be deduced from the terms of Labour's amendment, which emphasized that the White Paper proposals were 'inconsistent with the letter and spirit of the mandate . . . ' and that 'Parliament should not be committed pending examination of the proposals by the Permanent Mandates Commission of the League of Nations.'[8] The Commission had time before the outbreak of war to register its rejection of the White Paper – by a single vote. By the end of 1939 nearly half the 75,000 quota had been used up, whereas the land restrictions were not put into immediate effect. Early in 1940, as a result of Arab pressure, the Chamberlain Government decided to go ahead – despite the protests of one Cabinet minister, Winston Churchill.[9] Attlee tapped out to the PM on his own battered typewriter his objection. He set aside the question of whether the land transfer regulations were just or not to the Jews; that was 'a matter for a difference of opinion which [could] be debated without heat and without raising any wide repercussions'. The point he was concerned to make was the attitude that the White Paper (particularly in regard to the land regulations) revealed to the League of Nations and to the acceptance of international law. In taking the proposed action the Government, in his opinion, was claiming to be judge in its own case and treating Palestine as a colonial territory. He was convinced that untold harm would be done to the moral issue of the war, in the UK and neutral countries, 'especially the USA', if the Government proceeded without taking a month or two to obtain the opinion of the League's members.[10] He expressed these views publicly, in the form of a parliamentary question to the Colonial Secretary in February 1940,[11] and, not being satisfied with the answer, raised a motion on the subject in March.

For the next two and a half years or so the war was the dominating factor. Once in the War Cabinet, Attlee and Greenwood for Labour, as well as Churchill, lost no time in indicating their disapproval of the White Paper; they were joined in this view by Sinclair, the Liberal leader. With equal speed, they all agreed that June 1940 was no time to revise the Paper's policy.[12] Churchill, however, made it clear 'that for him the White Paper was a temporary expedient, a moral burden that he would discard as soon as he was politically and strategically able to do so'.[13] Though decidedly not a romantic Zionist like Churchill, Attlee certainly felt by the summer of 1943 that the time was ripe for a reconsideration of British policy. The position, he wrote in a Cabinet memorandum in June, could not be left where it was: the evidence seemed to show that 'there is every probability of our being faced with violent action by either, or both, Jews and Arabs. We shall have the thankless task of keeping order and will be blamed by both sides.' He particularly worried that the Zionist movement in Palestine had apparently 'fallen under the control of reckless fanatics'. If they attempted to gain their ends by violence, he warned, the results would be disastrous to the Jews all over the world. 'No one but a visionary,' he insisted, 'imagines that Palestine can absorb all the Jews, even if they were willing to go. Millions will desire and be obliged to live in Gentile lands in Europe, America and other continents. They will depend for their restoration to their old homes, for their continuance in their present or for their settlement in new homes on the goodwill of the United Nations, especially of Britain, the US and Russia. We should, I think, endeavour to bring to bear on the Zionists the influence of those Jews who intend to live in Gentile lands.'

To the extent that these views failed to anticipate the effect of the holocaust – on Jews and non-Jews alike – they may be thought unimaginative. But it should be stressed that Attlee had recognized Nazism as an absolute evil from the beginning. His profound repugnance to and anger at the perpetrators of the genocide – and with those who had allowed it to happen – did not affect his rejection of Zionism in its messianic form. To a man of his cast of mind it was inconceivable that the vast majority of Jewish people would not, with the extinction of Nazism, continue to live – in security and civil equality – in the several states of the Diaspora. To admit otherwise would be a concession to racialism of the worst sort.

Still, the question of Palestine remained: in June 1943, he thought that the Cabinet should settle on a definite policy, not only as concerned 'the relationship between Jews and Arabs in that country, but as part of the larger question of the future of both Jewish and Arab races'. The whole problem, he was certain, should be discussed with the US and as a first step, he suggested that a Cabinet Committee be set up to consider and report on the issue.[14] Nine other ministers also produced papers for the Cabinet meeting on 2 July 1943, but Attlee's June memorandum commanded as large a measure of support as any. The Cabinet decided that it was desirable to deal with Palestine on a wider basis than previously, that early consideration had to be given to long-term policy, and that a Cabinet Committee be appointed. There was also general agreement in favour of partition and, as well or alternatively, Jewish settlements in other areas such as Cyrenaica, Tripolitania or Eritrea. It was now Churchill's turn to become cautious. Though restating his well-known opinion that the White Paper was contrary to Balfour, the Prime Minister indicated that he too favoured a Joint Declaration with the US on the subject, a statement that need not go into details. The Cabinet extended the period in which Jewish immigration to Palestine would be permitted, but retained the 75,000 limit.[15]

Churchill and Attlee, despite their very different emotions on the subject, had no difficulty in persuading the moderate Dr Weizmann in

October 1943 that they remained 'staunch Zionists';[16] but Attlee's detached and circumspect approach would not have appealed very much to several Labour Party members. Since the outbreak of the war the Party had become increasingly Zionist. The Palestine Resolution at the 1940 annual conference had ostensibly reaffirmed Party policy, but the emphasis had definitely shifted to the Jewish side; an amendment insisting on Arab rights too was easily defeated. By the summer of 1943, the scarcely credible news of what was happening to European Jewry had begun seeping into general consciousness. The result was that pro-Zionist feelings became passionate. The annual conference that year accepted a resolution from the Jewish Socialist Labour Party (Poale Zion) reaffirming 'the traditional policy of the British Labour Party in favour of building Palestine as the Jewish National Home' – a significant departure from previous policy. On the other hand the NEC felt obliged to reject a motion calling for unrestricted entry to shelter for all genuine refugees in territories under British control, and the establishment of a Ministry for Refugees and Post-War Relief. Harold Laski, who was deputed to explain the NEC's position, confined his argument to a technical point: the creation of a separate ministry for a particular problem would, he said, be a grave error of judgment, 'administratively and in many other ways'.[17] A couple of weeks later, just before the Cabinet meeting on Palestine, Laski wrote privately to Churchill saying how deeply hurt he had been at the realization 'that among my own colleagues in your Government Dr Goebbels had induced a spirit of caution [on the Jewish refugee problem] when you have so amply shown that audacity is the road to victory'.[18] Laski's indiscretion was indicative of the degree of feeling on the Jewish – and now therefore Palestine – issue in the Party at large.

These feelings found their fullest expression in the NEC's statement, *The International Post-War Settlement*, which received overwhelming support at the Party's 1944 annual conference, held in December. The document was specific only in regard to two subjects, Germany and Palestine. Just as Germans who were not prepared to become loyal citizens of other States had to go back to Germany, so too in Palestine was there a case 'on human grounds' and in order to promote a stable settlement, for 'transfer of population'. Hitherto on Palestine the Party had 'halted half-way, irresolute between conflicting policies', the document admitted; but now, the NEC stated, 'there is surely neither hope nor meaning in a Jewish National Home unless we are prepared to let the Jews, if they wish, enter this tiny land in such numbers as to become a majority'. The statement continued:

> Let the Arabs be encouraged to move out as the Jews move in: let them be compensated handsomely for their land and let their settlement elsewhere be carefully organized and generously financed.[19] The Arabs

> have many wide territories of their own; they must not claim to exclude the Jews from this small area of Palestine, less than the size of Wales. Indeed, we should re-examine also the possibility of extending the present Palestinian boundaries, by agreement with Egypt, Syria or Transjordan. Moreover, we should seek to win the full sympathy and support both of the American and Russian Governments for the execution of this Palestine policy.[20]

Attlee, an infrequent attender of NEC meetings that year, moved a long resolution asking Conference to support the international policy statement as a whole; but he made no specific mention of Palestine in his speech and there were no references to the subject, either, in the ensuing debate. It also happened that the War Cabinet's Palestine Committee was one of the few ministerial groups in whose deliberations he played no part. The chair was taken by Herbert Morrison, who had been 'passionately pro-Zionist since his first visit ... to Palestine in 1935'.[21] In December 1943 the Committee recommended partition, along the lines of the Peel Commission's Report of 1937, leaving open the question of ownership of the Negev.[22] And despite the launching in early 1944 of terrorist attacks by the Irgun and others against the British authorities on the spot, a majority of the Cabinet – which certainly included Attlee – still favoured some kind of partition in June 1944. In addition, all members of the Cabinet agreed that the White Paper policy would not continue after the war.[23] Given Roosevelt's 'unequivocal pro-Zionist statement' during the presidential election campaign in October 1944 – which seemed to many British observers to carry an implication of future American involvement in the area[24] – it seemed as though most of the factors for a solution were finally present. Morrison's Committee, in a further report that same month, was clear that partition should be carried through whatever the opposition: when the time came the Government should act with unhesitating decision. Further negotiations with either Jews or Arabs, the Committee believed, would not produce agreement.[25]

But when the sole opportune moment for an imposed settlement by the British arrived, Labour was no longer in the Government. At the end of May 1945, French and Syrian forces came into conflict and Churchill virtually ordered a cease-fire. For once, British prestige in Arab circles ran high. Churchill, however, did nothing about Palestine – an omission for which Attlee later bitterly reproached him.[26] According to Nicholas Bethell, a former junior Conservative Minister and well-known writer on contemporary history who has investigated the subject, the Prime Minister's erstwhile ardour for the Zionist cause had languished after the assassination of Lord Moyne in November 1944. Mourning his friend in the Commons, Churchill had warned: 'If our dreams for Zionism should be dissolved in the smoke of the revolvers of assassins, and if our efforts for its future should provoke a new wave of banditry worthy of the Nazi Germans, many persons like myself will have to reconsider the position that we have maintained so firmly for such a long time.' Discussion of the Cabinet Committee's recommendations was put off for four months, and within weeks of Churchill agreeing with Morrison to place them on the full Cabinet's agenda, Roosevelt died. Towards the end of April 1945, Churchill decided that he could not ask the existing Parliament to deal with the matter. The question would, anyway, soon become one for the Peace Conference. Churchill's last note about Palestine to his Colonial Secretary and Chiefs of Staff, written on 6 July, 'bore the mark of a tired and disillusioned man, whose enthusiasm for the cause had turned into anguish at yet another insoluble post-war conflict. Why, he asked ... should Britain carry on being responsible for 'this very difficult place' while the United States sat back and criticized? Perhaps the Americans should take the problem over.'[27] The legacy that the disillusioned Zionist now bequeathed to Attlee also included a letter from Truman, written just before the election results. The President wanted to know the Prime Minister's 'ideas on the settlement of the Palestinian problem'. Attlee must have been sorely tempted to ask the same of Truman. Instead, from Potsdam, Attlee diplomatically replied that early and careful consideration would be given to the American request.[28]

The obvious person to appoint as chairman of the Labour Cabinet's Committee on the question was Morrison. Attlee duly named him on 22 August to preside over a group that included Bevin, Dalton and the Secretaries of India and Burma, the Colonies, War and Air. Attlee took the view that the problem could not be considered in the isolation implied by Truman's letter. Bevin had already indicated that the problems of the Middle East should be looked at from the angle of the peasants rather than the pashas,[29] but far from wishing to relinquish British influence he wanted to extend it. In part, Bevin's policy was a reaction to Russian interest, expressed by Stalin at Potsdam, in the fate of the Italian colonies. But it also represented an automatic reaction on the part of the Foreign Office officials and military chiefs to the Mediterranean area, a reaction which took little account of Britain's lack of resources or the change in the strategic value of the Middle East that the war had revealed. A joint memorandum by Bevin and George Hall, the new Colonial Secretary, on 25 August, argued in terms of imperial communications, defence, resisting Russian influence and response to American refusal to accept responsibility for Cyrenaica and Somalia.[30]

Attlee recorded his dissatisfaction with this line of reasoning. Quite apart from the advent of the atomic bomb which, in his view, should affect all considerations of strategic area, he did not believe that the British Commonwealth and Empire could be defended by itself. Air power alone had transformed the situation: in an air age the neutrality, if not the support, of all countries contiguous to the Mediterranean route was needed. The Empire could now only be defended because of its membership in the UN. If the organization was a reality it did not matter who held Cyrenaica or Somalia or who controlled the Suez Canal. If it was not a reality then they had better be thinking of the defence of England, for unless the home country was protected no strategic positions elsewhere would suffice. In any case, he saw no possible British advantage in assuming responsibility for the former Italian colonies. They could not pay for themselves and the more the British did for them the more they would be faced with demands for self-government. The British had enough of these 'awkward problems' already and simply could not afford any more. Attlee was tired of listening to 'outworn conceptions', and made some caustic detailed comments. British Somaliland, for instance, had always been a 'dead loss and nuisance to us. We only occupied it as part of the scramble for Africa'.[31]

However, although the Cabinet agreed with Attlee that further consideration of British policy was needed,[32] some in British circles seemed to think that the scramble for Africa was still on. A conference of ambassadors and other high officials called by Bevin in early September agreed, in general terms, that British influence resting on military or political props would not be enduring and that an economic and social policy making for the prosperity and contentment of the Middle East should be developed. It also agreed, however, that British influence should be predominant in the area and that American economic penetration should be resisted.[33] The Cabinet procrastinated: Bevin was to tell the Council of Foreign Ministers that ultimately the World Organization should decide about the trusteeship of the Somalilands and Cyrenaica; but until the Organization was ready, both might be kept under British military government. It is noteworthy that Morrison particularly agreed, because he thought that some part of those territories might be used for Jewish settlement.[34] As with Churchill, Morrison's formerly wholehearted Zionism was apparently abating. When Bevin arrived at the Council of Foreign Ministers, he found that there was general agreement that the territories should be placed under international trusteeship. The question was whether that trusteeship should be by an individual State, or collective, as favoured by the Americans. The cat was now fairly placed among the would-be imperialist British pigeons, and Attlee could turn the lengthy Cabinet discussion to his advantage. He declared that the general sense of the Cabinet was clearly in favour of collective trusteeship. Naturally, the assumption was that if the US plan was accepted, the US would play its full part: that was vital.[35]

Meanwhile, on 31 August, Truman had written again to Attlee about Palestine. The President enclosed a report by his special envoy, Earl G. Harrison, on the problems of Jewish refugees, particularly displaced persons. Calling Attlee's attention to the fact that the available certificates for immigration to Palestine would soon be exhausted, Truman suggested that 'the granting of an additional 100,000 of such certificates would contribute greatly to a sound solution for the future of Jews still in Germany and Austria, and for other Jewish refugees who do not wish to remain where they are or who for understandable reasons do not desire to return to their countries of origin ... '[36] On 8 September, Morrison's Committee was ready with an interim report: the immediate issue was precisely what should be done between the time the White Paper's quota would be exhausted and the promulgation of a new long-term policy. The Committee advised that the maximum figure that could be admitted without prejudice to future policy would be a temporary continuation of immigration at the current rate of about 1,500 a month beyond the 75,000 limit. But in this case, consultation with the Arabs, both of Palestine and the other Arab League states, would be imperative. The Committee recommended that the White Paper policy be maintained and that no further immigration should be allowed for the time being unless Arab acquiescence had been obtained. The Middle East was a region of vital consequence for Britain and the British Empire. With the exception of Cyprus, all other territories in the area either had or would shortly obtain full independence; protection of Britain's vital interests depended on the collaboration of those states. Before approaching the Arabs, the British should inform the US of the British position and that the Government eventually intended to refer its long-term policy for Palestine to the World Organization.[37]

At its meeting of 11 September, the Cabinet did not disagree with the Committee's short-term recommendations: these recommendations had, indeed, been unanimous, approved even by Morrison and Dalton, both known Zionists and the Committee's senior members. Attlee emphasized the strength of the arguments for a Government statement of policy and its intention in due course to put the matter to the World Organization. Timing was critical, and he suggested that he, Bevin, Morrison and Hall should make the arrangements about the statement. He also wanted the Chiefs of Staff to review the security aspect again.[38] But within three days of the Cabinet meeting, the US Secretary of State, Byrnes, told Bevin that Truman was thinking of issuing a statement about Palestine, including Harrison's report. Bevin retorted that such an action could not fail to do harm to Anglo-US relations.

Attlee was aroused. In a personal and top secret telegram to Truman on 14 September, he fully endorsed Bevin's warning. He had been glad to learn that Byrnes had recommended that Truman should not make his statement. The position in the Middle East was 'already one of great danger and difficulty' and Attlee feared that, had the action been taken, it would have precipitated a grave crisis which 'would indeed be a lamentable start to the work of reconstruction to which we are now devoting ourselves'. He pointed out to Truman that the Jews were not using the numbers of certificates which were being made available to them. It appeared they were insisting on the complete repudiation of the White Paper and the immediate granting of 100,000 certificates, regardless of the effect this would have on the Middle East situation.[39] Two days later in another personal and top secret cable, Attlee sent a more detailed reply. The Control Commission in Europe had tried to avoid treating people on a racial basis. If the Jews were placed in a special category there would be violent reactions from other people who had been in concentration camps. The effect would be disastrous for the Jews. After all, the situation in the whole of Central Europe was appalling: the number of displaced persons, the refugees from concentration camps, the violent driving of people from one territory to another, were some of the most horrible events in human history. The British had been taking steps to try to prevent epidemics arising and spreading to other countries. For immediate relief there was a camp at Philippeville, North Africa, capable of taking 30,000 and another one at Felada with a capacity of 5,000. He suggested that these two places be used. He reminded Truman that Arabs as well as Jews had to be considered, and that Truman himself, Roosevelt and Churchill had each given solemn undertakings that, before they came to a final decision, the Arabs would be consulted. Attlee thought it would be very unwise to break these pledges and so set aflame the whole Middle East. He knew that Truman realized that the responsibility for preserving order with all the consequences involved rested entirely with Britain. There was also the question of India with its ninety million Muslims, who were easily inflamed.[40]

Attlee's arguments appeared to have some effect. Perhaps also influenced by his own State Department whose assessment of the situation was similar to the British, Truman temporarily backed down.[41] He would take no further action on the matter until Byrnes returned to Washington.[42] But the matter leaked anyway to the American press[43] and on 29 September Truman deliberately made public Harrison's report. The President intimated that he had appealed to Attlee to open up Palestine to the estimated 100,000 Jews remaining in Germany and Austria, and was waiting for an answer. Attlee's response was to inform Truman on 1 October that he felt bound to make it known that he *had* replied.[44]

Thus within a few months of Labour taking office, the Palestine problem had assumed new proportions. Attlee had had his first experience of American duplicity – and it would not be his last. The vital negotiations for the US loan were scarcely under way and he had to reckon with, on the one hand, what he considered to be irresponsible American tactics on Palestine and, on the other, what he considered British delusions of grandeur about the Middle East in general. He could not ignore the potential Soviet threat to the stability of the area, while he personally was engrossed in the attempt to bring the Indian connection to a reasonable end. And the UN was nowhere near ready to exercise any effective political authority. All the elements of the dilemma that would defy resolution were now present.

When the Cabinet discussed the Middle East on 4 October, Bevin took the opportunity to explain his view that it was essential to broaden British influence there by developing an economic and social policy which would make for prosperity and contentment. No one had any objections to this idea, but Bevin did not say how it might be done. Apart from the threatening situation in Palestine, there was agitation in Egypt for British withdrawal and difficulties with France in the Levant. Attlee pointed out that since the circulation of the various memoranda on the Palestine problem there had been a marked increase in agitation on the question in the US; British difficulties in regard to immediate immigration were not understood. It was no longer possible to postpone a statement on the issue beyond the end of the month, and difficult to postpone it even for two more weeks. Bevin asked that he be allowed to take another look at the question; he indicated that, though the long-term problem should of course be referred to the UN, the Government had to do more than that lest they be accused of avoiding the urgent issues. What he had in mind was the immediate establishment of an Anglo-American Committee to consider how to ameliorate the position of Jews presently in Europe and how much immigration to allow into Palestine in the near future, and also to examine the relief of the situation in Europe by emigration to other countries, including the US and the Dominions. The Commission would be instructed to consult Arabs and Jews.[45]

Bevin's suggestion was formally proposed to the Cabinet on 11 October 1945 by Morrison on behalf of the Palestine Committee. Though still insisting that a solution for Palestine had to be found in terms of British policy for the entire Middle East, Bevin conceded that it had become essential to allay the agitation in the US which was poisoning Anglo-American relations in other fields. But he did not accept the view that none of the Jews in Europe could ever find a permanent home there; he also thought that the US should make an offer to take those Jews who had to be removed from Europe. Attlee strongly supported his Foreign Secretary. It had to be made clear that the establishment of a joint Anglo-American Commission constituted an entirely new approach to the problem, though any announcement that was made, he urged, should also state the extent to which the US Government was committed to consult the Arabs.[46] After 'some hectoring',[47] the US agreed to take part. However, Truman insisted that the US would participate only if Palestine was made the focus of the inquiry, and not if it was considered simply as one among other potential places of settlement for European

Jews. When he met Truman in Washington in November, Attlee had to accept the condition:[48] getting the Americans directly involved was his primary concern.

While the Commission was investigating, attacks by Jewish terrorists in Palestine were stepped up, but the Cabinet refused to be provoked. A distinction was made between the extremists and the Jewish Agency; no action was to be taken against the latter, despite the advice of the High Commissioner. Moreover, immigration at the rate of 1,500 a month beyond the White Paper quote was to continue, though the Arab states were to be informed.[49] Negotiations with Egypt for a revision of the Anglo-Egyptian Treaty of 1936 were begun, with the aim of moving away from the idea of British forces of occupation towards a conception of joint Anglo-Egyptian measures of defence.[50] In February 1946, the Cabinet received a solemn warning from Dalton, Chancellor of the Exchequer, that unless overseas military expenditure was reduced drastically and radically, there would be no alternative but to cut rations and reduce employment. There was no way round the arithmetic and all overseas policy had to be conditioned by it.[51] In March an alliance was concluded with the newly independent Transjordan and that same month the Americans were persuaded to act diplomatically against the Russians in Iran. Attlee resumed his efforts to educate his colleagues, this time on the Defence Committee, to the realities of the British position in the Middle East. Trying to reduce the numbers of the British troops in Egypt became 'the perfect plague' of his life.[52] In a memorandum ostensibly devoted to the Future of the Italian Colonies, he refuted the assumption in 'all those Chiefs of Staff and Foreign Office papers that the passage through the Mediterranean and the Suez Canal is a life line absolutely essential to the British Commonwealth and Empire'. Not only had the advent of air-power made former assumptions obsolete, but Britain could no longer afford the great sums of money needed for the maintenance of large forces just on the chance of being able to use the Mediterranean route in wartime. He agreed that the development of oil resources in Iraq and South Persia was vital, but Britain was unable to defend this area from a determined land attack from the north. 'In the changed conditions of the world and in the modern conditions of three-dimensional warfare,' he concluded, 'it [was] . . . necessary to review with an open mind strategic considerations that we have held for many years.'[53]

Attlee's overall view may be expressed as follows: henceforth, the Middle East was mainly important to Britain on account of its oil resources. These could no longer be assured by military power; the area's political stability had to be obtained by other means. The first requirement was to come to terms with Arab nationalism, and here the Palestinian issue was paramount. Russian hostility and American commercial penetration had also to be reckoned with. Some kind of political agreement with the US, especially over Palestine, was essential.[54] He and Bevin were probably encouraged in their continued optimism by the sympathetic opinion of the State Department's experts, but they miscalculated the impact of domestic political pressures upon the President; and it was Truman who, in the final analysis, called the American tune.

At first, accord between the British and American governments appeared possible: Bevin wanted joint consultation before the Anglo-American Commission's Report was published and Truman agreed.[55] The Report was completed on 20 April 1946 and, as Bevin desperately desired, was unanimous. Partition was rejected in favour of a bi-national state; but the 100,000 refugees should be admitted and the land regulations abolished. Pending the execution of a UN trusteeship agreement, the British Mandate should continue, but the Commissioners were sure that the US would help Britain discharge the responsibility. Bevin told Byrnes (who was in Paris for the Council of Foreign Ministers' meeting) on 26 April that the 100,000 refugees would be admitted if the Jews in Palestine were disarmed.[56] More British soldiers had just been killed by Jewish terrorists. He repeated his offer to another high American official on the following day, mentioning the possibility of a complete British withdrawal and Russian penetration into the area.[57]

Bevin was not bluffing: three days previously, the Cabinet had decided to offer to withdraw all British troops from Egypt in five years, hoping that Egyptian opinion might in the meantime become more favourable to Britain.[58] British weakness was daily becoming more apparent. Keynes, in his inimitable fashion, had pointed out in February that Britain was paying the cost of British forces in Egypt by borrowing the money from Egypt! What would the British reply, he had asked, if Egypt were to say – 'as, of course, she will' – that she was no longer prepared to provide the necessary funds?[59] While Bevin was talking to the Americans in Paris, a committee of top officials and military chiefs informed the Government that implementation of the Report would be disastrous for the British position in the Middle East – militarily impossible and enormously costly. If the Report was accepted, the officials could envisage only two alternative courses: (a) to invite the Americans to become completely involved or (b) to arrange for the Report to be discussed in the first instance by the UN Security Council.[60] Nevertheless, perhaps because of what he had gathered from the Americans in Paris, Bevin was still optimistic on 29 April, when the Cabinet discussed the Report, about the prospects for a reasonable settlement – if the US would participate. The Cabinet was certain that military and financial aid, as well as political support, would be required from the US. It criticized the Commission for not having grappled with the problem of the Jews in Europe; the whole world had a responsibility to Jewish victims of Nazi persecution. Bevin's tactic of consulting the Americans before any statement was made on the Report was approved, and the leaders of the Opposition were to be given advance copies.[61]

All the signs of Anglo-American harmony risked being nullified on 30 April when Truman unilaterally announced his support for the recommendation about the 100,000 refugees. Attlee reacted at once. Calling his Cabinet together on 1 May, he declared that a Government statement would have to be made. It should stress the current difficulties of absorbing such a large influx, which could not in any case be accepted unless the illegal organizations had first been disarmed and disbanded. The statement should also raise directly the question to what extent the Mandatory Power could rely on the active collaboration of the US Government in giving effect to the policy of the Report. The Prime Ministers of the Dominions agreed with the proposed statement,[62] which Attlee made himself to the Commons. He reiterated that the Report had to be considered as a whole in all its implications, and that Jews and Arabs in Palestine had to disarm completely.[63] The strength of Attlee's feeling may be gathered from the fact that Britain was still waiting for US ratification of the Loan. The Americans were impressed by the weight of the Arab protests that followed the publication of the Report, and on 8 May Truman asked Attlee for concurrent action in initiating consultation with Jews and Arabs.[64] Attlee was encouraged: perhaps the Americans were going to show some responsibility in the matter after all.

Cabling his agreement to Truman on 10 May, Attlee expressed the hope that in view of the delicate negotiations with Egypt, an approach to the parties concerned could be postponed until 29 May at the earliest. In any case, he thought the suggested period of two weeks was too short for 'the Arab Government [sic] and Jewish Organizations to prepare and submit their views on the Anglo-American Committee's recommendations, and that it would be preferable to allow them one month'. He also wanted time for British and American experts to study the military and financial liabilities which would be involved in the adoption of the Report. Finally, he suggested the convening of a conference with Arab, Jewish, British and American representatives to consider the results of the preliminary discussions: the US and UK would then be in a position to make known their decisions, on the basis of the largest possible measure of agreement between all parties.[65] Attlee's intervention appeared to be successful: Truman accepted his proposals. Bevin told the Cabinet on 20 May that the Americans 'now seemed to be willing to remove this question from the realm of propaganda and to study its practical implications on a business-like footing.' He thought that the British declaration of policy in regard to Egypt had had a salutary effect on the attitude of the US Government towards co-operation in the Middle East.[66] Attlee was determined to keep the British point of view directly before Truman; on 26 May he set out in a telegram no less than forty-five points which he considered the joint sets of experts should study before any decision on the Report was reached.[67] Truman doggedly held to his emphasis on the 100,000; equally stubbornly, Attlee countered that this was only one aspect of the problem, and that the Report had to be viewed as a whole.[68]

At the Labour Party conference, held on 10–12 June, some misgivings about the Palestinian situation were expressed. Laski, in his chairman's address, specifically asked that the 100,000 be given swift and direct access to Palestine, though he did not ask for a Jewish State there; the situation was too complex for so simple a formula. The representative of the Poale Zion Jewish Socialist Labour Party put a motion reaffirming the 1944 policy statement in its entirety. In his reply, Bevin managed at once to exacerbate the issue and to put it in a wider context. The reason why there had been so much agitation in the US and particularly New York about the 100,000 was that 'They did not want too many Jews in New York'. But the 100,000 did not touch the fringe of the European refugee problem; to admit them to Palestine would necessitate sending another division of British troops there, and he was not prepared to do it. The British Exchequer, moreover, could not support any further expenditure on Palestine. He agreed with the creation of some kind of Palestinian State, but not a 'Jewish State' because he did not believe in absolutely exclusive racial states. In particular, he could not bring himself to accept the theory that had been adumbrated in America and elsewhere that because a man is a Jew he must be hounded out of Europe to some other country. His goal as Foreign Secretary 'was to bring him back again, after all the terror he has had, on terms of equality with the other citizens throughout Europe'. The Poale Zion's resolution was withdrawn, in the hope that the short-term recommendations of the Anglo-American Commission would soon be implemented. One of the delegates who had been a member of the Commission, Richard Crossman, pointed out that the Commissioners had been unanimously against the creation of either an Arab or Jewish state in Palestine.[69]

At this juncture, renewed acts of violence in Palestine resulted in British action against the Jewish Agency and the illegal organizations, an operation which was necessarily kept secret. Attlee informed Truman about it a few hours beforehand[70] on 29 June – and Truman publicly regretted the action. Hall, the Colonial Secretary, now thought that the Anglo-American plan would prove unworkable: he proposed the creation of two semi-autonomous provinces, one Jewish and one Arab, under a central trustee government. The way would be left open for either future partition or a federation. On 11 July the Cabinet decided that the Commission's recommendations offered no practical prospect of success, and that the time was not ripe for outright partition. If US support could be obtained, Hall's plan should be recommended to the

Jews and Arabs. Bevin, who was not present, was favourably disposed, but doubted whether it would provide a lasting solution. He suggested that the Foreign and Colonial Offices, with the Chiefs of Staff, consider a long-term scheme under which the major part of the proposed Arab province would be assimilated into the adjacent Arab States of Transjordan and the Lebanon, and the Jewish province established as an independent Jewish State, with perhaps a somewhat larger area than that of the proposed province. He hoped that Jerusalem would become an international area under the UN. He was still anxious not to be put in the position of opposing the Americans over the 100,000, and thought that Arab opposition would be reduced if the Americans would announce that a substantial number of European Jewish refugees would be admitted to the US American financial aid should be sought both for assisting Jewish immigrants to Palestine and for raising the standard of living of Palestinian Arabs. The US should also be told that the British were unwilling and unable to impose a solution by force. The Americans might then join the British in trying to obtain Arab and Jewish agreement to a solution that would not require force.[71]

When the British and American experts met in London in July, they agreed to the Hall plan with only minor variations. After the explosion at the King David Hotel on 22 July, Attlee resisted great pressure from the British authorities in Palestine either to break up the Jewish resistance movement or to announce a settlement of the political problem. It would be a mistake, in his opinion, to alienate all sections of Jewish opinion or to rush into long-term policy before negotiations with the US were completed.[72] Similarly, Attlee resisted for as long as he could official and military pressures to divert illegal immigrant ships from Palestine. These pressures soon gained majority support in the Cabinet, but in deference to Attlee's views, and in the hope that Truman would support the experts' plan (recommended to him by his own Secretary of State, Byrnes), it was only on 7 August that the Cabinet agreed in principle that further illegal arrivals should be trans-shipped and removed to Cyprus or other suitable areas.[73] Then, on 12 August, Truman informed Attlee that he could not give his support to the Hall plan which had been revised and agreed to by his own experts.[74] Attlee had been dumbfounded by Truman's cavalier treatment of the Anglo-American Commission's Report; this new blow shook his 'habitual placidity' to the core.[75] He grimly warned Truman that any solution proposed by the forthcoming Arab-Jewish Conference would have to be one that the British could put into effect with their resources alone.[76]

The conference opened on 2 October and was at once adjourned: the public gulf between the parties was too wide and further discussions were needed. But on 4 October Truman again openly declared, in effect, for partition and insisted that immigration should begin before any solution.

Attlee had been given advance warning of Truman's statement and had asked for time to consult Bevin in Paris; Truman had refused. The New York election was only a month away. Attlee was insulted; he telegraphed Truman: 'I have received with great regret your letter refusing even a few hours grace to the Prime Minister of the country which has the actual responsibility for the government of Palestine in order that he might acquaint you with the actual situation and the probable results of your action. These may well include the frustration of the patient efforts to achieve a settlement and the loss of still more lives in Palestine.' He was 'astonished' that Truman did not wait to learn the reasons for the suspension of the conference with the Arabs. Truman did not seem to have been informed that 'so far from negotiations having been broken off, conversations with leading Zionists with a view to their entering the conference were proceeding with good prospects of success.'[77]

Attlee's annoyance with Truman did not prevent him on the very next day from appointing Arthur Creech Jones, well known as a Zionist sympathizer, as Colonial Secretary in place of Hall. At a time when the British were trying to get the US involved in Europe, they could not afford to push the Palestinian issue to an open break. Neither could they afford to let the Anglo-Egyptian negotiations collapse. Attlee overruled Foreign Office policy on 14 November 1946, when he bluntly told the Cabinet that there was little doubt about Egypt's sovereignty over the Sudan; plans for the Anglo-Egyptian treaty should proceed regardless of the risk of disorders in the Sudan.[78] Bevin went to New York later in the month for the Council of Foreign Ministers meeting. He was also to see Jewish and American representatives, with three possible courses in mind if negotiations failed: (1) an imposed solution acceptable to one of the two sides – the CoS had advised that Britain did not have the means to impose a solution resisted by both sides; (2) to surrender the Mandate and withdraw; and (3) to propose a partition scheme which might provide for the Arab part of Palestine to be merged into Transjordan.[79] Attlee told the Cabinet that, though there were indications in various quarters that opinion was moving towards partition, it was important that the Government should not commit itself before all the alternatives had been explored in the Palestinian Conference when it resumed. It might well turn out that no agreed settlement could be reached and that the Government would be compelled to impose a solution, but it was essential that this result should arise from the Conference itself, and that the Government should not prejudice issues not yet fully discussed with the Arabs and Jews. Thus Bevin's discussion in New York should continue to be purely exploratory.[80]

Nothing definite came of the talks and, shortly after he returned to London, Bevin again put the issue before the Cabinet. Attlee prefaced the discussion in January 1947 by saying that it might become necessary to impose a solution which would be actively resisted by one or both communities there. The Chief of the Imperial General Staff commented that resistance from one side could be handled by the forces available in Palestine. Resistance by both communities would necessitate military reinforcements which could be provided in the last resort, without delaying the demobilization scheme. Traditional attitudes died hard. Another military chief insisted that in the event of a war the Middle East was essential to British defence, that Egypt would be the key position, and that as the British had undertaken to withdraw from Egypt, Palestine was necessary as a screen for Egypt. From the military angle, if one of the communities had to be antagonized, it was better not to incur Arab hostility, which would extend to the whole of the Middle East. Bevin began the ministerial debate by saying that, legally, either a partition solution or a Provincial Autonomy plan would have to have the prior approval of the UN; partition, he believed, would not secure the necessary two-thirds majority. After a long review of the issue since the last stage of the war, Bevin stated that he would still like to explore with the resumed Palestine Conference the possibilities of a bi-national state containing provisions for future secession. Dalton, Bevan, Shinwell and the new Colonial Secretary all declared themselves in favour of partition.[81] Perhaps influenced by these opinions, Bevin told the Cabinet on 22 January that he was not opposed to partition in principle, but was impressed by the difficulty of imposing any solution against the active opposition of either community. A further effort ought to be made by negotiation to bring the parties somewhat nearer together; if this attempt failed the question would have to be brought in some form to the UN. The Cabinet agreed but was doubtful whether the internal situation in Palestine could be held until the next meeting of the UN in September: a special meeting might have to be called earlier.[82]

Attlee had now concluded that there was little possibility of anything useful coming from the Americans;[83] he was resigned to letting events take their course. The Palestine Conference held at the end of January convinced Bevin and Creech Jones that there was no prospect of finding a settlement acceptable to both communities. But there was a possibility of another solution which could be defended in Britain and in the UN. The two ministers explained this possibility in a Cabinet Memorandum on 6 February. The object was the establishment of self-government in Palestine, leading to independence after five years of trusteeship. Both Arab and Jewish areas would have a substantial measure of autonomy during these years but would also be enabled 'to collaborate at the centre'. The 100,000 Jews would be admitted over two years, with subsequent immigration by agreement or through UN arbitration. Bevin and Creech Jones did not expect that the two communities would accept their plan. The question the Cabinet had to decide – if it accepted the proposal –

was whether the Government would be justified in bringing the plan into operation on its own authority, pending a UN Trusteeship arrangement, or whether to submit the problem without any recommendations directly to the UN.[84]

Creech Jones confessed to the Cabinet that he too had modified his Zionist opinions: the longer he had examined the detailed implications of partition, the more he was impressed by its practical difficulties. It would also involve conditions of rebellion and disorder in Palestine for a considerable time – beyond British military capacities. Bevin urged that the joint plan be put to the Arabs and Jews before handing over the entire problem to the UN. Wearily, the Cabinet decided to try one more time.[85] But within a week Bevin and Creech Jones had to report failure: no peaceful settlement on any basis whatsoever was possible, except with the backing of the UN. The problem had to be handed over as soon as possible, though in the meantime Britain should continue to administer the Mandate. They specifically rejected 'what some of the Arabs appear to wish', namely that Britain should evacuate the country immediately. That would be 'a humiliating course'.[86] On the following day the Cabinet agreed with Bevin and Creech Jones; Attlee insisted that there should be no concessions on Jewish immigration pending the next UN assembly, and that soundings should be taken to see if that meeting could be held earlier than September.[87] The decision to refer the issue to the UN was announced to the Commons on 17 February and, when he addressed it on 25 February, Bevin did not conceal his bitterness at American diplomatic tactics: 'In international affairs', he said, 'I cannot settle things if any problem is made the subject of local elections.'[88]

Many Zionists did not believe that Attlee and Bevin were sincere in their decision to hand Palestine over to the UN.[89] Yet during the first two months of 1947, the evidence of retreat from Empire was unmistakable: the British were on their way out of India, Greece, Turkey and Egypt (though the Anglo-Egyptian negotiations broke down later). The end of the Palestinian story need not concern us much further. While the administrative problems grew steadily and violently worse, the UN on 15 May set up a fact-finding committee, the USSR suddenly reversed its policy – indicating that it might be necessary to consider partition – and the US position remained as obscure as ever. The UN committee, composed of eleven 'neutral' states, could only agree to produce two reports, the majority one favouring partition. On 20 September, Bevin warned the Cabinet that when the reports came to the UN some countries might be tempted to put forward unworkable proposals, relying on Britain to implement them. He thought the Government should announce their decision to surrender the Mandate and, failing a satisfactory settlement, to plan an early withdrawal of British forces and administration.

Attlee concluded the Cabinet's many discussions of the issue by saying that there was a close parallel between it and India. That the British administration should, under the circumstances, continue in Palestine was unreasonable. He hoped that a clear announcement of the British intention to withdraw might produce a salutary result.[90] Despite the view of his military advisers who had consistently argued that 'full control' in Palestine was essential to the protection of vital British interests in the Middle East,[91] Attlee had all along considered that British withdrawal was inevitable. Britain, he was convinced, neither needed nor had the capacity to maintain its interests in the area by force. The only questions to be settled were those of the method and timing of British withdrawal. But in Palestine, unlike India, there was a vacuum or, as Attlee put it, 'the conflict of two imperialisms, Jewish and Arab'.[92] No one imagined that the two imperialisms were of equal strength; in the event of a concerted Arab attack on the Jews, perhaps provoked by the sudden admission of 100,000 refugees, the result could have been a massacre. Premature British withdrawal in the absence of a negotiated settlement or American involvement also threatened to bring about this disaster. Bevin had been much more influenced than Attlee by the Foreign Office and military chiefs, and by his fear of Russian influence in the area. Both Attlee and Bevin had hoped that the US could be persuaded to step in, and both came to feel – as Bevin expressed it to the British Ambassador to the US on 12 October – that the US 'had been thoroughly dishonest'. The Jews had indeed suffered terribly, and this had thrown up a number of problems which President Truman and others had exploited for their own purposes.[93] Attlee's feelings went deeper: to him, the Americans had committed the cardinal political sin – they had run away from responsibility.

XV

Possibly India

Asked in 1959 what he thought he would be best remembered for as Prime Minister, Attlee replied with his usual diffidence: 'I don't know. Possibly India.'[1] In fact, his were indisputably the hands which removed 'the brightest jewel' from the imperial crown. He was his Party's leading authority on India, and his knowledge plus his position ensured that his views on the subject predominated in the Cabinet.

The path that led him to his historic deed was almost as circuitous as that which took him from his public school to the Cabinet Room. The battle for Indian Independence was certainly not won on the playing fields of Haileybury; neither, as we have seen, did the question have anything to do with his becoming a socialist. At the beginning of the century, Keir Hardie and Ramsay MacDonald had made separate visits to India and had concluded that there was no practical alternative to British rule for years to come.[2] And although Attlee soon discarded the crude imperialistic attitudes of his youth, his own tours of the subcontinent in the late 1920s did not cause him to deviate sharply from the views of his two Labour predecessors. He naturally wanted to see major reforms in the way Britain ruled India, and in the preparations made for eventual self-government. But for some time in the 1930s he could not rid himself entirely of the assumption of a generation of high-minded Englishmen: no people ought to be free until they were fit to use their freedom properly. As he put it in 1937, he considered that 'India for the Indians' was a 'simple slogan': there would be 'no particular gain in handing over the peasants and workers . . . to be exploited by their own Capitalists and landlords. Nationalism was a creed that could be sustained by great self-sacrifice and idealism, but it was not enough . . .'[3] Attlee, however, changed his mind in 1938, well before the war had reversed the imperial relationship of creditor to debtor (a development which affected the opinions of all but the most fanatic imperialists).

His interest in India may be traced back to the beginning of his political career. One of his first parliamentary questions, and one of his first speeches as well, concerned that country. He wanted to know, in February 1923, exactly how many persons had been imprisoned there for political offences;[4] and in July he roundly condemned the economic policy by which India 'was forced to buy in a single market in which there were rings and combines in every kind of goods'.[5] Nevertheless, prior to his appointment to the Simon Commission in 1927 he did not give any 'serious attention to the Indian problem', and had met few Indians. He believed that he was chosen for the Commission because he was known to have no preconceptions on the matter.[6]

The Commission's initial visit to India in the winter of 1928 was in the nature of a general tour designed to give the members a preliminary impression of the country plus a detailed survey of the district administration in two provinces, Madras and the Punjab.[7] In the course of the three months, the Commission was greeted by hostile demonstrations everywhere and it was boycotted by the Congress Party. But Attlee and his Labour colleague Hartshorn contrived to meet secretly the Congress Party's vice-chairman; they found him (as Attlee had found the leader, Motilal Nehru, in London before embarking) 'quite impossible and not co-operative'.[8] Attlee was not impressed, either, by some of the moderate Indian members of the Viceroy's Council of State. On this first visit he was more receptive to the Viceroy's views and those of some old university friends who had attained high administrative positions in India.

His second visit, a much more extensive one from October 1928 to April 1929 which included Burma, left him perplexed. The Commission held a large number of hearings and took evidence from people of all communities, though the Congress Party's continued boycott proved a serious disadvantage. As a result, the Indian historian Partha Gupta has pointed out, 'even a potentially sympathetic member like Attlee got a picture of India being just a medley of provincial and sectional interests'.[9] Attlee later acknowledged that the Commission 'tended to hear more about the communal differences than otherwise would have been the case'.[10] An Indian journalist who travelled with the Commission for two months recalled that 'Attlee frankly admitted that the more he studied the situation the more puzzled he became'. India seemed to him too big a country to be brought under the British system of parliamentary democracy. The Commission's terms of reference ruled out the projection of schemes like the presidential system in the US. Further, Attlee said that it was very difficult 'to see how hundreds of states, big and small, could remain islands of autocracy in a country with parliamentary institutions'.

He confessed 'that the inquiry had raised more question marks than it had found answers to'.[11]

Attlee believed, as he indicated to his brother Tom, that India's real disabilities were social and economic rather than political, whereas the Commission's task was limited to dealing with political change.[12] Golant has observed that Attlee usually preferred to cross-examine witnesses 'rather as an intelligent researcher than a socialist critic of injustice'.[13] The wealthy were an object of his questions, and with his municipal background he could hardly help being appalled by the corruption, inefficiency and irresponsibility of the Indian local administration. The local government units, he wrote to Tom, were 'awful'. Many people at home did not realize that India was not 'a tabula rasa, but a paper that has been much scribbled over'. Moreover, the British, he believed, had been trying to put an Anglo-Saxon façade on to a Mogul building and the two pieces were not structurally connected. He had no doubt the 1919 constitution had failed, and the reason for its failure lay in its non-acceptance by the Indians. In any case, the Hindu-Muslim dispute seemed to him to be insoluble.[14] He became sick of hearing the same old story at the provincial hearings. When the second volume of the Commission's Report appeared, it proposed among other things that a similar Commission to measure the progressive stages of the development to 'responsible government' should never again be sent out.[15] This, the most important section in the volume, was largely written by Attlee.

Before the Simon Commission's Report was completed, the political ground was cut away from under its feet. The Viceroy – in consultation with the British Government – announced that the natural issue of India's constitutional progress would be the attainment of Dominion status and that an attempt would be made to face the problem of the Indian States without waiting to hear what the Commission had to say; to this end a Round Table Conference would be convened immediately. The Government's hand had been forced by events in India. Late in 1929 the Indian National Congress had demanded complete independence, and in March 1930 Gandhi launched his famous civil disobedience campaign, the 'salt march'. The Commissioners, including Attlee, vainly protested at the Government's move[16] and proceeded to write their Report as if the announcement had not been made.

Volume I, published in May 1930, was mainly composed by Simon and consisted of a descriptive and analytical survey which Attlee considered 'masterly'.[17] Volume II, published the following month, contained the Commission's recommendations. They proposed the establishment of a federal type of constitution at the centre, including British India and the Native States, though the latter should not be compelled to join. The central government's responsibilities, over which Britain would retain final control, should be limited to those of defence, internal security and the protection of minorities. The provincial governments, on the other hand, should be given wider powers and an extended franchise.[18] This approach can fairly be described as one of enlightened paternalism, and as such was hotly rejected by majority Indian opinion as represented in the Congress, and by a strong section of Labour opinion.

Attlee, however, argued in retrospect that the recommendations were realistic and pointed with some pride to the fact that 'India was governed on the Simon Commission plan from 1935 onwards, and it was on our recommendation that Burma gained its freedom from India'. A very great advance in self-government, he insisted, had been recommended at the provincial level. If little progress was possible at the centre it was for three good reasons: (1) the communal tension, (2) the separate position of the Indian States, and (3) the question of the Armed Forces, which had the double role of external defence and internal security. It would have been 'quite wrong and contrary to all precedent' to have placed British troops at the disposal of a government not responsible to the House of Commons and, at that time, very few Indian officers had reached field rank.[19] In a private memorandum to MacDonald, in August 1930, Attlee was quite explicit: the Indians were ready neither for independence nor for the degree of self-government that they demanded. Some provinces even lacked the personnel to fill the ministerial posts adequately, and all the evidence seemed to suggest that there was exceedingly little likelihood of stable parties arising.[20] He would have postponed Indian participation in the central government rather than have diarchy, which he detested. He did not consider that rapid Indianization of the Army was possible and believed that it was necessary to retain the British Army to control the North-West Frontier and communal troubles. He reiterated his support of the Commission's view that the Army should be made an imperial responsibility, with a subvention from the British Treasury, under the Governor-General and the Commander-in-Chief, and not accountable to the Indian legislature. This arrangement would remove a constitutional obstacle to the achievement of Dominion status, as and when India developed her own defence capability.[21]

These views were no longer acceptable to the Labour Left or even to MacDonald. The Prime Minister ordered that Attlee's name be removed from the memorandum[22] and for many years Attlee was held, in some Labour circles, to be a reactionary on Indian questions.[23] This was far from being the case; he realized the defects of the Commission's Report, he admitted to his brother in June 1930, but how to support any alteration that would fit all the facts? 'It may be,' he suggested with a flash of insight, 'that there is no answer to the problems which we had to face. The real difficulty in dealing with the Central Government is that there is no feasible transitional stage between a government responsible to Britain and a government responsible to the Indian people.'[24] Fifteen years were to elapse before he was in a position to act on this insight.

After the failure of the Round Table Conference, in which Congress had not participated, but which had secured a conditional undertaking from the Princely States to join a future all-India Federation,[25] Attlee's views began to evolve. Congress and Gandhi agreed to participate in a Second Conference, though by the time it took place in September 1931 the Labour Government had given way to the National Government. The Indian journalist who had previously spoken to Attlee in India discovered a 'refreshing change'; he found that Attlee 'revealed a broader vision and spoke with self-confidence'. The party that mattered in India, Attlee readily conceded, was Congress, and how he wished that Congress had struck a deal with Labour while it was in power. Now he feared that the Tories would exploit the Second Round Table Conference to set up obstacles to India's advance to self-rule. They would play up the grievances of the Muslims and the depressed classes in their bid to thwart the Congress. The Muslims were the Tories' Crescent Card much as Ulster had served as their Orange Card in Ireland. They were also planning to drag the Princes into the cockpit to delay, if not to sabotage, the transfer of responsibility at the centre.[26]

In August 1931, of course, Attlee was very much caught up in domestic politics. But although the failure of the Second Round Table Conference was due as much to the impasse among the Indians as to British machinations, there were some indications that 'the British Government was already veering from the way of experimenting with partnership towards the old imperial ways of paternalism, collaboration and repression'.[27] From Attlee's point of view all that could be said was that during the Conference Baldwin repudiated Churchill and the Tory die-hards, pledging himself and his party to work for an agreed solution with the goal of an all-India Federation,[28] which had been one of Attlee's aims.[29] For this change in British attitude, Baldwin, MacDonald, Simon and Irwin (the Viceroy) have received their due measure of praise, Attlee and Hartshorn much less so. Their participation on the Commission may have made little immediate impression on the Labour Party, but it certainly contributed to the creation of a more informed Conservative opinion.

The fact that Baldwin did not deliver on his promise – 'the method and timing of the devolutionary process exacerbated divisions within India'[30] – can hardly be attributed to Attlee. He did his best to widen the split between extremist and moderate Conservative opinion. 'India . . . must be allowed to make her own mistakes,'[31] he told the Commons in November 1931. The following month, in his first major parliamentary speech on India since his appointment to the Simon Commission, he stressed that the essential point was the demand for equality of status: henceforth the method of negotiation as used in the Round Table

Conference was the only way to proceed. The situation had changed since the writing of the Simon Report; the Indians had become more self-conscious politically and the timing had become important: the path of safety now was the path of bold advance. The problem was enormously complex, but Britain could do little to help solve the social and economic evils.[32] Attlee's main targets in this speech were those Tories led by Churchill. Churchill's reply combined selective praise for the Commission's Report with a furious attack on the Round Table procedure and a condemnation of the very idea of Dominion status: 'England, apart from her Empire in India,' Churchill fulminated, 'ceases forever to exist as a Great Power.'[33] His attempt to divide the House was defeated by 369 votes to 43 and in the majority could be found Attlee and Aneurin Bevan, Baldwin and Neville Chamberlain, MacDonald and Simon, though a wide gap still existed between the main British parties. Buffeted at home by the die-hards and in India by the nationalists, the Government quickly returned to a policy of repression. Gandhi's arrest in particular, on 4 January 1932, marked a further deterioration in relations between the Raj and the Indians.[34]

Attlee's own political position was complicated in the New Year by the formal opening of the debates on the protection-imperial preference issue. He had made his scepticism on this question known in 1930, in his memorandum 'The Problems of British Industry'. His argument was that Britain should consciously aim at decreasing dependence on the old staple exports of coal and cotton while at the same time planning the modernization and rationalization of production, distribution and credit so as to take full advantage of the twentieth-century industrial revolution. It had to be recognized 'that the Dominions are not prepared to sacrifice their nascent industries in the interests of Great Britain, while we have no right to make the interests of other parts of the Empire subservient to our own'.[35] But in view of the economic crisis some trade union leaders were not so sure: the TUC, it has been observed,[36] would have preferred an imperial bloc rather than the further unemployment that rationalization might have led to. Fortunately for Attlee, as Labour remained in opposition the potential dispute with the trade unionists did not materialize. He was also able to minimize his differences with other Labourites over India by emphasizing his larger disagreement with the Government. Nevertheless, he later considered that his greatest service to his Party between the Simon Report and the third Labour Government was 'educating the Party into a greater sense of realism on the problem [of India] and in bringing them [*sic*] to realize that there were other views than those of Hindu congressmen which deserved their attention'.[37]

He often combined his criticism of Government policy with this effort to 'educate' Labour opinion. He was not taken in, he stated in February 1932, by the many democratic professions of people who did not know what democracy was, or by the 'wonderful love of mankind' professed by people who had a very shrewd idea of their own interests. He feared that Government policy was driving all Indians into the Congress Party which, though enjoying widespread support, did not represent all Indians. At the same time, Congress could not be ignored; he recognized the position of the Muslims and the depressed classes but there was a danger that, in seeking to placate the minorities, the majority would be estranged.[38] The Government had to come to terms with Indian nationalism, he repeated a year later: he believed that the greatest thing for the success of the next stage in India would not be the meticulous accuracy of the reforms in every detail, but the release of the political prisoners and a frank invitation to Congress to come in again. On the other hand it would be absurd to imagine that Congress was the only party that believed in Indian self-government.[39]

But Attlee's main political task between 1933, when the Government published its White Paper on the subject, and 1935, when the India Act was passed, was to try to influence the Government's policy. The White Paper made no mention of Dominion status, which the Simon Report had done, though an all-India Federation along with provincial autonomy was recommended. Attlee, also, still ruled out the prospect of self-government in the near future, but thought that the White Paper's proposals did not go far enough. His preliminary speech on the topic, in March 1933, established his reputation as Labour's foremost parliamentary authority on India, and might be said to mark a first step in his ascension to the Party's leadership.

He began by reaffirming the official Labour Party position laid down at the 1927 annual conference. The Indian people had a right to full self-government and self-determination. British policy ought to be one of continuous co-operation with the Indian people, with the object of establishing India at the earliest possible moment and with her consent as an equal partner in the British Commonwealth. Labour believed that a new constitution for India should contain provisions for its own development, as the Simon Commission had stated. Such safeguards as were necessary should be in the interests of India: the reserved powers should not prejudice the possibility of advance to self-government. No settlement could be reached without the co-operation of all sections of the Indian community; political prisoners not guilty of violence should be immediately released. He praised the previous Labour Government's initiative and condemned its successor's dismissal of the Second Round Table Conference, the policy of repression which had followed and the quite unrepresentative Third Conference (which had been held at the end of 1932). The Secretary of State (Sir Samuel Hoare) had tried, Attlee charged, to hold the balance between two sets of unreasonable people – Churchill with his friends, and many members of the Indian Congress

23 Attlee on the election trail in the 1950s

24 Attlee with his successor as Party Leader, Hugh Gaitskell, who never became Prime Minister

25 (*left*) Prime Minister Nehru greets Attlee in India, after Independence

26 (*below*) With President Tito in Yugoslavia, 1953

27 (*opposite above*) With Chou En Lai in China, 1954. (Attlee, Chou En Lai, interpreter, Bevan and Morgan Phillips, Secretary of the Labour Party)

28 (*opposite below*) A tribute from Durham miners in Bishop Auckland, the constituency of Hugh Dalton (second left)

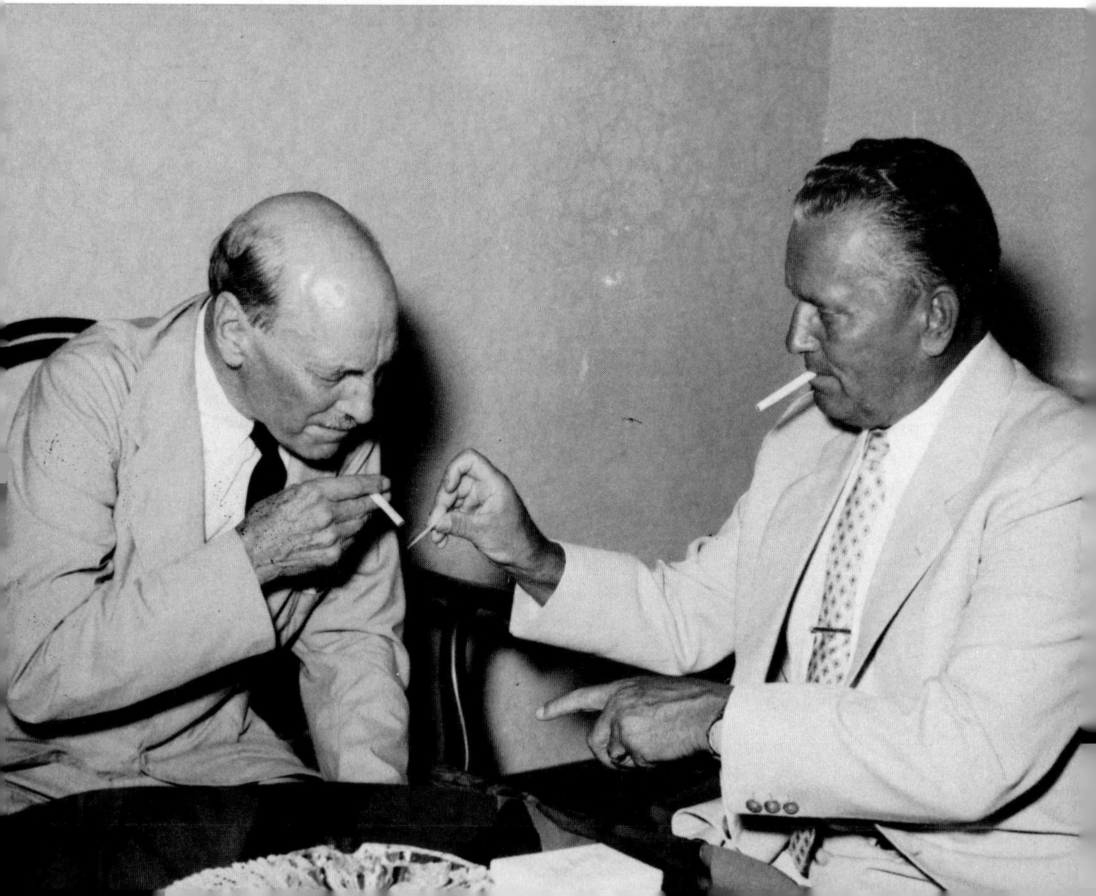

NATIONAL UNION OF MINEWORKER
DURHAM AREA
BRUSSELTON LODGE
MR. C.R. ATTLEE M.P.

29 Attlee's statue unveiled in the House of Commons in the presence of four Prime Ministers: Callaghan, Wilson, Thatcher and Heath, November 1979

Party: but the White Paper, in effect, favoured the Churchill faction. He did not wish to underestimate the difficulties. The 'facts of the situation' ruled out the immediate establishment of self-government on the Dominion model. Yet on the basis of the White Paper proposals, there was very little hope of getting full co-operation in India. The whole idea of Dominion status had gone and there was no concept of a progressive advance towards full, responsible government.

Anyone who knew anything about Indian constitutional matters, he continued, knew that the biggest obstacle to self-government was the existence of the Army in India. Yet there was no suggestion as to when that Army might be Indianized. Attlee was critical of the 'extremely vague time at which the Constitution at the centre' was to come into force; an extraordinary series of obstacles had been put in the way. He was particularly struck by the financial prerequisites – including the creation of a Reserve Bank, a balanced budget, the reduction of short-term credit, the accumulation of a surplus and the restoration of an export surplus. No modern state could pass such an examination; why should India? He insisted that the date and the conditions of the inauguration of federation should be made much clearer and nearer than they were in the White Paper. He again damned the diarchy system at the centre, evident from the scope of the Governor-General's discretionary powers; diarchy was 'a lesson in irresponsibility'. He also scorned the franchises on which the Council of State and Assembly of the Legislature would be based, and deplored those envisaged for the provinces, which gave too much representation to landlords and not enough to women. He concluded by saying that the only possible basis for an interim Constitution would be complete agreement with 'the politically-minded people in India'. It was no good suggesting that the latter were seditious, or that one admired the peasantry. He recognized the point of view of civil servants who feared that if the peasants and workers of India were handed over to an entirely Indian government they would be exploited. But in view of the current nationalist movement it was impossible to continue on the old lines of an imperial benefactor helping the people of India in their distress and protecting them from the oppressor. He had no illusions about nationalism – 'the illegitimate offspring of patriotism out of inferiority complex' – which was nourished by alien rule. Only responsibility and freedom would get rid of nationalism, but the White Paper contained no suggestion of any progress towards full responsibility. Unless great alterations were made, he feared very much for the future of peace in India.[40] The parliamentary struggle went on for over two years. The main reason for the prolonged debate over the White Paper and the Bill introduced in 1934 was not so much Labour's as the Churchill group's opposition. The Bill was fought at every stage and sometimes without scruple.[41] Attlee took a major part in all the debates, developing the criticisms made in March 1933. He also submitted his own minority report to a Joint Select Committee consisting of Lords and Commoners, of which he was a member. He agreed with the Government's proposal to link the central government with a new Indian federation, but thought that a definite date for federation should be given, that there was no need for a prior agreement with the Princely States and that there should be no preconditions about 'sound finance'. The reserved powers of the Government over finance in the transitional stage should be curtailed by setting a ten-year limit to the tenure of the financial adviser and by limiting the Governor-General's powers of interference to specific points. He did not think that the investment of British money provided any justification for special safeguarding, and the Reserve Bank of India should be nationalized. In any case it should be made clear that India's currency and credit policy would be decided in accordance with her needs and not by the influence of external financial interests of foreign creditors. He recommended tariff autonomy on the Dominion pattern.[42]

Explaining, in December 1934, the reasons why he had differed from the Joint Committee's majority recommendations to the Commons, Attlee said that they betrayed a distrust of the active political forces in India; a grave mistake had been made in the way in which the legislatures were to be formed, there was no adequate provision for constitutional development at the centre and a definite term – he suggested ten years – should have been laid down for the Indianization of the Army. He also differed from his fellow Labour members on the Committee: they thought the central government should be formed by direct election. Attlee had already pointed out that in India direct election would involve constituencies of a million people. In such circumstances there could be no proper contacts between electors and elected. But the Committee's proposed method of indirect election was even worse. Attlee believed that it would be possible to have indirect election by proportional representation from the provinces to the centre, whereas the Committee had based the election on communalism.[43] The eventual Act fell far short of what Attlee would have liked to have seen but it did contain some features that he approved. Diarchy disappeared and the provinces were given a very large measure of self-government. Provisions were made for the federal union of British India with the Princely States, after separate negotiations, and Burma was detached from India. To this extent, the work of the Simon Commission had been vindicated.

Attlee's primary objection to the India Bill, as he stated in one of his final speeches, was that it had been deliberately framed to exclude as far as possible the Congress Party from effective power.[44] During and after 1932, Congress had wilted under the weight of repression and the defeat of the civil disobedience movement,[45] but in the mid-1930s the Party staged a revival and found a new leader, Jawaharlal Nehru, who appeared to agree with Attlee that nationalism was not enough.[46] In November 1934, Attlee interceded with the Secretary of State to secure Nehru's release from prison (in order to take his sick wife to Europe).[47] Between 1935 and 1940 Nehru, an evolutionary socialist, was able to forge new links with Labour leaders. He made a number of visits to Britain, establishing ties with Labour politicians and intellectuals, especially on the Left. Attlee, together with Cripps, took a prominent part in these discussions, which testifies to the sincerity of Attlee's desire to find a way out of the difficulty which he described in 1937: 'the long period of British rule,' he wrote, had created a situation in which many rights had been acquired by particular sections of the Indian people; it would not be 'right to abandon control without taking care to see that these rights will be respected'.[48]

What has been called the 'high-water mark of Congress-Labour co-operation'[49] was reached in June 1938, when Nehru and Krishna Menon met Attlee and other Labour leaders at Cripps's country house. The discussion focussed on the terms of a treaty by which power would be transferred to India when Labour took office. The terms agreed included: a constituent assembly elected on universal suffrage, with acceptance of existing communal constituencies, to decide the future constitution; only those Princely States which accepted these bases would be allowed to send their elected representatives to the assembly; Britain would announce that all her treaties with the Princes would lapse as soon as the constitution had been passed; the question of the Indian debt was to be solved in a manner favourable to India, though India would undertake to settle the external part of the debt by buying British manufactured goods over a period of years.[50] The origin of these terms had to be kept secret at the time, though some of them were reproduced in a book published in 1939.[51] In the meantime Congress had considerably broadened its strength in India, ending its previous, almost exclusively middle-class character. It took an active part in the newly established provincial governments from 1937 to 1939. Unfortunately this participation had two disruptive effects; a rift opened up between the Congress's right and left elements, and tension increased between the Hindu and Muslim communities.[52] Then, on 3 September 1939, the Viceroy, in India's name, declared war on Germany.

Lord Linlithgow's action was by proclamation; his subsequent justification of it to the Central Indian Legislature provoked the abstention of the Congress Party. Its terms for co-operation in the war effort soon became clear; Congress wanted admittance to the Viceroy's Executive Council and British recognition of India's right to self-determination on the basis of a constitution drafted by an Indian assembly.[53] Labour alone favoured acceptance of these terms and, in October, Attlee attacked the Viceroy for his lack of tact in not seeking to bring India into the war on an equal footing with Britain. He called for a more imaginative approach to dealing with the Indian people.[54] Linlithgow's response later that month merely reiterated the long-term British aim of Dominion status, though he added that the 1935 Act would have to be reconsidered after the war. Congress thereupon asked its representatives to withdraw from the provincial governments, which alarmed the Conservative Government as well as the Viceroy. It was then decided to invite Indian leaders on to the Executive Council, on four provisos: that the Viceroy would retain his supreme power, that British freedom to deploy forces in India would not be affected, that there would be no constitutional change during the war, and that no promises would be made binding the post-war British Parliament. The author of these provisos was Winston Churchill,[55] now a member of the Chamberlain Government.

Churchill's return to power was to put the Labour Party, and Attlee in particular, into the apparent dilemma of whether to break with the Coalition, or temporarily to accept a compromise to the Party's approach to India. There was never any doubt as to what either the Party or Attlee would do, though the issue was to provoke the sole heated personal discord between Attlee and Churchill during the war.[56] By April 1940, Congress had definitively rejected the revised British offer and the Muslim League had opted for the creation of separate and sovereign Muslim nations.[57] That month, Labour's parliamentary spokesman put the main emphasis in his speech on an appeal to Congress not to threaten civil disobedience while Britain was fighting fascism. He also rejected the idea of a separate Pakistan and said that within a year from the end of the war Indians would be asked to frame their own constitution. At a meeting of the NEC, Attlee stated that the spokesman, Wedgwood Benn, had said all that needed to be said and that no useful purpose would be served by making any further announcements.[58]

Attlee's attitude did not mean that once the Coalition had been formed he abandoned his effort to seek a more positive British attitude towards India. Cripps had returned from a personal visit to India (in December 1939) convinced that Britain would have to choose between conciliation or coercion of Congress. He told the incoming Secretary of State, Leo Amery, that conciliation might take the form of an announcement of India's right to settle its own future and the dispatch of a negotiating team to try to bring the Indian parties together.[59] The war crisis proved a powerful reinforcement to Cripps's arguments, and Amery tried to persuade the War Cabinet to support full and immediate post-war Dominion status, provided the Indians could agree on a constitution.[60] Attlee alone supported Amery.[61] The offer made to the Indians in August 1940 was rejected by all Indian parties. It merely repeated the invitation to Indian party representatives to sit on the Executive Council and proposed the establishment of a War Consultative Committee.

British responsibilities to minorities were emphasized as an essential preliminary to any contemplation of the transfer of power.[62] Indian rejection was followed by British repression, which aroused widespread Labour misgivings, including those of Bevin and Attlee, who expressed their disapproval directly to Amery.[63] In the summer of 1941 the Viceroy's Executive Council was enlarged to contain a majority of Indians for the first time, though the Viceroy retained his special powers and no Indians were given ministerial posts. This Executive Council immediately recommended the release from prison of those Indians who had supported Gandhi's campaign for individual civil disobedience and, in view of his Cabinet's favourable attitude, Churchill was obliged to agree.[64]

However, the Prime Minister's insistence, in September 1941, that the Atlantic Charter did not apply to India reopened the wounds. By December 1941, when the entry of both Japan and the USA into the war transformed India's strategic situation, the Cabinet – presided over by Attlee in Churchill's absence in Washington – concluded that a further general discussion was needed.[65] Attlee prepared the ground for meeting Churchill's inevitable opposition by casting doubt on the Viceroy's advice to Churchill of 'standing firm and facing the music': it was worth considering, Attlee wrote to Amery, whether someone should not be charged with a mission to try to bring the Indian leaders together. A lot of British opinion, Conservative as well as Labour, was not satisfied that the only thing that could be done was 'to sit tight on the declaration of August 1940'.[66]

Attlee presented a memorandum on the Indian political situation to the War Cabinet on 2 February 1942. He challenged Linlithgow and Amery's conclusion that nothing could or should be done at that time. Britain, Attlee argued, could no longer afford a Eurocentric view of the world. Alliances had been found necessary with China and 'semi-oriental Russia' against an Asiatic nation (Japan) enjoying success in opposition to Britain and America. The changed relations between Europeans and Asiatics had to be reflected in Britain's relations with India, if Britain was not to store up trouble for the future. The formation of a pan-Asiatic bloc of Britain's allies was possible in the post-war world. The Viceroy's reference (in his advice to Churchill) to India and Burma as an alien and conquered element in the Empire was astonishing, reading like an 'extract from an anti-imperialist propaganda speech'. It was a great achievement of British rule to have planted in India British principles of justice and liberty, 'the very ethical conceptions' upon which India's condemnation of that rule were based. Britain should appeal to the principles of democracy and liberty to rally Indians to the war for a common cause. The Viceroy's crude imperialism was unacceptable. A do-nothing policy might enable Britain to weather the present storm. But 'what of subsequent storms? Such a hand-to-mouth policy was not statesmanship.' Now was 'the time for an act of statesmanship. To mark time is to lose India. A renewed effort must be made to get the leaders of the Indian political parties to unite. It is quite obvious from his telegram that the Viceroy is not the man to do this. Indeed his telegram goes far to explain his past failures.' The alternatives were to entrust a person of standing with wide powers to negotiate a settlement in India, or to bring over Indian representatives to discuss a settlement. The first seemed to offer greater flexibility in negotiations. The chosen representative would have 'very wide powers both as to the future and to the present', though the latter seemed less important than the former. There was a precedent for such action: 'Lord Durham saved Canada to the British Empire. We need a man to do in India what Durham did in Canada . . . A representative with power to negotiate should be sent to India now, either as a special envoy or in replacement of the present Viceroy, and . . . a Cabinet Consultative Committee should be appointed to draw up terms of reference and powers.'[67]

Confronted by this formal proposition from the leader of the indispensable political element in his Government, Churchill compromised. He put forth a plan of his own: the Indian Defence Council should be expanded into an elective body of one hundred, representing the provincial assemblies and the Princes. But that was not all: the Council's function would not only include the discussion of the war effort; after the war it would be the body to frame the new constitution.[68] Churchill, in effect if not intention, had been forced to recognize that the Empire in India would not long survive the war, even if the British won. As he told the Canadian Prime Minister in March 1942: 'We have resigned ourselves to fighting our utmost to defend India in order, if successful, to be turned out.'[69]

Churchill's plan was not realistic, and in fact was scuttled by the Viceroy as being unworkable. Neither Congress nor the Muslim League would accept it. Political reality was slow to dawn, but after British military failures in Singapore, Malaya and Burma, further Cabinet changes became inevitable. Attlee was named Deputy Prime Minister and Secretary of State for Dominion Affairs, and Cripps, who had still not been re-admitted to the Labour Party, was made a member of the War Cabinet. Amery, the Conservative Secretary of State for India, was the first to shift ground. Pressure for change in British Indian policy also came from Chiang Kai-shek and Roosevelt. On 26 February 1942, a War Cabinet Committee under Attlee and including Cripps was appointed to consider the form and content of a new declaration of policy.[70] Other Conservative ministers still attempted to preserve British power in India, and a dangerous impasse along party lines developed. It was broken by Cripps's offer to go to India with full power to discuss with Indian leaders an agreed Cabinet scheme. The new proposal 'guaranteed India the freedom immediately after the war to make its own constitution in the form of dominionhood or independence', though dissenting provinces might achieve their freedom separately. As one commentator, R. J. Moore, has said: 'This sharp departure in policy was the consequence of the overthrow of the formerly dominant Conservative influence in the War Cabinet.'[71] It was greatly facilitated by Attlee's presence, as well as the necessities of war.

Attlee, too, compromised, but much less so than Churchill. He yielded to the demand of the Muslim League for separate Muslim states, and did not insist on a resolution of the Princely States' problem. He reckoned that, in the war situation, the Indians would be more interested in obtaining clear guarantees of post-war independence than immediate benefits.[72] The Cabinet's India Committee gave a great deal more attention to the former than to the latter,[73] but the British assumption proved false: the Congress insisted on immediate and full self-government. Attlee put the blame for the failure of the Cripps mission on Gandhi[74] though, in any case, the Congress's demand was unacceptable to Attlee as it appeared to be detrimental to the British war effort. When the Congress began a campaign of mass civil disobedience in August 1942, Attlee reacted promptly: he presided over the Cabinet meeting which ordered the arrest of Gandhi, Nehru and other Indian leaders. 'It was necessary,' was his curt, retrospective comment.[75] Nor, when a new Viceroy, Lord Wavell, suggested a year later that Indian party representatives be again invited to sit on the Executive Council, did Attlee revise his attitude to the Indian politicians. He was now 'disinclined to reform the executive by introducing party representatives, and preferred to build up the centre out of elements derived from the provinces and the Indian states'.[76] And though, at the end of 1944, his India Committee and the War Cabinet agreed that the time had come for a comprehensive and fundamental analysis of the alternative methods of dealing with the Indian problem, he was still smarting at the wartime behaviour of the Indian party leaders.[77] He could take some consolation here in an older Labour tradition of hostility to oligarchic party leaders who might or might not be representative of the Indian masses.[78] The improvement in the British war situation in the second half of 1942 had also strengthened the Churchillian forces in the Coalition, and Attlee could hardly risk jettisoning Labour's hard-won stature for an issue that was peripheral to domestic politics.

Of his broad anti-imperialist stance within the Coalition there can be no doubt. He could be found protesting, in September 1942, along traditional Labour lines, against the holding of colonies for the financial advantage which 'mainly accrued to a capitalist group. The maintenance of national sovereignty over colonies required the maintenance of national armaments . . . and the political views which he shared were in favour of the substitution of an international system of responsibility and control.'[79] He proved 'a formidable adversary of the Tory view of proper colonial development',[80] though for the sake of Cabinet solidarity, he and other ministers were willing to bridge their differences – especially as against Americans.[81] Sensing rather more than his Conservative colleagues that the war was transforming the power basis of the British Empire, he could afford to be patient. By the end of 1942, the British regime in India had become a creditor of the British Government and would become ever more massively so as the war continued. The Cabinet Committee discussions in the Coalition's final months, which broke up along party lines, were overshadowed by a growing sense of financial reality. It was feared that the British electorate would not be content to go on bearing a financial burden in India. This fear probably explains why Churchill's caretaker Cabinet so readily accepted a set of proposals by Viceroy Wavell based largely on the Cripps offer of 1942. The Cabinet did not believe in any case that Wavell could obtain the consent both of Congress and of the Muslim League.[82] But acceptance of the proposals would keep the Indian question out of the general election.

The crux of the problem that Attlee had to face when he assumed the premiership in 1945 was that 'India' was on the point of becoming ungovernable – either by British or Indians. One of the results of the wartime internment of Congress leaders had been to give the Muslim League a free rein to consolidate its authority over the Muslims. And what the League, led by Mohammed Jinnah, wanted – even before the ejection of the British – was partition. Wavell's offer of June 1945 to include party representatives on the Executive Council fell foul, among other things, of Jinnah's refusal to budge on the recognition in principle of a separate Pakistan. The war had also brought about a social and economic revolution. The Indian Civil Service and Army had become increasingly Indianized; the latter's officer corps had expanded from a pre-war figure of under 100 to over 10,000 in 1945. The Navy and Air Force had undergone a similar development, though the races and religions were intermingled. Moreover, Indian industry had greatly increased: the Indian debt to Britain had been eliminated, and India had built up a credit of over $1240 million.[83] The cardinal feature of Attlee's actions was his grasp of these facts.

He determined to oversee the negotiations personally. As Secretary of State for India he appointed the experienced but elderly F. Pethick Lawrence, whom he had not recommended for office in the Coalition. Of the sixteen Standing Cabinet Committees which he set up on 13 August 1945 he retained the chairmanship of only two, the Defence Committee and the India and Burma Committee.[84] The ex-social worker's object in both was to do himself out of a job. He would hand over Defence in

December 1946 to the department's Minister when some degree of co-ordination between the Services had been effected. Similarly the purpose of the India and Burma Committee was to wind up British sovereignty as soon as possible.

Attlee approached the ending of the British Raj from his oft-stated premise that only the Indian (or Burmese) leaders could tackle the business of framing a constitution and that British policy should be to compel them to do so. When his India Committee met for the first time Wavell's offer had been rejected, but the Japanese war had ended earlier than expected. Attlee proposed that new elections should be held during the cold season, at the Centre and also in the provinces, and that they should be regarded primarily as providing an electoral college.[85] An announcement to this effect should be made at once, though the Indian leaders should also be invited by the Viceroy to discuss any alternative method they might prefer. Failing agreement, however, Britain would arrange for a Constitutional Assembly along the lines of the 1942 Cripps offer.

The Viceroy was opposed to any immediate announcement, but Attlee was adamant that there was no point in any more talks about talks, as so many meetings had already proved useless. Cripps agreed, adding that the only hope of making progress was to bring the parties up against a definite plan of action which would force them to face realities and come to agreement.[86] The announcement was duly made, and elections were held for the Central Legislature in December 1945 and for the provinces in the spring of 1946. At both levels they demonstrated the League's control of the Muslim vote and its antagonism to the Congress. The League, in effect, demanded that the British divide India and then quit, the Congress that the British quit and then it would divide the country.[87] As unrest in the country mounted alarmingly – among Indians themselves as much as between Indians and the British regime – Attlee did what he could to preserve a measure of accord.[88] Already, in December 1945, he had despatched an all-party parliamentary delegation to assess the situation. In February 1946, he made one final effort: a Cabinet Mission, he announced, would be sent to India to assist the Indian leaders in drawing up a new constitution and, as an interim measure, the Indians would be given *de facto* responsibility by the creation of a new Executive Council representing the main parties. India had to choose what her future constitution would be.

The charges that the decision to send the Mission was made mainly because of the threat of a mutiny in the Indian Navy, or that the eventual decision to accept partition was a deliberate attempt to keep the subcontinent weak in British strategic and economic interests, have been adequately refuted.[89] Similarly, the story of just how close the Cabinet Mission actually did come to drawing up a plan embracing overall unity with wide minority autonomy at local levels lies outside the scope of this book. Suffice it to say that, before the Mission left India at the end of June 1946, both Congress and the League appeared to have accepted a long-range plan. But renewed trouble between the factions soon broke out and the League reversed its position. The League, it is true, did join the new Council in October 1946, but there was a complete impasse on the question of the Constitutional Assembly which was to meet in December. Civil war became as much a probability as rebellion against British rule, and in either case British powerlessness was apparent.[90]

In desperation, Attlee summoned five Indian representatives to meet him in London, two each from Congress and the League, one from the Sikhs. Nothing came of the meeting, and Wavell proposed to the India Committee on 11 December 1946 that Britain announce a definite date for withdrawal. In the Viceroy's opinion, it would be impossible to enforce British rule beyond 31 March 1948. A previous suggestion by the Cabinet Mission in June that a specific withdrawal date in the event of a breakdown in negotiations be announced had been rejected by the Cabinet; the Mission itself had not favoured such a course.[91] Now, on 20 December 1946, after much hesitation the India Committee decided to recommend Wavell's proposal to the Cabinet.[92] It was Attlee who turned the scales; not only had he already made up his mind, he had also concluded that the new approach would require a new Viceroy.[93] After heated debate the full Cabinet agreed on 31 December 1946 to put a final date on the British Raj. The timing and actual terms of the announcement, which Attlee suggested should be approved by Parliament, were put off for further consideration. Bevin was among those ministers who expressed great concern over the serious repercussions any such statement might have on British policy in the Middle East, but Attlee, summing up the 'general feeling of the Cabinet', overbore this objection. It was too late to reverse the general direction of British policy, even if they desired to. The announcement might have the effect of bringing the communities together, which was the main objective. Withdrawal was, in any case, inevitable.[94]

Attlee's decision to replace the Viceroy was based partly on his assessment of Wavell's personality and partly on a disagreement over policy aims. Wavell, Attlee said afterwards, though 'a very good Viceroy in many ways ... was not quite the man to deal with politicians, particularly Indian politicians. He was a soldier and a singularly silent soldier ... and I don't think silent people get on very well with Indians, who are very loquacious. His mind wasn't subtle enough ... ' By the time Attlee decided on a time limit Wavell had become 'pretty defeatist ... I came to the conclusion that Wavell had shot his bolt and that I must find somebody else'.[95] To the Cabinet on 8 January 1947, Attlee explained that the reason why Wavell attached so much importance to the announcement of a definite plan was because he favoured a phased withdrawal of British authority along the lines of a military evacuation from hostile territory. But the India and Burma Committee thought the aim should be to secure a friendly transfer of power; it was even probable in this case that Britain might be asked to give continuing assistance in various forms to the Indian Governments. Until the Muslim League indicated whether they would collaborate in the work of the Constitutional Assembly, there was no occasion for an immediate announcement such as the Viceroy wanted.[96] Although Attlee was resolved that the hand-over of power would take place within a fixed period, he wanted to ensure that this would be done in the most amicable fashion possible.

Attlee's choice as replacement for Wavell was, however, extremely concerned that a precise date should be given very soon. Attlee had 'thought very hard' about his choice before having a 'sudden inspiration'. Lord Louis Mountbatten, he remembered, 'had an extraordinary facility for getting on with all kinds of people, as he'd shown when he was Supremo in South-East Asia. He was also blessed with a very unusual wife.'[97] When Attlee informed him on 9 January 1947 that to name a precise day would be inadvisable, Mountbatten became worried. Attlee reassured him on 16 January that, though to fix an exact day of the month so far ahead would be unwise, there was no intention of leaving an escape clause. Meeting Attlee at Buckingham Palace on 24 January, Mountbatten said that the proposed date of 'the middle of 1948' left too wide a margin, but Attlee convinced him that no date closer than a month should be given. For the record, Mountbatten put this in a letter to Attlee on 11 February.[98] Two days later, Attlee told the Cabinet that the India Committee was now satisfied that the time had come to make the statement, with one change; the date for the transfer of power should be given as June 1948. The Cabinet concurred, despite the Secretary of State's lingering fear that June 1948 might be too soon to effect the transfer smoothly. If the Indians were not ready the date could be postponed.[99]

At the last minute Wavell got cold feet, confirming Attlee's estimation of him. He urged that instead of announcing that power would be transferred by June 1948, British authority should be progressively withdrawn, with the announcement delayed to June 1947 (saying that power would finally be transferred at the end of 1948). Mountbatten was considerably perturbed and wrote urgently to Attlee on 17 February, declaring that Attlee's proposal provided 'the only condition' under which 'a new Viceregal period could be started at that stage with a reasonable chance of success'.[100] The letter, written in Mountbatten's own hand, clearly pointed to the possibility of Mountbatten backing out, and Attlee minuted that it was to be put in a special secret file. When the Cabinet met on the following day. Attlee made no bones about the matter. The India Committee – read Attlee[101] – was convinced that the Viceroy's alternative plan was totally impracticable. Quite apart from that, Attlee thought that the most disturbing element in the situation was the complete change in the Viceroy's attitude to the announcement of a definite date for the transfer of power. Attlee coldly traced the history of the Viceroy's previous support for the latter proposal, the better to condemn his last-minute change of mind. He now informed the Cabinet that the announcement would be accompanied by a statement of the appointment of a new Viceroy, who would proceed forthwith to India for the specific purpose of arranging the transfer of power. The change of Viceroy, he added, was an essential element in the final attempt to induce a spirit of co-operation between the two political parties in India, and the new Viceroy had accepted his appointment on the understanding that the announcement of a definite date would be made before he left for India. There were only one or two minor hesitations, and the Cabinet approved the Prime Minister's policy, authorizing the Secretary of State to take unobtrusive steps to ensure that increased shipping facilities would be made available to Europeans wishing to leave India in the next few months.[102] This was the Cabinet Meeting that ended the British Raj.[103]

Attlee made his announcement in the Commons on 20 February, and wrote to Mountbatten on 18 March 1947 that the date fixed for the transfer of power was flexible to one month, but Mountbatten should aim at 1 June 1948. It was the Government's definite policy to obtain a unitary Government for British India and the Indian States, if possible within the British Commonwealth. But since the Cabinet Mission's plan could only become operative in British India by agreement between the major parties, there could be no question of compelling either major party to accept it.[104] Mountbatten was sworn in as Viceroy on 24 March 1947, and the rest of the story belongs to Indian history. A note in the Cabinet files drily records on 13 October 1947 that, by direction of the Prime Minister, the India and Burma[105] Committee was abolished.

One last point about Attlee's role must be made. It has sometimes been alleged that the eventual decision to advance the date of Indian independence to 15 August 1947, instead of June 1948, was precipitate and may have contributed to the turmoil that ensued.[106] Associated with the allegation – which cannot be proved one way or the other – is the notion that Indian unity might somehow, and in spite of all the evidence to the contrary, have been preserved. That Attlee tried and hoped to achieve this will be obvious from the foregoing, and his efforts have been testified to by at least one Indian observer.[107] But he had also, from the time of his original visit, been highly conscious of the cultural and religious divisions. The advent of Nehru's leadership had momentarily given him renewed hope that unity could be preserved, yet he had conceded in 1942 that the Muslim provinces should have the right to opt out if they so desired. The failure of his further efforts after 1945 to achieve a unified settlement, together with Mountbatten's recommendation that partition was the only solution acceptable to both sides, convinced Attlee that Indian political unity was not possible. He rejected the argument that British policy as a whole was responsible for the minorities problem. The difficulties in India, he wrote to Lord Salisbury in December 1946, were primarily due 'to the failure of the Indians to agree among themselves'.[108] Whatever the difficulties and dangers, he told his Cabinet in May 1947, there was no alternative to partition.[109] Such was also the view advanced by Lord Halifax (in what Attlee believed to be a great speech, preventing any division)[110] in the Lords debate on the India Bill in July 1947. Partition was acceptable, as it had not been in Palestine, to both major groups in India. Indeed, the Viceroy's Interim Council was unanimous that, should any communal disorder break out when partition was announced, it was to be put down ruthlessly using all the force required, including tanks and aircraft, and given wide publicity.[111]

Attlee had a further reason for allowing Mountbatten the liberty of accelerating the date. Mr Jinnah, he explained to his Cabinet in May, had always claimed that Pakistan would wish to remain within the British Commonwealth, while the policy of the Congress Party had been to make India a sovereign, independent republic. The prospect of one part of India inside the Commonwealth and one part outside had involved issues of great complexity. But now there had been 'a development of major importance which put the whole matter in a new light'. Some of the Congress leaders had become increasingly apprehensive about the difficulties which the grant of immediate independence would involve. Pandit Nehru and Sardal Patel had suggested to the Viceroy that in the event of partition Hindu India should be granted Dominion status, at any rate as a temporary measure. They had explained that they would hope to secure the agreement of their followers to this course by arguing that acceptance of Dominion status would enable power to be transferred to Indian hands at a date substantially earlier than June 1948, and India would be free to secede at any time from the Commonwealth. Attlee strongly favoured such a settlement. If Dominion status were conferred on the two successor States it would greatly ease the difficulties inherent in partition: it could also be supposed that the Indian States, after experiencing the practical advantages of Dominion status, would later be slow to relinquish it, and India's decision might influence Burma and Ceylon. The Cabinet found these reasons persuasive, though Attlee agreed that they would entail a comprehensive review of the constitutional relations between the various parts of the British Commonwealth.[112]

Suitably, it was Attlee who introduced the last India Bill to the Commons. The Bill went through all its stages in two weeks of July 1947, receiving unanimous support. Independence for India and Pakistan came into force in August 1947, to be followed by Burma in October and Ceylon in February 1948. The verbal habits of a lifetime took a little longer to eradicate. In October 1948, the Cabinet tactfully agreed that it would be useful to establish, without any formal change, a convention of describing the Commonwealth as 'the Commonwealth of Nations' and not the British Commonwealth of Nations.[113] At the end of the year Attlee confessed that he still found himself occasionally using the old term, which was not incorrect in certain circumstances; but in case of doubt, he advised his colleagues, the shorter term should be preferred.[114] The next year the King was recognized as the Head of the Commonwealth, a symbol of the free association of its entirely independent member nations. The Prime Ministers of India, Pakistan and Ceylon were among the Commonwealth Prime Ministers gathered in London in April 1949. Their joint declaration noted India's desire to become a sovereign independent republic and effectively brought to a close British imperial history in the first half of the twentieth century.[115] Attlee was in the chair.

XVI

The Maximum We Can Do

February 1950 was the Labour Party's fiftieth anniversary. It was also the date of the general election, and a Special Jubilee Conference had to be abandoned. To mark the anniversary, Francis Williams wrote a popular history of the Party entitled *Fifty Years March* containing a Foreword by Attlee; the PM described the story as 'very characteristic of Britain, showing the triumph of reasonableness and practicality over doctrinaire impossibilism'.[1] To mark the election, the British public gave Labour the highest number of votes any party had ever received – and one of the smallest majorities. This result was neither characteristic nor very practical. Attlee found himself in a situation for which there was no historical parallel. There had been small majorities before, he observed, but in the days when political affiliations had been fluid.[2] The 1950 election was significant for another reason. Although Attlee did not realize it, Labour's fifty year march had effectively been brought to a halt. Shortly after his return to the premiership, he would be obliged to summon a special session of Parliament in order to announce heavy increases in defence expenditure. These, he explained, constituted 'the maximum we can do'.[3] His point was that further increases of the same sort were beyond the capacity of the economy, but in retrospect his phrase has a far wider application: it may serve as an epitaph for his Party's half-century of struggle to reshape British society.

The ending of Attlee's 'revolution without tears' owed a great deal, if not everything, to the rearmament programme and what it signified – a tense international era. Labour's attempt to lay the foundations of socialism had all along been hindered by the defence burden. It was Attlee himself who in November 1946 had had the unpleasant task of justifying National Service to the Commons. Britain, he said, was part of the Continent and the country had to have trained reserves.[4] Neither his Party nor many other Englishmen had been very enthusiastic about the proposal, which was unique for peacetime. Some seventy-odd Labour MPs voted against the National Service Act in April 1947, and a similar number abstained. The revolt was the largest during Attlee's term of office and forced the Government to reduce the proposed period of conscription from eighteen months to twelve. But the Act proved the first of a series of bitter pills. Although the Government tried hard to stabilize defence expenditure, the eighteen-month period had to be reimposed and, by 1948–49, Britain was spending more on defence than all the other Brussels Treaty Powers put together – more, proportionately, than the US.[5] A chain reaction was thereby set up; shortage of skilled manpower and demands on scarce materials, as well as the cost of armaments, inevitably affected the availability of domestic goods and services. When these factors were added to Britain's long-term economic difficulties and the dollar shortage, it became clear that no second instalment of socialism would be possible for some time to come.

In any case, in 1949 the electorate was mainly concerned about housing, food and the cost of living.[6] Labour had to recognize that the wartime sense of social solidarity and spirit of sacrifice could not be prolonged indefinitely. Consequently, despite certain differences between those advocating 'consolidation' and those favouring 'advance', broad Labour agreement on domestic issues prior to the 1950 election was not very difficult to achieve. If some left-wingers preferred larger schemes of nationalization, they were prepared to settle for a short list of industries (including cement, sugar-refining and meat distribution), state-ownership of which could be (and was) justified on grounds of efficiency as much as of socialism.[7] It was generally accepted that other such developments would depend on economic growth, and that exports would have to come before further socialist measures. Indeed, given the precarious financial situation and the unexpected pressure on social services from both ends of the age spectrum, it was widely believed that the biggest challenge in the immediate future would be to maintain the Welfare State. The eventual election manifesto, *Let Us Win Through Together*, clearly reflected what was an essentially conservative stance, though one which could also be viewed as a tribute to the Party's success. Labour at last had something to defend.

This was the line taken by Attlee when he presented the Parliamentary Report (for the fifteenth time) to the Party's 1949 annual conference held in June. He stressed that the Report had to be seen in the context of a programme that had almost been carried out. Much remained to be done but, at the next election, Labour would be standing (primarily) on a great record. The final year in office would be especially testing. The Opposition would become more active, grievances would be magnified and attempts to sow dissension would be made. To his mind, the moral for Labour was plain: 'to carry on and preserve our unity'.[8] This position was more radical than it sounded; and if it lacked the emotional appeal of the past, it had the advantage of coming from a leader whose reputation in the Party had never been higher. Morrison, who had played a large part in the formulation of the new programme,[9] admitted that the task had not been as simple as in 1945. Behind *Let Us Face The Future* had been forty years of thought and propaganda. The new programme had had to be shaped to fit in with the policies of the last five years. The first priority now was increased production. He rightly insisted that the coming election would be the most important in Labour's history; when it was won, they should be able to 'go on for quite an indefinite time'.[10] Aneurin Bevan loyally supported Morrison, declaring that the kind of society Labour envisaged, and would have to live in, would be 'a mixed society, a mixed economy . . . [and that] . . . the language of priorities [was] the religion of Socialism'.[11] Hugh Dalton added that one of the most remarkable features of the debate on foreign affairs had been an almost complete absence of criticism of Ernest Bevin.[12] Thus to all intents and purposes Attlee took a united Party into the crucial final year of his mandate, just as he had taken a united Party out of the coalition. But in 1950 unity did not prove enough to win the election with a sufficient majority.

Up to the 1949 conference, the economic recovery – thanks to Marshall Aid and controls – had appeared to be making good headway after the setback in 1947. Industrial production by volume during the first six months of 1949, for instance, was 30 per cent above that of 1938; and output per man-hour had increased since the war faster than in the US.[13] Under Cripps's direction, the emphasis had begun to shift from direct to budgetary controls. There had been some de-rationing, and the 1949 Budget provided significant tax incentives to stimulate private investment. At the same time, ceilings had been imposed on food subsidies and social service expenditures;[14] in these areas the maximum had been done already. Trouble began as soon as the conference ended. A rail strike in June and a docks strike the following month had to be dealt with in firm fashion, with Attlee taking a leading role in the settlement at the docks. More serious was the economy's underlying fragility. Cripps had emphasized in his 1949 Budget speech that Marshall Aid provided only a limited time in which to improve the country's export performance,[15] but the breathing space was less than the cautious Chancellor had anticipated. During the second quarter of the year the dollar deficit doubled[16] because of a recession in the US and the partial convertibility of the drawing rights of the Marshall Plan's OEEC debtors. The consequent run on the pound brought about the devaluation crisis. It was '1931 all over again', Attlee remarked to Dalton in June.[17] To counter the inflationary pressures following the devaluation of the pound on 18 September,

Attlee had to announce in October a series of cuts in Government spending to reduce home demand. They included defence, agricultural subsidies and housing; he also announced a potential charge on Health Service prescriptions. The balance of payments was restored,[18] but the Government's popularity was hardly enhanced. The cuts also provoked brisk clashes within the Cabinet[19] that required all Attlee's diplomatic skills to resolve.

Such was the economic background to the crucial decision that was Attlee's sole prerogative to take, the date of the election.[20] A cynical politician, knowing that devaluation would entail unpopular measures, might have been tempted to go to the country as soon as the decision to devalue was made. The question was first discussed on 19 July 1949, when it appears that Attlee and Morrison had already 'broadly come round' to the idea of devaluation.[21] Cripps, who had not, wrote from a clinic in Zürich that he favoured an early election anyway; Attlee discounted the advice, saying that Cripps was evidently not in good shape when he wrote it. Bevan also favoured an early, if not immediate, election. Morrison, highly regarded as Labour's best electoral tactician, was uncertain: he feared that the country might think Labour was running away from responsibility if it dissolved Parliament then, an argument certain to impress Attlee. He, Bevin and Dalton were agreed on the need to dissolve before the next Budget, which meant February 1950 at the latest. Further discussion of the subject took place after devaluation, on 12 October. Again, Attlee, Bevin and Morrison favoured delay; Attlee in particular, despite the contrary opinions of Bevan, Cripps and Gaitskell, 'strongly urged' that they should wait until 1950.[22] And so it was decided, and announced. All ministers present at a meeting on 7 December, except Morrison who had doubts about the weather, then opted for February.

One other reason for not going to the polls in 1949 had been the passage of the Parliament Bill, which could not be completed until November. The new Act was necessary to overcome the Lords' veto on the Steel Nationalization Bill. Still, Morrison's hesitations about February were based upon shrewd experience; they were ignored because Cripps could not be moved. Further postponement would have meant having the Budget first, something that according to Attlee 'went against [Cripps's] sense of rectitude'. Attlee entirely agreed: 'It is dangerous to play politics with the Budget. It opens the way to every possible kind of stunt.'[23] (In 1955 the Conservatives would be untroubled by similar scruples.) When he subsequently explained the somewhat paradoxical result of the 1950 election, Attlee could also point to seat redistribution, instituted by his own Government, as 'the most important' factor which told against Labour. His own constituency had been among those eliminated; elsewhere, he noted, 'the tendency ... [had been] ... to transfer Labour votes in marginal constituencies to solid Labour seats. Undoubtedly this honest attempt to give one vote one value hurt Labour very severely.'[24] Had the Conservatives obtained Labour's lead in votes they would have gained an overall majority of 69.[25] Perhaps it is not too much of an exaggeration to suggest that Labour's effective period of power came to an end partly because of the Victorian integrity of its leaders.

Attlee's stamina during the campaign, one of the last in which television did not count, was reminiscent of a bygone era. He averaged seven or eight meetings a day, in different cities, being driven by his wife and escorted solely by a detective and a journalist. He spoke without notes, continued to deal with official business and made the final broadcast for Labour.[26] The tone of the campaign was quiet. The Conservatives, having improved their organization, equipped themselves with a manifesto that apparently differed from Labour's only in so far as it stressed personal initiative and freedom, and promised to de-nationalize road transport and steel. They still relied heavily on the appeal of an ageing Churchill, which suited Attlee well enough: 'Mr Churchill,' he joked, '[was] like a cock that crows and thinks it has produced the dawn.'[27] The strong Liberal intervention, with more candidates than at any time since 1929, also promised to help Labour. Attlee neatly defined his Party's claim to the middle of the road: 'Communism denies the dignity of the individual, Conservatism ranges the individual in classes'[28] – and jogged Liberal memories by saying that he knew 'of no one more loyal to the party to which he was attached for the time being than Mr Churchill.'[29]

The end result was a disappointment to all parties, despite the electoral turnout of 84 per cent, a record under the universal franchise. Of the 625 seats (15 fewer than in 1945), Labour took 315, the Conservatives and their allies 298, the Liberals 9, and Others 3. Labour polled 13.26 million votes, the Conservatives 12.5 million, the Liberals 2.6 million. Labour's percentage of the poll was 46.1 (compared with 48.0 in 1945), the Conservatives' 43.5 (39.6), and the Liberals' was unchanged at 9.0 (9.1).

At the time Attlee, naturally, was impressed by the 1.25 million increase in the Labour vote, 'a remarkable achievement'.[30] So it was, yet the creation of a majority Socialist electorate had eluded his Party. Some 30 per cent of the working-class vote continued to go to the Conservatives. It has been pointed out that a mere 5 per cent increase in what might be thought of as Labour's natural constituency would have enabled the Party to win on any or no programme, and to have established a virtually permanent majority.[31] Just as significant, the small overall swing to the Conservatives of 2.9 per cent concealed substantial regional variations. In industrial Scotland and Wales, Labour representation actually increased; but in Attlee's beloved Southern England and the Home Counties, as well as in the suburbs of London and other big cities, there was a distinct falling away in Labour support.[32] Attlee, Cripps and others largely held Bevan to blame.[33] Viewed as a whole, the election was a gloomy portent for Labour's future prospects in a society poised on the threshold of 'affluence'. The old rule still applied: the more prosperous the area, the less tendency to vote Labour. Paradoxically, if it did well in government, the Party stood to work itself out of a job.

However, Labour had *won* the election, as Attlee reminded the annual conference later in the year.[34] The Party itself had never been stronger; individual and affiliated membership reached new heights.[35] The only danger from the voting point of view in the House, Attlee added in October, was not a question of opinion but one of the health of Labour's MPs.[36] Still, he took it for granted that his second administration would not be able to embark 'on any major controversial measures'. Under the new Parliament Act a veto by the Lords could still delay any such legislation by up to a year. But 'the King's Government had got to be carried on',[37] and it was better that Labour should do it than the Conservatives! Few may have shared his optimism,[38] yet Labour would survive for another twenty months.

Indeed, for some months after the election, Labour's and the country's fortunes rose together. The small majority helped maintain Party discipline[39] and the Gallup polls recorded a slight but steady Labour lead until October.[40] Cripps's April Budget pursued the same responsible and deflationary course as the previous year, while aiming to preserve full employment, food subsidies and the social services. There was a large surplus and Cripps budgeted for another. He could afford some reduction in income taxes and, though the petrol tax was increased, the standard ration was doubled.[41] Industrial production during the year continued to improve; Britain's share of world manufactured exports was 21.5 per cent;[42] wages and prices were fairly stable; gold and dollar reserves increased; and 'unemployment' stood at 1.5 per cent.[43] The Party's chairman, Sam Watson, could jubilantly proclaim to the October conference that 'Poverty has been abolished, Hunger is unknown. The sick are tended. The old folks are cherished, our children are growing up in a land of opportunity.'[44]

Party unity, at least in public, prevailed up to the 1950 conference. After the election, Herbert Morrison had drawn the appropriate lessons. More attention had to be paid to consumer needs and to the problems of the housewife; better electoral organization was required and had to be concentrated on the marginal constituencies. He found few major faults with the Party's economic policy, so long as controls and nationalization were not insisted on for their own sakes.[45] This was also Attlee's view, though inside the Cabinet in March he judged it best to curtail Morrison's over-zealous proposals for improving the efficiency of the nationalized industries, which promised to upset Board chairmen[46] and possibly impair Government unity. Despite some wrangling over future domestic policy orientation,[47] the NEC was able to publish by the summer of that year an agreed statement on *Labour and the New Society*. Its most notable feature was the enunciation, in effect, of the principle, 'nationalization if necessary, not necessarily nationalization'; the shopping list of industries was deliberately dropped. Otherwise the philosophy and policy on which Labour had fought the election held good. Morrison ably introduced the document to the conference and Bevan concluded the debate for the NEC. Bevan's speech pointedly contained two specific, highly favourable references to Attlee, one Attlee remark – 'We are always better when we are getting on with the job' – and one aphorism which could have pleased no one more than the Prime Minister: 'There is no immaculate conception of socialism.' The statement was carried without need of a vote.[48]

All the same, the writing was already on the wall for the Labour Party. The Korean War had broken out in late June and the Americans had at once pressed Britain to spend more on defence.[49] Raw materials prices began to take off; further inflationary pressures and a balance of payments crisis were only a matter of time. At the October conference, Attlee was obliged to repeat his 'maximum-we-can-do' admonition of the previous month, but now in regard to domestic policy. The whole position established by the April Budget, he warned, had been 'overshadowed by increasing need for strengthening our defences'. Unpleasant as it was to have to devote so much of the country's resources to defence, he believed that the course of the next few years could well decide the future of civilization for decades or centuries.[50] The annual report of the Party's International Department referred to the sombre prospect of having to postpone some advances in the social services and in living standards.[51] These forecasts alarmed the idealists. An NEC supplementary report on the gloomy international situation, defended by Bevin in his last speech to the conference, was challenged. And though the bloc votes of the unions prevailed (by 4,861,000 against 881,000), the combination of internal dissension and external economic pressure that would decide Labour's electoral fortunes and, as a result, the character of British politics for a long time to come, was established. The twelve months between the conference and the next election also took a heavy toll of the Party's leadership. Bevin died; Cripps was dying; Morrison was discredited; Dalton remained on the sidelines; and Bevan resigned. Practically alone among his generation, Attlee managed not merely to hang on but to enhance his position in the Party and country. To him must go a good deal of the credit for Labour, amazingly, receiving in the 1951 election the highest vote given to any party in British history.

Inside the Cabinet, disputes had arisen before the Budget of April 1950 and had been smoothed over only after great patience on Attlee's part. Cripps had wanted to keep the economy on an even keel, Bevan to preserve the 'free' Health Service despite mounting costs. Attlee could readily sympathize with the desires of both men; the difficulty was the impossibility of accurately estimating those costs. He had therefore set up a weekly Cabinet Committee to act as a watch-dog.[52] Although hotly resented by Bevan,[53] the move can be seen in part as a prime ministerial shield to protect him. Bevan's reputation had diminished considerably in certain Labour circles after a speech in which he referred to the pre-War Tories as 'lower than vermin', and made other intemperate remarks. Just before the final Budget decisions Hugh Gaitskell acted as Cripps's representative on the Committee, and an ominous incident at once occurred: 'the Minister of Health', Gaitskell recorded in his diary, 'provoked by something I had said, slammed his papers down and started to walk out of the room. The PM, however, summoned him back and smoothed him down ...'[54] The day was thus saved for Harold Wilson to effect a compromise,[55] largely in Bevan's favour: a ceiling on costs was arrived at, but no charges were imposed.

Attlee's instincts were always left of centre and, besides, he liked Bevan much more than he did Gaitskell. Despite his impulsiveness, Bevan exerted on Attlee the same fascination that another former member of the working class, Bevin, had. 'When Bevan meets people he charms them,' Attlee told a journalist.[56] Even after Bevan had broken ranks, Attlee still considered that Bevan 'had the leadership on a plate' and, what was more, wanted him to have it.[57] That Attlee appointed Gaitskell, in October 1950, to succeed the ailing Cripps as Chancellor was mainly on account of Gaitskell's technical expertise; Bevan, in Attlee's view, would not have inspired confidence abroad.[58] Gaitskell was also recommended by Cripps, Bevan's former mentor, and Gaitskell's nomination was supported by Bevin and Morrison, whereas the choice of Bevan was opposed by senior ministers and trade union leaders.[59] Gaitskell did not threaten Bevan politically at this point,[60] yet the Welshman again allowed his fiery temperament to get the better of him, remonstrating directly to Attlee.[61] Gaitskell turned out to have an equal conceit of himself and it was not long before the conflict between the two men became critical, when Attlee was ill.

To appreciate the futility of the dispute that became public in 1951, it has to be stressed that Bevan, and the Left generally, had accepted British involvement in the Korean War[62] just as all sections of the Party applauded Attlee's efforts in Washington, in December 1950, to limit it.[63] It was also apparent that a certain price would have to be paid to reinforce British influence on US policy. The American preoccupation with the Far East could have caused the US to reduce its commitments in Europe unless the Europeans manifested their will to resist any aggression. In practice everything depended on the British attitude; NATO only existed on paper and the other West European countries lagged behind Britain in economic recovery and political stability. However, trebling the extra load on British resources between August 1950 and January 1951 did not satisfy the Americans, who requested defence expenditures in the region of £6,000 million.[64] Ridiculous as the figure was, the Cabinet had to appear to accept it. In January an increase from Attlee's 'maximum-we-can-do' figure of £3,600 million (spread over three years) to £4,700 million was approved with little dissension. Bevan actually defended the latter figure to the full in the Commons.[65]

Attlee very carefully posited both figures on certain conditions. In September 1950 he had specified that, before the exact amount of British rearmament could be decided, the amount of US assistance had to be known.[66] In January 1951 he deliberately told the Commons that, '*If* the programme is fully achieved, the total defence budget in the next three years ... *may* be as much as £4,700 million.' He added that '... limitations on production ... may make it impossible to spend this sum within that period'.[67] Nevertheless, the colossal sums had been 'accepted' in order to get Congress to vote supplies. The need to impress American opinion over rearmament was probably strengthened by Labour's reluctance to get too politically and economically involved in Europe, a reluctance that would be shared by the Conservatives when they returned to office. Attlee's approach to the question of rearmament represented a calculated effort to find a path through the maze of higher international considerations, which included anxiety about both Russian and US policy (where Britain would soon, and successfully, be attempting to soften the terms of the 'Brand China' resolution in the UN), practical economic realities and domestic politics (where Churchill was berating the Government for not doing enough on defence).

In sharp contrast, the pomposity and pride displayed by Bevan and Gaitskell in their quarrel over the 1951 Budget was on a distinctly lower level of statesmanship. Years afterwards, referring to Bevan, Attlee was reminded of something said by an old Labour stalwart: 'You know, when I was young I was always talking about my conscience. But I thought it over and came to the conclusion that what I called my conscience was just my own bloody conceit.'[68] A dispassionate reading of Gaitskell's biographer's detailed account of the episode strongly suggests that the remark applies in Gaitskell's case too. And the more Morrison's role in the affair is considered, the more dubious that also becomes. One point deserves to be stressed before any other: in 1951 Labour was in office with a tiny majority. Any action which risked splitting the Party was fraught with possible election consequences. Both protagonists, and a singularly indecisive Morrison, were prepared to court that risk. Bevan may have been the one who resigned, but as some commentators admit, Gaitskell was 'handling dynamite', and Morrison himself was 'far from depressed by the prospective resignations'.[69] Of course, preparing the rearmament

Budget was bound to be painful for all concerned, and for none more so than Attlee, who was actually nursing an ulcer throughout the prolonged discussions. Quite early on, he commented drily, 'Well, we shall not get many votes out of this!'[70] By mid-March 1951 Attlee's Committee had, without enthusiasm, largely agreed that health care costs would have to be contained by imposing some dental and optical charges, as well as the prescription charges. Attlee did not defend these proposals when they were questioned by Bevan and Bevin. Instead, a compromise suggested by Bevin was arranged between him, Attlee, Morrison and Gaitskell: prescription charges, which arguably bore more heavily on the sick, were eliminated.[71] On the very next day, Attlee had to go to hospital.

Until then, despite friction and strain, government solidarity was preserved. And though it is obviously impossible to say what the result would have been had Attlee remained on the daily scene, no better indication of his value to the Party may be found than the constant recourse to his hospital bed by all the disputants. Around that bed, at least for a time, some sense of proportion seemed to prevail. Away from it, inflexibility, intrigue and talk about principles flourished.[72]

The immediate issue boiled down to the question of optical and dental charges which, as Bevan did not fail to observe in his resignation speech,[73] involved the trivial sum of less than £30 million in a budget of £4,000 million. Yet that argument, from Attlee's point of view, could cut several ways. A case could and should, in his opinion, be made for the charges on grounds of preventing abuse, besides economy. Or they might be postponed until absolutely necessary, a course which Gaitskell stubbornly refused to accept. Or, Attlee recollected, 'If you really think that putting a charge for medicine entitles a man to wreck the whole party – if you have a sense of proportion you don't.'[74] When Bevan had piloted the Act authorizing prescription charges through the House in November 1949, he had in effect denied that any great principle was at stake.[75] At one point, in March 1951, thinking that Bevan had made a conciliatory gesture, Attlee wrote to him saying, 'The death of Ernie [Bevin, on 14 March] has rather overshadowed these differences and I hope that everyone will forget them.'[76] From his sick bed, Attlee also raised other arguments – the proximity of the election, the impact of MacArthur in the US and, finally, the golden rule of collective Cabinet responsibility. It was to no effect, except that Bevan in his letter of resignation widened his disagreement to include, apparently, the entire Budget.

Michael Foot may well explain that Bevan's act, as expressed in his speech to the Commons, was 'an explosion of the forces pent up in him over months, even years'.[77] The fact remains that, *while Attlee was actively present*, Bevan had brilliantly defended all the Government's policies, including rearmament. The Cabinet decision to accept charges, taken in Attlee's absence on 9 April, was the sole major issue settled on a vote in Labour's entire term of office.[78] Even after Gaitskell had presented his Budget to the Commons, there were proposals for a last-minute compromise along the lines that the 50 per cent charges on spectacles and dentures need not be permanent.[79] Some of Bevan's own friends were distressed at his tactics.[80] His resignation proved to be the prelude to a period of internal strife in the post-election period comparable to that of the 1930s. It was as if part of Labour's nerve, Labour's will to govern, had cracked. Attlee's retrospective feeling that, possibly, he might have prevented the fateful resignation was, as noted earlier, shared by Harold Wilson. In any event, although Attlee did not think Bevan's reasons for walking out were valid,[81] he did not blame Bevan so much as Morrison (who had presided over the Cabinet during Attlee's absence); and to Gaitskell he became 'pretty cool'.[82]

The open dissension in the Party's ranks, Attlee considered, necessarily weakened the position of the administration[83] and, as he had indicated, few votes would be *gained* by the 1951 Budget. The effect of either the dissension or the Budget on Labour's traditional working-class supporters was probably insignificant in 1951. Bevan's followers could be counted upon to vote Labour, and if the Budget further reduced consumer spending, the taxation increases – on income, purchases, petrol and entertainment – were relatively minor. There were various compensations for lower wage earners; pensions were increased, social services expenditure and food subsidies remained about the same. And those members of the working class who continued to vote Conservative were surely a lost cause for Labour by now. The major electoral problem was how to attract voters from the other social groups. The Budget contained little to excite the material interest of these people and it came after eleven years of austerity. Moreover, the extra £500 million devoted to defence wiped out the previous year's surplus and left no safety margin to counter the effects of the sudden balance of payments crisis in the autumn. Prices and wage pressures increased, some food rations were cut and some controls reimposed. The sombre economic outlook was compounded by the threat of an interruption or of an increase in the price of Iranian oil. In short, the election that Attlee called for on 25 October could have hardly come at a more unfavourable time for Labour.

Yet if there were difficulties ahead Labour had to have a larger majority in the House. Attlee had spoken of the health problem in October 1950; by the spring of 1951 it had become acute. 'It was not pleasant,' he recalled, 'to have Members coming from hospital at the risk of their lives to prevent a defeat . . . '[84] There was also the constitutional consideration that the King was due to embark on a lengthy tour of Australia and New Zealand early in the new year. Attlee therefore wrote to Morrison on 27 May, soon after the Budget and before the balance of payments and foreign crises had come to a head, that the election should be held that year. He added that October was the best month. The Party needed time to prepare, the holiday period was obviously not good and, in the meantime, the meat supply might improve and the foreign situation change. Most ministers approved and, though Morrison had his doubts, his biographers admit that he did not make a firm stand for a later date.[85]

Over the summer, although the economic and foreign situations deteriorated, the constitutional factor became more pressing. The King wrote to Attlee that it would be 'disastrous' if his tour had to be postponed or even interrupted on account of political upheaval at home, that the people of Australia, New Zealand and Ceylon 'would never understand the reasons for such a postponement or interruption . . . and would never forgive it'. These words were perhaps exaggerated, but when the King put his signature to them he was a very sick man, far sicker than he realized. Attlee thoroughly admired the King's sense of duty and was a strong partisan of Commonwealth ties. He replied to the King on 3 September that one of the factors to which he had given particular attention was precisely the one His Majesty had raised. Attlee had decided that 'the right course' would be a dissolution in the first week of October. The King, however, learned from his doctors on 11 September that his left lung had to be removed, and informed Attlee on 18 September.[86] The news did not prevent Attlee on the following day from broadcasting that election day would be 25 October; it may even have sharpened his concern about the effects of Conservative procedural tactics in the Commons on the health of several Labour MPs.[87] And the imperative need for a larger majority remained.

Soon after his resignation, Bevan's friends had felt a curious need 'to engage in propaganda, to recruit, to organize'.[88] In July, *Tribune* published *One Way Only*, a pamphlet written by Michael Foot and Jennie Lee[89] (Bevan's wife), which held the West's 'hysterical fear of Russian aggression' responsible for the excessive arms programme and emphasized the importance of constructive relations with the Third World. Bevan contributed an introduction saying, quite gratuitously, about the defence problem that 'all or nothing [was] a silly slogan'; too much wealth and energy should not be devoted to war machines though Britain should not deprive itself of the means of effective defence or fear would supervene.[90] Two days after Attlee's announcement of the election date, *Tribune* came forth with another pamphlet, *Going Our Way*, which repeated the criticism of the Government.[91] How these pamphlets were expected to help Labour win the election was unclear. Attlee rather sadly remembered that 'you never had an intellectual paper that wasn't violently critical, always run by your left-wingers with no sense of practicality about them at all.'[92] Bevan's standing even with Labour voters had diminished by 44 per cent since his resignation according to a Gallup Poll.[93] Just before the election, Bevan tried to redeem himself. At the

Party's annual conference held in early October he stated that he was frightened at the prospect of Winston Churchill replacing Attlee on the front bench in the House of Commons. 'The quiet, moderate, balanced approach of Clem Attlee', he added in a sudden burst of enthusiasm, 'is more adjusted to the international situation than the romanticism of Winston Churchill.'

There was a poignant moment at the conference. A great-grandmother from Poplar who had been in the Labour Movement for forty-eight years got up and declared that her London slum had 'found Clem first'. She recalled how Attlee had come knocking at the door in 1907. Bevan was so moved that he said he was prepared to hand over his engagement diary to 'Grandma Cressall', and that she had made one of the best speeches he had ever heard. The only new point that Attlee could contribute to the proceedings was that, though the last eighteen months had been difficult and not very spectacular, Labour's advance had been continued in the field of administration. It was superficial to think of that advance mainly in terms of Acts of Parliament.[94] Attlee, at least, never had any difficulty in distinguishing between Labour's purposes and priorities and those of the Conservatives.

Had he not resigned, Bevan would have had good cause to support Attlee in a more tangible fashion. The Iranian oil crisis, which was to dog Labour's footsteps right up to the election campaign, made Attlee realize that his appointment of Herbert Morrison as Foreign Secretary had been a mistake.[95] Attlee would have preferred another trade unionist in the post,[96] but no outstanding figure was available and Morrison was easily the senior member of the Cabinet. Attlee had no idea that Morrison was 'so ignorant'; and he had turned down every other position that Attlee had offered him. Attlee also thought that Morrison wanted the job badly.[97] Morrison himself had some doubts but overruled them, as he 'saw the appointment as a final step necessary to complete his qualifications for the leadership', and to keep Bevan out.[98] Iran's nationalization of the Anglo-Iranian Oil Company was not in itself objectionable to the Government; the dispute turned on the method and the question of compensation. When negotiations failed, Morrison wanted to use force.[99] Attlee refused. He was opposed in principle to the use of force by a big power against a small one (except in so far as needed to protect British lives), but he had other cogent reasons. He believed that quick and decisive action on the scale required was impracticable, that such action would alienate world opinion and might prove politically and militarily disastrous.[100] The US, for its own reasons, would not have assisted Britain.[101] In fact, the episode was astonishingly similar to the Suez crisis of 1956. There was one great difference: under Attlee, the question was submitted to the Security Council of the UN, and the British technicians withdrawn.[102] But the affair triggered a wave of nationalism throughout the Middle East and the election campaign had also to be conducted against the background of Egypt's decision to abrogate the Anglo-Egyptian Treaty over the Suez Canal Zone.[103]

Although the Conservatives were thus enabled to sound the patriotic drum, the election results would again disappoint them.[104] Labour was still on the defensive, in so far as the Party's election manifesto made no mention of socialism. But it also addressed itself in some detail to what it described as 'the four major tasks for the nation – peace, full employment and increased production, reduction of the cost of living and the building of a just society'.[105] These were respectable if unexciting aims. The campaign was perhaps most noteworthy for the introduction of television electioneering.[106] Attlee did not use the device; he stuck to the old formula, making fifty-four speeches on his tour (nine in a single day), and the final radio broadcast. Patrick O'Donovan of the *Observer* wrote a vivid impression of Attlee on the hustings in his own constituency: 'He stood quite still, smiling. The tiredness left his face and he looked affectionately at his loyal electors. He spoke for half an hour, slowly and carefully, never fumbling a sentence, his voice high and unstrained. He spoke of faraway issues like Persia and he poured a little gentle mockery over the Conservative manifesto. He held a paper in his left hand, and with his right played with a gold chain that shone across his waistcoat. He did not have that air of being more than lifelike that surrounds many British politicians, nor did he display that spurious cheerfulness that suggests that everything is fine, just fine. He looked like a great headmaster, controlled, efficient, and above all, good.'[107] In his broadcast, Attlee reminded the electorate that 'the Tories always want a bogy man. It was the late Mr Laski in 1945 and it is Mr Bevan today.'[108] That Attlee's calm approach was, from Labour's point of view, the correct one, would be confirmed by the Party's record poll.

The decisive factor in the election result was the voting behaviour of many former Liberal supporters. Their party could only manage to put up 109 candidates compared with 475 in 1950, and the Liberal percentage of the vote declined from 9.1 to 2.5, in actual votes from 2.6 million to 0.73 million. Attlee noted that the Liberals in most areas tended to give two or three votes to the Conservatives for every one they gave to Labour.[109] The total poll declined slightly from the record 84 per cent in 1950 to 82.5 per cent. The Conservatives took 13.71 million votes (48.0 per cent) and 321 seats. Labour had 13.94 million votes (48.8 per cent) for its 295 seats. Less than one in a hundred voters had actually swung to the Conservatives, but the fraction proved sufficient to bring Labour's forward march to a close. The tragic irony for Labour was that had it managed to remain in power for only a year or so longer, until the terms of trade had moved back in Britain's favour, it could probably have won the support of the former Liberal voters.

As it was, return to opposition proved a disaster for the Party, and turned Attlee's subsequent career into something of an anti-climax. Freed from the always irksome constraints of government, the intellectual and emotional Left enjoyed a field day. But if the publicists seemed never so happy as when in opposition, Attlee was doubly shackled by it. He had no further opportunity to use his executive talents and he was forced once more to preside over a bitterly squabbling party. The 'Left' provoked a counter-reaction from the 'Right'; and, as Labour's most authoritative spokesman on foreign affairs (after Morrison's rapid disengagement from that area),[110] Attlee's status also suffered because of the very large measure of bi-partisanship and moderation that he (apparently) shared with Eden. On international affairs, the Bevanite zeal for over-definition made Attlee's position particularly difficult. In addition, he became an even lonelier political figure than before: the deaths of Bevin (which meant that the unions no longer had a recognized champion in the Commons) and Addison in 1951, followed by that of Cripps in 1952, deprived him of his few cronies. He also felt 'a real sense of personal loss'[111] at the death of George VI in 1952.

Attlee would have been quite content to resign the leadership after the 1951 election, but there were three good reasons why he did not. The Party wanted him to stay on: he was re-elected leader by acclamation in October.[112] Secondly, he feared that his most obvious successor, Morrison, might cause an irrevocable split.[113] Morrison had conceived a deep, personal animosity towards Bevan[114] and, after his unsuccessful stint as Foreign Secretary, Attlee was concerned about Morrison's standing in the Party.[115] James Griffiths, a prominent middle-of-the-road figure, was among those who urged Attlee to remain; he did so because he believed that only Attlee could hold Labour together. Otherwise Griffiths and his colleagues would have been glad to support Morrison.[116] Finally, there was in 1951 and 1952 (when Labour made large gains in the local elections) a feeling that the Party might very soon be offered a favourable opportunity of returning to office. A leadership contest would scarcely have facilitated that prospect.

Attlee's supposed procrastination[117] in regard to the fierce disputes that were to rage within Labour ranks between 1951 and 1955 owed little to fatigue (though he was sixty-nine in January 1952), and nothing to weakness. As Prime Minister, he could choose his colleagues, as Leader of the Opposition he had to accept an NEC chosen by the Party. His conception of leadership differed accordingly. To govern effectively meant taking decisions with a minimum of talk; to lead his turbulent Party in opposition, that is, to try to keep it together, meant suspending judgment until opinions had had the chance to work themselves out. In his time he had seen many divisions and feuds come and go; the same could well happen to the Bevanite disputes.

However, though necessarily detached, he was neither a passive spectator nor entirely neutral. Believing, as he still did, that 'The thing which does more harm than anything else is the lack of unity among Socialists and the bitterness which is imported into these discussions,'[118] Attlee would have occasion to reprimand the protagonists of both Left and Right. Nevertheless he made a subtle distinction. Up to a point, left-wing deviations were almost normal; he and his colleagues had demonstrated that they could be handled – within a framework of agreement on ultimate goals. Public challenges to Labour unity from the Right were much rarer and more difficult. Attlee's motives, in attempting, at considerable pains, to keep Bevan in contention for the leadership between 1951 and 1954[119] were not merely personal, though it can certainly be said that he 'inclined to Bevan, ignored Gaitskell, and ... turned even more against Morrison'.[120] It was Bevan, 'the greatest natural orator in the Party',[121] who best articulated the traditional Labour faith which continued to inspire Attlee; and Bevan had given some indications that he could build a bridge between the Labour generations. Attlee also made a distinction between Bevan's personal associates and Bevan himself plus the mass of humble Bevan followers in the constituencies, members of the rank and file on whose idealism, devotion and intelligence, he had written in 1937, the Party's future depended.[122] But Bevan did not come up to Attlee's expectations and destroyed his own chances for the leadership. He wanted, Attlee wryly commented in 1955, 'to be two things simultaneously, a rebel and an official leader, and you can't be both'.[123]

Bevan's ambivalence became evident just after the 1951 election. He refused either to stand for membership of the Shadow Cabinet (which would have indicated that he was prepared to close the pre-election quarrel), or to challenge Morrison for the Deputy Leadership (which would have openly revived it). Richard Crossman, who was all for 'a constructive Socialist policy', noted that Bevan was an 'extraordinary mixture of withdrawnness and boldness', and that he could 'never be persuaded to have any consistent or coherent strategy ...' In January 1952, Crossman had the impression that Bevan was 'a somewhat reluctant Bevanite'.[124] The Bevanites never did produce 'a constructive Socialist policy'. Bevan's book *In Place Of Fear* (published in April 1952) was a general statement of principles and contained nothing with which Attlee would have disagreed.[125] At a Fabian dinner that same month, Crossman heard Bevan give 'the philosophical case against any form of Socialist blueprints or programmes'.[126] Attlee had much in common with Bevan as a theorist. It was the revisionism of the Right, culminating politically in 1960 with Gaitskell's attempted assault on Clause Four of the Party's Constitution, that would earn Attlee's intellectual disapproval.[127] Unfortunately, between 1952 and 1954 Bevan and his followers addressed themselves more often to the most intangible and therefore most unprofitable of political issues, defence and foreign policy. Even here, the differences with the Labour establishment were more apparent than real. After Attlee's retirement and Gaitskell's succession to the leadership, Gaitskell and Bevan patched them up and Bevan became Labour's Shadow Foreign Secretary. Before then, the dispute basically turned on the old question of Britain's relationship with the US. Ironically the new American administration's verbal aggressiveness gave the Churchill Government almost as much trouble, in private,[128] as it caused the Labour Party in public.

At some cost to himself, Attlee bent over backwards to give Bevan time to rehabilitate his claim for the succession. The task would have been easier had Churchill and his colleagues made the expected assault on the Welfare State and mixed economy. Instead, Attlee found that he had to defend Labour policies more from the criticism of Labour dissidents than from Conservative attacks. Attlee himself had no new ideas to contribute; he did not believe they were necessary. Publicly, the Bevanite revolt began in the spring of 1952 over defence, a topic on which the Bevanites could indulge their self-righteousness to the full, as Churchill had discovered that the Labour Government's figures had indeed been too high for the country's economic capacity. In the House the Labour Shadow Cabinet introduced a formal amendment on 2 March approving the Government's reduced defence programme though critical of the Government's capacity to carry it out. Some fifty-seven Labour MPs refused to support this amendment, despite a three-line whip signed by Attlee, Morrison and the Chief Whip. At the subsequent Party meeting, Attlee, under considerable pressure from outraged loyalists, moved a resolution bringing back standing orders and also deploring the dissidents' behaviour. But he did not speak very strongly for the reprimand and a compromise proposal limited to the restoration of standing orders was passed in its place.[129] The Bevanite tumult continued, reaching a climax in the autumn at the annual conference when the group's candidates all but swept the board in the constituency section elections for NEC membership.[130] Attlee had great difficulty trying to justify the Party's position on rearmament as being based on the concept of collective security. A critical resolution received 2.28 million votes to 3.64 million for the NEC.[131] Soon after the conference, which had been conducted in an exceedingly rancorous atmosphere, Attlee made a public statement to the effect that the existence of a party within a party, with separate leadership, separate meetings and supported by its own press, was intolerable.[132] Bevan, though not many of the Bevanites, seemed to agree. He told Crossman that to perpetuate the group would be to perpetuate schism; 'If you were to continue the group in these conditions and I were the leader', Bevan added, 'I would have you expelled.' With the Bevanites' institutional success at the conference, there was no longer any need for the group.[133] At a PLP meeting on 23 October Attlee demanded as a matter of confidence that unofficial groups be disbanded and personal attacks ended. The Churchill Government was doing badly and the only strength it had was Labour's divisions. He added that the previous year had been the unhappiest in his seventeen years of leadership.[134]

Attlee's tactics were initially effective. A hint of a reaction to the Bevanites had been felt at the 1952 annual conference when Morrison, after being voted off the NEC, had – in Michael Foot's words – 'recaptured the sympathy of the whole place with a valiant display of sportsmanship'.[135] Attlee's 'counter-attack' appeared to Crossman also to be 'extremely successful'. By the end of the year he was noting in his diary the 'quite extraordinary rapidity' of the change in mood in the PLP; 'everyone [was] rather shamefacedly aware that both sides are on the same side after all'.[136] Bevan did stand against Morrison for the Deputy Leadership (receiving a respectable 82 votes to Morrison's 194), but this contest 'was really no more than a gesture'.[137] Bevan's decision to stand for membership of the Shadow Cabinet, on the other hand, allowed Attlee to continue to regard him as a possible successor. The differences between the Labour and Conservative attitudes to economic policy, which became clearer in 1953, also contributed to Labour's relative harmony. Butler's Budget took advantage of the temporarily improved terms of trade to increase consumption among the better-off rather than to increase investment.[138]

Labour found that general agreement over domestic policy could still be obtained. During the NEC discussions on the subject, Attlee surprised everyone by 'strongly supporting' Bevan's proposal for land nationalization,[139] though it was rejected by the majority. The resulting document, *Challenge to Britain*, was approved almost unanimously, with only minor changes, by the 1953 annual conference (held from 28 September to 2 October). The nation was asked to 'face the facts' of economic life. Britain had failed to pay her way as a trading nation since the Great Depression and her best prospects lay in the export of goods requiring a high degree of technical skill and experience. The whole emphasis of production and export effort had to be changed, which would involve sacrifices not only of material benefits but of many cherished habits and traditions. A series of industrial and financial proposals was made, together with suggestions for changes in the education system and the abolition of all charges on the health service. The only specific industry selected for nationalization was that of chemicals, though steel and road haulage would be renationalized. Attlee concluded the debate, in which Bevan, Wilson and Barbara Castle had spoken for the NEC, by underlining that Labour had to get a majority in the country to put the programme through. People who wanted more would get nothing unless they were prepared to work with everyone else in the Party. It was no good having a tremendous freight on the train if the engine was not strong enough to pull it. Labour was a responsible Party, expecting to have charge of the Government in a very short time; priorities had to be considered.[140] Once again, Labour had a detailed, agreed domestic programme and even, with the re-appointment of Morrison to the NEC (as an *ex officio* member),[141] a façade of personal accord.

The same was not true in regard to international policy, but in 1953 affairs were relatively quiet; there was a large measure of agreement between the parties and each party had its dissidents. Attlee was a convinced middle-of-the-roader, and his even-handedness paid political dividends for a time. His hostility to what he regarded as traditional Russian imperialism in modern totalitarian form was undiminished. The Soviet Union was responsible for the East-West division of Europe and the Russians, he believed, respected only strength.[142] After the death of Stalin in March 1953, neither Attlee nor Eden shared Bevan and Churchill's somewhat romantic hope that top-level talks might produce substantial changes,[143] though Attlee did not object to Churchill's call for them in May. Attlee had not objected, either, to a 1952 NEC resolution favouring such talks, limited in the first instance to the exceedingly unlikely possibility (in his opinion) of free elections throughout Germany.[144] His scepticism towards the USSR received a certain justification in mid-1953 when the Russians ruthlessly suppressed a workers' uprising in East Berlin. Attlee's approach to international affairs also took into consideration the new, strident tone in US policy which was hardly conducive to diplomacy. In 1952 he had chided Churchill for trying to woo extremist American politicians.[145] In 1953 Attlee and Eden were also troubled by the advent of McCarthyism and the impact of Secretary of State Dulles's rigid approach.[146] Attlee used the greater freedom of opposition to criticize openly Dulles's attitude to the negotiations in Korea[147] which, fortunately, concluded in a truce.

The lengthy resolution on foreign policy which Attlee presented to the annual conference in October 1953 required no vote to secure acceptance. On behalf of the NEC, including the solid contingent of Bevanites, he defined Labour policy as support for the UN, NATO and the Commonwealth. The Party favoured a Four Power meeting; it did not favour any forceful liberation of Eastern Europe. There should be peaceful co-operation through the Council of Europe, the OEEC, the Economic Commission for Europe and the Brussels Treaty Organization. No obstacles should be put in the way of the European Coal and Steel Community. Germany should be re-unified on the basis of free, democratic elections, and there should be no German rearmament before further efforts had been made to secure the peaceful re-unification of that country. Finally, Labour supported the truce in Korea, recognition of China, and the admittance of China to the UN. The destiny of Formosa should be decided by the people there and, meantime, it should be neutralized.[148] Despite his own critical views, Crossman was impressed by Attlee's speech supporting the resolution: '. . . he sounded like a Prime Minister and made it sound like a policy . . .'[149]

The NEC's pronouncement on German unification, however, was clearly a compromise. Attlee, for one, did not believe it to be a practical proposition. Indeed, before leaving office he had indicated that Western Germany would have to make a contribution to Western defence. The Americans insisted on it and, in view of the Soviet rearmament of Eastern Germany, it would sooner or later become essential. The other Western countries could not undertake the defence of West Germany by themselves. The prospect, of course, was hardly one to gladden Attlee's heart and he was well aware of its potential effect on his Party. He had, therefore, in February 1951, stipulated that four conditions needed to be satisfied prior to any German rearmament: (1) the rearmament of the Atlantic Treaty countries had to precede that of Germany; (2) the building up of forces in the democratic States should precede the creation of German forces; (3) German units had to be integrated into the defence forces in such a way as to preclude the emergence again of a German military menace; (4) there had to be agreement with the German people themselves.[150] A year later, Attlee again warned that neither the British nor any other people were prepared indefinitely to go on paying for German defence while the Germans did nothing,[151] though he approved in April 1952 a further stipulation by the NEC that, in order to satisfy his fourth condition, fresh elections should be held in Western Germany prior to any commitment by the Adenauer Government to the European Defence Community.[152] But these niceties were overtaken soon after the 1953 conference by the news that the British and American Governments had decided, in any case, to rearm Western Germany.

Neither Attlee's 'conditions' nor the eventual announcement of the *fait accompli* could entirely quell Labour turmoil over the issue. To some extent, it cut across Left-Right divisions. For the Left it also proved an irresistible temptation to resurrect the old cause of a 'Socialist foreign policy' which, during 1954, was reinforced by anxieties about the H-bomb and the proposed SEATO. Inevitably, the 'war of Attlee's succession'[153] was resumed, and Bevan made the mistake of openly attacking Attlee. There was little that he could do to save Bevan from himself, but he again contrived to shield him from the right-wing counter-attacks which, in the spring of 1955, aimed at expelling Bevan from the Party. By then, Bevan had lost any opportunity he might have had of succeeding Attlee. Gaitskell, too, came perilously close to excluding himself from serious consideration. The clash between the contenders and their supporters did great harm to Labour's reputation as a potential government, with the result that the nearer the approach of the next election, the more necessary Attlee's continued leadership became. Whereas Churchill had practically to be forced out of high politics,[154] Attlee was virtually constrained to stay in.

He managed to keep his Party in contention for a return to office until the spring of 1954. In February the NEC declared that, as the Soviet Union showed no sign of willingness to permit the re-unification of Germany through free elections, Labour was prepared to support 'a West German contribution to European defence' subject to the Attlee condition. It added, in April, that the best way of precluding the emergence of a German military menace would be by the establishment of the EDC within the NATO framework.[155] Before the Party had had time to digest the implications of these pronouncements, Attlee achieved another resounding parliamentary success over the visibly declining Churchill. The explosion of the American H-bomb on 1 March had created widespread British concern which Attlee (and Churchill for that matter) fully shared. Attlee decided that this was the subject, above all others, on which Three Power talks were required; his hands shook with emotion as he told the PLP so.[156] He then addressed the Commons in deliberately non-partisan terms that aroused the admiration of friend and foe alike, while Churchill bungled the occasion.[157] The Budget shortly afterwards did little to boost Conservative popularity and some by-elections indicated the beginning of a swing to Labour. These were the circumstances in which Attlee was publicly contradicted by Bevan on the floor of the House in a fashion which Bevan's admirer Foot admits could hardly have been sharper or ruder.[158] The issue was the proposed SEATO arrangement to which Attlee had offered a cautious qualified support. 'Just when we were beginning to win the match,' Attlee ruefully commented, 'our inside left has scored against his own side.'[159]

Further Labour conflict followed. After Bevan's resignation from the Shadow Cabinet, the NEC ruled on 18 May that majority decisions were binding unless the NEC decided otherwise. A week later the NEC was obliged to exempt the issue of German rearmament as regards the expression of individual opinion.[160] By the time of the 1954 annual conference in late September, the German rearmament issue had been complicated by French rejection of the EDC. It fell to Attlee to introduce a tortuous NEC resolution which stated that the NEC would consult with other European Socialist Parties as to how the German Federal Republic could best contribute to collective security. Attlee, declaring that he was not in the least likely to underrate the danger of a resurgent, militarist, nationalist Germany, added that the matter was one on which the delegates should not be swayed by emotion. He believed that his conditions for German rearmament had been substantially fulfilled.

However, tumult reigned, and the NEC resolution was approved by only 3,270,000 votes to 3,022,000, despite Morrison's warning that if the Party was in a state of confusion on the matter it would hear about it at the next election. A motion opposing SEATO as then constituted was rejected by the hardly more convincing figure of 3.66 million to 2.57.[161] There can be no doubt that as a result of this conference, Labour's credibility on foreign policy was undermined. Although the NEC decided after the conference that there should be no further deviation from Party policy on Germany,[162] Attlee and the PLP Executive had to recommend in November, when the question of German rearmament was debated in the Commons, that Labour's best course was to abstain. By then the Western Powers had agreed on German sovereignty and had invited West Germany to join NATO. Emotions on the subject soon drained away, but the electoral damage had been done. A by-election on 18 November in a marginal seat recorded a small swing to the Conservatives.[163]

Attlee vainly attempted to restore some measure of vigour and coherence to Labour's foreign policy. In the summer of 1954 he had visited China as head of a Labour Party delegation which had included Bevan. Attlee did not conceal his dislike for the Chinese regime which, he said, kept the people there behind a curtain of ignorance thicker and more dangerous than the Iron Curtain.[164] On the other hand he also told the press that the sooner Chiang Kai-shek and his troops were eliminated the better. In January 1955 Attlee stepped up his criticism of official American opinion about the Far East, then waxing hot over Formosa, by repeating what he had said about Chiang Kai-shek and suggesting that Formosa should be excluded from America's 'island defence ring'. The people in Formosa should be allowed to decide by plebiscite whether or not they wanted to join Communist China.[165] There was little new in his attitude, which reflected the view he had personally expressed to Truman that Western policy should aim at detaching China from Russia, but it pleased the Labour left.[166] Bevan's final public altercation with Attlee succeeded merely in splitting the Bevanites and in removing the Labour whip from Bevan; it was over the purely hypothetical question whether the H-bomb, production of which had been decided on by the Government and not opposed by Attlee, might be used to repel an attack by conventional methods. By March 1955 Attlee had to recognize that Bevan had destroyed his chances for the succession. It had taken all of Attlee's experience and finesse at Labour committee meetings to prevent Bevan being expelled altogether from the Party.[167]

To what extent these issues of foreign policy and defence affected Labour's support in the election is debatable. The decline in the Labour vote was greatest in safe Labour seats whether contested by Bevanites or not.[168] But while Labour wrangled, the Conservatives proceeded to score on the issue that certainly counted, domestic policy. Butler's income tax 'give-away' Budget of April 1955 had the merit, from the Labour point of view, of allowing Gaitskell to develop his reputation as a debater[169] (and so eventually to settle the leadership dispute), but no other. Gaitskell's prophecy that the Chancellor would have to eat his words in the autumn, though correct, could not attract votes. The Budget, as one of Eden's biographers has commented, was the first of many electioneering Budgets of the post-war era, yet because it was the first it may not have been identified as such by the electorate.[170] The country had also benefited from the easing of import prices after the Korean War and the Conservatives did not hesitate to claim that the ending of rationing, austerity and crisis was due to their economic and fiscal policies. To clinch matters for the Conservatives, Austrian neutrality was agreed on 15 May, and Soviet assent to a Four Power Meeting was received on polling day itself. Prosperity, peace and relaxation seemed just around the corner – a make-believe situation that might have reminded Attlee, in certain respects, of what he had had to face when he came in as Labour's leader.

In 1955 neither party had anything particularly new to offer. This did no electoral harm to the Conservatives. Labour's manifesto, *Forward With Labour*, was a rewritten version of *Challenge to Britain*,[171] with the emphasis on exports, investment and welfare as opposed to consumerism and commercialism. Labour could also announce that Lady Megan Lloyd George had joined its ranks. Otherwise the Conservatives had everything going for them – an opposition with a well-publicized recent history of division, a new Leader, the Budget, 'peace' and a further redistribution of seats, raising the total at stake to 630. The combination of full employment and internal strife had also weakened Labour's local organizations.[172] Attlee had little television appeal, though that medium was sparingly used, and he made only one radio broadcast.[173] On the hustings in his usual fashion, he gave forty-one addresses between 12 and 14 May.

The wonder was that Labour lost only 25 seats, obtaining 277 to the Conservatives' 344, with 6 going to the Liberals and 3 to Others. The Conservatives received 13.28 million votes (49.7 per cent), Labour 12.4 million (46.4 per cent) and the Liberals 0.72 million (2.7 per cent). Compared with 1951, the Conservative vote declined by 0.5 million and Labour's by 1.5 million, while the total poll fell from 82.5 per cent in 1951 to 76.8 per cent. Most significantly, the regional and sociological trends that had appeared in 1951 repeated themselves. Politically the country was split between South and North, between rural areas and industrial cities. The forward march of Labour gave way to the forward march of the suburbs. For the first time since 1935 Labour did not increase its vote, while the Conservatives regained the largest share. For Attlee, the political wheel had turned full circle. His vision of a nation-wide Labour consensus, cutting across geographical and class divisions, was shattered.

The final irony was that the result was judged 'a Labour failure rather than a Conservative success'.[174] Attlee was the least to blame. It had been a close-run thing and he had come nearer than any other Labour leader could have done to bringing it off. Under him, Labour had achieved the maximum it could, or would, do in changing the political face of Britain.

XVII

Times and Seasons

Attlee abruptly resigned from the leadership of the Labour Party in December 1955. He was nearly seventy-three and had held the post for twenty years; no leader of any major party in recent history has lasted as long. The question of his successor had been resolved and he hardly needed to account for his action. Pressed on the point by a provincial journalist, he merely remarked: 'Well, one has to watch times and seasons, you know.'[1]

Churchill had also retired earlier that year, though not from the Commons, at the age of eighty. His and Attlee's joint passing from the centre stage marked the ending of a political epoch, one in which politics had been strongly influenced by moral visions of one kind or another. They were the last of those brought up in Queen Victoria's reign to hold the post of Prime Minister. Their respective creeds had stemmed from the same broad and confident psychological roots. They belonged, in Attlee's words, 'to a generation which [had] believed that the world was more or less settled, that it had become to a greater or less extent civilized'.[2] Both Tories in their youth, neither had ever doubted the value of the English contribution to civilization and each, in his own way, had sought to extend it.

By the mid-twentieth century, the cultural soil in which they had been nurtured was exhausted; during their final years in office the two Victorians were confronted with the sombre reality of Britain's decline in an alien world. That world had changed faster than had Britain. International economic competition had become the rule. The relative British decline that had begun at about the time of Attlee's birth became absolute. Churchill's and Attlee's political philosophies were inevitably questioned. Churchill's liberal imperialism was virtually barren before he became Premier; but before Attlee left office, his brand of socialism also appeared to have lost much of its former fertility. The grinding poverty which had stimulated the growth of evangelical socialism had disappeared almost as completely as Churchill's lost empire. Technological and other developments had weakened socialism's moral and aesthetic vitality.

Opening the William Morris Gallery in Walthamstow (his new constituency) in 1950, Attlee wryly observed that 'a machine-made world in which men were becoming more and more the slaves of their own inventions, with, in some places, a purely materialistic conception of Socialism'[3] would have made Morris uneasy. Two years later Attlee admitted to his own unease: much of the thinking that had been done in the Socialist Movement, he wrote, had been done a good many years ago, and conditions had changed.[4] He did not know the kind of thing that young people wanted, he added in 1953, and it was no good giving the young what the old wanted.[5] With the best will in the world, he concluded in 1955, 'it is almost impossible for a man born in one age to understand fully the mental background of those from another ... There is a difference in outlook between people who grew to maturity in what appeared to be the stable world before 1914 and those reared in the uncertainties and complexities of the last 40 years.'[6]

In terms of the life of a political party, forty years or so is a relatively short period, but they constituted most of Attlee's active years. In the course of them he had seen his Party come from the street corners to full possession of Downing Street; and accession to power meant that Labour lost its political virginity. That he became increasingly conscious of the emotional gap between himself and the latest recruits to Labour's cause is easy to understand. Before he resigned, a quite new breed of Labour MPs had arrived at Westminster, whose experience sometimes consisted solely of a university education, and who considered politics ambitiously from the start as a career. Attlee dated from the pre-1914 days when the movement had been little more than 'a voice crying in the wilderness',[7] sustained mainly by the 'wonderful spirit of comradeship'. More precisely, as a politician he regarded himself as 'a survivor of the generation which lost so many of its members in the Great War'.[8] He was the first of those who had seen continuously active service between 1914 and 1918 to attain a high position in politics. But he was an old survivor, and even in 1937 had thought that 'a new generation was about to take its part in shaping the future, one that had been subject to influences very different from his own'.[9] Because of the Second World War and the Labour victories, that did not happen: Attlee's generation remained at the helm, Attlee himself longer than anyone.

Although he was inevitably nostalgic towards the end of his career for the simpler days of the past, Attlee had personally stood up remarkably well to 'the uncertainties and complexities' of his time in politics. The mercurial Aneurin Bevan was impressed by how 'in defeat and victory, he was unperturbed'.[10] In the concluding sentence of his otherwise laconic autobiography (published in 1954), Attlee explained that he had been 'a very happy and fortunate man in having lived so long in the greatest country in the world, in having a happy family life and in having been given the opportunity of serving in a state of life to which [he] had never expected to be called'.[11] Typically, he said hardly a word about his own accomplishments.

The distinguished American historian, Crane Brinton, in a review of Attlee's book, put his finger on the key question about Attlee's career: 'Was he the real, the natural leader of his party, or did he rise because of incurable rivalries among abler men . . . were Bevin, Morrison, Cripps, perhaps even Laski, the great men, Attlee merely PM by default?'[12] The answer, it is hoped, is already clear in outline. Despite the element of luck which had contributed to his promotion, and rivalries that helped keep him in the leadership, Attlee indeed turned out to be Labour's 'natural' leader. The accidental was providential. He was the vital catalyst who held the Party together in opposition, who made it function effectively in office, and whose pragmatic yet unswerving devotion to Labour's ideals stood the test of time and seasons. It is true that he had nothing like the authority commonly attributed to the head of a political party. But it was the essence of his own and Labour's philosophy that he should not have it. He rose with the Labour Party and his progress to the premiership can be seen as the culmination of half a century of political change. In terms of a single lifespan, this was a slow change but it aptly reflected the relaxed pace of British political life. Not until 1945 did Labour manage to attain a sufficient degree of either internal unity or external credibility to win the confidence of the electorate. That it came about then was due in large part to Attlee's ability to unite the Party and take it into the wartime Coalition and bring it out again in a similar fashion. His success owed much to his personal qualities and the soundness of his judgments on most of the issues of the day.

As an individual, his most impressive feature was his moral probity: it was this which produced in others the feeling of respect for him as for a headmaster. Otherwise he was the Prime Minister who came in from suburbia, an outstanding one, but not 'a great man'. He owed his initial rise to the leadership partly to the fact that his Party had become wary of any marked individualism in its leader. No one ever accused Clement Attlee of vanity. His extraordinary diffidence made him the most profoundly private figure who has ever occupied that most public of offices. His modesty was proverbial. At the great turning-point in his career, in May 1940, he carefully and needlessly explained to Churchill that he was joining the Cabinet not in a personal capacity but solely because he was leader of the Labour Party. The only ostentatious act of his lengthy time in politics was his acceptance of an earldom at the end of it; and the first use he made of his ennoblement was to plead the cause of the 'grossly overworked and underpaid' MPs.[13] He had very few, if any, of the aptitudes usually considered necessary for a public or political career. He was initially propelled into an active social role, almost against his will, by his revulsion at the situation he found in the London slums before the First World War. In many respects he became a socialist *malgré lui*, because of his conviction that neither conservatism nor liberalism could do anything significant about improving conditions in places like Stepney.

As a politician perhaps his most immediate appeal was to those who took the view that politics was a necessary evil: one could be certain that his actions would not gratify any personal ego. To him, politics was just a job, a prosaic business of compromises, qualified judgments and questions of priorities which were impossible to glorify in personal terms. In an age of committees, nothing was settled by speeches, however stirring; power in the Labour Party and in the country was too diffuse, a situation which was very much to his liking, except in emergencies. The exercise of political authority, of course, meant taking decisions that would affect people's lives, but so did the exercise of authority in other professions. At the same time, he was much too aware of the need for legitimate authority to succumb to the lure of utopianism. Government to Attlee was the art of what was possible for reform and improvement.

As a leader, he derived his strength from the representativeness of his opinions, not from their originality, or from his non-existent charisma. He gained several other advantages from his 'deficiencies'. Though incapable of creating political excitement, he could create political atmosphere of a sort – reasonableness and calm. He was undoubtedly better at getting people to change their minds, or at least suspend judgment, than at preaching to the converted; and he came closer to voicing the aspirations of a broad section of the British people than any other Labour leader. Unlike many other middle-class Labourites, he was not an intellectual. His respectable ordinariness arguably did more to reconcile the middle class to Labour[14] than the efforts of more dramatic figures who tended to frighten or repel.

Attlee was not in revolt against his background. His upbringing gave him an easily recognizable English aesthetic sensibility, essentially historical, literary and visual in kind.[15] When he discovered that the most hideous places in the country produced the most wealth, consumed disproportionately by a small minority, this sensibility received a terrific jolt; but that was all. He did not subsequently, for example, make the middle-class rebel's mistake of idealizing the working classes, though his attachment to the cause of improving the conditions in which they lived became the driving force of his life. On this point Attlee was unshakeable.

For himself he demanded little from life.[16] He had great courage but was overawed by, even frightened of, the grandiose. On the other hand he had a high regard for custom, tradition and ceremony;[17] if reasonable and inoffensive, they should be preserved. This conservative temperament proved a great asset to him as a leader and to his Party. It accounted for his astonishing self-control, his detachment in personal relations and his ability to keep apart from current party passions. It freed him from undue speculation and allowed him to concentrate upon practical affairs. It was an invaluable antidote to the feverish enthusiasms and unbalanced judgments sometimes to be found in his colleagues.

Next to moral probity, loyalty was the strongest trait in his character: he could be relied upon absolutely. His unassuming and tolerant nature was widely recognized to be genuine and not a façade. In fact he depended for his influence on the personal respect which he enjoyed and, among many of those who knew him, on the love and devotion which he inspired. Apart from his safe parliamentary seat, he did not possess a political base in the Party. He was committed to no single group or point of view. Incapable of provoking personal animosity, extremely difficult to misrepresent, he offered few (if any) verbal hostages to fortune; he was thus an almost impossible target for organized conspiracy. And just as his socialist opinions disarmed criticism from the Left, so did his patriotism and respectability procure him immunity from the Right. He was perhaps the most redoubtable Labour opponent the Conservatives ever had to face. No one seemed further from the irresponsible rebel and yet he was unsurpassed in his profound and sustained determination to bring about social reform. After 1945 it was the Conservatives, or some of them, who changed, not Attlee: in his unassertive way, he came to represent an historical force that they had no alternative but to accept.

His odd combination of socialist views and conservative temperament made it easy for him to love the Labour Party, 'warts and all'. He could resist the temptation to become impatient with its cumbersome procedures, awkward federal structure and innate tendency to criticize the leadership. Allowances had to be made for the way in which the Party had grown, and criticism was natural to the Left. He was proud that Labour was rooted in the British historical experience whose major theme, he believed, had been the struggle for liberty. Labour, he considered, belonged to that tradition. It sought 'to free the human spirit', though its immediate objectives were dictated by modern conditions.[18] His temperament was peculiarly well fitted to cope with Labour's basic weakness, the difficulty in maintaining unity, in action and aim. At the very outset of his career, at the local level, he had demonstrated how to deal with the problem: 'cut the cackle and get on with the job'. His reaction then had been instinctive; but he repeated the method with equal success when he became Prime Minister. Opposition called for different tactics, but here again he was able to show the way by precept and example.

As Labour changed into one of the two main political groupings in a primarily two-party system, the penalty for dissension became heavier. Acceptance of majority decisions within the Party was the indispensable preliminary to winning majority support outside it; and a party which seriously and constitutionally aimed at making a new society had a special obligation to present its positions calmly and coherently. These conditions suited Attlee's style of leadership perfectly. He made it clear that he 'was not prepared to arrogate to [himself] a superiority to the rest of the movement'. He was ready to submit to its will, even if he disagreed. He would do all he could to get his views accepted but, unless acquiescence in the views of the majority conflicted with his conscience, he would fall into line, for he had great faith in the wisdom of the rank and file.[19] Attlee personified this democratic socialist approach* to the problem of unity to an exceptional degree.

He was none the less a staunch partisan of Labour's distinctive identity. He considered that democratic socialism was more than a middle way between capitalism and communism: it was a political philosophy with its own principles. These principles were fully compatible with the institutional framework of the British liberal state, and no kind of socialism other than the democratic was worth having. Labour was the only Party capable of implementing socialism in British society. Yet though himself committed to Clause Four of the constitution, he was well aware that historically the mainsprings of the Party had been the trade unions and the nonconformist conscience rather than socialist theory. If pushed, he might even have agreed that the adoption of a socialist programme in 1918 had not been a cause so much as an effect of the break with the Liberals, accepted by the union partly in return for effective control of the Party. Certainly he knew that without the great growth in trade union membership Labour could not have flourished as it did and, furthermore, that only the strength of the unions could keep the Party together. A bridge between the unions and the politicians, therefore, had to be made and maintained. It was the alliance between the Party's political and industrial wings, symbolized or consecrated by the relationship between him and Bevin, that made possible the breakthrough in 1940. But Attlee remained adamant that the Labour Party was not 'a mere political expression of Trade Unionism . . . it was a national party with a Socialist objective.' The politicians had to grasp that 'Socialism was not just State Capitalism', and the unions had to understand that, in a socialist system, unionism would be changing from an antagonistic to a co-operative

*In the Party as a whole freedom of debate was preserved, while in the parliamentary wing there was freedom of conscience (to abstain from, though not on major issues to vote against, Labour).

position in industry.[20] He was quite clear that, in case of conflict, the will of the State had to prevail. A Labour Government stood for control of the economy by the people, and not by the unions or any other interest group.*

That he also fully subscribed to the residual British suspicion of State power was not a paradox. Even under capitalism the use of that power required the explicit consent of the majority and had to be exercised with due regard to individual liberties. Socialism, he felt, made far greater, though not impossible, demands on the individual. Labour's final triumph would not and could not be achieved by legislation alone; it also needed 'the demonstration by Socialists in their own lives that they have a high ideal and live up to it'.[21] Ultimately, socialism had 'to be built in the minds and hearts of men and women for it is not just an economic theory but a way of life'.[22] There could be no true socialism without a sufficient number of socialists. It followed that he was a gradualist: 'Revolutionary changes in a democratic society,' he wrote, 'though brought about by the active impulsion of one political party, must, if they are to have any chance of permanence, be generally acceptable and in effect express a change of view in the mental make-up of society.'[23] Violence along class lines would be worse than useless.

Socialism to Attlee was a moral creed, not a doctrine: it gave a sense of purpose, not a blueprint for action. It was not an end in itself but a continuing process with the aim of making the fullest possible life available to everyone. It meant fellowship of the sort he had experienced at the beginning of his political life. Such fellowship could not make people perfect, merely better. It was only possible in an orderly country and an orderly world. Order implied authority, but a limited, prosaic, responsible authority whose purpose was primarily to make fellowship possible. Authority could not create fellowship. The actual details of socialism would emerge – and change – over the course of time by discussion, trial and error, and agreement. Once people got the ethics right the practical consequences would look after themselves.

Attlee's insistence on the moral values of Socialism also had the tremendous practical advantage of being the sole way by which Labour could be kept together: far from being ambiguous, these values provided an emotional dynamic to policy-making and winning power. He abhorred perfectionism. His socialism was roughly a secular equivalent of Anglican Christianity – short on dogma, long on English tradition. Rampant capitalism, in his view, had betrayed that tradition; socialism sought to return to it. The challenge of the twentieth century, for

*It may be that after 1951 a conflict between the unions and a Labour Government bent on restructuring the economy was inevitable, and that Attlee did not realize this. But in 1951 he still possessed the support of a majority of the trade union leaders.

practical as well as ethical reasons, was to convert the historic English sense of patriotic fellowship into social fellowship. Nothing else could arrest British decline. Industrial capitalism was divisive in its social influence, whereas socialism unified. Industry existed for man, not man for industry.

But his gradualism had its limits. It was a proper function of the State to counterbalance the individual acquisition of wealth; a Labour Government had a duty to accelerate social and economic change by democratic methods. Attlee had a great desire to begin the socialist process, and was certain that an interventionist party was far more suited to redressing social and economic problems than a non-interventionist one. He believed in careful planning and did not fear to use democratically sanctioned authority. Political, religious and personal liberty had to be supplemented by economic liberty which – given technological and other developments – could no longer be assured by the extension of private property, only by collective control. Large-scale, private ownership of capital had to be transferred to the community; how this was to be done was a matter of convenience, not of principle. The essential point was governmental responsibility for the overall co-ordination of the economy and the broad development of society.

He had no thought that private property should be completely abolished; people in a socialist society would still own houses and small businesses. It was the grotesque differences in wealth and income that were a hindrance to individual freedom, not the minor ones. He showed very little interest in economic explanations of the existing differences between rich and poor. Theoretical discussions about the sources of wealth, the different kinds of income and their relative merits left him cold. To Attlee, great material inequalities between individuals were simply wrong and socially undesirable. No doubt individuals differed greatly in their capacities and were naturally competitive. But if it was silly not to accept that material self-interest was one of the primary human motivations, it was equally short-sighted for society to favour individual greed. The trouble with economic competition for its own sake was that it tended to be demoralizing and anti-social. The aim of a Socialist government was to reduce and control those effects, and encourage the sense of public spirit. Service to the community was a better ideal than the profit motive and had to be stimulated by every possible means. He did not object to competition or leadership so long as they were conducted in a spirit of fellowship, which was more important than absolute equality. Altogether, his was an uncomplicated set of socialist values, coupled with an acute sense of what was realistic and possible.

Labour's primary task, in Attlee's view, was to persuade a majority of the population of the soundness and relevance of these values. Once a national consensus of more or less socialist opinion – cutting across class or even party lines – had been established, Labour (whether in or out of office) would become the effective party of government. By 1944 it seemed that this goal had been attained. He could explain to Harold Laski that much of what they had cried for in the wilderness a generation ago had become part of the assumptions of the ordinary man and woman. There was another reason for his confidence in 1944. During the First World War there had also been some indications of an urge for social reform, but they had petered out. During the Second, Attlee had made it his business to ensure that this should not happen again. He had deliberately paved the institutional way for social reconstruction. Thus although somewhat surprised at the result of the 1945 election, Attlee was nevertheless fully prepared mentally for the task ahead. Labour could at last move on from indirect pressure to direct action, and Attlee himself embodied the strength and solidity of his Party's triumph. The calm, unruffled manner with which he then tackled the colossal difficulties of rebuilding the war-torn economy, his matter-of-fact introduction of the Welfare State, his caustic puncturing of Churchillian bombast and left-wing nitpicking, all gave the electorate the reassurance it sought. Under Attlee, Labour found the formula for political success. Despite the inevitable post-war austerity, there has never been any comparable period of reform since 1906 or even 1832. Attlee's revolution may, as he much preferred, have been quiet; it was a revolution all the same. When he relinquished the premiership he left behind him almost a festival of a Britain. The country was constitutionally governed and reasonably united. It was also healthier, more secure and prosperous, with full employment and more equality of opportunity than ever before. Above all, it was more optimistic about its future than for several decades.

As he had foreseen, the conduct of a 'Labour' foreign policy proved a different matter. British economic weakness precluded much in the way of new initiatives. Attlee's contribution, especially in the early post-war years, was primarily his exercise of an almost stoical patience. Confronted by Soviet intransigence, American vacillation and unrealistic criticism from his own backbenchers, he did not yield to panic. He had no desire to embark on an anti-Russian crusade or to romanticize the so-called special Anglo-American relationship. He had no illusions about the possibility of Britain setting herself up as the head of a Third Force or about the Commonwealth's potential as a power bloc. Indeed, he retained all his old scepticism about power politics in general, and not merely because of Britain's manifest powerlessness. Lasting peace, he believed as strongly as ever, could only be secured by some kind of world authority. Two new factors had come out of the Second World War, the UN and the atomic bomb: yet the failure of the one and the further development of the other did not affect his basic premise.

At the beginning of his premiership he thought that there was just a chance that the UN, appearances notwithstanding, might be made to work; he was eager to give it that chance. He was willing, as well, to accept the international results of the war as sketchily defined in the Yalta and Potsdam Agreements, though he hoped for something better. Loathing the Soviet system, he was nevertheless sympathetic to Russian fears of a revived Germany and to Russian reparation claims. Anxious for American involvement in Europe and elsewhere, he knew that a price for US aid would have to be paid. His mistrust of the Soviets and his misgivings about certain aspects of American policy-making were amply confirmed, in the case of the former over Germany and the latter over Palestine, the atomic bomb and China. In the end, failing world-wide collective security, he had to be content with a mixture of partial collective security in NATO, and possible British diplomatic influence in the British bomb. But he regarded both as stop-gap solutions to the fundamental problem of international relations – anarchy.

In retrospect, it is difficult to see that Attlee had many choices in international policy. Though freer than most British politicians, including some of his colleagues, from traditional myths about foreign and imperial policy, he was not a Little Englander. He considered that Britain had an important, independent role to play on the international stage, preferably in a UN setting and not submerged either in an amorphous West European political grouping or as the junior partner in an Anglo-American relationship. He believed that British influence, if not power, still mattered in the world. He took a particular interest and pride in the Commonwealth as an example of how very different peoples could meet together to discuss subjects of mutual concern in an amicable and co-operative spirit. His handling of the Indian question alone is sufficient to put him in the first rank as a statesman, and gives a good indication of what he might have achieved in other areas had he had the power and time.

Attlee, however, found the USSR intractable. The former Czarist ambitions in regard to surrounding satellite States, he considered, had been complemented by a new kind of imperialism based on Soviet hostility towards all those who did not share the communist creed.[24] The only prospect he could see was that, in time, by a combination of patience and strength on the part of the Western democracies, the Soviet regime would be modified and tension eased. Germany stuck in his throat. He was in no immediate hurry after the war to do much more than to keep Germans from starving and those in the Western zones from being thrown in the arms of Stalin. But economic necessities soon prevailed, and plans for the internationalization or nationalization of the Ruhr industries had to be abandoned on account of American opposition. He did what he could to modify what he thought to be awkwardness or ignorance in American policies.

On Palestine, the Attlee-Bevin approach was much criticized but, arguably, these criticisms have lost much of their force in the light of history. The same may be said about Attlee's warning of a possible breakdown in collective security if the US became too enmeshed militarily in the Far East. The soundness of his attitude to China is beyond dispute. He was clear about the need to resist aggression in South Korea though, until that conflict erupted, he fully endorsed the effort to stabilize British defence expenditures. Of all his decisions, the implications of the one to build atomic weapons probably caused him the most anguish, yet it followed logically from his reservations about American policies.

Another decision not previously mentioned, for which Attlee took particular credit, was his strong personal support for the Ireland Act of 1949. The independence of the Irish Republic was formally recognized, but the Act also stipulated that Northern Ireland was to remain part of the UK unless the Belfast Parliament decided otherwise. Despite the serious difficulties of recent years, it is worth noting that recent Irish governments have accepted Attlee's basic contention that unification without the consent of Northern Ireland would not be worth having.

Attlee devoted much of his energy during his last years to the cause of world government. As usual, any suggestion of utopianism was rigorously excluded from his arguments. He was concerned only with that surrender of sovereignty necessary for international security; national identities were to be safeguarded in all other respects. He did not think that tyranny and freedom could be reconciled, though differences could no longer be resolved by conquest. Western democracies were in a better position to understand the reality of co-existence than the totalitarian powers, but these too would have to accept it. His hope was, if war could be avoided, that 'gradually, intercourse will soften asperities'. The nuclear deterrent only perpetuated 'a state of anarchy tempered by fear'. National defences had become obsolete. He did not argue that the advent of a world authority would herald the dawn of a new age; he simply said it was necessary for the survival of civilization. Perhaps the best way might be the establishment of an international police force, together with disarmament.[25] He had said it all, of course, many times, and in his old age he had nothing of any substance to add. But he did not mind repeating himself: the main task for him remained that of creating the right atmosphere for change. Just as Labour had had to be weaned away from its class basis, so the world had to be persuaded to give up the more lethal aspects of its nationalisms.

Attlee's was a quiet, still voice in an age of unreason; perhaps he expected too much. The kind of consensus he sought, at home and abroad, proved elusive. It was meant to be dynamic; it turned out to be somewhat sterile. The England that Attlee saw coming into being in his final years was one with which he was increasingly out of sympathy. He did not condemn it out of hand, but neither did he altogether understand it. On the international scene the lessons he had learned after the slaughter and madness of the First World War still seemed relevant, if anything more relevant. The sole conceivable remedy for anarchy was government. Deterrents, ever more awesome and uncontrollable, might bring a breathing space; they would not suffice to ensure peace in the end. The cause of world government could obviously be supported by non-socialists, though for Attlee such government was an integral part of his socialist creed. In this sense, his career was all of a piece.

Attlee's political and personal legacies are equally impressive. He very nearly achieved a consensus in the nation, as well as in the Labour Party. And he remains an example of selfless, calm and rational devotion to the betterment of the human condition which deserves to stand the test of time and season.

Notes

Introduction

1 Lord Salter, *Memoirs of a Public Servant*, 1961, p. 286.
2 M. Foot, *Aneurin Bevan: A Biography, Vol II: 1945–1960*, 1973, pp. 26 and 30.
3 R. J. Cruikshank in the *News Chronicle*, 28 March 1953.
4 Foot, op. cit., pp. 29–30.
5 F. Williams, *The Triple Challenge*, 1948, p. 60.
6 Foot, op. cit., p. 25.
7 C. R. Attlee to Harold Laski, 1 May 1944 in K. Martin, *Harold Laski: A Biographical Memoir*, 1953, pp. 152–3.
8 F. Williams in the *News Chronicle*, 5 February 1953.
9 Arthur Moyle, 'The Real Attlee – By His PPS' in the *Star*, 8 December 1955.

I Basically A Victorian

1 3 January 1883.
2 The allusions to Attlee's memories of the period covered in this chapter (and others) are taken from the unpublished version of his 'Draft Autobiography' in the Attlee Papers, Churchill College, Cambridge, unless otherwise noted.
3 In 1966, Harold Wilson invited the retired Attlee to spend a weekend at Chequers and asked him the following question: '"Clem, yourself excluded, and politics apart, who of all the Prime Ministers Britain has had since you became old enough to take an interest do you consider the best, as Prime Minister?" "Salisbury!" he replied.' (Harold Wilson, *A Prime Minister on Prime Ministers*, 1977, p. 128.)
4 T. S. Attlee, MA, ARIBA, *Man and His Buildings*, 1920, p. 144.
5 Ibid., p. 146.
6 *News Chronicle*, 10 October 1953.
7 C. R. Attlee, *The Labour Party in Perspective*, 1937, p. 140.
8 Quoted in W. Golant, 'The Political Development of C. R. Attlee to 1935',

unpublished B. Litt. thesis, Oxford, 1967, MS. d1263, p. 17. (Hereafter referred to as Thesis.)

9 Of the two other sisters, one married and the other died at the age of forty-two.
10 See *The Times*, 7 and 13 September 1958.
11 The eight Attlee children were: Robert (1871–1953), Bernard (1873–1943), Mary (1875–1956), Dorothy (1877–1920), Margaret (1879–1919), Tom (1880–1960), Clement (1883–1967), Laurence (1884–1969).
12 C. R. Attlee, op. cit., pp. 27–30.
13 Evidently the Attlees had a lively sense of humour, but that it could be tinged with snobbishness is apparent from another of Attlee's childhood recollections. While walking at the seaside someone shouted, 'Look at those kids walking on the rocks!' His brother Bernard instantly commented, 'Essence of vulgarity,' which was considered a very fine retort. Bernard trod a well-worn path, becoming a Tory as well as a parson.
14 BBC television broadcast, 'Facing the Future', 24 May 1977. Comment by Lord Shinwell.
15 David Low, *Autobiography*, 1956, p. 356.
16 J. Margach, *The Abuse of Power*, 1978, p. 91.
17 Wilson, op. cit., p. 296.
18 E. C. Mack, *Public Schools and British Opinion Since 1860*, 1941, p. 117.
19 D. Kelly, *The Ruling Few*, 1952, p. 51.
20 V. Ogilvie, *The English Public School*, 1957, p. 189.
21 Mack, op. cit., p. 124.
22 A. Sampson, *Anatomy of Britain*, 1962, p. 180.
23 Quoted in Kelly, op. cit., p. 9.
24 The boys were severely caned: 'Every one of us received twelve strokes,' recalled another victim, who provides an interesting insight into the psychology of the school; 'no suggestion was made that our treatment had been unfair – rather, we applauded our Headmaster as somebody who was a strong man and was ready and able to deal with an emergency of that kind.' (John Postlethwaite, *I Look Back*, 1947, p. 14.)
25 Ibid., p. 12.
26 Attlee to Gerald Strawson, Attlee Papers, Box 16, University College, Oxford.
27 Quoted in Golant, op. cit., p. 10.
28 As in the case of his preparatory school, Haileybury provides a striking example of Attlee's singular memory for names. Among his papers are to be found long lists of boys who had been with him in Lawrence House, Haileybury in 1896 and 1901. These lists were apparently compiled in 1940 and include references to the careers and distinctions won by his schoolmates (Haileybury was placed in Group I of the leading public schools between 1880 and 1902). Many of his friends, of course, were killed in the First World War. Attlee was one of those people who did not forget: alone among ex-Prime Ministers, he continued to attend the annual Remembrance Service at the Cenotaph on 11 November. In 1942 he found the time to concern himself with the fate of Lawrence House. The current Headmaster assured him that though the House had had to be temporarily closed, the recent amalgamation of Haileybury with the Imperial Service College would ensure its revival. 'All going well,' (CAB 118/74, 24 April 1942) concluded the Headmaster – at a time when little else was going well for either Britain, the Empire, Europe or the world. Attlee was no doubt reassured. 'There is nothing in most other countries,' one observer has noted, 'comparable to this devoted loyalty, this yearning to perpetuate schooldays.' (Ogilvie, op. cit., p. 182).

29 On the other hand, of the six former students of Haileybury who were elected to the House of Commons in 1945, including Attlee, no fewer than five were members of the Labour Party. One was in luck: he was highly favoured for a certain position, a Private Secretary reported; 'Yes,' agreed Attlee, 'and another advantage is that he was at my old school, Haileybury.' (J. Colville, *Footprints in Time*, 1976, p. 80.) In 1946 Attlee told his school that the country had changed, but it was the English way to change things gradually. He had no reason for thinking that the public schools would disappear. He thought the great traditions would carry on and might even be extended. (*The Times*, 29 January 1946.)

It should be added that though subscribing to the notion that only gentlemen were fit to govern, Attlee did not accept that the necessary qualities were the exclusive possession of a single class or the attribute of a single form of education. Though strongly in favour of an educational system which would break down the class barriers and preserve the unity of the nation, he supported educational variety. He was entirely opposed to the abolition of the 'old' tradition and the levelling of everything to a dull uniformity. (*The Times*, 25 February 1945.)

He did not send his only son, Martin, to Haileybury, but all four of his children attended private fee-paying schools.

30 Sir Ernest Barker, *Age and Youth*, 1953, p. 229.
31 Ibid.
32 Ross Terrill, *R. H. Tawney and His Times*, 1974, p. 25.
33 José Harris, *William Beveridge: A Biography*, 1977, p. 23.
34 Ibid.
35 Unlike Attlee, one of the most brilliant of University College's students, A. D. Lindsay, who subsequently also became a socialist as well as Master of Balliol College, developed a prejudice against public schools. (L. E. Jones, *An Edwardian Youth*, 1956, p. 39.)
36 Barker, op. cit., p. 22.
37 C. A. Alington, *Things Ancient and Modern*, 1936, p. 61.
38 Barker, op. cit., pp. 23–4.
39 Lord Beveridge, *Power and Influence: An Autobiography*, 1953, p. 9.
40 Sir Andrew McFadyean, *Recollected in Tranquillity*, 1964, p. 32. In 1919 Barker also was lecturing to packed halls on the new subject of 'Working-class Conditions and Movements in England during the last two centuries.' He could usefully have consulted his ex-pupil.
41 Eustace Percy, *Some Memories*, 1958, p. 12.
42 William Carr, *University of Oxford; College Histories: University College*, 1902, p. 204.
43 P. Johnson, *The Offshore Islanders*, 1972, p. 340.
44 Jones, op. cit., p. 181.

II Not Going Home To Tea

1 His last home was about 100 yards from Paper Buildings where he had his first chambers after being called to the Bar.
2 F. Williams, *The Triple Challenge*, 1948, p. 57.
3 R. C. Ensor, *England, 1870–1914*, 1936, p. 217.
4 Ibid., p. 301.
5 M. Bruce, *The Coming of the Welfare State*, 1961, p. 145.
6 Paul Thompson, *Socialists, Liberals and Labour: The Struggle for London 1855–1914*, 1967, pp. 11–12.

7 One sister, Dorothy, had married. An elder brother, Bernard the parson, had accepted an ecclesiastical living close to Oxford, where Attlee had often visited him.
8 W. Golant, Thesis, p. 17.
9 In 1905 the average number of people living in one dwelling was 9–10, often sharing one or two rooms: the infant mortality rate was 143 per 1,000. (Ibid. Source: Borough of Stepney, Report of Medical Officer, 1905.)
10 C. R. Attlee, *The Social Worker*, 1920, pp. 210–12.
11 William Beveridge made the same discovery: he, too, was surprised to find that, for all their poverty, the children of the East End were 'dreadfully intelligent and full of knowledge'. (José Harris, *William Beveridge: A Biography*, 1977, p. 53.)
12 See Helen Bosanquet, *Social Work in London, 1869–1912*, second edn, with an Introduction by C. S. Yeo, 1973.
13 Thompson, op. cit., p. 21.
14 Golant, op. cit., pp. 26–7 (Source: C. R. Attlee, 'The Haileybury Guild' in *The Haileyburian*, 31 August 1908.)
15 C. R. Attlee quoted by F. Williams in the Preface to *The Labour Party in Perspective – And Twelve Years Later*, 1949.
16 Thompson, op. cit., p. 140.
17 C. R. Attlee, *As It Happened*, 1954, p. 21.
18 Also in the early 1920s. W. Golant, 'The Early Political Thought of C. R. Attlee' in *Political Quarterly*, vol. 40, no. 3, July–September 1969, p. 426. (Hereinafter referred to as Article.)
19 C. R. Attlee in *Reynolds News*, 18 December 1955.
20 The SDF changed its name to Social Democratic Party in 1907 but as Attlee continued to refer to it as the SDF so shall we.
21 C. R. Attlee, 'Socialist Faith in the Past and the Future' in *Forward*, 5 July 1952.
22 R. E. Dowse, *Left in the Centre: The Independent Labour Party, 1893–1940*, 1966, p. 6.
23 Ibid.
24 The SDF had also been involved but, typically, it had severed itself from the LRC in 1901.
25 Dowse, op. cit., p. 12.
26 The pact had been 'absolutely vital in securing Labour success in the 1906 election'. (Chris Cook, 'Labour's Electoral Base' in *The Labour Party*, eds. C. Cook and I. Taylor, 1980, p. 84.)
27 Especially after 1910. See Dowse, op. cit., p. 17.
28 R. McKibbin, *The Evolution of the Labour Party, 1910–1924*, 1974, p. 28.
29 Thompson, op. cit., p. 69.
30 Ibid., pp. 68–72.
31 Ibid., p. 230.
32 Golant, Thesis, p. 52.
33 Ibid., p. 46, Source: *Wandsworth Boro' News*, 14 October 1910.
34 Ibid., pp. 62–3.
35 Ibid., pp. 39–40.
36 Thompson, op. cit., p. 226.
37 Ibid., p. 228.
38 *Reynolds News*, 9 September 1956.
39 C. R. Attlee, *The Labour Party in Perspective*, 1937, p. 7.
40 Thompson, op. cit., p. 230.
41 Attlee, *As It Happened*, p. 34.

42 McKibbin, op. cit., ch. xv.
43 Thompson, op. cit., p. 226.
44 Golant, op. cit., p. 64.
45 Harris, op. cit., p. 95.
46 Ross Terrill, *R. H. Tawney and His Times*, 1974, p. 35.
47 Attlee, *The Social Worker*, pp. 2, 132, 138, 155.
48 Attlee, *As It Happened*, p. 21.
49 B. Pimlott, *Labour and the Left in the 1930s*, 1977, p. 24.
50 Harris, op. cit., p. 95.
51 D. Frazer, *The Evolution of the British Welfare State*, 1973, pp. 148–9.
52 Ibid.
53 Ibid., pp. 155–6.
54 This poem was first published in full in the *East London Advertiser*, 16 July 1976. (Information from D. T. Elliott, Chief Librarian, Tower Hamlets, London.) It has subsequently been included in G. Dellar, ed., *Attlee As I Knew Him*, 1983, p. 3.
55 B. Donoughue and G. W. Jones, *Herbert Morrison: Portrait of a Politician*, 1973, p. 20.
56 He was nevertheless invited back, and lectured on 'The Industrial History of England' with some success. The Institute's newsletter commented that 'even the most bashful comrades feel inclined to ask questions of such a sympathetic teacher.' (F. Brockway, *Bermondsey Story*, 1949, p. 49.)
57 H. Wilson, *A Prime Minister on Prime Ministers*, 1977, p. 280.
58 H. Dalton, *Call Back Yesterday: Memoirs 1887–1931*, 1953, p. 71.
59 Beveridge remained in this post until 1937, when he became Master of Attlee's Alma Mater, University College, Oxford.
60 Quoted in Golant, Article.

III The Work Has To Be Done

1 C. R. Attlee to Tom Attlee, April 1918. Quoted in W. Golant, Thesis, p. 67.
2 C. R. Attlee, *As It Happened*, p. 61.
3 C. R. Attlee, *The Labour Party in Perspective*, 1937, p. 122.
4 Ibid., pp. 10–11.
5 159 *H. C. Deb.*, cols. 92–6, 23 November 1922.
6 Attlee, op. cit., p. 12.
7 Ibid., p. 23.
8 The only instance this writer can find of Attlee using his position as Prime Minister to do a favour for a member of his family concerned his sister, Margaret. In August 1948, she asked him if he could do anything about the re-hanging of the church bells at St Thomas's, Salisbury. The Ministry of Works had refused to grant a building licence. Attlee asked the Minister to look into the matter and, unsurprisingly, the Ministry reconsidered and granted the licence. Attlee's action was entirely consistent with that of a subscriber to *The Countryman*. One of his secretaries considered Attlee to exceed even Baldwin in his love of the (Southern) English countryside. (D. Hunt, *On the Spot: An Ambassador Remembers*, 1975, p. 42.)
9 C. R. Attlee, 'Written on Walney Island, Barrow, 1918', unpublished ms., Attlee Papers, Churchill College, Cambridge.
10 Attlee to Tom Attlee, 20 March 1918. Quoted in Golant, op. cit., p. 107.
11 C. R. Attlee, *The Will and the Way to Socialism*, 1935, p. 120.
12 J. M. Winter, *Socialism and the Challenge of War: Ideas and Politics in Britain*

1912–1918, 1974, p. 6.

13 By May 1915, Henderson had joined Asquith's coalition, though in the odd post of President of the Board of Education; two other Labour MPs were given junior posts. When Lloyd George formed his coalition in December 1916, Henderson was promoted to the War Cabinet, and several other trade union MPs secured ministerial and junior offices.

14 Winter, op. cit., p. 40. Also D. Marquand, *Ramsay MacDonald*, 1977, pp. 200–1, and R. McKibbin, *The Evolution of the Labour Party, 1910–1924*, 1974, p. 105.

15 R. Terrill, *R. H. Tawney and His Times: Socialism as Fellowship*, 1974, p. 52.

16 Marquand, op. cit., p. 184.

17 See H. Pelling, *A Short History of the Labour Party*, 1962, pp. 41–2.

18 Ibid.

19 Marquand, op. cit., p. 221.

20 Ibid.

21 Pelling, op. cit., p. 43.

22 McKibbin, op. cit., p. 91.

23 Pelling, op. cit., pp. 39–40.

24 Between 1914 and 1919, the total affiliated membership of the TUC grew from less than 2.5 million to more than 4 million, and that of the Labour Party from 1.6 million to more than 3 million. By 1920 the total membership of the trade unions affiliated to the TUC had reached 6.5 million, while Labour Party membership had reached over 4.3 million (Marquand, op. cit., pp. 194, 243.)

25 It was partly put in as a sop to the professional bourgeoisie; the Fabians argued that the latter were socialist by class interest as much as the proletariat and that the war had finally revealed this to them. Ibid., pp. 96–7.

26 S. H. Beer, *Modern British Politics*, 1969 edn, p. 151.

27 Quoted in Marquand, op. cit., p. 230.

28 Attlee, *The Labour Party in Perspective*, pp. 100–1, 279.

29 Philip M. Williams, *Hugh Gaitskell: A Political Biography*, 1979, p. 560.

30 Quoted in Golant, Thesis, p. 75.

31 Ibid., p. 85.

32 C. R. Attlee, *Metropolitan Borough Councils: Their Constitution, Power and Duties*, Fabian Tract No. 190, March 1920, p. 14.

33 Golant, op. cit., pp. 102–4.

34 Attlee, *As It Happened*, p. 71.

35 R. Jenkins, *Mr Attlee: An Interim Biography*, 1948, p. 91.

36 He was also nominated by the Stepney Labour Party and Trades Council to serve on the executive of the London Labour Party, which he did from 1921–22. His sojourn on this body was too brief to allow him to make any original contribution but it was to make a lasting impression on him in another way. The secretary of the LLP was Herbert Morrison who was actively preparing himself for his future role on the London County Council. Though not elected to the LCC until March 1922, Morrison had already become Labour's leading operator behind the scene. The opportunity arose to name Labour's first alderman to London's foremost governing body and Morrison approached Attlee who was keen to serve. For some unexplained reason, Morrison then changed his mind and invited a city financier and close friend, A. E. Davies, to stand instead. Davies was duly selected. Attlee did not forget the incident: in his view, according to Morrison's biographers, 'Morrison had condemned himself as not being straight.' Attlee abruptly ceased to have any further dealings with the LCC and remained highly suspicious of Morrison

ever afterwards. (B. Donoughue and G. W. Jones, *Herbert Morrison: Portrait of a Politician*, 1973, p. 92.)
37 *News Chronicle*, 28 March 1953. Article by R. J. Cruikshank.
38 Letter from Attlee to *The Times*, 12 April 1920.
39 C. R. Attlee, 'Guild v. Municipal Socialism: A reply' in *Socialist Review*, May 1923.
40 A. Marwick, *Clifford Allen: the Open Conspirator*, 1964, p. 74.
41 Ibid., p. 75. See also R. K. Middlemass, *The Clydesiders: A Left-Wing Struggle for Parliamentary Power*, 1965, p. 104.
42 Attlee, 'Guild v. Municipal Socialism', p. 214. My emphasis.
43 Attlee to Tom Attlee, 20 March 1918. Quoted in Golant, Thesis, p. 131.
44 Golant, Thesis, p. 132.
45 C. R. Attlee, *Economic History with Notes for Lecturers and class leaders*, ILP Information Committee, ILP Study Course no. 4. No date, probably 1922–3.
46 C. R. Attlee, 'History: Socialist and Liberal' in *The New Leader*, 12 January 1923.
47 C. R. Attlee, 'Labour and the Municipal Elections' in *The New Leader*, 13 and 22 October 1922.
48 Attlee, 'Guild v. Municipal Socialism', p. 216.
49 W. Golant, Article, p. 251.
50 Ibid., p. 252.
51 Attlee, 'Guild v. Municipal Socialism', p. 127.
52 C. R. Attlee, 'Socialism for Trade Unionists', ILP Programme Pamphlet, no. 4, p. 8. No date, probably late 1922 or 1923.
53 Attlee, 'Guild v. Municipal Socialism', p. 214.
54 Ibid., p. 217.
55 Ibid., p. 218.
56 Oddly enough, Violet Millar's twin sister also married a man who became pre-eminent in his profession – a future admiral and C-in-C of the British Navy in the Mediterranean, Admiral Willis.
57 *Reynolds News*, 6 January 1946.
58 *Torquay Express and Herald*, 8 December 1955.
59 Attlee, *As It Happened*, p. 234.
60 Lord Moran, *Churchill: Taken from the Diaries of Lord Moran*, 1966, p. 639.
61 Hunt, op. cit., p. 33.
62 Ibid., p. 47.
63 *Reynolds News*, loc. cit.

IV No More The Old Street Corner

1 I am indebted to Lady Attlee for the full text of this pre-war poem, which has four other stanzas.
2 Chris Cook, 'Labour's Electoral Base' in C. Cook and I. Taylor, eds, *The Labour Party*, 1980, p. 85.
3 D. Marquand, *Ramsay MacDonald*, 1977, p. 283.
4 Quoted in R. Jenkins, *Mr Attlee: An Interim Biography*, 1948, p. 99.
5 Marquand, op. cit., p. 285.
6 E. Shinwell, *I've Lived Through It All*, 1973, p. 133.
7 Marquand, op. cit., p. 287.
8 W. Golant, Article, p. 254.
9 A. Marwick, *Clifford Allen: The Open Conspirator*, 1964, p. 80.

10 R. E. Dowse, *Left in the Centre: The Independent Labour Party, 1893–1940*, 1966, p. 124.
11 159 *H. C. Deb.*, col. 96, 23 November 1922.
12 160 *H. C. Deb.*, cols 2087–9, 28 February 1923.
13 161 *H. C. Deb.*, cols 1897–1900, 15 March 1923.
14 162 *H. C. Deb.*, cols 979–80, 9 April 1923.
15 157 *H. C. Deb.*, col. 707, 29 November 1922.
16 166 *H. C. Deb.*, cols 2085–6, 17 July 1923.
17 H. Nicolson, *King George V: His Life and Reign*, 1952, p. 380.
18 K. Middlemas and J. Barnes, *Baldwin: A Biography*, 1969, p. 212–33.
19 H. Pelling, *A Short History of the Labour Party*, 1961, p. 55.
20 David Butler and Jennie Freeman, *British Political Facts*, 3rd edn, 1969, p. 142.
21 Pelling, op. cit., pp. 55–6.
22 Nicolson, op. cit., pp. 383–4.
23 Marquand, op. cit., p. 298.
24 C. R. Attlee, *The Labour Party in Perspective*, 1937, p. 52.
25 Earl Attlee, 'Labour in this Changing Age' in the *Evening Star*, 23 January 1956.
26 C. R. Attlee, *The Labour Party in Perspective*, p. 49.
27 C. R. Attlee, *As It Happened*, 1954, p. 61.
28 171 *H. C. Deb.*, col. 111, 17 March 1924.
29 Ibid., cols 111 and 1382, 17 and 26 March 1924.
30 Golant, Thesis, p. 151.
31 Jack Lawson, *A Man's Life*, 1932, p. 268.
32 Attlee, *The Labour Party in Perspective*, p. 207.
33 Nicolson, op. cit., p. 393.
34 A. J. P. Taylor, *English History: 1914–1945*, 1965, p. 217.
35 Attlee, op. cit., p. 207.
36 The Campbell case arose from an article by a Communist, J. R. Campbell, in which he urged soldiers not to fire on their fellow workers in industrial disputes. There was nothing unusual about such articles but the Labour Attorney General decided to prosecute on grounds of sedition. Then he changed his mind. The Government was defeated on a combined Liberal-Conservative motion for an inquiry. The Zinoviev letter purported to be an instruction from the President of the Communist International to the British Communist Party for further forms of seditious activity. It was published during the election campaign and used to portray Labour as being the dupe of the Communists. The letter, many years afterwards, was shown to be a forgery.
37 Taylor, op. cit., pp. 219–20.
38 197 *H. C. Deb.*, cols 2425–6, 9 July 1926.
39 182 *H. C. Deb.*, cols 771–7, 21 May 1925. By 'prime movers' Attlee meant transport and electricity, etc.
40 192 *H. C. Deb.*, cols 626–630, 24 February 1926.
41 198 *H. C. Deb.*, cols 1440–1, 12 November 1926.
42 H. B. Lees-Smith, ed., *The Encyclopaedia of the Labour Movement*, 1928. Article by C. R. Attlee on 'Electricity' vol. 1.
43 Source: 188 *H. C. Deb.*, col. 817, 1925.
44 Jenkins, op. cit., pp. 114–15.
45 Golant, op. cit., p. 164. Source: interview with Attlee.
46 *The Times*, 11 December 1926.
47 Golant, op. cit., p. 165.

48 192 *H. C. Deb.*, cols 782–8, 25 February 1926.
49 196 *H. C. Deb.*, cols 1868–9, 11 June 1926.
50 185 *H. C. Deb.*, cols 85–90, 15 June 1925.
51 Lees-Smith, op. cit.
52 Attlee also published, in collaboration with W. A. Robson, *The Town Councillor*, 1925. It was essentially a text book that Attlee had begun in 1923. The book was taken over and mostly written by Robson though Attlee no doubt subscribed to the suggestion in the last chapter that local government most needed 'a reconstruction of the whole conception of civic pride, civic duty and civic glory', p. 121.
53 P. S. Gupta, *Imperialism and the British Labour Movement, 1914–1964*, 1971, p. 111.
54 Ibid., p. 96.
55 Golant, op. cit., p. 173.
56 191 *H. C. Deb.*, cols 2277–82, 18 February 1926.
57 Taylor, op. cit., p. 254.
58 Gupta, op. cit., p. 113.
59 C. R. Attlee, Draft Autobiography, 'India' and 'India and Burma'.
60 Gupta, op. cit., p. 114.
61 One telling point was a report by some English trade unionists after a visit to India that Indian union leaders appeared almost exclusively middle-class; doubt was cast as to whether the leaders of the Indian boycott of the Commission, equally bourgeois, were really concerned about the Indian working class. In the end, ILP criticism of the way the Labour Party had conducted itself on the whole matter of the Commission was resoundingly beaten at Labour's 1928 annual conference. (Ibid., pp. 114–16.) The Labour Party was more concerned with domestic affairs.
62 See e.g., 216 *H. C. Deb.*
63 A. Havighurst, *Twentieth Century Britain*, 2nd edn, 1962, p. 208.
64 Pelling, op. cit., p. 63.
65 Cook and Taylor, op. cit., p. 89. By 40.1 to 43.9 per cent (Labour MPs sponsored by local parties). The ILP had put up 54 candidates and elected 37 MPs, but 17 of these were from Scotland. (C. L. Mowat, *Britain Between The Wars*, 1955, p. 351.)
66 Taylor, op. cit., p. 263.
67 Pelling, op. cit.
68 R. Terrill, *R. H. Tawney and His Times: Socialism As Fellowship*, 1947, p. 63.
69 Attlee, *The Labour Party in Perspective*, p. 53.
70 Pelling, op. cit.
71 MacDonald had been partly responsible for the deliberate blurring of Labour's domestic policy. (Marquand, op. cit., pp. 474–81.)
72 Ibid., p. 452.
73 Taylor, op. cit., pp. 264–5.
74 Attlee, *The Labour Party in Perspective*, p. 57.
75 Marquand, op. cit., pp. 458–60.
76 C. R. Attlee, *The Will and the Way to Socialism*, 1935, p. 111.
77 Attlee, *The Labour Party in Perspective*, pp. 55–6.
78 Attlee to Tom Attlee, 20 March 1918: quoted in Golant, op. cit., pp. 135–6.
79 Following the General Strike of 1926, Baldwin had forced through a Bill which stipulated that members of a trade union who wanted to pay the political levy to the Labour Party had to do so specifically: this system of 'contracting-in' had reduced the Party's income by more than a third. (Taylor, op. cit., p. 251.)

80 Attlee, *The Labour Party in Perspective*, p. 57.
81 244 *H. C. Deb.*, cols 620–4, 3 November 1930.
82 245, 247 and 248 *H. C. Deb.*, (Attlee spoke on several occasions, viz: 18 and 26 November 1930, 29 January, 4, 5 and 10 February 1931, on the Agricultural Bill.) Though passed by the Commons, the Bill, which aimed at providing small holdings for unemployed men, was seriously amended in the Lords and eventually vetoed by the Treasury from being put into effect. (Golant, op. cit., pp. 226–7.)
83 Mowat, op. cit., pp. 356–7.
84 Attlee to Tom Attlee, 16 July 1930: quoted in Golant, op. cit., p. 217.
85 In January 1930, MacDonald had created, for instance, an Economic Advisory Council composed of far more brilliant and experienced economic minds than Attlee possessed: they included Keynes, Tawney, Cole, Bevin, Citrine, Hubert Henderson, V. H. Hodson and Colin Clark (who also served Attlee), and several prominent business men. (Mowat, op. cit., p. 359.)
86 Marquand, op. cit., pp. 519, 521.
87 Attlee to Tom Attlee, loc. cit.
88 Golant, op. cit., pp. 218–23.
89 M. Cole, *The Life of G. D. H. Cole*, 1971, p. 175 and M. Cole, *The Story of Fabian Socialism*, 1961, Mercury Books edn, pp. 222–6.
90 Quoted in Marquand, op. cit., p. 560.
91 C. R. Attlee, Draft Autobiography, '1931'.
92 Quoted in Jenkins, op. cit., p. 137.
93 254 *H. C. Deb.*, col. 1075, 30 June 1931. Attlee replied 'No!'
94 *The Times*, 21 September 1931: Letter by C. R. Attlee. *New Statesman*, 7 November 1931: Article on the Post Office by C. R. Attlee.

V What About The Rentiers?

1 C. R. Attlee, *The Labour Party in Perspective*, 1937, p. 59. Attlee's comment was literally true: 'Only 99 Labour candidates faced both Conservative and Liberal opponents [in the 1931 election], compared to 447 in 1929.' (C. Cook and I. Taylor, eds, *The Labour Party*, 1980, p. 91.)
2 Though not that of the rank and file. See R. Eatwell and A. Wright, 'Labour and the Lessons of 1931' in *History*, vol. 53, no. 207, February 1978, p. 39.
3 Philip Guedalla quoted in Robert Rhodes James, *The British Revolution: Volume 2; 1914–1939*, 1977, p. 164.
4 A motion asking the NEC to 'go fully into the details of the Mosley Memorandum', for instance, was only barely defeated by 1,251,000 votes to 1,046,000 (*LPCR, 1930*).
5 D. Marquand, *Ramsay MacDonald*, 1977, p. 569.
6 Quoted in Marquand, ibid. See *LPCR, 1930* for full text.
7 A. J. P. Taylor, *English History: 1914–1945*, 1965, p. 288.
8 Marquand, op. cit., p. 605.
9 Ibid., 636.
10 R. Jenkins, *Mr Attlee: An Interim Biography*, 1948, p. 139.
11 H. Dalton, *Call Back Yesterday: Memoirs 1887–1931*, 1953, p. 272.
12 E. Shinwell, *I've Lived Through It All*, 1973, pp. 113–14.
13 Dalton, op. cit., p. 273.
14 Marquand, op. cit., p. 645. See also B. Donoughue and G. W. Jones, *Herbert Morrison: Portrait of a Politician*, 1973, pp. 164–8.

15 Marquand, op. cit., p. 634.
16 As Marquand asserts, ibid., p. 625 and p. 641.
17 Ibid., p. 645.
18 B. Pimlott, *Labour and the Left in the 1930s*, 1977, p. 15. The Chairman of the Labour Party's 1931 annual conference, held after the political crisis, also declared that, 'No Party in the State stands for an unbalanced budget.' (*LPCR, 1931*, p. 156.)
19 Trevor Lloyd, *Empire to Welfare State: English History 1906–1976*, 2nd edn, 1979. p. 173.
20 257 *H. C. Deb.*, cols 705, 712–3. 725, 771–3, 706, 2 October 1931.
21 Lady Lawson, quoted by W. Golant, Thesis, p. 235.
22 Attlee to Tom Attlee, 18 December 1931, ibid., p. 236.
23 267 *H. C. Deb.*, col. 1385, 23 June 1932.
24 269 *H. C. Deb.*, cols 176–185, 19 October 1932.
25 *Morning Post*, 31 October 1935. (Quoted in Golant, op. cit., p. 236.)
26 Eatwell and Wright, op. cit., p. 50.
27 Ibid., p. 40.
28 Attlee to Tom Attlee, 16 November 1931. Quoted in Golant, op. cit., p. 235.
29 C. R. Attlee, *The Labour Party in Perspective*, 1937, pp. 59–60.
30 Attlee to Tom Attlee, 25 April 1932. Quoted in Golant, op. cit.
31 Ibid., 8 August 1932, p. 247.
32 B. Pimlott, 'The Socialist League: Intellectuals and the Labour Left in the 1930s' in *Journal of Contemporary History*, vol. 6, no. 3, 1971, p. 15. (Article.)
33 Ibid., p. 16.
34 P. Seyd, 'Factionalism Within the Labour Party: The Socialist League, 1932–37' in A. Briggs and J. Saville, eds, *Essays in Labour History, 1918–1939,* 1977, p. 206.
35 Pimlott, op. cit., pp. 19–20, 25–6.
36 *LPCR, 1932*, 3–7 October, p. 204–5.
37 In their Parliamentary Report to the 1932 Conference, Attlee and Lansbury expressed the same feeling of bitter determination. The House of Commons, they sarcastically wrote, had 'proved itself a very good machine for carrying out the will of the nation . . .' The arrangements by which 'new taxes [were] imposed without any previous discussion; the administration of Unemployment Benefit . . . and the . . . repulsive and cruel Means Test; the creation of a tribunal consisting of three men to investigate and if necessary insist on reorganization of a drastic character for great industries such as the iron and steel trade . . .' could be equally used by a Socialist Government. Once Labour had its majority, 'courage and grit [would] do the rest.' (Ibid., p. 99.)
38 Pimlott, op. cit., p. 2.
39 Seyd, op. cit., p. 211.
40 B. Pimlott, *Labour and the Left in the 1930s*, 1977, p. 99.
41 C. R. Attlee, *Local Government and the Socialist Plan*, Forum Series no. 7, Socialist League, 1933.
42 *Sunday Pictorial*, 25 August 1956.
43 C. R. Attlee and S. Cripps, 'The Joint Stock Banks', A Confidential Labour Party Document. Finance and Trade Committee. Policy no. 102. January 1933.
44 *LCPR, 1933*, October, p. 159.
45 Ibid., p. 162.
46 Pimlott, Article, p. 31.
47 K. Martin, *Harold Laski: A Biographical Memoir*, 1953, p. 87.

48 Pimlott, op. cit., p. 30.
49 Ibid., p. 26.
50 Pimlott (ibid., p. 27) says the number rose from 70 in March to 100 in August 1933: Seyd (op. cit., p. 208) claims that the increase reached 74 by March 1934, with a membership of about 3,000.
51 Donoughue and Jones, op. cit., pp. 182, 188, 186.
52 Quoted in Golant, op. cit., p. 276.
53 Though not for the same reasons as Attlee: Bevin and the TUC's General Secretary, Walter Citrine, were 'expansionists by instinct': they denied that the devaluation of the pound would bring about ruin. (Marquand, op. cit., p. 622.)
54 Pelling, *A Short History of the Labour Party*, 1961, p. 71.
55 The votes were:

Morrison	2,134,000
Dalton	1,893,000
Attlee	1,593,000
Dallas	1,255,000
Cripps	1,187,000

56 Eatwell and Wright, op. cit., pp. 38–53.
57 *LPCR, 1934*, p. 174.
58 R. Terrill, *R. H. Tawney and His Times: Socialism As Fellowship*, 1947, pp. 78, 17.
59 Pimlott, *Labour and the Left*, pp. 38, 54.
60 *LPCR*, 1934, pp. 261, 263.
61 C. R. Attlee, 'Cabinet Reconstruction', 12 October 1932, Golant, op. cit., pp. 289–91.
62 Attlee, *The Labour Party in Perspective*, 136, 103.
63 MacDonald to Attlee, 24 August 1931. Attlee Papers, Churchill College.
64 Attlee, Draft Autobiography.
65 At £400 p.a. It was raised in 1937 to £600, when a pension fund for MPs was also established.
66 Up to August 1931 Attlee had held the following posts: Parliamentary Private Secretary to the Prime Minister; Under-Secretary of State at the War Office; Member of the Statutory Commission on India; Chancellor of the Duchy of Lancaster and Postmaster-General. In January 1932, he toyed with at least two schemes for increasing his income. But whether he seriously entertained the idea of leaving politics, as Golant suggests, is a moot point. (W. Golant, 'The Emergence of C. R. Attlee as Leader of the Parliamentary Labour Party', in *The Historical Journal*, vol. XIII, no. 2, 1970, pp. 319–20.)
67 Attlee, Draft Autobiography.
68 Eatwell and Wright, op. cit., p. 38.
69 The shrinking of its geographical base in British society was perhaps more important: 'The West Midlands, which include Birmingham, returned no Labour member in 1931, against 25 in 1929; Lancashire and Cheshire showed a decline from 44 to 5, Scotland from 37 to 3 (excluding the ILP).' (J. Saville, 'May Day 1937', in A. Briggs and J. Saville, eds, *Essays in Labour History 1918–1939*, 1977, p. 234.)
70 Dalton, op. cit., p. 297.
71 Pelling, op. cit., p. 74. See also Saville, op. cit., pp. 235–6.
72 Pimlott, 'The Socialist League . . .', op. cit., p. 17. See also Marquand, op. cit., p. 645.
73 M. Foot, *Aneurin Bevan: A Biography; Vol. 1: 1897–1945*, 1962, p. 164.
74 Pelling, op. cit., p. 75.

75 Foot, op. cit.
76 Ibid.
77 *LPCR, 1935*, p. 173.
78 Golant, op. cit., p. 274.
79 259 *H. C. Deb.*, cols 121–9, 11 November 1931.
80 The newspaper was quoted in the debate by George Lansbury, ibid., col. 55.
81 Churchill went on to say how he had been a life-long supporter of Free Trade and an opponent of Socialism, though he had now changed his mind about the former: the rejoinder was quickly made (but not by Attlee) that he might yet do the same about the latter.
82 261 *H. C. Deb.*, col. 301.
83 Attlee to Tom Attlee, 18 December 1931. Quoted in Golant, Thesis, p. 252.
84 Ibid.
85 261 *H. C. Deb.*, col. 301, 4 February 1932.
86 270 *H. C. Deb.*, col. 140, 7 November 1932.
87 261 *H. C. Deb.*, col. 301, 4 February 1932.
88 267 *H. C. Deb.*, col. 638, 16 June 1932.
89 267 *H. C. Deb.*, col. 267, 14 June 1932.
90 N. Davenport, *Memoirs of a City Radical*, 1974, pp. 75–6.
91 272 *H. C. Deb.*, col. 379, 25 November 1932.
92 270 *H. C. Deb.*, col. 144, 7 November 1932.
93 Attlee, *The Labour Party in Perspective*, p. 13.
94 277 *H. C. Deb.*, cols 107 and 111.
95 Ibid., col. 1307, 8 May 1933.
96 209 *H. C. Deb.*, col. 958–9, 6 June 1934.
97 See e.g. 276 *H. C. Deb.*, 20 March 1933. Attlee spoke for forty-five minutes on an Agricultural Marketing Bill and demonstrated a sound command of the subject.
98 The attitude of the TUC towards unemployment, Saville has noted, was 'half-hearted and certainly ineffectual'. The National Unemployed Workers Movement was organized by Communists. Yet despite the opposition of the Labour leadership to several national hunger marches and various Party bans on association with Communists, Attlee spoke at the 1936 Hyde Park reception for one of the marches. (Saville, op. cit., p. 240.)
99 289 *H. C. Deb.*, col. 1572, 14 May 1934.
100 315 *H. C. Deb.*, cols 900–903, 26 July 1936.
101 R. M. Martin, *TUC: The Growth of a Pressure Group, 1868–1976*, 1980, p. 206.
102 Such as C. R. Attlee, 'Economic Justice Under Democracy' in E. D. Simon, ed., *Constructive Democracy*, 1938; C. R. Attlee, 'Why I Am A Democrat' in R. Acland, ed., *Why I Am A Democrat*, 1939.
103 E. D. Simon, ed., *Constructive Democracy*, 1938, pp. 117–19.
104 C. R. Attlee, *Labour's Method*, A Labour Party Pamphlet, 1937.
105 One of the effects of the change was to strengthen the PLP's representation on the NEC, though it had little effect on Party policy which was still in the bloc vote hands of the trade unions, who had a majority on the NEC and NJCL.
106 *LPCR, 1937*, pp. 25–8.
107 Ibid., pp. 181–3.
108 Ibid., Appendix x, pp. 277–9.
109 Pimlott, *Labour and the Left* . . ., op. cit., p. 155.
110 Ibid., p. 160. Pimlott adds that Attlee was always the most sympathetic of the 'respectable' Labour leadership to the campaigns of the extreme Left.

111 Hugh Thomas, *John Strachey*, 1973, p. 157.
112 Pimlott, op. cit.
113 Attlee, Draft Autobiography.
114 C. R. Attlee, *As It Happened*, 1954.
115 Attlee, *The Labour Party in Perspective*, 1949 edn, pp. 9–13.
116 Ibid., Original edn, p. 22.
117 Ibid., p. 139.
118 Ibid., 1937 edn, pp. 31–2.

VI Collective Security

1 The occasion occurred in July 1944 when he presented a memorandum to the War Cabinet on 'Foreign Policy and the Flying Bomb' – the first minister to address himself officially to the topic: he argued that, within a general system of collective security, there should be a close military alliance of Britain, France, Norway, Denmark and Holland, which would serve – and thereby involve – the US as an outpost. (CAB 65/53, W. P. (44), 26 July 1944.) To Attlee, the menace of the flying bomb in 1944 was similar to the fear in the 1930s 'that the bomber would always get through' (270 *H. C. Deb.*, col. 534, 10 November 1932), and his conclusions were virtually identical in both cases.
2 H. Pelling, *A Short History of the Labour Party*, 1961, p. 29.
3 M. R. Gordon, *Conflict and Consensus in Labour's Foreign Policy*, 1969, p. 20.
4 G. D. H. Cole, *A History of the Labour Party Since 1914*, cited in P. Stansky, ed., *The Left and War: the British Labour Party and World War I*, 1969, pp. 73–4.
5 Pelling, op. cit., p. 35.
6 J. F. Naylor, *Labour's International Policy: The Labour Party in the 1930s*, 1969, p. 11.
7 Ibid., p. 7.
8 See Chapter VII.
9 313 *H. C. Deb.*, col. 1709. Figures cited by Hugh Dalton, 23 June 1936. In 1932 the National Government actually reduced the Army Estimates below the figure sanctioned by the Labour Government.
10 C. R. Attlee, *The Labour Party in Perspective*, 1937, p. 207.
11 305 *H. C. Deb.*, col. 33. 22 October 1935.
12 Attlee, op. cit., p. 208.
13 Naylor, op. cit., p. 6.
14 Attlee, op. cit., p. 209.
15 Pelling, op. cit., p. 78.
16 262 *H. C. Deb.*, cols 1665–8, 8 March 1932.
17 263 *H. C. Deb.*, cols 228–30, 15 March 1932.
18 267 *H. C. Deb.*, col. 1378, 23 June 1932.
19 268 *H. C. Deb.*, col. 911, 11 July 1932.
20 C. L. Mowat, *Britain Between The Wars*, 1955, p. 422.
21 The French, in view of the fact that Germany was already rearming beyond the provisions of the Versailles Treaty, wanted security – while the British strove for reconciliation. To this end the British were prepared to allow Germany to catch up with the other powers, but the French refused. Hence Germany withdrew from the Conference. (Ibid.)
22 The League, on British initiative, was to accept the Lytton Report in

February 1933 and Britain proposed an arms embargo the same month – after Japan had extended its aggression in China. (A. J. P. Taylor, *English History: 1914–1945*, 1965, p. 371.)

23 270 *H. C. Deb.*, cols 526–34, 10 November 1932; my emphasis.
24 Attlee to Tom Attlee, 1 January 1933, quoted in W. Golant, Thesis, pp. 264–5..
25 Naylor, op. cit., p. 32.
26 275 *H. C. Deb.*, col. 46, 27 February 1933.
27 Ibid.
28 Naylor, loc. cit.
29 Pelling, op. cit., p. 78.
30 275 *H. C. Deb.*, cols 1382–3, 9 March 1933.
31 Ibid., col. 1405 and 276 *H. C. Deb.*, cols 205, 207, 21 March 1933.
32 Ibid., col. 203.
33 Ibid., cols 2740–7, April 1933; my emphasis.
34 Ibid., cols 2756, 2775 and 2786.
35 279 *H. C. Deb.*, cols 33–6, 13 June 1933.
36 Attlee to Tom Attlee, 18 August 1933; quoted in M. Cowling, *The Impact of Hitler: British Politics and British Policy, 1933–1940*, 1975, p. 23.
37 Naylor, op. cit., pp. 58–9.
38 Ibid., p. 62–4.
39 Attlee to Tom Attlee, 6 November 1933; quoted in Golant, Thesis, p. 272.
40 Naylor, op. cit., p. 70.
41 Ibid., pp. 48, 59.
42 284 *H. C. Deb.*, cols 474–7, 13 December 1933.
43 Ibid., col. 1503, 21 December 1933.
44 285 *H. C. Deb.*, cols 1000–4, 6 February 1934.
45 287 *H. C. Deb.*, cols 465–6, 14 March 1934.
46 C. R. Attlee, *As It Happened*, 1954, p. 139.
47 287 *H. C. Deb.*, col. 466, 14 March 1934.
48 Ibid., col. 679, 15 March 1934.
49 Ibid., cols 1221–7, 21 March 1934.
50 Ibid., col. 1241.
51 C. R. Attlee, 'An International Police Force', *The New Commonwealth*, Series B, no. 3, 1934.
52 292 *H. C. Deb.*, cols 684–9, 13 July 1934; my emphasis. Russia was admitted to the League in September 1934.
53 Naylor, op. cit., p. 76.
54 *LPCR, 1934*, Appendix II, 'War and Peace', p. 244.
55 Naylor, op. cit., p. 79.
56 Ibid., p. 78.
57 Ibid., p. 79.
58 B. Pimlott, *Labour and the Left in the 1930s*, 1977, p. 72.
59 *LPCR, 1934*, p. 174.
60 Naylor, op. cit., p. 78.
61 299 *H. C. Deb.*, cols 41–3, 11 March 1935.
62 NEC, *Minutes and Memoranda*, 1935. Special Report to the NEC by the Scottish Secretary on the West Edinburgh By-Election, 2 May 1935.
63 301 *H. C. Deb.*, cols 672–6, 2 May 1935.
64 Especially the TUC representatives. Dalton, Diaries, May 1935.
65 NEC *Minutes*, 21–2 May, 1935.
66 Dalton, Diaries, May 1935.
67 Ibid., and NEC, op. cit.

68 302 *H. C. Deb.*, cols 374–8, 22 May 1935.
69 Ibid., cols 2194–5, 7 June 1935.
70 NEC *Minutes and Memoranda*. Advisory Committee on International Questions. Note concerning the present position with regard to the Italo-Abyssinian dispute. July 1935.
71 304 *H. C. Deb.*, cols 534–40, 11 July 1935.
72 Naylor, op. cit., p. 65.
73 Ibid., pp. 65–7; Taylor, op. cit., p. 379; Mowat, op. cit., pp. 541–2.
74 Naylor, op. cit., p. 93.
75 Quoted in ibid., p. 94.
76 *LPCR, 1935*, p. 179.
77 Ibid., p. 177.
78 He still admired Lansbury personally, 'whose old time pacifism', as Attlee later put it, 'could not stomach the needs of a new era of barbarism'. (Earl Attlee, 'The Nation's Defence' in *Socialist Commentary*, June, 1956.)
79 *LPCR, 1935*, p. 136.
80 Ibid., pp. 173–4.
81

Dalton	2,096,000
Morrison	2,011,000
Attlee	1,964,000
Dallas	1,641,000
Toole	888,000

82 Naylor, op. cit., p. 109.
83 Ibid., p. 110.
84 Golant, Thesis, p. 280.
85 305 *H. C. Deb.*, col. 29, 22 October 1935.
86 Ibid., col. 45.
87 Mowat, op. cit., p. 553. That Baldwin was motivated by expediency in the timing of the election is convincingly argued in T. Stannage, *Baldwin Thwarts the Opposition: The British General Election of 1935*, 1980, p. 123.
88 Naylor, op. cit., p. 115.
89 Taylor, op. cit., p. 383.
90 Ibid.
91 Stannage, op. cit., p. 237.
92 Ibid., pp. 140–8.
93 Ibid., pp. 66–8, 74–6, 180–90, 242–3, 245.
94 Dalton, Diaries, 31 May 1935.
95 Naylor, op. cit., p. 114.
96 305 *H. C. Deb.*, cols 44–6, 22 October 1935.
97 M. Cowling, *The Impact of Hitler: British Politics and British Policy, 1933–1940*, 1975, p. 45.
98 In any case, though a seat in the Commons had been found for him in 1933, Henderson had devoted his last years almost exclusively to the World Disarmament Conference and for his work had received the Nobel Peace Prize in 1934.
99 Pimlott, op. cit., p. 73.
100 B. Donoughue and G. W. Jones, *Herbert Morrison: Portrait of a Politician*, 1973, pp. 236–7.
101 Ibid., p. 242.
102 Dalton, Diaries, 26 November 1935.
103 Lord Williams, *Digging for Britain*, 1965, p. 101.
104 See Special Report to the NEC on the West Edinburgh by-election, 2 May 1935. (NEC, *Minutes*, 1935.) Also Dalton, Diaries, May 1935.

105 Dalton, op. cit., 26 November 1935.
106 Donoughue and Jones, op. cit., p. 241.
107 Dalton, op. cit., 26 November 1935.
108 Pelling, op. cit., p. 80.
109 Cowling, op. cit., p. 25.
110 Taylor, op. cit., p. 385.
111 307 *H. C. Deb.*, cols 2017–29, 19 December 1935.
112 Austen Chamberlain replied to Attlee: 'I venture to say that when, across that table, he pointed to the PM and said, "It is your honour that is at stake," he made it certain that no supporter of the Government would abstain from the vote.' (Ibid., col. 2040.)
113 Ibid., col. 586, 3 December 1935.

VII Too Late

1 Laval was reluctant and a committee of League experts reported in February that, even with universal application by League members and a limitation of US exports to a pre-1935 level, an oil sanction would require at least three months to become effective. J. F. Naylor, *Labour's International Policy: The Labour Party in the 1930s*, 1969, p. 129.)
2 309 *H. C. Deb.*, cols 150–3, 24 February 1936.
3 310 *H. C. Deb.*, col. 1531, 26 March 1936.
4 Naylor, op. cit., p. 128.
5 330 *H. C. Deb.*, col. 1830, 21 December 1937.
6 Earl Attlee, 'The Nation's Defence' in *Socialist Commentary*, June 1956.
7 A. J. P. Taylor, *English History: 1914–1945*, 1965, p. 390.
8 Labour Party Defence Advisory Committee, *Minutes*, (1), 4 February 1936.
9 Attlee and Dalton were also privately informed about Service developments by senior officers, as was Churchill.
10 In NEC, *Minutes and Papers*, 4 March 1936.
11 C. R. Attlee, *As It Happened*, 1954, p. 140.
12 C. R. Attlee, 'Votes in Supply', Labour Party Memorandum, 1936; my emphasis. (In Dalton, Papers, Part II, Section 2, 3/1.)
13 Attlee, *As It Happened*, p. 98.
14 In 1935–6, defence expenditure totalled £137 million; the estimate for 1936–7 was for £158 million and actual expenditure came to £186 million. (C. L. Mowat, *Britain Between The Wars*, 1955, p. 571.)
15 The NEC, the General Council of the TUC and the executive committee of the PLP. Between 2–4 March 1936, the Labour Party's executive organs were in almost constant session. Dalton attended nine meetings in these three days. (H. Dalton, *The Fateful Years: Memoirs 1931–1945*, 1957, p. 87.)
16 Sir Thomas Inskip, the man appointed, was known as a 'nonentity' (Mowat, op. cit., p. 570), and he had little power to co-ordinate anything.
17 309 *H. C. Deb.*, cols 1843, 1846, 1849, 9 March 1936.
18 Naylor, op. cit., p. 155.
19 NEC, *Minutes and Papers*, 19–20 March, 1936. The voting was 18 to 1, with 7 abstentions.
20 Mowat, op. cit., p. 565.
21 See Taylor, op. cit., pp. 387–8 on this point.
22 A. Bullock, *Hitler: A Study in Tyranny*, revised edn, 1962, p. 345.
23 310 *H. C. Deb.*, cols 1532–6, 26 March 1936.
24 Churchill agreed with Attlee that international issues 'should not be settled

by any single power, but by all those Powers, or all who matter at Geneva, and within the circle and under the authority of the League of Nations'. (Ibid., col. 2478, 6 April 1936.)

25 313 *H. C. Deb.*, cols 1608–15, 1719, 23 June 1936.
26 Taylor, op. cit., p. 389.
27 Mowat, op. cit., p. 569.
28 Ibid., pp. 562, 566.
29 CAB, PREM 1/93, 28 July 1936: transcript of Parliamentary Deputation to Baldwin, Halifax and Inskip. Quoted in M. E. Ceadel, 'Pacifism in Britain, 1931–1939', Oxford D. Phil., 1976.
30 Naylor, op. cit., pp. 171–2.
31 319 *H. C. Deb.*, cols 115, 117, 19 January 1937.
32 Naylor, op. cit., p. 155.
33 Dalton, Diaries, 22 July 1936. Several Labour MPs, however, including Dalton, did not comply with the PLP's decision and consistently abstained in the Commons. (Naylor, op. cit., pp. 155–6.)
34 B. Pimlott, *Labour and Left in the 1930s*, 1977, p. 102.
35 Ibid., pp. 94–8.
36 As were Dalton, Morrison, James Walker and Susan Lawrence. (Naylor, op. cit., p. 158.)
37 NEC, *Minutes and Papers*, 4 September and 2 October 1936.
38 See Naylor, op. cit., pp. 159, 161. The same happened to Attlee in regard to his often quoted statement in 1937 that 'there is no agreement on foreign policy between a Labour Opposition and a Capitalist Government'. (C. R. Attlee, *The Labour Party in Perspective*, 1937, p. 227.)
39 *LPCR, 1936*, pp. 182–4.
40 Ibid., pp. 192–4.
41 Ibid., pp. 202–4.
42 Ibid., pp. 205–6.
43 See Naylor, op. cit., pp. 142–4.
44 Ibid., pp. 145–6.
45 NEC *Minutes*, 4 October 1936.
46 Naylor, op. cit., p. 145.
47 *LPCR, 1936*, pp. 179–80.
48 Ibid., pp. 258–9.
49 Pimlott, op. cit., pp. 94–8.
50 Attlee to H. Laski, 22 February 1937. (K. Martin, *Harold Laski: A Biographical Memoir*, 1953, pp. 100–1.)
51 Pimlott, op. cit., p. 104.
52 Ibid., p. 107.
53 Attlee, *The Labour Party in Perspective*, p. 9.
54 Naylor, op. cit., p. 172.
55 313 *H. C. Deb.*, cols 1608, 1614, 23 June 1936.
56 NEC *Papers*, Memorandum on Factors in the International Situation to be considered in relation to any new Security Agreement. December 1936.
57 Ibid., 'Some Notes on Europe and the Covenant of the League of Nations' by William Gillies, 28 April 1937.
58 325 *H. C. Deb.*, cols 1550–4, 25 June 1937.
59 *LPCR, 1937*, pp. 89–90.
60 Naylor, op. cit., pp. 194–5. Dalton, who organized the rebellion, believed that greater participation would only have increased the margin of victory. (Ibid.)
61 Ibid., p. 196.

62 *LPCR, 1937*, p. 4.
63 Ibid., p. 208.
64 Laski, Cripps and D. N. Pritt were elected, but so too was Dalton. The results:

Morrison	348,000
Dalton	306,000
Laski	276,000
Noel-Baker	267,000
Cripps	260,000
Dallas	187,000
Pritt	155,000

65 R. Jenkins, *Mr Attlee: An Interim Biography*, 1948, pp. 175–6.
66 Ibid., pp. 180–1.
67 330 *H. C. Deb.*, cols 882–4, 844, 13 December 1937.
68 There were several demands between March and May 1938, mostly by constituency bodies, for special Party conferences of one sort or another in regard to international issues, but they were rejected by the NEC. The annual conference in 1937 had also accepted the idea of separating the date of its meeting by a longer interval from that of the TUC. Faced with the alternative of convening an annual conference within either six or eighteen months, the NEC decided in favour of the latter. Thus no annual conference was held in 1938.
69 *Clem Attlee: The Granada Historical Records Interview*, 1967, p. 17. Attlee added: 'He [Chamberlain] always treated us like dirt.'
70 According to the monthly Gallup poll started in October 1938, Chamberlain regularly had the support of the majority of the electorate. (H. Pelling, *Britain and the Second World War*, Fontana edn, 1970, p. 34.)
71 Martin, *Laski*, p. 111.
72 333 *H. C. Deb.*, col. 99, 14 March 1938. By September 1938, the Labour hierarchy was no longer speaking so much about collective security as about collective defence. (NEC, *Papers*, *Declaration*, 8 September 1938: 'Labour and the International Situation'.)
73 332 *H. C. Deb.*, cols 64–5, 21 February 1938.
74 Naylor, op. cit., pp. 221–3.
75 332 *H. C. Deb.*, col. 227, 22 February 1938.
76 333 *H. C. Deb.*, cols 54–5, 14 March 1938.
77 Ibid., cols. 98–9.
78 Ibid., cols 1417–21, 24 March 1938.
79 Cowling, op. cit., p. 245.
80 In November. M. Gilbert, *Winston S. Churchill: The Prophet of Truth, 1922–1939*, 1977, p. 807.
81 P. Addison, *The Road to 1945*, 1975, p. 46.
82 Attlee had been made a PC in 1937.
83 PREM 1/238.
84 332 *H. C. Deb.*, col. 1059, 7 March 1938.
85 Naylor, op. cit., p. 229.
86 335 *H. C. Deb.*, cols 1793–1895, 12 May 1938. In the division, Churchill abstained but Harold Macmillan sided with Labour.
87 PREM 1/251.
88 Naylor, op. cit., p. 238.
89 310 *H. C. Deb.*, col. 1541, 26 March 1936.
90 Attlee, *As It Happened*, p. 145.
91 *LPCR, 1939*, p. 10.

92 NEC, *Minutes and Papers*: Advisory Committee on International Questions: 'Guarantees to Czechoslovakia in relation to Spain'; April, 1938.
93 Naylor, op. cit., p. 241.
94 PREM 1/264. 17 September 1938.
95 Dalton, Diaries, 11 April 1938.
96 Ibid., 12 April 1938.
97 Ibid., 7 July 1938. Attlee nevertheless had to reckon with the French and British deal which had been reluctantly accepted by the Czechs.
98 Ibid., 18 September 1938.
99 *LPCR, 1939*, p. 10.
100 Dalton, Diaries, 20 September 1938.
101 Ibid., 8 April 1938. Dalton's informant was Kingsley Martin.
102 Ibid., 21 September 1938.
103 NEC, *Minutes and Papers*, 21 September 1938.
104 PREM 1/264.
105 H. Nicolson, *Diaries and Letters, 1930–39*, 1966, p. 364.
106 Naylor, op. cit., p. 246.
107 338 *H. C. Deb.*, col. 26, 28 September 1938.
108 F. Williams, *A Prime Minister Remembers*, 1961, p. 18.
109 One of the rare tributes to Attlee's Munich speech, oddly enough, has come from a Conservative historian and MP: Robert Rhodes James, *The British Revolution, Vol. 2: 1914–1939*, 1977, p. 322.
110 339 *H. C. Deb.*, cols 50–66, 13 October 1938. Attlee spoke for an hour less two minutes, one of the longest speeches he ever made in the Commons.
111 Williams, op. cit., p. 20.
112 Naylor, op. cit., pp. 254, 255.
113 Labour Party, Policy Committee, 'Labour Policy After Munich', no. 8, 8 October 1938.
114 Labour Party, Policy Sub-Committee, 'General Policy No. 3 and Notes of Policy Committee Discussion'. (No date, but by internal evidence after 26 October 1938.) Found in Dalton, Papers, 4/3, 49.
115 The minority consisted of Cripps himself, Ellen Wilkinson and D. N. Pritt. (M. Foot, *Aneurin Bevan: A Biography*, vol. 1, p. 287.)
116 *LPCR, 1939*, p. 10.
117 Ibid., p. 303.
118 Labour Party, *Defence Committee Minutes and Papers*, 25 October 1938; January 1939.
119 340 *H. C. Deb.*, col. 6607, 1 November 1938.
120 343 *H. C. Deb.*, col. 84, 31 January 1939.
121 344 *H. C. Deb.*, cols 99–109, 28 February 1939.
122 Information supplied by Mr (now Lord) P. J. Noel-Baker.
123 344 *H. C. Deb.*, cols 99–109, 28 February 1939.
124 346 *H. C. Deb.*, cols 13, 15–19, 13 April 1939.
125 Naylor, op. cit., 284.
The Labour leaders were also influenced by Liddell Hart who believed that the defence held an overwhelming advantage over attacking forces. (See Jenkins, op. cit., p. 200.)
126 *LPCR, 1939*, p. 216.
127 Ibid., p. 303.

VIII Not With A Flourish Of Trumpets

1 P. Addison, *The Road to 1945: British Politics and the Second World War*, 1975, p. 270.
2 355 *H. C. Deb.*, cols 22–3, 28 November 1939.
3 *Foreign Relations of the U.S., 1940*, vol. 1, p. 81.
4 NEC *Minutes*, 26 March 1942.
5 Attlee to Laski, 29 January 1941: Laski Papers, Hull University.
6 Attlee to Laski, 1 May 1944: quoted in full in K. Martin, *Harold Laski: A Biographical Memoir*, 1953, pp. 152–3.
7 NEC *Minutes*, 10 May 1940.
8 Sir Henry Channon, a loyal Chamberlain supporter, noted in his diary that the day was 'Perhaps the darkest day in English history' and he was not thinking entirely of the international developments. (R. Rhodes James, ed., *Chips: The Diaries of Sir Henry Channon*, 1967, p. 248.)
9 If one accepts that the Liberal victory in 1906 owed something to the reaction to the Boer War.
10 Dalton, Diaries, 6 September 1939.
11 Attlee Papers, University College, Oxford, Box 8.
12 Addison, op. cit., p. 62.
13 *LPCR, 1940*, p. 123.
14 L. S. Amery, *My Political Life*, vol. III, 1955, pp. 371–2.
15 Morrison, A. V. Alexander and Cripps, according to A. J. P. Taylor, *English History: 1914–1945*, 1965, p. 100. Also Dalton, according to Addison, op. cit., p. 101.
16 Taylor, op. cit. Privately, Attlee regarded Halifax as a 'Queer bird . . . Very humorous, all hunting and Holy Communion.' (*Clem Attlee: The Granada Historical Records Interview*, 1967, p. 20.)
17 Amery, op. cit.
18 Lord Attlee, 'The Churchill I Knew' in Lord Attlee et al., *Churchill By His Contemporaries: An Observer Appreciation*, 1965, p. 33.
19 *LPCR, 1940*, p. 123.
20 W. S. Churchill, *The Second World War, Vol. II: Their Finest Hour*, 1962, p. 10.
21 Eden, A. V. Alexander, Sinclair (Liberal).
22 February 1942 to September 1943.
23 'I have some reason to believe,' Chamberlain wrote privately, 'that my colleagues [including Attlee] have considerably revised their ideas of my value in the government.' (Quoted in Addison, op. cit., pp. 112–13.) He was right. 'Always very business-like. You could work with him,' said Attlee of Chamberlain later. (Quoted in H. Pelling, *Britain and the Second World War*, Fontana edn, 1970, p. 78.)
24 The Act gave the Government 'practically unlimited authority over all British citizens and their property'. (Taylor, op. cit., p. 479.) The significance of the Act and the speed of its passage may, as Taylor suggests, have been largely symbolic. But symbols were important at that point, and the Act took Labour left-wingers' breath away for a moment. (*Tribune*, 24 May 1940.)
25 Addison, op. cit., p. 116. Attlee, naturally, was chairman.
26 Attlee Papers, Churchill College. 2/2. No date, probably 1943. Draft of memo, Attlee to Churchill. My emphasis.
27 For example, Hugh Dalton. Though Churchill himself was against Dalton taking over the new Department of Political Warfare, Addison notes, Attlee 'fought doggedly through an epic Whitehall intrigue' to see that Dalton got

his additional department. (Addison, op. cit., p. 113, and D. Dilks, ed., *The Diaries of Sir Alexander Cadogan, 1938–1945*, 1971, p. 312.) Beaverbrook opined in 1942 that Attlee's 'chief idea nowadays is to stick obstinately for positions in the Government for Labour people'. (A. J. P. Taylor, ed., W. P. Crozier, *Off The Record; Political Interviews 1933–1943*, 1973, p. 285.)

28 Such as Chamberlain.
29 Attlee, Papers, Churchill College, Cambridge. 1/5/4.
30 Addison, op. cit., p. 124.
31 Dalton, Diaries, 18 September 1939.
32 Ibid., 8 May 1941.
33 For example, Lord Chandos, *The Memoirs*, 1962, p. 293 and Lord Ismay, *The Memoirs*, 1960, p. 133.
34 Attlee to Laski, 1 May 1944; op. cit.
35 H. Laski, 'Epitaph on a System' in the *New Statesman*, 11 July 1942.
36 Chuter Ede to Attlee, 14 February 1941; Attlee Papers, (U.), Box 8.
37 *Tribune*, 21 June 1940.
38 27 October 1940.
39 NEC *Minutes*, 5 November 1940; and see Dalton, Diaries, 5 November 1940.
40 See T. Burridge, 'A Postscript to Potsdam: The Churchill-Laski Electoral Clash, June 1945' in *Journal of Contemporary History* 12, 1977, pp. 728–9.
41 *LPCR, 1941*, pp. 132–4. The conference was held in London, from 2 to 4 June 1941.
42 CAB 21/1581.
43 CAB 87/9, 4 October 1940.
44 N. Nicolson ed., H. Nicolson, *Diaries and Letters*, vol. II, 1967, pp. 102–3, 139, and 139n.
45 CAB 65/17, 20 January 1941.
46 Attlee may also have been influenced by the consideration that any detailed statement of British war aims might have encouraged the Free French to make extreme statements, with the effect of consolidating German support for Hitler.
47 Nicolson, op. cit., p. 99.
48 W. S. Churchill, *The Second World War*, vol. III, *The Grand Alliance*, 1950, p. 374.
49 Sir E. L. Woodward, *British Foreign Policy During the Second World War*, vol. II, 1970, p. 200.
50 CAB 66/20, 282, 24 November 1941.
51 See T. Burridge, *British Labour and Hitler's War*, 1976, pp. 14–15.
52 J. Griffiths, *Pages from Memory*, 1969, p. 69. The committee consisted of twelve members.
53 A. Calder, *The People's War: Britain 1939–1945*, Panther edn., 1971, p. 314. Cripps, however, became a member of the War Cabinet at the end of February 1942, and his public criticism ceased.
54 Taylor, *English History*, pp. 542–3.
55 See Burridge, 'Postscript to Potsdam', p. 729.
56 6 June 1942.
57 See NEC *Minutes*, 28 October 1942.
58 Dalton, Diaries, 12 October 1942.
59 *Tribune*, 2 October 1942.
60 Nicolson, op. cit., p. 192.
61 *LPCR, 1942*, pp. 52–3.
62 Nicolson, op. cit., p. 237.

63 NEC *Minutes*, 26 March 1942.
64 Ibid., 9 April 1942.
65 380 *H. C. Deb.*, col. 63, 19 May 1942.
66 *LPCR, 1942*, p. 100.
67 CAB 66/22, WP (42) 311, 21 July 1942.
68 Dilks, op. cit., p. 440.
69 By 2,319,000 votes to 164,000.
70 Calder, op. cit., p. 632.
71 K. Young, *Churchill and Beaverbrook: A Study in Friendship and Politics*, 1966, p. 228.
72 A. J. P. Taylor, *Beaverbrook*, 1972, pp. 507–8, 515.
73 385 *H. C. Deb.*, col. 461, 18 November 1942.
74 Ibid., col. 1395, 3 December 1942.
75 Dalton, Diaries, 8 December 1942.
76 José Harris, *William Beveridge: a Biography*, 1977, p. 412.
77 Burridge, *British Labour*, p. 78.
78 Addison, op. cit., p. 224.
79 Ibid., and see Calder, op. cit., p. 612.
80 Calder, ibid.
81 See Griffiths, op. cit., pp. 70–2.
82 Addison, op. cit., pp. 225 and 249.
83 Ibid., p. 221.
84 Calder, op. cit., p. 613.
85 F. Williams, *A Prime Minister Remembers*, 1961, p. 57
86 CAB 66/34, 15 February 1943; Addison, op. cit., p. 223; Harris, op. cit., p. 424.
87 Addison, op. cit., pp. 227–8.
88 To Laski, Attlee provocatively argued that the Beveridge Report was not a fully-fledged socialist one – the flat rate contribution idea alone precluded that. (Attlee to Laski, 1 May 1944. Quoted in Harris, op. cit., p. 448.)
89 See Harris, op. cit., pp. 368, 369, 375, 383, 435.
90 Addison, op. cit., p. 225; Harris, op. cit., p. 425.
91 Addison, op. cit., p. 222; Harris, op. cit., p. 426.
92 Williams, op. cit., p. 57.
93 Lord Beveridge, *Power and Influence: An Autobiography*, 1953, p. 332.
94 Harris, op. cit., p. 448. In some respects, the Labour Government's measures did not come up to Beveridge's proposals: family allowances were introduced at a much lower rate; old age pensions contained no commitment to build up towards subsistence; industrial assurance was never nationalized; and some of Beveridge's fringe benefits, such as the furnishing allowance and domestic service benefits for sick housewives, were quietly dropped. (Harris, op. cit., p. 449.)
95 CAB, WP (43) 255, 26 June 1943.
96 Attlee Papers, Churchill College, 2/2. No date; almost certainly 1943; Attlee's use of the word Empire in his approach to Churchill may be noted.
97 Addison, op. cit., p. 233.
98 WP (43) 255, 1 July 1943.
99 WP (43) 324, 20 July 1943.
100 Addison, op. cit., pp. 234–6.
101 CAB 65/40, WM (43) 140 conclusions, 14 October 1943.
102 Ibid., WM 144 (43).
103 CAB 87/5R. (44) 3rd meeting. 10 January 1944.
104 CAB 87/6.

105 Quoted in Addison, op. cit., p. 236.
106 Dilks, op. cit., p. 697. Note by Dilks.
107 *Churchill by his Contemporaries*, (Attlee), pp. 19–20.
108 Attlee Papers, Churchill College, Attlee to Churchill, undated, probably early January 1945.
109 Attlee's opinion is corroborated by Sir Henry Channon (*Diary* p. 376). By November 1943, Channon recorded serious unrest among Conservative MPs at Beaverbrook's growing influence and power (p. 380).
110 See Chapter IX.
111 Addison, op. cit., p. 234.
112 Taylor, ed., *Off The Record*, p. 371.
113 NEC *Minutes*, 5 May 1943.
114 NEC *Minutes*, 8 June 1943.
115 H. Pelling, 'The 1945 General Election Reconsidered' in the *Historical Journal*, vol. 23, 2 June 1980, p. 400.
116 Addison, op. cit., p. 249.
117 NEC *Minutes*, 26 and 27 February 1944.
118 A. V. Alexander Papers, Churchill College. AVAR 569/6 a. and b. Attlee to Alexander, Papers 1 March 1944. My emphasis.
119 Dalton, Diaries, 20 April 1944.
120 Ibid., 19 July 1944.
121 Attlee Papers, Churchill College. Undated typescript. 1/24.
122 NEC *Minutes*. Middleton's draft dated 27 April 1944: Attlee's reply 1 May 1944. My emphasis.
123 See Chapter IX.
124 NEC *Minutes*, 16 May and 26 July, 1944.
125 See *LPCR, 1944*.
126 *Clem Attlee:, The Granada Historical Records Interview*, 1967, p. 23.
127 Lord Moran, *Churchill*, 1966, p. 266.
128 Pelling, op. cit., p. 401.
129 PREM 4/64/4, 12 May 1945. Churchill was determined that he should play the British hand at Potsdam himself, whoever won the election. Writing privately to Attlee, on 2 June, inviting the Labour leader to participate in the Conference, Churchill added: 'If your Party is successful, I should remain Prime Minister until my resignation is accepted by the King, which may be before or after an expression of the will of the New House.' (Burridge, 'Postscript to Potsdam', p. 734.)
130 Dalton, Diaries, 16 May 1945.
131 PREM 4/65/4, 18 May 1945.
132 Dalton, Diaries, 18 May 1945.
133 Addison, op. cit., p. 257; Pelling, op. cit., p. 402; B. Donoughue and G. W. Jones, *Herbert Morrison: Portrait of a Politician*, 1973, pp. 333–4. Only three members of the NEC, all trade unionists, were willing to support Attlee – out of a total Executive of twenty-seven. Morrison may have already had in mind the possibility of challenging Attlee for the leadership.
134 Attlee's letter to Churchill is quoted in full in Williams, *A Prime Minister Remembers*, pp. 64–7.

IX No Mistake This Time

1 See e.g. Keith Sainsbury, 'British policy and German unity at the end of the Second World War' in *The English Historical Review*, vol. XCIV, no. 373,

October 1979; and also T. Burridge, 'Great Britain and the Dismemberment of Germany at the end of the Second World War' in *The International History Review*, vol. III, no. 4, October 1981.

2 T. Sharp, *The Wartime Alliance and the Zonal Division of Germany*, 1975, p. 52.

3 *LPCR, 1940*, pp. 8–9.

4 J. F. Naylor, *Labour's International Policy: The Labour Party in the 1930s*, 1969, p. 5.

5 Dalton, Diaries, 5 January 1943.

6 T. Burridge, *British Labour and Hitler's War*, 1976, p. 18.

7 Ibid., pp. 19–24.

8 *Daily Herald*, 18 September 1939.

9 351 *H. C. Deb.*, col. 1862, 3 October 1939.

10 352 *H. C. Deb.*, cols 568–70, 12 October 1939.

11 H. Nicolson Diaries, Balliol College, Oxford, 17 October 1939. It had been resolved that, before any statement of war aims could be issued, consultation with the French Socialist Party and the Labour and Socialist International would be necessary. (NEC, *Minutes*, 27 September 1939.)

12 The statement was subsequently published as a pamphlet by the Labour Party, under the title *Labour's Peace Aims*, 5 December 1939.

13 A. Calder, *The People's War: Britain 1939–1945*, Panther edn, 1971, p. 75.

14 See e.g. Burridge, op. cit., p. 37.

15 Noel-Baker went instead.

16 H. Dalton, *The Fateful Years: Memoirs 1931–1945*, 1957, pp. 290 and 292, and NEC, *Minutes*, 20 March 1940.

17 *Daily Herald*, 2 April 1940.

18 Dalton, Diaries, 'Middle of February. 1940'. He was, however, prepared to subscribe to a communiqué a few days later, at an Anglo-French Socialist meeting, which stated that the two Parties were resolved 'from now onwards to work for an ever closer unity of the French and British peoples because they are convinced that this unity will form the essential basis of the new order' (NEC *Minutes*, 20 March 1940). He also had no objection to Churchill's celebrated proposal of a Franco-British constitutional union in June 1940 (F. Williams, *A Prime Minister Remembers*, 1961, p. 43). The object, in both cases, was clearly to stiffen French morale.

19 For full text see *LPCR, 1940*, pp. 188–90.

20 356 *H. C. Deb.*, cols 1415–22.

21 *Daily Herald*, 22 April 1940.

22 P. Addison, *The Road to 1945: British Politics and the Second World War*, 1975, p. 60.

23 Elizabeth Barker, *Churchill and Eden at War*, 1978, pp. 141–4.

24 *Churchill By His Contemporaries: An Observer Appreciation*, 1965, p. 14.

25 Williams, *A Prime Minister Remembers*, p. 46.

26 Ibid., p. 14.

27 *Churchill By His Contemporaries*, pp. 16, 14.

28 Williams, op. cit., p. 14.

29 Ibid.

30 Lord Attlee, 'Jumping the Gun' in the *Observer*, 1 November 1958. (The other two, in Attlee's opinion, were Marshall and McArthur.)

31 Williams, op. cit., pp. 46–50: also Attlee, op. cit.

32 W. Golant, Thesis, p. 72. Re Attlee's 1914–18 War Diary, Golant remarks: 'The memoirs studied as a personal document show the writer to be completely

without sentimentality.' Attlee was primarily interested in composing an 'unembellished record of events'.

33 Attlee, op. cit. Attlee did not seek to evade his part in Cabinet responsibility for the mass air attacks on German cities, but he confessed, retrospectively, to having had doubts about 'Bomber Harris'; '. . . I thought that concentration on strategic targets such as oil installations would have paid better. That at any rate was my impression at the time though there were technical difficulties which I hadn't fully realized.' (Williams, op. cit., p. 49.) There is evidence that he objected to the bombing plan in connection with Overlord (the invasion of Europe) in 1944. 'Both Attlee and Eden held that it was militarily unsound, and that great hostility would be caused among the French if the offensive was to proceed along the lines proposed.' Their objections were to the high rate of casualties envisaged among civilians. (See Solly Zuckerman, *From Apes to Warlords: The Autobiography, 1904–1946*, 1978, p. 250.)

34 CAB 65/13. May and June 1940, especially WM (40) 153 conclusions, Minute 5, 3 June. In fact the Cabinet, on 15 May, 'after long discussions' had authorized an attack on the Ruhr and the Strategic Air Offensive had begun. (J. R. M. Butler, *Grand Strategy*, vol. II, HMSO, 1957, p. 182.)

35 CAB 118/74. Memo from Attlee to Churchill, 28 November 1940; with a letter from Attlee and reply from 10 Downing Street on 7 January 1941.

36 D. Dilks, ed., *The Diaries of Sir Alexander Cadogan, 1938–1945*, 1971, p. 313.

37 *Clem Attlee: The Granada Historical Records Interview*, 1967, p. 24.

38 Quoted in C. Hassall, *Edward Marsh: Patron of the Arts*, 1959, p. 631.

39 380 *H. C. Deb.*, col. 64, 19 May 1942.

40 A. J. P. Taylor, *Beaverbrook*, 1972, pp. 475–6. In Moscow, Cripps also had doubts.

41 A. J. P. Taylor, *English History: 1914–1945*, 1965, p. 536.

42 See Keith Sainsbury, '"Second front in 1942" – a strategic controversy revisited' in *British Journal of International Studies*, 1978, vol. 4, pp. 50–1.

43 CAB 65/30, 54 conclusion, 29 April 1942.

44 CAB 69/4, Defence Committee (Operations), 1940–1945, 14 April 1942.

45 CAB 65/30, 73 conclusion, 11 June 1942.

46 *Churchill By His Contemporaries*, p. 26.

47 *Tribune*, 20 December 1940.

48 See *New Statesman*, 23 and 30 August, and *Tribune*, 22 August and 5 September 1941.

49 NEC *Minutes*, 25 January 1940.

50 *Daily Herald*, 17 November 1941.

51 Dalton, Diaries, 18 and 23 October 1939.

52 H. Dalton, *Hitler's War: Before and After*, March, 1940, p. 145.

53 Dalton, Diaries, 17 November 1942.

54 *LPCR, 1943*, p. 39.

55 PREM 4, 21/5, 23 May 1943.

56 CAB 65/29, WM (42), 17 conclusion, Minute 5, 6 February 1942.

57 CAB 66/29, WP (41), 282, 24 November 1941.

58 CAB 66/39, WP (43), 321, 19 July 1943.

59 PREM 4, 30/3, 15 June 1943.

60 David Stafford, *Britain and European Resistance: 1940–1945*, 1980, p. 91.

61 Ibid., p. 34.

62 Ibid., p. 35.

63 Ibid., p. 207.

64 Barker, op. cit., pp. 51–3.
65 CAB 65/38, 75 conclusions, minute 1, 23 May 1943.
66 Barker, op. cit., p. 107.
67 Ibid., p. 109.
68 CAB 65/38, 75 conclusions, minute 1, 13 April 1943.
69 CAB 87/65, 322, July 1943.
70 CAB 78/11.
71 CAB 65/40, 147 conclusions, 27 October 1943 and 150 conclusions, 4 November 1943.
72 CAB 87/65, PS (43) 2, 11 August 1943.
73 Sir E. L. Woodward, *British Foreign Policy During the Second World War*, 1962, pp. 446–7.
74 CAB 65/38, WM (43), 155 conclusions, minute 5, 16 November 1943.
75 CAB 87/83, COS (43), 311, 12 December 1943.
76 Sharp, op. cit.
77 Barker, op. cit., pp. 176, 178, 181, 199, 207.
78 Ibid., p. 161.
79 CAB 65/47, WM (44), 103 conclusions, minute 1, 9 August 1944.
80 CAB 65/48, WM (44), 162 conclusions.
81 W. S. Churchill, *The Second World War*, vol. VI, *Triumph and Tragedy*, 1962, p. 253.
82 Ibid., p. 197; 9 October 1944.
83 See e.g. Dilks, op. cit., p. 689.
84 Dilks, op. cit., p. 689. Re Cabinet meeting of 21 December 1944.
85 Barker, op. cit., p. 197.
86 Ibid., p. 194.
87 Calder, op. cit., p. 651.
88 Quoted in Addison, op. cit., p. 255.
89 406 *H. C. Deb.*, cols 1859–61.
90 PREM 4, 81/4, 15 January 1945.
91 407 *H. C. Deb.*, cols 397–8, 18 January 1945.
92 Ibid., col. 493.
93 Ibid., col. 585.
94 PREM 4, 19/8.
95 Dalton, *Fateful Years*, p. 431.
96 Sharp, op. cit., p. 7.
97 CAB 21/1614(2), also COS (44), 248 meeting, minute 14, 26 July 1944.
98 See CAB 80/97, COS (44) 'O' memoranda, 9 September 1944; and CAB 21/1614, P.H.S. (44), 15 (0), Revised Final, 15 November 1944.
99 Sir Llewellyn Woodward, *British Foreign Policy in the Second World War*, vol. II, 1971, pp. 469–70.
100 CAB 87/66, 1 and 8 June 1944.
101 Attlee was more sceptical at this time about the prospects for a World Security Organization than Bevin, although Attlee was in favour of an attempt to create one. Bevin was clear that the only World Organization worth having would be one backed by force. (CAB 87/66, 27 April 1944.)
102 PREM 4, 30/7 (APW, WP (44), 106, 24 July 1944).
103 CAB 66/53, 414, 26 July 1944.
104 See Burridge, *British Labour and Hitler's War*, pp. 144–9.
105 CAB 87/67, 43, 11 July 1944. 'Policy Towards Germany' by C. R. Attlee.
106 Quoted in Barker, op. cit., p. 209.
107 Burridge, op. cit., pp. 132–3.
108 CAB 87/69 A.P.W. (45), 11 January 1945, and ibid., 25 January 1945.

109 CAB 65/51, 16 conclusions, 8 February 1945, and PREM 4, 78/1, Fleece 324 (part 2), 9 February 1945.
110 CAB 65/51, 18 conclusions, 12 February 1945.
111 PREM 4, 78/1, Fleece 449, 15 February 1945.
112 408 *H. C. Deb.*, col. 1267, 27 February 1945.
113 Ibid., cols 1421–2.
114 *Tribune*, 16 February 1945; *New Statesman*, 17 February 1945.
115 408 *H. C. Deb.*, cols 1616–19.
116 *New Statesman*, 27 January 1945.
117 *Tribune*, 12 January 1945.
118 *New Statesman*, 1, 8, 15 and 22 January 1944.
119 Ibid., 24 March, 21 April, 1945.
120 *Tribune*, 7 and 14 April 1944.
121 *Tribune*, 23 February 1945.
122 *LPCR, 1945*, p. 119.
123 See Burridge, op. cit., pp. 156–8.
124 Piers, Dixon *Double Diplomat: The Life of Sir Pierson Dixon, Don and Diplomat*, 1968, p. 155.

X Getting On With The Job

1 R. Eatwell, *The 1945–51 Labour Governments*, 1979, p. 36.
2 Ibid., pp. 41 and 38.
3 *Churchill By His Contemporaries: An Observer Appreciation*, 1965, pp. 31–2.
4 These figures are taken again from David Butler and Jennie Freeman, *British Political Facts*, 3rd edn, 1969. They vary slightly in other accounts.
5 C. Cook and I. Taylor, eds, *The Labour Party*, 1980, pp. 96–7.
6 H. Pelling, 'The 1945 General Election Reconsidered' in *The Historical Journal*, vol. XXIII, no. 2, 1980, p. 411.
7 Pelling, op. cit., p. 414.
8 A. Salter, *Memoirs of a Public Servant*, 1961, p. 285; F. Williams, *The Triple Challenge*, 1948, p. 63.
9 C. R. Attlee, *As It Happened*, 1954, p. 151.
10 Quoted in F. Williams, *A Prime Minister Remembers*, 1961, p. 81.
11 For example, Lord Chandos, *The Memoirs*, 1962; Lord Ismay, *The Memoirs*, 1960.
12 Several sources have been found for this often-used quotation: perhaps the most likely is K. Martin, *Harold Laski: A Biographical Memoir*, 1953, p. 149.
13 H. Pelling, *A Short History of the Labour Party*, 1961, p. 95. (Pelling notes that the trade-union sponsored members were now less than a third of the total.)
14 *Cambridge Daily News*, 13 November 1948.
15 C. R. Attlee, 'The Office of Prime Minister' in *Municipal Review*, March 1965.
16 C. R. Attlee, 'What Sort of Man Gets to the Top?' in the *Observer*, 7 February 1960.
17 J. Chuter Ede, 'Diaries', British Library MS. 128.
18 Cripps, Bevan, Laski and E. Wilkinson. (F. Williams, *Nothing So Strange: An Autobiography*, 1970, p. 211.)
19 Attlee Papers, Churchill College, 1/17/1.

20 Attlee, 'What Sort of Man Gets to the Top?'
21 *Manchester Guardian*, 15 May 1954.
22 Williams, op. cit., p. 80. For much of the time, however, his son Martin was away at sea as a midshipman. Attlee arranged to have weekly reports of the movements of the ships on which Martin served. (Attlee Papers, University College, Box 2.)
23 Attlee, *As It Happened*.
24 *Manchester Guardian, loc. cit.*
In view of the housing shortage, Attlee sold his house in Stanmore, Middlesex, in February 1946. He invested the proceeds of £5000 equally in 2 per cent Defence Bonds and 2½ per cent Savings Bonds. This sum represented the greater part of his personal savings; he was not concerned about the interest so much as 'prompt reconvertibility without loss' – so as to be able to buy another house. (Attlee Papers, op. cit.)
25 Williams, *A Prime Minister Remembers*, p. 81.
26 David Hunt, *On the Spot: An Ambassador Remembers*, 1975, pp. 42–3; Williams, loc. cit.; John Colville, *Footprints In Time*, 1976, p. 80.
Attlee was abstemious: his favourite drink was a glass or two of claret with a meal; brandy was to be used only 'in extremis'. (F. Williams, *The Triple Challenge*, p. 56.)
27 *Municipal Review*, op. cit.
28 Ibid.
29 Arthur Moyle, 'The Real Attlee – By His PPS' in the *Star*, 8 December 1955.
30 Robert E. Dowse, 'Clement Attlee' in *British Prime Ministers In The Twentieth Century*, ed. J. P. Mackintosh, vol. 2, 1978, p. 45.
31 Moyle, op. cit. Moyle added that in sport Attlee could recall at will almost every celebrity in the past 50 years. His great love was cricket. He used to meet visiting Test players, have demonstrations of the latest leg-break bowling ideas, and then regale the players with stories of the giants of the past.
32 Ibid.
33 A. Bevan, 'Clem Attlee' in *Tribune*, 16 December 1955.
34 Chuter Ede, op. cit.
35 Attlee, *As It Happened*, p. 156.
36 B. Donoughue and G. W. Jones, *Herbert Morrison: Portrait of a Politician*, 1973, p. 343.
37 Williams, *A Prime Minister Remembers*, p. 5.
38 Ibid., p. 85.
39 Ibid., pp. 80–1, 84.
40 *The Times*, 15 June 1957.
41 C. R. Attlee, 'Bevan As Hero' in the *Observer*, 21 October 1962.
42 Williams, op. cit., p. 8. She remained to testify that Attlee was essentially 'a team leader and a team worker. Far from wanting all the limelight for himself, anyone can have the tiresome notoriety provided he is willing to work in the team ... He is the only public man I know who casually gives away quite brilliant remarks to whoever is sitting beside or behind him in the House of Commons ... It is this casual generosity which makes it easy to work with him as leader ...' (C. Clemens, *The Man From Limehouse*, Introduction by E. Wilkinson, 1946.)
43 G. Brown, *In My Way*, 1972, p. 46.
44 Donoughue and Jones, op. cit., p. 419.
45 Attlee, 'What Sort of Man Gets to the Top?'
46 Chuter Ede, op. cit.

47 Attlee, *As It Happened*, p. 155: *The Times*, 15 June 1957.
48 Douglas Jay, 'The Quiet Master At No. 10' in *The Times*, 26 April 1980.
49 *Municipal Review*, op. cit.
50 In the 1930s he had written that 'the essence of the Premiership ... [is] ... that there must be someone to take a decision. The decision that he must take is not that a certain course should be followed but that a decision must be come to.' (Attlee Papers, Churchill College, 2/1.)
51 *The Times*, 15 June 1957.
52 Ibid. See also Williams, op. cit., p. 81; *Manchester Guardian*, 21 January 1959.
53 Donoughue and Jones, op. cit., p. 361.
54 J. Margach, *The Anatomy of Power*, 1979, p. 14.
55 G. Mallaby, *From My Level*, 1965, p. 57.
56 *Manchester Guardian*, 21 April 1963.
57 Williams, op. cit., p. 81.
58 H. Wilson, *The Labour Government, 1964–1970*, 1971, p. 481.
59 J. Griffiths, *Pages From Memory*, 1969, p. 128: Brown, op. cit., p. 239.
60 M. Foot, *Aneurin Bevan: A Biography*, vol. II: 1945–1960, 1973, p. 223.
61 PREM 8/434, CP (45) 306. 4 December 1945. He advised chairmen, among other things, to keep discussion to the point, not to hesitate to check irrelevance or repetition and, when summing-up, to avoid framing conclusions in a way which would require further discussion by Ministers, if that was not necessary. In September 1946, however, he felt obliged to stress again the importance of effective chairmanship. (Ibid., CP (46) 357. 26 September 1946.)
62 R. Rose, *Politics in England*, 1965, p. 105.
63 Dowse, op. cit., p. 50.
64 PREM 8/432, CP (47) 288, 18 October 1947. 'Cabinet Business and Procedure: Note by the Prime Minister.'
He took his time about it, but when he informed Morrison (who was away resting) of his proposed changes, Attlee's letter was 'strikingly authoritative in tone and informative in detail'. (Donoughue and Jones, op. cit., p. 421.)
65 J. H. Brookshire, 'Clement Attlee and Cabinet Reform, 1930–1945' in *The Historical Journal*, 1981, 24, 1, p. 185.
The great exception to the pattern was the question of atomic energy – see Chapter XII: 'It was to remain so under the Conservatives.' (M. Gowing, *Independence and Deterrence*, 1974, vol. I, pp. 55–6.)
66 Attlee Papers, Churchill College, 1/5/4.
67 J. P. Mackintosh, *The British Cabinet*, 3rd edn, 1977, p. 503.
68 Williams, *The Triple Challenge*, p. 49. 'The key to his character,' Williams added, 'lies in the fact that he is a true solitary. He requires less than most men the support of others. He will listen, he will consider other points of view, but once he has decided on a course to be followed he is completely sustained by his own inner strength.' (Ibid., p. 60.)
69 Foot, op. cit., p. 30.
70 Williams, *A Prime Minister Remembers*, p. 150.
71 W. Golant, 'Clem and Ernie' in *The Times*, 29 November 1980.
72 H. Dalton, *High Tide and After: Memoirs 1945–1960*, 1962, p. 51.
73 Williams, *Nothing So Strange*, p. 222.
74 For example, over steel nationalization. See Chapter XI.
75 Attlee's sense of public rectitude was so strong that he was also capable of risking Bevin's irritation over trivialities. The Foreign Office, for example, was extremely keen in July 1947 that Bevin have the use of a plane to attend a

miners' gathering. He was returning to London from Paris in an RAF plane and his speech would deal with foreign policy which he regarded as essentially non-partisan. Attlee vetoed the proposal. (PREM 8/616.)

76 K. and I. Morgan, *Portrait of a Progressive*, 1980, p. 239.
77 Attlee, 'What Sort of Man Gets to the Top?'
78 Morgan, op. cit.
79 Donoughue and Jones, op. cit., pp. 348–61.
80 *Clem Attlee: The Granada Historical Records Interview*, 1967, p. 55.
81 Donoughue and Jones, op. cit., p. 391.
82 Williams, op. cit., p. 227.
83 Attlee, *As It Happened*, pp. 197–8.
84 *Clem Attlee, Interview*, p. 43.
85 Attlee, Draft Autobiography.
86 Foot, op. cit., pp. 25–7.
87 A good example occurred in October 1945 when the Cabinet discussed memoranda by Morrison and Bevan on the proposed Health Service. Morrison argued that Bevan's proposals would dangerously weaken the fabric of local government, as the Government were already committed to take gas, electricity and transport functions from local authorities. Attlee said the differences between Bevan and Morrison were probably less fundamental than they appeared. On either alternative the major part of the expenditure would fall on the Exchequer, and the regional and district committees proposed by Bevan would in all probability consist of the same persons as would be members of the joint committees under Morrison's scheme. Whichever course was adopted there would inevitably be controversy. The predominant feeling in Cabinet seemed to Attlee to favour Bevan's solution. (CAB 128/1, 43 conclusions, 18 October 1945.) All Attlee's qualities as chairman are evident here; his succinct summing-up, the reconciliation of differences and a decision indicating the line of action.
88 Foot, op. cit., pp. 237–8.
89 The incident took place on the day before the Government's Social Security Act was to come into operation. While Attlee on 4 July 1948 made a non-polemical broadcast paying tribute to all political parties for their co-operation in the passage of the Act, Bevan made a speech in Manchester asserting that so far as he was concerned the Tories were 'lower than vermin'. The resulting furore was not limited to the Tory press; over a year later Attlee was still receiving letters from old Labour stalwarts urging that Bevan be muzzled as he lost thousands of pendulum votes. Attlee agreed. (Attlee Papers, University College. Lord Calverley to Attlee, 11 November 1949.)
90 *Clem Attlee, Interview*, p. 46; H. Wilson, *A Prime Minister on Prime Ministers*, 1977, p. 298.
91 H. Morrison, *Government and Party*, 1954, p. 123. In addition, the practice of encouraging smaller groups of Labour MPs to specialize in particular subjects was continued. (Ibid., p. 130.) This worked out well, except in the case of foreign policy. (See Dalton, *High Tide and After*, p. 23.)
92 Dalton, Diaries, 30 July 1947.
93 *LPCR, 1946*, p. 125. Attlee had no cause in subsequent speeches to the conference to modify significantly his general satisfaction with the PLP.
94 S. H. Beer, *Modern British Politics*, 2nd edn, 1969, p. 179.
95 For example, after his intervention in the 1945 election campaign, Harold Laski was bluntly informed that a period of silence on his part would be welcome. (Martin, *Laski*, p. 173.) Konni Zilliacus, who in 1946 sent Attlee a long memorandum on foreign policy, was thanked for the document which

seemed to Attlee 'to be based on an astonishing lack of understanding of the facts'. (Attlee Papers, University College. Attlee to Konni Zilliacus, 17 February 1946.)

96 Attlee: reported in *The Times*, 15 January 1957.

97 L. Minkin, *The Labour Party Conference*, 1978, p. 23.

98 Ibid., p. 22.

99 C. R. Attlee *The Labour Party in Perspective*, 1937, p. 109.

100 H. Morrison, *Herbert Morrison: An Autobiography*, 1960, p. 249; Bevan, 'Clem Attlee'.

101 Bevan, ibid.

102 CAB 128/10, 3 June 1947.

103 *LPCR, 1948*, p. 214.

104 Williams, *A Prime Minister Remembers*, pp. 90–1.

105 PREM 8/673. Knowledge of the plan was limited to senior Whitehall officials.

106 P. Hennessy, 'Hard lessons learnt during blizzards and transport strike' in *The Times*, 6 January 1978.

107 CAB 128/9. CM (47) 36 conclusions, 14 April 1947; 37 conclusions, 17 April 1947.

108 PREM 8/455.

109 CAB 128/1. 23 conclusions, 16 August 1945.

110 P. Hennessy and K. Jeffery, 'How Attlee stood up to strikers' in *The Times*, 21 November 1979.

111 Quoted in P. Hennessy, 'Waterfront Troubles Plagued Attlee from 1945' in *The Times*, 3 January 1980.

112 The Act had forbidden civil service unions from affiliating to the TUC, had placed restrictions on picketing and intimidation, and prohibited closed shops in local or public authorities as well as General Strikes or sympathetic strikes which were not purely industrial. It had also stipulated that individual union members had to 'contract in' to the union's political levy which had a direct and adverse effect upon Labour Party finances. As a result of the repeal of the Act, affiliated membership of the Labour Party rose from 2.5 million in 1945 to about 5 million in 1950. In the same period, individual membership rose from 487,000 to 900,000. (Eatwell, op. cit., pp. 134–5.)

113 TUC, *Annual Congress Report, 1949*, p. 212.

114 H. Pelling, *A History of British Trade Unionism*, 1963, p. 231.

115 Attlee, *The Labour Party in Perspective*, p. 66.

116 CAB 128/5, 24 conclusions, 14 March 1946; 33 conclusions, 11 April 1946.

117 G. A. Dorfman, *Wage Politics in Britain 1945–1967: Government Vs the TUC*, Iowa, 1973, p. 48. The TUC also recommended that the trade union movement had to be free to function without State interference and be left to represent its members as it saw fit, especially in determining wages, hours and conditions of work. (Ibid.)

118 CAB 128/5, op. cit.

119 Ibid., 42 conclusions, 6 May 1946.

120 Dorfman, op. cit., p. 57.

121 R. M. Martin, *TUC: The Growth of a Pressure Group 1868–1976*, 1980, p. 297.

122 CAB 128/10, 62 conclusions, 17 July 1947.

123 Dorfman, op. cit., pp. 58–62.

124 Ibid., pp. 62–6.

125 Ibid., p. 65. The eventual bargain also included strong price controls and a

limitation on profits and dividends. But the pound had, anyway, to be devalued in September 1949.

126 Attlee, *The Labour Party in Perspective*, p. 74.

127 The number fell to four in 1950, though the proportion of trade-union sponsored MPs had increased. Some trade union ministers proved incompetent and many unions didn't send their best men to Parliament. (Eatwell, op. cit., p. 132.)

128 CAB 129/16. CP (47) 46. 30 January 1947.

129 The visit was to Arthur Deakin, the leader of Bevin's former union (the Transport and General Workers). Deakin had taken a prominent part in resisting Communist pressure in the unions.

130 The order was withdrawn in August 1951.

131 Pelling, op. cit., p. 225; Martin, op. cit., pp. 297–8. The significance of the Order was symbolic or psychological: in its 2½ years' existence only 29 individuals were directed to take new jobs, and only 688 were required to remain in agriculture or coal-mining. (A. Havighurst, *Twentieth Century Britain*, 1962, p. 402.)

132 Pelling, op. cit., p. 231. The figures were: 1946 – 2.1 millions; 1947 – 2.4; 1948 – 1.9; 1949 – 1.8; 1950 – 1.3; 1951 – 1.6.

133 CAB 128/10, 71 conclusions, 17 August 1947; 74 conclusions, 25 August 1947.

134 Hennessy and Jeffery, op. cit.

135 Pelling, op. cit., p. 226.

136 Attlee Papers, Churchill College, 1/5/4.

137 A. Gamble, *The Conservative Nation*, 1974, p. 38.

138 Havighurst, op. cit., pp. 379–80.

139 J. D. Hoffman, *The Conservative Party in Opposition, 1945–1951*, 1964, p. 235.

140 One of them, Harold Macmillan, even wanted to re-name the Conservative Party in 1946. (D. Carlton, *Anthony Eden: A Biography*, 1981, p. 268.)

141 Havighurst, op. cit., p. 381.

142 In the pamphlet, *The Right Road for Britain* (ibid., p. 424).

143 Butler and Freeman, op. cit., pp. 159–60.

144 Hoffman, op. cit., p. 230.

145 416 *H. C. Deb.*, cols 2552–65, 6 December 1945.

146 *The Times*, 7 December 1945.

147 *Manchester Guardian*, 1 July 1947.

148 Attlee Papers, Churchill College, 1/5/4.

149 In the electoral campaign of 1951, Attlee would have bigger meetings than he had ever had, amounting in some cases to 30,000 or more. (Williams, *Nothing So Strange*, p. 285.)

150 *News Chronicle*, 30 May 1950.

151 J. Hall, *Labour's First Year*, 1947, p. 165.

152 P. Gregg, *The Welfare State*, 1967, p. 44.

153 430 *H. C. Deb.*, col. 44, 12 November 1946.

154 Hunt, op. cit., pp. 40–1.

155 D. Jay, 'The Quiet Master at No. 10' in *The Times*, 26 April 1980.

156 Williams, *The Triple Challenge*, p. 48.

157 Ibid.

158 434 *H. C. Deb.*, cols 1333–4, 12 March 1947.

159 See Chapter XI.

160 434 *H. C. Deb.*, cols 1429–38, 12 March 1947.

161 *The Times*, 13 March 1947.

162 Hoffman, op. cit., p. 241.
But the private relationship between Attlee and Churchill, which was one of great mutual respect and courtesy, was quite unaffected by the parliamentary duels. Churchill thought nothing of writing in his own hand to Attlee on 5 May 1948, for example, telling the Prime Minister how much he admired Attlee's May Day speech. (Attlee Papers, University College.)
163 J. Margach, *The Abuse of Power*, 1978, p. 86.
164 Eatwell, op. cit., p. 127.
165 Ibid., pp. 126–7.
166 He was correct. The British Embassy in Washington reported that the 1945 election result had aroused more interest in the US than any previous British or other foreign election. (H. G. Nicholas, ed., *Washington Despatches, 1941–1945*, University of Chicago Press, 1981, pp. 595–6.)
167 F. Williams, *Nothing So Strange*, p. 215.
168 Ibid., p. 226. In fact, Attlee in December 1945 had expressly warned his ministers to be careful in their dealings with the press: 'such activities should be kept to a minimum', he had advised. (CAB 129/5. CP (45) 306. 4 December 1945.) Dalton had clearly ignored this advice.
169 Williams, op. cit., pp. 218–19.
170 Margach, op. cit., p. 91.
171 Ibid., p. 87.

XI Revolution Without Tears

1 Earl Attlee, 'Is Peaceful Change Possible?' in *The Emerging World: Jawaharlal Nehru Memorial Volume*, 1964, p. 28.
2 Dalton, Diaries, 27 October 1951.
3 C. R. Attlee, *As It Happened*, 1954, p. 166.
4 Ibid., p. 233.
5 See e.g. P. Gregg, *The Welfare State*, 1967, p. 4; W. N. Medlicott, *Contemporary England, 1914–1964*, 1974, p. 479.
6 C. R. Attlee, *The Labour Party in Perspective*, 1937, p. 31.
7 P. Addison, *The Road to 1945: British Politics and the Second World War*, 1975, p. 273.
8 Ibid., p. 272.
9 H. Hopkins, *The New Look: A Social History of the Forties and Fifties in Britain*, 1963, pp. 479–80.
In fact, Attlee had written in 1937 that the aim of socialism was to give greater freedom to the individual. British Socialists had never made an idol of the State. Progress was not towards, but away from the herd. (*Labour Party in Perspective*, p. 139.) In 1949 he rebuked those who still thought that the communists were the left wing of the socialist movement: 'They are not. The socialist movement was always a movement for freedom. (Quoted in *The Labour Party*, eds C. Cook and I. Taylor, 1980, p. 172.)
10 J. Frankel, *British Foreign Policy, 1945–1973*, 1975, p. 181.
11 Hopkins, op. cit., p. 479.
12 Attlee, *As It Happened*, p. 229.
13 Attlee, *The Labour Party in Perspective*, p. 153.
14 H. Pelling, *A History of British Trade Unionism*, 1963, p. 223.
Attlee sought to modify this arrangement in February 1948. (See CAB 129/24, CP (48) 53, 17 February 1948. Note by PM on 'Political Activities of Members of the Public Boards'.)

15 'By 1951 the central and regional boards of all nationalized industries contained 44 members possessing 'some previous connection with the Trade Union Movement' – but that was out of a total of about 350 members, most of whom were former directors and senior executives of the original companies.' (R. R. Martin, *TUC: The Growth of a Pressure Group*, 1980, p. 290.)
16 F. Williams, *A Prime Minister Remembers*, 1961, p. 93.
17 Attlee, *As It Happened*, p. 163.
18 *The Times*, 2 January 1951.
19 C. A. R. Crosland, *The Future of Socialism*, 1956, p. 59.
20 That is, after 1947.
21 A. Havighurst, *Twentieth Century Britain*, 1962, p. 420.
22 Quoted in *The Diaries of Sir Alexander Cadogan*, 1938–1945, ed. D. Dilks, 1971, p. 335.
23 P. Kennedy, *The Realities Behind Diplomacy: Background Influences on British External Policy, 1865–1980*, 1981, p. 316.
24 Quoted in T. Lloyd, *Empire to Welfare State: English History, 1906–1976*, 1979, p. 271.
25 Gregg, op. cit., pp. 39–40; Havighurst, op. cit., pp. 382–3; F. Williams, *Fifty Years March: The Rise of the Labour Party*, 1951, pp. 360–1. During the war something like one-third of British overseas investments were sold and a good deal of the rest were in enemy hands, damaged and producing no income. Material destruction in the UK was valued at approximately £1,500 million, shipping and cargo losses at £700 million. Internal disinvestment, through failure to replace plant and machinery, totalled some £900 million. The Government liquidated £152 million of the gold and dollar reserves and sold foreign assets valued at £4,200 million. (Quoted in F. S. Northedge, *British Foreign Policy*, 1962, p. 33n.)
26 Kennedy, op. cit., p. 318.
27 Quoted in R. Jenkins, *Mr Attlee: An Interim Biography*, 1948, p. 256.
28 Quoted in Gregg, op. cit., p. 45.
29 Lloyd, loc. cit.
30 Frankel, op. cit., p. 183.
31 L. Minkin, 'Radicalism and Reconstruction: The British Experience' in *Europa*, tome 5, no. 2, 1982, p. 208.
32 Lloyd, op. cit., p. 298.
33 Kennedy, op. cit., p. 320.
34 Harold Macmillan considered it to be 'one of the most able governments of modern times'. (H. Macmillan, *Tides of Fortune: 1945–1955*, 1969, p. 49.)
35 After 1948 the Cabinet Minutes become much less specific.
36 CAB 129/1, CP (45) 112, 14 August 1945.
37 In fact the Cabinet was forced in October 1945 to deplete UK stocks of wheat in order to send 112,500 tons to Germany and Austria. A similar decision had to be taken in December. (CAB 128/1, 47 conclusions, 30 October, 45 and 61 conclusions, 10 December 1945.)
38 CAB 128/1, CP (45) 112, 23 conclusions, 16 August 1945.
39 See e.g. CAB 128/1, 39 conclusions, 9 October 1945; ibid., 57 conclusions, 29 November 1945.
40 CAB 129/3, CP (45) 223, 12 October 1945.
41 CAB 129/2, CP (45) 186 and 187, 20 and 21 September 1945.
42 CAB 128/1, 36 conclusions, 28 September 1945.
43 H. S. Truman, *Memoirs: Vol I; Year of Decisions*, 1955, pp. 508–9.
44 R. Eatwell, *The 1945–51 Labour Governments*, 1979, p. 71.
45 CAB 128/4, CM (45), 50 conclusions, 6 November 1945.

46 Ibid., 57 conclusions, 29 November 1945.
47 Ibid.
48 Ibid., 58 conclusions, 3 December 1945.
49 Ibid., 59 conclusions, 5 December 1945.
50 Attlee, 1961. Quoted in *The Times*, 4 January 1978.
51 *Clem Attlee: The Granada Historical Records Interview*, 1967, p. 35. There was also a supplementary loan from Canada, also at 2 per cent, of $1.25 billion.
52 Eatwell, op. cit., p. 72.
53 CAB 129/6, CP (46) 32, 30 January 1946.
54 CAB 129/7, CP (46) 53, 8 February 1946 and CP (46) 58, 8 February 1946.
55 CAB 128/5, 22 conclusions, 8 March 1946.
56 Ibid., 27 conclusions, 25 March 1946.
57 Ibid., 17 May 1946.
58 B. Donoughue and G. W. Jones, *Herbert Morrison: Portrait of a Politician*, 1973, p. 383.
59 H. Thomas, *John Strachey*, 1973, p. 234.
60 Bread had a symbolic importance for Bevin whose 'roots were in a time when bread was the staff of life'. During the agonizing discussions on devaluation in September 1949, Bevin's main concern was its effect on food prices, particularly bread. He believed that the British working man would accept an increase in the price provided the extraction rate was raised and a whiter loaf produced. Cripps, then Chancellor, accepted Bevin's concern about the price but didn't believe in white bread: a 'terrible argument' ensued. (P. Hennessy and M. Brown, 'Cripps and the search for a white loaf' in *The Times*, 4 January 1980.)
61 CAB 128/8, 70 conclusions, 21 July 1946: PREM 8/502.
The obvious setback to Morrison is absent from Donoughue and Jones's account and naturally not mentioned in Morrison's *Autobiography*. Eatwell's explanation of the 21 July decision is that it 'owed as much to personality as rationality' (op. cit., p. 73).
62 CAB 128/8, 80 conclusions, minute 2, 9 September 1946; PREM 8/502.
63 PREM 8/502.
64 Clem Attlee, *Interview*, p. 36. There were at least two other interesting if minor examples of Attlee's use of his executive authority in 1946. He insisted, in August, despite the objections of several Cabinet ministers, that 6 Boeing Strato-Cruisers be bought for BOAC at a cost of £12 million: it was essential, in his opinion, that Britain retain a reasonable share of the North Atlantic traffic. In the same month he became annoyed about the question of squatters in Army camps, as he had given clear instructions that redundant camps were not to stand empty: he ordered that squatters who had occupied camps designated as Training Centres for teachers and others should be evicted forthwith. (CAB 128/5, 77 conclusions, 7 August, and 78 conclusions, 14 August 1946.)
65 Havighurst, op. cit., p. 399.
66 The Cabinet agreed in April to reduce the period of National Service from 18 to 12 months, which Montgomery, the CIGS, had said was only feasible if a satisfactory solution to the Palestine situation was found and if there were no military commitments in India. (CAB 128/9, 35 conclusions, 3 April 1947.)
67 Macmillan 'was never conscious at any time from the moment [Attlee] became PM until the day he retired from the leadership of the party that Attlee was not in full command of the situation.' (Macmillan, op. cit., p. 53.)
68 PREM 8/443, 12 February 1947. The main trouble about coal production at

this time was that young men in the coal mining areas increasingly refused to go into the pits. Who could blame them?

69 CAB 128/9, 31 conclusions, 21 March 1947.
70 J. D. Hoffman, *The Conservative Party in Opposition, 1945–1951*, 1964, p. 241.
71 PREM 8/444, 1 March and 18 August 1947.
72 Attlee Papers, University College, Oxford (April 1947).
73 CAB 128/9, 11 conclusions, 22 January 1947.
74 CAB 128/9, 21 conclusions, 13 February 1947.
75 Quoted in Eatwell, op. cit., p. 85.
76 Quoted in Havighurst, op. cit., p. 401.
77 Ibid.
78 Bevan conceded that it was no longer possible to ask the country to make heavy sacrifices to avoid the need for a US loan, though he still insisted that it would have been possible in 1945. (CAB 128/10, 52 conclusions, 5 June 1947.)
79 It was not formally approved by the US Congress until April 1948.
80 PREM 8/495, 17 June 1947.
81 CAB 128/10, CM 67 (47), 1 August 1947.
82 Havighurst, op. cit., p. 402.
83 Hoffman, op. cit., p. 245.
84 Attlee, *As It Happened*, p. 165.
85 Donoughue and Jones, op. cit., p. 400.
86 Addison, op. cit., p. 273.
87 H. Dalton, *High Tide and After*, 1962, p. 136.
88 G. Hodgson, 'The Steel Debates' in *The Age of Austerity, 1945–51*, 1964, eds, M. Sisson and P. French, p. 312.
89 For example, Donoughue and Jones, op. cit.
90 Dalton, op. cit., p. 135n.
91 Quoted in Havighurst, op. cit., p. 412.
92 Attlee, *As It Happened*, p. 164.
93 Donoughue and Jones, op. cit., p. 401.
94 CAB 128/9, 30 conclusions, 20 March 1947.
95 Ibid., 37 conclusions, 17 April 1947.
96 CAB 128/10, 24 and 28 April 1947.
97 Dalton, Diaries, 8 August 1947.
98 Morrison's autobiographical recriminations against Attlee in this connection are vitiated by his biographers, who point out that Attlee's suggestion was subsequently approved by the Cabinet. (See H. Morrison, *Autobiography*, 1960, pp. 296; Donoughue and Jones, op. cit., p. 402.)
99 CAB 129/20, CP (47) 212, 21 July 1947.
100 CAB 128/10, CM 64 (47), 24 July 1947.
101 Ibid., 31 July 1947.
102 Quoted in K. and I. Morgan, *Portrait of a Progressive*, 1980, p. 261.
103 CAB 128/10, CM 70 (47), 7 August 1947. See also Donoughue and Jones, op. cit., pp. 402–3.
104 Ostensibly, Bevan agreed because of the decision taken at the same meeting to introduce the Parliament Bill; but the Cabinet was also informed that almost all the parliamentary time for 1947–48 was already occupied. (CAB 128/10, CM (70), 47, 80 conclusions, 14 October 1947.) Bevan had already had his own experience of compromising with Labour 'principles' and Conference decisions: it was he who had urged the Cabinet in June 1947 that it would be inexpedient to introduce equal pay then; nor could the tied

cottage system be immediately abolished. (CAB 128/9, 51 conclusions, 3 June 1947.)

105 See Donoughue and Jones, op. cit., pp. 412–25, for a good, detailed account.

106 Dalton, Diaries, 26 July 1947.

107 Donoughue and Jones, op. cit., p. 421.

108 C. R. Attlee, 'Local Government and the Socialist Plan' in Forum Series no. 7, Socialist League, 1933.

109 Attlee, Draft Autobiography, 'The Constitution'.

110 Attlee, 'The Office of Prime Minister', op. cit.

111 S. H. Beer, 'The Future of British Politics: An American View' in *The Political Quarterly*, vol. XXVI, no. 1, 1955 (January–March), p. 43.

112 Attlee, 'The Role of the Monarchy' in the *Observer*, 13 August 1958.

113 J. W. Wheeler-Bennett, *King George VI: His Life and Reign*, 1958, pp. 685–7. Attlee argued that cancellation of the tour would only serve to magnify the domestic difficulties, especially in foreign eyes.

114 The signatories to the Declaration were the UK, Canada, Australia, New Zealand, S. Africa, India, Pakistan and Ceylon. The document has been described 'as important as any in the history of the development of the British Empire'. (Ibid., p. 730.)

115 The change was made in December 1946. (Ibid., p. 756.)
Attlee's love of traditional ceremony also extended to the Lord Mayor of London's annual banquet. He indicated to the Cabinet in October 1947 that he wanted this held, despite the Government's ban on public banquets of more than 100 persons. He got his way, though 300 people were to be invited. (CAB 128/10, 78 conclusions, 2 October 1947.)

116 Attlee, 'The Role of the Monarchy'.

117 Ibid.

118 K. Middlemas and J. Barnes, *Baldwin: A Biography*, 1969, pp. 988, 999 and 1003.

119 R. R. James, ed., *Memoirs of a Conservative: J. C. C. Davidson's Memoirs and Papers*, 1969, p. 416.

120 Attlee, Draft Autobiography, '1937'.

121 M. Foot, *Aneurin Bevan: A Biography*, vol. II, 1973, p. 349n.
Attlee heard the news of the King's death at a PLP meeting: R. H. S. Crossman described him as 'looking as though he had had a stroke'. Crossman reckoned that Attlee was moved more by the death of the King than anything in the previous four years. (J. Morgan, ed., *The Backbench Diaries of Richard Crossman*, 1981, pp. 70, 72.)

122 R. Lacey, *Majesty: Elizabeth II and the House of Windsor*, 1977, p. 119.

123 'At the outset, the Prime Minister's audiences were marked by long silences', though this did not last. (Wheeler-Bennett, op. cit., p. 651.)

124 CAB 128/0, 95 conclusions, 15 December 1947. Many Labour MPs voted against the increase.

125 Attlee, 'The Role of the Monarchy'.

126 PREM 8/492, the King to C. R. Attlee, 26 August 1947.

127 Ibid., C. R. Attlee to the King, 28 August 1947.

128 Attlee, 'The Role of the Monarchy'.

129 Ibid.; see also Wheeler-Bennett, op. cit., p. 792.

130 Attlee, *The Labour Party in Perspective*, pp. 171–3.

131 *LPCR, 1942*, p. 56.

132 Morgan, op. cit., p. 236.

133 Ibid.

134 CAB 128/5, CM 60 (46), 20 June 1946.
135 Attlee, *As It Happened*, p. 167.
136 Morgan, op. cit., p. 261.
137 CAB 128/12, CM 48, 1 conclusion, 6 January 1948.
138 Ibid., 29 January 1948.
139 CAB 128/21, 11 March 1948. It was agreed, for instance, that the Second Chamber should be complementary to and not a rival of the Commons, that there should be no permanent majority for any one political party, that hereditary peers should not *ipso facto* have the right to attend and vote, that Life Peers should be created, including women, etc. (H. Morrison, *Government and Parliament*, 1954, p. 188.)
140 Ibid. and CAB 128/28 (48), 15 April 1948.
In 1953 Attlee would reject an offer by Churchill to continue informal party talks, on the grounds that the difference of opinion between Labour and Conservative parties about the House of Lords' constitutional role was too great. (Morrison, op. cit., p. 191.)
141 The same ideal, he believed, predominated among MPs, though here he granted that there were many exceptions. Earl Attlee, 'The Attitudes of MPs and Active Peers' in *The Political Quarterly*, 1959, vol. 30, pp. 31–2. By the time this article was published the Life Peerages Act of 1958 had been passed.
142 Morrison, op. cit., p. 194.

XII Not as Simple as That

1 *LPCR, 1945*, pp. 80, 107.
2 413 *H. C. Deb.*, col. 661, 22 August 1945.
3 *The Times*, 11 October 1945.
4 PREM 8, 515, 19 February 1946.
5 *LPCR, 1945*, p. 107.
6 Ibid., p. 118.
7 Ibid., p. 108.
8 CAB 66/63, 146, 7 March 1945.
9 *LPCR, 1945*, p. 118.
10 The line of the Western Neisse included the 9,700 sq. km. of Upper Silesia (pre-war population about 1½ million) as well as the 26,000 sq. km. of Lower Silesia (pre-war population about 3½ million). Silesia also produced coal. It may be noted that the Russians handed over this territory to the Poles on 25 April 1945.
11 H. Feis, *Between War and Peace*, 1960, pp. 259–67.
12 See Sir Llewellyn Woodward, *British Foreign Policy in the Second World War*, 1962, pp. 561–3, for much of this paragraph.
13 The final compromise at Potsdam was 15 per cent on the exchange basis and 10 per cent on the free transfer, from the Western zones (ibid., pp. 1485–6).
14 However, it is noteworthy that in conversation with the US Secretary of State, Byrnes, on 29 July 1945, Molotov mentioned two billion dollars as a reparations figure from the Ruhr. (United States, *Foreign Relations of the US: Diplomatic Papers: The Conference of Berlin 1945*, vol. II, 1960, p. 473.) Byrnes wasn't interested, but it makes a striking contrast with the 10 billion dollars mentioned at Yalta (even though that figure was to be applied to the whole of Germany) – considering that the Russians only got something like one-third of the poorest part of Germany, to be shared with the Poles for reparations purposes.

15 This last stipulation was at Bevin's insistence: it was not to apply to the equipment and products specifically allocated to the USSR from the Western zones.
16 CAB 128/1, 7 August 1945.
17 CAB 129/2, CP (45) 160, 10 September 1945.
18 CAB 128/1, 13 September 1945.
19 *The Times*, 13 September 1945.
20 CAB 128/1, CM (45), 45.
21 From 11 September to 2 October 1945.
22 For full text see F. Williams, *A Prime Minister Remembers*, 1961, pp. 151–3.
23 C. R. Attlee, *As It Happened*, 1954, p. 146. Years later, Truman told Acheson that the sudden ending of Lend-lease had been 'a grave mistake'. The Americans, Acheson writes, took two years to understand the seriousness of the European situation. (Dean Acheson, *Present At The Creation*, 1969, p. 122.)
24 J. Byrnes, *Speaking Frankly*, 1947, p. 97.
25 B. von Oppen, ed., *Documents on Germany under Occupation, 1945–54*, 1955, pp. 66–8. The first sign of the French preventing any attempt to establish central German agencies appeared in the Finance Directorate of the Control Commission on 21 September 1945. (Roy Willis, *The French in Germany 1945–49*, 1962, p. 27.)
26 'The new German authorities appointed by the British lacked experience, prestige and, above all, resources...' The British Control Commission 'grew in a matter of weeks from almost nothing to the government of 23 million people ...' (M. Balfour and J. Mair, *Four Power Control in Germany and Austria*, 1956, pp. 69, 99.)
27 Hynd was a 'soft-liner' on Germany. During the debate which followed Attlee's foreign policy speech at the 1945 annual conference, Hynd alleged (without mentioning Attlee's name) that there had been a good deal of talk about the collective responsibility of the German people for the concentration camps, etc. If that could be said of the Nazi regime, he asked, then what was the British responsibility for what had happened in India? (*LPCR 1945*, p. 113). He was appointed Chancellor of the Duchy of Lancaster in August 1945 and made responsible for the day-to-day administration of the British zones of occupation in Germany and Austria in October 1945, though ultimate parliamentary responsibility was retained by the Secretary of State for War. Hynd did not have a seat in the Cabinet and in Whitehall he had to hold a balance between the War Office, Foreign Office and Treasury: inevitably, his organization became known as the Hynd quarters. The reasons for his abrupt and ignominious dismissal by Attlee in April 1947 have remained unclear.
28 *New Statesman*, 22 September 1945.
29 Ibid., 6 October 1945.
30 414 *H. C. Deb.*, cols 2377–86, 26 October 1945.
31 CAB 128/5, 22 conclusions, 8 March 1946.
32 *Manchester Guardian*, 22 March 1946.
33 CAB 128/5, 17 April 1946.
34 CAB 128/7, 43 conclusions, minute 1, 7 May 1946.
35 Ibid. Though Attlee certainly agreed with Bevin's earlier definition of British interests in the future of Germany and the Ruhr as being: (1) Security from a revival of German aggression; (2) Reasonable economic well-being in Germany and Europe; (3) Reduction of British cost of occupation and feeding of Germany; (4) A democratic and Western-minded Germany; (5) Restriction

of predominating Soviet influence to as far East as possible; (6) Recovery of France. (CAB 129/9, CP (46) 156, 11 March 1946.)

36 CAB 128/4, 56 conclusions, 6 June 1946.
37 Lucius D. Clay, *Decision in Germany*, 1950, pp. 136–7.
38 CAB 128/4, 68 conclusions, 15 July 1946.
39 Ibid.
40 D. Carlton, *Anthony Eden: A Biography*, 1981, p. 266.
41 423 *H. C. Deb.*, cols 2036–8, 5 June 1946.
42 CAB 128/4, 89 conclusions, 21 October 1946.
43 Ibid., 102 conclusions, 2 December 1946.
44 PREM 8/524 contains the telegrams mentioned in this paragraph. The first two were marked by Attlee for distribution to the King only.
45 Attlee's antipathy to Crossman was notorious. In 1965 he described Crossman as belonging to the lunatic fringe. (*Clem Attlee: The Granada Historical Records Interview*, 1967, p. 39.)
46 430 *H. C. Deb.*, cols 544–5.
47 The Conservative candidate lost his deposit. *The Times*, 20 November 1946.
48 Ibid. *Tribune* put the figure at 82. Attlee was particularly concerned with the fact that about half-a-dozen Parliamentary Private Secretaries had signed the amendment. (CAB 128/8, CM (46), 97 conclusions, 18 November 1946.)
49 430 H. C. Deb., cols 577–90.
50 Duff Cooper, *Old Men Forget*, 1953, p. 371.
51 CAB 128/9, CM (16) 47, 4 February 1947.
52 432 *H. C. Deb.*, cols 1826–38, 27 February 1947.
53 CAB 128/9, CM (25) 47. Ironically, while the American administration's economic fusion proposals were undergoing the usual tortuous process of ratification and final formulation, it was the British who had to carry the dollar costs of supplies to *both* zones! Dalton, an increasingly desperate Chancellor, would complain to his diary in May that 'we are still wasting our substance and dollars on those bloody Germans!' (Dalton, Diaries, 2 May 1947.)
54 Labour Party, *Cards On The Table: an Interpretation of Labour's Foreign Policy*, 1947.
55 For example, *Tribune*, 9 May 1947; *New Statesman*, 17 May 1947.
56 437 *H. C. Deb.*, cols 1718–37, 15 May 1947.
57 *LPCR, 1947*, p. 119.
58 PREM 8/514: Bevin to Attlee, 19 March 1947; Attlee to Bevin, 23 March 1947.
59 CAB 128/9, CM (43) 47.
60 For instance, *Tribune*, 13 June 1947; *New Statesman*, 14 June 1947.
61 Attlee Papers, University College, Oxford.
62 PREM 8/495, CP (47) 209, 22 July 47, and CAB 128/9, CM (47) 63 conclusions, 23 July 1947.
63 441 *H. C. Deb.*, cols 1091–4, 4 August 1947.
64 *The Times*, 22 October 1947.
65 Leonard Woolf, *Foreign Policy: The Labour Party's Dilemma; with a critical comment by W. N. Ewer*, November 1947.
66 CAB 128/10, 95 conclusions, 15 December 1947.
67 445 *H. C. Deb.*, cols 1874–82, 18 December 1947.
68 CAB 129/23, CP (48) 5, 5 January 1948.
69 CAB 128/13.
70 *The Times*, 5 January 1948.
71 Ibid., 3 May 1948; 11 April 1949; 13 September 1950; 27 January 1951.
72 Williams, op. cit., p. 172.

XIII The Bomb Became Essential

1 Margaret Gowing, *Independence and Deterrence; Britain and Atomic Energy, 1945–1952*, vol. I, *Policy Making*, 1974, p. 27.
2 Margaret Gowing, 'Britain, America and the Bomb' in David Dilks, ed., *Retreat From Power; Studies in Britain's Foreign Policy of the Twentieth Century*, vol. II, *After 1939*, 1981, p. 121. The following chapter is – as, indeed, any study of the history of the British atomic energy project must be – greatly indebted to the work of Professor Gowing and her assistant Lorna Arnold.
3 Alfred Goldberg, 'The Atomic Origins of the British Nuclear Deterrent' in *International Affairs*, vol. 40, July 1964, no. 3, p. 426.
4 Gowing, *Independence and Deterrence*, vol. I, p. 19. Gowing added that 'the machinery for governing the atom became more, rather than less irrational' under Churchill in 1951 (Ibid., p. 429). The Atomic Energy Authority was set up in 1954.
5 Ibid., p. 5.
6 Goldberg, op. cit., p. 417.
7 PREM 8/113. Attlee to Churchill, 28 September 1945; Churchill to Attlee, 6 October 1945.
8 In response to a question about progress in the development of the most modern type of weapons, the Minister of Defence (Alexander) stated that all types, including atomic weapons, were being developed. The announcement caused little stir in the Commons or elsewhere. (Goldberg, op. cit., p. 420.)
The same policy was applied to information about the continuation of biological warfare research in peacetime, which the Defence Committee approved in October 1945. This project also came under the Ministry of Supply, and the Medical Research Council refused to have anything to do with it. When the Defence Committee learned in November 1945 that the Americans were about to make a public statement on the subject, it decided that a British statement, subject to Attlee's approval, was necessary. The British announcement on 14 November 1945, referring to the wartime work, said that the research had accumulated much knowledge concerning fundamental problems in biology, including new techniques applicable to the study of preventive medicines and of value to agriculture. It was the Government's intention to make the results of fundamental studies available to scientific workers generally. (PREM 8/140.)
9 For example, CAB 128/2, CM 58(45), Minute 2, 3 December 1945: CAB 129/3, CP (45) 249, 26 October 1945: CAB 129/4, CP (45) 282, 9 November 1945: CAB 129/9, CP (45) 168, 29 April 1946.
10 M. Gowing, *Independence and Deterrence, Britain and Atomic Energy, 1945–1952*, vol. II, *Policy Execution*, 1974, p. 116.
11 Ibid., p. 117.
12 Gowing, *Independence and Deterrence*, I, p. 279.
13 Ibid., p. 182n. Morgan has noted that Dalton and Cripps who, in 1946, had protested fiercely, on financial grounds, against developing a British nuclear weapons programme, were significantly excluded from this meeting. (Kenneth O. Morgan, *Labour in Power, 1945–51*, 1984, p. 282.)
14 Ibid., p. 184.
15 Ibid., pp. 186–7.
16 Ibid., pp. 184–6.
17 F. Williams, *A Prime Minister Remembers*, 1961, pp. 118–19.
18 *Clem Attlee: The Granada Historical Records Interview*, 1967, p. 34.

19 Gowing, *Independence and Deterrence*, I, p. 233.
20 Gowing adds two points in support of this conclusion: (1) that the Labour Government feared a situation where the use, or threat of using, atomic weapons might be essential for the country's defence, but where the Americans would refuse to help; and (2) the 'clear belief that by demonstrating her capacity to make her own fissile material and bomb, Britain would impress the US and enhance her own special status as an ally.' (Gowing, *Independence and Deterrence*, II, pp. 499–500.)
21 Gowing, 'Britain, America and the Bomb', p. 120.
22 Gowing, *Independence and Deterrence*, I, p. 2.
23 Williams, op. cit., p. 113.
24 Gowing, 'Britain, America and the Bomb', p. 126.
25 Gowing, *Independence and Deterrence*, I, pp. 6–7.
26 *Clem Attlee, Interview*, pp. 31–2.
27 Ibid.
28 Full text in Gowing, *Independence and Deterrence*, I, pp. 14–18.
29 Williams, op. cit., pp. 95–6.
30 Ibid., p. 96 and see Goldberg, op. cit., p. 411.
31 Gowing, *Independence and Deterrence*, I, pp. 64–5.
32 Full text in ibid., pp. 78–81.
33 Goldberg, op. cit., p. 411.
34 Gowing, *Independence and Deterrence*, I, p. 66.
35 Ibid.
36 CAB 129/4, CP (45) 272, 5 November 1945.
37 Gowing, *Independence and Deterrence*, I, pp. 67–9.
38 Ibid., p. 65.
39 CAB 128/4, CM (45) 51 conclusions, Minute 4, 8 November 1945.
40 Gowing, *Independence and Deterrence*, I, p. 72.
41 Ibid., p. 73.
42 Ibid., p. 69.
43 CAB 128/4, loc. cit.
44 Full text in Gowing, *Independence and Deterrence*, I, pp. 82–4.
45 Ibid., p. 76.
46 Williams, op. cit., p. 109.
47 Goldberg, op. cit., p. 413.
48 Goldberg, op. cit., p. 414.
49 Gowing, 'Britain, America and the Bomb', p. 132.
50 Full text in Williams, op. cit., pp. 112–17.
51 Ibid., p. 119.
52 Gowing. *Independence and Deterrence*, I, p. 115.
53 Ibid., p. 241.
54 Ibid., p. 265.
55 Ibid., p. 228.
56 Ibid., p. 241.
57 Attlee to Truman, 6 July 1950 (Williams, op. cit., pp. 230–1).
58 H. S. Truman, *Memoirs*, vol. II, *Years of Trial and Hope*, 1956, p. 396.
59 Williams, op. cit., p. 235.
60 Truman, op. cit., pp. 396–413.
61 Dean Acheson, *Present At The Creation*, 1969, p. 481.
62 Gowing, *Independence and Deterrence*, I, p. 313.
63 Quoted by Gowing, ibid., pp. 314–15.
64 Truman, op. cit.
65 Gowing, *Independence and Deterrence*, I, p. 315. In October 1951, the

Americans, at the official level, did agree that the use of bases and facilities in Britain in an emergency 'naturally remains a matter for joint decision in the light of the circumstances at the time'; but they would 'admit no curb on their right to drop atomic bombs from other bases in non-NATO wars ... even though this might call forth the same retribution on Britain for harbouring U.S. Air Force bases'. (Gowing, ibid., pp. 317, 318 and 412.)

66 Ibid., I, pp. 209–10.
67 Ibid.
68 Ibid., p. 163.
69 Ibid., pp. 209–10. Only one month after Britain exploded her atomic bomb in 1952 the Americans exploded their first thermo-nuclear device, followed in 1953 by the Russians.
70 Ibid., p. 172. Complete text, pp. 194–206.
71 Ibid., pp. 183–4.
72 Ibid., p. 228. Tizzard wanted increased conventional forces and reliance on American atomic weapons. The British should continue with research and development on long-range aircraft and atomic weapons, but should not produce any. (Ibid., pp. 229–30.)
73 British public opinion, measured in 1952, strongly approved of Britain's atomic bomb: in percentage terms: – 60 for, 22 against, 18 don't knows. (Gowing, *Independence and Deterrence*, II, p. 489.)
74 Gowing, *Independence and Deterrence*, I, p. 438.
75 Truman, op. cit., p. 397.

XIV The Irresponsible Americans

1 *Clem Attlee: The Granada Historical Records Interview*, 1967, p. 40.
2 Ibid.
3 A. Koestler, *Promise and Fulfilment: Palestine 1917–1949*, 1949, p. 8.
4 Nicholas Bethell, *The Palestine Triangle: The Struggle between the British, the Jews and the Arabs, 1935–48*, 1979, p. 24.
5 *LPCR, 1937*, p. 95.
6 326 *H. C. Deb.*, col. 2362, 21 July 1937.
7 *LPCR, 1937*, pp. 218–19.
8 347 *H. C. Deb.*, col. 1954, 22 May 1939.
9 Bethell, op. cit., p. 82.
10 CAB 118/74, undated.
11 357 *H. C. Deb.*, cols 2057–8, 28 February 1940.
12 Bethell, op. cit., p. 89.
13 Ibid.
14 CAB 66/38, WP (43) 266, 23 June 1943.
15 CAB 65/39, WM (43), 92 conclusions, Minute 2, 2 July 1943.
16 Bethell, op. cit., p. 150.
17 *LPCR, 1943*, pp. 190–1.
18 Quoted in Bernard Wasserstein, *Britain and the Jews of Europe, 1939–45*, 1979, p. 33.
19 Dalton, who drafted the statement, was rather less inclined as Chancellor to favour overseas expenditures!
20 *LPCR, 1944*, p. 9
21 B. Donoughue and G. W. Jones, *Herbert Morrison: Portrait of a Politician*, 1973, p. 435.
22 Bethell, op. cit., p. 151.

23 Ibid., p. 166.
24 Ibid., p. 167.
25 Ibid., pp. 177–8.
26 460 *H. C. Deb.*, cols 1051–60, 26 January 1949.
27 Bethell, op. cit., pp. 183–6, 197–9, 201.
28 F. Williams, *A Prime Minister Remembers*, 1961, pp. 183–4.
29 Ibid., p. 176.
30 CAB 134/594, 25 August 1945.
31 CAB 129/1, CP (45) 144, 1 September 1945. Memo by Attlee.
32 CAB 128/1, 27 conclusions, 3 September 1945.
33 CAB 129/91, CP (45) 174, 17 September 1945.
34 CAB 128/1, CM 30 (45), 5.
In regard to Tripolitania Bevin thought that if Italian trusteeship claims were pressed, the British should not oppose them.
35 CAB 128/3, CM (45), 32 conclusions, 15 September 1945.
36 PREM 8/89. But 'the message does not seem to have been conveyed to the PM personally until September 10 by James Byrnes.' R. Ovendale, 'The Palestine Policy of the British Labour Government 1945–1946' in *International Affairs*, July 1979, p. 414.
37 CAB 129, CP (45) 156, 8 September 1945.
38 CAB 128/3, CM (45), 30 conclusions, Minute 7, 11 September 1945.
39 PREM 8/89, Attlee to Truman, 14 September 1945.
40 Ibid., Attlee to Truman, 16 September 1945.
41 Ovendale, op. cit.
42 PREM 8/89, Truman to Attlee, 17 September 1945.
43 See e.g. *The Times*, 25 September 1945.
44 PREM 8/89, Attlee to Truman, 1 October 1945.
45 CAB 128/1, 38 conclusions, 4 October 1945.
46 CAB 128/1, CM 40 (45), 11 October 1945.
47 Ovendale, op. cit., p. 415.
48 Williams, op. cit., p. 193.
49 CAB 128/5, CM 1 (46), 1 January 1946.
50 Ibid., 7 conclusions, 22 January 1946.
51 CAB 128/7, CP (46) 58, 8 February 1946.
52 Williams, op. cit., p. 177.
53 PREM 8/515, 19 February 1946. The file contains Attlee's original notes and the final memorandum; both have been used in this summary.
54 Attlee put these views, in part, to Dalton. See Dalton, Diaries, 18 February 1946.
55 Ovendale, op. cit., p. 419.
56 Bethell, op. cit., p. 234.
57 Ovendale, op. cit.
58 CAB 128/5, CM (46), 37 conclusions, 24 April 1946. (Attlee made the decision public in the Commons on 6 May: the Opposition insisted on a division.)
59 CAB 128/7, CP (46), 58, 8 February 1946.
60 CAB 128/9, CP (46), 173, 27 April 1946.
61 CAB 128/5, 38 conclusions, 29 April 1946.
62 CAB 128/5, 39 conclusions, 1 May 1946.
63 *The Times*, 2 May 1946. Churchill said that the Opposition would not press for a debate.
64 Ovendale, op. cit., p. 420.
65 Williams, op. cit., pp. 194–5.
66 CAB 128/5, 50 conclusions, 20 May 1946.

67 Williams, op. cit., p. 196.

68 Bethell, op. cit., p. 243.

69 *LPCR, 1946*, pp. 107, 153–4, 165–6, 169, 161. Crossman had had an interview with Attlee on 6 May 1946. In a follow-up letter to Attlee on the next day, Crossman alleged that Attlee had said that he and his colleagues on the Commission had let the Government down badly: the Report, Attlee had said, was 'grossly unfair to Great Britain'. Crossman protested that no indication had been given to the British members 'that you desired us to push responsibility on to the Americans'. (PREM 8/302, Crossman to Attlee, 7 May 1946.) But that was not the understanding of the British co-chairman of the Commission, who had seen Anglo-American partnership as the most important of the mission's aims. (Ovendale, op. cit., p. 416.)

70 Text of telegram in Williams, op. cit., pp. 197–8. The text was shown to Opposition leaders, and Churchill agreed that yielding to terrorism would be a disaster. At the same time he wrote to Attlee that several of his friends were far from abandoning partition and he was very much inclined to think this might be the sole solution. (Churchill to Attlee, 2 July 1946, Attlee Papers, University College, Oxford.)

71 CAB 128/6, 67 conclusions, 11 July 1946. Bevin's views were given to the Cabinet by Sir Norman Brook whom Attlee had sent to Paris to get Bevin's opinion.

72 CAB 128/6, 72 conclusions, 23 July 1946.

73 Ibid., 74 conclusions, 29 July; 75 conclusions, 30 July; 76 conclusions, 1 August; 77 conclusions, 7 August. Attlee subsequently had to agree that the camp guards could use force, if necessary, to restrain the refugees in the camps: at the same time he was ordering that squatters in former Army camps in England should be evicted forthwith! While Jewish refugees were trying to fight their way out of camps in Cyprus, some of the British were trying to force their way into camps in Britain! (CAB 128/6, 78 conclusions, 14 August 1946.)

74 Ovendale, op. cit., p. 426. Truman gave as his reason the strength of the American opposition to the plan. Attlee gained some personal experience of American opinion five days later when he received La Guardia, then Director-General of UNRRA, who wanted him to admit Polish Jews to the British Zone of Germany (of all places!). La Guardia obviously saw this move as a preliminary to settlement in Palestine. Attlee curtly replied that to believe it was impossible for Polish Jews to remain in Poland would be to adopt the Nazi view that there was no place for them in Central and Eastern Europe. The British Zone was already over-full with genuine refugees and the housing and food situation there was critical. (PREM 8/384.)

75 F. Williams, *Nothing So Strange: An Autobiography*, 1970, pp. 249–50.

76 Williams, *A Prime Minister Remembers*, pp. 199–200.

77 Ovendale, op. cit., p. 428.

78 CAB 128/6, 96 conclusions, 14 November 1946.

79 Ovendale, op. cit., p. 429.

80 CAB 128/6, 101 conclusions, 28 November 1946.

81 CAB 128/11, 6 conclusions, Minute 3 & 4, 15 January 1947.

82 Ibid., 11 conclusions, Minute 2, 22 January 1947.

83 R. Ovendale, 'The Palestinian Policy of the British Labour Government 1947: The Decision to Withdraw' in *International Affairs*, January 1980, p. 82.

84 CAB 129/16: *Palestine*, Joint Memorandum by the Secretaries of State for Foreign Affairs and the Colonies, 6 February 1947.

85 CAB 128/9, 7 February 1947.

86 CAB 129/16, CP (47), 59, 13 February 1947.

87 Ovendale, 'The Decision to Withdraw,' p. 86.
88 433 *H. C. Deb.*, col. 1901, 25 February 1947.
89 Bethell, op. cit., p. 310.
90 CAB 128/16, CM 76 (47), 20 September 1947.
91 CAB 129/11, CP (46) 267, 11 July 1946.
92 *Clem Attlee, Interview*, p. 39. He was probably thinking of Arab as well as Jewish immigration into Palestine.
93 PREM 8/627. Bevin's telegram to Ambassador in Washington, 12 October 1947.

XV Possibly India

1 *News Chronicle*, 20 April 1959.
2 D. Marquand, *Ramsay MacDonald*, 1977, p. 118.
3 C. R. Attlee, *The Labour Party in Perspective*, 1937, pp. 245–6.
4 160 *H. C. Deb.*, col. 779, 20 February 1923. The answer was 1112.
5 166 *H. C. Deb.*, cols 2085–6, 17 July 1923.
6 C. R. Attlee, Draft Autobiography, 'India' and 'India and Burma'.
7 W. Golant, Thesis, p. 174.
8 Attlee, Draft Autobiography, loc. cit.
9 Partha Sarathi Gupta, *Imperialism and the British Labour Movement, 1914–1964*, 1971, p. 117.
10 C. R. Attlee, *As It Happened*, 1954, p. 94.
11 Durga Das, *India from Curzon to Nehru and After*, 1970, p. 131.
12 Attlee to Tom Attlee, 25 November 1928, (quoted in Golant, op. cit., p. 190).
13 Ibid., pp. 194–5.
14 Ibid., pp. 190–9. Attlee's letters to Tom, quoted by Golant, reveal the seriousness of Attlee's approach to his duties on the Commission.
15 Ibid., p. 108.
16 R. Jenkins, *Mr Attlee: An Interim Biography*, 1948, p. 121.
17 Attlee, *As It Happened*, p. 96.
18 See Golant, op. cit., p. 210; Jenkins, op. cit., p. 121–2.
19 Attlee, *As It Happened*, pp. 96–7.
20 Golant, op. cit., p. 254.
21 Gupta, op. cit., p. 210 and 210n.
22 Ibid., p. 209. MacDonald had already, after the 1929 election, passed over Attlee and Hartshorn in forming the Government.
23 Jenkins, op. cit., p. 123.
24 Attlee to Tom Attlee, 27 June 1930 (quoted in Golant, op. cit., p. 211).
25 Marquand, op. cit., p. 582.
26 Das, op. cit., p. 152.
27 R. J. Moore, *The Crisis of Indian Unity, 1917–1940*, 1974, p. 315.
28 Marquand, op. cit., p. 582.
29 Golant, op. cit., p. 199.
30 Moore, op. cit., p. 316.
31 260 *H. C. Deb.*, col. 416, 25 November 1931.
32 260 *H. C. Deb.*, cols 1120–28, 2 December 1931.
33 Ibid., cols 1191–6, 3 December 1931.
34 Moore, op. cit., p. 250.
35 Quoted in Gupta, op. cit., p. 152–3.
36 Ibid., p. 161.

37 Attlee, Draft Autobiography, op. cit.
38 262 *H. C. Deb.*, cols 840–3, 29 February 1932.
39 274 *H. C. Deb.*, cols 1772–3, 16 February 1933.
40 276 *H. C. Deb.*, cols 718–31, 27 March 1933.
41 Moore, op. cit., p. 297.
42 Quoted in Gupta, op. cit., p. 256.
43 296 *H. C. Deb.*, cols 61–72, 10 December 1934.
44 Quoted in Das, op. cit., p. 168.
45 T. Waller Wallbank, *A Short History of India and Pakistan*, 1958, p. 176.
46 Attlee, *The Labour Party in Perspective*, p. 246: Wallbank, op. cit., p. 177.
47 Gupta, op. cit., p. 257.
48 Attlee, op. cit., p. 245.
49 Gupta, op. cit., p. 258.
50 Ibid., p. 259. See also R. J. Moore, *Churchill, Cripps and India, 1939–1945*, 1979, p. 4.
51 Gupta, loc. cit.
52 Wallbank, op. cit., pp. 178, 181.
53 Moore, *Churchill, Cripps and India*, p. 5; J. Nehru, *The Discovery of India*, 1959, pp. 344–7.
54 Moore, op. cit., p. 7.
55 Ibid., p. 22.
56 *Clem Attlee: The Granada Historical Records Interview*, 1967, p. 23.
57 Moore, op. cit., p. 30.
58 Gupta, op. cit., p. 267.
59 Moore, op. cit., p. 31.
60 Ibid., p. 33.
61 Ibid., p. 34.
62 Ibid., p. 36.
63 Gupta, op. cit., pp. 268–9.
64 Moore, op. cit., pp. 41–2.
65 Ibid., p. 47.
66 Quoted in ibid., p. 53. (Attlee to Amery, 24 January 1942.)
67 Quoted in ibid., pp. 55–6.
68 Ibid., p. 57.
69 Quoted by Eric Stokes, 'Cripps in India' in *The Historical Journal*, vol. 14, 1971, p. 427.
70 Moore, op. cit., pp. 61– 2.
71 Ibid., p. 75.
72 Stokes, op. cit., p. 432; Gupta, op. cit., pp. 270–1.
73 Stokes, op. cit., p. 430.
74 F. Williams, *A Prime Minister Remembers*, 1961, p. 206; C. R. Attlee, *Empire into Commonwealth*, 1961, p. 37. Nehru vehemently disagreed. (Nehru, op. cit., p. 372.)
75 Williams, op. cit., p. 205.
76 Moore, op. cit., p. 139.
77 Ibid., p. 142.
78 Ibid.; Gupta, op. cit., p. 272.
79 Quoted in W. Roger Louis, *Imperialism At Bay*, 1978, p. 193.
80 Ibid., p. 195.
81 Ibid., pp. 212, 250.
82 Moore, op. cit., pp. 142–3.
83 Wallbank, op. cit., pp. 208, 214–15, 219.
84 CAB 129, XMO6287, CP (45) 110, 13 August 1945. He also presided over

the Committee on Atomic Energy and, later, the Economic Policy Committee, and some *ad hoc* committees such as one on Fuel.

85 CAB 134, IB (45), 1st meeting, 17 August 1945.

86 Ibid., 2, 3, 4 Meetings, 29 August, 4 and 6 September 1945.

87 Wallbank, op. cit., p. 220.

88 Oddly enough, Stalin also indicated his dislike of separation and expressed the hope that India would remain in the British Commonwealth (CAB 128/7, CM (46) 1st conclusion, 1 January 1946.)

89 See Gupta, op. cit., p. 294–6. The decision to send the Cabinet Mission was taken on 24 January 1946, three weeks before the naval mutiny. The partition of the sub-continent was not in British strategic interests.

90 CAB 128/7, CM (46) 59 conclusions, Minute 3, 17 June 1946.

91 Ibid., 55 conclusions, 5 June 1946.

92 CAB 134, IB (46), 10 and 13 Meetings, 19 and 20 December 1946.

93 Attlee seems first to have contacted Lord Louis Mountbatten on 18 December 1946. (Hugh Tinker, 'Preparing to Withdraw' in *Times Literary Supplement*, 26 September 1980.) But Mountbatten thought they first met on 20 December (PREM 8/563, Mountbatten to Attlee, 17 February 1947). Attlee consulted R. A. Butler regarding Mountbatten; Butler approved. (R. A. Butler, *The Art of the Possible*, 1972, p. 104.)

94 CAB 128/8, CM (46) 108 conclusions, 31 December 1946. Bevin's argument was: Britain claimed it impossible to withdraw from Egypt before 1949. How to reconcile this claim with withdrawal from India by the spring of 1948? More generally he maintained that withdrawal without solution would weaken British influence in the world – as would premature withdrawal from Germany, Italy, Greece or the Middle East.

95 Williams, op. cit., pp. 208–9.

96 CAB 128/11, 4 conclusions, Minute 1, 8 January 1947.

97 Williams, loc. cit. Attlee had also consulted Mountbatten about Burma in 1946.

98 PREM 8/557, Mountbatten to Attlee, 11 February 1947.

99 CAB 128/11, 21 conclusions, Minute 4, 13 February 1947.

100 PREM 8/563, Mountbatten to Attlee, 17 February 1947.

101 The India and Burma Committee had in fact come to no decision but had left it to the full Cabinet – precisely because Attlee had said it was for Cabinet to decide (CAB 134/343, IB (47), 10 Meeting, 17 February 1947). Attlee's leadership in the matter is thus beyond dispute.

102 CAB 128/11, CM (47), 23 conclusions, Minute 1, 18 February 1947.

103 There was still no mention of Mountbatten. It is not clear when Attlee informed his colleagues of his choice for this crucial post – but he had consulted a Conservative representative. (See note 93.)

104 PREM 8/557, Attlee to Mountbatten, 18 March 1947.

105 Burma became independent on 4 January 1948.

106 For example, Roger Eatwell, *The 1945–1951 Labour Governments*, 1979, p. 92.

107 For example, Das, op. cit., p. 255.

108 Attlee to Salisbury, 21 December 1946. Attlee Papers, University College, Oxford, Box 7.

109 CAB 128/10, CM 50 (47), 23 May 1947.

110 See e.g. C. R. Attlee 'What Sort of Man Gets to the Top?' in the *Observer*, 7 February 1960: '. . . the Lords knew that Halifax knew India, and they knew that he would tell them the truth'. Also Attlee, *As It Happened*, p. 184.

111 CAB 128/10, loc. cit.

112 Ibid.
113 CAB 128/13.
114 CAB 128/31, CP (48) 307, C. R. Attlee, 'Commonwealth Nomenclature', 30 December 1948.
115 A. Havighurst, *Twentieth Century Britain*, 1952, p. 395.

XVI The Maximum We Can Do

1 F. Williams, *Fifty Years March: The Rise of the Labour Party*, 1950, p. 5.
2 *LPCR, 1950*, p. 98.
3 Quoted in Philip Williams, *Hugh Gaitskell*, 1979, p. 229.
4 C. J. Bartlett, *The Long Retreat: A Short History of British Defence Policy, 1945–70*, 1972, p. 25.
5 Ibid., p. 52.
6 Or so the NEC was informed by its Policy and Publicity Sub-Committee. (R. Eatwell, *The 1945–51 Labour Governments*, 1979, p. 121.)
7 Ibid., p. 122.
8 *LPCR, 1949*, p. 137.
9 B. Donoughue and G. W. Jones, *Herbert Morrison: Portrait of a Politician*, 1973, pp. 441–3.
10 *LPCR*, 1949, pp. 153–4.
11 Ibid., pp. 170–2.
12 Ibid., p. 197.
13 Philip Williams, op. cit., p. 195.
14 Eatwell, op. cit., p. 102.
15 Ibid.
16 Philip Williams, op. cit., p. 199.
17 Dalton, Diaries, 15 June 1949.
18 C. Cook and I. Taylor, eds, *The Labour Party*, 1980, p. 132.
19 See M. Foot, *Aneurin Bevan: A Biography*, vol. II, 1973, p. 276; Philip Williams, op. cit., p. 204; Donoughue and Jones, op. cit., p. 447.
20 This paragraph is taken largely from Philip Williams, op. cit., pp. 204–6; Donoughue and Jones, op. cit., pp. 448–9.
21 Philip Williams, op. cit., p. 199.
22 Ibid., p. 206.
23 F. Williams, *A Prime Minister Remembers*, 1961, p. 228.
24 C. R. Attlee, *As It Happened*, 1954, p. 194.
25 Philip Williams, op. cit., pp. 208–9. Labour had fifty of the sixty seats with the largest majorities. The introduction of the postal vote also probably helped the Conservatives. (See Eatwell, op. cit., p. 129.)
26 Attlee, *As It Happened*, p. 195; Philip Williams, op. cit., p. 208.
27 *Daily Herald*, 16 February 1950.
28 *The Times*, 16 February 1950.
29 *Evening Star*, 15 February 1950.
30 Attlee, *As It Happened*, p. 196.
31 Bernard Crick, 'The Future of the Labour Government' in *Political Quarterly*, vol. 38, no. 4, October-December 1967, p. 385.
32 Cook and Taylor, op. cit., p. 98.
33 Philip Williams, op. cit., p. 208.
34 *LPCR, 1950*, p. 98.
35 David Butler and Jennie Freeman, *British Political Facts*, 3rd edn, 1969, p. 108. Although, from 1931 to 1951, manual workers declined as a percen-

tage of the work-force from 70.3 to 64.2, while white-collar workers rose from 23.0 to 30.9, Labour more than doubled its membership. It was only after 1953 that individual membership began to decline. (S. H. Beer, *Modern British Politics*, 1969, pp. 414, 416).

36 *LPCR, 1950*, p. 98.
37 Attlee, *As It Happened*, p. 196.
38 See Eatwell, op. cit., p. 133 and Philip Williams, op. cit., p. 209.
39 Donoughue and Jones, op. cit., p. 461.
40 Butler and Freeman, op. cit., p. 160.
41 Philip Williams, op. cit., p. 216.
42 V. Bogdanor and R. Skidelsky, eds, *Age of Affluence, 1951–1964*, 1970, p. 122.
43 Eatwell, op. cit., pp. 141, 142.
44 *LPCR, 1950*, p. 77.
45 Donoughue and Jones, op. cit., p. 455.
46 Ibid., pp. 459–60.
47 See Foot, *Bevan*, vol. II, p. 289 and Donoughue and Jones, op. cit., p. 457.
48 *LPCR, 1950*, pp. 130–2.
49 Philip Williams, op. cit., p. 226.
50 *LPCR, 1950*, p. 99.
51 Ibid., p. 27.
52 Philip Williams, op. cit., p. 213.
53 Foot, op. cit., p. 294.
54 Philip Williams, op. cit., p. 214.
55 Foot, loc. cit.; Philip Williams, op. cit., p. 212.
56 *News Chronicle*, 20 April 1959. Frank Barber, 'Interview with Attlee'.
57 Janet Morgan, ed., *The Backbench Diaries of Richard Crossman*, 1981, p. 397.
58 Attlee on Gaitskell, in W. T. Rodgers, ed., *Hugh Gaitskell 1906–1963*, 1964, p. 150; F. Williams, *A Prime Minister Remembers*, p. 245.
59 Philip Williams, op. cit., pp. 236–7.
60 Bevan headed the poll for membership of the NEC (constituency section) in 1950.
61 In his letter to Attlee, Bevan expressed his 'consternation and astonishment' at Gaitskell's appointment, which Bevan considered '. . . a great mistake'. Quoted in Foot, op. cit., p. 300.
62 Ibid., p. 302.
63 Foot describes them as 'a major achievement of his premiership'. (Ibid., p. 309.)
64 Philip Williams, op. cit., p. 246.
65 Ibid., p. 248.
66 Ibid., pp. 229–30.
67 483 *H. C. Deb.*, col. 583, 29 January 1951. (My emphasis.) Attlee had also told Bevan in private discussions 'that the rate by which we achieved the defence programme was bound to be conditioned by availability of raw materials and machine tools and the level of prices, it wasn't one of those issues where you were left with no flexibility.' (F. Williams, op. cit., p. 246.)
68 *Clem Attlee: The Granada Historical Records Interview*, 1967, p. 47.
69 Donoughue and Jones, op. cit., pp. 485 and 489.
70 Philip Williams, op. cit., p. 249.
71 Ibid., p. 250.
72 See especially Philip Williams, Donoughue and Jones, and Foot, op. cit., passim.

73 Quoted in Foot, op. cit., p. 337. Bevan referred to £13 million; the savings to the Exchequer in a full year from the optical and dental charges were reckoned by Gaitskell to be £23 million; the sick, the needy and children were to be exempt from the charges. (Philip Williams, op. cit., p. 263.)
74 *Clem Attlee, Interview*, p. 47.
75 Philip Williams, op. cit., p. 263. Bevan was then more concerned with reductions in provision for housing which came under his jurisdiction as Minister of Health. (Foot, op. cit., pp. 276–7.)
76 Quoted in Foot, op. cit., p. 330.
77 Ibid., p. 334.
78 Eatwell, op. cit., p. 145. Only Bevan and Wilson were opposed.
79 Philip Williams, op. cit., p. 256.
80 Foot, op. cit., pp. 333–4.
81 *Clem Attlee, Interview*, p. 46.
82 Philip Williams, op. cit., p. 268. In Attlee's view, 'there was no real difference of principle between Nye [Bevan] and the rest of the Cabinet and I was sorry it was allowed to develop into one.' (F. Williams, op. cit., p. 246.)
83 Attlee, *As It Happened*, p. 206.
84 Ibid.
85 Donoughue and Jones, op. cit., pp. 501–2.
86 J. W. Wheeler-Bennett, *King George VI: His Life and Reign*, 1958, pp. 788–93. On 21 September, the King's Private Secretary wrote a Personal and Secret letter to Attlee (to avoid any misinterpretation of events by future historians) confirming that the King had had no conception that his physical condition might make it necessary for him to abandon the tour. (Ibid., p. 793.)
87 Attlee, *As It Happened*, p. 206.
88 Foot, op. cit., p. 344.
89 Morgan, op. cit., p. 26.
90 Foot, op. cit., p. 346.
91 Morgan, op. cit., p. 26.
92 *Clem Attlee, Interview*, p. 56.
93 *News Chronicle*, 24 September 1951. Attlee's own position in the country had also declined, from 57 per cent who preferred him as PM in May 1950, to 44 per cent in September 1951; it still out-ran that of his Government. (Ibid.)
94 *LPCR, 1951*, pp. 122, 114–15, 120, 86.
95 *Clem Attlee, Interview*, p. 49.
96 Donoughue and Jones, op. cit., p. 467. The obvious replacement for Bevin (and perhaps Attlee himself later on) would have been Sam Watson of the Durham miners' union. Watson was 'a personal friend of Bevan as well as Gaitskell, keen on adult education, a man of broad interests and great intellectual ability.' He was on the NEC and chaired the International Sub-Committee. But 'he was no power-seeker and repeatedly refused to move from Durham to London.' (Philip Williams, op. cit., p. 336.)
97 *Clem Attlee, Interview*, loc. cit.; F. Williams, op. cit., p. 243.
98 Donoughue and Jones, op. cit., p. 468.
99 Philip Williams, op. cit., p. 271.
100 F. Williams, op. cit., pp. 254–5.
101 Philip Williams, op. cit., pp. 271–2.
102 Attlee would describe Eden's Suez action as 'very odd'. His reaction to the argument that the only thing wrong with Suez was that the British did not go

through with it was: 'Oh well, that's the old Tory line. Force. It's led them up the garden so often.' (*News Chronicle*, 20 April 1959.)

103 As Egypt also proclaimed her sovereignty over the Sudan, the Government was able to register a formal protest, before the election.

104 H. Macmillan, *Tides of Fortune: 1945–1969*, 1969, p. 361.

105 *LPCR, 1951*, pp. 209–11.

106 The first television election broadcast in Great Britain was made on 16 October 1951, by Lord Samuel for the Liberal Party. (*The Times*, 17 October 1951.)

107 *Observer*, 7 October 1951.

108 *The Times*, 22 October 1951.

109 Attlee, *As It Happened*, p. 208.

110 Donoughue and Jones, op. cit., p. 518.

111 Attlee, *As It Happened*, p. 209.

112 Morgan, op. cit., p. 28.

113 Attlee, in the spring of 1952, said: 'I'd go at once if I thought Morrison could hold the party together, but I don't think he can. He is too heavy-handed . . .' (Quoted in Philip Williams, op. cit., p. 300.)

114 Donoughue and Jones, op. cit., p. 518.

115 Philip Williams, op. cit., p. 255.

116 J. Griffiths, *Pages From Memory*, 1969, p. 129. Griffiths denies Morrison's view that Attlee stayed on in order to deprive Morrison of the leadership.

117 'Attlee . . . gave little guidance or direction' (Donoughue and Jones, op. cit., p. 522); Attlee in opposition gave 'no lead at all'. (Philip Williams, op. cit., p. 300.)

118 C. R. Attlee, *The Labour Party in Perspective*, 1937, p. 286.

119 It is significant that Foot has no criticism to make of Attlee's leadership from 1951 to 1954.

120 Philip Williams, op. cit., p. 300n.

121 H. Dalton, *High Tide and After: Memoirs 1945–1960*, 1962, p. 363.

122 Attlee, *The Labour Party in Perspective*, p. 286.

123 Morgan, op. cit., p. 406.

124 Ibid., pp. 27, 30, 47, 63.

125 Attlee would certainly have subscribed to Bevan's celebrated conclusion: 'Democratic Socialism is a child of modern society and so of relativist philosophy. It seeks the truth in any given situation knowing all the time that if this be pushed too far it falls into error. It struggles against the evils that flow from private property, yet realizes that all forms of private property are not necessarily evil. Its chief enemy is vacillation, for it must achieve passion in action in the pursuit of qualified judgments. It must know how to enjoy the struggle, while recognizing that progress is not the elimination of struggle but rather a change in its terms.' (A. Bevan, *In Place of Fear*, 1961, edn, p. 202.)

126 Morgan, op. cit., p. 98.

127 Rodgers, op. cit., 1964, p. 151.

128 See D. Carlton, *Anthony Eden: A Biography*, 1981, pp. 299–367.

129 Philip Williams, op. cit., p. 299.

130 The only exception was James Griffiths. Morrison and Dalton were among the former NEC members who lost their seats, Hugh Gaitskell among those candidates not elected.

131 *LPCR, 1952*, pp. 152–3.

132 *The Times*, 11 October 1952.

133 Morgan, op. cit., p. 157.

134 Ibid., pp. 163–8; Philip Williams, op. cit., p. 307.

135 Foot, op. cit., p. 381.
136 Morgan, op. cit., pp. 169, 186.
137 Foot, op. cit., p. 386.
138 Philip Williams, op. cit., p. 315.
139 Morgan, op. cit., p. 225.
140 *LPCR, 1953*, pp. 206–7.
141 The way in which this was arranged caused several union leaders to lose confidence in Morrison, who 'no longer had any institutional base of popular support in the mass party'. Morrison again beat Bevan in the 1953 election for the Deputy Leadership but the falling away in the votes for both men indicated an 'increasing irritation with the endless warfare'. (Donoughue and Jones, op. cit., pp. 524, 529.)
142 Attlee, 'The Best Way To Peace in Europe' in *Daily Herald*, 6 March 1952.
143 See Carlton, op. cit., pp. 330–2, and Foot, op. cit., pp. 400–1.
144 NEC, *Minutes*, 30 April 1952.
145 Attlee, 'Two Matters of Policy: Labour's View,' in *The Listener*, 28 February 1952. Attlee was always sceptical of Churchill's conception of a super-special Anglo-American relationship, which Eisenhower himself considered to be 'completely fatuous'. (Carlton, op. cit., p. 332.)
146 Carlton, ibid., pp. 342–4. (Carlton argues that the most plausible explanation of Eden's contretemps with Dulles in April 1953 was that Eden was trying to help Attlee politically. But it is clear from Carlton's account that Eden shared Attlee's views.)
147 *The Times*, 31 July 1953.
148 *LPCR, 1953*, p. 164.
149 Morgan, op. cit., p. 269.
150 *The Times*, 13 February 1951.
151 *Daily Herald*, 6 March 1952.
152 NEC *Minutes*, 30 April 1952.
153 Philip Williams, op. cit., p. 289.
154 Carlton, op. cit., p. 365.
155 NEC *Minutes*, 24 February 1954, 28 April 1954.
156 Morgan, op. cit., p. 305.
157 See Moran's vivid account, in *Churchill*, 1966, pp. 569–73.
158 Foot, op. cit., p. 431.
159 Quoted in Philip Williams, op. cit., p. 326.
160 NEC, *Minutes*, 18 May 1954, 26 May 1954. The latter resolution was only carried by 12 votes to 11.
161 *LPCR, 1954*, pp. 92–106.
162 NEC, *Minutes*, 29 September 1954.
163 Morgan, op. cit., p. 369n.
164 *New York Times*, 10 September 1954.
165 *Daily Herald*, 31 January 1955.
166 Morgan, op. cit., p. 382.
167 Details of Bevan's final dispute with Attlee and its repercussions are given in Philip Williams, op. cit., pp. 337–47; Foot, op. cit., pp. 455–80; Morgan, op. cit., pp. 385–414. Williams argues that Attlee could have stopped the move to expel Bevan from the beginning, but from Williams' own account it is clear that Attlee indicated his opposition to the move throughout the convoluted proceedings. Attlee was quite aware that it was the Party (and not he) who was on borrowed time, and would have to live with the decision; and that the expulsion of Bevan would have torn Labour asunder at the roots. Given the

passions involved, Attlee's handling of the issue is quite explicable and, of course, was justified by the result.

168 Morgan, op. cit., p. 421.
169 Philip Williams, op. cit., p. 352.
170 Carlton, op. cit., p. 372.
171 Morgan, op. cit., p. 420.
172 See 'Report of Sub-Committee on Party Organization' in *LPCR, 1955*.
173 Compared to Macmillan's post-TV Gallup poll rating of 41 per cent, Attlee only scored 28 per cent. (A. Sampson, *Macmillan: A Study in Ambiguity*, 1968, p. 106.)
174 Morgan, op. cit., p. 421.

XVII Times and Seasons

1 *Torquay Herald and Express*, 8 December 1955.
2 Earl Attlee, *Collective Security Under the United Nations*, 1958, p. 3.
3 *The Times*, 23 October 1950.
4 C. R. Attlee, 'Socialist Faith – The Past and Present' in *Forward*, 5 July 1952.
5 *News Chronicle*, 1 October 1953.
6 *Reynolds News*, 18 December 1955.
7 *Cambridge Daily News*, 13 November 1948.
8 C. R. Attlee, *The Labour Party In Perspective*, 1937, p. 11.
9 Ibid., p. 273.
10 A. Bevan, 'Clem Attlee' in *Tribune*, 16 December 1955.
11 C. R. Attlee, *As It Happened*, 1954, p. 217.
12 Reported in the *Manchester Guardian*, 24 May 1954.
13 *Sunday Express*, 29 January 1956. Attlee subsequently described the House of Lords as being like a glass of champagne that had stood for five days. (*Sunday Times*, 7 December 1958.)
14 A contemporary commentator wrote: 'For a long time Mr Attlee sold the Socialist Party to the middle class far more successfully than Herbert Morrison.' (Colm Brogan in the *Daily Express*, 28 December 1949.)
15 But not musical. In the twentieth century the appreciation of music became an important feature of English sensibility but Attlee missed out on it completely. His wife, however, loved music. Attlee described his literary tastes in a charming essay, 'The Pleasure of Books' in the *National and English Review*, January 1954. His favourite author was Jane Austen.
16 The biographer has cause to be grateful that, to supplement his income, Attlee wrote a number of book reviews and articles later in life. He also made several strenuous lecture tours in North America and recorded some conversations, later published as *A Prime Minister Remembers* and *Clem Attlee: the Granada Historical Records Interview*. In 1959 he was very short of money to pay his expenses. (Attlee to Francis Williams, 8 May 1959. *Francis Williams Papers*, Box 8, Churchill College, Cambridge.) Attlee was concerned to make adequate provision for his wife should he die first, which was the much more likely event. At that time, no pension was paid to an ex-Prime Minister's widow. As it turned out, Mrs Attlee died in 1964, three years before her husband.
17 On receiving the honorary freedom of the City of London in 1953, Attlee referred to his love of ancient things: he liked to keep old institutions and to see them turned to new uses. He also liked some pageantry. 'Take away all colour from our public life,' he remarked, 'and we may find the void filled, as

happened in Germany, with something very evil. We must never let the devil get all the best tunes.' (*Daily Herald*, 21 November 1953.)

18 Attlee, *The Labour Party in Perspective*, p. 22.
19 Ibid., p. 136.
20 Ibid., pp. 66, 74.
21 Ibid., p. 285.
22 *Reynolds News*, 18 December 1955.
23 Earl Attlee, 'Is Peaceful Change Possible?' in *The Emerging World*, 1964.
24 *Daily Herald*, 6 March 1952.
25 *Davies Memorial Lecture*, 9: *Manchester Guardian*, 14 June 1961.

Bibliography of Sources Cited

(Place of publication, unless otherwise noted, is London. Original British and/or hardback publisher appears at the end of a reference where relevant.)

Works by Attlee

BOOKS

The Social Worker, Geo. Bell & Sons, 1920.
The Town Councillor, with W. A. Robson, Labour Publishing Co., 1925.
The Will and the Way to Socialism, Methuen, 1935.
The Labour Party in Perspective, Gollancz, 1937.
The Labour Party in Perspective – And Twelve Years Later, Gollancz, 1949.
As It Happened, Heinemann, 1954.
Collective Security Under the United Nations, David Davies Memorial Institute, 1958.
Empire Into Commonwealth, OUP, 1961.

BOOKS BASED ON INTERVIEWS WITH ATTLEE

F. Williams, *A Prime Minister Remembers*, Heinemann, 1961.
Clem Attlee: The Granada Historical Records Interview, Panther Books, 1967.

PAMPHLETS

Metropolitan Borough Councils: Their Constitution, Power and Duties, Fabian Tract no. 190, March 1920.
Socialism For Trade Unionists, ILP Programme Pamphlet, no. 4. No date, probably late 1922 or 1923.
Economic History with Notes for Lecturers and Class Leaders, ILP Information Committee, ILP Study Course no. 4. No date, probably 1922–3.

Local Government and the Socialist Plan, Forum Series no. 7, Socialist League, 1933.
An International Police Force, The New Commonwealth, series B, no. 3, 1934.
Labour's Method, The Labour Party, 1937.
Labour's Peace Aims, The Labour Party, 5 December 1939.

ARTICLES (in books)

'Air Force', 'Army', 'Conscription', 'Compensation and Confiscation', 'Electricity', 'Local Government', 'London Government' and 'National Defence' in H. Lees-Smith, ed., *The Encyclopaedia of the Labour Movement*, 3 vols, Caxton Publishing Co., 1928.
'Economic Justice Under Democracy' in E. D. Simon, ed., *Constructive Democracy*, Geo. Allen & Unwin, 1938.
'Why I Am A Democrat' in R. Acland, ed., *Why I Am A Democrat*, Lawrence and Wishart, 1939.
'Is Peaceful Change Possible?' in *The Emerging World: Jawaharlal Nehru Memorial Volume*, Asia Publishing House, 1964.
'Hugh Gaitskell' in W. T. Rodgers, ed., *Hugh Gaitskell, 1906–1963*, Thames & Hudson, 1964.
'The Churchill I Knew' in *Churchill By His Contemporaries: An Observer Appreciation*, Hodder and Stoughton, 1965.

ARTICLES (in journals of opinion)

'Labour and the Municipal Elections' in the *New Leader*, 13 and 22 October 1922.
'History: Socialist and Liberal' in the *New Leader*, 12 January 1923.
'Guild v. Municipal Socialism: A reply' in *Socialist Review*, May 1923.
'Post Office Reform' in the *New Statesman and Nation*, 7 November 1931.
'Two Matters of Policy: Labour's View' in the *Listener*, 28 February 1952.
'Socialist Faith in The Past and The Future' in *Forward*, 5 July 1952.
'The Pleasure of Books' in *The National and English Review*, January 1954.
'Civil Servants, Ministers, Parliament and the Public' in *The Political Quarterly*, vol. 25, 1954.
'The Office of Prime Minister' in *Municipal Review*, March 1955.
'The Nation's Defence' in *Socialist Commentary*, June 1956.
'The Attitudes of MPs and Active Peers' in *The Political Quarterly*, vol. 30, 1959.

JOURNALISM

'The Best Way to Peace in Europe', *Daily Herald*, 6 March 1952.
'Labour in this Changing Age', the *Evening Star*, 23 January 1956.
'Ernie Bevin', *Reynolds News*, 12 August 1956.
'The Role of the Monarchy', the *Observer*, 13 August 1958.
'Jumping the Gun', the *Observer*, 1 November 1958.
'What Sort of Man Gets to the Top?' the *Observer*, 7 February 1960.
'Bevan As Hero', the *Observer*, 21 October 1962.

Unpublished Sources

PRIVATE MANUSCRIPTS

A. V. Alexander Papers, Churchill College, Cambridge.
C. R. Attlee Papers and Draft Autobiography, Churchill College, Cambridge.

C. R. Attlee Papers, University College, Oxford (now at the Bodleian Library, Oxford).
Hugh Dalton Diaries and Papers, British Library of Political and Economic Science (LSE).
J. Chuter Ede Diary, British Library, MS. 128.
H. Laski Papers, University College Library, Hull.
H. Nicolson Diaries, Balliol College, Oxford.
F. Williams Papers, Churchill College, Cambridge.

PUBLIC RECORDS

Cabinet Papers; CAB 21, 65, 66, 69, 78, 80, 87, 118, 128, 129 and 134.
Prime Minister's Office; PREM 1, 4 and 8.

LABOUR PARTY RECORDS

NEC Minutes, Memoranda and Papers (including Sub-Committees), 1933–1954.

THESES

M. E. Ceadel, 'Pacifism in Britain, 1931–1939', D. Phil (Oxford) 1976.
W. Golant, 'The Political Development of C. R. Attlee to 1935', B. Litt. (Oxford), MS. d1263.

Published Sources

OFFICIAL DOCUMENTS

Great Britain, *House of Commons, Official Report*, fifth series, 1922–1951, vols 159–483.
Labour Party, *Reports of the Annual Conference*, 1930–1955.
H. G. Nicholas, ed., *Washington Despatches, 1941–1945*, University of Chicago Press, 1981.
B. von Oppen, ed., *Documents on Germany under Occupation, 1945–1954*, OUP, Oxford, 1955.
United States, *Foreign Relations of the US: Diplomatic Papers (1) 1940, Vol. I: (2) The Conference of Berlin in 1945, Vol. II*, Washington, 1959 and 1960.
Trades Union Congress, *Report of the Proceedings of the Annual Conference, 1949*.

PAMPHLETS

The Labour Party, *Cards On The Table: an Interpretation of Labour's Foreign Policy*, 1947.
Leonard Woolf, *Foreign Policy: The Labour Party's Dilemma: with a critical comment by W. N. Ewer*, Fabian Publications Ltd, Fabian Research Series no. 121, November 1947.
The Conservative Party, *The Right Road For Britain*, July 1949.

AUTOBIOGRAPHY, DIARIES AND MEMOIRS

Acheson, Dean, *Present At The Creation: My Years in the State Department*, W. W. Norton, New York, 1969.
Alington, C. A., *Things Ancient and Modern*, Longmans Green & Co., 1936.

Amery, L. S., *My Political Life; Vol. III: The Unforgiving Years*, Hutchinson, 1955.

Barker, Sir Ernest, *Age and Youth*, OUP, Oxford, 1953.

Beveridge, Lord, *Power and Influence: An Autobiography*, Hodder and Stoughton, 1953.

Brown, George, *In My Way*, Penguin, 1972. (Gollancz.)

Butler, R. A., *The Art of the Possible*, Gambit Inc., Boston, 1972.

Byrnes, J., *Speaking Frankly*, Harper Bros., New York, 1947.

Chandos, Lord, *The Memoirs*, The Bodley Head, 1962.

Churchill, W. S., *The Second World War, Vol. II: Their Finest Hour*, Bantam Books, New York, 1962. (Collins.)

—*The Second World War, Vol. III: The Grand Alliance*, Bantam Books, New York, 1962. (Collins.)

—*The Second World War, Vol. VI: Triumph and Tragedy*, Bantam Books, New York, 1962. (Collins.)

Clay, Lucius, *Decision in Germany*, Heinemann, 1950.

Colville, J., *Footprints in Time*, Collins, 1976.

Cooper, Duff, *Old Men Forget*, Rupert Hart-Davis, 1953.

Dalton, Hugh, *Call Back Yesterday: Memoirs 1887–1931*, Frederic Muller, 1953.

—*The Fateful Years: Memoirs 1931–1945*, Frederic Muller, 1957.

—*High Tide and After: Memoirs 1945–1960*, Frederic Muller, 1962.

Davenport, N., *Memoirs of a City Radical*, Weidenfeld and Nicolson, 1974.

Dilks, D., ed., *The Diaries of Sir Alexander Cadogan, 1938–1945*, Cassell, 1971.

Griffiths, J., *Pages From Memory*, J. M. Dent & Sons, 1969.

Hunt, D., *On The Spot: An Ambassador Remembers*, Peter Davies, 1975.

Ismay, Lord, *The Memoirs*, Heinemann, 1960.

James, R. R., ed., *Chips: The Diaries of Sir Henry Channon*, Weidenfeld and Nicolson, 1967.

—*Memoirs of a Conservative: J. C. C. Davidson's Memoirs and Papers*, Weidenfeld and Nicolson, 1969.

Jones, L. E., *An Edwardian Youth*, Macmillan, 1956.

Kelly, Sir David, *The Ruling Few*, Hollis and Carter, 1952.

Lawson, J., *A Man's Life*, Hodder and Stoughton, 1932.

Low, D., *Autobiography*, Michael Joseph, 1956.

McFadyean, Sir Andrew, *Recollected in Tranquillity*, Pall Mall Press, 1964.

Macmillan, H., *Tides of Fortune: 1945–1955*, Harper and Row, New York, 1969. (Macmillan.)

Mallaby, G., *From My Level: Unwritten Minutes*, Hutchinson, 1965.

Morgan, J., ed., *The Backbench Diaries of Richard Crossman*, Holt, Rinehart and Winston, New York, 1981. (Hamish Hamilton and Jonathan Cape.)

Morrison, H., *Herbert Morrison: An Autobiography*, Odhams, 1960.

Nicolson, H., (ed. by N. Nicolson), *Diaries and Letters: Vol. I; 1930–1939*, Collins, 1966.

—*Diaries and Letters: Vol. II; 1939–1945*, Collins, 1967.

Percy, Eustace, *Some Memories*, Eyre and Spottiswoode, 1958.

Postlethwaite, J., *I Look Back*, T. V. Boardman, 1947.

Salter, A., *Memoirs of a Public Servant*, Faber and Faber, 1961.

Shinwell, E., *I've Lived Through It All*, Gollancz, 1973.

Truman, H. S., *Memoirs: Vol. I, Year of Decisions; Vol. II, Years of Trial and Hope*, Doubleday, New York, 1955–6.

Williams, F., *Nothing So Strange: An Autobiography*, Cassell, 1970.

Williams, Lord, *Digging For Britain*, Hutchinson, 1965.

Zuckerman, S., *From Apes to Warlords: The Autobiography, 1904–1946*, Hamish Hamilton, 1978.

BIOGRAPHY

Brockway, F., *Bermondsey Story: The Life of Alfred Salter*, Geo. Allen and Unwin, 1949.
Carlton, D., *Anthony Eden: A Biography*, Allen Lane, 1981.
Cole, M., *The Life of G. D. H. Cole*, Macmillan, 1971.
Dixon, Piers, *Double Diplomat: The Life of Sir Pierson Dixon, Don and Diplomat*, Hutchinson, 1968.
Donoughue, B., and Jones, G. W., *Herbert Morrison: Portrait of a Politician*, Weidenfeld and Nicolson, 1973.
Foot, M., *Aneurin Bevan: A Biography, Vol. I: 1897–1945*, MacGibbon and Kee, 1962.
—*Aneurin Bevan: A Biography, Vol. II: 1945–1960*, (Davis Poynter, 1973).
Gilbert, M., *Winston S. Churchill: The Prophet of Truth, 1922–1939*, Houghton Mifflin, Boston, 1977.
Harris, José, *William Beveridge: a Biography*, OUP, Oxford, 1977.
Hassall, C., *Edward Marsh: Patron of the Arts*, Longmans, Green & Co., 1959.
Jenkins, R., *Mr Attlee: An Interim Biography*, Heinemann, 1948.
Lacey, R., *Majesty: Elizabeth II and the House of Windsor*, Harcourt, Brace, Jovanovich, New York, 1977. (Hutchinson.)
Marquand, D., *Ramsay MacDonald*, Jonathan Cape, 1977.
Martin, K., *Harold Laski: A Biographical Memoir*, The Viking Press, New York, 1953. (Gollancz.)
Marwick, A., *Clifford Allen: the Open Conspirator*, Oliver and Boyd, 1964.
Middlemas, K., and Barnes, J., *Baldwin: A Biography*, Weidenfeld and Nicolson, 1969.
Moran, Lord, *Churchill: Taken from the Diaries of Lord Moran*, Houghton Mifflin, Boston, 1966.
Morgan, K. and I., *Portrait of a Progressive: The Political Career of Christopher, Viscount Addison*, OUP, Oxford, 1980.
Nicolson, H., *King George VI: His Life and Reign*, Constable & Co., 1952.
Sampson, A., *Macmillan: A Study in Ambiguity*, Pelican, 1968.
Taylor, A. J. P., *Beaverbrook*, Hamish Hamilton, 1972.
Terrill, R., *R. H. Tawney and His Times: Socialism as Fellowship*, André Deutsch, 1974.
Thomas, H., *John Strachey*, Eyre/Methuen, 1973.
Wheeler-Bennett, J. W., *King George VI: His Life and Reign*, Macmillan, 1958.
Williams, P. M., *Hugh Gaitskell: A Political Biography*, Jonathan Cape, 1979.

GENERAL AND DESCRIPTIVE WORKS

Addison, P., *The Road to 1945: British Politics and the Second World War*, Jonathan Cape, 1975.
Attlee, T. S., *Man and His Buildings*, Swarthmore Press, 1920.
Balfour, M., and Mair, J., *Four Power Control in Germany and Austria*, OUP, Oxford, 1956.
Barker, E., *Churchill and Eden at War*, St Martin's Press, New York, 1978. (Macmillan.)
Bartlett, C. J., *The Long Retreat: A Short History of British Defence Policy, 1945–1970*, Macmillan, 1972.
Beer, S. H., *Modern British Politics*, Faber and Faber, 1969 edn.

Bethell, N., *The Palestine Triangle: The Struggle between the British, the Jews and the Arabs, 1935–1948*, André Deutsch, 1979.

Bevan, A., *In Place of Fear*, MacGibbon and Kee, 1961 edn.

Bogdanor, V., and Skidelsky, R., eds., *Age of Affluence, 1951–1964*, Macmillan, 1970.

Bosanquet, H., *Social Work in London, 1869–1912*, The Harvester Press, Brighton, 2nd edn, with an Introduction by C. S. Yeo, 1973.

Bruce, M., *The Coming of the Welfare State*, B. T. Batsford, 1961.

Bullock, A., *Hitler: A Study in Tyranny*, Harper Torchbooks, New York, revised edn, 1962. (Penguin.)

Burridge, T., *British Labour and Hitler's War*, André Deutsch, 1976.

Butler, D., and Freeman, J., *British Political Facts*, 3rd edn, Macmillan, 1969.

Butler, J. R. M., *Grand Strategy, Vol. II: September 1939–June 1941*, HMSO, 1957.

Calder, A., *The People's War: Britain 1939–1945*, Panther edn, 1971. (Jonathan Cape, 1969.)

Carr, W., *University of Oxford; College Histories: University College*, F. E. Robinson, 1902.

Cole, G. D. H., *A History of the Labour Party from 1914*, Routledge and Kegan Paul, 1948.

Cole, M., *The Story of Fabian Socialism*, Mercury Books edn, 1961.

Cook, C., and Taylor, I., eds, *The Labour Party*, Longman, 1980.

Cowling, M., *The Impact of Hitler: British Politics and British Policy, 1933–1940*, CUP, Cambridge, 1975.

Crosland, C. A. R., *The Future of Socialism*, Jonathan Cape, 1956.

Crozier, W. P., ed. A. J. P. Taylor, *Off The Record: Political Interviews, 1933–1943*, Hutchinson, 1973.

Dalton, H., *Hitler's War: Before and After*, Penguin, 1940.

Das, Durgo, *India from Curzon to Nehru and After*, The John Day Co., New York, 1970.

Dorfman, G. A., *Wage Politics in Britain, 1945–1967: Government Vs the TUC*, Iowa University Press, Iowa, 1973.

Dowse, R. E., *Left in the Centre: The Independent Labour Party, 1893–1940*, Northwestern University Press, Evanston, 1966.

Eatwell, R., *The 1945–51 Labour Governments*, Batsford Academic, 1979.

Ensor, R. C., *England, 1870–1914*, OUP, Oxford, 1936.

Feis, H., *Between War and Peace*, Princeton University Press, Princeton, 1960.

Frankel, J., *British Foreign Policy, 1945–1973*, OUP, Oxford, 1975.

Fraser, D., *The Evolution of the British Welfare State*, Macmillan, 1973.

Gamble, A., *The Conservative Nation*, Routledge and Kegan Paul, 1974.

Gordon, M. R., *Conflict and Consensus in Labour's Foreign Policy*, Stanford University Press, Stanford, 1969.

Gowing, M., *Independence and Deterrence: Britain and Atomic Energy 1945–1952*; vol. I, *Policy Making*; *vol. II, Policy Execution*, Macmillan, 1974.

Gregg, P., *The Welfare State*, Geo. Harrap, 1967.

Gupta, P. S., *Imperialism and the British Labour Movement, 1914–1964*, Macmillan, 1971.

Hall, J., *Labour's First Year*, Penguin, 1947.

Havighurst, A., *Twentieth Century Britain*, Harper and Row, New York, 2nd edn, 1962. (Hamish Hamilton.)

Hoffman, J. D., *The Conservative Party in Opposition, 1945–1951*, MacGibbon and Kee, 1964.

Hopkins, H., *The New Look: A Social History of the Forties and Fifties in Britain*, Secker and Warburg, 1963.
James, R. R., *The British Revolution: Vol. II; 1914–1939*, Hamish Hamilton, 1977.
Johnson, P., *The Offshore Islanders*, Weidenfeld and Nicolson, 1972.
Kennedy, P., *The Realities Behind Diplomacy: Background Influences on British External Policy, 1865–1980*, Fontana, 1981.
Koestler, A., *Promise and Fulfilment: Palestine, 1917–1949*, The Macmillan Co., New York, 1949.
Lloyd, T., *Empire to Welfare State: English History, 1906–1976*, OUP, 2nd edn, 1979.
Louis, W. R., *Imperialism At Bay: The United States and the Decolonization of the British Empire, 1941–1945*, OUP, New York, 1978. (OUP, Oxford.)
Mack, E. C., *Public Schools and British Opinion since 1860*, Columbia University Press, New York, 1941.
McKibbin, R., *The Evolution of the Labour Party, 1910–1924*, OUP, Oxford, 1974.
Mackintosh, J. P., *The British Cabinet*, Stevens & Sons Ltd., 3rd edn, 1977.
Margach, J., *The Abuse of Power*, W. H. Allen, 1978.
—*The Anatomy of Power*, 1979.
Martin, R. M., *TUC: The Growth of a Pressure Group, 1868–1976*, OUP, Oxford, 1980.
Medlicott, W. N., *Contemporary England, 1914–1964*, Longman, 1974.
Middlemass, R. K., *The Clydesiders: A Left-Wing Struggle for Parliamentary Power*, Hutchinson, 1965.
Minkin, L., *The Labour Party Conference*, Allen Lane, 1978.
Moore, R. J., *The Crisis of Indian Unity, 1917–1940*, OUP, Oxford, 1974.
—*Churchill, Cripps and India, 1939–1945*, OUP, Oxford, 1979.
Morgan, K. O., *Labour in Power, 1945–1951*, OUP, Oxford, 1984.
Morrison, H., *Government and Party*, OUP, Oxford, 1954.
Mowat, C. L., *Britain Between The Wars*, Methuen, 1955.
Naylor, J. F., *Labour's International Policy: The Labour Party in the 1930s*, Weidenfeld and Nicolson, 1969.
Nehru, J., *The Discovery of India*, Anchor Books, New York, 1959.
Northedge, F. S., *British Foreign Policy*, Geo. Allen and Unwin, 1962.
Ogilvie, V., *The English Public School*, B. T. Batsford, 1957.
Pelling, H., *A Short History of the Labour Party*, Macmillan, 1961.
—*A History of British Trade Unionism*, Penguin, 1963.
—*Britain and the Second World War*, Fontana edn, 1970.
Pimlott, B., *Labour and the Left in the 1930s*, CUP, Cambridge, 1977.
Rose, R., *Politics in England*, Faber and Faber, 1965.
Sampson, A., *Anatomy of Britain*, Hodder and Stoughton, 1962.
Sharp, T., *The Wartime Alliance and the Zonal Division of Germany*, OUP, Oxford, 1975.
Stafford, D., *Britain and European Resistance: 1940–1945*, University of Toronto Press, Toronto and Buffalo, 1980.
Stannage, T., *Baldwin Thwarts the Opposition: The British General Election of 1935*, Croom Helm, 1980.
Stansky, P., ed., *The Left and War: The British Labour Party and World War I*, OUP, New York, 1969.
Taylor, A. J. P., *English History: 1914–1945*, OUP, Oxford, 1965.
Thompson, P., *Socialists, Liberals and Labour: The Struggle for London, 1885–1914*, Routledge and Kegan Paul, 1967.

Wallbank, T. W., *A Short History of India and Pakistan*, Scott, Foresman & Co., A Mentor Book, New York, 1958.

Wasserstein, B., *Britain and the Jews of Europe, 1939–45*, OUP, Oxford, 1979.

Williams, F., *The Triple Challenge*, Heinemann, 1948.

—*Fifty Years March: The Rise of the Labour Party*, Odhams, 1951.

Willis, R., *The French in Germany 1945–1949*, Stanford University Press, California, 1962.

Wilson, H., *The Labour Government, 1964–1970*, Weidenfeld and Nicolson, 1971.

—*A Prime Minister on Prime Ministers*, Weidenfeld and Nicolson, and Michael Joseph, 1977.

Winter, J. M., *Socialism and the Challenge of War: Ideas and Politics in Britain, 1912–1918*, Routledge and Kegan Paul, 1971.

Woodward, Sir E. L., *British Foreign Policy During The Second World War*, HMSO, 1962.

—*British Foreign Policy During the Second World War, Vol. II*, HMSO, 1971.

Young, K., *Churchill and Beaverbrook: A Study in Friendship and Politics*, Eyre and Spottiswoode, 1966.

ARTICLES

Beer, S., 'The Future of British Politics: An American View' in *The Political Quarterly*, vol. XXVI, no. 1, 1955.

Bevan, A., 'Clem Attlee' in *Tribune*, 16 December 1955.

Brookshire, J. H., 'Clement Attlee and Cabinet Reform, 1930–1945' in *The Historical Journal*, vol. 24, no. 1, 1981.

Burridge, T., 'A Postscript to Potsdam: The Churchill-Laski Electoral Clash, June 1945' in *Journal of Contemporary History*, vol. 12, 1977.

– 'Great Britain and the Dismemberment of Germany at the end of the Second World War' in *The International History Review*, vol. III, no. 4, 1981.

Crick, B., 'The Future of the Labour Government' in *The Political Quarterly*, vol. XXXVIII, no. 4, 1967.

Dowse, R. E., 'Clement Attlee' in Mackintosh, I. P., ed., *British Prime Ministers in the Twentieth Century*, vol. 2, Weidenfeld and Nicolson, 1978.

Eatwell, R. and Wright, A., 'Labour and the Lessons of 1931' in *History*, vol. 53, no. 207, 1978.

Golant, W., 'The Early Political Thought of C. R. Attlee' in *The Political Quarterly*, vol. XXXX, no. 3, 1969.

– 'The Emergence of C. R. Attlee as Leader of the Parliamentary Labour Party' in *The Historical Journal*, vol. XIII, no. 2, 1970.

– 'Clem and Ernie' in *The Times*, 29 November 1980.

Goldberg, A., 'The Atomic Origins of the British Nuclear Deterrent' in *International Affairs*, vol. 40, July 1964.

Gowing, M., 'Britain, America and the Bomb' in David Dilks, ed., *Retreat From Power; Studies in Britain's Foreign Policy of the Twentieth Century: Vol. II; After 1939*, Macmillan, 1981.

Hennessy, P., 'Hard lessons learnt during blizzards and transport strike', in *The Times*, 6 January 1978.

– 'Waterfront Troubles Plagued Attlee from 1945' in *The Times*, 3 January 1980.

Hennessy, P., and Brown, M., 'Cripps and the Search for a white loaf' in *The Times*, 4 January 1980.

Hennessy, P. and Jeffery, K., 'How Attlee stood up to strikers' in *The Times*, 21 November 1979.

Hodgson, G., 'The Steel Debates' in Sisson, M., and French, P., eds, *The Age of Austerity, 1945–51*, Penguin, 1964.
Jay, D., 'The Quiet Master at No. 10' in *The Times*, 26 April 1980.
Laski, H., 'Epitaph on a System' in the *New Statesman*, 11 July 1942.
Minkin, L., 'Radicalism and Reconstruction: The British Experience' in *Europa*, tome 5, no. 2, 1982.
Moyle, A., 'The Real Attlee – By His PPS' in the *Star*, 8 December 1955.
Ovendale, R., 'The Palestine Policy of the British Labour Government, 1945–1946' in *International Affairs*, July 1979.
– 'The Palestine Policy of the British Labour Government, 1947: The Decision to Withdraw' in *International Affairs*, January 1980.
Pelling, H., 'The 1945 General Election Reconsidered' in *The Historical Journal*, vol. XXIII, no. 2, 1980.
Pimlott, B., 'The Socialist League: Intellectuals and the Labour Left in the 1930s' in the *Journal of Contemporary History*, vol. 6, no. 3, 1971.
Sainsbury, K., '"Second Front in 1942" – a strategic controversy revisited' in *British Journal of International Studies*, vol. 4.
– 'British Policy and German Unity at the end of the Second World War' in *The English Historical Review*, vol. XCIV, no. 373, 1979.
Saville, J., 'May Day 1937' in Briggs, A., and Saville, J., eds, *Essays in Labour History 1918–1939*, Archon Books, Hamden, USA, 1977. (Croom Helm.)
Seyd, P., 'Factionalism Within The Labour Party: The Socialist League' in Briggs, A. and Saville, J., *Essays in Labour History, 1918–1939*, Archon Books, Hamden, USA, 1977. (Croom Helm.)
Stokes, E., 'Cripps in India' in *The Historical Journal*, vol. XIV, 1971.
Tinker, H., 'Preparing to Withdraw' in *The Times Literary Supplement*, 26 September 1980.

NEWSPAPERS, JOURNALS OF OPINION, TV BROADCAST

BBC Television Broadcast, 'Facing the Future', 24 May 1977.
Cambridge Daily News
Daily Express
Daily Herald
East London Advertiser
Evening Star (London)
Forward
Listener
Manchester Guardian
Morning Post
Municipal Review
New Leader
New Statesman
New York Times
News Chronicle
Observer
Reynolds News
Socialist Commentary
Socialist Review
Sunday Express
Sunday Graphic
Sunday Pictorial
The Sunday Times
The Times
Torquay Express and Herald
Tribune
Wandsworth Borough News

Index

abdication crisis, 125, 215
Abyssinia, 107, 108–11, 116, 128, 130
Acheson, Dean, 245, 246
Acland, Sir Richard, 148
Adamson, W., 58
Addison, Lord, 189, 208, 217, 218, 234, 236, 303
Addison, Paul, 141, 143, 149
Adenauer, Konrad, 308
Advisory Committee on International Questions, 108, 125, 131
Africa, 166, 255
Aid to Finland Fund, 162
Air Ministry, 129
Alanbrooke, Viscount, 164, 166
Albania, 137
Alexander, A. V. (Lord), 208, 234, 236, 242
Allen, Clifford, 51, 57
Allied Control Council, 223, 226
Amery, Leo, 278–9, 280
Anderson, Sir John, 142, 143, 151, 235, 243
Angel, Norman, 51
Anglican Church, 32, 319
Anglo-Egyptian Treaty, 259, 302
Anglo-German Naval Treaty, 134
Anglo-Iranian Oil Company, 301
Anglo-Italian Agreement, 130
Arab League, 256
Arabs, 249–53, 256, 257, 259, 261–7
Arcadia Conference, 165
Armistice and Post-War Committee, 175–6, 177
Armistice Terms and Civil Administration Committee, 172, 175
Armstrong, E., 18
Army Act, 63
Arnold, Matthew, 12
Arnold, Thomas, 13
Art Union of London, 10
Athens, 173, 174
Atlantic Charter, 145, 166, 178, 180, 223, 279
atomic bomb, development of, 234–44, 246–7, 254, 321, 322, 323
Atomic Energy Officials Committee, 235
Attlee, Bernard (Attlee's brother), 11
Attlee, Clement (Earl)
private life: character, 1–5, 23, 315–17; honours, 2, 218–19, 316; autobiography, 3, 49; early life, 7–21; religious attitudes, 10–11, 15, 19; love of family life, 12; education, 12–21; love of cricket, 12–13; legal career, 19, 20, 21, 24–5, 37; poetry, 38, 39–40; marriage, 54–5; children, 54, 61, 66; ill-health, 137, 138, 185, 298; private life as Prime Minister, 184; aims and achievements, 315–21
early political life: political conversion, 22, 25–40; at Haileybury House, 26–9, 35–6, 47; in Fabian Society, 30, 50–1; and the ILP, 32–5, 39, 51–3, 57, 59; social work, 35–9; in First World War, 41–4; patriotism, 42–3; parliamentary candidate for Limehouse, 48; Mayor of Stepney, 48–50; elected to Parliament, 43, 54, 55, 57–61; PPS to MacDonald, 58, 62
first Labour Government, 1924: Under-Secretary for War, 62–4; 1924 election, 65
in opposition, 1924–9, 65–7; on Indian Statutory Commission, 59, 61, 68–9, 72,

269–72; in the General Strike, 66–7; 1929 election, 69
second Labour Government, 1929–31, 71–4; Chancellor of the Duchy of Lancaster, 72–3; Postmaster General, 72, 74
National Government, 1931–5: 1931 financial crisis, 77–80; and the Socialist League, 80–4, 86; 'Local Government and the Socialist Plan', 81–3; and Indian constitutional reform, 84; relations with trade unions, 85; membership of NEC, 85; 1931 election, 88; deputy chairman of PLP, 89, 111; economic policies, 90–3; writes for the Left Book Club, 93–4; foreign and defence policies, 96–112, 117–38; 1935 election, 112–13
Labour leader, 1935–9: 75, 87, 113–15, 116; visits Soviet Union, 127; Czech crisis, 130–5; abdication crisis, 215
Second World War, 139–81; war aims, 144–5, 165; and Beveridge Report, 148–51; post-war reconstruction, 151–4, 157; and future of the wartime Coalition, 154–8; German policies, 159–68, 170–2, 175–81; on conduct of the war, 164–6; distrusts Soviet Union, 168, 181; formation of post-war policy, 168–9, 171–2; support for de Gaulle, 169–70; and Greek civil war, 173–5; 'Foreign Policy and the Flying Bomb', 177; 1945 election, 156, 182–3
as Prime Minister, 1945–51, 183–91, 213–14; formation of Government, 185–90; relationship with Bevin, 188–9, 214; and Christopher Addison, 189; 1950 election, 289, 290–4; 1951 election, 216–17, 295, 299–302; relationship with Bevan, 296, 309, 310; and Bevan's resignation, 298–9
as Prime Minister – home affairs: labour relations, 191–5, 202; economic policies, 193–4, 197–8, 204; debating ability, 196–8; popularity, 196–7; press relations, 198–9; Welfare State, 200–1, 203–4; nationalization, 200, 201–3, 211–13; economic crises, 205–6, 209–11, 291–2, 295–6, 299; food shortages, 206–9, 226; admiration for the monarchy, 214–17; and House of Lords, 217–19
as Prime Minister – foreign and defence policies: rearmament programme, 289–90, 295, 297–9; Soviet Union, 220–1, 233, 321, 322; Germany, 221–31, 322; relations with America, 229–30, 248–67, 322–3; Berlin crisis, 233; atomic bomb, 234–44, 246–7, 254, 323; Korean War, 244–6; Palestine, 248–67, 323; India, 268–88, 322; Iranian oil crisis, 301–2
in opposition, 1951–5: and Bevanite revolt, 303–12; domestic policy, 306–7; foreign policy, 307–10; German rearmament and reunification, 307–10; 1955 election, 310–12; resignation, 313
Attlee, Dorothy (Attlee's sister), 47
Attlee, Dorothy (Tom's wife), 40
Attlee, Ellen Bravery Watson (Attlee's mother), 10, 47
Attlee, Felicity (Attlee's daughter), 66
Attlee, Henry (Attlee's father), 9–10, 11, 21, 24, 25, 37
Attlee, Laurence (Attlee's brother), 11, 25
Attlee, Martin, Earl Attlee (Attlee's son), 66
Attlee, Mary (Attlee's sister), 11
Attlee, Robert (Attlee's brother), 11, 25
Attlee, Tom (Attlee's brother), 9, 24–5, 35, 40, 110; childhood, 7, 8; on the Attlee family, 10; career, 11; at Haileybury, 14, 15; at Oxford, 19; joins Fabian Society, 30; in First World War, 41, 42; Attlee's letters to, 47, 51, 71, 73, 79, 80, 84, 100, 270, 271
Attlee, Violet Helen (Attlee's wife), 1, 10, 54–5, 185, 293
Attlee Memorial Appeal, 26–7
Australia, 206, 216, 299, 300
Austria, 102, 106, 128, 181, 231, 232, 311

Badoglio, Marshal, 173
Baldwin, Stanley, 215; 1923 election, 61; 1929 election, 69; National Government, 96; foreign policies, 103, 109, 114, 120–1; 1935 election, 112, 118; and India, 272, 273
Balfour, Arthur, 37
Balfour Declaration (1917), 249, 251
Balliol College, Oxford, 17, 19, 27
Bank of England, 70, 83, 86, 93, 201, 202
Bannerman, H. Campbell, 18
Barker, Sir Ernest, 16, 18, 19
Barnes, George, 45–6
Barrow-in-Furness, 43, 52
Bavaria, 170
Beaverbrook, Lord, 143, 146, 147, 151, 154, 182
Beer, Samuel, 46, 215
Belgium, 21, 42, 160, 181, 235
Benes, Dr, 130
Benn, Anthony Wedgwood, 278
Berlin, 164, 166, 227, 307
Berlin crisis, 233, 244
Bermondsey, 39, 228
Bethell, Nicholas, 253
Bevan, Aneurin, 3; defence policy, 123, 126; in Second World War, 144, 146; 1945 election, 156; and Greek crisis, 157, 174, 175; and post-war Germany, 166,

Bevan, Aneurin (*cont.*)
179–81; on Attlee, 185, 315; in Attlee's Government, 190, 191–2, 214; and economic crises, 205–6, 295–6; and food shortages, 207, 208; and iron and steel nationalization, 212–13; and Palestine, 265; and India, 273; 1950 election, 291, 292, 294; 1950 party conference, 295; resignation, 295, 297–9, 300, 301; rivalry with Gaitskell, 296, 297–8; relationship with Attlee, 296; and increased defence spending, 297, 298; 1951 election, 300–1, 302; and leadership of the Labour Party, 304–5, 306, 308, 310; Bevanite revolt, 304–6; proposes land nationalization, 306; and Soviet Union, 307; publicly argues with Attlee, 309, 310
Beveridge, Sir William (later Lord), 17, 19, 35, 37, 39, 150
Beveridge Report, 38, 148–51
Bevin, Ernest, 83, 87, 182, 183, 215, 315, 318; chairman of SSIP, 80, 81; attacks Lansbury, 110; and leadership of the Labour Party, 113; defence policy, 121, 122, 123, 126; in War Cabinet, 142, 145; Committee on War Aims, 144; and Beveridge Report, 150, 151; and post-war reconstruction, 151–2; and future of wartime Coalition, 154; and Greek crisis, 157, 174; attacks Tories, 157–8; and post-war Germany, 167, 181, 222, 223–4, 226, 228–9, 230–3; support for de Gaulle, 169; on Attlee, 184; in Attlee's Government, 185, 187, 193, 194; relationship with Attlee, 188–9, 214; and economic crisis, 205, 210; and food shortages, 208; and iron and steel nationalization, 212–13; as Foreign Secretary, 216, 220–1; and atomic bomb, 234, 236, 241–2; and Palestine, 248, 254, 255, 258, 260–7, 323; and India, 279, 284; 1950 election, 291, 292; 1950 party conference, 295; and increased defence spending, 298; death, 295, 298, 303
Bidault, Georges, 225
The Bitter Cry of Outcast London, 24
Black Country, 43
Blackett, P. M. S., 247
Blum, Léon, 162
Board of Guardians, 28, 33, 37, 49, 65
Board of Trade, 190
Boer War, 14
Bonomi, Ivanoe, 173
Booth, Charles, 24
Bournemouth, 126, 140
Bow, 34
Bracken, Brendan, 154
Brazil, 235
Bretton Woods Agreement (1944), 206
Bridges, Sir Edward, 209
Brighton, 110, 111
Brinton, Crane, 315
British Army, 60, 63, 99, 101, 271
British Communist Party, 52, 68, 93, 112, 124
British Empire, 91, 103, 105, 151, 173, 254–5, 256, 259, 282
Bromley, 34
Brown, Ernest, 129
Brown, George, 186, 187
Brussels Treaty, 233, 290, 307
Bulgaria, 223
Burma, 269, 271, 279, 280, 283, 287–8
Butler, R. A., 306, 311
Buxton, Noel, 132
Byrnes, James, 226–7, 256, 257, 260, 263

Cable and Wireless, 202
Cadogan, Edward, 147, 173
Campbell, J. R., 64
Canada, 145, 207, 208–9, 237, 239, 243, 244, 246, 280
Castle, Barbara, 306
Central Office of Information, 198
Ceylon, 287–8, 300
Challenge to Britain, 306, 311
Chamberlain, Sir Austen, 102
Chamberlain, Joseph, 18
Chamberlain, Neville, 160; National Government, 96; foreign policy, 120; and Spanish Civil War, 123; appeasement, 127–8, 131, 133, 134; Attlee critical of, 127; defence policy, 129–30; Czech crisis, 132–5; visits Mussolini, 137; loses power, 140–1; in War Cabinet, 141; death, 142; in Second World War, 163–4; trade-union relations, 194; and Palestine, 249–50; and India, 273
Charity Commissioners, 39
Charity Organizational Society (COS), 28, 29
Chequers, 184, 189
Cherwell, Lord, 143, 152, 154, 235
Chiang Kai-shek, 280, 310
Children's Act, 202
China, 100, 101, 127, 128, 230, 244–6, 279, 297, 308, 310, 322, 323
Christian Social Union (Oxford), 19
Church Commission, 39
Churchill, Lord Randolph, 12
Churchill, Sir Winston, 2, 12, 90, 105, 117, 202, 209, 225, 297, 313–14; on Attlee, 3; relations with Attlee, 67–8; and 1931 financial crisis, 76; on Attlee's foreign policy, 102; foreign and defence policies, 116, 120, 125, 127, 129, 159; and 'Arms and the Covenant', 121; and Czech crisis, 132–3, 134, 135; new Coalition proposed,

133; wartime Government, 141–5, 163–4; Atlantic Charter, 145; in Second World War, 147; and Beveridge Report, 149–50; and post-war reconstruction, 151–4; and future of wartime Coalition, 154–8; wartime by-elections, 154–5; Bevin attacks Tories, 157–8; 1945 election, 158, 182, 215; conduct of the war, 164–6; and Soviet Union, 168, 307; and post-war France, 169; and post-war Germany, 170, 176, 178, 179, 222; and Italy, 173; and Spain, 173; and Greek civil war, 173–5; trade-union relations, 194; in opposition, 196, 197–8, 209, 216; and House of Lords, 217; Yalta Conference, 222; proposes Anglo-American alliance, 227; and atomic bomb, 235, 237, 239; and Palestine, 249–54, 257; and India, 272–5, 278–82; 1950 election, 293; 1951 election, 301; relations with America, 305; retirement, 309, 313
Citrine, Walter, 107–8, 111, 119, 130, 131, 132
The Civil Servant (poem), 56
Civil Service, 183, 205, 210
Clark, Colin, 73
Clydesiders, 57, 58, 71, 77
Clynes, J. R., 58, 86, 113
Coalition Government (Second World War), 139–58, 159, 163, 278–82
Cold War, 233
Cole, G. D. H., 52–4
collective security, 96–115, 116
Comintern, 168
Committee on War Aims, 144–5
Common Market, 20
Commonwealth, 168–9, 171, 173, 177, 215, 233, 254–5, 259, 274, 286, 287–8, 300, 307, 321, 322
Commonwealth Party, 148, 149
Commonwealth Prime Ministers' Conference (1949), 215
Communist Party, 34
Congress Party (India), 269, 272, 274–8, 280–4, 287
Conservative Party, and Tariff Reform, 6–7; 1922 election, 56–7; 1923 election, 61–2; 1924 election, 64; 1929 election, 69; in National Government, 88; 1935 election, 112–13; defence policy, 127–8; and Czech crisis, 135; proposed Popular Front, 135–6; and Beveridge Report, 149; and post-war reconstruction, 153–4; and future of wartime Coalition, 154–8; 1945 election, 182–3, 195; relations with Attlee Government, 195–6; social welfare, 195, 200; popularity, 196, 209; opposition to nationalization, 211; and India, 272–3, 278–9, 280–2; 1950 election, 293; 1951 election, 300, 302; 1955 election, 292, 310–12
Control of Engagement Order, 194, 195
Cooper, Duff, 144, 299
Corpus Christi, Oxford, 19
Council of Europe, 307
Council of Foreign Ministers, 225, 226, 227, 229, 230, 231, 232, 255, 260, 264
Cowling, M., 113
Cranbourne, Viscount, 128
Creech Jones, Arthur, 264, 265–6
Cressall, Grandma, 301
Criminal Justice Act (1948), 219
Cripps, Sir Stafford, 3, 81, 83–4, 86, 89, 90, 102, 182, 183, 315; NEC membership, 85; foreign policy, 99, 110; defence policy, 108, 122, 129; resigns from NEC, 109; and leadership of the Labour Party, 114; and Spanish Civil War, 123–4; Unity Campaign, 135, 136, 138; in Second World War, 146, 148; readmitted to Labour Party, 157; Ambassador to Moscow, 165; and post-war Germany, 181; in Attlee's Government, 186, 187, 190; and economic crises, 206, 210, 291, 295–6; and food shortages, 208; and iron and steel nationalization, 212; suggests Bevin take Attlee's place, 214; and India, 277, 278, 280–1, 282, 283; 1950 Budget, 294; 1950 election, 292, 293–4; death, 295, 303
Crosland, Anthony, 202
Cross, Lord, 20
Crossman, Richard, 225, 228, 230, 262, 304, 305–6, 308
Cyprus, 256, 263
Cyrenaica, 251, 254, 255
Czechoslovakia, 130–5, 137, 163, 167, 226

Daily Herald, 144, 160, 162, 167, 198, 199, 228
Daily Mirror, 3
Daladier, Edouard, 134
Dalton, Hugh, 3, 39, 77, 89, 150, 158, 160, 291; and Palestine, 65, 254, 256, 259; NEC membership, 84, 85; foreign policies, 97; and Labour Party leadership, 113–14; defence policy, 118, 122, 123, 129; and 'Arms and the Covenant', 121; and Czech crisis, 130, 131–2, 135; on Attlee, 143; in Second World War, 143, 188; and future of wartime Coalition, 154, 156; German policies, 162, 167, 175; and Soviet invasion of Finland, 162; Special Operations Executive, 165; in Attlee's Government, 185, 187, 191; 1947 Budget leak, 198; and economic crisis, 205, 206, 210; and food shortages, 207, 208; and

Dalton, Hugh (*cont.*)
iron and steel nationalization, 211–13; and post-war Germany, 226; and atomic bomb, 234; 1950 election, 291, 292
Damaskinos, Archbishop, 173–4
Darlan, Admiral, 170
Davies, H. W. C., 18
Dawes Plan, 97
Dawson, Christopher, 19
de Gaulle, Charles, 169–70
Defence Committee, 142, 164, 165, 235, 259, 282–3
Denmark, 177, 214
Devon, 40, 41
Disarmament Conference, Geneva, 100–3
Disraeli, Benjamin, 1
Douglas-Home, Sir Alec, 20
Dulles, John Foster, 307
Dunkirk, Treaty of, 230
Durham, Lord, 280

East India Company, 14
East London Observer, 48–9
East Prussia, 172
Eastern Europe, 168, 307, 308
Economic Commission for Europe, 307
Economic Policy Committee, 212
Economic survey for 1947, 193, 210
Ede, Chuter, 208
Eden, Sir Anthony, 20, 128, 133, 143, 158, 170, 172, 173, 178, 197, 220, 303, 307, 311
Edinburgh, 34, 122–3
Edward VIII, King, 215
Egypt, 253, 258, 259, 260, 261, 264, 265, 266, 302
Eire, 184, 323
Eisenhower, Dwight D., 164, 166, 170, 180
El Alamein, 148
Electrical Trades Union, 66
Elizabeth, Princess, 216
Emergency Powers Act, 192
Emergency War Measures Bill, 142
The Encyclopaedia of the Labour Movement, 67–8
Ensor, R. C. K., 32
Eritrea, 108, 251
Essex, Attlee family house in, 9, 12
European Advisory Commission, 172, 175, 223
European Coal and Steel Community, 307
European Defence Community (EDC), 308, 309

Fabian Society, 30, 39, 50–1, 232, 304
Fascism, 93, 103, 119, 121, 137, 171, 174
Feiling, Keith, 19
Fifty Years March, 289
Finland, 161–2, 171, 223
First World War, 41–7, 50, 91, 97, 116, 129, 159–60, 166, 167, 170, 321, 324
Firth, Charles, 18
Fisher, H. A. L., 18
Fletcher, C., 18
Food Committee, 142
Foot, Michael, 3, 89, 187, 190, 215, 230, 298, 300, 306, 309
Foreign Office, 98, 147, 168, 175, 176, 177, 199, 221, 254, 259, 263, 264, 267
Foreign Policy: the Labour Party's Dilemma, 232
Formosa, 308, 310
Forster, 20
Forward With Labour, 311
France, 21, 76, 184; and the Ruhr, 64; Dawes Plan, 97; withdraws from Rhineland, 98; and occupation of the Rhineland, 119–20; Popular Front Government, 121, 123; and Czech crisis, 131, 132, 133, 135; in Second World War, 163, 165, 168; planned Allied invasion, 166; role in post-war Europe, 169–70, 176, 177, 181; proposed invasion of, 172; and post-war Germany, 179, 223, 226, 229, 231; Treaty of Dunkirk, 230; and Middle East, 258
Franco, General, 137, 173
Free French, 169–70
Free Trade, 61, 62, 73, 90–1, 92
French Air Force, 61, 132
Friendly Society of Iron Founders, 45
Front Populaire, 123
Fulham, 67

Gaitskell, Hugh, 292, 296, 297–8, 299, 304, 305, 308, 311
Gallipoli, 42, 66, 68, 134
Gallup Polls, 154, 195, 196–7, 294, 300
Gandhi, Mahatma, 270, 272, 273, 279, 281;
general elections: January 1906, 33; January 1910, 34; December 1910, 34, 50; December 1918, 47, 48, 50, 56; November 1922, 56–7, 59; December 1923, 59, 61–2; October 1924, 64–5; May 1929, 69, 72; October 1931, 78, 79, 88, 90; November 1935, 85, 91–2, 109, 112–13, 115; July 1945, 1–2, 156, 158, 182, 195, 217; February 1950, 289, 290–4, 295; October 1951, 216–17, 295, 299–301, 302; May 1955, 292, 310–12
General Strike (1926), 65, 66–7
Geneva Protocol, 98
George V, King, 61, 62, 215
George VI, King, 2, 141, 184, 215–17, 245, 288, 299–300, 303
German Air Force, 107, 132
Germany, 21, 96, 101, 106, 209; in First World War, 41–2; socialists, 45;

disarmament, 63; Labour's foreign policy, 64; banking crisis, 76; reparations, 97, 221–5; and League of Nations, 98; rearmament, 99, 100, 102, 103–4, 107–8, 120, 122, 126, 130; Hitler's rise to power, 101–2; withdraws from League of Nations, 103; naval pact with Britain, 109; occupation of Rhineland, 116, 119–20; Labour's defence policy and, 118; occupation of Austria, 128; Czech crisis, 130–5; in Second World War, 140, 144, 155; attacks Russia, 147, 165, 166; Attlee's wartime policy, 159–68, 170–2, 175–81; food shortages, 206–7, 208, 224–5, 226, 228; *Keep Left* pamphlet, 230; Berlin crisis, 233, 244; and atomic bomb, 241; reunification and rearmament proposals, 307–8, 309–10
Gibbon, Edward, 184
Gibraltar, 108, 163
Gilbert, Sir William Schwenck, 7
Gillies, William, 126
Giraud, General, 170
Gladstone, William Ewart, 7, 20
Glasgow, 192
Glazier, Bruce, 34
Goebbels, Dr, 252
Goering, Hermann, 167
Going Our Way, 300
Golant, W., 58, 67, 270
gold standard, 76, 78, 91, 93
Goldberg, Alfred, 234, 244
Gollancz, Victor, 93
Gowing, Margaret, 234, 235–6, 237, 242, 243, 246–7
Grace, W. G., 13
Graham, William, 68
Grayson, Victor, 33–4
Greece, 66, 157, 173–5, 209, 230, 266
Greenwood, Arthur, 113, 123, 133; in War Cabinet, 141–2, 144, 160; on Labour's support for war effort, 146–7; and Beveridge Report, 150; and Greek civil war, 174; and post-war Germany, 180; in Attlee's Government, 187, 191; and atomic bomb, 234; and Palestine, 250
Gregory, Sir Philip, 24
Grenfell, David, 113, 188
Griffiths, James, 174, 175, 187, 303
Groves, General, 243
guild socialism, 51, 52–3
Gupta, Partha, 269

H-bombs, 308, 309, 310
Haileybury College, 14–16
Haileybury House, 26–9, 35–6, 47
Halifax, Lord (Lord Irwin), 133, 137, 141, 144, 164, 169, 269, 270, 272, 287
Hall, George, 158, 208, 254, 256, 262–3, 264
Hansard, 69, 90
Hardie, Keir, 34, 38, 268
Harriman, W. Averell, 243
Harrison, Earl G., 255–6, 257
Hartington, Marquess of, 78–9
Hartshorn, Vernon, 69, 269, 272
Hazlitt Essay Club, 24
Henderson, Arthur, 44, 45, 57; foreign policies, 45–6, 97, 98, 100, 103, 108; and Russian Revolution, 45; as Foreign Secretary, 72; and Socialist League's challenge, 81; death, 113
Herbert, A. P., 3
Hindus, 270, 277, 287
Hiroshima, 237
Hitler, Adolf, 98, 100, 119, 122, 159, 167, 181; rise to power, 101–2; rearmament, 107, 108, 120; *Mein Kampf*, 125; Munich crisis, 128; Czech crisis, 130, 131–5, 137; Chamberlain visits, 131, 133, 134; Second World War, 147; peace proposals, 160; Labour Party attitudes towards, 163; advances on Russia, 165; assassination plots, 170
Hoare, Sir Samuel, 109, 111, 114, 116, 274
Hoare-Laval Pact, 114, 117, 128
Hobson, J. A., 51
Holland, 177, 181, 235
Home Office, 119
Hoover, President, 76
Hore-Belisha, Leslie, 129
House of Commons, Attlee's maiden spoeech, 43, 59; Attlee's speeches in, 59–61, 90; and Beveridge Report, 148–9; and Greek civil war, 174; Attlee's success in, 196–8; and post-war Germany, 224; and atomic bomb, 235; and India, 272–3
House of Lords, 82, 83–4, 86, 189, 217–19, 287, 292
Hungary, 171, 223, 226
Hutchinson, Miss, 12
Hynd, John, 225

Imperial Defence College, 118
In Limehouse (poem), 38
Independent Labour Party (ILP), 30–1, 39, 45, 78, 124; in London, 32, 34–5; Attlee and, 32–5, 39, 51–3, 57, 59; Grayson affair, 33–4; National Administrative Council, 34; in First World War, 41; relations with Labour Party, 58, 59; and 1923 general election, 62; supports Indian independence, 68; *Socialism in Our Time*, 70; and second Labour Government, 72; and 1931 financial crisis, 77; breaks links with Labour Party, 81; 1931 election, 88; foreign policies, 97; 1935 election, 112

India, 61, 98, 132, 190, 257; Simon Commission, 59, 61, 68–9, 72, 269–73, 274, 276; constitutional reform, 84; Second World War, 165; food shortages, 207, 208; independence, 209, 258, 266, 267, 268–88, 322
India Act (1935), 274, 276, 278
India Act (1947), 287
India and Burma Committee, 282–6
India Committee, 281, 282
Indian Army, 271, 275, 276, 282
Indian Civil Service, 282
Indian Defence Council, 280
Indian National Congress, 270, 271
Indian Navy, 282, 283
Industrial Charter, 195
Inns of Court Officers' Training Corps, 42
International Brigade, 127
International Federation of Trade Unions, 99, 119
International Policy and Defence, 126
International Socialist Congress, 45
International Trade Secretariat, 119
The International Post-War Settlement, 252–3
Iran, 259, 299, 301–2
Iraq, 68, 259
Ireland, 32n., 48, 272
Ireland Act (1949), 323
Irgun, 253
Iron and Steel Federation, 212
iron and steel industry, nationalization, 211–13, 218
Irwin, Lord, *see* Halifax, Lord
Isaacs, George, 194, 208
Italy, 60–1, 64, 106, 126, 131, 132, 175; Attlee visits, 54, 66; Abyssinian crisis, 107, 108–11, 114, 120, 130; invasion of Albania, 137; and Attlee's post-war policy, 171–2; defeat of, 173; post-war role, 181; peace settlement, 223; and atomic bomb, 241; colonies, 254, 255, 259

Japan, 100, 106, 126, 130, 131, 132; invasion of Manchuria, 98; Sino-Japanese dispute, 100, 101, 102, 112, 127; and Attlee's view of world security, 101; in Second World War, 158, 279, 283; defeat of, 205, 237; and atomic bomb, 241, 246
Jerusalem, 165, 263
Jewish Agency, 259, 262
Jewish Board of Guardians, 60
Jewish Socialist Labour Party (Poale Zion), 252, 262
Jews, 48, 168, 248–67
Jinnah, Mohammed, 282, 287
Joachim, Harold, 16
Johnson, Arthur, 17–18, 19
Joint Disarmament Conference, Zurich (1932), 99
Joint National Council, 126
'The Joint Stock Banks', 83
Jowitt, William, 150, 151–2, 208

Keep Left, 230
Kellogg Pact (1927), 108
Kennedy, Tom, 34
Keynes, John Maynard, 205, 206, 260
Keynesianism, 85, 91, 93
King, Mackenzie, 209, 239, 243
Kipling, Rudyard, 13, 27
Kitchener, Lord, 41
Korean War, 230, 244–6, 295, 296, 307, 308, 311, 323

Labour, The War and The Peace, 162
Labour and the Nation, 69, 86
Labour and the New Society, 295
Labour and Socialist International, 99, 119, 162
Labour League, Stepney, 33
Labour Party, formation of, 30, 31; relations with Liberals, 31, 33, 34; electoral advances, 33–4; and First World War, 44–7, 97; and trade-union movement, 45, 46–7, 85, 318–19; reactions to Russian Revolution, 45; constitution, 46–7, 304, 318; Clause IV, 46–7, 304, 318; 1918 election, 47, 48, 50; in London, 47–8; Stepney borough elections, 48; rejects Communist Party, 52; 1922 election, 56–7; and the ILP, 57–8; 1923 election, 61–2; forms Government, 62–4; 1924 election, 64–5; Indian policies, 68–9, 272, 273–4, 277–9; 1929 election, 69–70, 72; second Government, 71–4, 75; and *Socialism in Our Time*, 70; 1931 financial crisis, 76–80, 87; formation of National Government, 77; 1931 election, 78, 88, 90; and Socialist League, 81, 84; 1935 election, 85, 91–2, 109, 112–13, 115; and disarmament, 86; economic policies, 90–3; democracy in, 92; foreign policy, 96–112, 114–15; recognizes Soviet Union, 98; foreign and defence policies, 104–5, 117–38; 1935 conference, 110–11; Attlee becomes leader, 75, 113–15; and Second World War, 124; Defence Committee, 129–30, 136–7; and Czech crisis, 130–5; Policy Sub-Committee, 135; proposed Popular Front, 135–6; in wartime Coalition, 139–58; Beveridge Report, 148–50; and post-war reconstruction, 151–3; and future of wartime Coalition, 154–8; German policies, 159–68, 170–2, 175–81, 230;

support for de Gaulle, 169; and Greek civil war, 174–5; attitude towards Soviet Union, 181; 1945 election, 182–4; and Attlee Government, 188, 191; popularity, 195–6; and House of Lords, 217; 1945 election, 217; and atomic bomb, 245; and Palestine, 249–50, 252–3, 262; 1950 election, 289, 290–4, 295; opposition to National Service, 290; Bevan's resignation, 295, 297–9; 1951 election, 295, 299–301, 302; and Korean War, 296; Iranian oil crisis, 301; in opposition (1951–5), 303–10; Bevanite revolt, 305–6; and German rearmament, 308, 309–10; 1955 election, 310–12; Attlee's resignation, 313; Attlee's leadership of, 315–21; *see also* National Executive Committee
The Labour Party in Perspective, 43, 94, 125
Labour Representation Committee, 31
Labour's Call to Action, 78, 86
Labour's Immediate Programme, 85, 92–3, 127, 135, 139
Lambert, George, 78
Lancashire, 43
Lancaster, Duchy of, 72
Lansbury, George, 59, 62, 72, 83, 84, 90, 102, 103, 113; 1910 election, 32, 34; and India, 69; 1931 election, 89; pacifism, 93, 98–9; foreign and defence policies, 101, 107–8, 109, 111; and 'War and Peace', 106; Bevin attacks, 110; resignation, 111, 113; and leadership of Labour Party, 114; death, 167
Laski, Harold, 4, 19, 124, 140, 143, 162, 302, 315, 321; visit to Moscow, 84; introduces Attlee to Left Book Club, 93; in Second World War, 144, 146, 147, 150; and the Greek civil war, 174; and Labour's foreign policy, 232; and Palestine, 252, 262
Laval, Pierre, 114
Law, Andrew Bonar, 75
Law Society, 9
Lawrence, T. E., 19
Lawson, Jack, 63–4, 79, 207
Lawson, Lady, 79
League of Nations, 46, 97–111, 114–17, 120–2, 125, 126, 128, 130, 131, 138, 249, 250
League of Nations Union, 109
Lebanon, 258, 263
Lee, Jennie, 300
Left Book Club, 93–4
Legal Aid Act, 202
Lend-lease, 203, 205, 223
Leo X, Pope, 184
Let Us Face the Future, 183, 291
Let Us Win Through, 290
Liberal Association, Stepney, 33
Liberal Party, 318; and Irish Home Rule, 6, 32; electoral pact with ILP, 31, 33, 34; and Poor Law reform, 37; National Insurance Act, 38; split, 56; 1922 election, 56–7; 1923 election, 61–2; 1924 election, 64; 1929 election, 69; and second Labour Government, 71; 1935 election, 112; and future of wartime Coalition, 158; 1945 election, 183; 1950 election, 293; 1951 election, 302, 1955 election, 311
Limehouse, 25, 28–9, 47, 48, 55, 57, 61, 65, 88, 203
Linlithgow, Lord, 277–8, 279–80
Lloyd George, David, 58, 61, 70, 71, 75; social welfare, 37, 200; National Insurance Act, 38; and Russian Revolution, 45; Coalition Government, 56; 1929 general election, 69; and 'Arms and the Covenant', 121; and Beveridge Report, 148, 149
Lloyd George, Lady Megan, 311
'Local Government and the Socialist Plan', 81–3
London, 22–4, 31–2, 34–5, 47–8, 61, 133–4, 192, 195, 293, 316
London and Home Counties Electrical Authority, 67
London County Council (LCC), 34, 48, 66, 84, 114, 125
London Hospital, 66
London Labour Party, 35
London Progressive Movement, 32
London School of Economics (LSE), 39, 47, 58, 150
Lord President's Committee, 142
Low, David, 13
Lyttleton, Edward, 15
Lytton Commission, 100

MacArthur, General, 245, 298
McCarthyism, 307
MacDonald, Ramsay, 44, 51, 63, 90, 105, 185; resignation from NAC, 34; in First World War, 46; relations with trade unions, 46–7, 194; as leader of Labour Party, 58; forms government, 62; foreign policies, 64, 97, 98; Indian policy, 68–9, 268, 271, 272, 273; second Government, 70–4; formation of National Government, 77–8, 79, 88, 96; 1931 financial crisis, 77–80, 87; 1931 election, 88; economic policies, 92; loses Labour leadership, 75–6, 113, 114; and Palestine, 249
McKibbin, R., 35
McMahon Act, 244
Macmillan, Harold, 2, 3, 143, 173–4
Madras, 269

Malaya, 244, 280
Malta, 163
Manchester Guardian, 5, 90, 196
Manchuria, 98, 100, 128
Manpower Bill, 146
Margach, James, 199
Marriott, Sir John, 18
Marquand, David, 58, 73
Marshall, General, 244
Marshall Aid, 204, 210, 231, 244, 291
Martin, Kingsley, 4, 161
Marx, Karl, 29
Marxism, 30, 51–2, 97
Masaryk, Jan, 130
May, Sir George, 76
May Committee, 76, 79
Mediterranean, 163, 166, 174, 254, 255, 259
'Memorandum on War Aims', 46
Menon, Krishna, 277
Mesopotamia, 42
Message to the German People, 159
Middle East, 165, 203, 225, 254–5, 256; *see also* Palestine
Middleton, J. S., 156–7
Millar, Cedric, 54
Millar, Mrs, 54
Ministerial Atomic Energy Committee, 235
Ministry of Defence, 104–5, 136–7
Ministry of Food, 208–9, 225
Ministry of Health, 50
Ministry of Information, 198
Ministry of Labour, 150, 194
Ministry of Supply, 148, 235
Ministry of Transport, 74
Mr Churchill's Declaration of Policy to the Electors, 183
Molotov, V. M., 166, 225, 232
Montgomery, Field-Marshal, 54, 166, 226
Moore, R. J., 281
Morel, E. D., 51
Morgenthau Plan, 179
Morris, William, 16, 20, 25, 29, 314
Morrison, Herbert, 35, 89, 158, 182, 183, 294–5, 307, 310, 315; on Attlee, 3, 186; and 1931 financial crisis, 77; LCC elections, 84; NEC membership, 84, 85; and leadership of Labour Party, 113, 114; defence policy, 122; Czech crisis, 131, 132, 135; and Beveridge Report, 150, 151; and post-war reconstruction, 151–2; and future of wartime Coalition, 154, 158; German policies, 162; support for de Gaulle, 169; challenges Attlee for leadership, 184; in Attlee's Government, 186, 187, 189, 190, 191; wage controls, 194; industrial relations, 202; and economic crisis, 206, 210; and food shortages, 207–8; and iron and steel nationalization, 211–13; and House of Lords reform, 219; and atomic bomb, 234, 236; and Palestine, 253, 254, 255, 256, 258; 1950 election, 291, 292; discredited, 295; and Bevan's resignation, 297, 299; and increased defence spending, 298; 1951 election, 299–300; as Foreign Secretary, 301; Iranian oil crisis, 301; in opposition, 303; and leadership of the Labour Party, 303, 304, 306; and Bevanite revolt, 305, 306
Moscow, 84, 146
Mosley, Oswald, 72, 73
Mountbatten, Lord Louis, 190, 285–7
Moyle, Arthur, 5, 184, 185
Moyne, Lord, 253
Munich Agreement, 128, 134–5, 137, 229
Muslim League, 278, 280, 281, 282, 283–5
Muslims, 270, 272, 274, 277, 281, 282, 283, 286
Mussolini, Benito, 107, 108–9, 114, 120, 125, 130, 134, 135, 137, 163, 173

Nagasaki, 237
Nathan, Lord, 213
National Coal Board, 209
National Council of Labour (NCL), 85, 101, 111, 130, 132, 133, 137, 149, 159, 162, 174
National Executive Committee (NEC), 62; elections, 45, 92; in First World War, 46; Indian policy, 68, 69, 278; and Socialist League, 81, 84; Finance and Trade Committee, 83; Attlee's membership of, 85; and disarmament, 86; *For Socialism and Peace*, 86; foreign and defence policies, 101, 104–11, 119, 121–4; Defence Committee, 117–18; and proposed Popular Front, 136, 138; in Second World War, 140–1, 147–8; and future of wartime Coalition, 154, 156–7; German policies, 162, 168; and Greek civil war, 174; nationalization policy, 211, 295; and Palestine, 252–3; and Bevanite revolt, 305, 306; and Soviet Union, 307; and German reunification and rearmament proposals, 308, 309–10; *see also* Labour Party
National Government, 77–9, 88, 96, 99, 135, 136
National Health Service, 202, 211, 292
National Health Service Bill, 195
National Insurance Acts, 38, 197, 203–4
National Joint Advisory Council, 193
National Parks Act (1949), 202
National Party, 112
National Service, 289–90
National Service Act (1947), 290
National Union of Clerks, 34
nationalization, 74, 83, 86, 93, 146, 195,

196, 198, 200, 201–3, 211–13, 218, 290, 295, 306
NATO, 233, 236, 244, 246, 296, 307, 309, 310, 322
Naval Staff College, 118
Naylor, J. F., 106
Nazi-Soviet Pact, 161, 162
Nazis, 101, 107, 118, 128, 137, 160, 161–2, 164, 166, 167–8, 170, 174, 178, 179, 180, 233, 251, 260
Nehru, Jawaharlal, 276–7, 281, 286, 287
Nehru, Motilal, 269
New Fabian Bureau, 73
New Statesman, 3–4, 146, 161, 180, 181, 225–6, 230
New York, 76
New Zealand, 206, 216–17, 299, 300
Nicolson, Harold, 144, 146, 161
Nield, Sir Herbert, 60
1922 Committee, 196
Noel-Baker, Philip, 121
Non-Intervention Agreement, 123
Northaw Place, 12
Northcote, Sir Stafford, 20
Northern Ireland, 323
Norway, 177, 184, 214
Nussey, Cecil, 26–7

Observer, 4–5, 302
O'Donovan, Patrick, 302
OEEC, 291, 307
The Old World and the New Society, 156–7
Oman, Charles, 18
One Way Only, 300
Order of the Garter, 215
Ottawa Agreements, 79
Overseas Reconstruction Committee, 223
Owen, Robert, 11
Oxford Union, 17, 20, 101
Oxford University, 14, 15, 16–21, 22, 24

Pakistan, 278, 282, 287–8
Palestine, 132, 209, 229, 248–67, 287, 322, 323
Palestine Committee, 253, 258
Palestine Conference, 263, 264, 265
Palestine Resolution (1940), 252
Paris, 76
Parliament Act (1911), 217–18
Parliament Act (1949), 292, 294
Parliamentary Labour Party (PLP), 45, 47, 61, 62; in 1920s, 57; weaknesses, 63; Attlee in, 65; and 1931 financial crisis, 78; Attlee as deputy chairman, 89; defence policy, 107, 118, 121, 122, 126; and Czech crisis, 134; in Second World War, 145; and Attlee as Prime Minister, 190–1; and iron and steel nationalization, 213; and Bevanite revolt, 306; and German rearmament, 310
Parliamentary Problems and Procedures, 86–7
Patel, Sardar, 287
Patterson, Alec, 18
Peel, Lord, 249
Peel Commission, 249, 253
Pelling, Henry, 192–3
Percy, Eustace, 19
Permanent Court of International Justice, 98
Persia, 68, 259
Pethick-Lawrence, Lord, 208, 282
Philip, Prince, 216
Phillips, Morgan, 174
Plymouth, 121
Poland, 118, 130, 137, 159, 160, 163, 167, 172, 177–8, 179, 222, 228
Pollard, Professor, 18
Ponsonby, Arthur, 51
Poor Law, 28, 37–8, 60
Poplar, 32, 301
Post Office, 72, 73–4, 90, 91, 202
Potsdam Conference, 177, 181, 182, 185, 222–3, 225, 226, 227, 229, 230, 237, 238, 254, 322
Prague, 137
Pre-Raphaelites, 20
Punjab, 269
Putney, 8, 24–5, 28, 47

Quebec Agreement, 237, 241
Queen's London Regiment, First Cadet Battalion, 26, 27, 28, 42

Reconstruction Committee, 152–4
Red Army, 176
Representation of the People Act (1918), 35
Reynaud, Paul, 163–4
Reynolds News, 146
Rhineland, 98, 116, 119–20, 128
Robertson, Charles Grant, 18
Roman Catholic Church, 32
Roosevelt, Franklin D., 145, 157, 163, 169, 173, 237, 253–4, 257, 280
Rosebery, Lord, 18, 20
Royal Air Force, 97, 105, 107, 118, 129, 163
Royal Commission on the Poor Law, 37
Royal Navy, 105, 108–9
Ruhr, 64, 222, 229, 322
Rumania, 137, 171, 223, 228
Ruskin, John, 25, 29
Ruskin College, Oxford, 39
Russian Revolution (1917), 45, 51, 98, 143

St Pierre and Miquelon, 169
Salisbury, 3rd Marquis of, 7, 20
Salisbury, 5th Marquis of, 287

Salvation Army, 28
San Francisco, 239
Scotland, 57, 293
SEATO, 308, 309, 310
Second Front, 146, 147, 149, 165, 166
Second International, 97
Second World War, 2, 96, 139–58, 159–81, 237, 277–8, 314, 321–2
Selborne, Lord, 20
Service Estimates, 104, 118–19, 120, 126, 129
Sforza, Count, 173
Sharp, T., 176
Shaw, Bernard, 30
Shinwell, Emanuel, 3, 58, 205–6, 208, 209, 265
Short Programme, 211
Sikhs, 284
Simon, Sir John, 101, 129, 270, 272, 273
Simon Commission, 59, 61, 68–9, 72, 269–73, 274, 276
Simpson, Mrs, 215
Sinclair, Sir Archibald, 250
Singapore, 280
Sino-Japanese dispute, 100, 101, 102, 112, 127
Smethwick, 112
Smith, A. L., 18
Smith, Sir Ben, 206, 207
Smyrna, 61
Snowden, Philip, 34, 57, 71, 73, 76, 77, 78–9
Social Democratic Federation (SDF), 30, 32, 33, 34, 35, 51, 93
The Social Worker, 27, 36
The Socialism and Peace, 86
Socialism in Our Time, 70
Socialist League, 81, 83–4, 86, 92, 103, 106, 108, 121, 124–5, 127
Socialist Review, 50
Society for Socialist Inquiry and Propaganda (SSIP), 73, 80–1, 83
Somalia, 108, 254, 255
South Africa, 215
South Lancashire Regiment (6th), 42
Southport, 138
Soviet Union, 67, 101; British recognition of, 51–2, 98; Labour's foreign policy, 64; purges, 93, 124, 131; Attlee visits, 127; and Czech crisis, 132, 133, 135; Second World War, 146, 147, 148, 168; post-war relations with West, 157–8, 168; and Attlee's plan for Germany, 159, 176–7; invasion of Poland, 160; invasion of Finland, 161–2; Germany attacks, 165, 166; Labour Party attitude towards, 167, 181; Attlee's attitude towards, 171–2, 233, 307, 321, 322; occupation of Germany, 172, 222; Yalta Conference, 177–8, 179; and United Nations, 220; and post-war Germany, 220–1, 225–7, 231, 232; and atomic bomb, 236, 241–4; and Korean War, 245; and Palestine, 253, 254, 266; and German reunification proposals, 309
Spain, 21, 93, 127, 132, 137, 173, 181
Spanish Civil War, 121, 123–4, 125, 127, 128, 130, 131
Special Operations Executive, 165
Stafford, David, 169
Stalin, Joseph, 131, 161–2, 165, 168, 172, 173, 181, 225, 237, 242, 254, 307, 322
Stalingrad, 148, 168
Stanmore, 88
Steel Nationalization Bill, 292
Stepney, 25–9, 30, 33, 35, 47–9, 56, 60, 61, 66, 87, 88, 248–9, 316
The Stepney Worker, 33
Stockholm, 45
Strachey, John, 94, 207, 208–9
Strauss, George, 234
Stresemann, Gustav, 102
Sudan, 264
Suez Canal, 108, 255, 259, 302
Suez crisis (1956), 301
Supplies and Services (Emergency Powers) Bill, 216
Sweden, 214
Swinburne, Algernon Charles, 20
Swindon, Lord, 129

Tawney, R. H., 19, 35, 39, 45, 70, 86
Taylor, A. J. P., 68
Taylor, F. H., 16
Teheran Conference, 178
Temple, William, Archbishop of Canterbury, 19
Thomas, J. H., 68
Thompson, Paul, 32, 34
Thorne, Will, 34
Tillet, Ben, 34
Time, 1–2
The Times, 50, 60, 67, 196, 198, 199, 210, 228
Tizzard, Sir Henry, 247
Tolstoy, Count Leo, 50
Tower Hamlets, 32
Town and Country Planning Act (1947), 202
Toynbee Hall, 35, 37, 47, 150
Trade Disputes Act (1927), 154, 192
trade unions, 53–4; ILP and, 31; relationship with Labour Party, 45, 46–7, 85, 318–19; Attlee's relations with, 85; support for League of Nations, 99; and Attlee Government, 192–5
Trades Union Congress (TUC), 62, 87, 162, 224; and ILP, 31; in First World War, 46; General Strike, 66; and 1931 financial

crisis, 77, 78, 85; opposition to Socialist League, 84; foreign and defence policies, 101, 107–11, 119, 121, 126, 129–30; and post-war reconstruction, 152; and Greek civil war, 175; and Attlee Government, 192–5; rejects workers' participation, 202; and iron and steel nationalization, 211
Transjordan, 253, 259, 263, 264
Treasury, 74, 142, 151, 186, 262, 271
Trevelyan, Sir Charles, 81
Tribune, 125, 146, 180, 181, 230, 300
Truman, Harry S., 205, 207, 237–44, 245–6, 247, 248, 254, 255–64, 267, 310
Truman doctrine, 230
TUC and Labour Party Research Department, 113
Turkey, 209, 230, 266
Tyneside, 43

Ulster, 272
unemployment, 43, 61, 72, 76–7, 82, 85, 91–2
Unemployment Act (1934), 113
Union of Democratic Control (UDC), 45, 97
Union of Stepney Ratepayers, 33
United Front Campaign, 124
United Irish League, 48
United Nations (UN), 230, 255, 297, 307, 321–2; Attlee and, 220, 228, 231, 233; and atomic bomb, 239, 242–4, 247; Korean War, 245–6; Security Council, 240; and Palestine, 258, 260, 263, 265–6; and China, 308; and Iranian oil crisis, 301
UN Atomic Commission, 235–6
United States, 61, 101, 130; and 1931 financial crisis, 76; relations with Britain, 98, 305, in Second World War, 145, 147, 172, 279; German policy, 159, 170, 178–9, 180, 222, 226–8, 230–1; conduct of the war, 164, 165–6; and post-war security, 168, 169, 171; opposition to de Gaulle, 160–70; unconditional surrender doctrine, 170; occupation of Germany, 172; and Italy, 173; and Attlee's plan for Germany, 176; economic aid to Britain, 197–8, 203, 223, 257, 261; and Britain's economic crisis, 205–6, 225, 226; and British food shortages, 207, 208; and the United Nations, 220; and Attlee's foreign policy, 220–1; Attlee's relations with, 229–30, 248, 322–3; Truman doctrine, 230; Marshall Plan, 231, 244, 291; Berlin crisis, 233; and atomic bomb, 236–44, 246; Korean War, 244–6, 295, 296, 307; and Palestine, 248, 251, 253–4, 255–67; asks Britain to increase defence spending, 295, 297; and Iranian oil crisis, 301; rearms Germany, 308; H-bombs, 309
University College, Oxford, 17, 19–20

Versailles Treaties, 98, 120, 160, 170
Victoria, Queen, 7, 18, 24

Wales, 184, 214, 293
Wall Street Crash (1929), 72
Walpole, Sir Robert, 39
Walsh, Stephen, 63, 68, 69
Walthamstow, 314
Wandsworth Common, 8–9
'War and Peace' (NEC policy document), 106–7
War Cabinet (First World War), 45
War Cabinet (Second World War), 141–2, 144, 152–3, 159, 163–6, 168, 171–3, 187, 221–2, 250, 253, 278, 280–1
War Office, 62–4
Washington, 165
Washington, Treaty of, 99–100
Washington Declaration, 243
Watson, Sam, 294
Watson, T. S. (Attlee's grandfather), 10
Wavell, Lord, 281, 282, 283, 284–6
Webb, Beatrice, 37, 148
Webb, Sidney, 30, 37, 39, 46, 148, 249
Wedgwood, Colonel, 102
Weizmann, Dr, 251–2
Welfare State, 38, 195, 200–1, 290, 305, 321
Welles, Sumner, 170
Wells, H. G., 30
West Germany, 232–3, 308, 309–10; *see also* Germany
Western Desert, 168
Westminster Abbey, 3
Wheatley, John, 62, 63, 72
Whiteley, William, 208
Wilhelm II, Kaiser, 170
Wilkinson, Ellen, 186
Williams, Francis, 3, 4, 94, 198–9, 289
Williams, Tom, 113, 208
Wilmot, John, 213, 214, 234, 236
Wilson, Harold, 13, 20, 187, 190, 296, 299, 306
Wood, Kingsley, 133, 151
Woodford, 55, 66, 88
Woolton, Lord, 143, 151
World Economic Conference, 100

Yalta Conference, 177–8, 179–80, 222, 223, 230, 322
Yorkshire, 43
Yugoslavia, 175

Zinoviev letter, 64
Zionism, 249–54, 255, 256, 264, 266
Zurich, 99